SO-AJC-260

The Abolitionist Legacy

James M. McPherson

The Abolitionist Legacy

From Reconstruction to the NAACP

PRINCETON UNIVERSITY PRESS, PRINCETON, NEW JERSEY

JUN 1 1978

for my MOTHER *and* FATHER

Contents

Acknowledgments

Although writing a book is ultimately a lonely enterprise, it cannot be done without help from a great many people. I have been particularly fortunate in both the quantity and quality of assistance I have received from friends, colleagues, and librarians. I wish it were possible to thank all of them by name here, but to do so would lengthen this book by the equivalent of another chapter. Nevertheless, several people who gave generously of their time and resources deserve more than a blanket nod of anonymous thanks. Foremost among them is my wife Patricia, who shared thousands of hours of research with me in libraries from Maine to California. My undergraduate research assistant, Ronald W. Davis, helped with the laborious task of searching through newspapers for material. Among the scores of librarians, archivists, and historians who helped us find material, four went far beyond the call of duty to provide the kind of special service and friendship that can make research a pleasure. Clifton H. Johnson, Executive Director of the Amistad Research Center at Dillard University (formerly at Fisk University), put his unparalleled knowledge of the American Missionary Association Archives and the assistance of his cheerful staff at our disposal during two visits to the rich resources of the Amistad Center. John Ness, Director of the Commission on Archives and History of the United Methodist Church, did the same during my visit to Lake Junaluska, North Carolina, to consult the archives of the Freedmen's Aid Society of the Methodist Episcopal Church. Elizabeth S. Duvall, Bibliographer of the Sophia Smith Collection at the Smith College Library, was especially helpful to our research in the William Lloyd Garrison, Jr., Papers. And finally, Herbert Aptheker kindly let me consult the W. E. B. Du Bois Papers in his custody, before these papers were turned over to the University of Massachusetts at Amherst.

The directors and staffs of the following libraries and institutions were also very helpful: the American Antiquarian Society; the American Baptist Historical Society, housed in the library of the Colgate-Rochester Theological Seminary, Rochester, New York; the Atlanta University Archives; the Department of Special Collections, Hutchins Library, Berea College; the Manuscript Division of the Boston Public Library; the Bowdoin College Library; the Chautauqua County Historical Museum, Westfield, New York; the Chicago Historical Society; the Cincinnati Historical Society; the Columbia University Library;

the Concord (Mass.) Public Library; the Cornell University Library; the Frederick Douglass Memorial Home in Washington, D.C., which formerly housed the Frederick Douglass Papers; the Drew University Library, Madison, N.J.; the Essex Institute Library, Salem, Mass.; the Manuscript Division of the Baker Library, Harvard Business School; the Harvard University Archives; the Houghton Library, Harvard University; the Widener Library, Harvard University; the Quaker Collection, Haverford College Library; the Rutherford B. Hayes Library, Fremont, Ohio; the Moorland Foundation Library, Howard University; the Henry E. Huntington Library, San Marino, California; the Interdenominational Theological Center affiliated with Atlanta University; the Manuscript, Newspaper, and Stack and Reader Divisions of the Library of Congress; the Massachusetts Historical Society; the Mississippi Department of Archives and History; the New York Historical Society; the New York Public Library, including the Newspaper Annex and the Schomburg Library; the Manuscript Division of the Oberlin College Library; the Department of Western MSS., Bodleian Library, Oxford University; the Speer Library, Princeton Theological Seminary; the Firestone Library, especially Eleanor V. Weld of the Interlibrary Loan Division, Princeton University; the Department of Special Collections, University of Rochester Library; the Schlesinger Library, Radcliffe College; the Syracuse University Library; the Union Theological Seminary Library, New York City; the Western Reserve Historical Society, Cleveland, Ohio; the Wilberforce University Library; the State Historical Society of Wisconsin; and the Yale University Library.

The resources of these libraries provided most of the material for this book, but in addition the following friends, colleagues, and students kindly allowed me to read and cite their own unpublished studies or shared items uncovered by their own research: William M. Armstrong; Clarence A. Bacote; Philip Benjamin; Thomas C. Cox; Daniel W. Crofts; Tilden G. Edelstein; John Hope Franklin; David A. Gerber; Victor M. Glasberg; William B. Gravely; William B. Hixson, Jr.; Thomas C. Holt; Donald Gene Jones; Jacqueline Halstead; Ralph E. Luker; Howard N. Meyer; Carl R. Osthaus; Joe M. Richardson; May Miller Sullivan; Barbara Myers Swartz; Nancy J. Weiss; and Ronald C. White. I am especially indebted to Timothy Bird, who gave me access to his large collection of black college catalogues dating back to 1867.

Much of the research for this book would not have been possible without fellowships and grants from the John Simon Guggenheim Memorial Foundation, the National Endowment for the Humanities, the Procter and Gamble Foundation, the Shelby Cullom Davis Center for Historical Studies, and the Princeton University Committee on Research in the Humanities and Social Sciences. My warmest thanks go to these institutions, which financed three academic leaves plus additional released time from teaching duties as well as providing research funds.

No author dares to send his book into the world without first passing it through the screen of critical readings by colleagues. Those who read early drafts of this book proved their friendship by their fruitful criticisms and by giving me leads to additional sources I would otherwise have missed. For such help I am profoundly grateful to William B. Gravely, William B. Hixson, Jr., August Meier, Willie Lee Rose, Elliott Rudwick, Nancy J. Weiss, Ronald C. White, Raymond Wolters, and C. Vann Woodward. Several students in my graduate seminar on black history in the fall of 1973 also read an early draft and contributed helpful suggestions. Members of the Shelby Cullom Davis Seminar on the History of Education, especially James McLachlan and Lawrence Stone, criticized versions of several chapters and helped to shape my thinking about Negro education. At the Princeton University Press, Miriam R. Brokaw and Lewis Bateman helped smooth the way for publication of the book while Gail Filion, my copy editor, has saved me from egregious comma faults. The expert and patient counsel of these people has made this book much better (and shorter) than it would otherwise have been; only my own lack of ability or energy to carry out all of their suggestions has kept it from being still better.

JAMES M. McPHERSON

Princeton, New Jersey
March 1975

Abbreviations

For the sake of brevity, the following abbreviations are used for frequently cited sources in the footnotes:

ABHMS	American Baptist Home Mission Society Archives, American Baptist Historical Society, Colgate-Rochester Theological Seminary, Rochester, N.Y.
AM	*American Missionary* (magazine of the American Missionary Association)
AMA Archives	American Missionary Association Archives, Amistad Research Center, Dillard University, New Orleans
BC	*Boston Commonwealth*
BET	*Boston Evening Transcript*
BTW Papers	Booker T. Washington Papers, Library of Congress
CIO (D)	*Chicago Inter Ocean* (daily edition)
CIO (W)	*Chicago Inter Ocean* (weekly edition)
FASME Archives	Archives of the Freedmen's Aid Society of the Methodist Episcopal Church, Interdenominational Theological Center, Atlanta; microfilm copies at the Commission on Archives and History, United Methodist Church, Lake Junaluska, N.C.
Annual Reports, FASME	Published annual reports of the Freedmen's Aid Society of the Methodist Episcopal Church
FGV Papers	Fanny (Helen Frances) Garrison Villard Papers, Houghton Library, Harvard University
HMM	*Home Mission Monthly* (magazine of the American Baptist Home Mission Society)
HW	*Harper's Weekly*
Mass. Spy	*Massachusetts Spy* (weekly edition of the Worcester *Spy*)

xii

NWCA	*Northwestern Christian Advocate* (Chicago)
NYEP	*New York Evening Post*
NYT	*New York Times*
NYTrib.	*New York Tribune*
OGV Papers	Oswald Garrison Villard Papers, Houghton Library, Harvard University
SWCA	*Southwestern Christian Advocate* (New Orleans)
WLG Papers	William Lloyd Garrison Papers, Boston Public Library
WLG, Jr., Papers	William Lloyd Garrison, Jr., Papers, Smith College Library
WPG Papers	Wendell Phillips Garrison Papers, Houghton Library, Harvard University
ZH	*Zion's Herald* (Boston)

The Abolitionist Legacy

Introduction

This book challenges the prevailing assumption that most abolitionists abandoned the battle for Negro rights after 1870. My earlier study, *The Struggle for Equality: Abolitionists and the Negro in the Civil War and Reconstruction* (1964), argued that abolitionists led the campaign for equal rights after emancipation and launched the movement for education of the freedmen. *The Struggle for Equality* ended with the adoption of the 15th Amendment in 1870, but the abolitionist struggle for racial equality did not then end. Hence this book, which carries the story down to the founding of the neo-abolitionist NAACP in 1909-1910. Its thesis runs contrary to such statements as August Meier's assertion that "since the white abolitionists . . . were not, for the most part, genuinely committed to a belief in the essential human dignity of Negroes" they found it easy "to pay the price of sectional reconciliation [which was] the rejection of the idea of a racially egalitarian society. . . . Many of the abolitionists deserted and betrayed the southern Negroes." Other historians have made the same point. Philip Foner maintained that by the 1870s "northern reformers were finished with the Negro"; C. Vann Woodward wrote that by 1877 "a whole generation" of "Northern liberals and former abolitionists [were] mouthing the shibboleths of white supremacy regarding the Negro's innate inferiority, shiftlessness, and hopeless unfitness for full participation in the white man's civilization."[1]

If my findings are correct, these statements are wrong—or at least partly wrong. As Part I of this book shows, while a minority of former abolitionists did become disillusioned with radical Reconstruction and approved its demise, the majority did not. But those in the former category did not necessarily abandon the Negro. Many of them were active in freedmen's education, hoping that with such help black people could struggle up to the equality that legislation and force had failed to achieve during Reconstruction. Negro education was in many ways the most important and positive abolitionist legacy. The schools and colleges founded mainly by abolitionists trained the black leaders who have led the struggle for equality in the twentieth century, and the

[1] Meier, "Negroes in the First and Second Reconstructions of the South," *Civil War History*, XIII (1967), 126, 128-29; Meier and Elliott M. Rudwick, *From Plantation to Ghetto*, rev. ed., New York, 1970, p. 176; Philip Foner, *Frederick Douglass, A Biography*, New York, 1964, p. 317; Whitelaw Reid, *After the War: A Southern Tour*, ed. with an Intro. by C. Vann Woodward, New York, 1966, p. xx; Woodward, *The Strange Career of Jim Crow*, 3rd rev. ed., New York, 1974, p. 70.

values instilled by those schools helped prepare them for the struggle. Part II treats this crusade for education.

Despite its successes, Negro education did not immediately improve race relations. Instead, things got worse after 1890, dashing the hopes built up during the optimistic 1880s. With the hardening of racial lines came a revived neo-abolitionist militancy that eventually produced the NAACP. Part III traces the twisting path that led to this result.

This book reflects my interest in the role of white liberals in the evolution of American racial attitudes and practices. Thus it focuses on the *race question* from 1870 to 1910 rather than on the part—often an important part—that former abolitionists played in other reform movements. An interesting book could be written about the diffusion of the antislavery impulse into the temperance movement, civil service reform, the women's rights movement, labor reform, and a host of other causes.[2] But this is not that book. The racial rather than reform legacy of abolitionism is my theme. Such activities as women's rights, civil service reform, and anti-imperialism are discussed only as they affected racial attitudes.

Anyone writing about abolitionists confronts the problem of defining the term, and this becomes more difficult for the period after 1865. Even before emancipation, of course, the antislavery movement was beset by factionalism. At times it seemed as if there were almost as many kinds of abolitionists as there were individuals in the movement. In *The Struggle for Equality* I defined "abolitionist" as one who before the Civil War had agitated for the immediate, unconditional, and total abolition of slavery in the United States. The same general definition will serve again here (with the addition, as explained below, of "second generation" and "third generation" abolitionists). It encompasses those people who founded or joined the American Anti-Slavery Society or its auxiliaries in the 1830s plus those who founded or joined any of the numerous offshoots of these societies as the movement fragmented after 1840: the Liberty party; the American and Foreign Anti-Slavery Society; the American Missionary Association; the Church Anti-Slavery Society; and so on.

Most abolitionists could be classified in one of three groups by 1840: the Garrisonians, whose anticlericalism, antistatism, and radicalism on such issues as women's rights had driven most church-oriented and politically inclined abolitionists out of the American Anti-Slavery Society; the evangelicals, who continued to work through their churches

[2] Two studies that emphasize the role of former abolitionists in postwar reform movements are Robert Winston Mardock, *The Reformers and the American Indian*, Columbia, Mo., 1971, and David J. Pivar, *Purity Crusade: Sexual Morality and Social Control, 1868-1900*, Westport, Conn., 1973.

for emancipation; and the political abolitionists, who hoped to achieve abolition through the political process. This three-tiered classification is somewhat artificial, for in practice the three types frequently shaded into each other, especially the latter two and especially after 1860. On the ideological spectrum, from immediate abolition on the Left to conservative antislavery on the Right, it is often hard to tell where "abolition" (which demanded unconditional emancipation and usually envisaged civil equality for the freed slaves) ended and "antislavery" or "free soil" (which desired only the containment of slavery and was ambivalent on the question of equality) began. In New England particularly, many free soilers were abolitionists at heart; in the mid-Atlantic states and even more in the old Northwest, political abolitionists tended to submerge their abolitionist identity in the broader but shallower stream of free soil. Fully recognizing the difficulty of separating abolitionist from antislavery at the middle of the spectrum, this book concentrates on abolitionists in the belief that by studying the post-1870 actions of those in the vanguard of racial liberalism, we can arrive at a better understanding of the post-emancipation history of black people and race relations.

Not all of the white people active in racial reform were abolitionists, of course; one did not need to be born into an abolitionist family to teach in a black school or to join the NAACP or to participate in other enterprises herein described as part of the "abolitionist legacy." And it may seem a bit awkward to use the word abolitionist when discussing developments a generation or more after emancipation—hence the introduction of the term "neo-abolitionist" in Part III dealing with the period after 1890. On the other hand, contemporaries described themselves or others as "abolitionists" even into the 1910s, and the NAACP proudly called itself the New Abolition Movement. This book is based on the premise that not only did former abolitionists provide much of the leadership for post-emancipation racial reform, but also that their attitudes provide a perspective for viewing the successes and failures of those efforts and a mirror reflecting both the triumphs and tragedies of the age.

The abolitionists did not function in a cultural vacuum, and I have paid considerable attention in this book to political developments, social and intellectual currents, and other matters that formed the context of their activities. In *The Struggle for Equality*, I examined the roles of black as well as white abolitionists. In the present book the actions of black leaders are compared and contrasted with those of white abolitionists. But the focus is on whites, and black abolitionists are not included in the definitional, quantitative, and qualitative generalizations herein made concerning "abolitionists." This is not because the only "men who have a right to that title were born free" and therefore were not "periling everything but honor for the freedom of others," as Frederick Douglass put it in 1874.[3] Rather it is because this book is primarily a study of white racial attitudes. There are a number of good books about black ideology and leadership during the two generations after Reconstruction, while the role of former white abolitionists is relatively unknown or misunderstood.

In my research I have read the letters, articles, editorials, speeches, and other writings of several hundred whites concerned with racial matters from 1870 to 1915. Something over 300 of these people were identifiable as abolitionists or the children or grandchildren of abolitionists. Of these, 284 were important and active enough to form the basis of this study. This number does not include several dozen persons active in Negro education who probably had an antislavery background but whom I have not been able definitely to identify as abolitionists. The 284 are listed alphabetically in Appendix A with accompanying information for most of them on the following variables: dates of birth and death; principal place(s) of residence during this period; occupation; education; religion; the abolitionist faction to which they belonged; their degree of importance in this study; and designation as first-, second-, or third-generation abolitionists.

For our purposes, a first-generation abolitionist was one who joined the movement before 1860 and whose parents are not known to have been active in the post-1830 phase of militant abolitionism; a second-generation abolitionist was the son or daughter of such a person; and a third-generation abolitionist was the grandson or granddaughter of a first-generation abolitionist. The 284 persons on this list are *not* a representative or random sample of all the abolitionists and their descendants who lived during this period. The bases for their selection were their functional importance and the survival of evidence for their ideas or activities. Thus the list is biased toward activists and leaders. Most of the children and grandchildren born to first-generation abolitionists are not on the list because either they were not prominent in the ancestral cause or no evidence of their activities has come to light. At the same time, the parents or grandparents of some of the second- and third-generation activists cannot be found on my list of first-generation abolitionists.

Of the 284 abolitionists, 191 were first generation, 70 second generation, and 23 third generation. Since the parents of some of those listed

[3] Letter from Douglass to an antislavery reunion convention in Chicago, June 1874, quoted in Larry Gara, "Who Was an Abolitionist?" in Martin Duberman, ed., *The Antislavery Vanguard: New Essays on the Abolitionists*, Princeton, 1965, pp. 41-42.

as first generation *may* have been abolitionists, these figures probably overstate the proportion of first-generation abolitionists. Of the 284, I have designated 48 (35 first generation, 12 second generation, and 1 third generation) as "important" in this study and 29 (16 first generation, 9 second generation, and 4 third generation) as "very important." These 77 persons formed the nucleus of post-1870 abolitionism; they were editors of newspapers and periodicals, secretaries of freedmen's education societies, presidents of black colleges, prominent public figures, and the like.

We are dealing with a hardy group of people who had many years of life ahead of them after the war. In 1870 the average age of the 163 first-generation abolitionists for whom birth dates were found was 52.9 years and the average number of years they had still to live was 24.5. The comparable averages for 62 second-generation abolitionists in 1890 were 49.2 and 29.1 years, and for 18 third-generation abolitionists in 1910 were 46.9 and 29.0 years.

I have been able to identify the faction of the abolition movement to which 253 of the 284 belonged. If we keep in mind that such identification is sometimes hazardous because of overlapping between groups and the tendency of some individuals to move from one group to another, 79 (31 percent) were Garrisonians, 116 (46 percent) were evangelicals, and 57 (23 percent) were political abolitionists. Since most overlapping occurred between the last two groups, another way of stating the distinction is that 69 percent of the identifiable abolitionists in this study were non-Garrisonians. In the case of second- and third-generation abolitionists who reached their adult years after 1860 when factional divisions became blurred, I have identified them with one group or another only if their ancestral loyalties are clear from their own words or deeds. Most of the non-identifiables are from the second and third generations.

Data on the education and occupations of these people confirm generalizations about the middle- and upper-middle class nature of the leadership of moral/social reform movements in America. Of the 248 for whom I found information regarding education, an extraordinary 139 (57 percent) had graduated from college and another 21 (9 percent) had attended college without graduating—and this at a time when fewer than 3 percent of the population attended college and fewer than 2 percent graduated. Occupationally our sample was top-heavy in the professions, especially teaching, preaching, and journalism—which reflects in part the functional bias of the sample toward those active in Negro education and in the molding of public opinion. The occupations of 278 of the 284 are known. Since many of them had more than one occupation during their lives, I have selected the principal occupation of each individual during the main period under consideration. Thirty-nine (14 percent) were clergymen, 42 (15 percent) were "clergymen/educators" (ordained ministers whose most important work was in education), and 45 (16 percent) were "educators" (teachers, school principals, college presidents, etc.). The total of those concerned with education is 87, or nearly a third of the sample. Next to educators, journalists were the largest category with 45 (16 percent). Another 12 (4 percent) are classified as "writers" (of books and of articles for periodicals), one as an editor for a book publisher, and 17 (6 percent) as "lecturer/reformers"—persons who made a living as lecturers, usually in behalf of a reform cause such as women's rights. Grouping together the journalists, writers, and lecturers as "publicists" we have a total of 75 (26 percent). If we classify all of the categories mentioned so far as persons involved in the communication of information and ideas, we get a grand total of 201, or 71 percent of our sample. The remaining 29 percent were scattered mainly among other professional and white-collar occupations—lawyers, physicians, social workers, businessmen, and others (for a detailed breakdown, see Appendix A).

Most of those listed as journalists were editors of daily or weekly newspapers or of monthly or quarterly magazines. In addition, several who are classified in other occupations edited or wrote for religious and missionary publications. Major sources for this study were 33 newspapers and periodicals edited by abolitionists. Some of these journals have been researched for the 50-year period from 1865 to 1915; most for a shorter period; the average length of time for the 33 journals consulted was 17 years.

Of the 284 abolitionists listed in Appendix A, 68 (24 percent) were women. As one might expect, the largest group of women was found among the Garrisonians—exactly half of the 50 whose affiliation could be identified. Or to put it another way, 32 percent of the Garrisonians in our sample were women, compared with 19 percent (mostly teachers) of the evangelicals and 11 percent of the political abolitionists. Occupationally the women abolitionists were concentrated in three areas: 24 educators, 11 lecturer/reformers, and 10 social workers.

The regional patterns of residence tend to confirm the image of New England as the cradle of abolition. Determination of the place of residence for a given member of the sample was often difficult, since many people moved from place to place and more than a quarter of the sample were teachers in the South but natives of the North. The *principal* place of residence listed in Appendix A, therefore, refers to the city or state in which an individual lived for the longest and/or most important part of his career in the period covered by this book. For those working in the South, notation of their home cities or states in the North is also included. Of the 284 in the sample, 95 (33 percent) lived in New England, 84 (30 percent) lived in the mid-Atlantic states including Maryland, Delaware, and the District of Columbia, 31 (11 percent) lived in the rest of the North, and 74 (26 percent) lived in the South including Kentucky. Only two of the latter were natives of the South, another 10 were northerners whose home states could not be determined, 25 were from New England, 12 from the mid-Atlantic states, and 25 from the rest of the North. If one assigns those living in the South to their home states and adds them to the totals for those states, New England becomes the home for 120 (42 percent) of the 284 (at a time when fewer than 8 percent of all Americans lived in New England), the mid-Atlantic states of 95 (34 percent), and the rest of the North of 56 (20 percent). This actually understates New England's predominance, since many persons residing elsewhere had been born in New England. The Garrisonians and political abolitionists were concentrated mainly in New England, while the evangelicals lived mostly in other sections. This reflects the Unitarianism and anti-clericalism of the New England abolitionists and the tendency of political abolitionists elsewhere to lose their abolitionist identity in anti-slavery political parties. The 284 abolitionists were predominantly urban—about three-quarters of them lived in what the census defined as urban areas (cities of 2,500 or more population) at a time when about one-third of all Americans lived in cities. Sixty-four of the abolitionists in our sample lived in metropolitan Boston, 49 in New York, 18 in Philadelphia, and nine each in Washington and Chicago.

Information on religious affiliation was the hardest to obtain and the least reliable of the variables in this collective biography. Not only do the biographical directories, obituaries, and other sources consulted frequently fail to designate an individual's religion, but many persons changed denominations at least once in their lives, others attended churches of which they were not formal members, and still others were only nominal members of a denomination or not affiliated formally with any church. The designation of a few individuals as belonging to a particular denomination was surmise—for example, I have listed some teachers and clergymen affiliated with the American Missionary Association as Congregationalists although they may have been Presbyterians before and even during their connection with this Congregational society. And the number of "Liberals" is understated, since several of those designated as Unitarians and Quakers also belonged to associations herein described as Liberal—the Free Religious Association, the Progressive Friends, the Ethical Culture Society, and the like. Recognizing the margin of error in any conclusions based on religious affiliation, I have data for 247 people, of whom 64 (26 percent) were Congregationalists, 51 (21 percent) Unitarians, 39 (16 percent) Quakers, 27 (11 percent) Methodists, 14 (6 percent) Baptists, and 14 (6 percent) Presbyterians. Of the remainder, 15 were "Liberals" and 12 were not affiliated with any denomination. While this sample is functionally biased toward leadership and toward the key role of the American Missionary Association in freedmen's education, the large number of Congregationalists and Unitarians (which together with the four Universalists comprise 48 percent of the sample) is nevertheless striking, since these denominations combined had barely 5 percent of the white church membership in the United States. It is another reflection of New England's predominance in abolitionism. The overrepresentation of the Quakers is equally notable, for with little more than 1 percent of national church membership they constituted 16 percent of the sample. The skewed distribution of denominational membership among the three abolitionist factions is also striking but not surprising. Among the Garrisonians only six of 70 can be identified as members of evangelical denominations—four Congregationalists, one Presbyterian, and one Baptist—while the other 64 were Unitarians (24), Quakers (18), non-affiliated (12), Liberals (7), and Universalists (3). Among the 38 political abolitionists whose religion could be established, a similar though less extreme pattern occurs—only 10 were traditional Protestants, while the remainder were Unitarians (19) and Quakers, Liberals, or Universalists. Among the evangelicals the reverse was true—no Unitarians, Universalists, or Liberals but 52 Congregationalists, 26 Methodists, 12 Baptists, 11 Presbyterians, 10 Quakers, and two others.

The "typical" abolitionist treated in this book, therefore, was a college-educated Protestant, a member of one of the professions concerned with the communication of ideas or information, a native of the Northeast and most likely of New England. Such a generalization, of course, belies the diversity and complexity of this group of men and women and tells us little about any given individual's ideas or behavior. And the collective story of their ideas and behavior regarding the race issue from 1870 to 1910 is far too complex to be encapsulated in any single generalization. To make some sense out of this complexity without oversimplifying it is the purpose of the pages that follow.

Part One

The Retreat from Reconstruction

Chapter One

Unfinished Task: The Civil Rights Act of 1875

On a brisk spring day in 1870, abolitionists convened in New York City to celebrate the ratification of the 15th Amendment and to dissolve their antislavery societies. "Capstone and completion of our movement," the 15th Amendment climaxed 40 years of agitation for the freedom and equal rights of black people. During the last 10 years of this period, change had come with revolutionary swiftness. Four million slaves had been emancipated by force of arms, their freedom and civil equality had been written into the Constitution, half a million had already achieved literacy, and hundreds of their leaders had won election to office in states where they had recently been slaves. Although the veteran crusaders who gathered in April 1870 had hoped all this would one day come to pass, most of them had not expected to see it in their lifetimes. Little wonder that they praised God for His marvelous providence and dismantled their societies in a mood of triumph.

Yet while congratulating themselves on a job well done, the old campaigners warned each other that eternal vigilance would remain the price of the black man's liberty. "While this generation lasts it is probable the negro will need the special sympathy of his friends," said Wendell Phillips. "Our work is not done; we probably never shall live to see it done." The day after the dissolution of the American Anti-Slavery Society, many of its members reconstituted themselves as the "National Reform League" to work against "social persecution of men on account of their color."[1]

Abolition of this "social persecution" was for abolitionists a vital unfinished task of Reconstruction in 1870. Many of them campaigned for civil rights legislation as the best way to accomplish the task. The National Reform League helped to push a public accommodations law through the New York legislature in 1873, and lobbied also for a federal statute. The Civil Rights Act passed by Congress in 1875 climaxed these efforts. But while this law seemed to complete the revolution of racial equality, the victory was more symbolic than real. Running counter to the general retreat from Reconstruction, the Civil Rights

[1] *National Anti-Slavery Standard*, Apr. 16, 1870; *National Standard*, 1 (May 1870), 46-48.

Act was passed mainly as a gesture to the departed spirit of Charles Sumner. Stripped of moral authority by the lukewarm commitment of its Republican sponsors, the law had little apparent impact on racial practices. Even its symbolic legal value came to an end in 1883 when the Supreme Court ruled it unconstitutional. Nevertheless the story of the abolitionists' role in events leading to its passage is the best starting point for understanding the part they played in the complex racial developments of the 1870s.

Although discrimination in housing, jobs, hotels, restaurants, and places of amusement long persisted in the North, Jim Crow on trains, steamboats, and streetcars had become rare by 1870. At the same time the visibility of segregation was growing in the South. Several cases were publicized in the antislavery press. In 1869 Lieutenant-Governor Oscar J. Dunn of Louisiana was denied admission to a first-class railroad car in his own state. In 1871 the captain of a Potomac river steamboat refused to allow Frederick Douglass into the boat's dining room. Gilbert Haven, the Massachusetts abolitionist who went south as bishop of the northern-based Methodist Episcopal Church, reported from Georgia that the second-class cars in which black passengers had to ride were "hideous pens."[2]

Abolitionists in the South worked to break down this color line. Haven made a habit of riding in the "Negro car" when traveling with black clergymen. After the Mississippi legislature passed an antidiscrimination law in 1873, Haven visited Vicksburg, where he took two black pastors to breakfast at the city's best hotel. The waiter tried to serve them at a corner table behind a screen, but Haven walked over to a central table and said "we'll take our breakfast here." The owner refused; Haven threatened to sue. The owner gave in and the three men enjoyed a good breakfast at the table of their choice.[3] Two abolitionist carpetbaggers in South Carolina, Gilbert Pillsbury and Reuben Tomlinson, helped persuade the commander of the federal occupying forces to abolish Charleston's streetcar segregation in 1867. The next year one of the first measures enacted by the new Republican legislature, which contained several former abolitionists, was a civil rights law forbidding discrimination in public facilities. This law was never fully enforced, but South Carolina blacks reportedly suffered less segregation than those of other southern states during Reconstruction.[4]

[2] *National Anti-Slavery Standard*, May 29, 1869; *National Standard*, Apr. 1, 8, 1871; article by Haven in *Independent*, Aug. 6, 1874.

[3] *ZH*, June 19, July 3, Oct. 16, 1873; George Prentice, *The Life of Gilbert Haven*, New York, 1883, pp. 444-45.

[4] *BC*, Apr. 27, 1867; *The Revised Statutes of the State of South Carolina*, Colum-

In Nashville, Fisk University's abolitionist president, Erastus M. Cravath, reacted swiftly when a ticket agent refused to sell him a dozen Pullman berths for the Fisk Jubilee Singers. Cravath telegraphed George Pullman himself, who wired a rebuke to the agent ordering him to sell Cravath the tickets. For the next quarter-century Pullman cars were officially nonsegregated.[5]

Most abolitionists considered public school segregation one of the worst forms of discrimination. In a democratic society, wrote one, "the majority have no right to exclude the children of the minority from the schools, even though they open others 'as good' for their use. Such a separation in childhood would breed two races of citizens, hostile in their interests." By 1874 all of the New England states plus Michigan, Iowa, Minnesota, and Kansas had prohibited *de jure* segregation in public schools. Abolitionists were active in the antisegregation movements in these and other northern states.[6] Freedmen's schools in the South established by abolitionist missionary societies were open to both races. In the early 1870s two Methodist abolitionists sat on the New Orleans school board, which presided over the desegregation of about one-third of that city's public schools and the assignment of black teachers to some of the mixed schools.[7] When Henry J. Fox, a northern Methodist clergyman and abolitionist, was elected president of the University of South Carolina in 1873, he ordered the admission of a black applicant. Three southern white faculty members promptly resigned. "We are victors—and are going on to greater conquests," wrote Fox, who appointed sympathetic professors to the vacancies. In 1874 a black man joined the faculty. Large numbers of Negroes entered the university, most white students left, and by 1875 nine-tenths of the students were black. One of the new students had been a slave who remembered "standing in the door of one of the [university] buildings and crying because I could not go to school. Now thank God

---

bia, 1873, pp. 739-41; Elizabeth Hyde Botume, *First Days Amongst the Contrabands,* Boston, 1893, pp. 268-71.

[5] Undated newspaper clipping, Joseph E. Roy Scrapbook, Amistad Research Center, Dillard University.

[6] *Right Way,* Feb. 23, 1867; James M. McPherson, *The Struggle for Equality: Abolitionists and the Negro in the Civil War and Reconstruction,* Princeton, 1964, pp. 228-29; McPherson, "Abolitionists and the Civil Rights Act of 1875," *Journal of American History,* LII (1965), 498-99.

[7] The two Methodist abolitionists were Joseph C. Hartzell and Lucius Matlack. Memoranda and miscellaneous materials in the Joseph C. Hartzell Papers, Drew University Library. See also Barbara Myers Swartz, "The Lord's Carpetbagger: A Biography of Joseph Crane Hartzell," Ph.D. Dissertation, S.U.N.Y. at Stony Brook, 1972, pp. 379-90; and Louis R. Harlan, "Desegregation in New Orleans Public Schools during Reconstruction," *American Historical Review,* LXVII (1962), 663-75.

there has been a great change, the mountains have been brought low and the valleys are exalted."[8]

Except in Louisiana and at the University of South Carolina, no public schools in the South were integrated during Reconstruction. In the North the schools in the states where most of the black population lived were segregated. And many other forms of discrimination persisted in both North and South. The failure of local and state efforts to banish these evils caused many abolitionists to call for national legislation. "Why sit supinely and let these insolent [hotel] proprietors virtually trample upon the great Constitutional guarantees?" asked one. "The hour for fawning, begging, and cringing has gone by. . . . It is necessary and proper that the *law* be appealed to."[9]

Senator Charles Sumner led the drive for a national civil rights law. On May 13, 1870, he introduced a bill to forbid discrimination by railroads, steamboats, public conveyances, hotels, restaurants, licensed theaters, public schools, juries, and incorporated church or cemetery associations. Offenders would be tried by federal courts and punished with fines or imprisonment.[10] When this bill became bottled up in the Senate Judiciary Committee, Sumner pushed for passage of an act to desegregate public schools in the District of Columbia as a pilot project for national legislation. Opponents maintained that integration would drive away white students and destroy public education in the District. Several abolitionists branded this argument specious. William Lloyd Garrison cited the success of desegregation in Boston and other northern cities despite the dire predictions of skeptics; after an initial shakedown period, he said, it would work as well in Washington. Even if white parents did threaten to take their children out of school, "surely it is not for Congress to grant them any indulgence." Arthur Edwards, young editor of the *Northwestern Christian Advocate* who had grown up as an abolitionist in the 1850s, thought that whites "afflicted with colorphobia" must "originate for themselves at their own expense select schools; the public schools must be for the public."[11]

Though the Senate also buried the District of Columbia bill, Sumner made a determined bid for passage of his national civil rights act at the next session of Congress. Abolitionist journalists tried to stir up

---

8 Joel Williamson, *After Slavery: The Negro in South Carolina during Reconstruction, 1861-1877*, Chapel Hill, 1965, pp. 232-33; Fox to Matthew Simpson, Oct. 13, 1873, Simpson Papers, Library of Congress; Simon P. Smith to Edward F. Williams, Dec. 26, 1873, Williams Papers, Amistad Research Center.

9 *National Standard*, Oct. 15, 1870.

10 *Cong. Globe*, 41 Cong., 2 Sess., pp. 3434, 5314.

11 *Independent*, Feb. 16, 1871; *NWCA*, Mar. 22, 1871.

support for the measure. Editor George William Curtis of *Harper's Weekly* insisted that its passage was required to "remove the last lingering taint of slavery." Theodore Tilton proclaimed that "it is not enough to provide separate accommodations for colored citizens, even if in all respects as good as those of other persons; equality is not found in equivalent, but only in equality." Blacks and abolitionists in both North and South circulated petitions in behalf of the bill; scores of such petitions bearing thousands of signatures soon found their way to congressional desks. The Republicans' landslide victory in the 1872 election gave the party a two-thirds majority in both houses of Congress. Though President Ulysses S. Grant opposed efforts to legislate "social equality," he did recommend "civil rights" legislation in 1873. Whatever this ambiguous endorsement may have meant, most Republicans by this time favored some kind of civil rights law.[12]

But two serious obstacles soon materialized, one legal and the other educational. In the *Slaughter-House* decision (April 1873) the Supreme Court ruled that the 14th Amendment applied only to the privileges and immunities of national citizenship, leaving protection of state citizenship to the states themselves.[13] Though the Court did not clearly define the respective spheres of state and national citizenship, opponents of civil rights legislation cited *Slaughter-House* when arguing against Sumner's bill as an unconstitutional extension of federal power into the realm of states' rights.

The ruling also raised the doubts of a few abolitionists. Although Henry C. Bowen of the *Independent* had been a strong supporter of civil rights legislation, he now stated that "an interpretation of the Fourteenth Amendment which . . . makes *all* the rights of citizenship subject to the legislative will of Congress" was never intended by the framers. When other abolitionists accused Bowen of backsliding, he replied that he did not abate a jot of his opposition to caste. "All such discriminations are oppressive, cruel, and unjust. We denounce them." But "we would not have Congress attempt to do even a good thing beyond the reach of its constitutional powers." Bowen tried to prove his sincerity by urging the states to pass civil rights laws, but a number of Negroes criticized him for deserting the cause. The black abolitionist George T. Downing told him that "the very nice concern you manifest

---

[12] *HW*, May 25, 1872; *Golden Age*, Nov. 4, 1871; James D. Richardson, ed., *Messages and Papers of the Presidents*, 20 vols., Washington, 1897-1913, x, 4175, 4209. The Charles Sumner Papers (Houghton Library, Harvard University) and the pages of the *Congressional Globe* are crowded with references to petitions for the bill. For the bill's fate in Congress from 1870 to 1872, see David Donald, *Charles Sumner and the Rights of Man*, New York, 1970, pp. 531-39.

[13] 16 Wallace 36.

for state rights might receive more consideration did it not oppose efforts in behalf of *personal rights.*"[14]

The second obstacle to Sumner's bill was a growing conviction, shared by some abolitionists, that any attempt to force school desegregation on the South would destroy public education there. As an "abstract question" integrated schools were desirable, wrote an abolitionist carpetbagger in Virginia, but as a "practical question" nothing was "more certain than the utter ruin of our free schools if mixed schools are attempted in Virginia." Even though opposition to integration was based on "unreasonable prejudice," added the *Independent*, we "have lived long enough to know that this prejudice, so far as it exists, is not to be corrected by the legislative coercion of a civil rights bill. It is far better to have both [races] educated, even in 'separate' schools, than not to have them educated at all."[15]

Although Bowen's belief that coercion could not abolish racism was spreading among former abolitionists, most of them still believed that race prejudice "will perish when the law refuses to sanction the distinction to which it leads." The phalanx of old crusaders remained fairly solid on the civil rights issue. Of the 83 abolitionists whose attitude is known, 73 (88 percent) supported Sumner's bill, while four of the 10 on the other side opposed only the school provision and favored the rest of the bill. Garrisonians were slightly more favorable to civil rights legislation (90 percent) than evangelical (81 percent) or political (82 percent) abolitionists.[16]

The bill's most influential supporter outside Congress was George William Curtis, editor of *Harper's Weekly* whose circulation of 150,000 made it the largest weekly in the country. An antislavery man from his youth, Curtis became even more closely identified with the movement in 1856 when he married Anna Shaw, daughter of the prominent abolitionist Francis G. Shaw. On the question whether law could curb prejudice, Curtis took an aggressive stand in 1874. By penalizing its consequences, he said, law would "clear the way for its disappearance." When "hotels and restaurants may turn respectable guests away because they are of the colored race, and theatres and cars, all doing business by legal licence, may refuse them entrance for the same reason, it is plain that the law fosters the prejudice." But when "the law enables the colored guest to call the offending host to

14 *Independent*, Feb. 5, Mar. 12, 19, June 18, 1874.

15 *Richmond State Journal*, Oct. 27, 1871; *Virginia State Journal*, Feb. 18, 1874; *Independent*, June 4, 1874.

16 Quotation from *Mass. Spy*, June 24, 1874. Evidence of abolitionists' opinions on this and other issues treated in subsequent chapters was gathered from various primary sources, chiefly articles and letters in newspapers and periodicals, and personal correspondence.

account . . . the prejudice will begin to wane." As for the argument that school desegregation would cripple public education in the South and was therefore a "false friendship" for the Negro, Curtis thought it "much wiser to take the risk of closing some of the schools now than of nourishing a prejudice of this kind indefinitely."[17]

Abolitionists mounted a journalistic barrage in 1874 to reinforce and amplify these propositions. Bishop Gilbert Haven insisted that "there is no cure for this evil except by law. . . . Moral suasion never killed so much as a mosquito sin." William W. Patton, a long-time abolitionist and future president of Howard University, considered it "to little purpose that we give the freedman other rights and privileges, if we are powerless to protect" his right to "go from place to place, to eat and drink and sleep, to be sheltered from the storm, to enjoy as do others the ordinary comforts of life." After a visit to Georgia a Methodist abolitionist declared that "there is nothing [the South] so much needs as good laws thoroughly enforced." Of course southern whites say "they don't want to be compelled to concede social equality to 'niggers,' they don't want this, and that and the other. Well, suppose they don't; what then? Are they to dictate and domineer as in the past? . . . We have had enough of that."[18]

Conceding that the "school argument is the only one used by the opponents of the bill which deserves the slightest respect," abolitionists realized that to answer it they would have to do more than point to the integration of a few black children in the Boston schools. Fortunately, more relevant examples existed. The experience of New Orleans, said one abolitionist, "strongly disputes" the assumption that desegregation would destroy public education in the South. And faculty members at abolitionist-founded Berea College, where 167 black and 117 white students attended classes together peacefully from the elementary to the college grades, insisted that what had been done there "can be done again elsewhere . . . if Christian men and women will stand for the right."[19]

Despite these efforts to mobilize support, Sumner's bill languished in Congress. On March 11, 1874, the senator died. On his deathbed he said to a close friend: "My bill, the civil-rights bill,—don't let it fail!" Two months later the Senate finally passed the measure (minus the provision on church associations). Several senators voted aye as

[17] *HW*, Jan. 10, Apr. 11, June 13, 1874.

[18] Haven in *Independent*, Feb. 26, 1874; Patton in *Advance*, Feb. 19, 1874; "John Brown" in *ZH*, Feb. 26, 1874.

[19] *Mass. Spy*, May 29, 1875; *Independent*, June 25, Oct. 15, 1874; lecture notes in the John G. Fee Papers, Berea College Library; article by Fee in *AM*, xviii (July 1874), 178.

a memorial gesture to their departed colleague; the House, perhaps less affected by Sumner's passing, adjourned without action.[20]

The 1874 congressional elections muddied the crosscurrents of civil rights pressures. The campaign produced fierce outbreaks of violence against black voters in several southern states. Commenting on this, the *Boston Commonwealth*, edited by political abolitionist Charles Wesley Slack, stated that "there has been too much shilly-shallying about the civil rights bill. It is seen everywhere that no Southern hate has been placated by deferring action on that bill. The Republicans had better stake the enhanced devotion of the blacks by passing that bill than longer hope to conciliate a set of worthless Southerners by refraining from so doing." But the Democrats made large gains in both North and South in November, winning control of the next House of Representatives. President Grant was reported to believe that popular hostility to the civil rights bill was partly responsible for Republican defeat (this may have been true in several districts) and it was rumored that he would veto the bill if it reached his desk.[21]

Since the outlook for civil rights legislation seemed bleak when Congress convened in December 1874, the bill's managers decided to amputate the school clause to save the rest of the measure. In response to radical protests against this surgery, some Republican congressmen suggested the addition of a provision requiring that any school district maintaining separate schools must insure their equality in every respect. But Curtis considered such a proposal "puerile." Anyone with "common sense knows that in a community where color prejudice is so strong as to abandon the whole school system rather than to provide for schools in common, schools of equal excellence are simply impossible." Wendell Phillips agreed that separate schools even if equal in theory were seldom so in fact. "Herd together the children of the poor, no matter whether the colored poor or those of any other race—whose parents have not the education to see defects, or the influence to secure attention to their complaint," and the schools would deteriorate. "The negro child loses if you shut him up in separate schools, no matter how accomplished his teacher or how perfect the apparatus." And Congressman James Monroe, a veteran abolitionist from Oberlin, opposed the separate but equal amendment as "a dangerous precedent. . . . If we once establish a discrimination of this kind we know not where it will end."[22]

[20] Edward L. Pierce, *Memoir and Letters of Charles Sumner*, 4 vols., Boston, 1877-1893, IV, 598; *Cong. Record*, 43 Cong., 1 Sess., pp. 3451, 4175-76.

[21] *BC*, Oct. 17, 1874; William B. Hesseltine, *Ulysses S. Grant, Politician*, New York, 1935, pp. 367-71.

[22] *HW*, Nov. 4, 1874; articles by Phillips in *Advance*, Nov. 5, 1874, and *Boston Advertiser*, Jan. 11, 1875; *Cong. Record*, 43 Cong., 2 Sess., pp. 997-98.

Despite abolitionist opposition, the House cut the school and cemetery provisions from Sumner's bill and then passed the emasculated civil rights act on February 4, 1875. The Senate concurred, and the measure became law when Grant signed it on March 1. Few observers seemed to take the Civil Rights Act seriously. The *Washington National Republican* described it as a "piece of legislative sentimentalism"; the *Nation* thought it "amusing . . . tea-table nonsense." Several officials in the Justice Department considered the law unconstitutional. And not only were many of the 162 Republican congressmen who voted for it in the House lukewarm if not skeptical, but 90 of them were lame ducks, having been retired by the voters at the previous election. Under such circumstances, prospects for enforcement were dubious.[23]

Abolitionists were far from jubilant over what they considered a hollow victory. Though the bill was "good as far as it goes," said one, the deletion of the school clause "simply postpones the question to the future." Curtis believed that "to say that half a loaf is better than no bread" was "absurd" because "the bill recognizes and indirectly authorizes the very prejudice against which it is supposed to be directed," while John D. Baldwin of the *Massachusetts Spy* considered its passage almost "a cause for regret [rather] than congratulation."[24]

But the Civil Rights Act may have had some initial impact in the South. Although abolitionist Anna Dickinson reported during a southern trip in the spring of 1875 that she found a tacit agreement among blacks to avoid trouble by refraining from testing the law, Gilbert Haven maintained that Negroes could now get into first-class cars on some railroads. When Thomas Wentworth Higginson traveled through the south Atlantic states in 1878, viewing matters with "the eyes of a tolerably suspicious abolitionist," he professed to find little overt discrimination. "I rode with colored people in first-class cars throughout Virginia and South Carolina," he said, "and in street cars in Richmond and Charleston." He added, almost as an afterthought, that "in Georgia, I was told, the colored people were not allowed in the first-class cars; but they had always a decent second-class car."[25]

[23] *Cong. Record*, 43 Cong., 2 Sess., pp. 996-1011; *U.S. Statutes at Large*, XVIII, 336-37; *Washington National Republican*, Mar. 1, 1875; *Nation*, Mar. 4, June 23, 1875. The complex political maneuvers that preceded House passage of the bill are described in Bertram Wyatt-Brown, "The Civil Rights Act of 1875," *Western Political Quarterly*, XVIII (1965), 771-74, and Alfred H. Kelly, "The Congressional Controversy over School Segregation, 1867-1875," *American Historical Review*, LXIV (1959), 556-62.

[24] *Index*, Feb. 11, 1875; *HW*, Mar. 20, 1875; *Mass. Spy*, Feb. 12, 1875.

[25] Dickinson to her mother, Apr. 25, 1875, Dickinson Papers, Library of Congress; *ZH*, Aug. 12, 1875; Higginson, "Some War Scenes Revisited," *Atlantic Monthly*, XLII (July 1878), 1-9, esp. 7.

Many Negroes in Georgia, however, did not consider the second-class accommodations "decent." "The fact is," reported a black clergyman whose duties made it necessary for him to travel widely, "pushing the colored people off to themselves is the practice of all the South. . . . In Atlanta everything is separate. You go to the depot, and you find three sets of rooms—*to wit*, 'Ladies' Rooms,' 'Gentlemen's Rooms' and 'Freedmen's Rooms'! You enter the cars, and the same heathen rule bears sway, only to be broken when white men wish to smoke, and then they come into the 'Freedmen's Car.' "[26]

One can find scores of such complaints in newspapers of the period. One can also find reports of nonsegregated public carriers similar to Higginson's. This seemingly contradictory evidence only confirms C. Vann Woodward's thesis that, before the onset of legalized segregation in the 1890s, uncertainty and fluidity characterized racial patterns in the South. It does appear that in the first months after passage of the Civil Rights Act some public facilities obeyed it, but as it became clear that the Justice Department intended to do little to enforce the law, practices reverted to local custom, which varied widely.[27]

After several cases had been appealed through lower courts, the Supreme Court in 1883 ruled the Civil Rights Act unconstitutional on the ground that the 14th Amendment gave Congress no power to legislate against discrimination by *individuals* (as opposed to states). The *Nation* noted that the public's general indifference to the decision showed "how completely the extravagant expectations as well as the fierce passions of the war have died out." Nevertheless several abolitionists denounced this "new Dred Scott decision." George B. Cheever, an old abolition warhorse whose rhetoric was still untamed at the age of 76, said that "a resurrected band of Ku-Klux savages could hardly have done worse" than the Court whose decision consigned the freedmen "back to the reign of contempt, injury, and ignomy." But some abolitionists who had advocated the Civil Rights Act a decade earlier viewed the Court's ruling with resigned acquiescence. The law had long been a dead letter, they said, so the Negro had lost only an empty symbol. William W. Patton thought that the Court's decision "leaves colored people as to legal protection just where it leaves white people." Most civil rights, said Patton, "including that of life itself," fell within the province of state law, and he urged blacks to keep up "a steady

26 Benjamin Tanner, in *Independent*, Aug. 17, 1876.

27 C. Vann Woodward, *The Strange Career of Jim Crow*, 3rd rev. ed., New York, 1974, chaps. 1-2; John Hope Franklin, "The Enforcement of the Civil Rights Act of 1875," paper delivered at the annual convention of the American Historical Association, Dec. 29, 1964, a copy of which was kindly supplied by the author; Valeria W. Weaver, "The Failure of Civil Rights 1875-1883 and Its Repercussions," *Journal of Negro History*, LIV (1969), 368-69.

agitation" for the passage of state civil rights laws. He also suggested a new federal statute based on the interstate commerce clause of the Constitution to guarantee equal treatment in interstate travel.[28]

Although several northern states did pass civil rights laws in the 1880s, they were weakly enforced. Abolitionist journalists continued to publicize Jim Crow incidents in both North and South, but never again did their militancy on this issue reach the level of 1874-1875. Experience seemed to confirm that laws alone could not change racial mores. And the question of segregation per se tended to lose significance as the whole edifice of Reconstruction began to collapse in the 1870s. Republican victory in the 1872 presidential election temporarily shored up the edifice, but the issues of the election alarmed many of those abolitionists who had gathered only two years earlier to celebrate the "consummation of the anti-slavery struggle."

[28] *Nation*, Oct. 18, 1883; clipping of a published letter by Wendell Phillips, dated Oct. 30, 1883, in the Stephen S. Foster Papers, American Antiquarian Society; Cheever to Elizabeth Cheever Washburn, Nov. 23, 1883, Cheever Family Papers, American Antiquarian Society; articles by Patton in *Independent*, Nov. 8, 1883, and *New Englander*, XLIII (Jan. 1884), 1-19. The Court's decision is in the *Civil Rights Cases*, 109 U.S. 3. Only the provision barring racial discrimination in the selection of juries survived the Court's ruling.

Chapter Two

Reconstruction Reconfirmed?
The Election of 1872

The Republican party had scarcely elected Ulysses S. Grant to the presidency in 1868 before it began to split into factions. The main cleavage developed between the party regulars or "Radicals" and those who called themselves "Liberal" Republicans. The Liberals derived their ideology partly from nineteenth-century Manchester liberalism, with its emphasis on individual liberty, limited government, laissez-faire economics, and free trade. In the American context, Liberals included tariff reformers and free traders, civil service reformers, and those who urged a policy of amnesty and "self-government" for the South. Although the flourishing spoils system during Grant's first administration gave the Liberal movement its initial impulse, the southern question soon emerged as the dominant issue. An educated elite, Liberals believed in the efficient administration of public affairs by men of good background—men like themselves. Their chief aim, as Carl Schurz phrased it in his keynote address to the Liberal Republican convention in 1872, was to create a government "which the best people of this country will be proud of." In their view, the patronage machines of Republican bosses Roscoe Conkling of New York, Benjamin Butler of Massachusetts, or Zachariah Chandler of Michigan—all of them closely allied with the Grant administration—were hardly composed of the best people. And when Liberals looked to the South they discovered that some of the "best people" there were former Confederates, many of them now disqualified from office or denied power by "corrupt Negro-Carpetbag governments."[1]

"The most striking feature" of the Liberal movement, wrote one historian, "was the large number of free soilers and founders of the Re-

[1] Useful studies of the Liberal Republicans include Earle Dudley Ross, *The Liberal Republican Movement*, New York, 1919; John G. Sproat, *"The Best Men": Liberal Reformers in the Gilded Age*, New York, 1968, esp. chap. 3; Matthew T. Downey, "The Rebirth of Reform: A Study of Liberal Reform Movements, 1865-1872," Ph.D. Dissertation, Princeton University, 1963; Downey, "Horace Greeley and the Politicians: The Liberal Republican Convention in 1872," *Journal of American History*, LIII (1967), 727-50. The Schurz quotation is from Frederic Bancroft, ed., *Speeches, Correspondence and Political Papers of Carl Schurz*, 6 vols., New York, 1913, II, 359.

publican party" among its leaders.[2] Thus one might also expect to find many former abolitionists in the Liberal camp. But three-fourths of the surviving abolitionists favored the re-election of Grant in 1872. They did so mainly because they feared that the Liberal program for conciliation of the South meant a sellout of the freedmen. While many former free soilers and some abolitionists believed that the new issues of civil service and tariff reform or the need for "good government" had superseded the question of Negro rights, most abolitionists still clung to this "old" issue. They may have been just as unhappy as the Liberals with Grant's patronage policy or even with the quality of southern state governments, but for them none of these questions took precedence over the need for continued federal protection of the freedmen.

The first abolitionist to join the Liberal movement was Theodore Tilton, the brilliant but mercurial editor of the *Independent* from 1863 to 1870. Nobody had been more radical than Tilton during those years. But in 1870 a series of personal and professional crises forced his resignation from the *Independent* and led to eventual obscurity. The *Independent* was owned by Henry C. Bowen, a New York merchant who had started his career as a clerk in Arthur Tappan's dry-goods firm and had married Lewis Tappan's daughter. Bowen took up the evangelical abolitionism of his employer and father-in-law; after going into business on his own he founded the *Independent* in 1848 as a Congregational antislavery weekly. Edited for a time by Henry Ward Beecher, the paper reached its greatest influence under Tilton during Reconstruction with a circulation of 75,000 by 1870. Increasingly liberal in his religious views, Tilton began to stray from the faith altogether after his wife confessed in 1870 to an affair with Beecher, Tilton's life-long idol. As his personal and religious problems grew worse, Tilton's editorial policy became erratic. At the end of the year Bowen fired him and took over editorial control of the *Independent* himself.[3]

In March 1871 Tilton started his own reform paper, the *Golden Age*, which soon became a vehicle to promote the presidential candidacy of his friend Horace Greeley. Though Tilton had supported the Reconstruction enforcement laws passed by Congress in 1870-1871, which authorized the president to declare martial law and use the army against southern terrorists, he now began to denounce carpetbag cor-

[2] Ross, *Liberal Republican Movement*, 61.

[3] Frank Luther Mott, *A History of American Magazines*, 4 vols., Cambridge, Mass., 1957, II, 367-82; Paxton Hibben, *Henry Ward Beecher*, New York, 1927, pp. 207-27; Oliver Johnson to William Lloyd Garrison, Dec. 17, 21, 1870, WLG Papers; Johnson to Anna E. Dickinson, Jan. 1, 1871, Dickinson Papers, Library of Congress; Tilton to Whitelaw Reid, Dec. 21, 1870, Reid Papers, Library of Congress; *Independent*, Dec. 22, 1870; *Golden Age*, Mar. 4, 1871.

ruption and urge conciliation rather than force in the South. "Bayonet rule" was "not the way to heal the wounds of a civil war," he wrote. "Peace, magnanimity, fraternal kindness—this is the spirit which we hope the North will . . . exhibit toward the South in the next presidential canvass." And who better than Greeley could exhibit that spirit?[4]

A year or two earlier the suggestion of Greeley for the presidency would have been a joke. But the quixotic editor's political stock rose as the Liberal Republican movement gathered momentum. Back in 1869 Greeley's *New York Tribune* had become the leading spokesman for "universal amnesty." Greeley believed that Reconstruction could not work without the voluntary cooperation of the "better class" of southern whites. To continue any longer a repressive southern policy, he said, would only drive all whites into the Democratic party and intensify anti-Negro terrorism, while amnesty would encourage the growth of a southern Republican party dominated by the region's "natural leaders," especially those who like Greeley had once been Whigs. In the spring of 1871 Greeley carried this message south on a well-publicized lecture tour of the former Confederacy. Although the *Tribune* editor later gave Tilton undeserved credit for "inventing" him as a presidential candidate, it was this southern tour that boosted him into serious contention.[5]

Most Liberals hoped at first to reform the Republican party from within, but as early as March 1871 Tilton hinted at a possible Liberal/Democratic coalition. To achieve such a coalition, he said, the Democrats needed only to repudiate their racist past, "accept the plan of reconstruction," and pledge to "carry out the fourteenth and fifteenth amendments." The *New York World*, a leading Democratic newspaper, had been urging such a "New Departure" for some time. In the spring of 1871 the onetime Copperhead Clement L. Vallandigham joined the *World* in persuading several northern Democratic county and state conventions to endorse the 14th and 15th Amendments. Tilton was delighted by the New Departure. Since the Democratic party now accepted Reconstruction, he wrote, "why not therefore let the better class of Democrats unite with the anti-Grant Republicans" and with Greeley as their nominee "take victorious possession of a government which President Grant has failed to administer."[6]

But most abolitionists agreed with George William Curtis that the New Departure was a ruse, since the Democratic party was still domi-

4 *Golden Age*, June 3, 24, 1871.

5 Glyndon G. Van Deusen, *Horace Greeley, Nineteenth-Century Crusader*, Philadelphia, 1953, pp. 380-84. Murat Halstead of the *Cincinnati Commercial* was the first to suggest Greeley as a presidential candidate, in November 1870.

6 Ross, *Liberal Republican Movement*, 68-69; *Golden Age*, Mar. 25, June 10, 1871.

nated by those "who hate the government, who hold to paramount allegiance to the State, who hunt and harass the colored race, who compose the Ku-Klux." Abolitionists did not necessarily oppose amnesty in its narrow sense of ending the remaining political disqualifications of former Confederates. But in the Liberal lexicon, "amnesty" was coming to mean much more than that: it connoted total forgiveness of rebels and a willingness to entrust to their stewardship the results of northern victory, including Negro rights. To most abolitionists this was unacceptable. As Bowen put it, since freedmen were still being "shot, hung, burned," the antislavery battle was "not yet fought out. . . . There is the old enemy to fight, the old cause to fight for. . . . It is no time to dream we have done."[7]

When it became clear that the Republican party would renominate Grant, Liberal leaders made the fateful decision to form a third party. The Liberal Republican convention at Cincinnati in May 1872 was a motley gathering. Free traders and civil service reformers vied with protectionists and out-of-office politicians seeking to recoup their fortunes. Although Charles Francis Adams was the leading presidential contender when balloting began, the dedicated labor of Greeley's managers Whitelaw Reid and Theodore Tilton plus the wire-pulling of ambitious politicos brought Greeley the nomination on the sixth ballot. While the platform pledged to support the "equality of all men before the law," it placed greater stress on amnesty and local self-government for the South. Of the Liberals' three main issues—tariff reduction, civil service reform, and sectional reconciliation—Greeley was hostile toward the first and indifferent toward the second, which left amnesty and home rule as the "chief issue" and "great watchword" of the party. Greeley announced in his letter of acceptance that he would make Grant's southern policy the main campaign question "in the confident trust that the masses of our countrymen, North and South, are eager to clasp hands across the bloody chasm which has too long divided them."[8]

When the Democratic convention endorsed Greeley, William Lloyd Garrison felt confirmed in his belief that the Liberal movement "is simply a stool-pigeon for the Democracy to capture the Presidency." Lydia Maria Child admitted that the Liberal/Democratic platforms, with their affirmations of equal rights, were cleverly framed in an effort to deceive "the very elect." But if examined closely they proved to be full of loopholes. The platforms "claim 'self-government for the

---

[7] *HW*, Nov. 11, 1871; *Independent*, Feb. 23, 1871.

[8] Ross, *Liberal Republican Movement*, 86-105; Downey, "Horace Greeley and the Politicians"; *Golden Age*, May 11, 1872.

States;' which means the 'State sovereignty' for which the Rebels fought," she wrote. They demand "the 'supremacy of civil over military authority,' which means that when the Ku Klux renew their plans to exterminate Republicans . . . they shall be dealt with . . . by judges and jurors who are themselves members of the Ku Klux associations."[9]

But a number of abolitionists did not see it this way. Tilton was from beginning to end the most active abolitionist Liberal. In *Golden Age* editorials and countless campaign speeches, he hammered away at the themes of carpetbag corruption, the need for sectional reconciliation, and the genuineness of the Democratic New Departure. "Disgraceful to civilization" were the "alien and carpetbagging governments which, in the name of liberty, tread justice and equity under foot," he said. "Every vote for Grant is a vote to sustain these villains. . . . Every vote for Greeley is a blow for their destruction." Since southern Democrats had pledged to accept the results of the war," the North must go half-way to meet them. There had never been "so noble, so advanced, so radiant a manifesto" as the Liberal/Democratic platform. "If the anti-slavery battle is not yet fought out, this fights it out."[10]

Greeley's most venerable abolitionist supporter was 73-year-old Asa Mahan, who had been a trustee of Lane Seminary in 1834, when the school prohibited students from discussing slavery. Mahan dissented from this action and left Lane to become the first president of Oberlin, which at his insistence welcomed black students and became America's first coeducational college. Mahan lost a son and a nephew in the Civil War; in 1872 he said that, though he had as much cause as anyone to hate southern whites, his religion taught forgiveness. "All the ends for which these brave boys lost their lives have been fully accomplished," he declared. Better now to end "carpet-bag misrule" before "party lines between the whites and blacks become so fixed and their hates as enduring as those between the Orangeman and Irishman." In states such as Virginia where Conservatives had already gained control there was "no quartering of our armies upon the people; no suspension of habeas corpus; no interference with the elections or State Legislatures, and there we find no war of races, no ruinous increase in State taxa-tion, and no Ku-Klux outrages, but general harmony and advancing prosperity." Federal withdrawal from the South would not leave the freedmen helpless, for as one-third of the South's voters "the colored people will visibly hold the balance of power, and their rights will be

[9] Garrison to Fanny (Helen Frances) Garrison Villard, July 11, 1872, FGV Papers; letter from Child in *NYT*, July 20, 1872; Child to Sarah B. Shaw, July ?, 1872, Child Papers, Cornell University Library.
[10] *Golden Age*, May 18, June 8, 29, 1872.

as safe in those States as are those of the Irishmen, Germans or colored men in these Northern States."[11]

Mahan's words presaged the tack that a growing number of abolitionists would take in subsequent years. It is hard to tell what proportions of genuine conviction, wishful thinking, and indifference to the fate of the freedmen went into this argument that if only the carpetbaggers would leave the South the white lion and black lamb would lie down together in peace and equality. Tilton and Mahan appear to have believed sincerely that the freedmen would benefit from the New Departure. For some other abolitionist Liberals, however, the question of racial equality was beginning to take second place to other causes, especially that of "good government." The Puritan values of efficiency, thrift, austerity, and an aristocracy of merit seemed to clash with "Grantism" in Washington, "Butlerism" in Massachusetts, and carpetbaggery in the South. If Negro rights could be purchased only at the cost of what they saw as wasteful, corrupt, demagogic government, it was time to count the cost.

Such considerations induced abolitionists Franklin B. Sanborn, Elizur Wright, and Anna Dickinson to join the Liberals in 1872. Though Sanborn had once been a supporter of John Brown, his radicalism was later tempered by a successful career in journalism and public service. In 1872 he confessed that, while he was "not quite convinced that the condition of the colored people would be safe under Greeley," Grant's "ignorance of the first principles of statesmanship" caused him to choose the lesser of two evils and to vote Liberal. Elizur Wright, one of the founders of the American Anti-Slavery Society four decades earlier, also thought that corruption was the main issue in 1872. "I spent a fortnight in the South last fall," he explained, "and became fully convinced that an administration which could not prevent its friends from robbing those poor states . . . cannot long maintain itself there by any fair means. It may suppress the *Ku Klux*, but what is the use of keeping people's throats from being cut if they are to be perpetually robbed?" Anna Dickinson was less defensive about her support for Greeley. A teenager when Fort Sumter fell, Dickinson had blossomed into a spectacular orator during the war, winning laurels as the American Joan of Arc. Although aggressively radical during the early Reconstruction years, her disillusionment with southern Republican governments and her friendship with Greeley's campaign manager Whitelaw Reid caused her to come out for the Liberals. In a well-publicized New York speech just before the election, she lambasted Grantism in the South: "The administrations in those States began in

[11] Speech at Oberlin, Aug. 20, 1872, printed in *Cincinnati Commercial*, Aug. 22.

corruption, and ended in rapine. (Cheers.)" As for the blacks, they had been granted legal equality with whites. If they "cannot defend themselves and exercise their rights at the polls, if . . . republican law and the forms of our old legislation . . . are to be destroyed to help them in fighting, we might as well confess that the experiment of republican Union is ended."[12]

But in the view of pro-Grant abolitionists, the Liberal movement was nothing but a stalking horse for a neo-Confederate revival. The trouble with Liberals, said Garrison, was that they were "most liberal toward all that has been traitorous" and "most illiberal toward all that is eminently loyal." Curtis asserted that a Liberal victory would "make justice toward Union men of any color a farce"; Phillips considered Greeley "a secession candidate"; and the *Independent* predicted that a Liberal/Democratic triumph would bring to power "the unrepentant Southern ex-rebels, the Ku-Klux Klans, the Tammany thieves and rowdies."[13]

Most abolitionists who had gone South as missionaries and teachers desperately hoped for Grant's re-election. The Massachusetts-born Charles Stearns, who bought a Georgia plantation after the war, was angered by the Liberal charge that Grant's use of federal troops in the South was "tyranny." Without troops, said Stearns, the Negro's freedom would be a farce because the Klan feared "no power on earth except the *military power* of the United States." Sallie Holley (daughter of Myron Holley, a founder of the Liberty party) wrote from her freedmen's school in Lottsburgh, Virginia, that "the triumph of Greeleyism . . . means gagging us all and driving us out of Virginia." And from Nashville came the plea of a man who had been "rotten-egged and mobbed in the North before the war" and had suffered worse since he came South. The New Departure was a satanic trick, he warned. Southern Democrats "will do anything, say anything, adopt anything, vote for anybody to get into power, and then farewell platforms and promises. . . . *These people are not changed.*"[14]

One of the campaign's early enigmas was Charles Sumner. His bitter quarrel with Grant over the administration's attempt to annex Santo Domingo made it impossible for him to endorse the president's re-elec-

---

[12] Sanborn in *Springfield Republican*, July 31, 1872, and *Atlantic Monthly*, III (Aug. 1872), 254; Wright to Sumner, July 13, 1872, Sumner Papers, Houghton Library, Harvard University; Dickinson's speech published in *NYTrib.*, Oct. 26, 1872.

[13] Garrison in *Independent*, Sept. 12, 1872; *HW*, Nov. 2, 1872; Phillips in *NYT*, May 25, 1872; *Independent*, Sept. 26, 1872.

[14] Charles Stearns, *The Black Man of the South, and the Rebels*, New York, 1872, pp. 405-406, 437-38; Holley to Gerrit Smith, Oct. 24, 1872, Smith Papers, Syracuse University Library; J. P. Rexford to Charles Sumner, Aug. 3, 1872, Sumner Papers.

tion. Yet Sumner refused to participate in the Liberal convention and took a long time to make up his mind whether to support Greeley. Most of his abolitionist friends urged him to remain neutral. Garrison told him that since the contest was "essentially the old conflict between Slavery and Anti-Slavery" it was "no time for the indulgence of personal dislikes." Sumner took such advice seriously. But he was also under pressure from New England Liberals; this plus his antipathy to Grant finally caused him to endorse Greeley. On July 11 a group of Washington blacks addressed a public letter to Sumner requesting his opinion of the candidates. The tortured reasoning of Sumner's reply revealed the tormented state of his soul. He argued that Grant's southern policy was not strong enough because it had failed to suppress violence; at the same time it was too strong because it had antagonized southern whites. Sumner asserted his faith in the goodwill of ex-Confederates whom he had recently denounced as incorrigible rebels, and stated that Greeley, as an earlier convert than Grant to the antislavery cause, was a better friend of the freedmen.[15]

The Liberal press hailed Sumner's letter as a bombshell that would explode Republican pretensions of superior concern for the freedmen. But pro-Grant abolitionists wheeled out their heaviest artillery and fired deadly salvos at Sumner's statement. In a letter carried by most Republican papers, Garrison implied that Sumner was a backslider and that Republican vice-presidential nominee Henry Wilson, the other senator from Massachusetts, was a better antislavery man than Sumner. As for Greeley, "he was not even a Free-Soiler, but always a Henry Clay Whig." The Liberal movement was "characterized by the grossest dissimulation," Garrison lectured Sumner, for its Democratic allies "have *not* become converts to the principles of the Republican party—they are simply in masquerade!"[16]

Many of Sumner's oldest abolitionist friends lamented his fall from grace. Samuel Gridley Howe feared that the senator had succumbed to "personal hate & envy" and "become morally insane." Curtis wrote that "since Webster's 'Seventh of March' speech nothing in our political history has seemed to me so sad." John D. Baldwin of the *Massachusetts Spy* told Sumner that "I would as soon curse my whole antislavery record and become a kuklux mourner for the 'lost cause' " as to "participate with you in a movement which uses Horace Greeley . . . to give the Copperheads and ex-rebels control of the government."[17]

[15] Garrison to Sumner, May 27, 1872, Sumner Papers; *The Works of Charles Sumner*, 20 vols., Boston, 1900, XX, 173-95.

[16] *Boston Journal*, Aug. 5, 1872.

[17] Howe to Andrew Dickson White, Aug. 8, 1872, White Papers, Cornell University Library; Curtis to Thomas Nast, Aug. 1, 1872, in Albert Bigelow Paine, *Thomas Nast: His Period and His Pictures*, New York, 1904, p. 243; Baldwin to Sumner, Aug. 6, 1872, Sumner Papers.

Wendell Phillips wanted Sumner to know that "whatever [public] criticism I make on your position will be made with the sharpest regret & wrung from me by the gravest conviction of duty to the negro race which your mistake exposes to such horrible peril." Phillips was soon called upon to discuss Sumner's position. On August 7 a committee of Boston Negroes, noting the conflicting counsel from Sumner and Garrison, asked Phillips' advice. He replied that Greeley's election "means the constitutional amendments neutralized by a copperhead Congress" and "the negro surrendered to the hate of the Southern States." Phillips told the freedmen: "Vote, every one of you, for Grant, if you value property, life, wife, or child. If Greeley is elected, arm, concentrate, conceal your property, but organize for defence. You will need it."[18]

Editor Horace White of the *Chicago Tribune*, describing himself as a "Western Abolitionist," undertook Sumner's defense. Turning Garrison's ad hominem arguments against him, White maintained that after 1854 Garrison was "a less conspicuous leader of the anti-slavery column" than either Sumner or Greeley and therefore less qualified to speak for abolitionists. But though White maintained that the Democrats' "honest and frank" promises to uphold the 14th and 15th Amendments ought to cause joy rather than despair among abolitionists, his reference to Negro-Carpetbag governments as an example of "ignorance and barbarism over intelligence and civilization" probably came closer to his real sentiments. Statements such as this only reinforced Garrison's conviction that abolitionists and free soilers who supported Greeley had sold their birthright.[19]

While some Liberals were reluctant to publicize their abolitionist support because of its potentially negative impact on Democratic voters, the Republican press enthusiastically solicited statements by old abolitionists. The Republican National Committee distributed thousands of copies of a pamphlet titled *Grant or Greeley—Which? Facts and Arguments for the Consideration of the Colored Citizens of the United States*, containing speeches by Garrison, Phillips, and the black abolitionists Frederick Douglass and John Mercer Langston. When Gerrit Smith attended the Republican national convention he was introduced as "the oldest pioneer in the cause of emancipation." The delegates responded "with great enthusiasm," according to reporters, rising in their places, cheering, and calling for Smith to come for-

[18] Phillips to Sumner, Aug. 4, 1872, Sumner Papers; *Boston Advertiser*, Aug. 16, 1872.

[19] Joseph Logsdon, *Horace White, Nineteenth Century Liberal*, Westport, Conn., 1971, pp. 241-42, 247, 248. Although White had supported John Brown and talked like an abolitionist in the late 1850s, he was really as much a free soiler as an abolitionist.

ward. The chairman left the podium and escorted Smith to the platform while the band played "Hail to the Chief." Smith spoke briefly, stating that "the Anti-Slavery battle is not yet fought out—and, until it is, we shall need Grant's continuing leadership." He returned to his seat amid another standing ovation. Eager to clothe themselves in the antislavery mantle, Republicans made much of the event. The *New York Times* praised Smith's speech as "the utterance of an unflinching Abolitionist of the old type," which "furnishes in a nutshell the political argument which today animates the Republican party." It was a "significant fact," added the *Times*, that all the original Anti-Slavery men . . . are now zealous supporters of Gen. Grant."[20]

The *Times* exaggerated, but not much. Of the 104 white abolitionists for whom evidence has been found, 77 favored Grant and 22 backed Greeley, while five others refused to support either candidate. The proportions of Garrisonian and evangelical abolitionists who joined the Liberal movement were almost the same (16 and 18 percent, respectively), while 26 percent of the political abolitionists did so. Though small, this difference reflects the tendency of political abolitionists, like free soilers, to give a lower priority to the issue of Negro rights than did Garrisonians and evangelicals.

Several pro-Grant abolitionists accused their Liberal comrades of backsliding and elitism. They were right in some cases. But it would be a mistake to write off all those who supported Greeley as deserters from the battle for racial justice. Some weight should be given to the words of a post-election editorial by Theodore Tilton. In the 1860s, said Tilton, he had worked to prod the Republicans toward equal rights; in the 1870s he considered it his mission to commit the Democrats to the same policy. Thus he felt great satisfaction "when the Democratic Convention, after fighting for years against the negro, at last in a body tossed up their hats and clapped their hands in honor of the fourteenth and fifteenth amendments." Tilton had given more than 100 speeches for Greeley, which were "as radical and ultimate in their statements of the negro's absolutest rights as I had ever made in those darker days when, for similar speeches, I had been hooted or hissed." Though Greeley lost, the one great achievement of the Liberal/Democratic coalition was that "*the negro is left without a political enemy.*"[21]

In retrospect this appears naive. The Cassandra-like warnings of Phillips and Garrison were more prophetic, for when southern Democrats achieved power they acted more as Phillips predicted than as Tilton hoped. But if one grants the sincerity of those like Tilton who protested that their Liberalism was not an abandonment of the Negro, then the disagreement among most abolitionists in 1872 was more one

[20] *NYT*, June 6, 24, Aug. 7, 1872.   [21] *Golden Age*, Nov. 16, 1872.

of means than ends. In a sense, this was a revival of the old dispute over the efficacy of moral suasion versus legal coercion as the best way to abolish slavery. When the abolitionists began their crusade in the 1830s they hoped to convert slaveholders to voluntary emancipation by Christian and humanitarian appeals. This failed, and some abolitionists turned to disunion, others urged emancipation by government fiat, and a few sanctioned insurrection. These methods also failed; it took a war to abolish slavery. Until 1871 all but a few abolitionists supported the radical Reconstruction program of equal rights enforced by the bayonet if necessary. But turmoil in the South soon began to convince some of them that this policy was a failure. In a way they had come full circle by 1872; they now urged an abandonment of coercion and a return to moral suasion. No law on earth, they said, could protect the equal rights of freed slaves until the hearts and minds of southern whites were converted. A majority of the abolitionists, however, remembering the earlier failure of moral suasion, held to their belief that only through a relentless enforcement of the law could equal rights be assured. Ironically the Garrisonians, antigovernment before the war, had more faith in law and force in 1872 than did the political abolitionists. The explanation of this seeming paradox lies in the greater radicalism of Garrisonians, who now saw the state as a stronger agency of reform than moral suasion.

If support for Grant was a test of continued faith in Reconstruction, three-quarters of the abolitionists passed the test. But those who did not formed the nucleus of a group that nearly doubled in size during the next four years. President Grant's second administration witnessed a growing northern disillusionment with the whole experiment of "radical" Reconstruction. The next two chapters will trace the involvement of former abolitionists in that process.

Chapter Three

Reconstruction Unravels, 1873-1876

Although Grant's landslide victory in 1872 seemed to confirm the northern commitment to Reconstruction, during the next two years the onset of economic depression, the revelations of scandals in government, the increase of disorder in the South, and the glare of publicity focused on "corrupt Negro-Carpetbag regimes" produced a reaction against the Republican party and its southern policy. Capitalizing on voter discontent, Democrats won control of the House in 1874 for the first time in 18 years. Some Republicans began to talk of jettisoning the dead weight of Reconstruction to avoid sinking in 1876. A consensus began to emerge that the federal government must leave the South alone to work out the race problem in its own way. "Our people are tired out with this worn out cry of 'Southern outrages'!!!" wrote one politician in 1875. "Hard times & heavy taxes make them wish the 'nigger,' 'everlasting nigger,' were in – – – – or Africa." "The whole public are tired of these annual autumnal outbreaks in the South," said the U. S. attorney general as he refused a request from the governor of Mississippi for federal troops to protect black voters in 1875. The Democrats carried Mississippi, and the attorney general's remark symbolized the indifference of most northerners to that event.[1]

Many veterans of the antislavery crusade were alarmed by these developments. "I fear a Counter-Revolution," Vice-President Henry Wilson told Garrison in 1874. The old abolitionists, said Wilson, "must call the battle roll anew, and arrest the reactionary movements." Frederick Douglass told a reunion meeting of Philadelphia abolitionists in 1875 that "we need you, my friends, almost as much as ever." Gilbert Haven wanted "the old Anti-Slavery Society revived. Let the old Abolitionists ring [the] bell in pulpit or platform, through the press, by revived organization, and through political parties," he said, "until we completely save the nation."[2]

[1] T. Wilson to Lucius C. Fairchild, Jan. 17, 1875, quoted in William B. Hesseltine, *U. S. Grant, Politician*, New York, 1935, p. 358; Attorney General Edwards Pierrepont quoted in Vernon Lane Wharton, *The Negro in Mississippi, 1865-1890*, Chapel Hill, 1947, p. 194.

[2] Wilson to Garrison, Dec. 17, 1874, WLG Papers; address by Douglass published in *Centennial Anniversary of the Pennsylvania Society for Promoting the Abolition of Slavery . . . April 14, 1875*, Philadelphia, 1875, p. 26; article by Haven in *Independent*, Aug. 26, 1875.

But most of the original abolitionists were too old to start up the machinery of organized agitation again. One veteran wrote in 1870 that "my age & infirmities unfit me for conflict"; another felt "too old to engage anew in controversy." Gerrit Smith told a younger radical who wanted to organize a new reform party that "were I twenty years younger (I am 76 years old) I might be working with you." Nearly half a century after he had written his first antislavery poem, John Greenleaf Whittier reminisced that he had "been fighting for 'causes' half my life. I suppose I am growing old, and am disposed to ask for peace in my day." Even if he had felt more energetic, said Whittier, the moral climate of his youth had disappeared. "The world seems to have drifted past me." Another elderly abolitionist who still felt up to "hard work for 'God and Humanity' as of olden time" nevertheless wrote poignantly: "The great changes political, moral & personal, leave me as a lonely bark beached high upon the drifted sands."[3]

The sordid materialism of the Gilded Age seemed a betrayal of everything the abolitionists had stood for. "The arduous struggle for the abolition of slavery, and the heroic self-sacrifices in the war that followed, seemed to lift the nation up on a higher plane," wrote Lydia Maria Child in 1873. "Who could have thought we should so soon sink deeper than ever in the mire of corruption?" Disgust with the "tainted, rotten . . . moral atmosphere" of national politics estranged some former abolitionists from the very element of the Republican party that backed a strong southern policy. If Benjamin Butler, John Logan, and Oliver Morton "are the true lights of the party," wrote one abolitionist, "I prefer to be counted out."[4]

At a deeper level, disillusionment with the postwar moral climate caused some reformers to lose faith in the improvability of man. "It is heart sickening to read in the News Papers and witness with our eyes and ears so much of crime, and ungodliness, and to know that the great mass of mankind are deeply overwhelmed in ignorance, superstition and guilt," said one old crusader. Such a hopeless prospect made it hard for him to "shake off my sloth" and rededicate himself to

3 William H. Brisbane, diary, entry of Oct. 19, 1870, Brisbane Papers, Wisconsin Historical Society; Joshua Leavitt to Elizur Wright, Nov. 15, 1870, Wright Papers, Library of Congress; Smith to George W. Julian, Sept. 23, 1873, Giddings-Julian Correspondence, Library of Congress; Whittier to Elizabeth Stuart Phelps, 1878, quoted in Albert Mordell, *Quaker Militant: John Greenleaf Whittier*, Boston, 1933, p. 259; Whittier to James T. Fields, June 5, 1879, Fields Papers, Huntington Library; James C. White to Samuel May, June 27, 1883, May-Goddard Papers, Schlesinger Library, Radcliffe College.

4 Child to Sarah B. Shaw, Apr. 13, 1873, Shaw Family Correspondence, New York Public Library; Frederick Douglass to Gerrit Smith, Sept. 24, 1874, Smith Papers, Syracuse University Library; Homer Johnson to James Monroe, Apr. 24, 1874, Monroe Papers, Oberlin College Library.

"the work of the world's moral & spiritual renovation." Franklin B. Sanborn, secretary of the American Social Science Association, wrote that the reform hopes of the association's founders (many of them abolitionists) had been dashed by the realities of the Gilded Age. "We must confess now that we rather overestimated our powers: perhaps even it must be said . . . 'We have thought too well of human nature.' "[5]

Most of the time, however, reformers did not take such a despairing view. While Sanborn found the outlook less hopeful in 1875 than 1865, this meant that "the need of our labors was never greater."[6] Many younger abolitionists enlisted in reform causes in the 1870s. A good number even of the older veterans, despite complaints of fatigue, could be galvanized into action by the threat of a counterrevolution against Reconstruction, as in the election of 1872. Because of their roles as editors of important newspapers, writers or speakers with access to large audiences, founders of black colleges, or members of southern governments, several abolitionists exercised greater influence in racial matters than ever before. Yet on the difficult problem of Reconstruction their counsel became increasingly divided. And the participation of several abolitionists in the civil service reform movement reduced their commitment to Negro rights. The crusade against "Grantism" that began with the Liberal Republican movement broadened after 1872 as the scandals of the second Grant administration and the corruption of southern Republicans came to dominate the headlines. The influential reform weekly the *Nation* became a bellwether of the northern retreat from Reconstruction.

In the South, Wendell Phillips Garrison told his father in 1875, "good government is first to be thought of and striven for. . . . The incidental loss which it may seem to occasion to either race is far less mischievous than the incidental protection accorded to either by bad government."[7] With these words Wendell Garrison showed how far he had strayed from the faith of his father. During the war Wendell had written for the *Liberator* and *Independent*, and his early views on Reconstruction were more radical than his father's. But when he joined the *Nation*'s editorial staff in 1865, young Garrison came under the spell of Edwin L. Godkin's personality and soon began to parrot Godkin's elitism and disenchantment with radicalism. Wendell Garrison's retreat from Reconstruction was an extreme example of what happened to some other abolitionists who became civil service reformers.

[5] William H. Brisbane, diary, entry of Dec. 31, 1869, Brisbane Papers; Sanborn in *Journal of Social Science*, VIII (1876), 23-24.
[6] *Ibid.*
[7] W. P. Garrison to W. L. Garrison, Feb. 7, 1875, WPG Papers.

The *Nation* was founded with financial support from abolitionists who expected it to become a spokesman for the freedmen's interests. The abolitionist backers accepted the young British-born Godkin as editor only after he had assured them of his radicalism on Reconstruction. Wendell Garrison became assistant editor, and his father blessed the *Nation* as heir of the *Liberator*.[8] But from its first issue of July 6, 1865, the *Nation* disappointed and ultimately enraged most of its abolitionist supporters. Although he endorsed Reconstruction in its early years, Godkin could not resist the temptation occasionally to deride radicals as "sentimentalists" (analogous to today's "bleeding-heart liberals"). One abolitionist said bitterly that the *Nation* "seems to be written very much in the same spirit as much that we had in the early days of anti-slavery: 'I am as much of an abolitionist as you are—*but*—.' " It soon became clear that Godkin's true inclination was conservative and that he did not conceive of the *Nation* as a champion of the freedmen but as an intellectual review of politics and the arts modeled on the English *Spectator*. Angry Boston abolitionists withdrew their capital, but this only allowed Godkin to reorganize the company and proceed in his own way.[9]

Following Godkin's lead, Wendell Garrison joined the *Nation*'s crusade for "good government" as zealously as his father had joined the abolitionist movement. The issues of "political corruption, party misrule, public dishonesty and dishonor," he told his father in 1876, should "take precedence at this time of all others." Years later he reminisced with "satisfaction in having helped edit the *Nation* from the beginning, continuing the moral mission of the *Lib[erator]*. . . . I really think the civil-service reformers or mugwumps come nearer to being lineal descendants of the abolitionists than any other existing manifestation of the national conscience."[10]

Garrison's words take on a bitter irony as one reads Godkin's editorials from the 1870s. The Negro-Carpetbag governments, he wrote, were "a disgrace to civilization." Black voters in South Carolina "are as ignorant as a horse . . . as regards the right performance of a voter's duty." Conditions in some areas were so bad that they justified the white counterrevolution: Godkin said of an uprising by New Orleans

[8] The best account of the *Nation*'s origins is William M. Armstrong, "The Freedmen's Movement and the Founding of the *Nation*," *Journal of American History*, LIII (1967), 708-26. See also Armstrong, ed., *The Gilded Age Letters of E. L. Godkin*, Albany, N.Y., 1974, pp. 29-143.

[9] Quotation from Sarah Pugh to J. Miller McKim, Dec. 20, 1866, McKim Papers, New York Public Library. See also Frank P. Stearns, *The Life and Public Services of George Luther Stearns*, Philadelphia, 1907, pp. 332-38.

[10] Garrison to W. L. Garrison, July 9, 1876, Garrison to Francis Jackson Garrison, June 24, 1894, Garrison to William Everett, May 2, 1893, WPG Papers.

whites that there had never been a "case of armed resistance to an established government in modern times in which the insurgents had more plainly the right on their side." Reconstruction was a failure, concluded the *Nation* in 1876, because it had undertaken "the insane task of making newly-emancipated field-hands, led by barbers and barkeepers, fancy they knew as much about government, and were as capable of administering it, as the whites." It was time to put an end to the policy under which "the negro has been made into a fetish for the worship of sentimentalists and impractical idealists."[11]

Such assertions did not go unchallenged by abolitionists. Their chief spokesman was one of the *Nation*'s original backers, Richard P. Hallowell, who accused Godkin in 1874 of "flagrant, wanton disregard of facts . . . mental or moral obfuscation" and "incorrigible stupidity." The *Nation*'s "shameless apostasy" to its founders' intentions had turned it into an ally of "Southern cutthroats," a "ready and reckless apologist for their crimes against the negro." Hallowell doubted whether "the history of journalism affords a more striking illustration of bad faith."[12]

The *Nation*'s course almost caused a breach in the close-knit Garrison family. The paper's defense of Ku Klux violence, Francis Garrison told his brother Wendell, "is simply atrocious." In reply, Wendell said that southern whites had been provoked by "bad government become unendurable." It was time for the freedmen to "drop back" and "refrain from taking a leading part in politics." They "need more than anything else to have the gospel of education, thrift, industry, and chastity preached to them." When the *Nation* endorsed the Democratic effort to organize the Louisiana legislature after a disputed election in 1874, William Lloyd Garrison rebuked his son for the paper's "lack of sympathy with and evident contempt for the colored race." Wendell replied that "it is useless for you and me to exchange arguments on this matter. You see in every Southern issue a race issue, and your sympathies are naturally [with the blacks]," while Wendell tried to view the facts objectively and found it impossible "to draw a moral line among conflicting opinions with absolute certainty." His father's inability to adopt this moral relativism was proof that he took "the narrow view and not the broad view." The elder Garrison was shocked by "such a letter from a son to a father!" If there was "anything that I may fairly claim to understand," he told Wendell, "it is that question to the solution of which, half a century ago, I consecrated my life." The ques-

[11] *Nation*, May 12, 1870, Feb. 22, 1872, Jan. 23, 1873, Sept. 24, Oct. 8, 1874, Aug. 24, 1876, May 24, 1877.

[12] *Index*, Sept. 24, Oct. 22, 1874.

tion "still remained to be settled on the basis of justice," and settlement would be all the harder because Wendell, in a position to influence public opinion, now sided with "those very forces and elements which were furiously arrayed against the anti-slavery movement."[13]

Dissension in the Garrison family was a microcosm of growing abolitionist divisions after 1872. While the *Nation* under Godkin was not an abolitionist paper (Wendell Garrison actually had a minor role in determining editorial policy), it did move in a direction that other important weeklies edited by abolitionists fitfully followed. No abolitionist retreated so far from radicalism as the *Nation*. In fact, a majority remained true to the old faith, and even those who retreated seldom did so unequivocally or in a straight line. Nevertheless, the abolitionist unity of the 1860s was gradually breaking down, helping to pave the way toward ultimate defeat of northern radicalism.

The focal points of abolitionist concern were Louisiana and South Carolina. In 1873 Louisiana became almost a synonym for chaos and violence. Former Republican governor Henry C. Warmoth had bolted the party in 1872 to organize a Liberal Republican coalition with the Democrats. The regular Republicans had nominated William P. Kellogg for governor. Both sides claimed victory in the election; the Warmoth-appointed returning board counted in the Democratic/Liberal coalition, whereupon a federal judge declared this returning board illegal and certified the results reported by the regular Republican board. When Grant sent federal troops to install Kellogg in office, Louisiana Democrats were infuriated. They formed "White Leagues," which attacked black and white Republicans and took scores of lives. In one bloody affray at Colfax in April 1873, 59 blacks were killed. The turmoil in Louisiana and the unsavory reputation of the regular Republicans there caused many northerners to turn against Grant's southern policy even as others demanded greater federal protection for the freedmen.[14]

The hard-line abolitionist position was best stated by the *Boston Commonwealth*, which admitted that the Kellogg administration was hardly a model government but considered the White Leagues far worse. The Colfax massacre proved the necessity for federal troops, said the *Commonwealth*, for "better a squad of soldiers in every township than such fearful slaughterings in a single one. Better military

---

[13] F. J. Garrison to W. P. Garrison, Dec. 29, 1874, W. P. Garrison to F. J. Garrison, Dec. 31, 1874, WPG Papers; W. L. Garrison to W. P. Garrison, Jan. 25, 1875, WLG Papers; W. P. Garrison to W. L. Garrison, Feb. 7, Mar. 28, 1875, WPG Papers; W. L. Garrison to Fanny Garrison Villard, Feb. 2, 7, 1878, W. L. Garrison to W. P. Garrison, Feb. 15, 1878, WLG, Jr., Papers.

[14] Hesseltine, *Grant*, 341-47.

dictation and rule for forty years than the South be given over to law-lessness and blood for a day."[15]

The *Independent* and *Harper's Weekly*, on the other hand, were upset by Republican methods in Louisiana. The Kellogg administra-tion was a "*bogus* government" resting on fraud, they declared. When Frederick Douglass accused the *Independent* of siding with the white man's party in Louisiana, editor Henry C. Bowen denied that "we are one whit less enthusiastic than we have been in our defense of the rights of colored men. But among those rights is not the right to forge tens of thousands of affidavits of rejected voters, or to canvass an elec-tion without any returns." Since it was unclear which party would have won in a fair election, the *Independent* and *Harper's Weekly* joined other northern newspapers in urging Congress to order a new election under federal supervision. But Congress failed to act, and when the White Leagues began killing Republicans, Bowen and Curtis endorsed the use of federal troops to uphold the Kellogg administra-tion. Kellogg remained in office four years while the state was wracked with violence.[16]

Even more than Louisiana, South Carolina became a symbol of Re-construction's potential for both good and evil. Black power was great-er there than in any other state. From 1868 through 1876 a majority of all elected state and federal officeholders were black. At first, aboli-tionists pointed with pride to South Carolina as a showcase of Recon-struction, but as time went on the national press began to publicize events there as proof of the Negro's incapacity for self-government.

The latter viewpoint was expressed most vividly by James Shepherd Pike's book *The Prostrate State*. A former free soiler whose opposition to slavery had been based on aversion to blacks, Pike wrote what be-came a classic description of the "Africanization" of a southern state. The readiness of some former abolitionists to accept Pike's portrayal was a measure of their disillusionment with Reconstruction. James Freeman Clarke visited South Carolina in 1874 and returned to tell his Boston Unitarian congregation that "the facts" presented by Pike "were confirmed by every man whom I saw." In a review of Pike's book for the *Atlantic Monthly*, William Dean Howells, whose boyhood hero had been John Brown, wrote that South Carolina had "so utterly" fallen "prey to the black and white thieves who 'govern it' " that it was a "dismembered and devoured State." Though Pike's assertions were "alarming and shocking" they were "supported by figures and in-stances, which do not permit us to doubt their truth."[17]

[15] *BC*, Apr. 19, 1873.

[16] *Independent*, Jan. 2, Feb. 6, 13, Mar. 27, May 15, 29, 1873; *HW*, Feb. 21, Mar. 14, 1874.

[17] *Christian Union*, June 3, 1874; *Atlantic Monthly*, XXXIII (Feb. 1874), 233-34.

But many abolitionists did doubt their truth. One who lived in the state said that Pike had "so much prejudice as to be an unsafe authority." Gilbert Haven, who knew southern affairs from his travels as a Methodist bishop, admitted that in South Carolina "taxes are heavy, trade and production are low, thieves in the government circles exist," but this was not the whole story. Offsetting it were new roads and schools, improved social services, a revived and desegregated state university, and greater opportunities for black men than in any other state. "The persistent efforts made to bring disgrace" on South Carolina, said Haven, were "the working out" of the old slaveocracy's purpose "to win at the ballot-box what was lost with the cannon." If South Carolina were only sustained "a few years" more "by the votes and the sympathy of the North, she will have made this experiment a permanent and glorious success. . . . But if she is assailed and deserted by her friends, and left to the mercy of her malignant and steadfast foes, she may succumb, and then comes chaos and black night again to all this Southern land."[18]

Although the editors of *Harper's Weekly* and the *Independent* were shaken by Pike's description, they came around to Haven's view by the summer of 1874. Curtis conceded that while the situation in South Carolina was indeed "deplorable," it was better than when "the whole nation was prostrate under the heel of slave-breeders." In any case, said Curtis, "the fundamental conditions of reconstruction, especially equal suffrage," must "of course remain unchanged." The *Independent* insisted that despite "plunder and fraud" that threatened to "stagger the faith and disappoint the hopes" of the Negro's "true friends," the "common people are advancing in education, in the acquisition of property, and in a general sense of the responsibility of citizenship." The Negro was "entitled to patience and charity—or, rather, justice— at the hands of his northern friends. He is the victim still of three centuries of the white man's enforced degradation. How can he be expected to rise above it all in ten years? . . . Of the complete success finally of the experiment of negro suffrage, even in South Carolina, we do not entertain a doubt."[19]

The *Independent*'s faith had been renewed by the nomination of Daniel H. Chamberlain for governor of South Carolina in 1874. To understand why, we must take a brief look at the politics of Reconstruction in the state. Several abolitionists who had come to South Carolina as "carpetbaggers" or as missionaries to the freedmen rose to high positions in the Reconstruction government. Reuben Tomlinson from Philadelphia served as state superintendent of education for the

---

18 *Index*, Nov. 2, 1876; Haven in *Independent*, Mar. 12, Aug. 6, 13, 1874.
19 *HW*, Feb. 14, May 2, 1874; *Independent*, Mar. 12, May 28, Aug. 24, 1874.

Freedmen's Bureau, as a state legislator, and as state auditor. Another Philadelphian, James G. Thompson, came to the sea islands during the war and remained afterwards as a Republican editor in Beaufort and Columbia. Gilbert Pillsbury from Massachusetts was chief organizer of the South Carolina Union League and mayor of Charleston for one term. The most prominent ex-abolitionist in state politics was Daniel H. Chamberlain of Massachusetts, whose youthful idol had been Wendell Phillips. After wartime duty as an officer in a black cavalry regiment, Chamberlain settled in South Carolina, where he served two terms as attorney general and was elected governor in 1874.[20]

Chamberlain, Tomlinson, and Thompson became leaders of an attempt to reform the South Carolina Republican party from within. In 1872 editor Thompson confessed disillusionment with the past four years of Republican rule. He looked back to 1868 when radicals had confidently set out to uproot "the abuses fostered by the pro-slavery spirit which had so long ruled the State." They had hoped to create "an honest, economical but liberal government" that would uplift "the children of those kept in ignorance by slavery." What was the result? The last session of the legislature was "an enormous swindle." Black politicians bore part of the responsibility for this graft, said Thompson, and their constituents were its main victims. Not only did peculation cripple schools and other social services but the enemies of freedom seized upon "every act of fraud . . . every job of extravagance and knavery" as an excuse for counterrevolutionary violence.[21]

Both Chamberlain and Tomlinson were reform candidates for the Republican gubernatorial nomination in 1872. When the nod went instead to Franklin J. Moses, a "scalawag" whom a careful historian has called "as blatant a swindler as ever sat in any gubernatorial chair," several reformers bolted the party and nominated Tomlinson on a rival ticket. A few black politicians backed Tomlinson, but most were hostile to "reform" because it smacked of concessions to white supremacy. Tomlinson appealed to black voters on the basis of his abolitionist record and his 10 years' work for education and equal rights, but the mass of Negroes voted for Moses, giving him more than a two-to-one majority.[22]

[20] See especially Willie Lee Rose, *Rehearsal for Reconstruction: The Port Royal Experiment*, Indianapolis, 1964; Joel Williamson, *After Slavery: The Negro in South Carolina During Reconstruction, 1861-1877*, Chapel Hill, 1965; Wilton B. Fowler, "A Carpetbagger's Conversion to White Supremacy," *No. Car. Hist. Rev.*, XLIII (Summer 1966), 286-88; Walter Allen, *Governor Chamberlain's Administration in South Carolina*, New York, 1888.

[21] Quoted in Rose, *Rehearsal for Reconstruction*, 383.

[22] *Ibid.*, 391. See also John S. Reynolds, *Reconstruction in South Carolina, 1865-1877*, Columbia, 1905, pp. 223-25.

Embittered by this outcome, Tomlinson said to a Negro friend that the black politicians "who assail us old time friends of freedom and good government as Democrats, have no more idea of true Republicanism than a pig has of music. Republicanism and politics to them are a means simply of getting a living without doing any work and of course they stand by the 'party' long after it ceases to represent . . . a single principle of honesty or decency." Nevertheless Tomlinson remained in South Carolina as an activist for both reform and equal rights until driven out by the Democratic restoration in 1877. In 1875 he told an abolitionist reunion that, while much of the "ignorance and vice bequeathed to us by slavery" still existed, "my faith is unfaltering" that the Negro will "yet make a self-respecting and useful citizen."[23]

Tomlinson's faith had been bolstered by the 1874 election. Both Republican factions had nominated reform candidates for governor, but Chamberlain, as the nominee of the regulars, won most of the black votes and the election. He entered office with two goals: to demonstrate that Republicans could govern honestly; and to win Conservative support for his regime as a step toward blurring racial divisions and recruiting whites into a purified Republican party. The first goal he achieved; the second eluded him.

The new governor moved quickly to make economy and efficiency a hallmark of his administration. He proposed measures to lower taxes, simplify their collection, speed up court procedures, streamline the educational system, and eliminate pork-barrel spending. The legislature balked at some of these proposals, which affected special interests and might reduce social services. But with the help of the Democratic minority, Chamberlain jammed through many of his bills. He lowered taxes and reduced expenditures while improving some programs (especially the schools) by eliminating the fraud that had previously plagued them.[24]

Chamberlain's reforms won acclaim in the Democratic press. The *Charleston News and Courier*, his most rabid opponent in the 1874 election, praised him in 1875 as "honest, capable, and fearless." But while earning Democratic plaudits, the governor further divided his own party. Spoilsmen had regarded the reform pledges of 1874 as

---

[23] Tomlinson to William Still, Apr. 14, 1874, quoted in Alberta S. Norwood, "Negro Welfare Work in Philadelphia, Especially as Illustrated by the Career of William Still," M.A. Thesis, Univ. of Pa., 1931, pp. 169-70; Tomlinson to Still, Apr. 12, 1875, printed in *Centennial Anniversary of the Pennsylvania Society for Promoting the Abolition of Slavery*, 73.

[24] Allen, *Governor Chamberlain's Administration*, passim; Williamson, *After Slavery*, 400-405. Thomas C. Holt ("The Emergence of Negro Political Leadership in South Carolina During Reconstruction," Ph.D. Dissertation, Yale University, 1973, pp. 331-34) maintains that some of Chamberlain's retrenchments did reduce public services for the poor.

nothing more than the usual window dressing and were appalled when Chamberlain took them seriously. Of greater concern was the opposition of black leaders who were alarmed by Chamberlain's overtures to Democrats and angered by his patronage policy, which removed a number of Negroes from minor positions. When Chamberlain took office he discovered that 200 of the trial justices (comparable to justices of the peace in other states) were illiterate. Describing this as "a farce and a fraud," he replaced many of them with educated men. He also overhauled the jury system by cleaning out corrupt jury commissioners and replacing them with able men. In December 1875, black legislators threw down the gauntlet by electing William J. Whipper and Franklin J. Moses as circuit court judges. A northern-born black politician, Whipper's reputation for corruption almost matched that of Moses. Because their elevation to the bench would jeopardize the reform image of his administration, Chamberlain refused to sign their commissions. Instead he certified the two sitting judges to serve out four-year terms. An infuriated Whipper appealed to the state Supreme Court, but it upheld Chamberlain's action.[25]

Some black leaders charged the governor with apostasy to the Negro. Several historians have echoed the charge. But this distorts what was apparently a sincere attempt by Chamberlain to overcome white resistance to Reconstruction by proving that interracial government could be "good government." Nevertheless a case can be made affirming Chamberlain's racial ambivalence. Later in his life he became an extreme white supremacist; while this does not prove his tendency in that direction in 1875, it does call into question the depth of his egalitarian convictions. At the height of the Whipper-Moses crisis, Chamberlain told the annual banquet of the New England Society in Charleston that "the civilization of the Puritan and the Cavalier, of the Roundhead and the Huguenot, is in peril"—which came close to echoing southern white fears that their civilization was threatened by "Africanization." Earlier in 1875 William Lloyd Garrison, Jr., had visited Chamberlain while on a trip south for his health. "The weight of the opinion of the strongest republicans I talk with," wrote Garrison privately, "coincides in a measure with the *Nation* talk. Their estimate of the 'niggers' or 'darks' as they call them is very low. Chamberlain does not speak so, but he feels similarly."[26]

[25] Allen, *Governor Chamberlain's Administration*, 106-107 (for the *News and Courier* quotation), 140-41, 194-201, 228-32; Reynolds, *Reconstruction in South Carolina*, 322-26; Holt, "The Emergence of Negro Political Leadership," 334-41.

[26] Allen, *Governor Chamberlain's Administration*, 200-201; Garrison to Ellen Wright Garrison, Feb. 22, 1875, WLG, Jr., Papers. Historians critical of Chamberlain are Lerone Bennett, Jr., *Black Power U.S.A.: The Human Side of Reconstruction, 1865-1877*, Chicago, 1967, esp. 147, 177-79, 372; Peggy Lamson, *The Glor-*

Whatever his feelings, Chamberlain continued to speak out for equal rights. In July 1876 he told a black audience that "if I had to choose between an ignorant ballot and an educated ballot controlled by prejudice, I would say give me the free ballot and I can make it an intelligent ballot." In his speech accepting renomination for governor, he said that while some Republicans had faltered in the faith, "my confidence in [the freedmen's] capacity has never been lost, and I have believed, through all the mismanagement, corruption, and wrongs of their leaders, that . . . the colored masses of South Carolina, were as loyal as any people in this country to the demands and necessity of good government."[27]

Chamberlain's administration helped to revive abolitionist confidence in Reconstruction. But even before Chamberlain took office, outbreaks of anti-Negro violence during the 1874 election had rekindled their radicalism. Democratic tactics in 1874, said William Lloyd Garrison, were a restoration of "the diabolical spirit of slavery" so blatant as to "stir a fever in the blood of age." Francis E. Abbot, abolitionist editor of the free-thought journal *Index*, insisted that southern whites could expect no sympathy from the North "until they drop the infernal cry of a 'white man's government.' . . . All talk of 'reconciliation' and 'clasping hands' is sheerest buncombe, until this stern lesson of the war is learned." Putting it in "the baldest and extremist way," George William Curtis preferred "the party of thieves in the Southern States to the party of murderers."[28]

The worst violence occurred in Louisiana, where the White League raised a rebellion that drove the "usurper" Kellogg from the capitol to take refuge in the federal customs house. From there he wired Washington for troops. Although Grant considered Kellogg "a first-class cuss," he put the army on alert and ordered the White Leaguers to disperse. Abolitionists applauded. The White League deserved no quarter, said the *Independent*. "Crush them, utterly, remorselessly." When the *New York Tribune* denounced the use of troops against "the people of Louisiana," Charles Wesley Slack of the *Commonwealth* deplored "this fashion of talking about 'the people' of the South as if the insurrectionary white leaguers and their supporters were the only people there." Black victims of terrorism "are actually 'people'" too.

ious Failure: Black Congressman Robert Brown Elliott and the Reconstruction in South Carolina, New York, 1973, esp. 153-58, 199, 208-49; and Holt, "The Emergence of Negro Political Leadership," chap. 7.

27 Allen, *Governor Chamberlain's Administration*, 346, 357.

28 Garrison to W. P. Garrison, Sept. 2, 1874, WLG Papers; *Index*, Aug. 27, 1874; *HW*, Sept. 19, 1874.

"Their rights are as real and as sacred as those of their political opponents."[29]

While federal troops maintained an uneasy peace in Louisiana, violence flared elsewhere. But northern voters evidently considered Republican corruption a greater crime than Democratic terrorism, for the Democrats won control of the House of Representatives. Although the economic depression was probably the Republicans' greatest liability in the North, several party leaders believed the "reform" issue had cost them many votes. They began to talk of "unloading" the carpetbaggers as part of a drive to clean up the party for 1876. As Republicans veered toward a southern policy of conciliation, an influential minority of abolitionists—including some who had just been urging draconian action against the White League—tilted in the same direction. The ghost of Horace Greeley had risen, and some of Greeley's 1872 detractors became belated converts to his viewpoint.

A new crisis in Louisiana caused several abolitionists to make an agonized reappraisal of Reconstruction in early 1875. The state election of 1874 had repeated the pattern of two years earlier. On their face the returns gave Democrats a majority in the lower house, but the Republican returning board threw out the results of several parishes on grounds of intimidation and certified the election of 53 Republicans and 53 Democrats, with five cases undecided and referred to the legislature itself. When this body convened in January 1875 the Democrats, in a well-planned maneuver, mustered a bare majority and amid confusion elected a speaker, swore him in, and passed a motion to seat their own contested members. Kellogg asked federal troops to eject the five Democrats who had no election certificates. Branding the White Leaguers "banditti," General Philip Sheridan upheld the conduct of his field commander who had marched into the capitol and expelled the Democrats. Grant in turn sent a special message to Congress endorsing Sheridan's action and requesting legislation to settle the Louisiana imbroglio.[30]

The affair provoked an unprecedented uproar in Congress. "If this can be done in Louisiana," asked Senator Carl Schurz, "how long will it be before it can be done in Massachusetts and Ohio? . . . How long before a soldier may stalk into the National House of Representatives and pointing to the Speaker's mace, say 'Take away that bauble!' "[31] Democrats and reform Republicans sponsored meetings all over the North that denounced Grant and Sheridan as military despots.

Several abolitionists also attacked "this last outrage on the American

---

[29] *Independent*, Sept. 24, 1874; *BC*, Sept. 26, 1874.
[30] Hesseltine, *Grant*, 350-53.
[31] *Cong. Record*, 43 Cong., 2 Sess., p. 367.

system of home-rule." The people of Louisiana, asserted Franklin Sanborn, "not only have the right to turn out Kellogg's government, 'returning board' and all, but it is plainly their duty to do so. . . . The shocking farce has gone on long enough." Although Francis Abbot had supported Grant up to this point, he now proclaimed that "the people of the North are sick of . . . this half-horse, half-alligator Kellogg monstrosity, begotten in fraud and suckled in corruption."[32]

But most abolitionists approved of the army's intervention. The administration's strongest support came from New England, where abolitionists helped to rally public opinion behind the president. The *Commonwealth* thought Sheridan's description of the White Leaguers as banditti was "the first bold and truthful words that have come up officially from this land of blood." In reply to those who said peace would reign in the South if federal troops were withdrawn, the *Massachusetts Spy* agreed that indeed it would, especially if black people would also "forget that they are citizens, abstain from voting, take their children out of school . . . and settle down quietly, content to work on the plantations for such wages as their masters chose to give them." With the backing of *Zion's Herald*, journal of the New England Methodist Conference edited by former abolitionist Bradford Peirce, Methodist ministers in the Boston area unanimously adopted a resolution endorsing Sheridan and Grant. William Lloyd Garrison proclaimed that the contest in Louisiana was "essentially the old [antislavery] conflict in another form." The "rebels" were "still as perfidious, as brutal, as law-despising, as disloyal, as before their treasonable revolt." Most of Garrison's old allies joined the chorus, praising their leader's "tremendous bugle blast" which had rallied the friends of freedom when it looked like "Grant and Sheridan would be left alone and swept away by the overwhelming tide of negro hate and party timidity."[33]

In a dramatic confrontation, Wendell Phillips almost turned an anti-Grant meeting at Faneuil Hall into an endorsement of the president. As speaker after speaker showered maledictions on the administration, Phillips sat quietly in the gallery. Several people in the audience spotted him and began calling for him to come forward. The chairman ignored the clamor as long as he could but was finally forced to invite Phillips to the podium. The scene resembled the early days of abolitionism. Once again the great orator mastered a hostile audience in Boston's hall of liberty. Amid catcalls and hisses, interspersed with a

32 *Springfield Republican*, Jan. 1, 8, 1875; *Index*, Jan. 21, 1875.
33 *BC*, Jan. 9, 1875; *Mass. Spy*, Jan. 1, 22, 1875; *ZH*, Jan. 21, 28, 1875; Garrison in *Boston Journal*, Jan. 13, 1875; Samuel Johnson to Garrison, Jan. 13, 1875, Abigail Kelly Foster to Garrison, Mar. 16, 1875, WLG Papers.

growing volume of applause, Phillips defended the legality and necessity of military intervention. "When the negro in the Southern States looks around on the State government about him and sees no protection," he said, "has he not a full right, an emphatic right, to say to the National Government at Washington, 'Find a way to protect me, for I am a citizen of the United States?' . . . I should deem myself wanting in my duty as an old Abolitionist (loud hissing and applause), if I did not do everything in my power to prevent a word going out from this hall that will make a negro or a white Republican more exposed to danger." "Men of Boston," Phillips concluded. "If these resolutions [against the administration] are passed, they will carry consternation and terror into the house of every negro in Louisiana. (Applause, hisses, and groans.) They will carry comfort to every assassin in New Orleans. (Hisses and applause.)" Phillips won a large minority and perhaps even a majority of the audience to his view. When a vote was taken on the resolutions, the chairman ruled that they had been adopted although some observers believed that the "nays" were louder than the "ayes."[34]

Phillips' speech received national publicity. From Peoria, Illinois, a reader reported that it had made a strong impact there even in cold print. "Wendell Phillips is a power in politics, outside the throne," he wrote, "and we would rather have him help rule the nation than nine-tenths that now do so." But the comment of the *New York Times* was closer to the truth. "Wendell Phillips and William Lloyd Garrison are not exactly extinct forces in American politics," declared the *Times*, "but they represent ideas in regard to the South which the great majority of the Republican Party have outgrown."[35] A number of abolitionists had also "outgrown" such sentiments. Of the 42 former abolitionists whose opinions on the Louisiana issue are known, 12 (29 percent) opposed the army's intervention while 30 agreed with Phillips and Garrison. The differences among the three groups of abolitionists were sharper than in 1872: while 87 percent of the Garrisonians and 80 percent of the evangelicals backed Grant in 1875, only 47 percent of the political abolitionists did so.

Although the 71-percent abolitionist support for the Grant-Sheridan policy demonstrated a strong continuing commitment to Reconstruction, it also indicated erosion of earlier solidarity, especially compared with the nearly united front during the 1874 elections. Particularly significant was the stand of *Harper's Weekly* and the *Independent*.

[34] Phillips, *Speech in Faneuil Hall on the Louisiana Difficulties*, Boston, 1875. See also *Boston Journal and Boston Advertiser*, Jan. 16, 1875, and *BC*, Jan. 23, 1875.

[35] *BC*, Feb. 20, 1875; *NYT*, June 1, 1876.

While Curtis and Bowen avowed their undiminished fidelity to Negro rights, by 1875 they were convinced that the policy of force must give way to a policy of conciliation.

Less than two months after it had demanded the crushing of White Leagues, the *Independent* did an about-face and proclaimed that southern violence had been exaggerated by the northern press and that federal intervention was an unconstitutional aggravation rather than solution of the problem. Unconscious of parallels with proslavery rhetoric, the *Independent* began to insist that "the difficulties of the social problem in Southern society must mainly be disposed of by Southern society itself, and not by any outside power." When Governor Adelbert Ames of Mississippi pleaded for federal troops to protect Republican voters during the crucial state election of 1875, the *Independent* scorned Ames (one of the ablest carpetbag governors) as "a poltroon and a humbug. . . . If this condition of things is the best that Republicans can achieve in Mississippi, then the sooner they step aside the better for both races." After the Democrats had "redeemed" Mississippi, the *Independent* declared that although "suffering and wrong" would occur before the race problem worked itself out, there was no longer any alternative. "The effort of the Republican party, by Federal legislation, to protect the local rights of the colored people . . . must be set down as a failure."[36]

Within two months of the 1874 election, Curtis of *Harper's Weekly* also reversed his field and moved away from militancy. Alarmed by the army's interference in Louisiana and by House passage in February 1875 of a "force bill" (buried in the Senate) giving the president authority to suspend the writ of habeas corpus in four southern states, Curtis wrote that if "the citizenship of the negro [can be] maintained only at the cost of the traditional securities of freedom," the cost was too high. It was a "fatal error . . . for a party devoted to freedom to put forward the bayonet as its symbol." No matter how "humane and generous" the motivation, it was "not wise to expect the national power to do by force of arms what can be done only by moral processes and by time." The backlash provoked by "the habit of invoking military force at every turn" would hurt blacks most of all, for it would bring the Democrats to power in 1876 and put an end to civil as well as military enforcement of Negro rights.[37]

A majority of abolitionists (albeit a dwindling one) disagreed with Curtis and continued to advocate military protection of the freedmen.

[36] *Independent*, Nov. 19, Dec. 24, 1874, Feb. 4, 25, Sept. 16, 1875, Feb. 24, 1876.
[37] *HW*, Jan. 23, 30, Feb. 20, 27, Mar. 6, 1875; Curtis to Thomas Nast, Feb. 7, 1875, quoted in Albert Bigelow Paine, *Thomas Nast: His Period and His Pictures*, New York, 1904, pp. 304-305.

Methodist editor Arthur Edwards still thought "gunpowder and bayonets" were needed for "reform work" in the South. The Mississippi Plan of 1875 convinced John D. Baldwin that no southern white man could be trusted. During the Mississippi election, said Baldwin, state Conservative leader L. Q. C. Lamar had given speeches in the North promising to respect the freedmen's rights if the Democrats won, while in Mississippi he condoned "terrorism, ballot-box stuffing, and fraudulent voting." Such would be the fruits of "home rule" everywhere if federal troops were withdrawn.[38]

But to James Redpath, the Scots-born journalist who joined the abolitionist movement after coming to America in 1850, the issues were not so clear-cut. In 1876 Redpath was secretary of a Senate committee investigating the Mississippi election of the previous fall. He wrote most of the majority report that detailed the methods by which Mississippi Democrats had converted a losing margin of 30,000 votes at the prior election to a majority of 30,000 in 1875.[39] In his report and in two series of newspaper articles, Redpath spared no adjectives in his denunciation of the "miscreants" who had "slain in cold blood . . . thousands of Negroes and Northern men and Southern white Republicans" in the South since 1865. The Mississippi election was a "military revolution" featuring "wholesale murders and midnight assassinations." But there was "another side to even the Mississippi question," said Redpath. Many of the county governments were "a farce." Men who could not count were county treasurers; men who could not read were members of school boards; men who knew nothing of law were justices of the peace. Slavery, not black people, was responsible for this situation, but blaming the past would not solve the problems of the present. Redpath insisted that abolitionists must discard "cant and sentimental philanthropy" and take a hard look at the facts. They must realize that "our black ward is in very truth a barbarian and needs our best efforts to uplift him in the scale of civilization, and that it is not by denunciations even of the Mississippi assassins, but by earnest and vigilant efforts to educate him, that we shall ever be proud of him."

Reconstruction as it had been carried out thus far, wrote Redpath, was a failure for which "we are to blame. We knew the Negro to be timid, unarmed, illiterate; and yet we left him in the midst of the fiercest fighters on this planet, and expected him to rule them. In Mis-

---

[38] *NWCA*, Oct. 20, 1875; *Mass. Spy*, Dec. 31, 1875.

[39] *Mississippi in 1875, Report of the Select Committee to Inquire into the Mississippi Election of 1875*, Senate Reports, #527, 44 Cong., 1 Sess., 2 vols., Washington, 1876. Redpath presented his correspondence as secretary of the committee to the Astor Library in New York with instructions to keep the collection closed for 10 years because publicity might endanger the lives of his informants. The collection is now in the manuscript division of the New York Public Library.

sissippi his power went down in violence and blood. So will it disappear, unless we act promptly, in South Carolina and Louisiana." But what could be done to solve this "most complex problem"? A "let-alone" policy "means massacre." On the other hand, "if we give complete military protection to the Negro in all elections . . . where there is a large black majority we shall establish a system of government which no white race on the face of this earth either ought to endure or will endure." The only policy with a chance of success was federal enforcement of equal rights *coupled with* "a system of compulsory education [for] black and white alike, disfranchising every adult, without regard to race, who is not able to read and write. If we had adopted this policy ten years ago, every adult male in the South would have been able to read and write to-day."[40]

Redpath was somewhat taken aback by the response to his articles, for Democrats cited them to justify the repressive methods he had condemned and the *Independent* lamented that "the problem is an absolutely insoluble one for the present generation. . . . Let the Negroes exercise their rights as citizens, and their government is almost sure to be corrupt; but the alternative is . . . virtual disfranchisement and slavery." When Redpath protested that he had not said the problem was insoluble, the *Independent* agreed that the solution lay in education. Yet this was "a very slow process. . . . The question we ask, with no little anxiety, is: Will religion and education . . . give us, at last, allowing them time enough, equality of political and social rights at the South? They *must*, for it is our only hope."[41]

For many abolitionists, especially those involved in freedmen's education, this formula of time, education, and hope became their creed well before Booker T. Washington appeared on the scene. A decade of experience had convinced them by 1875 that although black people were potentially equal to whites, the legacy of slavery had made the path to equality long and steep.

[40] Articles by Redpath in *NYT*, July 3, 8, 27, 1876, and *Independent*, Mar. 2, 23, Aug. 3, 31, 1876.
[41] *Independent*, Aug. 3, 31, Sept. 28, 1876, July 5, 1877.

Chapter Four

Time, Education, and Bootstraps

Antebellum reformers had expected rapid social change to be accomplished through the cumulative regeneration of individuals. This conviction sprang from evangelical Protestantism's emphasis on the immediate expiation of sin by conversion to God's truth. The evangelical revolt against predestinarianism produced the belief not only that individuals could voluntarily take the first steps to salvation by renouncing personal sins, but that once they stopped sinning, social evils like slavery, intemperance, prostitution, and war would also cease. This underlay the abolitionists' demand for *immediate* emancipation. When emancipation came, of course, it did so with startling suddenness but not through the agency of individual regeneration. Nevertheless in the excitement of victory, some abolitionists celebrated the triumph of immediatism as if the Battle of Armageddon were already won. "A nation has been born in a day," wrote one in 1869; another agreed that "in the near future" the freedmen "will outrank the majority of the Southern whites as much in mental attainments as they already do in the capacity for other kinds of work" and become "the ruling race in the South."[1]

But the experiences of Reconstruction undermined the immediatism of evangelical abolitionists while reconfirming their conviction that social reform could be achieved only through changes in the hearts and minds of men. "The joy that was felt in . . . the emancipation of the slaves, dazzled the imagination and blinded the mind to the immense complications involved in the new order of things," confessed the secretary of the American Missionary Association (AMA) in 1875. Right after the war, said the president of a Baptist freedmen's school in 1880, "we thought that the school and the mission might almost vie with the sword in the rapidity and completeness of their work." But "these illusions have been dispelled and the real nature of the work has become manifest." It "is a great work, and must require long years of patient, steady toil. A hurrah and a rush cannot effect anything permanent." After a decade in Alabama, an abolitionist professor at Talladega College concluded that "it will take as long to destroy the effects of slavery as it had to do its dreadful work of ruin." The racism of whites and the

[1] Linda Slaughter, *The Freedmen of the South*, Cincinnati, 1869, p. 177; *National Anti-Slavery Standard*, Dec. 18, 1869.

mark of oppression on blacks were "internal diseases," said the AMA, which could not be remedied by "external" forces. The Negro's "elevation and progress," agreed another Baptist educator, "like the elevation and progress of all others, are first internal, then external . . . first in character, then in environment; first intellectual, moral, spiritual, then industrial, financial, social."[2]

For secular abolitionists the impact of Darwinism also helped to modify immediatist convictions. The popularization of Darwin was well under way by the 1870s, and following the lead of Herbert Spencer many Americans began to apply the concepts of biological evolution to social problems. Social change, they argued, could not be effected overnight by the conscious agency of man but only gradually, over many generations, by the operation of natural forces beyond the control of man. In 1875 a journalist named Abram W. Stevens, who had been converted to abolitionism as a young man in the 1850s, confessed that his wartime expectations of a racial millennium had been naive. "The discovery of Evolution," he wrote, taught that "all our efforts at reform, all our struggle and striving, are for naught." Social change "that is hastened or brought about by violent means is, so far as true progress is concerned, a *stumble*, not a step. It may be questioned if even the anti-slavery reform were not at last consummated too precipitately; if a more gradual emancipation, including a preparatory education for freedom, might not have been better." Darwinism did not teach, said Stevens, that man should sit back and let nature do *all* the work. But man's efforts should be those that harmonized with evolution instead of those that tried to hurry it up or transcend it. Since education was a means of "*formation* rather than reformation," it was compatible with evolution and therefore the "most efficient means of promoting the moral improvement of society." But it would not bring change immediately. "For this work the 'eternal years of God' are needed, and all 'evils' incident to its gradual accomplishment we must be patient and brave to endure."[3]

Other abolitionists also acknowledged the influence of Darwinism, though less directly than did Stevens. Wendell Garrison reviewed books on evolution for the *Nation* and pronounced Darwin "*the* man of our epoch, the greatest scientist & the greatest theologian of recent times." Traces of social Darwinism can be seen in Garrison's assertion that the Negro like other races must travel "the dusty and rugged

---

[2] *AM*, xix (Nov. 1875), 242, xx (May 1876), 100-101; Seth T. Axtell, president of Leland University, in *HMM*, ii (July 1880), 149-50; George W. Andrews to Erastus M. Cravath, Jan. 13, 1874, AMA Archives; *Thirty-Sixth Annual Catalogue of the Officers and Students of Roger Williams University, 1899-1900*, Nashville, 1899, p. 29.

[3] *Index*, Mar. 18, Apr. 15, 1875.

highway of competition." It had taken the white race "four to five centuries to traverse the space in social progress through which the Republican party with its frantic law-making has been trying to project the colored man in two Presidential terms." In 1876 James Russell Lowell, poet and essayist of the antislavery movement, said that radical Reconstruction had been based on the mistaken notion, which he had once shared, that "human nature is as clay in the hands of a potter instead of being, as it is, the result of a long past & only to be reshaped by the slow influences of an equally long future."[4]

At least one antislavery veteran, former Congressman George W. Julian, explicitly challenged the relevance of Darwinism to social problems. The "plausible" but dangerous teaching that "social progress is to be wrought only by gradual development," he wrote in 1878, "is remarkably solacing to a certain order of minds" who "embrace it as a welcome scapegoat for their laziness or moral indifference." Although natural selection and the survival of the fittest might explain development in the animal world, said Julian, "social evolution is chiefly the result of efforts consciously put forth for the purpose." Reliance solely on natural forces "would substitute a sickly moral fatalism for those deeds of heroism and self-sacrifice which have . . . lighted the world on its way to higher truth."[5]

Missionary educators of the freedmen shared this conviction. Too many "good-natured people regard time [alone] as an efficient agent in reform," declared the American Missionary Association. "The lapse of time did not check the growing power of slavery. It required the courageous, toilsome, and dangerous martyr-age of the abolition struggle." But while chary of Darwinisn in either its social or biological forms, evangelical abolitionists nevertheless believed that time *plus* education and moral regeneration were necessary to cure "the political and social evils" of the postwar South. Laws had destroyed the "superstructure" of slavery but left the "foundation" untouched, said one. This foundation was the "antagonism of races, the ignorance of the blacks, and the prejudices of the whites," which were "embedded in the *minds and hearts* of men" and could "only be overcome by education" which in the end would prove a "far more radical remedy" than legislation.[6]

[4] Garrison to William Lloyd Garrison, July 8, 1877, WPG Papers; *Nation*, Feb. 10, 1870, Feb. 4, 1875; Lowell quoted in Martin Duberman, *James Russell Lowell*, Boston, 1966, p. 276.

[5] Julian, "Is the Reformer Any Longer Needed?" *North American Review*, CXXVII (Sept.–Oct. 1878), 237-39, 244. Ironically, in spite of this reaffirmation of the reform credo, Julian had already retreated from racial radicalism and joined the Democratic party in 1876. Patrick W. Riddleberger, *George Washington Julian, Radical Republican*, Indianapolis, 1966, chaps. 9-11.

[6] *AM*, New Series, I (Jan. 1, 1877), 1-3, XIX (Apr. 1875), 73-74.

This did not mean that laws were useless. The AMA and other missionary societies vigorously supported the Reconstruction enforcement acts of 1870–1871 and Charles Sumner's civil rights bill. But while the Negro's rights must be protected, said abolitionist Michael Strieby, AMA secretary for more than 30 years, he must also "be so enlightened as to use and not abuse these rights." The root of the race problem was not in the Negro's "color or party, but with the man himself—with his ignorance, his degradation." When the black voter became a virtuous citizen, an owner of property with a stake in the community, "he will need no soldiers to guard him to the polls, and his vote will represent the man and not the musket. . . . *The remedy, then, is not to change his color or his party, but his character.*"[7]

The *Independent's* conversion to this viewpoint was an important cause of its disaffection from radical Reconstruction by 1875. "Four millions of ignorant and imbruted serfs cannot be made into voters and officeholders by an edict," wrote managing editor William Hayes Ward, a second-generation abolitionist who became increasingly responsible for editorial policy as Bowen grew older. The "most urgent endeavor" was not to pass more civil rights laws, but to "lead these Negroes into a higher intelligence; to reform and elevate their standards of morality; to teach them industry, temperance, thrift; to preach to them the pure religion of Christ." Impatient souls were "beseeching us to take some quicker method than that of individual regeneration," wrote Ward, but there was no shortcut. The roots of black dependence and white racism were sunk so deep in the centuries-old soil of slavery that they could not be pulled out quickly. "Take time—half a century, at least—and spend these years in unwearied denunciation of this wicked prejudice. . . . Spend them in making the negro the equal in intelligence and virtue to his white neighbor. Make him worthy of freedom and able to maintain it, and by and by he will get his rights."[8]

Thus by 1875 many abolitionists had altered the priorities of the 1860s. At the end of the Civil War, the enactment of freedom and equal rights by law was their foremost concern; a decade later the uplift of freedmen to the level of the rights conferred on paper had become the most pressing need. The social and economic realities they witnessed in the South convinced some abolitionists that political Reconstruction had put the cart before the horse by granting the freedmen rights before they were capable of exercising or defending them. But despite the mocking gibes of their old enemies, abolitionist disillu-

[7] *Ibid.*, XXXIII (Jan. 1879), 1-2. Italics in original.
[8] *Independent*, Feb. 4, 25, 1875.

sionment with Reconstruction did not necessarily mean disenchantment with the goal of racial equality.

James Redpath was not the first abolitionist whose description of the freedmen caused Democrats to chortle "I told you so." In 1869 one of the most militant of the old Garrisonians, Parker Pillsbury, visited the south Atlantic states and wrote a series of controversial articles about them. His observations persuaded him that "reconstruction, so far, is a failure." Although a radical suffragist in principle, Pillsbury thought black people at this stage of their development needed "bread, clothes, education, houses, homes, fields, farms" more than the ballot. Appalled by the drunkenness, adultery, disease, squalor, destitution, and even infanticide he professed to have seen among the freedmen, he portrayed these things as the bitter fruits of bondage. "Slavery was the one sole cause of the terrible devastation and desolation under which the South reels to-day, and from which it cannot recover in a hundred years under any policy. Nor under the present policy in a thousand, if ever."[9]

Ignoring Pillsbury's condemnation of slavery, the Democratic press seized gleefully on his articles as evidence that he had finally seen the light and now realized how quixotic his crusade for the benighted Negro had been. Not at all, replied Pillsbury. "True, I did find the condition of most of the colored people much more deplorable than I expected. . . . But that is no reason why an abolitionist should repent of his labors and sacrifices in their behalf." Indeed, it only confirmed his "loathing" for those who "enslaved, degraded, brutalized them."[10]

Pillsbury had written his articles in the hope of stimulating greater efforts to overcome the freedmen's "moral and material depression." But for some readers his depiction of squalor and immorality only confirmed their image of the Negro as an inferior race. Several abolitionists rushed into print to repair the damage. Thomas Wentworth Higginson termed Pillsbury a prophet of gloom whose words must be taken with a grain of salt. "It is probably many years since he has been in any company of a hundred people," said Higginson, "of whom he did not honestly think it his duty to mention that they were steeped in corruption, immersed in iniquity, and likely in a few days to wade knee-deep in human gore." This trait made him "effective, though depressing, as an Abolitionist" but was out of place and even tragic now, for after "devoting half his life" to freeing the slaves he "seems ready to devote the rest of it to proving their unworthiness of freedom." Higginson branded as "wantonly false" Pillsbury's charges of widespread

9 *Revolution*, Oct. 14, 1869; *Independent*, Nov. 4, 1869.
10 *Revolution*, Nov. 11, Dec. 2, 1869, Feb. 17, 1870.

black intemperance, adultery, and infanticide. The general verdict of observers since emancipation had instead "been greatly to the credit of the freedmen." As colonel of a black regiment during the war, Higginson had marveled at their capacity for improvement. "Never was there a race so obstinately resolved to live and vindicate itself, in spite of croakers and calumniators."[11]

A Quaker abolitionist who had lived on the South Carolina sea islands since 1862 stated that Pillsbury's articles were based on a "hasty glance" at conditions and contained "more exaggeration" than anything else written on the subject. Another abolitionist, who had worked with the freedmen in Memphis since 1863, declared flatly that "as a result of six years' acquaintance with our colored people, I am disappointed in them only in their favor; they have done and are doing better than I, born an abolitionist, have dared to hope." And Parker Pillsbury's brother Gilbert, who had been in South Carolina for five years, published a statement countering many of his brother's assertions. "We have made *great general progress* on the whole," Gilbert Pillsbury told northern friends, "but don't leave us alone. . . . The old inclination to crush and rob and keep in ignorance the colored race, is as strong as ever. . . . If abandoned by their great northern deliverers . . . their liberty, which cost the nation so dear, would not long exist."[12]

The controversy over Parker Pillsbury's articles sheds light on a problem that faced abolitionists who worked with the freedmen. Many of them agreed privately with at least some of Pillsbury's statements, but to say so publicly might dismay friends and delight enemies. The monthly magazines of the mission societies regularly printed letters from teachers to keep patrons informed about the work. In response to a request for such a letter, one northern teacher in Georgia wrote that "I am almost afraid to write the truth, it is so discouraging." Another noted that "those who have been longest in the field hesitate the most about writing" for publication. "If we give *facts* as we see them, our Northern friends either entirely discredit us, or we are told that we make the picture so dark that the churches are discouraged and the collection of funds hindered." On the other hand, there was a danger in presenting only the bright side, for this encouraged unrealistic expectations that would produce greater disillusionment in the end. "We think that the churches should know something of the obstacles and

11 *NYTrib.*, Nov. 24, 1869; *Independent*, June 30, 1870.
12 John A. Hunn in *Independent*, Dec. 2, 1869; A. M. Sperry in *BC*, July 3, 1869; Pillsbury to John W. Alvord, Jan. 10, 1870, in Alvord, *Letters from the South, Relating to the Condition of Freedmen*, Washington, 1870, pp. 11-12.

58

discouragements of the work; else how can they appreciate its importance and its difficulties?"[13]

The mission societies and their friends in the northern press never fully resolved this dilemma. Usually they accentuated the positive, publishing letters from teachers who wrote that "this has been the pleasantest field of labor I have ever been in," or "the progress made is indeed encouraging." The president of the Methodists' Claflin University in South Carolina declared that, contrary to the numerous accounts of the Negro's "inability, indolence, and general want of thrift," the freedmen "exhibit, as a general rule, as much industry, intelligent thrift and earnest improvement" as working-class whites in the North. The *Independent*, which blew hot and cold in its estimate of the freedmen's condition, often cited such items as the accumulation of $7,000,000 of land by Georgia blacks or the success of Negro cooperatives in South Carolina as evidence of "most remarkable" advances. "Who shall longer doubt whether colored men have brains or whether they should possess and exercise all the rights of American citizenship?"[14]

These sentiments were for publication; the teachers' private letters were less optimistic. A niece of Lydia Maria Child teaching in Richmond lamented the venality of black politicians and the ignorance of their constituents. Even "if I am an anti Slavery New Englander," she wrote, "I think it would have been a great deal better for the colored people to have had nothing to do with office for the next ten years." The most frequent complaints by white teachers were of lying, petty thieving, and sexual promiscuity. An AMA official in Savannah wrote privately that "they do *lie* so! They *do* steal—I hope no Rebel will get hold of this—they do have as many women as Mormons!" The principal of the AMA's LeMoyne Institute in Memphis reported that sexual offenses had forced several students to leave school. Some of "our most promising girls" had been "ruined" in this way, and "we are all well nigh discouraged."[15]

On the principle that northern supporters should know the worst as well as the best, missionary magazines decided to publish letters from teachers reflecting discouragement as well as confidence. Many of these letters followed a format that became almost a formula: slavery

[13] Lizzie Parsons to Erastus M. Cravath, Mar. 1, 1871, Samuel S. Ashley to Michael E. Strieby, Dec. 8, 1876, AMA Archives.

[14] *AM*, XIV (Oct. 1870), 222-23; *ZH*, Dec. 17, 1874; *Independent*, Sept. 25, 1873, Sept. 2, 1875.

[15] Abby B. Francis to Ednah Dow Cheney, Feb. 13, 1870, Cheney Papers, Boston Public Library; W. L. Clark to E. M. Cravath, June 3, 1871, A. J. Steele to M. E. Strieby, Mar. 20, July 10, 1876, AMA Archives.

was even worse than abolitionists had realized; its vices persisted into freedom and would require long, hard work to overcome; those freedmen reached by the elevating influences of northern Christianity and education had already shown marked improvement; this was all the more reason to redouble our efforts.

One issue of the *American Missionary*, for example, printed letters lamenting the freedmen's lack of punctuality, their "persistent carelessness, their lack of desire for true religion." A teacher in Texas was "amost wholly in despair" because her charges were "so quarrelsome, unforgiving and revengeful; but their worst fault is their untruthfulness. . . . I have become so doubtful of their veracity that I dare not appeal to them when I wish to learn the truth of anything." In 1876 President E. O. Thayer of Bennett College in South Carolina, a Methodist freedmen's school, confessed that having been brought up as an abolitionist he had considered Negroes a "much-abused class of people who differed from white folks only in their tanned complexions." His southern experiences had "given me different, and perhaps less exalted, views of them, though the effect has been to greatly increase rather than diminish my interest in their welfare." Few physical marks of bondage were left, "but the scars made by the awful system of slavery on their moral natures seem almost indelible." Like other teachers, Thayer described the freed slaves less as docile, happy, childlike Samboes than as amoral tricksters whose traits of cunning, dissimulation, and theft had evolved as survival techniques in slavery. To function in the environment created by these vestiges of bondage, said Thayer, teachers had to be careful whom they trusted, even though "it is an uncomfortable thing to distrust those for whose welfare you are daily laboring." Fortunately, "where education has made any progress, this state of affairs becomes greatly modified for the better"; that was why "we urge so much the necessity of pushing forward this branch of our missionary service with increased zeal."[16]

One of the most ambitious efforts to analyze these problems was a book by Charles Stearns published in 1872, *The Black Man of the South, and the Rebels*. Stearns was a Garrisonian from Massachusetts who in 1854 had gone to Kansas where he soon abandoned his pacifism and took up a Sharp's rifle. In 1866 he bought a 1500-acre plantation in Georgia, planning to operate it as a cooperative with his black employees sharing the profits. By 1872 his experiences as a plantation owner had modified whatever "rose-colored views" he had brought south. "It is well for us that the future is not often revealed," he wrote,

[16] *AM*, XIV (Oct. 1870), 220; *ZH*, Nov. 16, 1876.

for "if I had then known what I know to-day, I should not have been likely to have engaged in this almost Quixotic enterprise."[17]

When he first arrived, Stearns was shocked by the disorderly condition of the plantation, with tools lying about, fences and buildings unpainted, dirt and garbage strewn aimlessly, animals allowed to wander anywhere. He soon imposed a degree of New England order on this chaos, but keeping things in order proved difficult. He was distressed by the freedmen's carelessness with tools, which he recognized as a product of slavery. Stearns also noted apathy and lack of perseverance among many blacks; they were content to do things in any old slipshod way and were indifferent toward self-betterment. "This listlessness of mind is one of the natural consequences of slavery," he wrote, "but it is none the less a tremendous obstacle in the way of their mental improvement." It was also an obstacle to the efficient running of a plantation, and Stearns almost gave up in despair. "I can never cultivate a farm successfully with the blacks as laborers," he wrote in his diary in 1870. "Nothing can be done without incessant and minute supervision of them, such as I am not able to give." But he stuck it out, and at the end of six years he evaluated the experiment as a qualified success. The freedmen were not yet up to New England standards, he admitted, but they were more skilled, industrious, and honest than when he had come.[18]

Despite Stearns' support for radical Reconstruction, he conceded that the freedmen's ignorance partly justified southern resistance. "Life long friend of the colored race as I have been," he wrote, "still with my present knowledge of the incapacity of the *uneducated* blacks I could not consent for them to be rulers over me and my children." Education thus became one of the chief priorities of his mission. Stearns had been appalled by the apparent stupidity of the freedmen when he first arrived. "Not a man, woman, or child knew a letter of the alphabet [or] how to count." Many of them looked at Stearns with an "idiotic stare and shame-facedness" when he asked them questions. "It seemed to have been the settled purpose of their masters to reduce these poor creatures as nearly to the condition of brutes" as possible. Stearns put his wife and mother to work as teachers, imported another abolitionist as schoolmaster, and after six years he could write that education had made a "vast difference. . . . In no respect do they seem the same individuals that they were on my first arrival."[19]

17 Stearns, *The Black Man of the South, and the Rebels,* New York, 1872, pp. 20-39, quotation from 28.

18 *Ibid.,* 72-86, 278-319, 338-39, quotations from 279, 339.

19 *Ibid.,* 59-71, 427, quotations from 427, 59, 60, 62.

Stearns admitted to less success in changing patterns of black behavior. He learned the hard way to lock up or nail down everything on the plantation. His New England propriety was shocked by the sexual mores in the quarters. Realizing that these things also were legacies of slavery, he had hoped that the children could be taught middle-class values, but in this he was disappointed. "Sickening as it is to contemplate," he wrote, "this 'rising generation' does not hold out a very alluring prospect of usefulness. It is true that they will be more intelligent than their parents, but I fear that their morals will be no better." They took their cues in these matters from parents and siblings rather than from white teachers. Stearns thought the only hope lay in the establishment of boarding schools where children would be free from their parents' contaminating influence.[20]

To friends of the freedmen who might be discouraged by his portrait, Stearns said that no good purpose would be served by describing the freed slave "as only an injured martyr, possessing all the virtues and none of the vices of our common manhood." Hoping to avoid Pillsbury's experience of seeing his writings quoted by Negrophobes as confirmation of their beliefs, Stearns emphasized repeatedly that the freedmen's shortcomings were neither inherent nor irredeemable. "We are all responsible for the black man's depravity," he declared, "for we all aided in consigning him to that eternal tomb of all virtues and graces—American Slavery." Stearns warned "those moral buzzards who are continually on the wing in quest of carrion" to "feast not upon the moral delinquencies" presented in his book, "for if you and others had not stoutly opposed the abolition of Slavery, the faults you now gloat over, and make an excuse for your satanic hatred of the black man, would have had many years less time in which to mature."[21]

Despite these caveats, Stearns' book was quoted by racists. Nevertheless, the strategy of telling the worst and blaming it on slavery prevailed increasingly in the 1870s. The Protestant mission-education societies applied this strategy especially to their descriptions of black religion. By portraying it as an amalgam of camp-meeting emotionalism, amoral pietism, and pagan occultism they hoped to divert part of the missionary donations of northern churches from the heathen abroad to the heathen in the South.

Stearns had touched on these themes in his book. The freedmen's notion of religion, he wrote, seemed to be "insane yellings, and violent contortions of body, totally disconnected from any kind of idea." An AMA missionary in Wilmington, North Carolina, said that unless one had attended a black church he "cannot conceive of the contortions,

[20] *Ibid.*, 119-24, 388-93, 173-74, quotation from 173-74.
[21] *Ibid.*, xi-xiii, 18.

the unearthly screams, the dire confusion." The missionaries all agreed that "Christian education is the only instrumentality for the removal of this alarming evil."[22]

Educators were particularly exasperated by what they considered the wide gulf between religion and morality in black Christianity. Ednah Dow Cheney of the New England Freedmen's Aid Society could see little value in a church that accepted shouting, groaning, and rolling on the floor as proof that a man had "got religion" even though "he may lie and steal the next day." The "grossly immoral" black preachers scarcely helped matters. "Many of the ministers who have great influence over their congregations are men of notoriously corrupt lives," said Cheney. "They owe their power to a certain rude eloquence which works upon the nerves of the hearers and produces the desired intoxication." An AMA representative in Savannah stated flatly that black ministers "are the curse of the colored people."[23]

Baptist and Methodist missionaries, whose own churches emphasized the immediacy of experience over the understanding of doctrine, were more tolerant of black worship styles than were Unitarians and Congregationalists. Although "the type of piety among the freedmen is extremely defective," said Secretary Richard Rust of the Methodist Freedmen's Aid Society, emotionalism "must not be indiscriminately condemned" and northern educators "must take care" that "we do not substitute cold formality . . . for an enthusiastic religious experience and a warm heart." Gilbert Haven thought that the "occasional shouting, jumping up and down, or moving around the house" in black churches was no more exceptionable than "the jerks of the Western Methodists." In his usual sarcastic manner, Haven said that once black Christians were educated up to a level with whites "the work of reform to dull decorum will speedily be accomplished. We shall find them as able to be silent in prayer . . . as the most refined and most worldly and most sinful of our Churches." And on the matter of amoral Christianity, an abolitionist teacher in South Carolina said that to label black religion "hypocrisy because it has not made a nation of slaves perfectly honest, truthful and moral, is as illogical as to call the religion of the Anglo-Saxon race hypocrisy because it has not made them cease from war and learn to do justice."[24]

Comments like these were exceptions; criticisms of black churches

[22] *Ibid.*, 345-78, quotation from 345; *Congregationalist*, Mar. 14, 1872; *ZH*, Feb. 8, 1877.
[23] Cheney in *Index*, Mar. 18, 1875, Jan. 13, 1872; "grossly immoral" from *Advance*, Apr. 16, 1874; Robert F. Markham to M. E. Strieby, Dec. 11, 1876, AMA Archives.
[24] *Eighth Annual Report FASME*, Cincinnati, 1875, pp. 9-11; Haven in *ZH*, Mar. 19, 1874; Ellen Murray in *AM*, New Series, 1 (Oct. 1877), 1.

were the rule. The cultural gap between Yankee missionaries trained at Yale or Andover or Oberlin and the Baptist or Methodist freedmen of the South was a wide one. Many of the missionaries were slow to understand the functional value of the black church and its folk preachers among an oppressed people. This misunderstanding was greater in the mid-1870s than at any other time; abolitionist discouragement with the freedmen's progress was also most vocal in those years.

The depression of the 1870s played a part in this discouragement not only because of its general dispiriting effect but also because it reduced contributions to the mission societies. In response, missionary educators tried to shock northern churches into greater generosity by issuing appeals that dwelt upon the lamentable backwardness of the freedmen and the need for greater efforts to uplift them. In 1875 both the AMA and the Methodist Freedmen's Aid Society published alarmist pamphlets declaring that since "ignorance and immorality still prevail to a fearful extent" among the freedmen, they were in danger of succumbing to "the lowest types of viciousness and the worst forms of crime" unless saved by "the elevating influence of a Christian civilization through the agency of Christian Churches and schools." Numerous editorials in the religious press written by missionary educators reiterated the point. The South was filled with black churches "in which drunkenness, theft, and whoredom are no bars to acceptable membership," stated one such editorial. To "wipe out the moral degradation of slavery . . . our missionary work should be multiplied a thousand fold."[25]

Such statements may have done the missionary cause more harm than good, for white racists turned them to their own advantage while several black leaders condemned the mission societies as false friends. Spokesmen for the African Methodist Episcopal Church branded the AMA's description of black churches "a most outrageous lie," all the more harmful because perpetrated by "the supposed friends of the colored race." The Cincinnati black leader Peter H. Clark snapped that "when white men begin to . . . practice before us a religion which shall have 'some relation to morality,' then will be full time to blame us for the alleged divorce between our religion and our morals." The black lawyer John Mercer Langston accused the AMA of giving currency to "cruel slanders of an inoffensive and confiding, struggling and comparatively helpless people." In an angry speech Frederick Douglass proclaimed that "we have been injured more than we have been

25 AMA, *The Nation Still in Danger*, New York, 1875; Freedmen's Aid Society of the M.E. Church, *An Appeal to Our People for Our People*, Cincinnati, 1875; *Independent*, May 6, 1875.

helped by men who have professed to be our friends. . . . We do not want, we will not have these second-rate men begging for us." Douglass urged blacks to build their own schools and "don't ask white people to pay for them."[26]

Stung by these criticisms, missionary educators reacted in a fashion that could hardly have mollified the critics. "The Negro ought not to be let alone," wrote one. "The Negro is an inferior race in opportunities, in education, in sound moral training, and in culture. To such a race the impulse and the guidance must come from without, and not from within." The *American Missionary* commented that in view of black ingratitude, some friends of Negro education might be tempted to say that "if this is all the thanks we get, we will waste no more [effort] on such a people." But "we intend to go on with our efforts. . . . With the abolitionists we endured persecution for the slave, and, now that he is free, we shall toil for his elevation and happiness, as undeterred by his fault-finding as we formerly were by the opposition of his foes."[27]

Several black spokesmen came to the AMA's defense, foremost of whom was Benjamin Tanner, a clergyman, editor, and future bishop of the African Methodist Episcopal Church. Tanner reminded Douglass that he had "become great" because "this same class of humane men" he now criticized had helped him to get his start. "There are scores of thousands in the land just as ignorant and as poor and as weak as you once were," Tanner told Douglass, "and, if it were needful for 'these second-rate men' to take you by the hand and administer to your disabilities, it is equally necessary to them." Since Douglass' speech might "button the pockets of the philanthropists" who supported black schools, Tanner branded it "criminally malicious." The Negro "wants education, and he wants it to-day." He should not "contend with the man that brings it, much less traduce him."[28]

Whether the abolitionists' harsh appraisal of slavery's impact on black people was accurate is currently in dispute. Their appraisal bears more than a passing resemblance to Stanley Elkins' portrait of the psychologically emasculated slave. But it contrasts sharply with recent studies that emphasize the stability and vitality of black society in slavery. If these studies are correct, the slave family was a strong institution, slave workers were skillful and efficient, the black church was a viable agency of community solidarity, and the freedmen

[26] AME Church quoted in *Independent*, June 3, 1875; Clark in *Index*, Dec. 10, 1874; Langston, *Emancipation and Enfranchisement. The Work of the Republican Party. Address at Chillicothe, Ohio, Washington*, 1875, pp. 7-8; Douglass' speech reported in *NYTrib.*, July 7, 1875, and *Weekly Louisianian*, July 17, 1875.

[27] *Independent*, July 29, 1875; *AM*, XIX (Sept. 1875), 197-98.

[28] *Independent*, July 29, 1875.

emerged from bondage with a considerable measure of self-esteem. Therefore, according to the authors of one of these studies, the abolitionist-missionary perception of benighted, crippled black victims of repression could only have been the product of racist preconceptions.

It is true that the missionaries viewed the freedmen from a paternalistic, neo-Puritan perspective—a matter discussed in chapter eleven. They probably exaggerated the "Sambo" syndrome in the black personality; they generalized too easily about the universally corrupting impact of slavery from the worst examples in their own experience; and their culture-bound perceptions inhibited an understanding of the positive values of some facets of black culture, especially the church. But most of the abolitionist missionaries were not racists; they believed the Negro inherently equal to the Caucasian and saw their mission as one of helping him to achieve this equality. They also had the advantage over modern historians of first-hand observation of the effects of slavery. Their conclusions, however biased by middle-class Victorianism, were probably sounder than historians' generalizations based on inferential analysis of incomplete quantitative data. And their portrayal of slavery as an oppressive institution whose victims deserved compassion and help is more convincing than any portrait of an institution that allowed the development of strong personalities and a vigorous culture.[29]

Like most Americans, abolitionists measured the freedmen's progress by "white" standards, but unlike most other white Americans, they believed blacks to be capable of meeting those standards. The argument that the Negro was an inferior race had been a major defense of slavery. Theologians had labored to prove that the race was descended from Ham and condemned by the curse of Canaan to per-

[29] The most unqualified and controversial depiction of the viability and strength of black culture in slavery and the racism of whites who described the victims of bondage as psychologically crippled is Robert William Fogel and Stanley L. Engerman, *Time on the Cross: The Economics of American Negro Slavery*, Boston, 1974. Much more balanced, subtle, and persuasive are two books that make clear the repressive nature of slavery but nevertheless maintain that many slaves managed to overcome its corrosive effects: John W. Blassingame, *The Slave Community: Plantation Life in the Antebellum South*, New York, 1972; and Eugene D. Genovese, *Roll, Jordan, Roll: The World the Slaves Made*, New York, 1974. Two important articles are Theodore Hershberg, "Free Blacks in Antebellum Philadelphia: A Study of Ex-Slaves, Freeborn, and Socioeconomic Decline," *Journal of Social History*, v (Winter 1971-72), 183-209, and Herbert G. Gutman, "Le phénomène invisible: la composition de la famille et du foyer noirs après la Guerre de Sécession," *Annales: Economies, Sociétés, Civilisations*, xxxvii (July–Oct. 1972), 1197-1218. The Fall 1975 issue of the *Journal of Interdisciplinary History* will publish several articles on the black family, including a revised version (in English) of Gutman's article cited above.

petual bondage. Ethnologists maintained that the Negro had been created as a separate species of mankind. Emancipation discredited the proslavery purpose of these theories, and Darwinism undermined their intellectual respectability. But the widespread conviction of Negro inferiority persisted after 1865, aided by the Darwinian concept of differential rates of evolution among varieties of the same species. Even if the Negro was not subhuman, he was far below the Caucasian on the evolutionary scale.[30]

Most abolitionists dissented from this belief, for they recognized that it hampered the struggle for equality just as it had once hindered the battle for freedom. But since "science" was on their opponents' side, abolitionist denials of the Negro's innate inferiority often seemed to be acts of faith with defensive overtones. This defensiveness was apparent in an article by Higginson in 1873 on "The Fetich of Science." During the antislavery crusade, said Higginson, both science and theology had been used against the abolitionists. "So long as Canaan was cursed, it made no difference whether it was according to Scripture, or according to the measurements of the facial angle." The success of emancipation had proved that "the dogmatism of science may be just as shallow and hasty as that of theology." Recently, however, Higginson had noted a revival of scientific racism backed by the new prestige of Darwin. But "there is more in man than the scientific method yet knows how to reach," so Higginson advised those who "discard the fetich of theology" not to "deliver themselves wholly over to the new *fetich* of science." Gilbert Haven agreed that "predestination in science is quite as faulty as predestination in theology. Men are not created by races but by individuals." And the *Independent* held in 1872 that no adequate evidence had yet been marshaled to prove either the Negro's inferiority or his equality, and that in any case the equal rights of all men were derived from God rather than science.[31]

Most abolitionists were environmentalists; nurture rather than nature, they believed, explained racial differences. The "facts" that one scientist cited to demonstrate the Negro's inferiority, said Higginson, were "not the facts of race, but of condition." Lydia Maria Child and William Hayes Ward insisted that the freedmen's shortcomings were the result not of "any inherent impotence of the colored race" or "any deficiency of their *nature*" but of "centuries of dependence, and the consequent total inaction of calculation and forethought." When "all the controlling circumstances are taken into consideration," said Rich-

---

[30] George M. Fredrickson, *The Black Image in the White Mind: The Debate on Afro-American Character and Destiny, 1817-1914*, New York, 1971, chaps. 1-6.

[31] Higginson in *Index*, Mar. 22, 1873; Haven in *ZH*, Mar. 18, 1869; *Independent*, Feb. 8, 1872.

ard Rust, black people "will not suffer in comparison with the more favored whites."[32]

Of course environmentalism did not preclude a belief in racial differences; that is, one could consider external factors mainly responsible for black deficiencies but still admit the existence of *some* innate variations. Among the minority of abolitionists who did believe in racial differences, a handful can be classified as scientific racists and a larger number as romantic racialists.

One of the few genuine abolitionists (as opposed to free soilers) who openly accepted scientific racism in the 1870s was Samuel Gridley Howe, a friend of the renowned scientist Louis Agassiz. The latter was one of the foremost exponents of the theory that the Negro race was a separate species. Though Howe could not accept all of Agassiz's ideas, his respect for the latter's learning did lead him in the direction of racism. A visit to Haiti and Santo Domingo in 1871 pushed him even further in this direction. "The Negroes of Hayti, as in other West India Islands, where they are left entirely to themselves, tend to revert toward barbarism," he wrote. The Negro "needs contact with more highly developed races. He imitates, rather than originates; and he may carry on and improve a civilization which he never could have initiated." (Interestingly, Frederick Douglass, who accompanied Howe on this trip to Haiti, was reported to have said that "if this is the outcome of self-government by my race, Heaven help us!")[33]

More common among abolitionists than outright racism was what George M. Fredrickson has termed "romantic racialism," a belief in racial *differences* but not necessarily in black inferiority. Romantic racialists contrasted the cold, rational, pragmatic, aggressive character of the Anglo-Saxon with the artistic, warm, emotional, Christian nature of the Negro. For romantic racialists, the Negro was in some respects superior to the Anglo-Saxon. He was "the most religious man among men," said Theodore Tilton. "Is not the religious nature the highest part of human nature? . . . In all those intellectual activities which take their strange quickening from the moral faculties—processes which we call instincts, or intuitions—the negro is superior to the white man—

[32] Higginson in *Index*, Mar. 22, 1873; Child to Anna Loring Dresel, Aug. 11, 1878, Loring Family Papers, Schlesinger Library, Radcliffe College; Ward in *Independent*, May 25, 1876; Rust in *NWCA*, Sept. 5, 1877.

[33] Howe, *Letters on the Proposed Annexation of Santo Domingo*, Boston, 1871, pp. 11-13; Douglass quoted in *Autobiography of Andrew Dickson White*, 2 vols., New York, 1905, I, 501. Douglass was assistant secretary of a U.S. government commission that visited Santo Domingo and Haiti in 1871 as part of President Grant's effort to annex the former. Howe and White were members of the commission. Howe reported Douglass to have said: "If this is all my poor colored fellow-men have been able to do in seventy years, God help the race!" Howe, *Letters on the Proposed Annexation*, p. 13.

equal to the white woman. The negro is the feminine race of the world." Ednah Dow Cheney maintained that, while differences between black and white "in intellectual characteristics are very slight and not easily defined," nevertheless "races, like nations and individuals, have their peculiarities." In the Negro "the poetic and emotional qualities predominate, rather than the prosaic, mechanical, and merely intellectual powers." Black aesthetic superiority, said romantic racialists, would enrich American culture. "Naturally musical," the slaves had created in their spirituals a unique and beautiful heritage. The race's "great sensitiveness to beauty, sensibility to religious emotion, warm affections, undoubting faith," wrote Cheney, "will add new power and grace to our civilization."[34]

Although the romantic racialist stereotype was benign, the implicit obverse of Negro superiority in "feminine" traits was inferiority in the masculine characteristics prized by most Americans. Some romantic racialists said this explicitly. George William Curtis (who during the 1870s wavered between romantic racialism and egalitarianism) conceded that the "mildness of the colored race has been accounted its weakness." Cheney admitted that "in the hardier qualities, perhaps in those which constitute greatness, preeminent distinction, the African is inferior to the Anglo-Saxon." And according to Charles G. Fairchild of Berea College, blacks would benefit from racial integration because "their emotional worship . . . needs the careful Anglo-Saxon estimate of good accomplished. . . . Their tangled oratory needs the pruning of a sharp Anglo-Saxon criticism. The tractableness which so easily sinks into a servile contentment with any lot needs the constant magnetism of an aspiring and resolute nature."[35]

Although romantic racialism was a potent recessive strain in abolitionist thought, egalitarianism was dominant. Evidence has been found for the racial ideas of 50 white abolitionists during the Reconstruction era; of these, 44 insisted that no convincing evidence of black mental inferiority existed, two accepted the thesis of Negro inferiority, and four were ambivalent. Of the 44 in the first category, 34 could be described as egalitarians and 10 as romantic racialists, but there was some overlap between the two groups, with a half dozen in each category occasionally expressing sentiments that seemed to place them in the other.

Stating the egalitarian position, Wendell Phillips said that "it is

[34] Theodore Tilton, *The Negro*, New York, 1863, pp. 11-13; Cheney in *Index*, Mar. 18, 1875, and *Freedmen's Record*, I (Aug. 1865), 121-22. See also ZH, Feb. 12, 1874. Fredrickson, *The Black Image in the White Mind*, chap. 4, is a perceptive discussion of romantic racialism.

[35] *HW*, Sept. 5, 1874; Cheney in *Freedmen's Record*, IV (Sept. 1868), 141; Fairchild in *Old and New*, IX (Feb. 1874), 230.

hardly possible to catalogue the merits, or to find out the deficiencies, of any great race without finally coming to the conclusion that God has made all blood, no matter whether Asiatic, or Greek, or Latin, or Saxon, or African . . . about equal." In the Western Hemisphere the Negro race had been "chilled and wilted by social contempt, shut out from all advantages of education . . . condemned to the most menial service," yet still produced such great men as Benjamin Banneker, Frederick Douglass, and Toussaint L'Ouverture. "Rarely, if even once, in history can be found a race which has done more for itself under such disadvantages."[36]

The egalitarians' best evidence was the performance of black students in freedmen's schools. The mission societies frequently published letters from teachers asserting that black pupils were as bright as white students they had previously taught. One teacher whose students ranged in color from octoroon to black stated that "our blackest are just as good scholars as the whitest. It's all stuff about their being an inferior race." President Edward H. Fairchild (Charles's father) of integrated Berea College declared that "there is no essential difference, other things being equal, between [the black students'] standing and that of the white students." And a professor at Talladega proclaimed in 1879 that "the day is past when we need to parade proofs that the negro has a brain capable of improvement. We can now quietly assume that the color of a man's skin does not necessarily affect his mental calibre, and there we may leave it."[37]

In their private letters, teachers were sometimes less positive. One said that "while the freedman's *ability to learn* is no longer a matter of experiment, his ability to learn *rapidly, to reach conclusions speedily, to reason in like manner,* is not equal to like ability in the students in Brooklyn." Applying the then-prevalent Lamarckian theory of the inheritance of acquired characteristics, this teacher explained the black pupils' slowness by lack of *"inherited* ability—whatever they may have is the result of their own limited education & drill. The children of those who were prohibited from ever *reading,* or *attempting to learn* to read, cannot, assuredly, be expected to be the equals of those whose ancestors have been for centuries . . . accustomed to reason, reflect, deduce, &c." One should not compare black students with New England children but "with the children of the *backwoods* & *frontiersmen"* who were similarly deprived of inherited culture.[38]

36 *BC,* Nov. 15, 1873; *National Anti-Slavery Standard,* June 19, 1869.
37 Fairchild quoted in Robert Samuel Fletcher, *A History of Oberlin College from Its Foundation Through the Civil War,* 2 vols., Oberlin, 1943, II, 909; the other two quotations are from *AM,* XIV (Jan. 1870), 7, and XXXIII (Aug. 1879), 238.
38 A. A. Safford to Erastus M. Cravath, Oct. 29, 1874, AMA Archives.

But since the school was a controlled environment, most missionary educators remained confident that it could overcome the deficiencies of a slave background. Most of the students in missionary schools came from achievement-oriented and upwardly mobile families whose middle-class aspirations stimulated educational achievement. These students provided a solid basis for egalitarian affirmations. After a tour of the New England Freedmen's Aid Society's schools in 1870, Ednah Cheney wrote that "neither the capacity nor the desire of the negro to learn has been overstated, and we were perfectly convinced that only time and a fair opportunity is needed to raise him to a level with the white race in culture and civilization." And as black students began to graduate from missionary colleges, the old notion that no matter how well they did in lower grades Negroes were incapable of higher education was also "thoroughly exploded." "No one who is acquainted with these colleges," wrote an abolitionist educator, "now pretends to set any limits to the capacity of the colored race."[39]

But abolitionists realized that classroom performance alone would not win equality and respect for the freedmen. They must cast off the habits of slavery, go to work, and fight their way upstream to success. Now that black people had equal rights in law, said John G. Whittier in 1875, mainly on "themselves depends the question whether, by patient industry, sobriety, and assiduous self-culture, they shall overcome the unchristian prejudice still existing against them, or by idolence, thriftlessness, and moral and physical degradation they shall confirm and strengthen it." Negroes must "conquer prejudice by the power of hard work and good morals," said the AMA, while John G. Fee, founder of Berea College, told Kentucky freedmen that "before public sentiment will cede to you equal positions, you must demonstrate not only equal capacity, but equal merit." Even Wendell Phillips told a black organization in 1873 that "the recognition of the colored race will never come from your claiming it; the world never yields to a claimant. The world worships but one thing—success. . . . Go and do something that nobody else can do. . . . From that moment the world will recognize your race."[40]

This belief in the Protestant Ethic as the route to success was widely shared in the nineteenth century, by blacks as well as whites. It was the basis of the antislavery conviction that all men must be free to make the most of their God-given talents. It motivated the self-help

[39] *Freedmen's Record*, v (Apr. 1870), 74; *AM*, xix (June 1875), 123-24.
[40] Whittier in *NYT*, Apr. 4, 1875; *AM*, New Series, 1 (Mar. 1877), 4; broadside by Fee, dated Oct. 16, 1869, copy in Negro Collection, Berea College Library; Phillips quoted in *BC*, Nov. 15, 1873.

societies of antebellum free Negroes. It was the taproot of the free-labor ideology described so lucidly by Eric Foner. In the hands of social Darwinists, of course, this ideology of equality of opportunity could become a callous rationalization for inequality of condition. As some abolitionists began to stress the need for blacks to raise themselves by their own bootstraps, they sounded increasingly like social Darwinists. But most of them never lost sight of the dual nature of the free-labor ideology: rights as well as duties, opportunity as well as work. The shift of rhetorical emphasis from rights to duties was a modification of tactics, not goals.

Black leaders similarly modified their rhetoric in the 1870s. The black abolitionist William Wells Brown wrote that "we need more self-reliance, more . . . manly independence, a higher standard of moral, social, and literary culture" to break down "the barriers of prejudice." In 1868 Frederick Douglass asserted that the freedmen "must acquire property, show themselves capable of carrying on business, of mastering the professions. . . . If, *within the next fifteen years*, they have not fully demonstrated this, they will be *unworthy of their freedom*." A decade later Douglass told blacks to "cultivate their brains more and their lungs less." In 1875 he apologized for his earlier attack on white philanthropists and praised the AMA for its efforts to help the freedmen overcome "ignorance, superstition and groveling sensuality." When the race possessed "a class of men noted for enterprise, industry, economy, and success," said Douglass on another occasion, "we shall no longer have any trouble in the matter of civil and political rights."[41]

Although black and white abolitionists alike urged the freedmen to lift themselves by their bootstraps, they also believed, in the *Independent*'s words, that "it is the duty of the whites to aid them in the process."[42] Abolitionists did help in several ways. Most important by far were the schools and colleges they founded, discussed in chapters 9–15 of this book. The 1870s also witnessed other white efforts to help the freedmen acquire education, capital, and land.

Many abolitionists had urged some form of federal aid to southern education as a corollary to the Reconstruction Acts of 1867. In 1871 a Mississippi Republican congressman introduced a bill to appropriate the proceeds from public land sales for schools, to be apportioned among the states on the ratio of their percentage of the illiterate popu-

---

41 Brown, *My Southern Home*, Boston, 1880, pp. 233-34; Douglass in *National Anti-Slavery Standard*, Feb. 15, 1868; *AM*, New Series, 1 (Aug. 1877), 4; AMA, *The Nation Still in Danger*, p. 12; Douglass, *Life and Times of Frederick Douglass*, Hartford, 1882, p. 506.
42 Jan. 20, 1881.

lation. Three-quarters of the funds would thus have gone to the South. The House passed this bill in 1872, with the strongest support coming from New England and the southern states under Republican control. The Senate took no action, but during the rest of the decade similar measures were introduced in both houses at almost every session, even though the economic depression and Democratic control of the House after 1874 dimmed hopes for their passage.[43]

Arguing that "ignorant suffrage" was responsible for Tweed-type "rings" in both North and South, some abolitionists proposed a constitutional amendment to make literacy a prerequisite for voting, to establish with federal aid a system of primary schools in every state, and to compel all children to attend school until the age of 14. More popular was a proposal that would allow unrestricted suffrage but impose compulsory education; "universal suffrage and universal education" became the slogan of abolitionists backing this plan. In 1877 the National Liberal League, a group of post-Transcendentalist religious liberals that included several abolitionists, petitioned Congress for federal aid and compulsory education. It was time for the government to recognize, said the League, that "the right to a good elementary education belongs to every child in the country."[44]

Although such comprehensive proposals had no chance of passage, the more limited aim of federal aid to the states on the basis of illiteracy remained alive in Congress, where its most earnest supporter was James Monroe, the Oberlin abolitionist elected to the House in 1870 and appointed chairman of the Committee on Education and Labor in the 1873–1875 Congress. "If emancipation was the logical consequence of the war," said Monroe, "and the right of suffrage the logical consequence of emancipation, then general education is the logical consequence of the right of suffrage." The 1880 Republican platform endorsed federal aid; outgoing and incoming Presidents Hayes and Garfield recommended legislation in 1880; in December of that year the Senate passed a bill distributing the proceeds of public land sales to states on the illiteracy ratio. But the Democratic House rejected the bill. The opposition of Roman Catholics and of some Protestant denominations, Democratic hostility to "centralization," fears of a "raid" on the federal treasury, and the tradition of local control and financing of public schools were too strong to be overcome. Nevertheless the

[43] Gordon Canfield Lee, *The Struggle for Federal Aid. First Phase. A History of the Attempts to Obtain Federal Aid for the Common Schools, 1870-1890*, New York, 1949, pp. 11-84.

[44] Quotation from *Index*, Nov. 8, 1877. See also *HW*, June 13, 1874; Anna E. Dickinson, *A Paying Investment*, Boston, 1876; *Index*, Mar. 18, 1875, Nov. 2, Dec. 14, 1876; and Dexter A. Hawkins, *Education the Need of the South*, New York, 1878, pp. 11-16.

movement for federal aid grew stronger in the 1880s, when it became a major political issue (see pp. 127-31).[45]

The most ambitious effort to encourage thrift among blacks was the Freedmen's Savings and Trust Company, commonly called the Freedmen's Bank. During the war, a few Union generals had established banks for the deposit of black soldiers' pay. Impressed by the success of these banks, the veteran abolitionist and army chaplain John W. Alvord conceived the idea of founding a national freedmen's bank. He secured a congressional charter in March 1865 and began to establish branches throughout the South. For five years Alvord was both superintendent of education of the Freedmen's Bureau and chief officer of the Freedmen's Bank. Though the Bank was a private corporation, Alvord's dual role fostered the impression that it was officially connected with the Freedmen's Bureau, a belief that strengthened black confidence in the Bank. During the nine years of the Bank's life more than 100,000 depositors maintained accounts that totaled $57,000,000. With understandable pride, Alvord said in 1871 that "the banks are doing more for the people than the schools."[46]

But even as Alvord wrote these words, the Bank's affairs were getting beyond his control. An old man suffering from illness and approaching senility, Alvord was a clergyman whose knowledge of banking was minimal. Several other officials were also better missionaries than bankers. The Bank's charter required it to keep one-third of its deposits in cash and invest the remainder in government bonds. In 1870 some of the Bank's Washington trustees, arguing that a higher rate of return than yielded by bonds was necessary, persuaded Congress to amend the charter to allow half of the deposits to be invested in realty mortgages. The Bank began making high-risk loans and was soon tied to the fortunes of real estate interests and speculators in the capital. There is clear evidence of fraud in some of these transactions. Southern branches also made speculative loans, some of them illegal even under the revised charter, and a few cashiers were later found guilty of embezzlement. The Panic of 1873 exposed the shaky condition of the Bank. In a desperate effort to restore depositor confidence and stem a run on the branches, the trustees named Frederick Douglass president, but it was too late and the Bank was forced to close its doors in the summer of 1874.

[45] Monroe in *Cincinnati Gazette*, July 1, 1875; Lee, *The Struggle for Federal Aid*, 60-61, 64-68, 84-85.

[46] Walter L. Fleming, *The Freedmen's Savings Bank*, Chapel Hill, 1927, pp. 22-42, quotation p. 47; Carl R. Osthaus, *Freedmen, Philanthropy, and Fraud: A History of the Freedmen's Savings Bank*, chaps. 1-4. I am grateful to Professor Osthaus for allowing me to read the manuscript of his excellent book, forthcoming from the University of Illinois Press.

The failure of the Freedmen's Bank was a sad ending to a hopeful beginning. But the extent and consequences of that failure have been exaggerated. For eight years the Bank functioned successfully, providing an opportunity for thousands of black people to accumulate capital for investment in homes, farms, and businesses. Of the $57,000,000 deposited during the life of the Bank, only $2,940,000 was due depositors when it collapsed, and of this, $1,733,000 was eventually paid. Thus only 2 percent of the total amount deposited was lost. Though the psychological consequences of the Bank's failure were serious, the success of the Bank during most of its history should perhaps modify the usual picture of its ultimate failure as a disaster for black thrift. Like many other white efforts to help blacks, the results of the Freedmen's Bank were mixed but probably more beneficial than if no effort at all had been made.[47]

The same was true of attempts to place freedmen on land of their own. Since early in the war, abolitionists had urged the federal government to expropriate land owned by Confederates and redistribute it among the freedmen. But doubts about the constitutionality as well as desirability of such a course prevented its adoption. While continuing to lobby for a government land program, several abolitionists undertook private efforts after the war to purchase and resell land to freedmen. Several of these projects succeeded on a small scale; others failed. The mission societies bought several thousand acres in the South for school property and eventually sold some of this land to blacks. Occasionally the societies acted as agents for northern philanthropists who bought southern property for resale to freedmen. In 1867 John Baldwin, a wealthy Methodist abolitionist from Ohio, purchased a 1700-acre sugar plantation in Louisiana, where he spent the winters for the rest of his life. He deeded part of the land to the Methodist Freedmen's Aid Society and later bought an adjoining plantation of 2500 acres, much of which he resold to Negroes on easy credit terms in tracts of 40 acres or more. Yardley Warner, a tireless Quaker abolitionist who established several freedmen's schools in North Carolina and Tennessee, bought land on the outskirts of Greensboro in the 1870s and resold it to black families; this later became the middle-class black section of the city. Other examples could be cited; their cumulative impact was modest but perhaps not insignificant.[48]

[47] Fleming, *The Freedmen's Savings Bank*, 40, 53-54, and passim; Osthaus, *Freedmen, Philanthropy, and Fraud*, chaps. 5-7; Abby L. Gilbert, "The Comptroller of the Currency and the Freedmen's Savings Bank," *Journal of Negro History*, LVII (1972), 125-43. The two full-length studies of the bank, by Fleming and Osthaus, portray the impact of the Bank's failure in more negative terms than I have done.

[48] *AM*, XIII (Feb. 1869), 34, 37 (Apr. 1869), 84, 85, XVI (Sept. 1872), 193, 194, 201; Amos R. Webber, *Life of John Baldwin, Sr., of Berea*, Cincinnati, 1925, pp.

Two of the most interesting attempts by abolitionists to promote black landownership encountered many setbacks. Edward Daniels originated one of these enterprises. A typical Yankee entrepreneur-reformer, the Boston-born Daniels had migrated to Wisconsin, where he became state geologist, invested in various business ventures, joined the abolitionist movement and was briefly jailed for his antislavery activities, and served as colonel of a cavalry regiment in the Civil War. In 1868 he purchased a run-down plantation on the Potomac near Mount Vernon that had once belonged to George Mason, author of the Virginia Declaration of Rights and a signer of the Declaration of Independence. Daniels worked hard to restore the property, to grow diversified crops, and to teach his black employees the latest methods of scientific farming. But bad weather, an epidemic of illness among his farm animals, and resistance by his hired hands to some of Daniels' new-fangled ideas caused him to lose several thousand dollars in his first three years. "Everything seems to be loss with me since I came to Virginia," he wrote in his diary in 1870. "Yet I have tried my best to do well. I see now that I undertook too much in a direction where I had no knowledge."[49]

Daniels hung on, however, and even expanded his activities. In 1871 he bought the *State Journal* and for the next few years he divided his time between the plantation and his editorial office in Richmond. From the latter he preached a brand of advanced Republicanism consistent with his abolitionist past, crusading for public education, prison reform, and the abolition of the whipping post. Confessing to his diary that "I have [been] neglecting farm for politics," Daniels ran unsuccessfully for Congress in 1872. Recognizing by 1874 that there was little political future in Virginia for a radical Republican, Daniels sold the *State Journal* and returned to his plantation, which despite his absence (or perhaps because of it) was operating more profitably than a few years earlier.[50]

In his youth Daniels had lived in a cooperative community at Ripon, Wisconsin. In 1876 he obtained a Virginia charter for the "Co-operative Industrial Association," a project by which he hoped to turn his plantation into a community owned by resident blacks who would share the profits according to their contribution of labor. Daniels also tried to establish a "George Mason Industrial University" to teach both

---

139-43, 175; Stafford Allen Warner, *Yardley Warner: The Freedman's Friend*, Abington, England, 1957, pp. 210, 212, 219.

[49] Quotation from Daniels' diary, entry of Nov. 14, 1870, in Daniels Papers, Wisconsin State Historical Society. See also David H. Overy, Jr., *Wisconsin Carpetbaggers in Dixie*, Madison, 1961, pp. 39-44, and an anonymous typescript biography of Daniels in the Daniels Papers.

[50] Overy, *Wisconsin Carpetbaggers*, pp. 44-45; diary entry, Apr. 14, 1873.

blacks and whites how "to manage farms, machine shops, mills, mines, and furnaces; to build roads, bridges, houses, and boats; to run steam engines and other machinery; to conduct commercial transactions, and to manage public and private business." Daniels had to sell off part of his land to keep his projects afloat, and the George Mason Industrial University evidently never got beyond the planning stage. In the 1880s he moved to New York, where he edited the labor reform journal *Our Country*. He returned to Virginia in the 1890s where he cultivated what was left of his farm, dabbled in Populism, and died quietly in 1916. Although his grand plans never materialized, he did sell part of his land to black farmers, so his enterprise was not a total failure.[51]

A similar conclusion applies to Charles Stearns's efforts in Georgia. His difficulties with slipshod black labor convinced him that the ownership of land could best motivate the freedmen to become good farmers. Only two dozen freedmen were able to scrape together down payments for the 25-acre tracts Stearns offered for sale, yet the achievements of these men encouraged him to continue the program. One field worked by a farmer who owned it yielded six times as much cotton per acre as an adjoining field worked by wage labor. "This contrast was seen in other fields," wrote Stearns, "showing that . . . ownership of land is by far the best educator of the colored people."[52]

In 1873 Stearns organized a "Laborers' Homestead and Southern Emigration Society" with a planned capitalization of $50,000. He persuaded Gerrit Smith and other abolitionists to invest in the society, and bought some property in Virginia for resale to blacks. The society set up a fund for loans to enable purchasers to buy tools, seeds, and implements. Stearns urged Congress to lend his association $1,000,000 per year for 10 years to finance additional purchases. Congress ignored his appeal, and the depression soon dried up Stearns's limited sources of private capital. But he did not give up; in the late 1870s he enlisted a wealthy northern investor in a project to buy land in Tennessee for a communitarian experiment. But the backer turned out to be more interested in land speculation than in a socialist community, so Stearns pulled out of the enterprise. He became a Christian Socialist, endorsed Edward Bellamy's vision of a cooperative commonwealth, and never stopped believing that "the world requires stirring up." Although Stearns, like Daniels, had succeeded in selling land to a handful of freedmen, his larger schemes never materialized.[53]

---

[51] Circulars, prospectuses, diaries, and the typescript biography, in the Daniels Papers.

[52] Stearns, *The Black Man of the South*, p. 518; letter from Stearns in *BC*, June 27, 1874.

[53] *BC*, June 27, Sept. 19, 1874; Stearns to Gerrit Smith, Feb. 17, 1873, Feb. 4, 11, 1874, Smith Papers, Syracuse University Library; Stearns to William Lloyd

The only government agency to carry out land redistribution was the South Carolina Land Commission. Several abolitionist carpetbaggers took part in the creation of this body by the state legislature in 1869. It was capitalized at $500,000 with power to buy land and resell it at cost with liberal credit terms in tracts from 25 to 100 acres. Though the commission was riddled with corruption and dissension it managed to sell land to about 14,000 families, most of them black. Democrats preserved the commission after Reconstruction but changed its purpose. The length of the mortgage was reduced from eight to four years, buyers who could not make their paymens were evicted (in contrast with lax enforcement under the Republicans), and much of the land was sold in large blocks to whites. By 1890, when the commission wound up its work, it had conveyed 68,000 acres to white purchasers and only 44,000 to blacks. Thus it did not fulfill its founders' hopes for land redistribution. But it did achieve modest success, and in 1910 more black farmers owned their land free of debt in South Carolina than in any other deep South state.[54]

Despite these piecemeal efforts for land reform, most black farmers became tenants or sharecroppers. Convinced that emancipation was incomplete so long as this economic bondage existed, some abolitionists continued to urge federal programs even when they knew they were fighting for a lost cause. In 1869–1870 Wendell Phillips lobbied for legislation to create a cabinet-level department to administer land redistribution, long-term loans, and agricultural extension services to southern farmers. In reply to the argument that blacks must lift themselves by their bootstraps like other Americans—must "root, hog or die"—Phillips said that the freedmen would be glad to root for their survival if given an opportunity. But slavery had deprived them of the means to compete without an initial boost. "The Negro's inability in this instance, his want of means, is not his fault, but ours," said Phillips. "This adult man, a husband and father, we have robbed him of wages for forty years. The 'root, hog or die' advice, to such a victim is the coolest impertinence. . . . Every Negro family can justly claim forty acres of land, one year's support, a furnished cottage, a mule and farm tools, and free schools for life."[55]

Garrison, Dec. 12, 1876, WLG Papers; Stearns to Edward Bellamy, Oct. 27, 1889, Bellamy Papers, Houghton Library, Harvard University. I am indebted to John H. Thomas for calling the letter to Bellamy to my attention.

[54] Carol K. Rothrock Bleser, *The Promised Land: The History of the South Carolina Land Commission, 1869-1890*, Columbia, S.C., 1969; *Negro Population 1790-1915*, Dept. of Commerce, Bureau of the Census, Washington, 1918, p. 587.

[55] *National Anti-Slavery Standard*, Jan. 29, 1870.

In 1869 both the New England and American Anti-Slavery Societies, believing that "the New England village must be introduced at the South," called for "the immediate enactment of laws that will . . . place a homestead within the reach of the humblest freedman." Several abolitionists petitioned Congress for the creation of a federal land commission capitalized at $2,000,000 to purchase and resell land to the freedmen in the manner already begun by the South Carolina Land Commission. But Congress did nothing.[56]

Some abolitionists, to be sure, opposed "special legislation" for the Negro. Believers in the laissez-faire version of the Protestant Ethic, they argued that only through hard work and thrift could a man acquire the self-reliance necessary for success. Government aid would dampen these tempering fires of adversity and teach the Negro to depend on others rather than himself. "It is not by constantly appealing to the government or to any exterior force," said George William Curtis, "but by relying upon themselves" that blacks would "finally conquer the difficulties of their situation."[57]

But most Garrisonians, at least, believed in some form of reparations for slavery, and in later years they insisted that Reconstruction's greatest mistake was its failure to achieve land reform. "I shall never cease mourning over the injustice and impolicy of Congress," wrote Lydia Maria Child, "in not taking away large tracts of land from rich rebels and selling it in small portions, cheap, to the freedmen and the poor whites." As Reconstruction began to break down in the mid-1870s, Phillips could not refrain from reminding "foolish and timid" Republicans of his advice 10 years earlier that "the only way to secure thorough and prompt reconstruction was to . . . break down the *land power* by confiscating the landed estates."[58]

As this chapter has tried to make clear, most abolitionists considered the freedmen potentially equal to whites but believed that slavery had dwarfed their intellects, degraded their morals, and crippled their ambition. Although the first step toward rehabilitation was equal rights, it was *only* a first step. Theoretically equal before the law, the freedmen were far from equal in fact. Real equality would come only with the acquisition of education, skills, property, and the values of the Protestant Ethic, and this could not be done overnight. By 1875 the watchwords of racial progress for those abolitionists disillusioned with political Reconstruction were *time* and *education*. In their minds, this

[56] *Ibid.*, May 15, 22, June 12, Dec. 18, 1860, Jan. 29, 1870.
[57] *HW*, Sept. 25, 1875.
[58] Child to Harriet Sewall, undated, 1871, Robie-Sewall Papers, Massachusetts Historical Society; Phillips in *Advance*, Nov. 5, 1874.

was not a repudiation of life-long convictions but a frank recognition of the hard realities of the race problem. For them, the aftermath of the crucial 1876 presidential election only confirmed this viewpoint even as it sharpened the militancy of abolitionists who had never lost faith in Reconstruction.

Chapter Five

The Compromise of 1877

At the beginning of 1876 all signs pointed to Democratic victory in the forthcoming presidential election. Depression, political scandals, and northern disillusionment with Reconstruction presaged the restoration to power of a party based on the "solid South." Though this prospect produced an upsurge of Republican "bloody shirt" oratory, the tainted triumph of Rutherford B. Hayes resulted in a solid Democratic South just as surely as if Samuel J. Tilden had won the disputed election. That nearly half of the surviving abolitionists endorsed Hayes's withdrawal of federal troops from southern capitals was a significant measure of radical disillusionment with political Reconstruction.

As the presidential campaign opened, "Reform" was the leading issue. Democratic candidate Tilden enjoyed a reform reputation for his role in overthrowing the Tweed Ring and cleaning up graft in the New York state government. The mood of nationalism associated with the centennial also helped Democrats. Shrewdly linking the issues of reform and reconciliation, the party urged voters to end corruption, heal sectional wounds, and march united and strong into the nation's second century under the Democratic banner.

The reform element of the Republican party countered with an effort to nominate a candidate of unblemished reputation on a platform of good government and sectional peace. Several abolitionists including George William Curtis, Thomas Wentworth Higginson, and James Freeman Clarke took part in a conference of Reform Republicans in New York on May 15-16 that outlined reform goals. On the southern question they fashioned a vague resolution that harked back to the Liberal Republicans of 1872, calling for both equal rights and an end to carpetbag rule. At the Republican convention the reform delegates threw their support to dark-horse Rutherford B. Hayes on the seventh ballot and thereby insured his nomination. The platform pledged "exact equality in the exercise of all civic, political, and public rights" as well as "permanent pacification" of the South by the removal of "any just causes of discontent." This was a plank on which anyone could stand. Writing to Hayes after the convention, Curtis advised him to phrase his letter of acceptance carefully, for it would serve as a more important statement than the platform. Not only should Hayes speak out "for impartial justice in the southern states," said Curtis, but he should declare that "the Republican being the party of equality, should be the party of the southern white as well as of the southern black." This was hardly less ambiguous than the platform, nor did Hayes's letter do much to clarify his position. If elected, he would "cherish" the "interests of the white and colored people both" by pursuing a "policy which will wipe out forever the distinction between North and South" and "protect all classes of citizens in their political and private rights."[1]

Republicans clearly meant to straddle the fence on the southern question, a strategy unacceptable to abolitionists suspicious of "reconciliation" as a code word for abandonment of Reconstruction. While Lydia Maria Child welcomed "all *real* kindliness of feeling toward the South," she deplored "artificial, diseased, sentimental magnanimity, which is dangerously confusing all distinctions between right and wrong; and the Centennial will furnish a capital opportunity for politicians to traffic in such spurious wares." Was there any good reason for national pride and reconciliation, asked William Lloyd Garrison? True, slavery no longer existed, but "the nation has never repented of its great transgression" and Negroes were still victims of the caste spirit. "Before God, is this a time for special jubilation? . . . If we rejoice at all, let it be with contrite hearts that we have not been utterly consumed."[2]

The "Hamburg Massacre" and the campaign's partisan momentum soon moved Republicans in a direction that Garrison approved. On July 4 a minor incident between a company of black militia and two white civilians at Hamburg, South Carolina, escalated into a pitched battle between the militia and armed whites. Afterwards five black leaders were shot "while attempting to escape." This "massacre," as Governor Chamberlain labeled it, blew the lid off a tense situation in South Carolina and set the stage for a violent campaign. These events provoked a hard-line response from all but a few abolitionists, including several who had only recently preached conciliation. Perhaps most significant were the words of Thomas Wentworth Higginson: "I have been trying hard to convince myself that the Southern whites had accepted the results of the war," he wrote. But the Hamburg massacre indicated otherwise. What would stop southern Democrats from nulli-

1 Curtis to Hayes, June 30, 1876, Hayes Papers, Hayes Memorial Library, Fremont, Ohio; Charles L. Williams, *The Life of Rutherford Birchard Hayes*, 2 vols., Boston, 1914, I, 444, 462. See also *BC*, May 20, 1876; Thomas Wentworth Higginson, diary, entry of May 15, 1876, Higginson Papers, Houghton Library, Harvard University. A useful study of the 1876 election is Keith Ian Polakoff, *The Politics of Inertia: The Election of 1876 and the End of Reconstruction*, Baton Rouge, 1973.

2 Child to John G. Whittier, Jan. 20, 1876, Child-Whittier Correspondence, Library of Congress; Garrison in *Independent*, July 6, 1876.

fying the 15th Amendment if Tilden were elected? asked Higginson. "For one, I do not propose to acquiesce in this."[3]

When the first wave of Republican oratory denouncing southern "outrages" subsided, party moderates urged the subordination of this theme to financial and reform issues. But abolitionists insisted on keeping the southern question to the front. "So long as it is uncertain whether a white or black Republican can sleep [safely] under his own roof," said Phillips in his campaign speeches, "there is no other issue for the American people." And Arthur Edwards could not understand how anyone could be concerned with other issues when "there has not been a time since the memorable winter of 1861, when the South has been so defiant and threatening as now."[4]

Abolitionists were scornful of the argument that southern states under Democratic control enjoyed "peace, order, security, and self-government" in contrast to the violence and misgovernment in Republican states. Peace and order also prevailed in Poland under Russian rule, pointed out the *Independent* and *Harper's Weekly*, but that was not necessarily a good thing for the Poles. "The question of the method of keeping order is hardly less important than that of order," said Curtis. "When the negroes were absolutely enslaved there were few massacres like those of Hamburg." Higginson agreed that "this assertion of peace and order in Southern States controlled by the whites is precisely like the old assertions of Northern travelers that the slaves were happy and well off."[5]

Reversing their attitude of a year earlier toward the Mississippi election, Bowen of the *Independent* and Curtis of *Harper's Weekly* endorsed the use of federal troops in South Carolina in 1876. Though they would not have admitted it in so many words, the main reason they did so was that while Democratic victory in Mississippi had not endangered Republican control of the national government, Democratic victory in the South in 1876 did, and both men were as much Republicans as abolitionists. The same was true of the Quaker abolitionist William Penn Nixon, who with his brother Oliver had acquired control of the powerful *Chicago Inter Ocean* in 1875. But Nixon's position in 1876 was consistent with his stand at other times. When "bands of outlaws drive back free citizens from the ballot-boxes," he wrote, an "awful emergency" confronted the nation. If Tilden won, "the fate of

[3] Higginson in *NYT*, Oct. 15, 1876. See also Joel Williamson, *After Slavery: The Negro in South Carolina During Reconstruction*, Chapel Hill, 1965, pp. 267-72, and Walter Allen, *Governor Chamberlain's Administration in South Carolina*, New York, 1888, pp. 322-26, 398-427, 461.

[4] *BET*, Oct. 28, 1876; *NWCA*, Oct. 18, 1876.

[5] *Independent*, Oct. 19, 1876; *HW*, Sept. 9, 1876; Higginson in *Woman's Journal*, Dec. 30, 1876.

the rebellion would be reversed" and "we would have unconditional surrender of national authority to the Confederacy."[6]

William A. Hovey of the *Boston Evening Transcript* was the only abolitionist editor of a major newspaper who did not take a consistently hard line in 1876. A second-generation abolitionist whose merchant father had helped to finance the Garrisonians, Hovey became editor of the influential *Transcript* in 1875. During the 1876 campaign his editorials wavered back and forth between militancy and conciliation. On the one hand, "the South has not yet arrived at the point of fully believing in the manhood of the colored race. . . . While such a feeling lasts, would it be safe to commit the country to the hands of a party which derives two-thirds of its strength from the South?" On the other hand, the *Transcript* blamed radicals of the Benjamin Butler stripe for keeping sectional hostility alive. The bloody shirt was "the whole political capital" of this "disreputable clique of demagogues." Only by "eliminating the corrupt element that has made use of the negro vote at the South, and by a conciliatory yet firm policy toward the whites" would peace and prosperity ever prevail there. The policy of forcing outside rule on the South "is plainly enough now seen to be against all possibility . . . with the result only of making [blacks] the victims of race hatred." But on the eve of the election the *Transcript* returned to a hard line and declared that "a free and uncontrolled vote should be secured throughout the South if it requires the whole United States army."[7]

The disputed outcome of the 1876 election plunged many abolitionists into gloom. "The doubt about the result," wrote one, "has worried me more than I imagined it could, given me a headache three consecutive days, & haunted my dreams at night." But the conflicting returns from the three southern states (South Carolina, Louisiana, and Florida) still nominally controlled by Republicans provided a ray of hope. If Hayes carried all three, he would win the presidency by one electoral vote. Abolitionists developed a line of argument on this question that also became Republican orthodoxy: although on the face of the returns the Democrats appeared to have carried Florida and possibly Louisiana, the "bull-dozing" of black voters had nullified thousands of votes that would have given Republicans a majority in these states as

6 *CIO* (W), July 20, Oct. 25, 1876. For the Nixons and the *Inter Ocean*, see A. T. Andreas, *History of Chicago*, 3 vols., Chicago, 1886, III, 698-99, and John Moses and Joseph Kirkland, eds., *The History of Chicago*, 2 vols., Chicago, 1895, II, 19-20, 59-60.

7 *BET*, Aug. 18, 25, 26, Sept. 29, Oct. 12, 16, 1876. Edward L. Clement, another son of an abolitionist father, was assistant editor of the *Transcript* from 1875 to 1881 and editor from 1881 to 1905. Joseph E. Chamberlin, *The Boston Transcript, a History of Its First Hundred Years*, Boston, 1930, pp. 147-62.

well as South Carolina if a fair election had been held. Thus the action of Republican returning boards in throwing out the results from bull-dozed districts was legitimate. The veteran abolitionist and champion of woman suffrage Henry B. Blackwell denounced "doughfaced" Republicans who "accept without hestitation the charges of fraud made by the opposite Party, forgetting the great underlying Democratic fraud of negro intimidation. . . . If the Anti-Slavery battle is really not ended . . . then let us close up our ranks and prepare for the final conflict."[8]

But the ranks of doughfaced Republicans included some abolitionists. Franklin Sanborn hoped that "the day of the carpetbagger has passed away, never to return," while Wendell Garrison would view "without regret" the "blacks deprived of a supremacy as corrupting to themselves as it was dangerous to society at large." In a widely quoted Thanksgiving Day sermon, James Freeman Clarke warned that the future of the democratic process was at stake. If what appeared to be Democratic majorities in two states were overturned by federal force, he said, the United States was a despotism. Abolitionist though he was, "I had a thousand times rather have the Republican party defeated by an honest vote than successful by a fraudulent one."[9]

William Lloyd Garrison published a long rejoinder to Clarke's sermon. Far from being fraudulent, he declared, "the Republican majority in Louisiana, Mississippi, South Carolina and Florida, by a fair election, is no more to be questioned than in Maine, Vermont, Massachusetts or Iowa." Of the many who applauded Garrison's statement, none did so more fervently than the wife of Daniel H. Chamberlain, beleaguered governor of South Carolina. "There are too many timid Republicans in Boston," she wrote Garrison from Columbia. When such men as Clarke say that "the country would be better with Tilden for President . . . we . . . despair of ever convincing the Northern Republicans of the brutal outrages that have been perpetrated to elect him." Clarke had spent the winter in Charleston three years previously, she recalled, where "he saw only the pleasant exterior of the Southern gentleman and not the savage within. . . . A long residence here would have shown him their true character."[10]

With the protection of United States soldiers, Republican legislators organized the official legislature of South Carolina on November 28 while the Democrats departed in a body to convene their own legisla-

---

[8] Francis J. Garrison to Fanny Garrison Villard, Nov. 12, 1876, FGV Papers; *Woman's Journal*, Dec. 30, 1876.

[9] Sanborn in *Springfield Republican*, Feb. 9, 1877; Garrison in *Nation*, Mar. 1, 1877; Clarke's sermon reported in *Boston Journal*, Dec. 1, 1876.

[10] *Boston Journal*, Dec. 4, 1876; Alice Chamberlain to Garrison, Dec. 26, 1876, WLG Papers.

ture in a private building. Chamberlain took the oath of office December 7; his rival, Wade Hampton, was inaugurated by the Democratic legislature a few days later. For the next four months South Carolina enjoyed the luxury of two state governments. Only the presence of federal troops kept Chamberlain in office, and, so long as the presidential election remained in doubt, his future was uncertain. As a friend later recalled, for weeks "Chamberlain left his wife in the morning without knowing whether he would see her again at night, and often left her in a hysterical condition. Wherever he went he was surrounded with a guard of soldiers." Chamberlain carried on with dignity and courage, refusing a Democratic offer of election to the U.S. Senate if he would give up his claim to the governorship. In his inaugural address he declared himself "appalled" by northern "Republicans who permit the errors which have attended the first efforts of this race in self-government to chill their sympathies to such an extent that they stand coldly by and practically say that the peace of political servitude is better than the abuses and disquiet which newly acquired freedom has brought." Despite threats on his life, he did not intend to "cease my most vigorous resistance to this attempted overthrow and enslavement of a majority of the people of South Carolina. 'Here I stand; I can do no other.' "[11]

Meanwhile back in Washington Congress finally moved to break the electoral deadlock by creating a special commission to canvass the returns. By partisan decisions the commission awarded all disputed votes to Hayes. Many southern Democrats were reconciled to this outcome only by assurances that the new president would withdraw the federal troops from Columbia and New Orleans, give patronage to southern Democrats, and recommend federal appropriations for southern internal improvements. This Compromise of 1877 ended the electoral crisis, and Hayes took office on March 4. A former Whig, the president began his administration with the hope that by substituting conciliation for coercion he could win erstwhile southern Whigs over to the Republican party, take the race problem out of politics, and create a national Republican coalition based on economic rather than sectional issues.[12]

[11] *Boston Traveller*, Oct. 31, 1877; Allen, *Governor Chamberlain's Administration*, 446-47. The offer of the senatorship was described in a letter from Chamberlain to B. O. Duncan, Aug. 25, 1882, printed in *ibid.*, 505-506.

[12] C. Vann Woodward, *Reunion and Reaction: The Compromise of 1877 and the End of Reconstruction*, rev. ed., Boston, 1956; Harry Barnard, *Rutherford B. Hayes and His America*, Indianapolis, 1954, pp. 346-91. Polakoff, *The Politics of Inertia*, disputes Woodward's thesis that the negotiations between Hayes's lieutenants and southern Democrats were essential to the outcome.

These sentiments would not become fully evident until Hayes withdrew the troops in April. In the meantime he did not lack advice from abolitionists, some of whom had a personal stake in the matter. Governor Chamberlain responded angrily to a hint from the White House that he should give up his office for the larger good of the nation. He informed the president that he would not sacrifice "my honor as a public man" or "my duty to the Republicans of this State" for a shameful compromise. From Louisiana, where rival governments also existed, an ex-Oberlin abolitionist who was a member of the besieged Republican legislature informed James Monroe, abolitionist congressman and friend of Hayes, that "the same spirit which existed in 1861 exists here today. Although slavery cannot again be instituted here still a worse [condition] than Slavery for the black People would be the result of Democratic rule."[13]

But Hayes was getting advice more compatible with his own views from the advocates of retreat, including several abolitionists. "The times are ripe for a complete reconstruction of parties at the South," declared the *Boston Transcript*, which applauded Hayes's appointment of Tennessee Democrat David Key as postmaster general. The administration soon made it known that Wade Hampton and Francis T. Nicholls, Democratic claimants to the governorships of South Carolina and Louisiana, had promised to protect Negro rights if they were allowed to take office. Since Republicans in Louisiana had "utterly failed to furnish the colored race protection," said editor Hovey of the *Transcript*, such assurances held out hope for a better future. Even if Hampton and Nicholls failed to keep their promises "the United States could interpose its power with stronger reason than ever before, and the Republicans would reap great advantages from the hypocrisy and treachery of their opponents." In a private letter to a friend that was sent on to the president, Oliver Johnson, one of the original Garrisonians and now editor of a weekly newspaper in New Jersey, wrote that whatever southern policy Hayes decided on, "it cannot be worse than Grant's. It is impossible to govern the South by a combination of ignorance and low cunning, with the bayonet behind them. The negroes and the whites *must* find a way of living together peaceably, and then *time* must work out slowly the problems that remain."[14]

After backing and filling for several weeks, a number of other abolitionists also came to this conclusion. As late as the first of April the *In-*

[13] Chamberlain to Stanley Mathews, Mar. 7, 1877, in Allen, *Governor Chamberlain's Administration*, 470; Homer Johnson to Monroe, Jan. 19, 1877, Monroe Papers, Oberlin College Library.

[14] *BET*, Mar. 1, 13, 15, 21, 23, 1877; Johnson to Maria Weston Chapman, Mar. 18, 1877, Hayes Papers.

dependent said that "nothing but fraud, or violence, or both" could make Hampton and Nicholls governors of their states. George William Curtis believed that surrender to the Democrats would bring "the practical extinction of the colored vote." But even as they wrote these words, the editors of *Harper's Weekly* and the *Independent* showed signs of wavering. By the end of March Curtis was ready to pronounce the old southern policy a failure. All but two states had been lost to the Democrats *under that policy*, and the two remaining Republican administrations could not survive a day without soldiers in the state house. It was plain that a policy "which has not effectually protected the negro, and which has imbittered the jealousies of classes and of race" must be changed. After Hayes had made clear his intention to withdraw the troops, the *Independent* also came grudgingly to his support. "The strong and intelligent will somehow rule, said the paper in what would seem to be a repudiation of abolitionist doctrine, "and it is fighting against Nature to try to prevent it. . . . We know this is a very bad state of things, an illegal and revolutionary state of things. We wish it were different," but in the circumstances the Negro's best strategy was to work out an accommodation with conservative Democrats who alone had the power to protect his rights, "and gradually secure and profit by the advantages of education and free labor. For the time has now about come when the Negro must . . . fight his own battle, win his own elevation, prove his own manhood, and accredit his citizenship."[15]

In Massachusetts the *Commonwealth* and *Spy* spoke for old political abolitionists while *Zion's Herald* represented antislavery Methodists. All three papers reacted similarly to Hayes's policy. Confessing that "the subject is beset with difficulties," the *Spy* nevertheless concluded that military Reconstruction had failed and Hayes's policy of conciliation "at worst . . . can do no more than fail." If "the wealth, the intelligence, the business activity [of the South] side with the minority, refusing to contribute to the taxes, and thus exhaust the vitality of the majority government," asked the *Commonwealth*, what could be done? "The problem, at best, is a grave one. President Hayes has sought to solve it in one way. He should have the good wishes, at least, of the country that it may be solved happily." Sounding a theme that would become louder in subsequent years, *Zion's Herald* predicted that once the race issue was removed from southern politics, white men would begin to divide politically on the tariff, monetary policy, internal improvements, and so on, as they did in the North. "Either side will welcome all the assistance it can obtain from the negro," and eventually

[15] *Independent*, Mar. 29, Apr. 5, 1877; *HW*, Feb. 17, Mar. 31, 1877.

the race would win its rights. This "may not come in our day, but it will in our children's."[16]

But this did not represent the predominant abolitionist view in 1877. William Penn Nixon was the leading midwestern spokesman for abolitionists who opposed Hayes's policy. Though there were many good men in the South who might respond constructively to the president's olive branch, said Nixon, the section also contained "thousands of the most treacherous scoundrels that ever escaped hanging. . . . Conciliation to them is another word for weakness and imbecility. Left without restraint, such men as these will make the South the charnel-house of liberty." As for the argument that radical Reconstruction was a failure, Nixon replied that like Christianity it had not failed because it had never been tried. Instead of withdrawing troops from the South, Hayes should send more in.[17]

The angriest condemnations of Hayes's policy came from William Lloyd Garrison and Wendell Phillips. Even before the president made public his decisions on the South, Garrison issued a warning against the "weak, timid, purblind compromising element in the Republican party, whose panacea for all our national divisions is 'conciliation'— meaning thereby a truckling to the South . . . and a stolid indifference to the fate of her colored population." On the matter of southern pledges to protect Negro rights, Phillips said contemptuously that "the whole soil of the South is hidden by successive layers of broken promises. To trust a Southern promise would be fair evidence of insanity." To a reporter who asked why he did not wait to see if the president's "experiment" would work, Phillips replied that "it is no experiment, but a treacherous bargain." The traitor Hayes had "sold us out."[18]

Most of the press came down hard on Phillips and Garrison. The *Boston Post* called Phillips a "crazy rhetorical buffoon" whose speeches were "a blue stream of hatred." The *New York Tribune* derided his "blackguardism" and "venom." A Unitarian weekly commented that "during the anti-slavery struggle and the civil war [Phillips's] talk was somewhat tragical. Now it is merely farcical." The *New York Times* branded Garrison's statements "premature and unjust." Hayes did not intend to abandon the freedmen, said the *Times*; on the contrary, his policy was designed to redeem the failure of Reconstruction. Garrison had confounded "conciliation with surrender" and ignored the recent

[16] *Mass. Spy*, Mar. 16, Apr. 27, 1877; *BC*, Apr. 7, 14, 1877; *ZH*, June 28, July 26, 1877.

[17] *CIO* (W), Mar. 8, Apr. 19, 26, May 23, 1877.

[18] Garrison to James G. Blaine, Mar. 8, 1877, published in *NYT*, Mar. 12; Phillips in *Boston Globe*, Mar. 28, 1877, and *BC*, Mar. 31, 1877.

"growth of a change favorable to the cultivation of friendly relations between North and South."[19]

But many Garrisonians praised their old leaders for speaking out. Embattled Republicans in the South also thanked Garrison for his words. The U.S. Marshal in Louisiana told him that his statement of the case "goes to the marrow of our grave question. . . . Men, like you, are each a legion to re-inforce us." The black lieutenant-governor-elect wrote Garrison that "you understand the situation in Louisiana thoroughly. . . . We all pray for you and the Hon. Wendell Phillips that God in His Providence will strengthen you that you may continue to advocate the rights of my race." But Governor Chamberlain feared that Garrison's praiseworthy efforts to rouse public opinion were futile. "I see plainly that there is little effective opposition to the policy of surrender," he wrote Garrison's son. "The North is *tired* of the Southern question, and wants a settlement, no matter what."[20]

When Hayes notified Chamberlain that on April 10 all federal troops would be withdrawn from Columbia, the governor wanted at first to stay at his post whatever the cost. But his supporters led by the four black cabinet officers persuaded him to give up peacefully to avoid bloodshed in which blacks would be certain losers. Chamberlain stepped down with a bitterly eloquent proclamation explaining his actions and enjoining South Carolina Republicans from violence. Despite their "heroic efforts and sacrifices" and his own "clear and perfect" title to office, "by the order of the President whom your votes alone rescued from overwhelming defeat, the Government of the United States abandons you."[21]

Garrison seconded Chamberlain's proclamation with another excoriation of Hayes's "policy of compromise, of credulity, of weakness, of subserviency, of surrender," a policy that "sustains might against right . . . the rich and powerful against the poor and unprotected." The president was troubled by these attacks. To a newspaper reporter he said that he endorsed Garrison's goals and was sorry they could not agree on means. Through a mutual friend, Hayes informed Garrison that he meant "to stand by the freedmen," and invited the old crusader to Washington for a personal conference. Though flattered, Garrison declined the invitation. "It would do no good for me to talk with Mr. Hayes," he explained. "I do not doubt his honesty of purpose. But he does not understand the South." Garrison probably felt that a visit to

19 *Boston Post*, Mar. 28, 1877; *NYTrib.*, Apr. 3, 1877; *Christian Register*, Mar. 31, 1877; *NYT*, Mar. 13, 1877.
20 J. R. C. Pilkin to Garrison, Mar. 27, 1877, Caesar C. Antoine to Garrison, May 2, 1877, Chamberlain to Francis J. Garrison, Mar. 18, 1877, WLG Papers.
21 *NYTrib.*, Apr. 11, 1877.

the White House would compromise his freedom to speak out against the administration.[22]

Although most Garrisonians backed their leader's stand, two of his oldest co-workers did not. The "use of federal troops" was "no longer *possible*, even if desirable," Samuel May told Garrison. Even though southern Republicans would become powerless for a time, "better, I must say, that the colored people generally vote with the Democratic party than to be slaughtered by hundreds." More distressing to Garrison than May's private reflections were his old friend Oliver Johnson's public endorsements of Hayes's policy. Racial hostility in the South, said Johnson, "can only be aggravated by the measures heretofore chiefly employed. It will be best, in the long run, to leave [the two races] face to face, with the slightest possible interference, and trust to moral influences chiefly to secure peace and good-will." Astounded by these statements, Garrison penned a rejoinder that Johnson published in his newspaper, the *Orange* (N.J.) *Journal*. "The Southern question stands at present essentially as it has stood from the beginning," said Garrison. "It is still 'the irrepressible conflict' between right and wrong, freedom and oppression, Christ and Belial." In a private reply to Garrison, Johnson admitted that "any policy in regard to the South is but a choice of evils." But he could see no alternative to Hayes's program. If it "fails to give substantial protection to the negro, then there is no policy that can avail to do it under our Constitution. To have trodden further in Grant's footsteps would have been madness."[23]

An analysis of the private and public statements of former abolitionists in 1877 discloses that, of 81 whose opinion is known, 45 (56 percent) opposed Hayes's policy while 36 (44 percent) supported it. Of the latter, 16 endorsed the president's actions with qualifications or reluctance; many of these later turned against the policy. There was considerable continuity between Liberal Republicanism in 1872 and approval for Hayes's program five years later: of the 36 supporting Hayes, 20 had backed Greeley for president while of the 45 who opposed Hayes only one is known to have supported Greeley. The greatest defection from radical Reconstruction occurred among non-Garrisonians. Whereas only 27 percent of the Garrisonians supported Hayes, 45 percent of the evangelicals and 74 percent of the political abolitionists did so.

[22] *Boston Advertiser*, Apr. 23, 1877; Barnard, *Hayes*, 423; Henry B. Blackwell to Garrison, May 7, 1877, WLG Papers; Blackwell's obituary of Garrison in *Woman's Journal*, May 31, 1879.

[23] May to Garrison, Apr. 28, 1877, WLG Papers; *Orange Journal*, Mar. 17, 31, 1877; Johnson to Garrison, May 1, 1877, WLG Papers.

These data tend to confirm Aileen Kraditor's thesis that Garrisonians were more radical than their non-Garrisonian counterparts. Kraditor argued that Garrison and his followers saw slavery as the most glaring symptom of a sick society, while many non-Garrisonians regarded slavery as an anomaly in an otherwise healthy society. A number of Garrisonians were *radicals* who wanted a fundamental restructuring of society; most non-Garrisonians were *reformers* who hoped to strengthen the existing order by getting rid of the one big evil that weakened it.[24]

Although Kraditor applied her analysis mainly to the 1830s, it sheds light on differences among abolitionists in 1877. Those who endorsed Hayes's removal of the troops believed that an uneducated, propertyless majority could not govern against the wishes of the educated, propertied minority. They subscribed to the middle-class assumption that education and material success were the instruments of social mobility and political power in an open society. Thus the pro-Hayes abolitionists in 1877 stressed the need for blacks to cultivate friendly relations with conservative whites, to acquire land and education, and to work their way up gradually into the middle class. On the other hand, while the Garrisonians who denounced Hayes's policy were hardly revolutionaries (though some, following Wendell Phillips, were active in radical labor movements of the 1870s), they did believe that the rights and political power of the black proletariat should be upheld by whatever force was necessary. They too subscribed to the Protestant Ethic, but they thought the freedmen would sooner lift themselves to equal status if protected by law than if dependent on the uncertain good will of southern paternalists.

Perhaps surprisingly, most black abolitionists embraced the gradualist, paternalist, pro-Hayes view in 1877. Critics later charged that the silence or approval of three leading black abolitionists was bought with government patronage: Hayes appointed Frederick Douglass Marshal of the District of Columbia and John Mercer Langston Minister to Haiti, while in South Carolina Hampton appointed Martin R. Delany, who had supported him in the 1876 election, as a trial justice. But though these appointments may have helped, most black abolitionists who supported Hayes probably did so for pretty much the same reasons as white abolitionists. Disillusionment with the failure of Reconstruction caused many Negro spokesmen to emphasize the need for self-help, education, and uplift rather than politics and protest. As the Florida black leader J. Willis Menard put it in 1876: "Inasmuch as

24 Aileen S. Kraditor, *Means and Ends in American Abolitionism: Garrison and His Critics on Strategy and Tactics, 1834-1850*, New York, 1969, chaps. 2-5.

troops and repressive laws have failed to establish permanent peace between the two races, we must seek elsewhere . . . for a remedy."[25]

Whatever their reasons, several black abolitionists endorsed Hayes's policy and not a single prominent one spoke out against it. Langston considered the president's removal of troops "a step in the direction of just and peaceful Reconstruction." If the freedmen were to "become self-reliant and self-supporting, said Langston, they "must have reconciliation. . . . With harmony and good neighborhood existing between [the Negro] and the white classes, his life . . . will prove, it may be, at times rugged and hard, but on the whole successful and profitable." George T. Downing conceded that black voters might have to accept Democratic domination for a while. "It is a fact chilling to look upon, but it must be made to have an inspiring effect." The race must "bide its time, get means, apply itself, struggle hard, become educated and skilled."[26]

In March 1877 Frederick Douglass let the president know that an appointment as Marshal of the District of Columbia would be "entirely agreeable" to him. Several days after receiving the appointment, Douglass wrote privately to a friend of Hayes that the president "is a just man, & his policy embraces the welfare of both races, & I rejoice at any evidences of support whether from the North or the South." In May, Douglass told a white abolitionist that "what was called the President's policy might rather be considered the President's necessity. . . . Statesmen often [are] compelled to act upon facts as they [are], and not as they would like to have them." Several blacks regarded Douglass' appointment as a symbol of the administration's commitment to Negro rights; as one well-wisher wrote to him, the honor demonstrated "a determination to sustain *you* and eventually the negro at the South."[27]

Although of course not all blacks endorsed Hayes's policy, the number who did is striking. The president received many letters and resolutions of commendation from black organizations and individual Negroes, including several political leaders. George Washington Williams, Union army veteran and noted historian of his race, informed

[25] Menard quoted in Vincent P. De Santis, *Republicans Face the Southern Question: The New Departure Years, 1877-1897*, Baltimore, 1959, pp. 24-25.

[26] Langston, *The Other Phase of Reconstruction, a Speech Delivered at Congregational Tabernacle, Jersey City, Apr. 17, 1877*, Washington, 1877, p. 9; Downing to Frederick Douglass, Mar. 19, 1877, Douglass Papers formerly at Douglass Memorial Home, Washington, D.C.

[27] Douglass to John Sherman, Mar. 13, 1877, Hayes Papers; Douglass to F. S. Stebbins, Mar. 26, 1877, Misc. Mss., Hayes Memorial Library; Douglass quoted by William W. Patton in *Advance*, May 31, 1877; Martha Greene to Douglass, June 13, 1877, Douglass Papers.

Hayes in 1878 that "I was the first colored man in the country to give [your] Southern policy a practical endorsement—and in more than eighty public speeches, urged the people to accept it as the judgment of an honest man, a genuine republican and a noble patriot." And Francis L. Cardozo, who had served four years as secretary of state and four as treasurer of South Carolina, wrote on the day that federal troops left the state house in Columbia: "Many evils connected with . . . Republicanism in South Carolina . . . seemed almost ineradicable, and I have no hesitation in saying that its internal defects had more to do with its failure, than any external causes. . . . I am willing to see [Hayes's policy] fairly tried, and hope it may succeed."[28] If the actions of those white abolitionists who supported the president were an abandonment of the Negro, then the similar actions of the race's own leaders were equally so.

By the summer of 1877, abolitionists had settled into one of three patterns of response to Hayes's southern policy. Those who opposed it lost no opportunity to proclaim its shortcomings; those who warmly approved it professed to see evidence that it was working; and those who had come reluctantly to support it hoped for the best. The last position was volatile, and some who held it would swing back to a hard line within a year. Their sense of perplexity and divided loyalties was best expressed by abolitionist Congressman James Monroe, a friend of the president, who told his Ohio constituents in June that while Hayes's policy was not one "I could have recommended," further opposition "can not recover the past and . . . might sacrifice the future." The president had made his decision; "that notch in the ratchet wheel is passed," and "the right course for us now to pursue is to aid him in making it a success."[29]

[28] Williams to B. K. Rogers (Hayes's private secretary), Dec. 5, 1878, Hayes Papers; Cardozo to Oliver O. Howard, Apr. 10, 1877, Howard Papers, Bowdoin College Library.
[29] Monroe, *Present Wants of the Nation, An Address*, Oberlin, 1877, pp. 3-5.

Chapter Six

Crosscurrents and Confusion, 1877–1880

Although Reconstruction died in 1877, there were many efforts to bring it back to life. The debate among former abolitionists over coercion versus conciliation persisted with only slightly abated vigor for several more years. The Hayes administration was plagued by party factionalism in which conflicts over southern policy played a major role. By 1880 the "bloody shirt" strategy had re-emerged, but after it had served its purpose in the presidential election the shirt was put away again.

During the first year of Hayes's presidency his abolitionist supporters proclaimed southern pacification a success. Secretary Michael Strieby of the American Missionary Association agreed with the president's statement in September 1877 that "there has been no other six months since the war when there have been so few outrages committed upon the colored people." Strieby was gratified that "the comparative freedom of the South from political agitations gives the opportunity for undisturbed effort" in the work of education. As the South became "peaceful, law-respecting, industrious" and "devoted to business first and politics afterwards," said William Hovey of the *Boston Transcript*, "the negroes are better treated than when the State governments were propped up by the United States military."[1]

Optimistic abolitionists detected signs in scattered local elections that southern whites were now dividing politically on issues other than race with each side appealing for black support. When Negro voters helped independents triumph over regular Democrats in Mississippi and Georgia, the *American Missionary* and *Zion's Herald* hailed "the beginning of a condition which . . . offers the best solution of the Southern question." James Freeman Clarke declared in April 1878 that abolitionists should rejoice "when Southern democratic governors appoint colored men to office, when Southern democrats count the votes of the colored people. . . . All attacks on the President and his policy retard this tendency to the peaceful union of whites and blacks."[2]

The cordial welcome given President Hayes on a brief visit to Tennessee in the spring of 1877 encouraged him to make a good-will trip

---

[1] *AM*, XXXII (Jan. 1878), 2; *BET*, July 16, 1877, Mar. 7, 1878.
[2] *AM*, XXXII (Jan. 1878), 5-6; *ZH*, Dec. 20, 1877; Clarke, *State of the Nation, Fast-Day Sermon*, Boston, 1878, pp. 7-8.

to other southern states in September, accompanied part of the time by Wade Hampton. Wherever they went, the party was greeted with cheers and praise. Hayes and Hampton both reiterated their pledges to preserve Negro rights; the *Transcript* considered Hampton's presence in the president's entourage "in some sense a hostage that the colored race shall receive no detriment because of the President's policy."[3]

A few months after Hayes returned from the South, Thomas Wentworth Higginson made his own way down the Atlantic coast to visit veterans of his wartime black regiment. He reported plenty of evidence of black prosperity under the Hayes policy. The former soldiers with whom he talked owned their land and were doing well. In his travels through four southern states he "never saw an act of violence or insolence between persons of different colors." Wade Hampton had kept his promises, said Higginson; blacks continued to vote and to hold office in South Carolina. Most of the men from his old regiment "agreed that wherever the Democratic party itself began to divide on internal or local questions, each wing was ready to conciliate and consequently defend the colored vote, for its own interest, just as Northern politicians conciliate the Irish vote, even while they denounce it."[4]

Most abolitionists who had been driven out of South Carolina by the Democratic restoration or who had stayed there despite it did not share Higginson's "rose colored" view. The missionary teachers Laura Towne and Martha Schofield wrote letters to northern newspapers publicizing the expansion of the convict lease system and the cutbacks in public school appropriations that were part of Hampton's "retrenchment" program in 1877. After being forced from office, Daniel H. Chamberlain left South Carolina and settled into law practice in New York. But he did not lick his wounds in silence. A well-publicized 4th of July address gave him the opportunity to denounce the president in words dripping with acid. Hayes's action was "unconstitutional and revolutionary, subversive of constitutional guaranties and false to every dictate of political honor, public justice, and good morals," said Chamberlain. It was "a crime more wanton and unpardonable than the crime against Kansas." Reuben Tomlinson, who had left the state with Chamberlain, told northern audiences that "the same spirit which before the war tried to stifle the anti-slavery agitation by cries of danger to the Union, and injury to the business interests of the country, now seeks to quiet the conscience of the North by talk about a reconciliation" that was "nothing but a . . . complete surrender to the South." Tomlinson hoped that "the friends of the colored man" would speak

[3] *BET*, Sept. 21, 1877.
[4] Higginson, "The Southern Outlook," *Woman's Journal*, Mar. 16, 1878; "Some War Scenes Revisited," *Atlantic Monthly*, XLII (July 1878), 1-9.

out as of old to rouse public opinion against "the utter abandonment and disbandment of the Republican party in the South."[5]

Several abolitionists did their best in this direction. Gilbert Haven published many articles and speeches accusing the administration of "treason to God and their fellow-man." The *Chicago Inter Ocean*, with a circulation of 100,000, continued to hammer away at Hayes's policy in an attempt to revive radicalism among midwestern Republicans. In his 1877–1878 lecture tour, Wendell Phillips excoriated the president in speeches heard or read by hundreds of thousands. Hayes was the "traitor in the White House," said Phillips, "an old fashioned Northern snob—that class which, before the war, believed all the honor and all the gentlemen resided in the South." Wade Hampton was a "liar" and a "cheat" who "knows perfectly well that it is utterly impossible for him to perform what he has promised, and while he and others like him use President Hayes as their convenient tool, they will vote so as to organize the Government to serve as a Southern machine."[6]

Just as for half a century he had been the leading abolitionist, William Lloyd Garrison was until his death in 1879 the foremost critic of Hayes's southern policy. To those who said that carpetbag governments had been riddled with corruption while their successors were honest, Garrison replied that the corruption issue was "incidental" compared with the "fundamental" question of equal rights. "All parties are more or less corrupt," he wrote, but "we have in Mississippi, South Carolina, and Louisiana, three governments . . . that are there by the shot-gun policy, by bloody usurpation." Hayes's hopes for the South exhibited "a childish credulity, a blindness of vision, and an imbecility of judgment.[7]

Garrison's prose had lost none of its sting with 50 years of practice, and the "stalwart" faction of the Republican party welcomed his assistance. The stalwarts were the Gilded Age's successors of the old radical Republicans. They opposed both Hayes's southern policy and his plans for civil service reform. Since Garrison considered civil service reform incidental and Negro rights fundamental, he was willing to ally himself with stalwarts even though their motives were quite different from his own. Hoping to lend an aura of righteousness to his campaign against Hayes, stalwart leader William E. Chandler asked Garrison in

[5] Rupert S. Holland, ed., *Letters and Diary of Laura M. Towne, Written from the Sea Islands of South Carolina, 1862-84*, Cambridge, Mass., 1912, pp. 273-74; *Nation*, Aug. 7, 1877; *Woman's Journal*, Mar. 2, 1878; Chamberlain's speech in *Independent*, July 12, 1877; Tomlinson in *Boston Traveller*, Oct. 31, 1877, and *Index*, Feb. 21, 1878.

[6] Speeches by Phillips reported in *Boston Journal*, Oct. 29, 1877, *BET*, Nov. 8, 1877, *NYTrib.*, Nov. 24, 1877, *Cleveland Leader*, Nov. 22, 1877.

[7] *Boston Traveller*, Oct. 31, 1877; *BC*, Nov. 3, 1877.

January 1878 to write a public letter endorsing Chandler's recent condemnation of the president. Garrison responded enthusiastically, ridiculing the descriptions of "peace" in the South. Of course there was peace, he said: "they who are in their graves excite no animosities." The freedmen had been "thoroughly 'bull-dozed'; their spirits are broken, their hopes blasted, their means of defence wrested from them: what need of killing or hunting them any longer?"[8]

Chandler had Garrison's letter published in several newspapers, and later reprinted it in a pamphlet with several of his own speeches. Garrison's letter evoked a large response; Chandler later told him that "in my own fight . . . against the Hayes policy . . . I have been encouraged and aided immeasurably by your steadfast and unqualified support." Garrison was doubtless flattered by these words, but may have enjoyed even more the comment of a southern newspaper, reminiscent of the old days, that "Old Garrison . . . has always been a traitor, and if he had his rights would be swinging this moment from the gable end of some sour apple tree." More sobering was the *New York Times*'s admonition to Garrison not to be "deluded . . . into the belief that something may be gained by fighting an issue which for all practical purposes is as dead as secession. . . . Outside of small and suspicious circles [no] real interest attaches to the old forms of the Southern question."[9]

Recriminations of faithlessness to the black man divided the "small and suspicious circle" of old Garrisonians in the winter of 1877–1878. When Oliver Johnson and Parker Pillsbury criticized Garrison for being "still bent on the bloody shirt," another Garrisonian made a thinly veiled reference to "back-sliding friends of the freedmen," and Garrison himself lamented that "some of the old abolitionists seem to have lost . . . their once vital interest in the fate of a race whose course they espoused with so much zeal." Such insinuations brought a pained response from Johnson. "In regard for the rights and welfare of the negroes," he told Garrison, "I yield nothing to anybody, not even to you." When he spoke favorably of the president's policy, said Johnson, "I mean more than the withdrawal of the troops." He meant "the purpose to win the better portion at least of the Southern people by kindness rather than by force or denunciation . . . to do justice to the negro."[10]

[8] Chandler to Garrison, Jan. 15, 1878, WLG Papers; *NYT*, Jan. 24, 1878.

[9] Chandler to Garrison, Jan. 27, Dec. 9, 1878, WLG Papers; *Petersburg Index-Appeal*, Jan. 28, 1878, quoted in *NYT*, Jan. 31; *NYT*, Jan. 27, 1878.

[10] Johnson and Pillsbury quoted in *BC*, Nov. 10, 1877, and *Cincinnati Commercial*, Nov. 2, 1877; Abigail Kelly Foster to Garrison, Nov. 18, 1877, Garrison to Samuel Johnson, Jan. 18, 1879, Oliver Johnson to Garrison, Nov. 28, Dec. 10, 21, 1877, WLG Papers.

But some abolitionists who had earlier shared Johnson's faith in this policy had begun to voice doubts before the end of 1877. Commenting on the murder of three Republicans in Mississippi, the *Commonwealth* conceded that it may have done wrong when it "encouraged the hope . . . that with the withdrawal of the national troops, the promises of fair dealing to white loyalists and colored people would be fulfilled." The *Spy* agreed sadly that the white South was "as intolerant and proscriptive as it ever was." Hampton had turned out to be only "a maker of phrases" rather than "a man who brings things to pass."[11]

Abolitionists who had opposed Hayes's policy from the start were encouraged by these defections and by the backing they now began to receive from some black leaders. Frederick Douglass broke his silence in November 1877 with a speech criticizing the president's approval of "the Shot-Gun Governments of South Carolina and Louisiana." A black woman told Garrison that she was glad he and Wendell Phillips were still clothed in their righteous armor, for "you are wanted nowadays as much as in the early days of the great struggle for liberty." Heartened by such support, Garrison hoped to make the "southern question" the major issue of the 1878 congressional elections. He scolded Republicans who thought that finance, labor, or civil service reform were more important. So long as "the freedmen at the South are, on 'the Mississippi plan' and by 'the shot-gun policy,' ruthlessly deprived of their rights," he proclaimed, "the old anti-slavery issue is still the paramount issue."[12]

As the fall elections neared, terrorism in the South transformed several more proponents of conciliation into hard-liners again. Samuel May admitted to Garrison that "events largely confirm your predictions & expectations, and—I may truly say—my own fears; though I *hoped* that we might have arrived at the point when a 'decent regard for the opinions of the civilized world' might touch even Wade Hampton." Theodore Bourne, son of the pioneer abolitionist George Bourne and a supporter of Hayes's policy in 1877, was converted by his experiences in South Carolina during the 1878 campaign. He had "gone to the extreme verge of conciliation in making excuses for the ex-Confederates," Bourne told the president, but "I have lost all confidence in the white citizens *ever being changed into Union men*." The once-hopeful Methodist editors Bradford Peirce and Arthur Edwards confessed themselves "rudely shaken" by the 1878 elections which were "scarcely more free from intimidation, outrage, and fraud than in pre-

---

11 *BC*, June 9, 1877; *Mass. Spy*, June 1, July 20, 1877.
12 Douglass quoted in Philip S. Foner, *The Life and Writings of Frederick Douglass*, 4 vols., New York, 1950-55, IV, 102-103; Ottilia Assing to Garrison, Oct. 30, 1877, Garrison to Wendell Phillips, Oct. 30, 1878, WLG Papers.

vious years." Edwards was ready to return to a policy of force. "The recent murderers in South Carolina and Louisiana must be brought to justice," he thundered a week after the elections, "if it requires one hundred thousand troops."[13]

Although George William Curtis was not ready to go this far, he conceded that the "Red Shirt revival of the Ku-Klux" had "embarrassed" northern defenders of Hayes. Editors Bowen and Ward of the *Independent* were more angry than embarrassed. Wade Hampton's covert approval of fraud and violence while mouthing platitudes of equal rights, they said, proved him "a liar and a hypocrite." Forgetting temporarily about time and education as solutions of the race problem, the editors called on the federal government to "exercise all the lawful powers to protect every citizen of the United States in his constitutional right of voting. . . . Whether this is in accordance with the so-called 'Southern policy' we do not care."[14]

The *Boston Transcript* underwent the most dramatic conversion during the 1878 campaign. At first unwilling to admit that "Hampton is a hypocrite and the cherished hope of a new era in the South is but a dream," the *Transcript* nevertheless conceded that "it is very trying to the Southerners' well-wishers at the North . . . to find them such slow learners in the rudiments of political equality." Editor Hovey still thought that "United States bayonets can't mend matters," but after the election he was not so sure. The "crimes against freedom" required "something more than the concentration of public opinion upon the guilty. . . . It calls for action on the part of the General Government to the utmost limits of its constitutional power."[15]

This sounded almost like William Lloyd Garrison. Indeed, after the election, many former defenders of Hayes's policy began to talk like Garrison—including the president himself. The returns made clear the failure of his program to achieve its two principal aims: protection of Negro rights by the "better class" of southern whites, and the creation of an indigenous Republican party led by whites of Whig antecedents. Republican strength in southern state legislatures dropped sharply in 1878. Only 62 of 294 counties with black majorities went Republican compared with 125 in 1876. In South Carolina, the most extreme case, the Republican vote declined from 90,000 in 1876 to 4,000 in 1878. One South Carolina county whose population was three-quarters black cast not a single Republican ballot. In the face of such evidence the presi-

[13] May to Garrison, Oct. 11, 1878, WLG Papers; Bourne to Hayes, Nov. 16, 19, 30, 1878, Bourne to W. K. Rogers, Oct. 23, Dec. 6, 1878, Hayes Papers, Hayes Memorial Library; *ZH*, Nov. 21, 1878; *NWCA*, Nov. 13, 1878.

[14] HW, Nov. 16, 1878; *Independent*, Oct. 24, 1878.

[15] *BET*, Aug. 16, Oct. 23, 31, Nov. 13, 1878.

dent admitted that his policy was "a *failure*," for events had "proved that fair elections with free suffrage for every voter in the South are an impossibility."[16]

The question was, what to do about it? In his annual message to Congress in December 1878, Hayes struck a note reminiscent of Reconstruction when he promised to use every possible means to enforce the Constitution. But he was not precise in describing the means. Several abolitionists came forward to suggest new legislation or to point to ways in which existing laws could be used. The *Transcript* urged the House to deny credentials to representatives elected by fraud or violence. Then, under the constitutional provision giving Congress the power to regulate the elections of representatives, "Congress could go into the minutest machinery of congressional elections and provide such regulations as to have the whole business from the registration of voters to the counting of the ballots . . . in its own hands." Several other abolitionist newspapers endorsed these proposals.[17]

But with both houses under Democratic control after March 4, 1879, there was no chance for the passage of new legislation. And as a president with a questionable mandate at the head of a divided party, Hayes could do little. Realizing this, the *Independent* and other abolitionist journals took a position that would become a familiar Republican stance during the next decade: since the aim of southern Democrats, as of the old slave power, was "not simply supremacy on [their] own soil, but . . . control of the General Government," a solid Republican North must confront the solid Democratic South. How would this help the Negro? Northern firmness would teach southern whites that they could not gain their goals by "intimidation, bulldozing [and] ballot-box stuffing. . . . We are not going to let any party rule this country that will not deal justly by the political rights of the Negro." Although for many politicos this strategy of waving the bloody shirt was mainly a device to win northern votes rather than to help the freedmen, the bloody shirt nevertheless became something of a symbol of egalitarianism. By the end of 1878 even Oliver Johnson agreed with Garrison's words: " 'The bloody shirt!' *In hoc signo vinces!*"[18]

A special session of the new Democratic Congress in March 1879 gave Republicans plenty of chances to wave the shirt. As the *Inter*

[16] Vincent P. De Santis, *Republicans Face the Southern Question: The New Departure Years, 1877-1897*, Baltimore, 1959, pp. 99-100; Stanley P. Hirshson, *Farewell to the Bloody Shirt: Northern Republicans and the Southern Negro, 1877-1893*, Bloomington, Ind., 1962, pp. 47-48; Hayes quoted in *ibid.*, 49.

[17] James D. Richardson, ed., *The Messages and Papers of the Presidents*, Washington, 1897-1913, x, 4445-4447; *BET*, Dec. 2, 1878, Jan. 1, 9, 10, 1879.

[18] *Independent*, Nov. 14, 21, Dec. 5, 12, 1878; letter from Garrison in *NYTrib.*, Jan. 4, 1879. See also *Orange Journal*, Dec. 14, 1878.

Ocean pointed out, 18 Confederate generals sat in the Senate, rebel brigadiers crowded the House aisles, a Confederate editor was secretary of the Senate, and the commander of a Confederate prisoner of war camp "where many a poor boy met an inglorious death at the hands of starvation and disease" was the chairman of the pensions committee. Pulling out all the stops, the *Inter Ocean* warned that if the Democrats won in 1880, they would repeal all federal elections laws, nullify the 14th and 15th Amendments by refashioning the Supreme Court, enact new black laws to reduce the freedmen to serfdom, pay southern war claims, and grant pensions to rebel soldiers.[19]

The "Rebel Brigadiers" played into stalwart hands by attaching riders to appropriations bills to repeal what remained of the 1870–1871 Reconstruction enforcement acts. Hayes won the respect of radicals by vetoing five such riders. Democrats finally backed down, and the enforcement acts, though virtually dead letters, remained on the books. These attempted repeals completed the reconversion of most abolitionists and Republicans to a hard-line attitude. By the spring of 1879, 55 of the 64 abolitionists whose opinion is known agreed that conciliation had failed; 15 of these had originally supported Hayes's policy. The *Inter Ocean* rejoiced that the Republican party "has at last become once more what it should never have ceased to be, a stalwart party. There is no longer any cant about harmonizing and tranquillizing and conciliating the South."[20]

In March 1879 the first boatloads of black migrants from the lower Mississippi valley began to arrive in Kansas. They were the forerunners of an "Exodus" of tens of thousands during the next two years whose coming more than doubled the state's black population. The Exodus furnished abolitionists with additional evidence of southern wickedness. Though the migration's main cause was economic, abolitionists usually emphasized the denial of civil and political rights in their analysis of the phenomenon. From his vantage point in New Orleans, Methodist missionary Joseph C. Hartzell wrote that while "hard times, continued poverty, the tenant system . . . the credit system . . . have much to do with the present discontent," the "real cause of the Exodus is that colored people are shot and murdered and terrified and persecuted." A Congregational minister who interviewed several refugees in St. Louis wrote to northern newspapers: "Robbed, stripped, peeled, insulted, the negro has looked in vain toward the North for the help that has not come. We were too busy 'conciliating' his late master to hear the cry of the slave. And now that the rebel flag is virtually

[19] *CIO* (W), Mar. 27, Apr. 3, 1879.   [20] *Ibid.*, Mar. 27, 1879.

floating over Congress the black man flees . . . leaving a land where he is shot for voting a Republican ticket."[21]

Abolitionists and Republicans did more than talk about the Exodus. They soon realized that migrants who brought with them little more than the clothes on their backs were "in danger of perishing in the wilderness" before they ever reached the Promised Land. After Democrats blocked a congressional move to provide emergency relief, Kansas Governor John P. St. John enlisted the aid of Quaker abolitionists Laura S. Haviland and Elizabeth Comstock to found the Kansas Freedmen's Relief Association in May 1879. All over the North, former abolitionists helped to organize auxiliary Kansas freedmen's societies in their own communities, with Quakers often taking the lead. In Boston, William Lloyd Garrison arose from his sickbed to make one last effort for the freedmen. He personally raised a thousand dollars for relief before his death on May 24. Out on the Kansas plains an abolitionist friend of Garrison who had not been in the public eye for nearly half a century, Prudence Crandall Philleo, used her brother's farm as a base for the distribution of supplies to migrants.[22]

The Kansas Freedmen's Relief Association continued its work for two years. Laura Haviland supervised its employment bureau, which found jobs and established homesteading colonies for the "Exodusters." The Association bought land and resold it to the blacks for $2.65 per acre with only one-tenth down, waived the first payment, and provided farm animals to help them get started. During the winter of 1879–1880 the Association built temporary barracks in Topeka to house hundreds of migrants stranded in the city. Several northern societies were organized to establish evening schools, libraries, and agricultural institutes for the refugees. A recent study of the Exodus has concluded that white efforts to assist the settlers were a reassertion of "abolitionist principle" which helped thousands of blacks begin a new life despite the hostility of many Kansans and the disillusionment of some "Exodusters" who found the harsh climate and alien customs a far cry from the Promised Land they had sought.[23]

---

[21] *SWCA*, May 15, 1879; *Advance*, May 1, 1879. For descriptions of the Exodus, see John G. Van Dusen, "The Exodus of 1879," *Journal of Negro History*, xxi (Apr. 1936), 111-29; Glen Schwedemann, "St. Louis and the 'Exodusters' of 1879," *ibid.*, xlvi (Jan. 1961), 32-46; and Hirshson, *Farewell to the Bloody Shirt*, 63-72.

[22] Laura S. Haviland, *A Woman's Life-Work*, Cincinnati, 1881, pp. 482-508; Francis C. Anscomb, "The Contributions of the Quakers to the Reconstruction of the Southern States," Ph.D. Dissertation, Univ. of No. Car., 1926, pp. 253-58; Comstock to Joshua L. Baily, Dec. 22, 1879, Feb. 23, 1880, Baily Papers, Quaker Collection, Haverford College Library; *Friends' Review*, Jan. 31, 1880, Mar. 4, 1881; *Boston Traveller*, Apr. 16, 24, 1879; Prudence Crandall Philleo to Garrison, Mar. 20, Apr. 20, 1879, WLG Papers.

[23] Haviland, *A Woman's Life-Work*, 506-507; *Friends' Review*, Aug. 20, 1881;

Whether or not the Exodusters were successful in their quest for a better life, the abolitionist effort to rouse northern anger toward "southern outrages" benefited from the movement. At a Boston meeting to raise funds for the refugees, Wendell Phillips electrified a large crowd with his opening words: "Are the negroes free? . . . Did Lee really drive Grant out of Virginia, and was it Jefferson Davis who pardoned Abraham Lincoln?" For 10 years the freed slave had "tried to do his duty as a citizen" but had been "plundered, hunted and shot for his opinions. At last, deserted by his Northern ally, disheartened, trampled in blood . . . he seeks safety in exile." If the country "had statesmen at Washington instead of quarrelsome boys," things would be different. But "we shall save the Nation in spite of Washington. The flag does mean liberty, and the half a million men who once carried it to the Gulf still live to see that the negro shall yet find it so."[24]

Phillips' speech inspired emotions as intense as those of Civil War days. A committee headed by abolitionist Henry Ingersoll Bowditch, who two years previously had approved Hayes's southern policy, reported resolutions to the meeting denouncing the government for allowing southern blacks to be "cheated out of their earnings, robbed of their property, denied the rights of citizens, and trampled mercilessly in blood." The crowd shouted its approval of the resolutions. And the *New York Tribune*, which a year earlier had condemned Phillips as an apostle of hate, now praised his "brilliant denunciation of Southern barbarism."[25]

During the rest of 1879 the bloody shirt was for most abolitionists "the banner of American liberty," as George William Curtis put it. In early 1880, however, a number of abolitionists including Curtis suddenly reverted to the theme of reconciliation. The reason for their turnabout was the emergence of a stalwart movement to nominate General Grant for a third term. Even during their quasi-alliance with the stalwarts on the southern question in 1879, abolitionists who favored civil service reform had sided with Hayes in his bitter patronage battle against stalwarts. The Grant boom seemed to threaten the modest good-government gains made under Hayes. Roscoe Conkling, arch-stalwart and leader of the third-term movement, was an implacable foe of Curtis and other reform Republicans. Frightened by the specter of a return

Congregationalist, Aug. 11, 1880; *Advance*, July 1, 1880; circular signed by Elizabeth Comstock, Apr. 15, 1881, in Joshua Baily Papers; Thomas C. Cox, "The Kansas Freedmen's Relief Association: Organization and Activity in Topeka, Kansas, 1879-1880," paper read at the annual meeting of the Association of Negro Life and History, Oct. 22, 1971, quoted with author's permission.

24 *NYTrib.*, June 25, 1879.   25 *Ibid.*; *NYT*, June 25, 1879.

to Grantism, these reformers hurriedly organized a countermovement and played down the southern issue.[26]

At the Republican national convention, stalwarts went down the line for Grant through 36 ballots but were finally beaten when "half-breeds" and reformers united behind dark horse James A. Garfield. The Democrats tried to neutralize the bloody shirt by nominating Winfield Scott Hancock, like Garfield a Union general in the war. But as the lackluster campaign dragged on, the southern question emerged as the Republicans' main issue. All factions of the party bore down on the necessity of a solid Republican North to counter the solid Democratic South. Even *Harper's Weekly* and the *Boston Transcript* waved the bloody shirt during the campaign. Although Curtis was the most prominent civil service reformer in the country, he now considered even this issue less important than the problem of bulldozing in the South: "Reform of this outrage . . . is the most urgent of all reforms." Using rhetoric he had recently condemned, Hovey warned in dozens of editorials that a Democratic victory would "restore Southern mastery in the country and postpone indefinitely the practical recognition of the rights of the negroes. . . . All men of liberal views, particularly those who fought in the field against red-handed treason," must rally to the Republican cause.[27]

With Garfield winning by fewer than 10,000 votes, the 1880 election was the closest in American history. Hancock carried every former slave state; Garfield carried all but three northern states. The Republicans' "solid North" strategy had paid off, but postelection comments left the party's future southern policy unclear. This uncertainty was mirrored by abolitionists. For a while, the pre-election momentum of the bloody shirt persisted. The *Independent* described the southern vote as "a monstrous outrage upon the whole electoral system." The Republican party, said the *Commonwealth*, had too long "been completely indifferent, except in sympathy, for these disfranchised and outraged men." It was a time for action rather than words. What kind of action? The *Independent* suggested the enforcement of Section 2 of the 14th Amendment requiring a reduction in a state's congressional representation in proportion to the number of adult males denied the ballot. Charles Slack of the *Commonwealth* urged the Republican majority in the new House of Representatives to deny seats to congressmen elected by fraud or violence, and advised Garfield to give patronage only to southerners who had proved faithful to equal rights. "With

---

[26] *HW*, Aug. 16, 1879; Robert D. Marcus, *Grand Old Party: Political Structure in the Gilded Age 1880-1896*, New York, 1971, pp. 22-39.

[27] *HW*, Aug. 2, Oct. 16, 1880; *BET*, Aug. 7, 25, 1880.

executive and Congressional purpose to resist this glaring wrong," said Slack, "we shall breathe a spirit of justice throughout the South."[28]

By the end of 1880, however, editors Slack, Bowen, Curtis, and Hovey—who were as much Republicans as abolitionists—were again stressing the theme of conciliation. Once the election was over and the Republicans victorious, there was no need to wave the bloody shirt, so it was gradually retired—until, perhaps, the next election. And as these journalists examined the 1880 returns closely, they discovered that, while the Republican vote in the former slave states was only 40.3 percent of the total (virtually the same as in 1876), the party had improved its standing in the upper South, sometimes through coalitions with independent factions. This suggested that the best strategy for the 1880s might be to encourage such coalitions rather than to wave the bloody shirt. Though this remained a minor theme among former abolitionists in the winter of 1880–1881, it foreshadowed the major theme of the next decade. The concepts of time, education, moral suasion, and a "natural" division of southern whites into two parties, plus a new emphasis on bi-racial progress through the economic growth of a "New South," re-emerged in the 1880s as abolitionist prescriptions for Negro advancement.

[28] *Independent*, Nov. 4, 18, 1880, Jan. 13, 1881; *BC*, Nov. 6, 1880.

Chapter Seven

The New South

The dominant tone in abolitionist rhetoric during the 1880s was optimism. Despite the overthrow of Reconstruction and the decline of black voting power, former abolitionists discerned many signs of racial progress. The traditional jeremiads of the movement gave way to hopeful prophecies. Of course many of the old Jeremiahs were dead or dying, but even such hard-liners as William Penn Nixon, who remained very much alive, succumbed occasionally to optimism. This attitude was nurtured by recovery from the depression of the 1870s, the popularization of a "New South" ideology of progress through industrialization, the spread of black education, the emergence of a small but articulate band of southern liberals, and the waning of sectional hatred and racial violence. As C. Vann Woodward has shown, while race relations in the 1880s hovered uncertainly between the promising chaos of Reconstruction and the racist reaction after 1890, confidence in progress was the hallmark of the decade. Abolitionist opinion mirrored both the uncertainty and the confidence.

According to legend, Garfield's victory in 1880 convinced farseeing southerners that they could not achieve sectional salvation by politics, whereupon they rolled up their sleeves and went to work to build a New South of commerce, cotton mills, and foundries. Like all myths, the legend of the New South embodies some truth. A new spirit of enterprise quickened southern life in the 1880s. Economic growth underwent a dramatic spurt beginning about 1879; the cotton crop of that year exceeded the previous record crop of 1859; railroad mileage doubled during the next decade; the manufacture of cotton textiles nearly trebled; and between 1876 and 1901 southern pig-iron production increased seventeenfold. Yet these statistics obscured some unpleasant realities. Since much of the new wealth was skimmed off by northern investors, little of it trickled down to the southern masses, most of whom still faced a life of poverty and ill health. Moreover, southern economic growth barely kept pace with that of the rest of the country despite the ballyhoo of the 1880s.[1]

Nevertheless, major changes in the southern ethos did take place,

[1] C. Vann Woodward, *Origins of the New South 1877-1913*, Baton Rouge, 1951, esp. chaps. 5-6; Paul M. Gaston, *The New South Creed: A Study in Southern Mythmaking*, New York, 1970.

and a new entrepreneurial leadership replaced the old planter elite. These changes underlay abolitionist optimism. In their most euphoric vision of the New South, abolitionists saw economic reconstruction supplanting political; the new reconstruction, like the old, was to be carried out partly under northern auspices, but this time with the eager cooperation of the southern elite instead of against its will. Prosperity would lift the masses of both races, soften racial asperities, and give blacks the leverage for upward mobility that politics had never done. The South would become more like New England. "With railroads and telegraphs traversing its domain should go schools, factories, shops, a better family and community feeling," said the *Boston Commonwealth*, and eventually there would be town hall democracy, Puritan Christianity, respect for labor, and middle-class liberalism.[2]

Among the most enthusiastic boosters of the New South were two antislavery northerners, Edward Atkinson and William D. Kelley. Atkinson was a self-made man who had gone to work at the age of 15 in a Boston dry-goods store and by the age of 30 was a board member of several textile firms. In the 1850s he embraced abolitionism of the radical free soil variety and served as treasurer of a committee that supplied John Brown with Sharp's rifles. During the war he played an important role in the New England Freedmen's Aid Society; in the 1870s he worked with southern farmers to produce improved cotton for New England mills. A Liberal Republican in 1872, Atkinson was an early advocate of sectional reconciliation. After a trip to South Carolina and Georgia in 1879, he reported "marked signs of improvement" in the freedmen's lot. The new southern spirit of "vigor and energy" was "creating new conditions" that would soon excise the "cancer of slavery" and guide the New South "in the direction of peace, order, stability, and prosperity."[3]

As part of his campaign to publicize southern resources, Atkinson in 1881 helped to organize the International Cotton Exposition at Atlanta, the first of several southern "Expositions" that spread the New South gospel to thousands of visitors. He returned from the Atlanta Exposition with greater enthusiasm than ever for the New South. He quoted a conversation with a grandson of John C. Calhoun, who said that "if my grandfather and his associates had known as much about the negro as I know, and could have had the same faith in his capacity for progress which I have attained from my own experience, there would have been neither slavery nor war." In view of such sentiments,

[2] *BC*, Mar. 19, 1881.
[3] Articles by Atkinson in *Nation*, May 8, 1879, and *International Review*, x (Mar. 1881), 200, 202. Biographical information from Harold F. Williamson, *Edward Atkinson, The Biography of a Liberal, 1827-1905*, Boston, 1934.

concluded Atkinson, "all animosity ought now to cease with the hearty effort of both sections to adopt a policy of 'vigorous prosecution of the peace.'" In 1889 the University of South Carolina awarded this one-time supporter of John Brown an honorary degree for his services in behalf of southern rehabilitation and sectional amity.[4]

An even more avid panegyrist of the New South was William D. ("Pig-Iron") Kelley, former radical Republican congressman from Pennsylvania. Kelley had married into a Quaker abolitionist family and absorbed their racial egalitarianism. By the 1880s, however, his radical fervor had cooled, and he now urged racial melioration through economic growth. In 1886 he toured the South celebrating the section's industrial progress. In a book published after his trip, *The Old South and the New*, Kelley waxed rapturously: "Wealth and honor are in the pathway of the New South. Her impulses are those which are impelling the advance of civilization. . . . She is the coming El Dorado of American adventure." Industry was the salvation of blacks as well as whites. New South factories needed skilled black labor; industrial workers earned higher wages than agricultural; intelligent labor required a good educational system. Most of the workers in the largest tannery in the world at Chattanooga were black, Kelley observed, "and it was in connection with the homes of these laborers that my attention was first drawn to the striking contrast between the[ir] neat, commodious, and well-painted homes . . . and the cabins in which the poor white growers of cotton live."[5]

Other abolitionists echoed Atkinson and Kelley. The *Boston Transcript*, edited by William Hovey until 1881 and thereafter by another second-generation abolitionist Edward H. Clement, welcomed "the separation of business from Bourbonism, seaming the 'solid South' with cracks and foretelling the fruition of Hayes's policy in a Southern progressive party." Southern ideals in the 1880s, wrote Clement, were different from those of slavery. "Work and money have brought into vogue new ideals, new tests and new ambitions in Southern society. Capital is, after all, the greatest agent of civilization. . . . Money is the great emollient for social abrasions, and the two races . . . will move kindly together when wealth is more evenly divided between them."[6]

In the 1880s George William Curtis settled permanently into a conciliatory attitude toward the South. In 1886 *Harper's* commissioned a

[4] Williamson, *Atkinson*, 166-76; Atkinson, "Significant Aspects of the Atlanta Cotton Exposition," *Century Magazine*, XXIII (Feb. 1882), 567.

[5] Kelley, *The Old South and the New*, New York, 1888, pp. 161-62, 5-6, 110-11; biographical information from Ira V. Brown, "William D. Kelley and Radical Reconstruction," *Pennsylvania Magazine of History and Biography*, LXXXV (July 1961), 316-29.

[6] *BET*, May 7, 1879, Aug. 11, Oct. 21, 1885.

team of journalists and artists to do a series on the New South. Their flattering portrait showed, wrote Curtis, that "political differences and the friction of races are yielding to the beneficent touch of healthy industrial enterprise." While the series was in progress, Henry Grady made his famous speech at a dinner of the New England Society in New York City. Rejoicing that the South of slavery and secession was dead, Grady urged his listeners to bury the past and join the New South in its march toward a glorious future. The address made a remarkable impact on northerners, not least upon Curtis, who praised Grady's New South of "free schools, and active industry, and generous and sincere patriotism." To receive Grady's "hand of amity in the spirit in which it is offered," said Curtis, "means no surrender of principle or of purpose, but the renunciation of mere prejudice and of blinding tradition."[7]

To abolitionists, the most encouraging development in the New South was the emergence of racial moderates. To be sure, George Washington Cable and Lewis Harvey Blair were too liberal for most southern whites, and Cable eventually moved to Massachusetts. But several others led by Atticus G. Haygood won a hearing for their pleas in behalf of education and fair treatment of the Negro. Abolitionists did their best to encourage and publicize southern moderates. The *Independent* became an important northern outlet for their writings, and Lewis Harvey Blair's book *The Prosperity of the South Dependent on the Elevation of the Negro* first appeared as a series of articles in that journal.[8]

More than anyone else, the Methodist clergyman-educator Haygood became for abolitionists the symbol of hope in the New South. The leading southern spokesman for noblesse oblige toward the freedmen, Haygood set forth in *Our Brother in Black* (1881) his ideas on the race question. He rejoiced in the overthrow of slavery, accepted the permanence of Negro suffrage while deploring the methods that brought it about, advocated education and uplift of the freedmen, and urged his fellow southerners to treat the black man as an unfortunate younger brother in need of kindly assistance. Since Haygood was critical of abolitionist "sentimentalism" (read egalitarianism), few abolitionists could agree with everything he said. Nevertheless, wrote Brad-

[7] *HW*, Dec. 25, 1886, Jan. 8, 1887.

[8] *Independent*, June 16, 23, 30, July 14, 28, 1887. For a critical appraisal of the racial paternalism of most southern liberals in the 1880s, see Gaston, *The New South Creed*, chap. 4, and George M. Fredrickson, *The Black Image in the White Mind*, New York, 1971, chap. 7. More sympathetic is H. Shelton Smith, *In His Image, But . . . Racism in Southern Religion, 1780-1910*, Durham, N.C., 1972, pp. 277-97.

ford Peirce of *Zion's Herald,* "we can only hope that there is an increasing number of intelligent citizens at the South who take such views. . . . The Haygoods and the Cables are as sure to multiply at the South as the years are to roll on . . . and this means emphatically 'a new South.' "[9]

Especially gratifying was Haygood's praise for the "perfect sincerity and profound conviction" of the "good people" from the North working for Negro education. Though many of these good people were "sentimentalists," they were willing to overlook Haygood's inconsistency and bask in his praise. As agent of the Slater Fund (a northern endowment for black education), Haygood worked with missionary educators in the 1880s; so did southerner Jabez L. M. Curry, agent of the Peabody Fund, another northern endowment. Indeed, a growing number of southern whites cooperated with the once-despised abolitionist missionaries. In 1880 Richard Rust found the South more receptive to "our educational work than at any former period." Although southerners emphasized industrial education for Negroes while most missionaries continued to stress academic higher education (see chap. 12), the American Missionary Association saw "much occasion for thanking God and taking courage" in the South's support for at least *some* kind of black schooling.[10]

These effusions of good will were part of a larger trend that Paul H. Buck has described as the road to reunion. Several abolitionists trod this road. A favorite symbol of reconciliation celebrated in dozens of novels was the intersectional marriage. In 1886 Maude Howe, daughter of Julia Ward and Samuel Gridley Howe, wrote a typical Victorian romance, *Atalanta in the South,* in which a New England girl married a New Orleans gentleman descended from a slaveholding family and converted him to a retrospective abolitionism. In 1890 one abolitionist carried out the reunion-through-matrimony theme in real life when Samuel J. May's grandson married Jefferson Davis's daughter.[11]

In 1881 Thomas Wentworth Higginson delivered the after-dinner address at a centennial celebration of the Revolutionary War Battle of Cowpens at Spartanburg, South Carolina. Returning to the state where he had led black troops against rebels two decades earlier, Higginson had a "delightful time" and was "warmly received and applauded" by his "old opponents." He told the all-white audience that "Time is the great healer." The race problem was a difficult one. "We of the North, believe me, are not ignorant of the difficulties . . . nor can we forget

[9] *ZH,* Mar. 31, 1881, Jan. 28, 1885.
[10] Haygood, *Our Brother in Black: His Freedom and His Future,* New York, 1881, chap. 14; article by Haygood quoted in *Independent,* Nov. 16, 1882; *Thirteenth Annual Report FASME,* Cincinnati, 1880, p. 13; *AM,* xxxix (Dec. 1885), 359.
[11] *Woman's Journal,* Apr. 26, 1890.

that the greater responsibility must rest upon the more educated and enlightened race. *Noblesse oblige!*"[12]

In 1886 James Redpath, whose lifelong hero remained John Brown, began a friendly correspondence with Jefferson Davis concerning an article by Davis for the *North American Review*, of which Redpath was managing editor. Two years later Redpath visited Davis in Mississippi to discuss some articles on the Confederacy. The two men took a liking to each other, and from then until Davis's death in 1889 the former John Brown abolitionist was a ghostwriter for the ex-Confederate president. Redpath spent the summer of 1889 in the Davis home helping the old man write his *Short History of the Confederate States* and his memoirs. After Davis's death, Redpath helped his widow finish and edit the memoirs. In a magazine article, Redpath explained the reasons for this remarkable collaboration. He had never met a man with more "intellectual integrity" and "refined and benignant character" than Davis. While "neither of us had changed our essential creed," each respected the other's convictions. Redpath wished their friendship could become a model for the whole country. Both sides in the war had fought honorably for what they believed, but "now that the war both of bullets and of ideas is over . . . it is time to drop, and drop forever, the old war-cant about Rebellion and Treason."[13]

Something of a national consensus emerged in the 1880s to smooth the road to reunion. Progressive southerners admitted that slavery had been wrong and its abolition (though not necessarily the abolitionists) a good thing. Meeting the southern viewpoint halfway, northerners conceded that Reconstruction had been ill-conceived, vengeful, corrupt, and a failure. Both sides agreed that the 15th Amendment, though unwise, was in the Constitution to stay but that white men would control southern governments for a long time to come.

Some abolitionists subscribed to at least part of this consensus. In 1888 George William Curtis declared that, though it had seemed necessary at the time, the wholesale enfranchisement of freedmen "who were notoriously and absolutely unfit for political responsibility" in 1867 was a mistake. The North finally "saw the impracticability of try-

<hr/>

12 Higginson to Sydney Howard Gay, May 13, 1881, Gay Papers, Columbia University Library; *Charleston News and Courier*, May 12, 1881.

13 Hudson Strode, *Jefferson Davis: Tragic Hero, 1864-1889*, New York, 1964, pp. 497, 501, 527; letters between Redpath and Davis reprinted in Dunbar Rowland, ed., *Jefferson Davis, Constitutionalist, His Letters, Papers, and Speeches*, 10 vols., Jackson, Miss., 1923, IX, 470, 491-92, X, 36, 108, 158; clipping of the *New Orleans Picayune*, Mar. 30, 1890, and letter from Redpath to John Dimitry, May 23, 1890, in the Dimitry-Stuart Papers, Mississippi Department of Archives and History; Redpath, "Neither Traitor Nor Rebel," *The Commonwealth*, II (Jan. 1890), 386-87, 392.

ing to subject intelligence and civilization to ignorance and barbarism led by local knavery, and decided that the solution of the question could be most wisely left to the communities themselves." The policy that Lincoln would have carried out and Hayes tried to put into effect was now functioning successfully, said Curtis. Although "in some Southern communities" the black vote "is not free," the remedy was time and education, which had already brought considerable progress.[14]

Although Daniel H. Chamberlain came eventually to similar conclusions, he began the 1880s still defending Reconstruction. Despite all the missteps and difficulties, he wrote in a *North American Review* article, the freedmen "earned by their conduct from 1868 to 1876 . . . the very highest title to exercise the rights and assume the duties of self-government." But as time went on, Chamberlain became increasingly elitist and conservative; gradually he changed his mind about Reconstruction. The southern problem, he wrote in 1886, stemmed not only from the "race prejudice and political ambition of whites," but also from "the want of intelligence, experience, and good judgment" among blacks compounded by what Chamberlain now considered "the insupportable corruption and maladministration of most of the Southern state governments from 1868 to 1876." His reading of Darwin and Spencer had convinced him that the race question could only work itself out over a long period of time. Nothing was "so unreasonable, as well as unphilosophical, as a certain feeling . . . of over-haste and impatience to solve the problem at once." Chamberlain refused to admit any abandonment of principle in coming to this view: "To make a virtue of necessity, to adjust methods to the necessary conditions of the problem, is not cowardice or betrayal of principle; it is wisdom and prudence; it is the very essence of practical statesmanship."[15]

Some blacks agreed. George Washington Williams wrote in his *History of the Negro Race in America* (1883) that during Reconstruction the government gave the Negro the "statute book when he ought to have had the spelling-book, placed him in the legislature when he ought to have been in the school-house." Such a state of affairs could not last. "Ignorance, vice, poverty, and superstition could not rule intelligence, experience, wealth, and organization." Even Frederick Douglass, in a moment of disillusionment, declared that Reconstruc-

[14] *HW*, Jan. 21, 1888.

[15] Chamberlain, "Reconstruction and the Negro," *North American Review*, CXXVIII (Feb. 1879), 172; Wilton B. Fowler, "A Carpetbagger's Conversion to White Supremacy," *North Carolina Historical Review*, XLII (Summer 1966), 295; Chamberlain, "Present Aspects of the Southern Question," *New Englander and Yale Review*, IX (Jan. 1886), 29-31.

tion had "carried the colored voter to an altitude unsuited to his attainments."[16]

But while some former abolitionists, black as well as white, wrote off Reconstruction as a failure, others more numerous defended it as necessary and at least a qualified success (15 of 24 abolitionists who wrote about Reconstruction in the 1880s fell into this category). Wendell Phillips insisted that, so far as it went, Reconstruction worked well. Indeed, it was the *success* rather than failure of Negro suffrage that the white South feared most. The few ignorant, bribe-taking black politicians did not inflame white hatred so much as did the large numbers of intelligent leaders whose effectiveness threatened to revolutionize the South. The ultimate downfall of Reconstruction, said Phillips, resulted not from black shortcomings but from "cowardice, selfishness, and want of statesmanship on the part of the Government."[17]

Other abolitionists emphasized the positive achievements of Reconstruction—schools, social services, modern constitutions, state aid to economic recovery, genuine democracy—and maintained that these far outweighed corruption and misgovernment. Edward H. Fairchild insisted that Negro suffrage gave the South "far better state governments, however complained of, than they ever had before, and far better than they would have had without the help of the negro, the 'carpetbagger' and the 'scalawag.'" Henry B. Blackwell believed that the results of black enfranchisement were "better than the most sanguine radical had a right to expect." As for corruption, "let us not forget that the worst legislature that was ever seen under negro rule was more honest than the best one ever seen before in any Southern State. It stole; but only money. Those high-toned Southern aristocrats stole men and women, and sold babies by the pound on the auction-block!"[18]

Abolitionists who defended Reconstruction tended to be skeptical of the racial liberalism of the New South. Their suspicions became stronger in the second half of the decade when evils such as convict leasing and Jim Crow seemed to grow worse instead of withering away. "The New South to many means simply a new South for white people," concluded the *American Missionary* sadly in 1887. The AMA's disenchantment deepened when the lower house of Henry Grady's own state passed the "Glenn Bill" imposing a sentence of up to one year on the chain gang for anyone who taught whites and blacks in the

---

16 Williams, *History of the Negro Race in America from 1619-1880*, 2 vols., New York, 1883, II, 527-28; Douglass, "The Future of the Negro," *North American Review*, CXXXIX (July 1884), 85.

17 Phillips, "Ought the Negro to be Disfranchised? Ought He to have been Enfranchised?" *North American Review*, CXXVIII (Mar. 1879), 257-62.

18 Fairchild, *God's Designs For and Through the Negro Race. An Address*, New York, 1882, pp. 13-15; *Woman's Journal*, Aug. 31, 1878.

same classroom. This bill was aimed at the AMA-founded Atlanta University, where several faculty children were students. What more evidence was needed, asked the *American Missionary*, to show that for Negroes the New South meant only "the right to be legislated against, to be branded with essential inferiority as a race, to be insulted?"[19]

More than anything else in the 1880s, the leasing of black convicts to private contractors marred the New South's image. The convicts lived in vermin-infested camps, worked long hours under brutal conditions, and were often beaten to death by sadistic guards. Part of the New South's industrial growth was fueled by the cheap labor of black convicts, many of whom had been imprisoned on trumped-up charges or for minor offenses.[20] Abolitionists condemned the system as "an outrage on civilization," a "system of slavery more abject and proportionately more fatal to human life" than bondage itself. Many who were otherwise friendly to the New South were appalled by the abuses of convict labor. William D. Kelley denounced the system as a "barbarism"; the *Nation* considered it "a state of things hardly credible in a civilized community"; and Curtis pronounced "this newest and most revolting form of human slavery" a "horrible disgrace."[21]

Segregation in public facilities also tarnished the New South's promise. In 1884 an AMA teacher called on "old-time abolition friends" to take up anew "the battle with caste. Other legislation must be invoked to take the place of the defunct [federal] Civil Rights statute. Public sentiment must be brought up the demand of decency and right."[22]

In the 1880s, however, the battle with caste took place more in the North than the South. A dozen northern states passed antidiscrimination laws in the decade after the Supreme Court's 1883 decision ruling the 1875 federal Civil Rights Act unconstitutional. But these laws were weakly enforced; segregation in hotels, restaurants, vacation resorts, and recreation facilities (to say nothing of housing and jobs) remained undisturbed in many parts of the North. This embarrassed abolitionists, who conceded that they could make little headway against the "odious caste devil" in the South so long as it existed in the North. Citing several cases of segregation in New England, the *Transcript* urged "our Northern communities to act as they talk, and set the

[19] *AM*, XLI (June 1887), 163 (Nov. 1887), 309-10. The Georgia Senate passed a milder version of the Glenn bill merely abolishing the state subsidy for Atlanta University; the House concurred.

[20] Fletcher M. Green, "Some Aspects of the Convict Lease System in the Southern States," in Fletcher M. Green, ed., *Essays in Southern History*, Chapel Hill, 1949, pp. 112-23.

[21] *Independent*, Nov. 6, 1879, Sept. 24, 1891; *AM*, XLI (Dec. 1887), 341; *SWCA*, Feb. 12, 1880; Kelley, *The Old South and the New*, 142; *Nation*, Apr. 4, 1889; *HW*, Sept. 6, 1890.

[22] *Congregationalist*, Jan. 31, 1884.

South the example of welcoming black men . . . to social equality." In 1889 the veteran Boston abolitionist Henry I. Bowditch refused to attend a protest meeting against southern racism, stating that "I do not believe in hypocrisy ever rebuking sin. . . . When we of the North treat the negro as he ought to be treated . . . then, and not until then, should we have 'mass meetings' against other people."[23]

It was all very well to demand that the North pluck the beam from its own eye before worrying about the southern mote, but southern whites all too often interpreted this as a vindication of the South. So did the editors of the merged *Nation* and *New York Evening Post*. Since "outside of anti-slavery circles a social gathering . . . of white and colored people" rarely occurred in the North, wrote E. L. Godkin in 1880, and since many examples of northern segregation could be cited (the *Post/Nation* repeatedly cited them), northern people should exercise "charity in judging the South." Francis Garrison finally told his brother Wendell that he was sick and tired of the *Post*'s "editorial scribbler" who kept saying that "the North is as proscriptive as the South, & that therefore we should all hold our tongues & mind our own business, & let the whites of the South pursue their methods in peace."[24]

Wendell half-agreed with his brother, and in the editorials he wrote for the *Nation* he drew a somewhat different moral from the comparison of northern and southern practices. While doing research for a biography of his father, Wendell became convinced that in its treatment of Negroes the North of the 1880s, despite continuing racism, had nevertheless improved since the 1830s. Thus there was hope for the South. Did southern whites in a few areas still destroy black schoolhouses or drive their teachers out of town? The whites of Canterbury, Connecticut, and Canaan, New Hampshire, had done the same a half-century earlier. "No white teacher of the freedmen has had an experience at all comparable in malignity, inhumanity, and unrelenting persistence to that of [Prudence] Crandall," said Garrison. "The South of today, after all, is not so hopelessly wrong as the Canterbury of 1833 appeared, and if Connecticut feels inclined to despair of Georgia, she can recall her own history and cheer up."[25]

Historical parallels of this kind strengthened the conviction that only time and education could ultimately solve the race problem. Even critics of the New South conceded that, in spite of such vestiges of

23 *BET*, Mar. 2, 27, 1885; Vincent Y. Bowditch, *Life and Correspondence of Henry Ingersoll Bowditch*, 2 vols., Boston, 1902, II, 346-48.

24 *Nation*, May 6, 1880; *NYEP*, June 28, 1887; Francis J. Garrison to Wendell P. Garrison, Oct. 27, 1887, WPG Papers.

25 *Nation*, Sept. 9, 1880, Nov. 26, 1885.

slavery as convict leasing, the Negro's educational and economic condition was improving in the 1880s. To be sure, missionary teachers still deplored the "superstition and impurity" of many black churches and complained that "their ministers are often as ignorant, and as immoral, too, as many of the members." Henry L. Morehouse of the Baptist Home Mission Society was distressed by the poverty and "wretchedness" of rural blacks shackled by sharecropping and the crop-lien system. But Morehouse also pointed to the growing number of Negroes who owned property and were striving for middle-class respectability. Describing the changes after only 16 years of freedom as "a marvel," Morehouse predicted: "In this is a hint, is high hope of what they will be sixteen years hence. Their progress will be in almost a geometrical ratio for the next half-generation."[26]

In sharp contrast to its hand-wringing over the freedmen's degradation in the mid-1870s, the *Independent* celebrated their achievements in the 1880s. The paper frequently published statistics, case histories, and anecdotes of black success. These examples proved that, "considering the condition in which long years of oppression" left him, the Negro "has done more than well." Editor William Hayes Ward doubted whether "so great a change was ever made on so large a scale, with so few evils and such complete success" and questioned "whether an equal number of white persons would, in like circumstances, have done better."[27]

To get the black viewpoint on southern conditions, the *Independent* sent questionnaires to 200 Negro leaders in 1886. The results of the survey, published in early 1887, only slightly dimmed Ward's optimism. While many respondents complained of run-down public schools, discrimination in travel facilities, and the white man's double standard of justice, most believed that the race was getting ahead. They agreed that the crop-lien system, which created a perpetual debt, was their greatest handicap. Nearly all of the replies stressed that property ownership and education were the keys to progress. Commenting editorially, Ward conceded that "wrongs are still numerous" and that "the indignity of the caste prejudices . . . is bitterly felt." Nevertheless he was impressed by the growth in education and material well-being and by "the spirit of hopefulness" among the respondents. "The progress of the past twenty-five years has been marvelous, and another similar period will, we think, find the caste question nearly settled."[28]

[26] *Congregationalist*, Apr. 23, 1879; *Independent*, Apr. 29, 1880; Morehouse in *HMM*, XI (Apr. 1889), 86-87, II (Nov. 1880), 221.

[27] *Independent*, Apr. 12, 26, 1883.

[28] Digests of the questionnaire replies published in *ibid.*, Jan. 6, 13, 20, 27, Feb. 3, 17, 1887; editorial comments in issues of Feb. 3 and 24, 1887.

This confidence was backed by a continuing conviction that the Negro race was capable of equal achievement with whites—a conviction increasingly untenable according to the established wisdom of the age. The belief in racial differences was becoming more pervasive everywhere in the Western world. A few abolitionists succumbed to this belief—at least in part. There are hints in some writings by Curtis, Chamberlain, and Wendell Garrison of doubts about the Negro's innate capacities. In 1885 James Russell Lowell, who had long since retreated from his antebellum abolitionism, said that full-blooded Negroes seemed to be "incapable of civilization from their own resources." Even the AMA, usually firm in its egalitarianism, announced in 1878 that "this Association does not affirm that races, any more than individuals, are equal in physical or mental fibre and development. . . . All that we claim is, that all men shall be regarded as equal before God and the Law."[29]

But most abolitionists who discussed this question continued to deny Negro inferiority. The "illusion" of such inferiority, said one of them in 1880, was "simply part of the penumbra that still hangs round us as we emerge from the eclipse of chattel-slavery. . . . It is only theorizers without knowledge of the facts who assume the intellectual inferiority of the negro." In a *North American Review* article on "The Future of the Negro," Oliver Johnson stated flatly that the Negro "in his essential being" was "endowed with the same attributes and capacities as his Anglo-Saxon brother."[30]

Darwinian racists emphasized the importance of heredity in determining character; some abolitionists responded with a version of what Eric F. Goldman has called, in another context, Reform Darwinism, or the reciprocity of heredity and environment. President William W. Patton of Howard University was one of the most articulate exponents of this thesis. Since evolutionary progress resulted from the reproduction of those organisms best adapted to their environment, wrote Patton, environment was obviously important in determining the nature of the organism. Therefore a controlled change of environment could modify individual traits. "Our natures are plastic, and easily take the impress of objects with which we come continually into contact," he declared. "Education is not merely that from books, but that also which is received from all manner of surrounding influences, as they exist in the home, in social intercourse, and in the community at large." Expressing the mixture of paternalism and egalitarianism that charac-

[29] Martin Duberman, *James Russell Lowell*, Boston, 1966, p. 357; *AM*, XXXII (June 1878), 162.

[30] "Brain Knows No Color," in *Advance*, Sept. 16, 1880, reprinted with endorsement by *Woman's Journal*, Sept. 25, 1880; Johnson in *North American Review*, CXXIX (July 1884), 94.

terized freedmen's education, Patton asserted that the black child's home environment in a one-room cabin with illiterate parents and no intellectual stimulation kept him at the same level as his parents. To get ahead, he must enter the new environment of missionary schools where "in addition to having access to books he goes where the entire conception and standard of living is different and elevated; where religion is intelligent; where morals are pure; where manners are refined; where language is grammatical." Patton had seen the character of hundreds of black youths transformed by this change of environment; when they returned to their own communities they "introduce the leaven of improvement into the mass." The cumulative effect of this process would "gradually work such changes of character and condition in the colored population" as to enable them to achieve "positions of honor, profit and power" equal to those held by whites.[31]

Other abolitionist educators made the same point. A teacher at Leland University, a black school in New Orleans, admitted in 1886 that her students were slow learners at first because they lacked the background "that our children were going over from the cradle up. . . . The real intellectual culture of our children depends nearly as much on their domestic environment as upon their schools." But the success of the mission schools proved "that the capacity for sound learning among that race only needs the same surroundings, and time, to place them on a level with other races." Reaffirming its traditional viewpoint, the AMA insisted in the 1880s that it was "the lack of developed intelligence, not of native ability," that kept the Negro race below the Caucasian. The adaptability of students to their new environment in mission schools "has been so quick and the growth so rapid as to prove their mental brotherhood with the white race. That question is settled."[32]

"Settlement" of the question fed the cycle of abolitionist optimism: Negroes were inherently capable of progress; the progress already made despite great odds proved it; this gave promise for the future. "All that we as abolitionists ever said in vindication . . . of this people [is] being more than justified," wrote one old crusader in 1885. And secretary Michael Strieby of the AMA asserted that the race's "simply wonderful" progress "demonstrates that the negro can enter every profession and calling in which the white man is found" if only "given a white man's chance."[33]

[31] Articles by Patton in *AM*, xxxvi (Aug. 1882), 228-30; *Independent*, July 7, 1887; and Patton, *The History of Howard University, 1867-1888*, Washington, 1896, pp. 7-9.

[32] Marsena Stone in *Christian Union*, Jan. 21, 1886; *AM*, xxxvi (Sept. 1882), 261, xxxix (Dec. 1885), 356.

[33] *Wesleyan Methodist*, Aug. 13, 1884; *AM*, xxxix (July 1885), 189-91.

Abolitionists remained aware that blacks were not given a white man's chance. While the voices of reassuring optimism pre-empted center stage in the 1880s, the voices of protest were never silent. Reconstruction made several attempts at a comeback during the decade, and two important bills to provide federal aid to education and to protect black voting rights came close to enactment. The next chapter will treat the role of former abolitionists in these matters.

Chapter Eight

Good-bye to the Bloody Shirt

The "Southern Question" remained important in national politics during the 1880s as Republican leaders searched for a way to keep their party alive in the South. Early in the decade, attempts to forge coalitions between southern Republicans and independents dominated Republican policy; later the growth of protectionist sentiment among New South industrialists aroused interest in trying to build a high-tariff Republican constituency in the South. The meager results of these efforts caused some Republicans and abolitionists to wave the bloody shirt again in the 1884 and 1888 elections. In 1884 this did not work, and a Democrat won the presidency for the first time in 28 years. In 1888 it appeared to work, and Republicans followed up their victory with a near-successful attempt to pass new voting rights legislation. By the beginning of the next decade, however, all hopes for a political solution of the southern problem were dead; time and education seemed the only alternatives left.

From 1878 to 1883, factionalism rent the Democratic parties of several southern states, with independents challenging "Bourbons" (regular Democrats) for control of state and local offices. In several elections, both sides courted black voters; Republicans in some instances formed coalitions with independents or advised their followers to vote for independent candidates. Many abolitionists welcomed these developments as a fulfillment of their prediction that, once federal troops were removed from the South, white men would divide politically and appeal for black support, thus assuring the indigenous protection of Negro voting rights.[1]

The outstanding example of a Republican-independent coalition was the Readjuster movement in Virginia, led by former Confederate General William Mahone. With the help of black voters the Readjusters won control of the legislature in 1879, sent Mahone to the Senate in 1881, and elected the governor the same year. The Readjusters had split with the regular Democrats ("Funders") over the issue of funding the state debt. Proposing to scale down the debt, they pointed out that the Funders had starved public services and milked poor taxpaying farmers to pay off dubious obligations to creditors. The Readjust-

---

[1] C. Vann Woodward, *Origins of the New South 1877-1913*, Baton Rouge, 1951, chap. 4.

ers fulfilled their promises to black voters: in a wave of progressive legislation in the early 1880s they abolished the whipping post, repealed the poll tax, enrolled blacks as jurors, and increased public school appropriations by 50 percent with most of the new funds going to black schools. The Readjusters also pushed through their debt adjustment program, which stood the test of court challenges.[2]

With few exceptions, abolitionists overcame their scruples against the Readjusters' debt-scaling proposals and endorsed Mahone's party. They convinced themselves, in the *Commonwealth*'s words, that the debt question "has assumed in this movement a position of secondary importance; the real principles on which the party plumes itself are equal rights, a free ballot, an honest count, and a thorough system of public education." It was the "clear duty" of Virginia Republicans to merge with the Readjusters even though this meant a loss of their identity as Republicans. "In the South the name of Republican is a shibboleth," said the *Commonwealth*, and since "there are more ways than one to kill a cat, this old Bourbon cat must be killed by a coalition. A rose under any other name will smell as sweet." Celebrating Mahone's success, the *Massachusetts Spy* and the *Boston Transcript* proclaimed that "the solid south is no longer a fact, but only a reminiscence," for the Readjusters had "inaugurated a new era in Southern politics" that would achieve "the wiping out of class and race distinctions."[3]

Readjuster success in Virginia did inspire a proliferation of independent movements elsewhere. But while these movements sometimes gave lip service to equal rights and appealed for black support, they were often led by spokesmen for lower middle-class whites notably lacking in ardor for the Negro's cause. The independent leader in Mississippi was James R. Chalmers, who had participated in the massacre of black troops after the Civil War battle of Fort Pillow. Abolitionists living in the deep South scoffed at the notion that blacks there would benefit from Democratic factionalism. "However the Democratic hosts may divide in their local contests," said one, "they are united in their prejudices against . . . the free exercise of Negro citizenship."[4]

By the fall of 1882 the adoption of complicated registration or election laws in several southern states and the perfection of extralegal means of controlling the black vote had disillusioned some abolitionists who had earlier considered Mahone's success a harbinger of better things. Whatever hopes they still had were destroyed by the 1883 state

[2] *Ibid.*, 95-96; Stanley P. Hirshson, *Farewell to the Bloody Shirt: Northern Republicans and the Southern Negro, 1877-93*, Bloomington, Ind., 1962, p. 108; Carl N. Degler, *The Other South: Southern Dissenters in the Nineteenth Century*, New York, 1974, pp. 270-91.

[3] *BC*, June 11, Aug. 20, 1881; *Mass. Spy*, Mar. 18, 1881; *BET*, June 6, 1881.

[4] L. P. Cushman, in *SWCA*, Oct. 25, 1883.

elections. A political brawl in Danville, Virginia, in which four blacks were killed climaxed a statewide Bourbon campaign of intimidation. The Democrats crushed the Readjuster-Republican coalition and regained control of the state. In Mississippi the assassination of a Republican county chairman kicked off a campaign in which independentism was similarly snuffed out. Results were the same elsewhere in the South. These events insured the revival of the "bloody shirt" in 1884. "We have been congratulating ourselves," said Charles Wesley Slack, that "the spirit of the whites had so improved as to have made cruelty entirely exceptional, and now it appears that . . . our confidence reflected rather Northern ignorance than Southern progress."[5]

Taking his cue from Republican presidential nominee James G. Blaine, however, even William Penn Nixon kept his bloody shirt in the drawer during the early stages of the 1884 campaign. Blaine hoped to win the votes of New South protectionists on the tariff issue; Nixon pursued the same line, though with some skepticism. If there really was a "new South, honestly seeking the equal political rights of white and black," Nixon would be glad to keep quiet. But by October it was clear that this strategy was going nowhere. Blaine switched over to the bloody shirt, and Nixon switched with him. "The old implacable, pro-slavery . . . anti-free school, anti-free labor, Bourbon South" was still in control, he wrote. A Democratic victory would "restore every policy that prevailed anterior to 1860, and destroy at a blow all the results of the war." Other abolitionists also fell into line, proclaiming the "political and moral conflict" of 1884 to be a continuation of the military conflict of 1861.[6]

But those abolitionists who became mugwumps in 1884 maintained that Negroes would be no better off with Blaine than Grover Cleveland in the White House. Heirs of the Liberal Republicans of 1872, the mugwumps despised Blaine for his murky connections with railroad land grants and other matters revealed by the famous Mulligan letters. Cleveland, on the other hand, had compiled a record as governor of New York that put him into the mugwumps' pantheon of heroes. The mugwumps influenced some thousands of votes in New York, and since Blaine lost the state and therefore the presidency by only 1,149 votes, their claim of credit for Cleveland's election seemed plausible.[7]

Several abolitionist journalists became mugwumps, including Curtis of *Harper's Weekly* and Edward Clement of the *Transcript*. Bolting the Republican party was not easy for them. As late as February 1884

[5] Degler, *The Other South*, 292-300; Hirshson, *Farewell to the Bloody Shirt*, 118-22; *BC*, Dec. 29, 1883.

[6] *CIO* (D), Oct. 3, 21, 22, 1884; *NWCA*, July 23, 1884.

[7] John G. Sproat, *"The Best Men": Liberal Reformers in the Gilded Age*, New York, 1968, chap. 5, is a concise treatment of the mugwumps in the 1884 election.

Curtis believed that Democratic methods in the South "should array every intelligent Northern voter" against the party. "The essential reasonableness and force of this view is not to be overcome by decrying the bloody shirt." But after Blaine's nomination, Curtis's view changed abruptly. In reply to a "young Republican" who asked how Curtis could renounce the party that abolished slavery, he wrote that the "real question is not whether [one] prefers the traditions and original principles of the Republican party, but whether he will vote for . . . a dishonest candidate." And while Clement conceded that southern states were "controlled by force or fraud," he also thought Blaine not a "fit or safe man" for the presidency. By the end of the campaign, Clement was virtually justifying the force and fraud. "The practical nullification of the negro vote in the South is not the naked and simple outrage" it would be in the North, he said. Massachusetts deprived illiterates of the ballot by a literacy test; in effect, the South was doing the same "by trick and intimidation." Though this was lamentable, moderates were working quietly for improved conditions in the South, and bloody shirt oratory only struck "an unfeeling and unpatriotic blow at the delicate and difficult beginning of a better understanding between the two races."[8]

Several abolitionist mugwumps zeroed in on the Republicans' weak point: despite the party's "cant" about Negro rights, it had done nothing for years and could do nothing to protect those rights. "How would the election of another Republican President put a stop to . . . Southern intimidation?" asked James Freeman Clarke. "The surest way to break up the solid South will be the breaking up of the solid North," for this would remove the outside threat that compelled all southern whites to stick together in the Democratic party.[9]

Republican abolitionists, on the other hand, accused the mugwumps of deserting the Negro. Numbering several mugwumps among his friends, the Boston wool merchant and abolitionist Richard P. Hallowell nevertheless denounced them as "perhaps the most dangerous political class in our community," for they had abandoned concern with "questions involving human wrongs and human rights." George F. Hoar, Charles Sumner's successor in the Senate, accused mugwumps of being "totally indifferent to the fate of the negro and the establishment of honest suffrage at the South [because they] have not much belief in the capacity of mankind in general for suffrage anywhere."[10]

This was not quite fair, but it did pinpoint an important element of

8 *HW*, Nov. 24, 1883, Feb. 19, Oct. 4, 1884; *BET*, July 16, Oct. 30, Nov. 6, 1884.
9 *BET*, Oct. 29, 1884.
10 Hallowell, *The Southern Question*, Boston, 1890, pp. 24-25; Hoar to Henry Cabot Lodge, Nov. 12, 1884, in Hirshson, *Farewell to the Bloody Shirt*, 131.

mugwump thinking. The enfranchisement of the freedmen and the simultaneous rise to power of northern political machines based on immigrant votes frightened native-born Protestants with the specter of "their" country being taken over by ignorant and alien forces. Immigration increased sharply in the 1880s; the "Irish conquest of the cities" proceeded apace; the 1880 census showed an increase since 1870 in the number of illiterate Americans of voting age. At the same time, scholars were arguing that historically only Teutonic peoples had demonstrated a capacity for representative government. All of these factors turned some mugwumps against universal suffrage; as they grew alarmed about Irish power in the North, they increasingly sympathized with the attempt to hold down black power in the South.[11]

Abolitionists who supported Cleveland in 1884 did not necessarily subscribe to the full range of mugwump ideas. Three sons of William Lloyd Garrison voted for Cleveland, but while Wendell was a thoroughgoing mugwump, his brothers William and Francis were not. Both continued to defend Reconstruction and to denounce the *Nation* for its position on the southern question. Their vote was largely an anti-Blaine gesture. And a substantial number of blacks also voted Democratic in 1884, sometimes on mugwump grounds but usually as a protest against Republican failure to protect the race's rights and as a warning that the party should not take the Negro vote for granted. T. Thomas Fortune dismissed black Republicans as "flunkies" and praised Cleveland for his efforts to make the Democratic party "more broad, liberal, and tolerant" on the race question.[12]

Thus the 1884 election was not a referendum on southern policy. Too many other issues were involved, and those who maintained that Cleveland would do as much for the Negro as would Blaine may well have been right. Nevertheless, since at least the rhetoric of the Republicans was militant, the election provided something of an index of abolitionist attitudes. Of the 44 former abolitionists whose position in 1884 has been discovered, 26 (59 percent) supported Blaine and 18 backed Cleveland. There was considerable continuity between support for Hayes's southern policy in 1877 and Cleveland's election in 1884: 70 percent of Cleveland's abolitionist backers had also sustained Hayes's policy, while only 36 percent of Blaine's supporters are known to have

---

[11] Sproat, *"The Best Men,"* chap. 8; Barbara Miller Solomon, *Ancestors and Immigrants: A Changing New England Tradition*, Cambridge, Mass., 1956, chaps. 2-4.

[12] *Nation*, Oct. 16, 1884; Francis J. Garrison to Fanny Garrison Villard, June 15, Nov. 10, 1884, FGV Papers; clipping of a speech by William Lloyd Garrison, Jr., June 1884, in WLG, Jr., Papers; August Meier, *Negro Thought in America, 1880-1915*, Ann Arbor, 1963, pp. 26-33; Fortune quoted in Seth M. Scheiner, *Negro Mecca: A History of the Negro in New York City, 1865-1920*, New York, 1965, pp. 180-81.

done so. Exactly half of the political abolitionists favored Cleveland, compared with 43 percent of the Garrisonians and none of the evangelicals (Cleveland's sexual transgressions were probably decisive with the latter).

After the election, Blaine charged that the Bourbons had robbed him of victory by disfranchising enough black voters to deny him at least four southern states he would otherwise have carried. Republican abolitionists agreed, but mugwump abolitionists said that Blaine's postelection speech only showed him up for the demagogue he was. Admitting that many blacks in the deep South had not voted, they insisted that "there is an immense amount of fiction and fudge about the suppression of the negro vote." The *Transcript* compiled data showing that Republicans had cast 1,203,000 votes in the former slave states, 41½ percent of the total and an increase of 150,000 or 1 percent since 1880. A party still this vigorous should have "strength enough to defy bulldozing, and inspire the hope of the termination of one-party rule." Republican abolitionists did not dispute the *Transcript*'s figures but pointed out that most of the Republican votes came from the upper South while black votes in the deep South were suppressed. What good was 40 percent of the vote, they asked, in states where potential Republican voters were in the majority?[13]

Although some Republican abolitionists expected "disaster to flow from the accession to power of a party . . . which hatched the rebellion,"[14] the worst that could be said of the Cleveland administration is that it did no better than its predecessors in enforcing Negro rights. But the bloody shirt would not disintegrate. In the close-fought Ohio state election of 1885, Republicans rang all the changes on southern outrages. Mugwump abolitionists swung into action to ridicule this new effort (as they saw it) to make political capital out of sectionalism. By now they had perfected three arguments that they repeated with endless variations: 1) Republicans could do nothing to remedy injustice in the South if they gained power, so they should shut up; 2) northern whites would not consent to be ruled by ignorance; 3) the race problem was "one of the most perplexing in the whole history of civilization," which southern moderates were doing their best to solve in the only way it could be solved—through uplift and education.[15]

"Bloody Shirt" abolitionists were hard put to reply to some of these arguments, especially to the question: "Yes, some Negroes are disfran-

[13] *BET*, Nov. 22, 24, 1884.

[14] Oliver Johnson to Fanny Garrison Villard, Feb. 2, 1885, FGV Papers.

[15] See especially a remarkable pair of letters from "An Old Abolitionist on the Negro Vote" (Thomas Wentworth Higginson), published originally in the *Boston Advertiser* and widely reprinted, e.g. *NYEP*, Sept. 30, Oct. 6, 1885.

chised, but what can the federal government do about it?" So long as the Democrats were in power, they admitted, the government could do nothing. But "earnest protest will be in order, and Republicans should make it an issue in political campaigns," agreed the *Independent* and *Inter Ocean*. "If telling the actual truth about public affairs is 'unfurling the bloody shirt,' the more it is unfurled the better." And the *Spy* remarked in 1885: "It may be true that no Republican now is prepared to answer the question: 'What are you going to do about it?' But that is no reason why we should say that nothing needs to be done. If the need is recognized and kept always in view the way will be found some time."[16]

There the argument pretty much rested for three years, until the 1888 election intensified it. Meanwhile a major legislative effort to help solve the southern educational problem fell just short of success. With the revival of prosperity after 1879 came a renewed drive for federal aid to education. The literacy data of the 1880 census gave the movement a strong impetus. Twenty percent of the country's 10 million eligible voters were illiterate; three-quarters of them lived in the South, where 70 percent of the black population could not read or write and over half of the voters in some states were illiterate. Most alarming of all was the national increase of more than half a million illiterates since 1870 (though the *percentage* of illiteracy had declined slightly). "Free institutions must have the light of knowledge," ran a typical abolitionist editorial in behalf of federal aid. "In the poisonous night of ignorance they wilt and rot." A committee of abolitionist educators lobbying for federal aid declared that the existence of "millions of voters who have no proper qualification for the duties with which they are charged . . . has created an emergency of such vast and urgent proportions that no power short of the national government can deal with it."[17]

Although this crisis rhetoric seems inconsistent with the missionaries' optimistic appraisals of Negro education in the 1880s, the contradiction is more apparent than real. The positive assessments usually referred to missionary schools, which concentrated on higher education and reached only a fraction of the black population. Their success demonstrated what the rest of the race could do if given the chance,

[16] *Independent*, Sept. 17, 1885; *CIO* (D), Sept. 6, 1885; *Mass. Spy*, Sept. 4, 1885.
[17] *ZH*, Feb. 27, 1884; Joseph C. Hartzell, ed., *Christian Educators in Council. Sixty Addresses by American Educators*, New York, 1883, p. 38. The fullest account of the drive for federal aid in the early 1880s is Daniel W. Crofts, "The Blair Bill and the Elections Bill: The Congressional Aftermath to Reconstruction," Ph.D. Dissertation, Yale University, 1968, pp. 29-59.

said abolitionists, but northern philanthropy could not alone uplift the masses. If public schools did not do their job, the promising beginnings of black education would go for naught; hence the note of desperation in discussions of the issue.

As part of their policy of retrenchment, Bourbon state governments cut public school expenditures. In 1880 the amount spent per pupil in nine southern states was only 60 percent of what it had been in 1875. Fewer than three-fifths of the white children and two-fifths of the black children of school age were enrolled. At best the school term in rural areas lasted three months (some schools continued on a tuition basis after the free term ended). Northern states spent three times as much per pupil as southern states. Thus the case for federal aid to the South was a strong one; those who questioned its constitutionality, said the *Transcript*, were like the "churchmen who debated in their cloisters how many angels could balance on a needle's point, while the Huns were thundering at the gate."[18]

By 1882 the supporters of federal aid had created a lobby that included the Commissioner of Education, the National Education Association, nearly all of the freedmen's mission-education societies, former President Hayes, and such southern spokesmen as Jabez L. M. Curry of the Peabody Fund and Atticus Haygood of the Slater Fund. Senator Henry W. Blair of New Hampshire placed himself at their head and introduced a bill to grant the states $105,000,000 over a 10-year period, apportioned on the ratio of illiteracy. As amended to reduce the appropriation to $77,000,000 over seven years and to require the states to match federal grants dollar for dollar (a later amendment also required the states to divide the money *pro rata* between white and black schools), the Blair bill was pushed through the Senate in April 1884 by Republicans with the aid of deep-South Democrats whose states would benefit most from it. But Democratic leaders in the House, suspicious that the measure was a protectionist device to get rid of the Treasury surplus that was causing demands for tariff reduction, kept the Blair bill bottled up in committee.[19]

Opponents of the bill advanced four major arguments: direct federal grants to states were unconstitutional; the bill was a threat to states' rights and to local control of schools; "paternalism" or a "gov-

[18] Woodward, *Origins of the New South*, 61-62; Horace Mann Bond, *The Education of the Negro in the American Social Order*, rev. ed., New York, 1966, p. 92; Gordon Canfield Lee, *The Struggle for Federal Aid . . . 1870-1890*, New York, 1949, pp. 30-33; *BET*, Oct. 30, 1883.

[19] Crofts, "The Blair Bill and the Elections Bill," 60-69; Crofts, "The Black Response to the Blair Education Bill," *Journal of Southern History*, XXXVII (Feb. 1971), 41-65; Allen J. Going, "The South and the Blair Education Bill," *Mississippi Valley Historical Review*, XLIV (Sept. 1957), 267-90.

ernment dole" would undermine local responsibility and "pauperize" the recipients; and since four-fifths of the funds would come from taxes paid by the North while three-quarters of the appropriations would go to the South, it was unfair to tax people who would get little benefit to help those who paid few taxes. Proponents of the bill replied that the general welfare clause of the Constitution provided authority for the bill while the Northwest Ordinance, the Morrill Act, the Freedmen's Bureau, and other acts distributing federal funds to states provided plenty of precedent; that a nation with a serious race problem could no longer afford to defer to states' rights; that the amendment to the Blair bill requiring states to match federal grants would prevent pauperization; and that most social services furnished by government reallocated wealth from the rich to the poor, and the Blair bill would only do on a national scale what was already done at the state and local level. "It is easy and cheap" to say that the South should pay for its own schools, commented one abolitionist, but the South could not do it. "With less than half the resources of twenty years ago they are called on to meet more than double the responsibilities." Moreover, said the *Independent*, "the North shared the responsibility for the sin of slavery, is responsible for emancipation and enfranchisement, and is therefore under a triple obligation to share the duty and the burden of equipping the emancipated Negro race for the duties of citizenship."[20]

One of the most influential opponents of the Blair bill was the merged *New York Evening Post* and *Nation*. If this seems a strange role for a periodical founded to represent the freedmen's interests, it need only be recalled that Godkin had long since abandoned the *Nation*'s original purpose. The *Post/Nation*'s crusade against federal aid was the special province of Edward P. Clark, a new editorial writer with no antislavery background. Clark launched his barrage against the bill in 1886 and never let up until its burial in 1890. Some of his editorials were collected into a pamphlet titled *A Bill to Promote Mendicancy*, a phrase that became almost a cliché in debates on the measure.

Although important, education was "not the most important thing" for the South, said Clark. "The vital element of any success that is worth achieving in this world is self-reliance." Clark pointed out that two-thirds of the illiterate southerners were above school age and could not be reached by the schools anyway, and the remaining third could be taken care of by a South that was growing rapidly in wealth and enterprise. By an adroit juggling of selected statistics, he "proved"

[20] *Advance*, Apr. 5, 1883; *Independent*, June 11, 1891.

that southern states had increased their educational appropriations by nearly 50 percent since 1880, that the same percentage of school-age children were enrolled in a half-dozen southern states as in six northern states of comparable population density, that the school term in the most progressive southern states was as long as in the three northern New England states, and that therefore the South was catching up with the North and should be left alone "to work out its own salvation in the good old self-reliant New England way."[21]

Clark's arguments and statistics had a surface plausibility that won over several former supporters of the Blair bill and forced the remainder to respond with better arguments and statistics. Several abolitionists played important roles in this counterattack, especially William Hayes Ward of the *Independent* and Edward Clement of the *Transcript*. Comparison of the wealthiest southern urban school districts with the poorest rural districts in New England, they maintained, was as specious as citing the length of the school term and total enrollment as evidence of the *quality* of education and the average *daily* attendance. Ward conceded that southern spending for schools had risen since 1880 and that enrollment, especially of black students (which doubled between 1877 and 1887) had also increased. But this was precisely the problem, for the growth in enrollment had caused a decrease in per student expenditure of nearly 8 percent between the depression year of 1877 and the prosperous year of 1887. Citing the Commissioner of Education's reports, the *Independent* showed that the North's per student expenditure was now nearly four times the South's and the average school term in the North was 70 percent longer than in the South. "These are conditions which are not to be overcome by argument or sophistry. The typical Southern free school is kept in a log house, with dirt or puncheon floor, without desks or blackboards." To portray such schools as equal to those of Maine or Vermont was a crime against millions of southern children. "It is desperately important that those children should be educated. The North is rich and can educate its children. The South is poor and cannot."[22]

Despite this counterattack, the campaign against the Blair bill continued to make converts among former supporters, including George William Curtis, who by 1888 subscribed fully to the self-help theory, which fit well with his mugwump limited-government ideology. These and other defections proved fatal to the Blair bill. Although the Senate

21 *NYEP*, Jan. 16, Feb. 11, Mar. 23, Apr. 27, 1886. For the impact of Clark's editorial crusade against the Blair bill, see Hirshson, *Farewell to the Bloody Shirt*, 194-97, and Crofts, "The Blair Bill and the Elections Bill," 148-55.

22 *Independent*, July 8, 22, 1886, July 4, 1889, Feb. 2, 1888; *BET*, Feb. 15, Apr. 20, July 27, Aug. 2, 1886, Aug. 7, 1888.

passed the measure a second time in 1886 and again two years later, the margin of passage was reduced in 1888 and the Democratic House as usual refused to consider it. When Blair brought his bill before the Senate a fourth time in 1890, three Republicans and four southern Democrats switched their affirmative votes of 1888 to negative, thus killing the measure for good. Congress passed a veterans' pension act in 1890 that got rid of the Treasury surplus that might otherwise have gone to education.[23]

The failure of the Blair bill was one more in the long line of missed opportunities of Reconstruction. Though the handful of former abolitionists who opposed the bill must bear part of the responsibility, if it had not been for the active support of a much larger number the bill would not have come as close to passage as it did. Surviving evidence indicates that 35 former abolitionists favored federal aid, several of them being leaders in the movement, while five (including Curtis, who turned against the Blair bill in 1886) opposed it.

Although President Cleveland's record on civil service reform disappointed mugwump abolitionists, his tariff and southern policies caused most of them to support him for re-election in 1888. As Curtis told Carl Schurz, even though Cleveland had not fully measured up to expectations it would be impossible to support the Republicans on "a platform of high protection and Southern interference."[24]

Thomas Wentworth Higginson not only campaigned for Cleveland; he also ran for Congress as a Democrat with the backing of William Lloyd Garrison, Jr., and several other abolitionists. A free trader, Garrison voted Democratic in 1888 on the tariff issue; as for the southern question, he said, "the colored voter has been no more defrauded of his legal rights [under Cleveland] than under Grant, and Garfield, and Arthur." Higginson went further, asserting that "the colored people have not lost but gained by the country having passed under a Democratic administration," for there had been fewer "outrages" and greater material progress for Negroes in the past four years than in any comparable period since the war. Higginson hoped to win the black vote in his Cambridge district on his abolitionist record, but Frederick Douglass campaigned against him, attacking mugwumps as "traitors not only to [the Republican party] but to the cause of liberty itself." (This was not a unanimous black viewpoint; several race spokesmen, including T. Thomas Fortune, Ida B. Wells, and a Harvard junior named W.E.B. Du Bois, supported Cleveland in 1888.) Higgin-

[23] Crofts, "The Blair Bill and the Elections Bill," 176-85; Lee, *The Struggle for Federal Aid*, 110-21.

[24] Curtis to Schurz, Apr. 4, 1888, Schurz Papers, Library of Congress.

son lost the election (it was a Republican district); most of the black vote went against him.[25]

Unlike Garrison, most surviving Garrisonians were Republican in 1888. With unconscious irony, Oliver Johnson rebuked Garrison in the same manner that Garrison's father had rebuked Johnson a decade earlier for supporting Hayes's southern policy. Conceding that the Republicans had failed to protect black voters, Johnson thought it all the more important "not to surrender our *moral* protest. . . . No Abolitionist can consistently take any other grounds. But for the outrageous suppression of the negro vote, Cleveland could not have been elected in 1884."[26]

Although several Republican politicians agreed with Johnson, the National Committee instructed campaign speakers to play down the race question and concentrate on the tariff. Many abolitionist Republicans refused to heed this edict. William Hayes Ward proclaimed the racial issue "a matter of momentous importance" that could not "be laughed out of court" by jeers about the bloody shirt or buried under statistics on *ad valorem* duties. And while William Penn Nixon was a staunch party man and protectionist, he insisted that Republicans must not "abandon the principle of fair elections and let the Southern whites trample upon and crush into serfdom the colored citizens" for the sake of the tariff.[27]

One of the campaign's more colorful features was Anna Dickinson's return to the hustings. After several years of obscurity, Dickinson once again burst into the headlines in June 1888 with a newspaper interview, really an oration, in which she revived the themes of her earlier triumphs. Whether her chief motive was a desire for renewed fame or

[25] Tilden G. Edelstein, *Strange Enthusiasm: A Life of Thomas Wentworth Higginson*, New Haven, 1968, pp. 376-81; speech by Higginson published in *Boston Globe*, Oct. 24, 1888 (I am grateful to Tilden Edelstein for this citation); speeches by Garrison published in *NYEP*, Aug. 28, 1888, and in clippings, WLG, Jr., Papers; Higginson to "Dearest Anna," Nov. 7, 1888, Higginson Papers, Houghton Library, Harvard University; speech by Douglass published in *Cambridge Chronicle*, Oct. 27, 1888 (I am grateful to Tilden Edelstein for this citation); Emma Lou Thornbrough, *T. Thomas Fortune: Militant Journalist*, Chicago, 1972, pp. 93-94; Elliott M. Rudwick, *W. E. B. Du Bois: A Study in Minority Group Leadership*, Philadelphia, 1960, p. 22. Wendell Garrison's son Lloyd, a student at Harvard, was a campaign worker for Higginson in a predominantly black ward. Reporting after the election that the Republicans had used bribery and chicanery to carry the ward, young Garrison told Higginson that "the view of the negro question I received there was one I never had had an opportunity of obtaining before; and I admit that my grandfather's sanguine expectations of the near triumph and glory of the negro race seem to me to have little prospect even of ultimate fulfillment." Lloyd McKim Garrison to Higginson, Nov. 15, 1888, Higginson Papers.

[26] Oliver Johnson to William Lloyd Garrison, Jr., Nov. 6, 1888, WLG, Jr., Papers.

[27] *Independent*, Aug. 23, 1888; *CIO* (D), Nov. 4, 1888. For the tariff strategy in 1888, see Hirshson, *Farewell to the Bloody Shirt*, chap. 7.

genuine concern for oppressed blacks is unclear; in any case the one-time radical spellbinder who had supported Greeley in 1872 returned to her original allegiance in 1888 and loosed a barrage of epithets against Cleveland, the Democrats, and the South. "We, the Republican party of the North," she declared, "mean to elect so overwhelming a majority that the South will understand once and for all that the provisions of the Constitution will be enforced."[28]

This interview attracted considerable attention; enough people remembered Dickinson's earlier career to make her newsworthy. Taking their cue from the *New York World,* Democratic newspapers jeered her as a "belated Joan of Arc just emerged from a Rip Van Winkle sleep" who did not know that the "negro question . . . is dead beyond resurrection." But several Republican papers endorsed her "electric" remarks and urged the National Committee to enlist her as a speaker. Perhaps recalling the role her perfervid oratory had played in Republican victories a quarter-century earlier, Benjamin Harrison himself pressed the committee to sign her on. With some reluctance they did so, and Dickinson went to Indiana in September for the first of 30 scheduled speeches in three closely contested states.[29]

Her tour of the Hoosier state was just like the old days, with overflow crowds entranced by a woman who though now a middle-aged spinster could still rouse strong political emotions. Her theme was unvaried: "The rebels of the South, unrepentant and unreconstructed," were trying to win back what they had surrendered in 1865. A vote for Cleveland was a "vote for degradation, Southern aristocracy, slavery, [and] the devil." Frederick Douglass, also campaigning in Indiana, thought Dickinson's speeches the best he had heard. But the Republican national chairman and many Indiana party leaders were unhappy with her bloody shirt hyperbole, which was unlikely to win converts among high-tariff Democrats. "While such a speech might have been in order during the anti-slavery and war period," said an Indiana Republican, "Miss Dickinson ought to know that no party can hope to live on the dead issues of the past." The National Committee canceled some of her speeches and sent her on a circuit of small towns in upstate New York, where she could do little harm. She soon faded back into obscurity.[30]

Whether the tariff, the southern question, or any other national issue

[28] *New York Press,* June 17, 1888, clipping in Dickinson Papers, Library of Congress. All subsequent newspaper citations concerning Dickinson's activities are from this clipping collection. Giraud Chester, *Embattled Maiden: The Life of Anna Dickinson,* New York, 1951, pp. 238-52, discusses the 1888 campaign.

[29] *New York World,* July 4, 1888; Chester, *Embattled Maiden,* 238-40.

[30] *Indianapolis Sentinel,* Sept. 23, 25, 1888; *South Bend Daily Times,* Oct. 2, 1888; Chester, *Embattled Maiden,* 244-52.

was mainly responsible for Republican victory in 1888 is uncertain; in any case Harrison won New York and Indiana and therefore the election. Abolitionists supported the winning candidate this time by a margin of two to one: of the 39 for whom evidence has been found, 26 endorsed Harrison and 13 voted for Cleveland. Once again half of the political abolitionists, compared with 36 percent of the Garrisonians and none of the evangelicals, backed the Democratic candidate. In a postelection analysis, the *Independent* pointed out that although Republicans had made gratifying gains in the upper South, the party had lost ground in the lower South. In South Carolina, with a population 60 percent black, the Republicans polled only 17 percent of the vote. Such a situation was "an open attack upon the Constitution. . . . We dare not ignore the challenge." With firm control of the presidency and both houses of Congress for the first time in 14 years, the Republicans, said the *Independent*, should pass a federal elections law to restore constitutional rights in the South.[31]

In its first year, however, the Harrison administration tried to build a southern constituency on the tariff issue by encouraging lily-white Republican factions. But elections in Louisiana and Virginia in 1889 demonstrated the futility of this policy, and the administration thereupon joined forces with those who were demanding a new enforcement act. The president's first message to Congress in December 1889 recommended an elections law based on the constitutional provision giving Congress the right to regulate the time, place, and manner of electing its members. Several such bills were soon introduced, setting the stage for the most impassioned sectional debate since Reconstruction.[32] Former abolitionists took a prominent part in this debate, supporting federal legislation by a margin of more than two to one. Of 37 abolitionists for whom evidence has been found, 26 endorsed an elections law and 11 opposed it. While all eight evangelicals whose opinion is known supported the bill, 73 percent of the Garrisonians and 56 percent of the political abolitionists did so.

Nixon of the *Inter Ocean* and Curtis of *Harper's Weekly* were, respectively, the most outspoken abolitionists for and against such legislation. Almost daily the *Inter Ocean* thundered fulminations against the South, until one southern editor complained that it was "par excellence the nigger apologist in newspaperdom, and . . . represents . . . the relentless hate still fondled in the breasts of some venomous radicals at the North." Nixon was unruffled by such attacks. If it took a regiment in every southern county to enforce the Constitution, he said, the cost would not be too great. Not only was disfranchisement a crime

---

[31] *Independent*, Dec. 20, 1888, Jan. 31, Feb. 21, 1889.
[32] Hirshson, *Farewell to the Bloody Shirt*, 168-89, 200-211.

against the Negro, but it enabled southern Democrats to wield national power disproportionate to their voting strength. "The North will not much longer submit to the elections of Presidents and Congressmen by suppression of the negro vote."[33]

Curtis argued, on the other hand, that the presence of federal supervisors at the polls would not prevent the kinds of social and economic pressures that were most effective in keeping blacks from voting. Even "if it were provided that every colored voter should be escorted to the polls by a United States soldier," he wrote, "it is wholly improbable that a considerable number of such voters would avail themselves of the protection, because they would know that they would be made to suffer for it in ways which United States soldiers could not prevent." In contrast to his position 15 years earlier on the Civil Rights Act, Curtis maintained that laws could not change the hearts and minds of men. "The attempts to promote temperance by prohibitive laws," he said, "signally illustrate the truth that reformatory legislation to be efficient must represent the average opinion and feeling of the community."[34]

When the new Congress met in December 1889, it was confronted with 17 contested election cases from the South. The House decided 11 of them in favor of the Republican claimants. The testimony in these cases convinced many Republicans of the necessity for an elections law. In April 1890 the House Republican caucus instructed Henry Cabot Lodge, one of the chief proponents of such a law, to report from committee a bill embodying the best features of the many measures in the hopper. Lodge's bill, passed by a straight party vote in July, provided for the appointment of federal supervisors from both parties in any congressional district upon petition of 100 voters or in any part of a district upon petition of 50 voters. The supervisors were empowered to inspect registration books, observe the voting, and inform voters of election procedures. U.S. circuit courts were authorized to appoint boards of canvassers to certify the results in each district and to initiate proceedings against those guilty of intimidation or fraud.[35]

Opponents of the Lodge bill criticized both its purpose and method. W. E. B. Du Bois agreed with those white abolitionists who thought education more important than law in the Negro's struggle. A black newspaper quoted Du Bois as saying that "a good many of our people . . . are not fit for the responsibility of republican government. When you have the right sort of black voters you will need no election laws."

[33] *CIO* (D), Oct. 19, 1888, Feb. 23, 1889.
[34] *HW*, Jan. 26, Aug. 3, Nov. 9, 30, 1889.
[35] Hirshson, *Farewell to the Bloody Shirt*, 203-33; Richard E. Welch, Jr., "The Federal Elections Bill of 1890; Postscripts and Prelude," *Journal of American History*, LII (Dec. 1965), 511-26.

Moreover, since the Lodge bill applied only to congressional elections (constitutionally it could apply to no others), it left untouched the elections for state and local office where matters most vital to black interests were decided—schools, property rights, labor laws, criminal procedures, and the like. Thus it would not help the Negro where he needed help, said abolitionist opponents; indeed, it would only make his situation worse by provoking a white backlash. After initially supporting the Lodge bill, Edward Clement turned against it when he became convinced that it would not work and that its real purpose was partisan rather than humane. Republican politicians, he said, "are working this hobby for effect on the North, and with no remarkable concern as to what becomes of the negro in the confusion and disorder that may prevail because of partisan and sectional legislation."[36]

Backers of the law were placed on the defensive by the argument that it would not work. "We can at least try the Lodge method," replied the *Independent* lamely, "and if it doesn't work we can try something else. We do not believe in pleading imbecility for our National Government." Richard Hallowell conceded that the measure might not change things much in the South, but it would at least force "despotism [to] skulk in dark corners until it has learned the lesson of self-restraint; political morality will [then] develop by natural growth."[37]

Democrats branded the Lodge act a "force bill," and the epithet stuck. This gave its abolitionist supporters a chance to go on the offensive. Of course it was a force bill: "any wise and beneficent enactment which has for its aim the suppression of wrong-doing must have force behind it." It was hypocritical for those who used force to break the law to decry its use to uphold the law. As for the assertion that the bill would revive the Reconstruction horrors of "Negro domination," this was a bugbear, said the *Independent*. Negro domination was not likely, but even if it were it would not be "as bad as southern fears make it. . . . The Negroes have gained immensely in intelligence and capacity" since Reconstruction, and in any case "between a government which is based on fraud and intimidation and a government in the hands of Negroes there should not be a moment's hesitation of choice."[38]

Left unresolved was the question whether the Lodge bill would actually work, but this became academic when the Senate first postponed consideration of the measure and then killed it. The McKinley tariff was more important to many Republicans than the elections bill,

---

[36] Du Bois in *New York Age*, June 13, 1891, quoted by Meier, *Negro Thought in America*, p. 192; *BET*, Aug. 19, 1890.

[37] *Independent*, Jan. 1, 1891; Hallowell, *The Southern Question*, p. 31.

[38] *Independent*, July 10, Sept. 4, 1890.

so to pass the former they postponed the latter in August 1890 until the next session of Congress. The *Spy* commented angrily that this was "another of those shameful victories of timidity and interest over courage and principle with which the country became sadly familiar in the old days of the conflict between slavery and freedom." Although Lodge's Senate colleague George F. Hoar worked hard for the measure at the next session, a bargain between western Republicans and southern Democrats who traded anti-Lodge act votes for pro-silver votes buried the elections bill for good in January 1891. Several abolitionists excoriated this "unpardonable surrender," but there was nothing they could do about it.[39]

The twin defeats of the Blair and Lodge bills in 1890–1891 marked the end of an era. The last, lingering legacy of Reconstruction was gone. Yet even some of those who mourned its passing believed that "the sure forces of education, thrift and religion" were more effective than legislation in the long run. The *Independent*, whose support for the Lodge bill had been second to none, nevertheless placed its "chief trust" in education, which would give the Negro the weapons to "conquer his rights at the polls." Even the *Inter Ocean* stated in the midst of its editorial battle for federal legislation: "We are sometimes persuaded" that education "is the only feasible . . . solution of the race problem."[40]

In 1890 the Quaker philanthropist Albert K. Smiley hosted a conference on the race problem at his Lake Mohonk resort hotel in the Catskills. Modeled on the annual Indian conferences at Mohonk, the Negro conference of 1890 and its successor of 1891 avoided political issues and concentrated on education. Invited speakers included several former abolitionists and Albion W. Tourgée, one of the country's most outspoken radicals on the race question. Except for Tourgée, they confined their remarks to the education/uplift theme of the conferences. Typical were the words of William Hayes Ward, who described in glowing terms the moral and material progress of black people. Although the evils of racism and ignorance still rested heavily upon the South, said Ward, "we can leave them to the sure influences of those slow and silent forces of education and religion. . . . We are to look forward only a few years more, and we shall have the great Negro problem settled."[41]

[39] *Mass. Spy*, Aug. 22, 1890, Jan. 9, 1891; *CIO* (D), Jan. 7, 1891.

[40] *AM*, XLIV (Oct. 1890), 299; *Independent*, Apr. 2, June 11, 1891; *CIO* (D), Feb. 26, 1890.

[41] Isabel Barrows, ed., *Second Mohonk Conference on the Negro Question . . . June 3, 4, 5, 1891*, Boston, 1891, pp. 108, 27. Evidently to avoid embarrassing southern white participants, Smiley invited no blacks to the conference, an omission roundly condemned by several black newspapers. Tourgée openly chided the

In hindsight it is easy to label such views fatuously optimistic. Much of the talk about the promising state of affairs in the South was probably wishful thinking subconsciously designed to assuage consciences that may have felt guilty about the compromises and retreats since 1876. On the other hand, there was some truth in the optimists' portrait of the South in the 1880s. Though far from ideal, the Negro's condition at least gave promise of a gradual broadening of rights and opportunities. As C. Vann Woodward and others have shown, blacks continued to vote and hold office in many areas, rigid codification of Jim Crow had not yet taken place, and not all doors to better race relations had been closed. Despite the defeat of the Blair bill, the school enrollment of Negroes grew faster than the black population, the mission-education societies enjoyed a prosperous decade and expanded their programs for higher education, and black illiteracy declined at a faster rate than in the 1870s. The hopefulness with which some abolitionists viewed the South in the 1880s was not entirely rooted in fantasy. As they saw it, the decade after Reconstruction was better in some respects than the decade *of* Reconstruction with its turmoil, violence, and hatred of which the freedmen were the chief victims.

But events after 1890 eroded much of this optimism. Not only did the legal status of blacks deteriorate after that date, but the national government retreated completely from its commitment to Negro rights. The increasingly savage style of lynchings, the growing frequency of race riots, the codification of Jim Crow, the disfranchisement of nearly all southern blacks, the rise to power of Negrophobic "redneck" leaders in southern politics, and growing racism in the North as well as South made a mockery of Ward's 1891 prediction of an imminent settlement of the race problem. At the same time the Populist and free silver crusades, the antitrust movement, industrial violence, and urban problems overshadowed the "southern question" as national issues.

The question nevertheless remained alive, and for some former abolitionists and their descendants the worsening racial situation made it a more crucial question than ever. Their concern led, after many twistings and turnings, to the founding of the NAACP in 1909–1910. The changing focus of racial reform in the two decades after 1890 will be

sponsors for failing to invite blacks; several of the abolitionist guests were privately critical. Although the *Independent* brought pressure on Smiley to invite Negroes to future conferences, none was asked to the second and last meeting in 1891. Leslie H. Fishel, "The North and the Negro, 1865-1900: A Study in Race Discrimination," Ph.D. Dissertation, Harvard University, 1953, pp. 410-11; Otto H. Olsen, *Carpetbagger's Crusade: The Life of Albion W. Tourgée*, Baltimore, 1965, pp. 306-307; *Independent*, June 12, 1890.

the subject of Part III of this book. The one constant theme running through the entire period from Reconstruction to the NAACP, however, was education. Former abolitionists not only talked about education as a solution of the race problem, they did something about it. Their contributions to black education were perhaps the most enduring legacy of the antislavery movement. Part II will describe and evaluate that legacy.

Part Two

Education for Freedom

Chapter Nine

The Roots of Freedmen's Education

Like most wars, the Civil War summoned forth idealism as well as brutality. The outstanding example of idealism in the 1860s was the crusade for freedmen's education. In less than a decade, northern missionaries established more than a thousand schools for emancipated slaves and sent three thousand teachers to the South. Their elementary schools became the foundation of public education for blacks; their "universities," colleges, academies, and normal schools provided most of the higher education for southern Negroes until well into the twentieth century. These institutions were the products of two interrelated impulses: the missionary energy of northern Protestantism and the abolitionist desire to uplift the freedmen.

The story of freedmen's education during the Civil War and Reconstruction is well known.[1] But a false impression exists that the missionary educators began "to melt away" as Reconstruction collapsed. If this were true, one might wonder how the 39 missionary colleges and secondary schools founded before 1880 had multiplied threefold by 1915, how the number of institutions offering college-level courses had grown from 9 in 1880 to 27 by 1915, or how the combined annual budgets of the four major freedmen's education societies had gone from $315,000 in 1876 to $1,360,000 forty years later, with the latter figure not including a half-dozen important schools that had become independent of the societies' support in the interval.[2]

To be sure, there is other evidence that at first glance appears to support the melting away thesis. The Freedmen's Bureau ceased to function in 1870, and, with the disappearance of the wartime sense of crisis that had inspired the drive for freedmen's relief, the generosity of northern donors to education societies tapered off. "The tide of enthusiasm which sustained the schools the first ten years is fast ebbing," lamented a Quaker educator in 1872. Officials of the American Mis-

[1] For a guide to the literature on the subject, see James M. McPherson et al., *Blacks in America: Bibliographical Essays*, New York, 1971, pp. 119-21. A welcome new study is William Preston Vaughn, *Schools for All: The Blacks & Public Education in the South, 1865-1877*, Lexington, Ky., 1974.

[2] The "melting away" thesis is stated in Henry Allen Bullock, *A History of Negro Education in the South*, Cambridge, Mass., 1967, p. 123; and Louis R. Harlan, *Separate and Unequal: Public School Campaigns and Racism in the Southern Seaboard States 1901-1915*, Chapel Hill, 1958, pp. 6-7.

sionary Association (AMA) reported that "many who gave when it was popular to do for the 'contrabands' or the 'Freedmen' are growing lukewarm. . . . The times are so hard and the subject of the negroes so stale. . . . I do not see any other way than to cut down somewhere."[3]

The larger freedmen's aid societies retrenched in the 1870s; the smaller ones died. By 1876 only the AMA (nominally nonsectarian but primarily Congregational), the Freedmen's Aid Society of the Methodist Episcopal Church, the American Baptist Home Mission Society, and the Committee on Missions to Freedmen of the Presbyterian Church in the U.S.A. were carrying on a major effort for freedmen's education, while the Quakers and the United Presbyterians sustained smaller undertakings and a few other denominations supported a handful of schools. The American Freedmen's Union Commission, which in 1866 had expended more than $400,000 and supported 760 teachers in the South, dissolved in 1869. Of its constituent societies, only the New England Freedmen's Aid Society continued after 1871, and by 1876 it too no longer existed. The large Quaker effort of the 1860s likewise declined to the point that by 1883 fewer than 40 of more than 100 earlier schools remained. Even the AMA, largest of the mission societies, was compelled to reduce its 170 schools with 21,848 students in 1870 to 37 schools with 7,229 students in 1878.[4]

But despite appearances the freedmen's education movement had not fallen into permanent decline; rather, it was on the eve of vigorous growth in 1878. The decrease in the number of schools supported by northern societies was more apparent than real. Most of their elementary schools had been absorbed into the South's public school system, a development promoted by the mission societies themselves. Several missionary educators were active in the Reconstruction governments that established this system, and some of them taught in the new public schools or became state or county superintendents of education. The northern societies had never conceived their task to be mass education; this was to be the function of the public schools, as it was in the North. The mission societies sustained common schools in the 1860s as a temporary crash program until the Reconstruction governments could get public education started. As the states took over these elementary

3 *Friends' Review*, Dec. 28, 1872; George Whipple to Gerrit Smith, Dec. 12, 1874, Smith Papers, Syracuse University Library; Whipple to Erastus M. Cravath, Aug. 19, 1874, Robert F. Markham to Michael E. Strieby, June 1, 1876, AMA Archives.

4 These statistics are compiled from the annual reports of the various freedmen's associations and from other data in *The American Freedman* (organ of the American Freedmen's Union Commission); *The Freedmen's Record* (New England Freedmen's Aid Society); the Records of the New England Freedmen's Aid Society in the Massachusetts Historical Society; and *Friends' Review*.

schools, the societies began to concentrate most of their resources on secondary schools and colleges to train teachers, ministers, doctors, and lawyers. The growth in the number of black students at the secondary, college, and professional levels is shown in Figure 1. And though the income of mission societies declined during most of the 1870s, it began to *rise* late in the decade with recovery from the depression and continued to increase thereafter except for temporary downturns in the depression of the 1890s and the recession of 1907–1908. By 1889 the combined budgets of the four principal societies (see Figure 2) had surpassed the previous highest annual income of *all* the freedmen's aid societies in 1866. In 1891 the amount these four societies spent for black education was double their former high of 1870, and in 1906 their combined budget was more than four times as large as in 1876.[5]

These statistics actually understate the growth of missionary education after 1878, for they do not include the increasing amount expended by the smaller Protestant denominations or the substantial and growing contributions to the following schools, which were independent of the mission societies: Howard University, much of whose initial and later funding came from the federal government but which lived largely on private support in the 1870s and 1880s; Berea College, Hampton Institute, and Atlanta University, which achieved independence from the AMA in the 1870s; Leland University in New Orleans, which cut the apron strings of the Baptist Home Mission Society in 1887; and a number of other independent schools including Tuskegee that received most of their support from the North.

Most histories of black education have slighted the role of the mission societies. Even the studies of philanthropy in Negro education have tended to concentrate on such well-publicized grants as the

[5] Since the cost of living declined for 30 years after the Civil War and the price index was virtually the same in 1906 as 1876, this increase of missionary income was real and not inflation-caused. For cost-of-living indexes, see *Historical Statistics of the United States: Colonial Times to 1957*, Bureau of the Census, Washington, 1960, p. 127. The graphs were constructed from data in the annual reports of the mission societies supplemented by the annual reports of the U.S. Commissioner of Education. The data on the number of students in 1915 was obtained from *Negro Education: A Study of the Private and Higher Schools for the Colored People in the United States*, ed. Thomas Jesse Jones, 2 vols., Washington, 1917, which used stricter criteria than earlier reports to determine whether students were actually studying secondary or college subjects—hence the decline from 1910. Figure 1 is calculated for five-year intervals; the data in Figure 2 is on a yearly basis. Although the AMA sustained missions and schools for other groups besides the freedmen and the Methodist Freedmen's Aid Society supported white schools from 1882 through 1906, the data for these two societies in the graph include only the budgets for black schools (and in the case of the AMA, black churches).

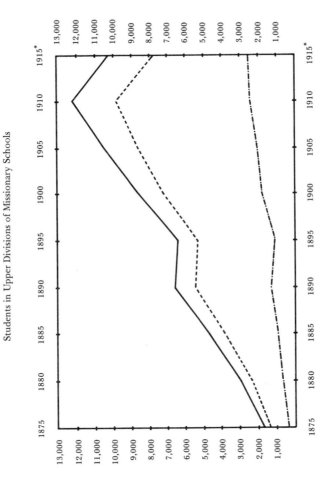

FIGURE 1.

Students in Upper Divisions of Missionary Schools

College and Professional ——·——·——

Secondary —— —— ——

Combined Total ————————

(Numbers before 1890 are estimates based on incomplete data)

Sources: See Note 5.

*The figures for 1915 are based on stricter criteria for classifying students in secondary and college classes; thus fewer students are placed in higher grades than if earlier standards had been applied.

Budgets of the Four Major Mission Societies

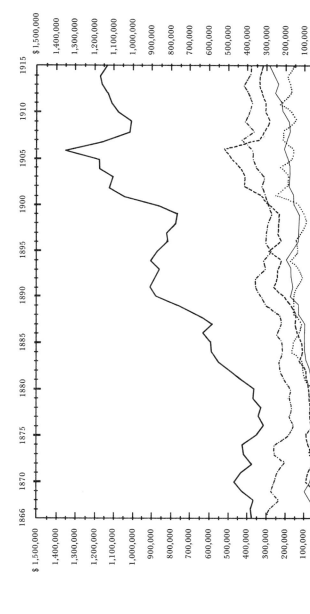

Total: Four missionary societies ───────

American Missionary Association ─ · ─ · ─

Freedmen's Aid Society of the Methodist Episcopal Church ─ ─ ─

Board of Missions for Freedmen, Presbyterian Church in the U. S. A. •••••••••

American Baptist Home Mission Society ───────

Sources: See Note 5.

George Peabody Fund (established in 1867), the John F. Slater Fund (1882), the Anna T. Jeanes Fund (1908), and the gifts of John D. Rockefeller, Andrew Carnegie, and Julius Rosenwald through various foundations. Such emphasis obscures the truth that before World War I the northern mission societies founded largely by abolitionists were by far the most important contributors to Negro higher education. Indeed, the largest single grant to black education during this period is virtually unmentioned in traditional accounts: the Daniel Hand Fund of $1,000,000 (later augmented by $500,000) established in 1888 and administered by the AMA, which applied the income to its schools.[6]

The surviving freedmen's education societies were able to expand after the depression of the 1870s because they were firmly rooted in the institutional structure of American Protestantism. Northern churches took up collections for the freedmen just as they did for other missions. The freedmen's societies were a *missionary* enterprise. The president of the Methodist Freedmen's Aid Society thought "the deliverance of the colored race from bondage" made the South "the most inviting field of our day for missionary and kindred beneficent labors." The AMA proclaimed in 1872 that "the anti-slavery discussions of the last forty years were a John-the-Baptist call to repentance, which was followed by the war laying the axe at the foot of the tree." Then came "the Christ-like mission of the teachers and ministers, instructing the emancipated slaves" in preparation for the day when "the Pentecostal baptism shall fall upon teachers, missionaries, and people . . . giving them a power . . . that shall break down all walls of caste-prejudice, so that there shall be no blacks and no whites, no North and no South, but when all shall be one in Christ Jesus."[7]

The AMA organized churches alongside its schools, but the Congregationalist style of worship appealed to few blacks, and by the mid-1870s the Association recognized the futility, as one official put it, of

[6] The Slater and Jeanes Funds were $1,000,000 each. The Peabody Fund totaled $2,000,000, but less than one-third of it was applied to black schools. From 1902 to 1914 Rockefeller gave $53,000,000 to the General Education Board, but only $700,000 of this went to Negro education. After 1914 the largesse of northern philanthropists toward Negro education grew enormously, and from 1923 to 1929 alone the General Education Board contributed nearly $14,000,000 to black schools. Raymond B. Fosdick, *Adventure in Giving: The Story of the General Education Board*, New York, 1962; Ullin W. Leavell, *Philanthropy in Negro Education*, Nashville, 1930. Leavell's book is an example of the slighting of the freedmen's mission societies; only one-fifth of the book is given to their work.

[7] Bishop D. W. Clark, president of the Methodist Society, quoted in Donald Gene Jones, "The Moral, Social, and Political Ideas of the Methodist Episcopal Church from the Closing Years of the Civil War through Reconstruction, 1864-1876," Ph.D. Dissertation, Drew University, 1969, p. 112; AMA Annual Report, quoted in *Friends' Review*, Feb. 22, 1873.

trying to win most of the freedmen away from "the noisy, excited, senseless practices in which their churches indulge." The AMA (and the Presbyterian society) therefore concentrated more on education than proselytization. Though some upper- and middle-class Negroes joined these denominations, in 1890 the Presbyterians had only 15,000 black members and the Congregationalists 7,000, which together constituted less than 1 percent of the total Negro church membership.[8]

In 1890, 53 percent of black church members were Baptists and 44 percent Methodists. Although the American Baptist Home Mission Society sent missionaries among the freedmen, they came not to convert the blacks nor to enlist them in northern-based churches, but to help existing Negro Baptist churches with financial aid and advice. By the 1880s the society devoted its resources almost entirely to education, leaving church affairs to black ministers, some of whom had been trained in missionary schools. Alone among northern denominations, the Methodist Episcopal Church recruited a sizable southern membership of both races after the war. The Methodist Freedmen's Aid Society devoted itself entirely to education; missionary efforts among the freedmen were carried on by the Missionary Society and the Church Extension Society. By 1893 the Freedmen's Aid Society had spent nearly $3,000,000 for black education (plus another $250,000 for white schools) and the Missionary and Church Extension Societies had spent $2,500,000 for both races in the South. For this effort northern Methodists could point to 5,000 black and 3,000 white students in their schools and a southern church membership of 269,000 whites (mostly in areas that had been pro-Union during the war) and 234,000 blacks, with another 20,000 black members in the North.[9]

---

[8] George Whipple to Erastus M. Cravath, July 24, 1874, AMA Archives. The data on black church membership in 1890 are from W. E. B. Du Bois, *The Negro Church*, Atlanta University Publication no. 8, Atlanta, 1903, p. 38. About 30,000 blacks also belonged to a Negro branch of the Cumberland Presbyterian Church, a small denomination located mainly in Kentucky and Tennessee that had split from the parent body in the early 19th century and carried its slave membership with it. The Cumberland Presbyterians were not active in education or mission work among blacks after the Civil War. The best accounts of Congregational and Presbyterian missionary efforts in the postwar South are Richard Bryant Drake, "The American Missionary Association and the Southern Negro, 1861-1888," Ph.D. Dissertation, Emory University, 1957, and Robert E. Thompkins, "A History of Religious Education Among Negroes in the Presbyterian Church in the United States of America," Ph.D. Dissertation, Univ. of Pittsburgh, 1951.

[9] Although each Baptist congregation was self-governing, most of them were loosely organized in one of three national "conventions" (in turn divided into state conventions): the American Baptist Convention (northern) with 800,000 members in 1894; the Southern Baptist Convention (white), with 1,200,000 members; and the National Baptist Convention (black), with nearly 1,500,000 members. Useful histories of the relationship between northern Baptists and their black brethren include James D. Tyms, *The Rise of Religious Education Among Negro*

In the modern era, education has always been a vital part of missions. Anglican missionaries founded the earliest school in North America in 1616 to Christianize the Indians. The Society for the Propagation of the Gospel and the Quakers established the first schools for Negroes a century later. From then until at least the 1830s most education for blacks took place under the auspices of church and mission groups. For more than two centuries, higher education for whites in America was also associated mainly with the church. The initial purpose of Harvard and the New England common schools was the training of clergymen and the education of the laity to understand the Bible and Puritan theology. Building on this foundation, other denominations sprinkled the land with academies and colleges. Of the 207 American colleges existing in 1860, 180 had been established by churches, most of them during the nineteenth century as a part of the missionary effort to preserve and expand the faith on successive frontiers.[10]

The founding of freedmen's schools was an extension of this missionary impulse to a new frontier. "The heart and conscience" of the freedmen, said the AMA, "must be quickened with the intellect. . . . Ignorance is a great hindrance to evangelization and intelligence is the handmaid of virtue. . . . The school and the Church must move on together at the South as they started together from Plymouth Rock." An official of the Methodist Freedmen's Aid Society explained that the teacher was "the right arm of the missionary." When the latter arrived in the South he found "just what all other missionaries find when they get to a foreign country, that they must begin at the bottom; that the school is the commencement of missionary work." It would be "a narrow conception of missionary effort," added Secretary Henry L. Morehouse of the Baptist Home Mission Society, "to suppose that it consists merely of inducing men to accept Christ." Jesus and His disciples were teachers; like them the missionary teachers must "mold character and sharpen the intellectual powers of students, that they may more clear-

Baptists, New York, 1965, and Lewis G. Jordan, Negro Baptist History U.S.A., 1750-1930, Nashville, 1930. At a time (1890) when 254,000 blacks were members of the Methodist Episcopal Church, the membership of the AME Church was 453,000, of the AME Zion Church 350,000, and of the Colored Methodist Episcopal Church 289,000. For studies of northern Methodists in the South, see Ralph E. Morrow, Northern Methodism and Reconstruction, East Lansing, Mich., 1956, and Frank K. Pool, "The Southern Negro in the Methodist Episcopal Church," Ph.D. Dissertation, Cornell University, 1939.

10 Bernard Bailyn, Education in the Forming of American Society, Chapel Hill, 1960, pp. 37-38; Carter G. Woodson, The Education of the Negro Prior to 1861, Washington, 1919; Donald G. Tewksbury, The Founding of American Colleges and Universities Before the Civil War (New York, 1932).

ly apprehend and more forcibly declare the great truths of the Christian system."[11]

Just as religion without education was an empty shell, education without religion would impart only information without conscience. "Right moral sentiment [can be] impressed upon this people," wrote an AMA teacher, only if "enough of Christianity [is] taught here in connection with the schools." The mission societies expected their teachers to "lead the youth to Christ as well as to the fountains of intelligence." Even nonsectarian Howard University required every trustee and faculty member to be "a member of some Evangelical Church."[12] In practice most schools taught the doctrines of their own denomination. Officially nondenominational, the AMA was a partial exception to this, but even so most of its teachers were Congregationalists. With few exceptions the other societies employed only members of their respective churches as teachers.

Largely because of denominational rivalry there was a surfeit of black schools bearing the name of college or university. By 1895 at least 54 such schools existed in the United States even though only 22 of them offered genuine college-level courses and scarcely 750 students were taking such courses. There were more "universities" for Negroes in America than universities of any kind in Britain and France combined. In several places the colleges of two or more denominations stood within walking distance of each other. In New Orleans and Nashville the AMA, the Baptists, and the northern Methodists each founded a black college, while in Atlanta these three denominations plus the AME Church sustained four separate institutions. Educational experts deplored this scattering of resources and urged the consolidation of many weak colleges into a few strong ones. But sectarian rivalry and the vested interests of each college prevented consolidation except in the cases of the Atlanta University Center (1929), Dillard University in New Orleans (1930), and Huston-Tillotson College in Austin, Texas (1951).[13]

[11] *AM*, New Series, I (June 1877), 4, xxxvii (Dec. 1883), 383; *Fourth Annual Report FASME*, Cincinnati, 1871, p. 27; *Baptist Home Missions in North America: Jubilee Volume, 1832-1882*, New York, 1883, pp. 416-17.

[12] Robert F. Markham to Michael E. Strieby, Jan. 11, 1878, AMA Archives; *Second Annual Report FASME*, Cincinnati, 1868, p. 11; Rayford W. Logan, *Howard University: The First Hundred Years 1867-1967*, New York, 1969, p. 28.

[13] The figure of 54 black colleges or universities was compiled from *Report of the U.S. Commissioner of Education for the Year 1894-95*, Washington, 1896, pp. 1338-45. See also W. E. B. Du Bois, *The College-Bred Negro*, Atlanta University Publications, no. 5, Atlanta, 1900, p. 112; Kelly Miller, "The Education of the Negro," in *Report of the U.S. Commissioner of Education for the Year 1900-01*, Washington, 1902, I, 837.

It should be kept in mind, however, that during the early decades of black higher education nine-tenths of the students in these schools were below the college level. Despite their names, the universities were founded mainly as grammar or normal schools to serve a local or regional constituency. Since public secondary schools for southern blacks were almost nonexistent before 1895, there were really too few instead of too many institutions for Negro higher education. Without the denominational zeal that inspired the founding of the missionary schools, there would have been fewer yet.

Freedmen's education was more than a purely missionary enterprise; it was the product also of continuing abolitionist concern for the freedmen. A decade after emancipation, Simeon S. Jocelyn, one of the founders of the AMA, declared that the freedmen "are still in a sense specially wards of the Abolitionists." Richard Rust of the Methodist Freedmen's Aid Society insisted that "the part we took in emancipation binds us with solemn obligations to educate, for education is the only completion of emancipation." And a Quaker abolitionist added simply: "Our duty is to *see the negro through.*"[14] Abolitionists took the lead in founding most of the freedmen's aid societies; in large part the story of *organized* abolitionism after 1870 is the story of their work for black education.

The anticlericalism of Garrisonian abolitionists has obscured the importance of evangelical Protestantism in the antislavery movement. The revivals of the Second Great Awakening left in their wake an army of reformers on the march against sin, especially the sin of slavery. In 1837 it was estimated that in New England two-thirds of the Methodist and Baptist clergy and one-third of the Congregational and Presbyterian ministers were avowed abolitionists. Seven-eighths of the members of antislavery societies were members of Protestant churches at a time when fewer than one in four adult Americans belonged to any church. But while most abolitionists were practicing Christians, most Christians were not abolitionists. A majority of northern Protestants were undoubtedly antislavery, but this meant only that they more or less disapproved of slavery without being sure what to do about it. Disappointed by the lukewarm response of most northern churches to their message of total, unqualified emancipation, Garrison and his followers denounced the clergy with increasing stridency after 1835. But evangelical abolitionists remained within their churches to try to abolitionize them. By 1840 the polarization became complete

---

[14] Jocelyn to Zebina Eastman, May 15, 1874, Eastman Papers, Chicago Historical Society; *Eighth Annual Report FASME*, Cincinnati, 1875, p. 4; *Friends' Review*, Dec. 28, 1872.

with the withdrawal of most evangelical abolitionists from the American Anti-Slavery Society. This split persisted even into the freedmen's education movement, for Garrisonians gave most of their support to the secular freedmen's aid societies while the evangelicals formed the mission-education societies in their denominations.

The four large evangelical churches (Methodist, Baptist, Presbyterian, and Congregational) suffered a series of schisms over slavery before the Civil War. In the Methodist and Baptist denominations, abolitionists were in the vanguard of movements that led to formal divisions into northern and southern churches in the 1840s. The split of the Presbyterians into "New School" and "Old School" factions in 1837 resulted from theological as well as sectional differences, but the New School became almost entirely a northern church with a sizable antislavery membership, while the Old School remained intersectional until its southern churches seceded in 1861. After the war the two northern factions reunited to form the Presbyterian Church in the U.S.A. Meanwhile two antislavery splinter groups had merged in 1858 to form the United Presbyterian Church. Although the Congregationalists had virtually no southern membership before the war, the slavery question plagued them also. After failing to win control of Congregational missionary societies, abolitionists in the denomination organized the American Missionary Association in 1846.[15]

When war came in 1861 the AMA established the first freedmen's schools, and from that time forward black education was its major function. Many of the AMA's executives until World War I were first-, second-, or third-generation abolitionists, among whom the most important were George Whipple, Michael E. Strieby, Augustus F. Beard, and Harlan Paul Douglass. Methodists initially contributed to black education through the AMA and the secular societies. But a concern that other denominations would win away black members unless Methodists founded their own association caused them to organize the Freedmen's Aid Society in 1866. Abolitionist Richard S. Rust was the society's secretary and dominating force until 1888, and his successors

[15] These two paragraphs are based on many secondary sources, among which the most useful are: Aileen Kraditor, *Means and Ends in American Abolitionism: Garrison and His Critics on Strategy and Tactics, 1834-1850*, New York, 1969; Bertram Wyatt-Brown, *Lewis Tappan and the Evangelical War Against Slavery*, Cleveland, 1969; Conrad J. Engelder, "The Churches and Slavery: A Study of the Attitudes toward Slavery of the Major Protestant Denominations," Ph.D. Dissertation, Univ. of Michigan, 1964; Charles Swaney, *Episcopal Methodism and Slavery*, Boston, 1926; Donald G. Mathews, *Slavery and Methodism: A Chapter in American Morality, 1780-1845*, Princeton, 1965; Robert A. Baker, *Relations Between Northern and Southern Baptists*, Fort Worth, 1948; Andrew E. Murray, *Presbyterians and the Negro—A History*, Philadelphia, 1966; and Clifton H. Johnson, "The American Missionary Association, 1846-1861: A Study of Christian Abolitionism," Ph.D. Dissertation, Univ. of North Carolina, 1959.

Joseph C. Hartzell, John W. Hamilton, and Wilbur P. Thirkield were also abolitionists.

The Baptists did not organize a separate freedmen's society, but grafted the southern work onto their existing Home Mission Society. Two Massachusetts abolitionists who had led the fight to expel slaveholders from the Baptist mission societies in 1844, Bartholomew T. Welch and Nathaniel Colver, also took the lead in organizing the freedmen's department of the Home Mission Society in 1862. Baptist freedmen's schools were sustained at first mainly by New England abolitionists in the denomination. When Henry L. Morehouse became secretary of the Home Mission Society in 1879, he made black education the society's main work. Morehouse served as executive secretary from 1879 to 1893, field secretary from 1893 to 1902, and executive secretary again from 1902 until his death in 1917; Thomas J. Morgan was executive secretary from 1893 to 1902. Both men came to maturity as abolitionists in the turbulent 1850s; Morgan commanded four regiments of black troops in the war.[16]

The tie between abolitionism and freedmen's education was less apparent among Presbyterians than in the other denominations. Both the New School and Old School factions organized freedmen's committees during the war. These were merged into the General Committee on Missions to Freedmen when the two northern halves of the denomination reunited in 1869 (this committee became the Board of Missions for Freedmen in 1883). No important abolitionist figure was an official of these boards, and from the meager biographical data available it is impossible to determine how many of the Presbyterians active in freedmen's education were abolitionists. At the same time the antislavery United Presbyterian Church, despite its small membership (only one-eighth that of the Presbyterian Church in the U.S.A.), did proportionately more for black education than the larger body, supporting Knoxville College and several secondary schools.[17]

Just as the Quakers had been the first religious group to oppose slavery, Friends' Yearly Meetings organized some of the earliest freedmen's societies during the war. By 1870 most of these societies had

[16] Drake, "The American Missionary Association and the Southern Negro"; Jay S. Stowell, *Methodist Adventures in Negro Education*, New York, 1922; minutes of the founding meeting of the Freedmen's Aid Society, Aug. 17, 1866, FASME Archives; Charles L. White, *A Century of Faith*, Philadelphia, 1932; *HMM*, I (Aug. 1879), 212. For biographical information on Morehouse and Morgan, see Lathan A. Crandall, *Henry Lyman Morehouse, a Biography*, Philadelphia, 1919, and the preface of Thomas J. Morgan, *The Negro in America and the Ideal American Republic*, Philadelphia, 1898.

[17] Murray, *Presbyterians and the Negro*, pp. 162-75; Lewis G. Vander Velde, *The Presbyterian Churches and the Federal Union, 1861-1869*, Cambridge, Mass., 1932, pp. 379-84.

been absorbed by the Friends' Freedmen's Relief Association of Philadelphia or the Indiana Yearly Meeting. These bodies were still supporting 47 elementary and six secondary schools in 1879, but the number declined thereafter. The Pennsylvania Society for Promoting the Abolition of Slavery, the oldest antislavery organization in existence (founded 1775), was also dominated by Quakers and devoted most of its resources after the Civil War to the support of black schools.[18]

Many of the first- and second-generation abolitionists who went South as founders, presidents, principals, and teachers of freedmen's schools spent the rest of their lives in this work. The two presidents who built Howard University from a struggling institution to the foremost black university in the country were lifelong abolitionists: William W. Patton was president from 1877 to 1889, and died in office; Jeremiah E. Rankin served from 1890 to 1903, dying a year after his retirement. Wilbur P. Thirkield was president of Howard from 1906 to 1912. Atlanta University's founder and first president (1867–1885) was Edmund Asa Ware, who had been converted to abolitionism as a young man by reading *Uncle Tom's Cabin* and hearing Wendell Phillips speak. Ware died in office and was succeeded by Horace Bumstead, who had grown up in a Boston antislavery family and fought in the war as a major in a black regiment. Bumstead's successor was Ware's son Edward, who served from 1907 to 1922. The founder and second president of Fisk University was Erastus M. Cravath, who held the office from 1875 until his death in 1900. Cravath had been brought up by an abolitionist father, attended two integrated colleges founded by abolitionists (New York Central College and Oberlin), and was an AMA district and field secretary for ten years before assuming the presidency of Fisk. His son Paul served for many years as chairman of the Fisk Board of Trustees. All of Berea College's founders and its first two presidents were abolitionists: Edward Henry Fairchild served from 1869 to 1889, dying in office; after an interim acting president, he was succeeded by William Goodell Frost (1892–1920), grandson of the prominent early abolitionist after whom he was named.

Abolitionists who headed Methodist schools included George Whipple Hubbard of Meharry Medical College (1876–1920); Wilbur P.

[18] Francis C. Anscomb, "The Contributions of the Quakers to the Reconstruction of the Southern States," Ph.D. Dissertation, Univ. of No. Car., 1926; *Centennial Anniversary of the Pennsylvania Society for Promoting the Abolition of Slavery . . . April 14, 1875*, Philadelphia, 1875, p. 40. Episcopalians organized the Protestant Episcopal Freedmen's Commission in 1865, but this body was much less active than the other Protestant societies and was dissolved in 1878. Thereafter the small Episcopal effort for black education, like that of the Roman Catholic Church, was sustained primarily by local parishes or dioceses. H. Peers Brewer, "The Protestant Episcopal Freedmen's Commission, 1865-1878," *Historical Magazine of the Protestant Episcopal Church*, XXVI (Dec. 1957), 361-81.

Thirkield of Gammon Theological Seminary (now part of the Interdenominational Theological Center of Atlanta University) from 1883 to 1900; Alonzo Webster, founder and first president of Claflin College (1870–1874); and E. O. Thayer, president of Bennett College (1875–1879) and Clark University (1880–1889). Among Baptist abolitionists, Nathaniel Colver started a Bible Institute for black preachers in a former slave jail at Richmond in 1867. He was succeeded as president by Charles H. Corey, a Canadian-born abolitionist who presided over the evolution of the school into Richmond Theological Seminary and eventually (1899) Virginia Union University. The first president of another institution that after one change of location and three changes of name became Morehouse College was Joseph Robert (1870–1884), a southerner who had left his native section in 1850 because he hated slavery.[19]

Among abolitionist founders of black secondary schools, Laura Towne and Ellen Murray deserve top rating. They came to the South Carolina sea islands in 1862 and established Penn School, remaining there until their deaths in 1901 and 1908. Another pair of lifelong abolitionists, Sallie Holley and Caroline Putnam, started a school at Lottsburgh, Virginia, in 1868 and stayed there for 25 and 49 years, respectively. Martha Schofield, a Hicksite Quaker who went to the sea islands as a teacher during the war, moved to Aiken, South Carolina, in 1867 where she founded the Schofield Normal and Industrial School and served as its principal until her death in 1916. Another Quaker abolitionist, Cornelia Hancock, started a freedmen's school in a shell-damaged church at Mount Pleasant, South Carolina, in 1866, and guided its development into the highly regarded Laing School named after a Quaker patron in Philadelphia. A husband-wife team of Indiana Quakers, Calvin and Alida Clark, followed the Union army into Arkansas in 1864 and started the Southland College and Normal Institute, which under their 22-year tutelage earned a reputation as one of the best black schools in the state.[20]

[19] The information in these two paragraphs was obtained from biographical dictionaries and obituaries, from the official reports and the magazines of the mission societies, and from the following secondary sources: Walter Dyson, *Howard University: The Capstone of Negro Education: A History, 1867-1940*, Washington, 1941; Myron W. Adams, *A History of Atlanta University*, Atlanta, 1930; Elisabeth S. Peck, *Berea's First Century, 1855-1955*, Lexington, Ky., 1955; Stowell, *Methodist Adventures in Negro Education*; Benjamin Brawley, *A History of Morehouse College*, Atlanta, 1917; and Charles H. Corey, *A History of the Richmond Theological Seminary*, Richmond, 1895.

[20] Information obtained mainly from the following: for Penn School, Rupert S. Holland, ed., *Letters and Diary of Laura M. Towne . . . 1862-84*, Cambridge, Mass., 1912; for Lottsburgh, John White Chadwick, *Sallie Holley, A Life for Liberty*, New York, 1899; for Schofield, Matilda A. Evans, *Martha Schofield: Pioneer Negro*

A number of abolitionists endowed Negro schools. In the 1880s Elijah Gammon, a farm machinery manufacturer who had been a Methodist clergyman before turning his talents to business, gave more than half a million dollars to found Gammon Theological Seminary. In 1881 Sophia Packard and Harriet Giles came from Massachusetts to Atlanta as representatives of the Woman's American Baptist Home Mission Society to start a school for black girls. On a fund-raising trip to the North in 1882, Packard met John D. Rockefeller, who pledged $250 to the school. Rockefeller's interest in Negro education was prompted by his wife, Laura Spelman, whose father Harvey was a Cleveland abolitionist active in freedmen's education after the war. In the 20 years after his first contribution, Rockefeller gave $200,000 to the school named in honor of his wife and father-in-law; in the twentieth century the Rockefellers have given millions to Spelman and to many other black colleges.[21]

Other abolitionist benefactions were on a more modest scale. One of the AMA's best secondary schools was LeMoyne Normal Institute in Memphis, founded in 1870 with a gift of $20,000 from Pennsylvania abolitionist Francis J. LeMoyne. LeMoyne gave several thousand dollars more to the school in the 1870s and left it a generous bequest at his death in 1879. Massachusetts abolitionist William B. Claflin and his father provided the initial endowment for the Methodists' Claflin College in Orangeburg, South Carolina. With the proceeds from lecture fees and special appeals, Bishop Gilbert Haven purchased land in Atlanta for Clark University. The hard-working Quaker abolitionist Yardley Warner traveled around the United States and Britain for many years raising money for several black schools, especially Maryville Institute and Jonesboro Institute in Tennessee.[22] Richard P. Hallowell endowed a large elementary school at Calhoun, Alabama, in the heart of the black belt where no other black schools existed. William Lloyd Garrison's daughter, Frances (Fanny) Garrison Villard, and

Educator, Columbia, S.C., 1916; for Laing School, Henrietta S. Jaquette, ed., *South After Gettysburg: Letters of Cornelia Hancock, 1863-1868*, New York, 1956; for Southland, Anscomb, "The Contributions of the Quakers," 183-90, 193-97, and many articles in *Friends' Review*, esp. Aug. 26, 1886.

[21] Willard Range, *The Rise and Progress of Negro Colleges in Georgia, 1865-1949*, Athens, Ga., 1951, pp. 57-59; Florence Matilda Read, *The Story of Spelman College*, Atlanta, 1961, pp. 30-33, 54-55, 85, 129, 136, 141, 175-86.

[22] Margaret C. McCulloch, *Fearless Advocate of the Right: The Life of Francis Julius LeMoyne*, Boston, 1941, pp. 205-10; LeMoyne to George Whipple, July 24, Sept. 21, 1870, Mar. 14, 1872, Feb. 2, 1874, AMA Archives; *AM*, LIV (July 1900), 149-54; Alphonse A. McPheeters, "The Origins and Development of Clark University and the Gammon Theological Seminary, 1869-1944," Ph.D. Dissertation, Univ. of Cincinnati, 1944, pp. 47-66; Stafford Allen Warner, *Yardley Warner: The Freedman's Friend*, Abingdon, Eng., 1957, esp. 70, 206-17.

her son Oswald were patrons of Manassas Industrial School, founded by the black Virginian Jennie Dean in 1894. Oswald served as chairman of the school's board of trustees and raised sizable sums for the institution, including two gifts from Andrew Carnegie.[23]

Abolitionists who gave money directly to black schools rather than to the mission societies had four favorite institutions: Berea College and Atlanta University, which stood for desegregated higher education (Atlanta had several white students during this period), and Hampton and Tuskegee Institutes, the foremost agricultural and industrial schools for Negroes.

Gerrit Smith donated about $10,000 to Berea; Elizabeth Cheever Washburn, sister of the militant Cheever brothers, George and Henry, gave the school $1,000 annually for several years; William Lloyd Garrison left a bequest to Berea in his will. When President William Goodell Frost went North on fund-raising trips for Berea in the 1890s, he received his warmest welcome from surviving abolitionists. The tradition of abolitionist support for Berea continued until its black students were driven out by Kentucky law in 1904.[24]

In its early years most of Hampton's support came from New England, with former abolitionists in the Boston area contributing a sizable share of the funds. But in the 1880s Principal Samuel C. Armstrong's success in selling the concept of black industrial education to businessmen-philanthropists shifted the major source of Hampton's income to New York and to a more conservative class of contributors. Tuskegee then became the chief beneficiary of abolitionist gifts to black industrial education. One of Tuskegee's first appeals for funds was a letter from Booker T. Washington's future wife Olivia Davidson to abolitionist Ednah D. Cheney, former secretary of the New England Freedmen's Aid Society and still a patron of black schools. Cheney publicized Tuskegee among her large circle of Boston friends, made regular gifts to the school, endowed a scholarship, and left Tuskegee $7,000 in her will. Two other abolitionist women also gave substantial amounts to the school. Emily Howland contributed $500 a year and donated several thousand dollars to an endowment fund. Mary E. Stearns (whose husband George had subsidized John Brown) endowed a Tuskegeee scholarship, gave $200 annually to the school, con-

23 The monthly magazine *Lend a Hand* and the OGV and FGV Papers contain a great deal of information and correspondence about the Calhoun and Manassas schools.

24 The Gerrit Smith Papers, Syracuse Univ. Library, and the Cheever Family Papers, American Antiquarian Society, contain correspondence concerning Berea College; Wendell P. and Francis J. Garrison, *William Lloyd Garrison 1805-1879*, 4 vols., New York, 1885-1889, IV, 239n.; William Goodell Frost, *For the Mountains*, New York, 1937, p. 101.

tributed much of the money for a new agricultural building in 1897, and left $50,000 at her death in 1901 to be divided equally among Tuskegee, Hampton, and Berea.[25]

Some prominent abolitionists also helped organize special fund-raising efforts for Tuskegee. Oswald Garrison Villard headed a drive that netted $157,000 for the endowment fund. William Lloyd Garrison, Jr., and his brother Francis persuaded a friend to bequeath $10,000 to the school. Richard P. Hallowell and his brother Norwood (a colonel of a black regiment during the war and later president of the National Bank of Commerce in Boston) acted as Tuskegee's financial agents in Massachusetts.[26]

Several abolitionists who helped Tuskegee were even more active in behalf of Atlanta University, whose egalitarianism antagonized conservative philanthropists. Cut off from this latter source of funds and independent of the mission-education societies, Atlanta relied on antislavery New Englanders for its very survival. The *Boston Transcript* under Edward Clement's editorship was the chief outlet of northern publicity for Atlanta; President Horace Bumstead considered Clement "one of our best friends." William Lloyd Garrison, Jr., organized an emergency appeal to northern donors to replace Georgia's annual $8,000 subsidy after Bumstead had refused in 1888 to bow to the state's demand for the expulsion of white students. Francis Garrison was president of the Atlanta University Association; three of the four vice presidents were also former abolitionists. Based in Boston, this association raised more than one-third of Atlanta's northern contributions in the 1890s. It also initiated a drive for an endowment fund in the early 1900s, headed by a $5,000 bequest from Richard Hallowell and a $10,000 gift from Josephine Shaw Lowell, sister of Robert Gould Shaw, the abolitionist colonel killed while leading the black 54th Massachusetts Regiment in the assault on Fort Wagner 40 years earlier.[27]

In 1915 the editor of the *Negro Year Book* estimated that over the past half-century northern sources had contributed $57 million to Negro education and blacks themselves had provided an additional $24 million. Though impressive, this was not enough. Missionary phi-

[25] The Cheney Papers, Boston Public Library, and the BTW Papers, contain a great deal of correspondence about these contributions; see also Francis J. Garrison to Fanny Garrison Villard, Dec. 8, 1901, FGV Papers.

[26] There is much correspondence on these matters in the BTW and WLG, Jr., Papers; see also the folder labeled "The Baldwin Memorial Fund" in OGV Papers.

[27] In addition to many letters in the WLG, Jr., Papers, the FGV Papers, the OGV Papers and frequent articles and editorials in the *BET*, see Horace Bumstead to W. E. B. Du Bois, Jan. 12, 1903, from the Du Bois Papers formerly in the custody of Herbert Aptheker, quoted with Dr. Aptheker's permission.

lanthropy and black self-help could not do the job alone; southern states and the federal government had done far less than necessary for adequate black schooling. A survey of Negro higher education in 1916 found most of the schools understaffed, meagerly equipped, and poorly financed.[28]

But without the efforts of northern mission societies, the situation would have been much worse. The 1916 survey found the best institutions to be those that had grown directly from the abolitionist-missionary impulse. These schools also earned warm praise from their alumni. "There is nothing in the annals of human history that out-rivals the unselfishness that founded and has maintained these schools for half a century," declared Talladega graduate William Pickens in 1923. And in his book *Black Reconstruction*, Fisk alumnus W. E. B. Du Bois concluded that the movement "to plant the New England college in the South" was "the salvation of the South and the Negro. Had it not been for the Negro school and college, the Negro would, to all intents and purposes, have been driven back to slavery."[29] Such quotations could be multiplied tenfold. They would have gratified Richard Rust and his fellow abolitionists who founded these schools on the belief that "education is the only completion of emancipation."

[28] Monroe Work, ed., *Negro Year Book, 1915*, Tuskegee, 1915, p. 235; Jones, ed., *Negro Education: A Study of the Private and Higher Schools.*
[29] Pickens, *Bursting Bonds*, Boston, 1923, p. 100; Du Bois, *Black Reconstruction . . . in America, 1860-1880*, New York, 1935, p. 667.

Chapter Ten

Between Black and White: Puritans in Babylon

Referring to his favorite professor at Fisk, Du Bois once said that "it did not make much difference whether the students were studying Greek or biology—the great thing was that they were studying under [Adam K.] Spence."[1] This observation that personal contact between teacher and student counts for more than the subject being taught is an educational truism. The heart of freedmen's education was human beings interacting with each other through good times and bad, success and failure, harmony and discord. Three groups of people played roles in this drama: the neo-Puritan missionary teachers who went South to uplift the lowly; the southern whites among whom they came as agents of a conquering power and bearers of an alien ideology; and the black community, recipients of a benevolent if sometimes repressive paternalism. This chapter will sketch the complex interplay between these three elements; the next will discuss the issue of paternalism.

Like abolitionism, the freedmen's education movement sprang mainly from the New England reform impulse. This was true not only of the Unitarian-dominated secular societies and the Congregational AMA, but of the Methodist and Baptist societies as well. Of 1,013 northern teachers in the 1860s whose homes have been located, 520 came from New England. Of the 82 white presidents of southern black colleges in the two generations after emancipation whose birthplaces have been identified, 40 had been born in New England. Thus at a time when 17 percent of the *northern* population lived in New England (1860 census; the percentage declined thereafter), that section furnished 51 percent of the northern teachers and 49 percent of the college presidents for whom data are available. In addition, many teachers who lived outside New England had been born there. One scholar estimated that at least 700 of the 1,013 teachers were from New England and areas settled by migrants from New England.[2]

[1] Editorial "Negro Education" in *Crisis*, Feb. 1918, reprinted in Meyer Weinberg, ed., *W.E.B. Du Bois: A Reader*, New York, 1970, p. 162.

[2] Henry Lee Swint, *The Northern Teacher in the South, 1862-1870*, Nashville, 1941, Appendix III, lists 1,048 teachers whose home towns and/or states Swint was able to discover, of whom 35 were from the South or foreign countries and have not been included in the sample of northern teachers. The estimate of more

New England contributed disproportionately to the financing as well as the personnel of freedmen's education. Residents of that region provided 60 percent of the AMA's funds from northern sources for randomly selected years in the 1870s and 1880s. The per capita contributions of the New England conferences to the Methodist Freedmen's Aid Society were consistently at or near the top for the entire Methodist Episcopal Church; the same was true for the New England collection districts of the Baptist Home Mission Society. With one-fourteenth of the membership of the northern Baptist Church, Massachusetts provided one-seventh of the amount of individual contributions and two-fifths of the amount of legacies to the Home Mission Society from 1882 to 1902. From 1870 through 1888, 68 percent of the individual contributors to Atlanta University and 61 percent of the money contributed came from New England; the figures for a comparable later period (1894–1912) were 63 and 53 percent.[3]

This New England pre-eminence was no statistical fluke; it was the result of a conscious effort by abolitionists and evangelicals to plant their neo-Puritan values in the reconstructed South. Gilbert Haven hailed the first wave of teachers departing from Boston for the South as the new "Pilgrim Fathers" sent on a nineteenth-century errand into the wilderness to create "a New South after the Puritan and perfect pattern." In 1865 the New England Freedmen's Aid Society urged the recruitment of "enough teachers to make a New England of the whole South." One of the founders of Talladega College conceived of his mission as the establishment in Alabama of "a real New England civilization." At Oberlin College, an outpost of New England culture beyond the Appalachians, students planning to become freedmen's teachers were told that "the South must be converted and puritanized" by "men who at heart hate slavery and oppression."[4] The AMA established a

---

than 700 teachers from New England plus areas settled by New England emigrants is Swint's, p. 50. Data on the birthplaces of college presidents were obtained from biographical encyclopedias, *Who Was Who in America*, *Who's Who in America*, obituaries, genealogies, and from information in the magazines and published reports of the mission societies.

[3] Data on contributions to the AMA are from the monthly or yearly breakdowns by states in *The American Missionary*. Per capita contributions to the Freedmen's Aid Society of the ME Church were tabulated for each state or regional conference in the annual reports of the Society. For the Baptists *The Home Mission Monthly* frequently reported the per capita contributions to the Home Mission Society by states: see esp. *HMM*, xxv (Mar. 1903), 59-60. The 1870-1888 data for Atlanta University are from the list of contributors published in the university's annual catalogues; the percentages for the 1894-1912 period are derived from a sampling of financial reports in the Atlanta University Archives for the fiscal years 1893-1894, 1898-1899, and 1911-1912.

[4] William B. Gravely, *Gilbert Haven, Methodist Abolitionist*, Nashville, 1973, p. 98; *Freedman's Journal*, 1 (Jan. 1865), 3; George W. Andrews to Erastus M.

black Congregational church in Charleston, the cradle of secession, and perhaps with a retributive sense of irony named it Plymouth Church.

This emphasis on Puritanism was more than rhetorical. While forging a theology in which God's grace and salvation were open to all who truly sought it rather than extended only to the predestined elect, nineteenth-century evangelical Protestantism preserved much of the ethical creed of New England Calvinism. Inspired by a zealous sense of mission, many evangelicals strove not only for the conversion of individual sinners but for the purification of society from such sins as intemperance, prostitution, and above all slavery. Westward-migrating sons of New England carried this creed through the Mohawk Valley of New York into the Western Reserve of Ohio and beyond. From these areas came most of the abolitionists as well as founders and teachers of freedmen's schools. As one reformer stated with only slight exaggeration: "The common school system, the temperance and the anti-slavery movements . . . have sprung from the exuberant Puritanic life of New England."[5] The army of New England schoolmarms who invaded the postwar South carried with them not only the Bible and Noah Webster's blue-backed speller, but also an amalgam of Puritan and "Yankee" values overlaid by evangelicalism and abolitionism. They were products of the nineteenth-century version of the Puritan commonwealth, a city on a hill serving as a model for all the world.

A Puritan-like emphasis on collective sin and divine judgment runs through the writings of missionary educators. "Slavery was a crime whose expiation must be by suffering and self-denial," declared the AMA. "We tore them from their native land, tortured them on the 'middle passage,' compelled them to unrequited toil and to shameful cruelties . . . and denied them knowledge and the written word of God." Thus "we owe the freedmen everything we can do for them"; whatever help "we bring them is to be reckoned not of grace, but of debt." A Methodist abolitionist insisted that the Church must continue its efforts for the freedmen "until the compensation should equal the injury." God was keeping the account between whites and blacks. "He will exact fair payment. If it is not made honestly, cheerfully, it will be wrung from our reluctant hands until the uttermost farthing is paid." The North was just as guilty as the South for the sin of slavery, said

---

Cravath, Jan. 13, 1874, AMA Archives; *Lorain County News*, Jan. 20, 1864, quoted in Robert Samuel Fletcher, *A History of Oberlin College From Its Foundation Through the Civil War*, 2 vols., Oberlin, 1943, II, 917.

[5] Quotation from Donald Gene Jones, "The Moral, Social, and Political Ideas of the Methodist Episcopal Church from the Closing Years of the Civil War Through Reconstruction, 1864-1876," Ph.D. Dissertation, Drew University, 1969, p. 150.

Richard Rust. "New England is steeped to the lips in guilt by her participation in bringing Negroes to this country and selling them into perpetual bondage." We can best "atone for our sins," he concluded, "by furnishing schools and the means of improvement for the children, upon whose parents we inflicted such terrible evils."[6]

Related to this conviction of sin and atonement was the Puritan doctrine of man's calling to serve God by serving mankind and thereby to achieve personal fulfillment while benefiting the commonweal. From this concept of the calling had stemmed much of the New England reform tradition. "The din of strife ceased long ago on the fields of our early effort," wrote an abolitionist faculty member at Berea College in 1874, "but *here* in the South is a life work." A New Hampshire teacher in South Carolina wondered in 1869 "how any one can lead the idle, useless life, that many do in this world of need. . . . What can life be worth to such?" A Mount Holyoke graduate who founded a black girls school in Mississippi wrote to a friend in 1872 about the problems confronting her, "yet when God calls I have no right to plead difficulties as a reason why I should not cheerfully and heartily respond."[7]

Ralph Barton Perry's portrayal of the Puritan as a moral athlete could have been written as a description of what was expected of freedmen's teachers. Commenting on the trials and discouragements faced by teachers, AMA officials stated that "whether the work is easy or difficult, *it must be done*, or woe to this nation. . . . It is no time . . . to sit down and cry. The voice we hear today, is Go! work—This people must be educated and may we rejoice that God permits us to aid in such a work." A visitor to the Baptists' Shaw University in Raleigh, North Carolina, in 1875 described the teachers as "the scrawniest, severest, primmest, ugliest most forbidding New England type,—with whom duty—in all matters,—is always a business and never a pleasure." She found such people unpleasant company, "but the truth is that a less cold, obtuse, self-reliant & determined set of people, would be worried & badgered & mortified almost to death, & be driven away in short order."[8]

[6] *AM* XVII (Oct. 1873), 228-29, XVIII (Aug. 1874), 182-83; Thomas Pearne, "The Freedmen," *Methodist Quarterly Review*, LIX (July 1877), 462, 476; *Fourth Annual Report FASME*, Cincinnati, 1871, p. 15; Joseph C. Hartzell, ed., *Christian Educators in Council: Sixty Addresses by American Educators*, New York, 1883, p. 55.

[7] William Hart, Jr., to Zebina Eastman, May 24, 1874, Eastman Papers, Chicago Historical Society; letter from Mary A. Hosley, in *Freedmen's Record*, v (Feb. 1869), 7; letter from Sarah Dickey, spring 1872, in Helen Griffith, *Dauntless in Mississippi: The Life of Sarah A. Dickey 1838-1904*, n.p., 1965, p. 73.

[8] *AM*, XIV (Oct. 1870), 227; Charles C. Carpenter to "Dear Friends," May 23, 1870, AMA Archives; Anne E. Dickinson to her mother, Apr. 25, 1875, Dickinson Papers, Library of Congress. For the Puritan as moral athlete, see Ralph Barton Perry, *Puritanism and Democracy*, New York, 1944, chap. 10.

Although these stern qualities of guilt, atonement, calling, and duty were important, they were not the only components of what contemporaries called the "missionary spirit." Also vital were the New Testament virtues of compassion and love. The AMA's secretary urged teachers to learn the 13th chapter of First Corinthians by heart, for they would need every ounce of faith, hope, and charity they could muster. Teachers also had to possess "great versatility" and "power of adaptation," explained one instructor, to cope with classes containing a greater variety in students' ages, backgrounds, and temperaments than anything in their previous experience. Classroom discipline was one of the hardest problems: the AMA specified that only teachers "whose experience, especially as disciplinarians has been crowned with marked success," should apply for jobs. But a heavy-handed, insensitive discipline was no good. A new teacher at the AMA's Ballard Institute provoked his class "to an open revolt," reported a fellow instructor in 1870. "They will not stand his impetuous words—when he gets angry—& he dont spare them—he is not gentlemanly in his wrath as Mr. Rockwell was, and they liken him to their Slave holders of old."[9]

Three-quarters of the missionary teachers were women, and about three-quarters of these were unmarried. Some were older spinsters; others were young women for whom missionary teaching gave at least temporary purpose to their lives. The AMA appealed to this motive in an 1874 pamphlet, *Woman's Work for the Lowly*, urging idle northern women to achieve fulfillment through service to the freedmen instead of remaining "merely ornaments in their fathers' parlors, dreaming, restless, hoping, till some fortunate mating shall give them a home and a sphere."[10] Even if they went into missionary work, however, many still dreamt of a fortunate mating, and those who married usually left the work except in the rare cases when they married another teacher. Most of the married women teachers had come South with their husbands. Married couples and unmarried women over 30 (very few of the male teachers were unmarried) were generally better teachers than the younger single women, among whom the "missionary spirit" was often fragile and who sometimes had trouble with discipline. The most rapid turnover of teachers was among this younger group. The

---

[9] Augustus F. Beard, *A Crusade of Brotherhood, A History of the American Missionary Association*, Boston, 1909, p. 169; A. N. Niles to Erastus M. Cravath, Oct. 24, 1871, AMA Archives; *AM*, x (July 1886), 152; E. E. Rogers to Edward P. Smith, Feb. 9, 1870, AMA Archives.

[10] Quoted in Jacqueline Halstead, " 'The Grand Opportunity': Wisconsin Yankees Teach the Freedmen, 1866-1876," unpublished seminar paper, Univ. of Wisconsin, 1971, pp. 22-23, cited with permission. The data and conclusions in the rest of this paragraph are based on a reading of missionary publications and correspondence in the archives of the mission societies.

average tenure of a freedmen's teacher in the 1860s and 1870s was about three years; in subsequent decades this average nearly trebled because most of the work was concentrated in the colleges and secondary schools where the faculty tended to be older and more stable. Unsuccessful teachers were usually weeded out after a year or two; the best teachers served for decades. It was the latter whom thousands of alumni remembered with fondness, respect, and gratitude.

The everyday problems of a teacher's life sometimes strained the missionary spirit to the breaking point. In the early days these problems were often physical. Teachers' letters in the 1860s and 1870s were full of complaints of discomfort, chills, fever, and exhaustion caused by an unfamiliar climate, poor food, and primitive santitation. Teachers in small towns sometimes roomed and boarded with black families because no white family would take in the "Yankee nigger teacher." The niece of one teacher who lived in a Negro home described "the little attic room where Miss [Emily] H[owland] slept, in company with all the wheezing, snuffing, coughing, ill smelling children of the family & where she was bitten by fleas & other vermin until she felt as tho she were scalded. She used to sit up in bed of a night & wonder why she should have got herself into such a scrape. . . . But when morning came, & school began, her enthusiasm for teaching chased the terrors of the night away, & she stayed on."[11]

If living accommodations were spartan, early school buildings were hardly less so. An alumnus of Atlanta University recalled the first school he attended, in Cuthbert, Georgia, where the "Yankee lady" nailed old army blankets to the windward side of a ramshackle building "packed as tightly with dusky children as a sardine box," and "taught as if she were in one of our modern school houses." Cornelia Hancock started Laing School in South Carolina in the ruins of a burned-out church with neither "a chair nor a table, a slate, pencil or book. The only thing that suggested itself to my mind was to take some coals from the improvised fire and make letters and figures on the large white pillars in the Church." The school that eventually became Virginia Union University began life in a former slave prison. The school that evolved into Atlanta University started out in a converted boxcar. Fisk University held classes for several years in a former Union army hospital "with the odor of disease still lingering about it," in Adam Spence's description, "floors that resound like a drum beneath your feet, seats that squeak at every motion, windows with tatters for blinds or no blinds at all." Yet "we toil on" even though, in the

[11] Sarah T. Miller to "Miss Kennedy," Feb. 18, 1896, Samuel May Papers, Mass. Historical Society.

words of Professor George W. White, "I am utterly discouraged in regard to our future."[12]

But when he felt the lowest, White conceived the idea of taking the best singers among his students on a concert tour to raise money, and the Fisk Jubilee Singers were born. By 1875 their earnings had built Jubilee Hall; by the 1880s most of the other schools had also moved into new buildings, and the primitive conditions of early days were a memory. But these things were not accomplished without hard work. Fatigue was a constant theme of teachers' letters. In the 1880s Sophia Packard and Harriet Giles, founders of Spelman, each taught 90 students in 10 classes daily for five and one-half days a week, conducted four prayer meetings and four Bible readings, taught two Bible classes each week, and made numerous visits to students' homes—besides administering the school and raising money for it. At the end of a typical day, Packard could find strength to write in her diary only "tired tired tired tired tired tired." The founder of a girls' school in Mississippi wrote to a friend: "Oh, what would not this tired mind and frame give for one brief week of entire rest from work and care. But just now the work seems to be rushing upon us like a great avalanche"—and it was seldom otherwise. In 1900 Martha Schofield complained that "I have never been under such pressure. . . . It would seem as if my 35 years of service in this work would have earned me heaven and rest," but she stayed on for another 16 years.[13]

The load carried by college presidents was a heavy one. Besides traveling a great deal to raise money, they taught much of the curriculum themselves. William W. Patton of Howard University taught Mental and Moral Philosophy, Logic, Science of Government, International Law, Natural Theology, Evidences of Christianity, and Hebrew plus conducting daily prayers and preaching every Sunday afternoon. As head of Gammon Theological Seminary, Wilbur P. Thirkield not only planned and taught many of the courses but also carried on correspondence without a secretary, borrowed money for the school on his own credit, and planted the magnolia trees lining the drive to the campus. In addition to the usual administrative, teaching, and fund-raising duties, President Edmund A. Ware of Atlanta University joined stu-

[12] Atlanta alumnus quoted in Willard Range, *The Rise and Progress of Negro Colleges in Georgia, 1865-1949*, Athens, Ga., 1951, p. 13; Henrietta S. Jaquette, ed., *South after Gettysburg: Letters of Cornelia Hancock, 1863-1868*, New York, 1956, pp. 186-87; Spence to E. M. Cravath, Apr. 6, 1871, White to Cravath, Apr. 7, 1871, AMA Archives.

[13] Joe M. Richardson, "History of Fisk University," unpublished manuscript, chaps. 2-3, cited with the author's permission; Florence Matilda Read, *The Story of Spelman College*, Atlanta, 1961, pp. 56-57; Griffith, *Dauntless in Mississippi*, 122; Schofield to Booker T. Washington, Oct. 3, 1900, BTW Papers.

dents in clearing trash from the site of the new campus in 1869, and reported three summers later that he had "put up about 50 bushels of blackberries, and am doing much garden work hoping to have a good late crop, that will help much in reducing table expenses" in the school's dining hall.[14]

For many missionaries the physical problems of overwork, illness, and poor facilities were less frustrating than their everyday dealings with the freedmen. A constant problem for teachers was student absenteeism; a pupil would attend school for a few days, disappear for a time, then come back again; multiplied by a factor of 40 or 50, this made classroom continuity difficult. This *"irregularity,"* said one teacher, was a *"positive vice"* of the freedmen. A related weakness was unreliability: "You can . . . never depend on any thing promised," went a typical complaint. Another "general failing among colored people," according to many teachers, was their tardiness at meetings, classes, church services, and so on. Whether caused by slavery or the unclocked rhythms of rural life, "it is certainly almost impossible for them to be promptly on hand at an appointed hour. . . . Much of their deplorable condition comes from always being behind time."[15]

More serious were sexual offenses, theft, and lying. The missionaries' private letters contained numerous oblique references to sexual scandals in church and school. Usually such matters did not become public, though in 1877 the Methodist Freedmen's Aid Society's annual report did state that "the most disheartening feature of the work is the readiness with which the more promising pupils are led astray—especially the older girls." Student theft was sometimes a problem; two teachers in the AMA's school at Montgomery were twice robbed by a student, but the principal "decided that it would injure the work here to have the girl accused or arrested." One of the teachers wrote: "I enjoy my school here and am much attached to many of the people but this treatment, I confess, has disheartened me."[16]

Some teachers blamed their own rather than the freedmen's inadequacies for the frustrations they encountered. "I have had a great

14 Patton, *The History of Howard University, 1867-1888*, Washington, 1896, pp. 28-29; Jay S. Stowell, *Methodist Adventures in Negro Education*, New York and Cincinnati, 1922, pp. 41-42; Elizabeth Ross Haynes, *The Black Boy of Atlanta*, Boston, 1952, p. 34; Ware to E. M. Cravath, July 17, 1872, AMA Archives.

15 J. W. Pratt to Ednah Dow Cheney, Feb. 3, 1872, in *Freedmen's Record*, v (Apr. 1872), 121; Robert F. Markham to Michael E. Strieby, May 28, 1877, A. N. Niles to Gustavus D. Pike, Mar. 25, 1871, A. W. Farnham to Strieby, June 20, 1877, AMA Archives; Henrietta Matson, *The Mississippi Schoolmaster*, Boston, 1893, pp. 107-108.

16 *Tenth Annual Report FASME* (Cincinnati, 1877), p. 32; C. E. Hulsart to M. E. Strieby, Dec. 22, 1875, AMA Archives.

many questions in my mind as to my fitness for this work," wrote a minister in charge of a black church and school in Chattanooga. An instructor at LeMoyne wondered "if others get as discouraged sometimes, as I do. . . . The fault is in myself, not in the place." An AMA teacher in Savannah felt that "I am a poor person for a Missionary. . . . I often fear I love business better than the souls of these people." After describing her inability to reach the freedmen, another teacher wrote: "It *is* trying to see what they might *be* and *do* and yet not be able to bring about better results."[17]

Self-doubt, exasperation, lack of a proper missionary spirit, and even fears for their own safety took a toll of missionary teachers. One AMA teacher in charge of a day school for children and a night school for adults on an Alabama plantation decided in 1873 that she had had enough. Two of her students had been killed and several hurt in razor fights during the past month. "I have almost come to the conclusion that I am not adapted to the work and when I have fulfilled my engagement here I think I will leave it for good," she informed the AMA secretary. A woman who had taught for several years on the South Carolina sea islands wrote an almost hysterical 30-page letter to her northern sponsor in 1873. She lived alone in a house near her school. "It is two weeks today since I have seen a white person," she wrote. "I have been so tired & half distracted with hard days & sleepless nights —that it seems to me—if I could have some new nerves—and a week for nothing but rest and sleep it would be all I would ask." She was beginning to fear that "I have lost my missionary or zealous spirit with which I came down here. . . . [Then] I had far more sympathy for—& faith in them—it took me a long time to believe in their many failings —yet after all I feel so differently from them. . . . I believe I *almost* have the blues." One day in school a girl fell to the floor in a convulsion; the teacher revived her, but the event caused a panic in class and "since then I have several times dreamed of fainting." She began to have headaches; terrified of living alone any longer, she moved into town to stay with a black family. But her troubles continued. An attempt to reduce enrollment below the 130 students she was trying to teach brought a delegation of angry parents to the school. "The man who made the most fuss had a little girl—who came two days last year —then staid away the rest of the time." She was so shaken by the experience that "after this the nights were a reign of terror. . . . I felt I was *alone in every sense of the word—& entirely at their mercy.*"

[17] Temple Cutler to M. E. Strieby, Oct. 3, 1876, May Merry to Delia E. Emerson, Mar. 6, 1877, Abby W. Johnson to E. M. Cravath, Apr. 24, 1877, K. K. Koons to Emerson, Oct. 26, 1876, AMA Archives.

Clearly the writer of this letter was on the verge of a nervous break-down; not surprisingly, she soon returned north.[18]

For successful teachers, on the other hand, the rewards of seeing students improve outweighed the discouragements. "It is worth doing—this work," wrote Laura Towne. "The schools are more interesting than ever—absorbing—thrilling." A teacher in Memphis reported that "eight years of culture has made its impress upon the people here so plainly that one can read at a glance the change in the countenances of those who have been under the influence of the mission work." Sometimes the satisfactions of success were slow in coming: one teach-er was "very much surprised, as well as gratified," at how well her for-mer students were doing as public school teachers in Virginia, since they "were not always a comfort and 'present reward' while I was teaching them in Alexandria."[19]

Expressions of gratitude from students often made up for the exas-peration they had caused their teachers. "I did not Appreciate untill now that you was so good & I am determined to learn all I can," wrote one pupil to her former teacher. "I think you had the most Patience of any Ladey I ever saw. . . . I think of you every day and will not soon forget you." When the AMA was considering whether to close its school in Athens, Georgia, an appeal signed by 15 students may have been a factor in the decision not to do so: "Our dear kind Teachers they are such good Teachers and we do want them so very bad to come back. . . . Thay did so much good for us, and if you please to send them back to us for we do love them so much . . . thay have been a Mother to some of us." A student at Straight University told the AMA's secretary that after much soul-searching "I have made up my mind to work for God all the days of my life. . . . I have done wrong in the past, but I will say to you as the prodigal son said to his Father: I am under many obligations to you and the hole Association for what aid they have give me I perpous to pay them in my labors." It was letters such as these, wrote one teacher, that made it all worthwhile. "Knowing that work in the past has not been wholly lost, gives me faith for future harvests."[20]

18 Mrs. H. F. Toadewall to E. M. Cravath, Nov. 10, 1873, AMA Archives; "S.M.L." to William C. Gannett, Dec. 20-21, 1873, Gannett Papers, University of Rochester Library.

19 Towne to W. C. Gannett, Dec. 10, 1872, Gannett Papers; Towne to Edward L. Pierce, Jan. 30, 1876, Pierce Papers, Houghton Library, Harvard University; Mrs. J. E. Cowan to M. E. Strieby, Oct. 11, 1875, AMA Archives; Mrs. B. L. Canady to Ednah D. Cheney, Jan. 12, 1874, Cheney Papers, Boston Public Library.

20 Mose Hume to Lucy Chase, Apr. 16, 1870, in Henry L. Swint, ed., *Dear Ones at Home: Letters from Contraband Camps*, Nashville, 1966, pp. 247-48; fifteen students to the AMA office, June 20, 1870, Thomas E. Hillson to E. M. Cravath, Jan. 23, 1875, Laura Parmelee to M. E. Strieby, May 12, 1877, AMA Archives.

A good many teachers found greater self-fulfillment in their work than they had ever known; perhaps this was the true definition of missionary spirit. After 10 years as principal of the AMA's Storrs School in Atlanta, Amy Williams hoped the Association would not turn the school over to the city board of education, which intended to get rid of northern teachers. If her job was abolished, she wrote in 1878, "I can go home and do nothing that is of real lasting benefit to anyone, or I can teach in the north, but I dislike to think of doing either. I was never so happy as I have been in this work and I have no desire to relapse into that selfish way of half living that used to be 'jist tolable' to me." The AMA kept control of the school and Williams, a popular teacher, remained at her post until she retired. Helen Morgan, Professor of Latin at Fisk and one of the ablest teachers on a good faculty, refused offers of higher salaries from other schools including Vassar and remained in what she considered a more rewarding career. Another well-liked teacher wrote that "though I have discovered the full meaning of two words—fatigue and hunger—I am not weary of it. . . . I used to think that it would be impossible to enjoy the work more than I then did, but *this*, I am sure, is perfect enjoyment."[21]

But when the work was not perfect enjoyment, when they were almost overwhelmed with weariness or despair, the missionaries fell back on their ultimate resource—religion. Here the Puritan ethos and the evangelical faith came together to give the missionary spirit its strength and endurance. "There is so much demand for "*patience* and wisdom*,*" wrote the head of the AMA's work in Savannah, that "I could not do the work here [except] as God bids me. . . . I know but little and am among a people that know less. . . . I can do no more than I can, and then I will trust God and let it slide." Alida Clark of Southland College thought many times of quitting, but she always persuaded herself to "labor on; it's for the Master." And on one occasion a Quaker educator wrote in his diary: "Wearily I close this day. . . . But as I looked toward the Help on High my heart was calmed with the secret assurance that I might rest all on the bosom of my God."[22] This faith gave many freedmen's teachers a staying power unmatched by secular educators or civil rights workers in that day or our own.

If in their relations with blacks the missionaries needed the patience of Job and the faith of St. Paul, in their encounters with southern

[21] Amy Williams to D. E. Emerson, Mar. 5, 1878, AMA Archives; Henry Hugh Proctor, *Between Black and White: Autobiographical Sketches*, Boston, 1925, p. 31; Mary Kildare to E. M. Cravath, Jan. 4, 1873, AMA Archives.
[22] Robert F. Markham to M. E. Strieby, Mar. 15, 1877, May 29, 1876, AMA Archives; letter from Alida Clark in *Friends' Review*, Feb. 3, 1875; Stafford Allen Warner, *Yardley Warner: The Freedman's Friend*, Abingdon, Eng., 1957, p. 236.

whites they needed sometimes to be bold as lions but more often wise as serpents and harmless as doves, for they knew that God had sent them forth as sheep in the midst of wolves. During Reconstruction the missionary schools were, to many whites, visible symbols of the destruction of the only world they had known. And the missionaries, some of whom were active in Reconstruction politics, sometimes forgot the precepts of charity toward "rebels" whom they considered even more benighted and in need of salvation than the freedmen. Yankee missionaries and southern rebels were a volatile mixture; explosions were not rare.

Southern feelings toward Yankee teachers most often took the form of ostracism. One teacher wrote that "we are shut out from white society, until it is really a treat to have a white child speak to us. My wife has spoken to but two white women since we came here, and that on business." When Mr. and Mrs. George W. Andrews celebrated their 25th wedding anniversary at Talladega in 1884 not a single southern white guest appeared, even though the Andrewses had been teaching there for 10 years. In the early 1880s some Atlanta merchants refused to deliver groceries to the door of Spelman Seminary and instead threw the boxes over a fence where students and teachers had to pick them up. Even southern Quakers sometimes ostracized their northern brethren who came down to teach the blacks; Yardley Warner and his wife frequently walked three miles to the Friends' meetinghouse in Springfield, North Carolina, looking "tired and bedraggled," because local Friends were reluctant to risk the hostility of other whites by offering them carriage rides.[23]

What southern whites disliked most of all was "that our workers recognize respectable colored men & women *socially*," wrote a teacher in Macon, Georgia. "We open our parlors to them; we invite them to our tables; we eat with them in their own homes." "You treat kitchen people as equals," one southern lady told the missionaries, "and we, of course, can not recognize you." Some teachers thought they should never give in to southern pressure on this matter, for it was "just where for a long time to come, we are to be of most benefit to the colored people at large—*as pioneers in securing to them their social rights*."[24]

Most missionaries would not have put it quite this way; they generally avoided the inflammatory words "social equality" or "social rights." Though they associated with blacks on terms that white south-

---

[23] Range, *The Rise of Negro Colleges in Georgia*, p. 39; Mrs. G. W. Andrews to James H. Fairchild, Mar. 24, 1884, Fairchild Papers, Oberlin College Library; Read, *The Story of Spelman*, 73; Warner, *Warner*, 296.

[24] *Sixteenth Annual Report FASME*, Cincinnati, 1883, p. 131; Frank Haley to E. M. Cravath, June 29, 1874, AMA Archives.

erners could only regard as social equality, they probably did not in any strict sense consider most of the freedmen socially equal to themselves. No matter how sincere their egalitarianism, missionary teachers could never completely bridge the racial gap. To the black community they were inevitably outsiders. And the teachers' frequent references to black people as "they" or "them" is evidence that they could not escape the consciousness of being outsiders.

Unmarried white teachers in urban schools often lived together in a house owned or rented by the mission society. Surrounded by southern whites who refused to recognize them socially and restrained by invisible but real barriers from full participation in black society, the teachers' social life was narrowly confined. This constriction plus the fatigue and irritability that built up in the classroom caused considerable bickering and backbiting among teachers. Wrote the male principal of one school in a fit of annoyance: "It is no holiday exercise to meet the varied traits of a given number of maiden ladies of a certain or uncertain age [full of] . . . asperities and positive opinions." Referring to squabbles among teachers at another school, an AMA official admitted that "missionary zeal has not burned out *all* the selfishness from any of us."[25]

Whether they lived alone, with a black family, or with colleagues, teachers often suffered from loneliness for friends and relatives. Though "I like my work very much," wrote a teacher at LeMoyne, "I am sometimes very tired, and a feeling of homesickness and loneliness will creep over me." Another reported that while she got along well with her fellow teachers, "owing to our being human, we *do become lonely at times.*" Whenever possible, teachers went north for summer vacations to renew their spirits. "I trust," wrote the exhausted principal of the AMA school at Athens, Alabama, in August 1876, "that a few weeks rest in the *north* will bring back my wonted strength." A native of Massachusetts, he needed to "breathe the briny air of the ocean . . . look upon the mountains and inhale the life-giving breezes—see and converse with cultivated men and women—be *recognized* by Christians of my own race—feel that I am no longer a leper."[26]

Even the prospect of a summer visit home did not equip some teachers to withstand loneliness. The woman who founded the AMA's Dorchester Academy in Georgia "labored here with no one to whom she could go for counsel," said a friend, "boarding in a colored family on fare unknown to the Northern palate," with her schoolhouse serving

[25] A. N. Niles to E. M. Cravath, May 3, 1871, Thomas N. Chase to Cravath, Nov. 13, 1878, AMA Archives.
[26] Emma C. Cook to M. E. Strieby, Mar. 24, 1877, S. C. Pierce to Strieby, Apr. 19, 1876, M. F. Wells to Strieby, Aug. 9, 1876, AMA Archives.

as "reception room, parlor, washroom, laundry and chapel. . . . There was no refined or educated person with whom to enjoy a moment's chat or spend a social evening." Two years of this life sent her home "broken in health and looked upon somewhat askance in consequence of her associations. But it made Dorchester Academy possible." A teacher at Milford, Delaware, was forced to live in a "noisy rumhole" of a hotel; not a single white person would speak to her; after a year of such treatment, according to a Freedmen's Bureau official, she lost her mind and was sent to an asylum in her home state of New York "hopelessly insane."[27]

Southern hostility to Yankee teachers sometimes went beyond ostracism and verbal abuse. In times of political excitement during Reconstruction many missionaries were threatened, beaten, and murdered. The AMA reported several incidents similar to the one in which a group of masked men took a teacher from his house in North Carolina in 1874, tied him up, and after threatening to kill him if he did not leave the state gave him 100 lashes with a bullwhip. The founder and president for nearly 30 years of Shaw University, Henry M. Tupper of Massachusetts, was often harassed by the Ku Klux Klan and once hid all night in a cornfield with his wife and two children to avoid an assassination attempt. The 1874 elections were a particularly tense time; as one teacher put it, "to be for weeks in constant expectation of being murdered or burned out, and without losing faith in God, is something of a strain on the nerves."[28] As the foremost practitioner of "social equality," Berea College suffered many threats and attacks. Drunken men frequently rode through the streets shooting at dormitory windows. In 1871 the college treasurer went to a nearby town on business, had dinner with a black family, and after leaving a prayer meeting at a Negro church was ambushed by five men who fired at him seven times and left him for dead. The shots had missed, however; the treasurer returned to his hotel, where at 3 a.m. 30 masked men dragged him from his bed, took him to the woods, and gave him 61 lashes with a hickory whip. In 1879 the northern Methodists compiled a list of 34 attacks on their missionaries and teachers in the past decade; 19 of the victims were white and 15 black; three of the whites and four of the blacks were killed.[29]

27 *AM*, LVI (May 1902), 230; Jacqueline J. Halstead, "The Delaware Association for the Moral Improvement and Education of the Colored People: 'Practical Christianity,'" *Delaware History*, XV (Apr. 1972), 31-32.

28 *Advance*, July 16, 1874; *HMM*, XX (Feb. 1898), 50; *Seventh Annual Report FASME*, Cincinnati, 1874, p. 11.

29 John A. R. Rogers, *Birth of Berea College. A Story of Providence*, Philadelphia, 1903, pp. 144, 163-64; affidavit by W. W. Wheeler in James Monroe Papers, Oberlin College Library; *SWCA*, July 3, 1879.

Arson was a favorite weapon of southern whites opposed to Negro education; in the 1870s they burned down countless black schools. Most of these were one-room country schoolhouses, but several large buildings in urban areas suffered the same fate. During the 1876 electoral crisis, arsonists destroyed Straight University in New Orleans and AMA secondary schools in Macon and Mobile. In Macon the firemen sprayed water on surrounding buildings but refused to make any effort to save the school. The AMA decided to rebuild all three schools immediately. "If burning out Yankees is the programme," wrote an AMA official, "the sooner our foes . . . are taught that they dont *stay* burned out . . . the safer all the A.M.A. property in the South will be."[30]

Some of the friction between missionary educators and southern whites was generated by experiments in joint support of Negro schools. The AMA tried for several years to cooperate with local school boards in such enterprises. The forms of this cooperation varied. Usually the mission society leased its school building to the city or county for a nominal sum, and the public agency paid all or part of the teachers' salaries. So long as Republicans were in power this arrangement worked reasonably well. But as Democrats began to regain control of the South the experiment of dual support foundered and eventually collapsed. In Memphis the Democrats dismissed all AMA teachers, forcing the association to withdraw from the jointly sponsored Lincoln School and to found LeMoyne Institute in its place. In Columbus, Mississippi, Democrats drove out Union Academy's northern teachers with threats of violence and then closed the school in 1877.[31]

Democratic boards of education in a few cities offered to continue their cooperation with the AMA on condition that the board appoint the principal and most of the teachers. This was a transparent attempt to "get rid of the Yankee teachers," as two members of the Savannah board admitted. Although some black leaders went along with this in the hope of replacing white teachers with blacks, in most cases the black community aligned itself with the AMA and implored the association to stand up to white pressures, for with good reason they feared that local boards would allow the schools to deteriorate. For several years an uneasy compromise prevailed, with the AMA and local

[30] Quotation from Thomas N. Chase to M. E. Strieby, Dec. 15, 1876, AMA Archives. See also Richard Bryant Drake, "The American Missionary Association and the Southern Negro, 1861-1888," Ph.D. Dissertation, Emory University, 1957, p. 226. Armed students and faculty guarded Talladega College around the clock for several weeks in early 1877 to prevent arson.

[31] There are many letters in the AMA Archives about various experiments in joint AMA-public schools. See also Drake, "The American Missionary Association and the Southern Negro," 296-302.

boards sharing the appointment of teachers. But this arrangement could not last. Most southern whites did not believe in secondary education for blacks, and if the AMA wanted to provide such education, as one missionary pointed out, it must do so in schools entirely its own. By 1878 the experiment of dual support had broken down, sometimes with bad feeling on both sides. A few days after the AMA terminated its contract with the Savannah school board, an arsonist burned down Beach Institute. The AMA promptly rebuilt the school. With recovery from the depression after 1878, the association was able to expand and multiply its secondary schools without public aid—or control.[32]

But as Democrats came to power, missionary educators of necessity toned down their rhetoric. "It's one thing to say what you think [in the] North, and another thing at the South," wrote an AMA teacher in Macon just after her school had been burned down. "We're in the den of lions and we would *prefer* that the lions should not be tantalized or aroused unnecessarily." An AMA principal in Alabama thought "we ought to establish cordial relations with the white people . . . so far as we can do so without compromising our principles." This meant, among other things, avoiding the word "rebel" to describe former Confederates and an effort not to "rail against the whites" in public.[33]

After Reconstruction it was a fact of life that black schools could not survive without the toleration of the "better class" of southern whites. The president of Fisk wrote: "I trust that I do not lack the courage to express my views, but so long as I know that Fisk is doing an uncalculable amount of good, I do not think it wise to jeopardize the existence of my work by an unnecessary exploitation of my private opinions." Although as a Methodist editor in New Orleans during the 1870s Joseph C. Hartzell had done his share of rebel-baiting, as secretary of the Methodist Freedmen's Aid Society 15 years later he wrote that, while "agitators, noble men, who are willing to sacrifice everything for the cause" were needed for the fight against racism, "men of that type are not the men to have in charge of our schools."[34] The tightrope act required of missionary educators to protect their institutions without sacrificing egalitarian goals accounts for their wavering back and forth between militancy and accommodation. At times they defied southern whites and provoked the hostile responses described on the preceding

[32] Quotation from Robert F. Markham to M. E. Strieby, Feb. 14, 1876, AMA Archives. See also *ibid.*, Feb. 14, 20, 1878, and a petition signed by 21 Negroes in Macon, sent to E. M. Cravath, June 30, 1874, also in AMA Archives.

[33] Mrs. P. M. Webster to Delia E. Emerson, Jan. 1, 1877, John Silsby to E. M. Cravath, Sept. 4, 1872, AMA Archives.

[34] James G. Merrill to the editor of *McClure's Magazine*, Jan. 8, 1904, copy in Carl Schurz Papers, Library of Congress; Hartzell to Isaiah B. Scott, Aug. 8, 1895, FASME Archives.

pages; at other times, and increasingly after 1876, they were compelled to speak softly.

This was especially true of presidents of missionary colleges receiving state aid—Claflin, Atlanta, and Tougaloo. Until 1890, southern states were not required to appropriate Morrill Act funds for black colleges, so these three schools (plus Hampton Institute) won state support only by cultivating the good will of white legislators. In 1886 Tougaloo's president found it necessary to apologize for an article in the school newspaper critical of local whites and to promise future censorship of the paper. In South Carolina the state-supported A. & M. Institute for Negroes was a part of Claflin but with a separate board of trustees appointed by the state. This arrangement lasted until 1896, when the two institutions were separated. During their united administration, the Claflin president had to tread carefully to avoid losing the annual $10,000 state appropriation. In 1876 President Edward Cooke did not deem it "prudent for me to take any active part in the political excitements." His prudence did not save him from a confrontation with Redshirts who called him a "damn son of a bitch Yankee nigger-lover" and gave him three weeks to leave the state. But Cooke remained and managed to establish correct if not cordial relations with the incoming Hampton government.[35] To protect Atlanta University's $8,000 annual state subsidy, President Edmund Ware spent a lot of time wooing moderates in the Georgia legislature. His tact and persistence paid off, but not without some compromises. He instructed teachers to be discreet in their statements about the South; when the state board of visitors raised a hue and cry about a few antisouthern Civil War books in the library, Ware had the offending books removed.[36]

The 1880s were the era of best feeling between southern whites and missionary educators. Atticus Haygood's sympathetic attitude seemed to be shared by a growing number of southern whites. As early as 1877 a group of AMA teachers attending a meeting at Marion, Alabama, were invited to tea by the local gentry. "This warm reception by the whites we had no reason—from past treatment—to expect," wrote one surprised teacher. "We all . . . praise God & rejoice that the old wall of prejudice, envy & hate . . . is beginning to crumble." Yardley Warner reported after an inspection tour of Quaker freedmen's schools in 1880

[35] Vernon Lane Wharton, *The Negro in Mississippi 1865-1890*, Chapel Hill, 1947, p. 233; *Zion's Herald*, Nov. 2, 1876; George B. Tindall, *South Carolina Negroes, 1877-1900*, Columbia, S.C., 1952, pp. 226-30.

[36] Ware to E. M. Cravath, Nov. 4, 17, Dec. 2, 5, 12, 1871, Feb. 11, 1874, AMA Archives; Ware to W. L. Brown, Apr. 9, 1872, Brown to Ware, Apr. 12, 1872, Ware Papers, Atlanta University Archives; Range, *Rise of Negro Colleges in Georgia*, 43-46.

that he was gratified by the "peaceful co-operation and cordial approval of our work" in communities where a few years earlier he had been shot at and threatened with hanging. In Memphis the leading newspaper publicized the work of LeMoyne, which "has nothing whatever to do with politics. . . . Their mission is one that every thinking person must endorse. It is to make boys and girls good, healthy-minded, self-supporting and self-respecting men and women."[37]

As this statement indicates, black schools would be tolerated so long as they confined themselves to education and left "politics" alone. Since missionary educators believed the Negro would advance more by education than politics, it was not hard for them to concentrate on the former. Nor did they regard this as a compromise of their principles, for they expected that as blacks demonstrated their capacity, racism would wane. The missionaries publicized every shred of evidence that supported this conviction. In 1871 the Georgia legislature created a board of visitors to attend public examinations at Atlanta University. The chairman of the first board of visitors was ex-slaveholder Joseph Brown, who reportedly said that he expected the examination to confirm the Negro's inferiority. But the recitations of former slaves in Latin, Greek, and geometry forced from him the confession that "we were impressed with the fallacy of the popular idea . . . that the members of the African race are not capable of a high grade of intellectual culture." And the Atlanta *Constitution* could hardly "believe what we witnessed. To see colored boys and girls fourteen and eighteen years of age, reading in Greek and Latin, and demonstrating correctly problems in Algebra and Geometry . . . appears almost wonderful." For more than a decade the visitors' reports were similarly enthusiastic, stating that "we have never seen . . . better teaching than we find done at the Atlanta University. . . . Who can doubt the wisdom of continuing the appropriation?" Such sentiments caused the AMA to rejoice in the "quiet and unostentatious" but "immense influence" of missionary schooling, which had "demonstrated the capacity of the Negro for education and improvement, and which has, therefore, tended to break down the prejudices against the colored race."[38]

But when it became apparent after 1890 that the South was growing more rather than less racist, some missionary educators expressed con-

[37] Joseph E. Smith to M. E. Strieby, May 2, 1877, AMA Archives; Warner, *Warner*, 183-84; *Memphis Daily Commercial*, quoted in *AM*, XLVI (Feb. 1892), 34-35.
[38] Clarence A. Bacote, *The Story of Atlanta University: A Century of Service*, Atlanta, 1969, pp. 46-53; Myron W. Adams, *A History of Atlanta University*, Atlanta, 1930, p. 24; Report of the Board of Visitors to Atlanta University, June 25, 1880, in Edmund A. Ware Scrapbook, Atlanta University Archives; *AM*, XLV (Oct. 1891), 348.

cern lest conciliation become capitulation. When a southern speaker at the second Mohonk Conference on the Negro (1891) told northern teachers that they would be more successful if they conformed to southern customs, several educators in the audience cried out "Never! Never!" Wilbur P. Thirkield insisted that "we cannot adopt the Southern ideas as to the nature and status of the negro. . . . Nor can we barter principle for peace, nor for apparent success." The danger confronting missionary educators was not, as southerners said, failure to "attune our work to the improved conditions of to-day," but retreat from a vision "that looks to the righteous solution of the graver problems of to-morrow."[39]

After a Chicago speech in 1890 on Negro education, Thirkield talked informally with reporters, who quoted him as denouncing southern racism in strong terms. This incident caused a "tremendous furor" in the southern press. Haygood threatened to resign from the board of Gammon Theological Seminary, of which Thirkield was president, and to withdraw Slater Fund grants from all Methodist schools. Both Thirkield and Secretary Hartzell of the Methodist Freedmen's Aid Society apologized privately to Haygood, alleging misquotation by sensation-seeking journalists. Hartzell said ruefully to a friend: "When these Southern fellows pitch into us for an occasional slip of the tongue, I think if they only knew what we do not say but could say truthfully, they would be mighty glad to keep still." Though it was hard to remain quiet in the presence of injustice, "our Church is in an enemy's land in the South and we can expect no favor."[40]

But no matter how hard they tried, missionary educators could not avoid stepping on southern sensibilities at one time or another. In 1888 a Virginian named Frank Ruffin published an article in a Richmond newspaper asserting the "permanent inferiority" of the Negro. President Lyman Tefft of the Baptists' Hartshorn College (later part of Virginia Union University) replied that Negroes were members of the human race "capable of the same ultimate development as any other portion of the race." Aha! exlaimed Ruffin. Tefft had stripped off his mask and revealed the true aim of Yankee education to be "absolute civil and social equality." "What is the greatest stimulus to the negro to reach that plane?" asked Ruffin rhetorically. "Miscegenation. . . . Professor Tefft . . . stands disclosed as the head of a miscegenation propaganda in this city."[41]

[39] Isabel Barrows, ed., *Second Mohonk Conference on the Negro Question,* Boston, 1891, p. 82; Thirkield in *ZH,* May 15, 1889.

[40] Quotations from Hartzell to George W. Gray, May 19, 1890, Hartzell to Bishop W. F. Mallalieu, Apr. 7, 1890, FASME Archives. See also Hartzell to Thirkield, Mar. 8, 1890, and Hartzell to Haygood, Mar. 8, 1890, *ibid.*

[41] *Richmond Dispatch,* Dec. 9, 1888, clipping in ABHMS Archives.

Clearly the social equality issue had not died with the end of Reconstruction; it remained the thorniest issue confronting northern teachers. "There should be an understanding as to what is meant by this term," wrote Henry L. Morehouse of the Baptist Home Mission Society in a memorandum to heads of the society's schools. "The schools should be conducted so as not to give unnecessary offense to the prejudice of the Southern people, but at the same time so as not to unnecessarily offend the pride of the Negroes. They should seek to awaken in the mind of the pupils self-respect and worthy ambition to excel in life." This masterpiece of ambiguity did little to clarify the problem. President Edward H. Fairchild of Berea College tried to meet the issue head-on. Southern whites, said Fairchild in an 1889 magazine article, saw an unbroken chain of relationships between blacks voting, holding office, serving on juries, riding with whites in trains, attending school with whites, and marrying their sisters. Thus they denied blacks *all* rights for fear that granting any would lead straight to "social equality." This being so, northern egalitarians should stop splitting hairs trying to define the difference between civil and social equality and should insist on the brotherhood of all men whether it suited southern prejudices or not.[42]

Secretary Michael Strieby of the AMA was disturbed by Fairchild's article, for Berea was still identified in the public mind with the AMA and "you know the danger of the commitment of a missionary society on delicate points." The term "social equality" was "a slippery one," conceded Strieby, but "we in our writings at this office . . . try to make out that we do not insist on *social* equality." While Strieby agreed with Fairchild on "the fundamental issue," he thought that "our best fight now is on the recognition of the equal manhood and rights of the Negro before the law, in the church, in the school, in the public conveyance, and in the public hotels, &c., leaving the question as to technical *social* equality to take care of itself."[43]

This semantic problem, if that is what it was, was never resolved. In any case, the alleged *practice* of social equality in missionary schools remained a source of tension. The issue of integrated classrooms will be treated in chapter 13. Equally controversial were the questions of interracial residential and dining facilities at the schools.

Southern whites seemed willing to tolerate the integration of faculties in black schools so long as it was confined to professional relations. But problems arose when the mission societies proposed to house unmarried black and white teachers together in "teachers' homes," espe-

---

[42] Undated memorandum, probably 1894, ABHMS Archives; Fairchild in *Advance*, Sept. 12, 1889.
[43] Strieby to James H. Fairchild, Sept. 17, 21, 1889, Fairchild Papers.

cially when the blacks were male and the whites female. On this matter, wrote an AMA official in 1878, "it is sometimes difficult to tell just how far we ought to go in opposition to the sentiments of the people among whom we live. Every sensible man knows that there is a limit that cannot be safely passed." Another AMA missionary said that "we are in a position where it is hard to avoid the breakers," for the black community would accuse the association of prejudice if it refused to board black teachers, while local whites threatened violence if it did. The societies usually resolved the problem according to local conditions. In most instances the issue did not arise because black teachers were married and/or already lived in the community where they taught. In 1878, however, the AMA asked an unmarried black missionary in Mobile to find his own housing when whites threatened to burn down Emerson Institute if he remained in the teachers' home. In Savannah, on the other hand, the AMA's Robert F. Markham decided to board a black minister with three white women teachers at Beach Institute even if "it does bring down the wrath of the whites. . . . I am of the old abolition stamp. I say stand by the principle of equal justice. . . . With one man if he is black and with God, we are in the majority." Markham's decision may have helped provoke the burning of Beach Institute in 1878.[44]

By 1900 the South's color line had grown so rigid that few missionary schools could maintain integrated faculty housing any longer, and after classes black and white teachers usually went their separate ways. One reflective white teacher wrote that while "professional integration was harmonious and successful," socially "both races were governed by Southern compulsion. . . . They left companionship when closing the schoolhouse door."[45]

Next to interracial marriage, southern whites considered interracial dining the most heinous manifestation of social equality. It was customary in several missionary colleges for the faculty to eat with the boarding students, one teacher at each table of ten or a dozen students. For some reason Atlanta University's practice of this custom attracted the most attention, jeopardizing the state appropriation on more than one occasion. But President Edmund Ware told the Georgia legislature that "we have come here to help these people and we cannot do it best at arm's length." Ware's integrity and candor carried weight with white Georgians, and so long as he lived the appropriation continued. As the pressure against integrated eating escalated around 1890, a

[44] Thomas N. Chase to M. E. Strieby, Apr. 19, 1878, William Ash to Strieby, June 10, 1878, Markham to Strieby, Mar. 15, June 15, 20, 1877, AMA Archives.
[45] Lura Beam, *He Called Them by the Lightning: A Teacher's Odyssey in the Negro South, 1908-1919*, Indianapolis, 1967, pp. 150, 154.

number of missionary schools gave in and established separate faculty dining rooms. At Hampton Institute, white teachers dined apart from their black colleagues as well as from students, a concession not only to southern sentiments but also to the prejudices of several white teachers themselves. But the faculty at Atlanta and most AMA and Methodist schools refused to take such action; they maintained the tradition of integrated faculty-student dining throughout the missionary era.[46]

Southern whites continued to ostracize Yankee teachers who ate with black people. The Atlanta University faculty in the 1890s included graduates of Harvard, Yale, Andover, Williams, and Oberlin; President Horace Bumstead belonged to an old New England family and had studied in Germany as well as at Yale and Andover. Yet they were sneered at on the street as "nigger teachers" and none of them was ever invited into a southern white home. A white teacher at the AMA's Gregory Institute in Wilmington, North Carolina, said that after a few months she learned to retreat into a shell of unconcern toward local whites and to avoid going into white sections of town. "The ostracized becomes the invisible one. . . . I lived behind Du Bois' 'Veil.' " The children of white teachers also lived behind the veil. Some of them attended the schools where their parents taught, which of course cut them off from the white community. If instead they attended a local public school or went north to boarding school the black community might resent the implication that black schools were not good enough for the missionaries' children. Howard University President John Gordon's decision to send his children to white schools in Washington rather than to Howard as previous presidents had done helped spark a successful drive by black faculty and alumni to force his resignation in 1906.[47]

Although antimissionary violence declined after Reconstruction, it did not disappear. The AMA's Emerson Institute was burned by an arsonist—for the second time—in 1882. When the association attempted to open an industrial school in Quitman, Georgia, in 1885, the local newspaper abused "meddling Yankee nigger teachers"; young toughs fired shotguns through the windows while classes were in session; and a few weeks later a mob burned down the school. In 1894 (the year Morehouse instructed Baptist teachers to avoid giving offense to southern prejudices), arsonists burned three of the Home Mis-

[46] *Independent*, Apr. 23, 1874; Edward K. Graham, "A Tender Violence: The Biography of a College," unpublished ms., cited by permission of the author.

[47] *Independent*, June 23, 1892; Albert Bushnell Hart, "Shall the Negro Be Educated?" in *BET*, Apr. 15, 1908; Beam, *He Called Them by the Lightning*, p. 34; Raymond Wolters, *The New Negro on Campus: Black College Rebellions of the 1920s*, Princeton, 1975, p. 80.

sion Society's school buildings. The lives of white teachers as well as those of black colleagues and students were in danger during the Wilmington and Atlanta race riots of 1898 and 1906. Such occurrences discouraged missionaries who had worked to enlist the sympathy of southern whites. Some gave up the attempt altogether, convinced that "the genus homo, a few years since called rebel, is just the same animal he used to be and men of underground railroad principles and slaveholding democrats cannot coalesce any more than oil & water."[48]

The instincts of southern whites who feared the egalitarian potential of black education were sound. Although real social equality between white teachers and the black community was rare, the ideology and thrust of missionary education was toward ultimate racial equality. But this ideology contained a fundamental ambivalence. Teachers came south intending to uplift the poor; like all missionary enterprises, this one implied the cultural inferiority of those to be uplifted. The next chapter will explore the paradox of paternalistic means for egalitarian ends.

[48] Drake, "The American Missionary Association and the Southern Negro," 226; *Friends' Review*, Dec. 26, 1885; *HMM*, xvi (July 1894), 306-307; Beam, *He Called Them by the Lightning*, p. 27; Thomas N. Chase to M. E. Strieby, Aug. 25, 1878, AMA Archives.

Chapter Eleven

Paternalism and Piety

In an 1883 speech on "The Negro in America," Henry L. Morehouse defined the goal of missionary education as "America in the Negro," which meant "American ideas of citizenship, of Church membership, of the family life, etc., incorporated into the Negro character." American ideas in this context were those of white native-born middle-class Protestants. Minority groups were expected to assimilate these ideas before they in turn could become assimilated as full-fledged Americans. The sociologist Milton Gordon calls this concept of Americanization "Anglo-conformity" and contrasts it with the melting-pot idea, which looks toward a blending of different cultures into one, and with cultural pluralism, which envisages the coexistence of several life-styles. Anglo-conformity prevailed almost universally among native-born Protestants in the nineteenth century, and the missionary educators were no exception. Though some of them achieved a sympathetic understanding of black culture from their experiences in the South, their principal purpose remained the transformation of the freedmen into ebony Puritans.[1]

From this standpoint the masses of freedmen a generation after emancipation still had far to go before they were ready for full assimilation. A questionnaire sent to AMA teachers in 1890 asking them to list the main obstacles to Negro progress produced a number of replies emphasizing white racism, such as "closed avenues to skilled labor," "low expectations of him by the whites as to intelligence and morality," "the credit and mortgage system," and "caste," but even more that stressed the race's own defects: "immorality," "want of home training," "perverted religion," "intemperance," "ignorance and conservatism of colored ministers who are often absolutely bad men," and "frivolity— no purpose in life."[2]

Missionary educators continued to blame slavery for these faults. Although by 1890 a majority of Negroes had been born in freedom, missionaries believed that the oppressive legacy of bondage still weighed heavily on the older generation and through them on their

[1] Morehouse in Joseph C. Hartzell, ed., *Christian Educators in Council*, New York, 1883, p. 71; Milton M. Gordon, *Assimilation in American Life: The Role of Race, Religion, and National Origins*, New York, 1964.

[2] *AM*, XLIV (July 1890), 208-209.

children. "The worst things abolitionists ever *wrote, spoke,* or thought about slavery are not half the truth," wrote one teacher. "No one knows the depth of degradation to which slavery has brought men that has never tried to lift up . . . one who has been a slave." At the turn of the century President William Goodell Frost of Berea College lamented that "it is now the fashion to varnish slavery." But those who had worked with the freedmen and their children could never subscribe to the romantic plantation myth. "True family life was impossible to the slave," said Frost. "Slavery was a school of laziness, deception, suspicion, and theft. . . . [It] removed the natural motives to ambition and self-improvement," leaving the race with psychological scars which those who "varnished" slavery could never understand.[3]

Since nineteenth-century Anglo-Saxon Protestants had achieved "the grandest heights ever attained by man," missionaries considered it their duty to reach down and lift less fortunate peoples up to the heights. Blacks could be "civilised [only] by close contact . . . with their fellow-citizens who are centuries ahead of them. . . . They need that those more favored should take them by the hand and lead them . . . up from debasement and misery into purity and joy."[4] At its best, this rhetoric of uplift reflected the humanitarianism of the Good Samaritan. "The black man needs what every human being needs, help from above," declared the *American Missionary.* "It is futile to say, he is free, let him alone. . . . The gospel of Christ is not a mere declaration of freedom; it is regeneration and help from above." The president of the Methodist Freedmen's Aid Society, answering affirmatively the question "Am I my brother's keeper?" proclaimed that "the colored man is our brother. . . . We must take care of him, educate him, help him, and lift him up into a higher life, that he may be a brother on whom we shall look with satisfaction and pride."[5]

But such fraternal expressions often slipped into the paternal mode. The missionaries believed slavery to have been an infantilizing process. They likened the most exasperating features they perceived in adult black behavior—unpredictability, unreliability, guile, petty quarreling—to the traits of children. "The colored people are yet children, and need to be taught everything," was a typical comment. An instructor of upper-level courses at the AMA's Avery Institute spoke in 1872 of the immaturity of even his adult students in "their manners,

[3] Robert F. Markham to Michael E. Strieby, May 2, 1877, AMA Archives; Mss. of convocation and chapel addresses by Frost, 1899 and 1904, in Frost Papers, Berea College Library.

[4] *Advance,* Feb. 25, 1875; *Independent,* Apr. 7, 1892; *Seventh Annual Report FASME,* Cincinnati, 1874, p. 8.

[5] *AM,* L (Apr. 1896), 125; *Fourth Annual Report FASME,* Cincinnati, 1871, p. 23.

morals even, their habits, their health, their notions of economy, of ten thousand little things that your child and mine learns before he is five years old." Missionary educators tended to think of the freedmen in generational metaphors: "This generation sees its infancy," wrote a teacher in 1874; "the next will see it in its youth; the next in the strength and vigor of its middle age."[6]

Since "the people are [yet] in infancy in virtue, truthfulness, self-control," said an AMA teacher in 1876, their "successful management" required kind but firm authority. Black adults did not always take well to such management. One white school principal complained of his problems with local black men who "think the colored people are competent to manage their own affairs in their own way." Robert F. Markham, the gruff, blunt AMA official in Savannah who supervised the association's black churches in the area, described his trials in frequent letters to Michael Strieby, the AMA's secretary. A professed egalitarian, Markham nevertheless felt it necessary to impose strict discipline on the black pastors under his jurisdiction. One of them, "brother Cuthbert," gave Markham trouble, telling him that "it was all nonsense he was not going to be catechised by me as though I was his master or he was my slave." Strieby evidently reprimanded Cuthbert, for Markham related that he "seems to have a different spirit since you wrote him"; he now worked hard and followed Markham's instructions. "I am getting all these colored preachers so I can manage them," Markham reported with satisfaction. "They all understand now when I decide a thing, that is the end." A month later, however, Markham had second thoughts; perhaps he realized that Cuthbert's master-slave analogy was too near the truth. He wrote that Cuthbert "yields too much, like a slave governed by a master that he feared. I do not like that, but if it is the only way then it will have to be so."[7]

For many freedmen, missionary teachers replaced slaveholders as the most "significant others" among the white people in their lives. As time went on, some teachers became increasingly aware of the danger of becoming surrogate masters. Since "our mission is not simply to educate Negroes, but also to obliterate race prejudice," said one, the "less consciousness of distinctions and classes in the minds of both worker and recipient, the better for the work." Another teacher deplored the tendency to refer to Negroes as "these people." "The way to win the hearts of 'These People,' " she said, "is not to talk down to them as if they were children; it is not to treat them as they know you

6 *Seventh Annual Report FASME*, Cincinnati, 1874, p. 9; M. A. Warren to Erastus M. Cravath, Aug. 27, 1872, AMA Archives; *AM*, xviii (May 1874), 104.

7 E. R. Sellers to M. E. Strieby, Mar. 10, 1876, A. N. Niles to E. M. Cravath, Oct. 26, 1870, Markham to Strieby, Nov. 8, 12, 17, Dec. 20, 1875, AMA Archives.

would not treat white pupils." But many, perhaps most missionaries never did fully reconcile the conflicting impulses of brotherhood and fatherhood. Their ambivalence was expressed by a teacher who wrote in 1892 that the chief remaining defect of the black man was dependence: "One thing above all others he must be taught [is] true independence." Yet in the very next paragraph, after praising black progress, the teacher concluded: "The ship is under sail, but as yet we can't step aside entirely and give the wheel" to Negroes themselves.[8]

Several black leaders resented the patronizing tone of missionary rhetoric, which "causes the country to look upon us as a poor and helpless people," in Frederick Douglass's words. Although the mission societies had been "of the most incalculable benefit" to blacks, said T. Thomas Fortune in 1884, it was an open question "whether the black man has any manhood left, after the missionaries and religious enthusiasts had done picturing, or, rather, caricaturing his debased moral and mental condition." A black Presbyterian clergyman asserted that the missionaries exhibited "too much pity and too little love" toward Negroes. They came to the freedmen as "the eminently high to the almost hopelessly low" and did more "to make him feel his degradation" than "to make him feel that he is a man and a brother."[9]

On the other hand, many middle-class Negroes expressed the same Anglo-conformity uplift sentiments as did the white missionaries. A Fisk graduate insisted that "the Christianization of the Negro must come from without his own institutions," while a black professor at Atlanta Baptist College wrote in 1896 that the freed slaves had been so degraded that without white help "progress would have been impossible." The talented-tenth theory of education, said Howard University Professor Kelly Miller, was based on the premise that "the choice youth of the race should assimilate the principles of [Western] culture and hand them down to the masses below." Miller praised the missionary teachers who "sowed the seeds of intelligence in the soil of ignorance and planted the rose of virtue in the garden of dishonor and shame. . . . Their monument is builded in the hopes of a race struggling upward from ignorance to enlightenment, from corruption to purity of life."[10]

[8] *Independent*, Feb. 21, 1884; *AM*, LXIII (Aug. 1909), 511, XLVI (Sept. 1892), 302-303.

[9] Douglass in *NYTrib.*, July 7, 1875; Fortune, *Black and White: Land, Labor and Politics in the South*, New York, 1884, pp. 78, 66; Matthew Anderson, *Presbyterianism—Its Relation to the Negro*, Philadelphia, 1897, pp. 128-29.

[10] *AM*, XLII (Mar. 1888), 58; *HMM*, XVIII (Jan. 1896), 34-35; Miller, "Howard University," in *From Servitude to Service*, Boston, 1905, p. 15; Miller, "The Education of the Negro," in *Report of the U.S. Commissioner of Education for the Year 1900-01*, Washington, 1902, I, 830-31.

The component of Anglo-American culture that blacks needed most, said Miller, was the Protestant ethic. "The Negro does not make provision because he lacks prevision. . . . He cannot see beyond the momentary gratification of his desires." Negro leaders had been making the same point for generations, and black as well as white missionary educators had been driving it home in their schools ever since emancipation. The Protestant ethic (or as it is often called, the Puritan ethic) formed the core of the values carried South by the neo-Puritan abolitionists who came to teach the freedmen. Described by Ralph Barton Perry as "austerity, reliability, energy, industry, self-control, marital fidelity, frugality, sobriety, thrift, self-reliance, and foresight," the Puritan ethic was the basis of reform movements growing out of evangelical Protestantism. As William McLoughlin has pointed out, these reforms were primarily missionary endeavors. Conversion of the poor, the intemperate, the depraved and deprived would "implant in them the virtues of true Protestantism—industry, sobriety, thrift and piety" —which would enable them to become prosperous and useful citizens.[11]

The opposite of the Protestant ethic virtues were wastefulness, idleness, unreliability, infidelity, hedonism, and lack of foresight. These were precisely the vices that abolitionists believed slavery had ingrained in its victims. To help them "unlearn the teachings of slavery," therefore, the freedmen's schools drilled students in "lessons of industry, of domestic management and thrift"; they taught that "industry is commendable and indispensable to freedom, and indolence both wicked and degrading." Freed slaves needed "the New England church and school . . . to civilize the people, beget order, sobriety, purity, and faith," and teach the freedmen to become "like Northerners, in industry, economy, and thrift."[12]

This message permeated all levels of black education. Several colleges informed applicants that "persons who have not a fixed purpose to improve their time, and an earnest desire to fit themselves for usefulness, should not seek admission." President William W. Patton of Howard sounded a common theme when he urged the graduating class of 1880 to emulate successful groups, especially New England Yankees and the Jews, who had achieved success through "industry, thrift, wealth, knowledge, culture, morality, and religion." And in 1902 Secretary Thomas J. Morgan of the Baptist Home Mission Society

11 *Ibid.*, 809-10; Perry, *Puritanism and Democracy*, New York, 1944, p. 302; Mc-Loughlin, ed., *The American Evangelicals, 1800-1900: An Anthology*, New York, 1968, p. 13.

12 *AM*, VII (June 1863), 128, XL (Mar. 1867), 59, XII (Dec. 1868), 274; Sallie Holley to Maria Porter, Sept. 30, 1887, in John White Chadwick, *Sallie Holley, A Life for Liberty*, New York, 1899, p. 252.

summed up the values that Baptist colleges tried to teach. The goals of education, he wrote, were the growth of knowledge, skills, and character, and of these the last was most important. "If a man goes out of the schools depraved in heart and deficient in will power," said Morgan, "all his learning and skill and intellectual qualities may be a curse and not a blessing." Students must "be trained to be . . . industrious, thrifty, faithful to the performance of duty. . . . Ignorance fosters idleness, thriftlessness, wastefulness and vagabondage; education encourages industry, thrift, frugality and home keeping."[13]

Piety and virtue were essential to the Protestant ethic. Missionary educators considered black churches deficient in these areas. Among the freedmen, wrote one northerner, "religion degenerates into mere wild-fire, with as little tendency to transform the character as the heathen rites of their ancestors in their native jungles." Since black clergymen were often the worst sinners, especially against the Seventh Commandment, little moral leadership could be expected from them. "The mass of Southern colored churches," declared an AMA teacher, were "travesties of Christianity. They must be reformed from without, by planting true churches, whose chief test shall be obedience to the Ten Commandments."[14]

Some of the strongest criticism of the Negro clergy came not from missionaries but from prominent black leaders. In 1890 Booker T. Washington wrote in a northern magazine that "three fourths of the Baptist ministers and two thirds of the Methodists are unfit either morally or mentally, or both, to preach the gospel to any one." Several other spokesmen including even some clergymen endorsed this statement. Bishop Daniel A. Payne, president of Wilberforce and the foremost figure in the AME Church, offered to cite names and places to prove the "shameful and painful facts" that "not more than one-third of the ministers, Baptist and Methodist, in the South are morally and intellectually qualified." And Francis J. Grimké, pastor of the leading black Presbyterian church of Washington, pronounced most black preachers "literally the blind leading the blind." Instead of instructing their congregations in the need for "honesty in business, truthfulness, purity, temperance, the duty of husbands and wives to their families and to each other," too many ministers were fleecing their flocks, seducing female parishioners, and covering their sins with frenzied rantings from the pulpit. "The thing most to be deplored in our condition today," concluded Grimké, "is not our poverty, nor our ignorance, but

[13] *Catalogue of Atlanta University, 1876*, New York, 1876, p. 21; Patton in *Independent*, Aug. 26, 1880; Morgan in *HMM*, XXIV (Jan. 1902), 14, 16 (Feb. 1902), 30.
[14] Gilbert Haven et al., *An Appeal to Our People for Our People*, n.p., 1875, p. 22; *Independent*, May 6, 1875.

our moral deficiencies, and for these deficiencies the Afro-American pulpit is in a very large measure responsible."[15]

Whether these indictments were accurate or were distorted by the middle-class Victorianism of their authors is uncertain. In any case, most missionaries agreed with the Baptist abolitionist who declared that "the education of colored preachers is the one great and crying need of the Freedmen!" Many missionary schools offered courses in theology and provided in-service training to black clergymen. Several Negro colleges evolved out of schools originally founded as Bible institutes. But although a trained clergy was the first priority of freedmen's education, less than one-sixth of the graduates of missionary colleges and secondary schools went into the ministry while three-fifths became teachers. Rather than lessening the importance of religious education, however, this heightened it, for teachers molded the values of rising generations. Thus the schools were "decidedly *Christian* institutions," said Henry L. Morehouse, "wherein the Bible is a daily textbook" and "the formation of right Christian character is an uppermost aim."[16]

Black colleges reproduced the religious requirements of northern institutions from which their founders had graduated, including daily or twice-daily prayer meetings or chapel services, compulsory Bible study, two church services on Sunday, and in some schools a prayer or scripture reading at the beginning of each class. Most colleges held a Week of Prayer during the school year, and the missionary magazines were full of news about revivals. "Salvation is the guiding purpose of this educational work," stated the AMA's executive committee, while a professor at Straight University explained that "the student is never allowed to forget that he has a soul to save as well as a mind to train." He carefully added that "our meetings are wholly free from feverish excitement, and their influence upon the scholarship and deportment of the students is marked and salutary." The AMA's secretary boasted

[15] Washington, "The Colored Ministry: Its Defects and Needs," in *Christian Union*, Aug. 14, 1890; Payne in *Indianapolis Freeman*, Nov. 29, 1890, and Payne, *History of the African Methodist Episcopal Church*, Nashville, 1891, p. 420; Grimké, "The Defects of Our Ministry, and the Remedy," *A.M.E. Church Review*, III (Oct. 1886), 154-57; Grimké, "The Afro-American Pulpit in Relation to Race Elevation," in Carter G. Woodson, ed., *The Works of Francis James Grimké*, 4 vols., Washington, 1942, I, 229-33.

[16] Charles H. Corey, *A History of the Richmond Theological Seminary, With Reminiscences of Thirty Years' Work Among the Colored People*, Richmond 1894, p. 112; *HMM*, I (July 1879), 204, IX (Mar. 1887), 62. In 1900 W. E. B. Du Bois tabulated the occupations of 1,252 black college graduates and found that 54 percent of them were teachers and 17 percent clergymen. An even higher percentage of secondary school graduates went into teaching and a lower percentage into the ministry. Du Bois, *The College-Bred Negro*, Atlanta University Publication no. 5, Atlanta, 1900, pp. 63-64.

in 1887 that since the founding of Fisk "there has not been a year without the conversion of from twelve to seventy of the students." The Methodist Freedmen's Aid Society also kept score of the students brought to Christ in campus revivals; the society's annual report of 1885 expressed special pleasure that during the past year "nearly every institution has been visited with special outpourings of the Holy Ghost." Not to be outdone, the Baptist Home Mission Society reported in 1886 that the number of conversions in its schools the previous year had been 234, led by Spelman with 55.[17]

Occasionally a faculty member voiced skepticism about the value of such heavy religious emphasis. "We have texts of scripture, prayers & singing every evening after supper before rising from the table, & a prayer meeting every other thing," wrote the wife of an Atlanta professor less pious than his colleagues. "Rather an excess of a good thing." Some alumni went further in their criticisms. "The requirements of the religious observances took up so much time as to leave little for the prescribed course of studies," said T. Thomas Fortune of his student days at Howard. E. Franklin Frazier thought that the content of missionary education was too much inspiration and too little information, while James Weldon Johnson believed that the main effect of the obligatory piety was "to put a premium on hypocrisy or, almost as bad, to substitute for religion a lazy and stupid conformity."[18]

A corollary of the middle-class piety that pervaded freedmen's schools was a rigid Victorian code of behavior. Liquor and tobacco were universally proscribed, with expulsion a frequent penalty for violation. Most colleges had rules similar to those of Fisk, which prohibited "profanity, card playing, betting, gambling, dancing, and whatever is immoral or opposed to true culture." Since 22 of the 29 missionary colleges were co-educational (and the remainder included two pairs of coordinate colleges), relations between the sexes were a central disciplinary concern of college authorities. The rules at Howard and Atlanta Universities were typical. Students at Howard were forbidden "to take rides, or walks, correspond, or engage in out-of-door games, with those of the other sex without permission from the proper authority." All letters coming to the girls' dormitory were subject to inspection by the matron. A boy who wished to visit a girl in her dorm-

[17] *AM*, XLV (Feb. 1891), 74 (Sept. 1891), 320-21, XLI (Nov. 1887), 318; *ZH*, Nov. 28, 1885; *HMM*, VIII (July 1886), 165.

[18] Julia Rollins Holt to "My Darling Burtie," Mar. 15, 1875, Holt-Messner Papers, Schlesinger Library, Radcliffe College; Fortune quoted in Emma Lou Thornbrough, *T. Thomas Fortune: Militant Journalist*, Chicago, 1972, pp. 25-26; E. Franklin Frazier, "A Note on Negro Education," *Opportunity*, II (Mar. 1924), 75-77; James Weldon Johnson, *Along This Way*, New York, 1933, pp. 80-81.

itory at Atlanta University had to present a written application, countersigned by the president or dean, to the matron before he was allowed to spend a maximum of 20 minutes in the parlor with the girl.[19]

Missionary educators justified these rules on the ground that they "are not more rigorous than the moral law; not more radical than is righteousness. . . . Christianity teaches that the body is a temple for the indwelling of the spirit, and that this temple must not be defiled." But while the regulations were intended to foster the development of Christian character, in practice they often encouraged the development of spying by faculty and students on each other, petty harassment, hypocrisy, and ingenious methods of evasion. James Weldon Johnson considered many of the rules during his student days at Atlanta University "humiliating" and did his best to outflank them. He frequently played cards in the evening "with the shades drawn, hat over key-hole, crack under door chinked, and muffled voices." Much faculty time and energy were expended in efforts to enforce parietal rules and to cope with the consequent student unrest.[20]

The inculcation of piety, morality, discipline, and industry was of course not unique to black schools. The transmission of middle-class values has always been an important function of American education. Lawrence A. Cremin has shown that "piety, civility, and learning" in that order were the major goals of colonial education. In setting aside one section of each township to support schools, the Northwest Ordinance of 1787 declared that "religion, morality and knowledge being necessary to good government and the happiness of mankind, schools and the means of education shall forever be encouraged." The Massachusetts Commissioner of Education wrote in 1857 that an essential purpose of schooling was "by moral and religious instruction daily given" to "inculcate habits of regularity, punctuality, constancy and industry." A study of leading American educators of the nineteenth and early twentieth centuries concluded that no purpose "played a larger role in the thinking and practice of educators than character training" backed by "religious sanctions."[21]

Required religious observances and restrictive parietal regulations were the norm in white as well as black colleges. In the late nineteenth century the rise of the university with its emphasis on a liberalized curriculum was accompanied by some relaxation of these requirements.

---

[19] AM, XLVII (May 1893), 158; Rayford W. Logan, Howard University: The First Hundred Years, 1867-1967, New York, 1969, p. 102; Johnson, Along This Way, 68.
[20] AM, XLVII (May 1893), 158; Johnson, Along This Way, 77.
[21] Cremin, American Education: The Colonial Experience, 1607-1783, New York, 1970; Michael D. Katz, The Irony of Early School Reform: Educational Innovation in Mid-Nineteenth Century Massachusetts, Cambridge, Mass., 1968, p. 43; Merle Curti, The Social Ideas of American Educators, New York, 1935, p. 584.

But such relaxation came slowly if at all to small, church-related colleges. Some of them dropped the mandatory prayer meetings, reduced the amount of Bible study in the curriculum, and gave students more freedom to leave campus during daylight hours. But at most denominational colleges—white as well as black—the old rules remained pretty much unchanged until at least the 1920s. "The supreme object" of our schools, declared the Home Mission Society proudly in 1905, was "still soul culture, not merely intellectual training." Knowledge without morality, said the AMA, could never be a "power for good. . . . Integrity, veracity, purity, educated conscience do not come in the multiplication tables. . . . Religious education is needed."[22]

Colleges took seriously their function *in loco parentis*. And since missionary educators believed that slavery had turned black adults into grown-up children, they felt a special obligation to substitute the school for the home as a moral training ground. The president of Fisk described AMA colleges as homes "where teachers & students all live together and form a family," a system that gave the faculty "close & direct" influence over "young men who need to have their whole character and lives moulded anew." The president of Roger Williams University in Nashville wrote that "I have endeavored to be a father unto" the students. An alumnus of Atlanta University recalled that when he first arrived on campus the president welcomed him "as though he were adopting me into what was his large family." Many black leaders approved of this foster-home environment. "It will not do in the South to leave moral training to individual homes," wrote Du Bois in 1905, "since their homes are just recovering from the debauchery of slavery."[23]

What Booker T. Washington later called the gospel of the toothbrush was first taught in missionary schools. "The irregularity of their habits of life, their lack of knowledge of all that pertains to neatness in person and neatness in dress," wrote an AMA teacher, made it necessary to teach the freedmen "habits of cleanliness, neatness, and order." In 1884 an instructor at Talladega College (then essentially a grammar school with a small secondary enrollment) explained that all students "are taught personal cleanliness most thoroughly; their wardrobes are examined, and suitable clothing provided when it is needed.

---

[22] *HMM*, XXVII (Feb. 1905), 48-49; *AM*, LVII (Mar. 1904), 67-69; LX (Jan. 1906), 1-2, LXII (Sept. 1908), 196. See also Lawrence R. Veysey, *The Emergence of the American University*, Chicago, 1965, and John Barnard, *From Evangelism to Progressivism at Oberlin College, 1866-1917*, Columbus, Ohio, 1969.

[23] E. M. Cravath to Oliver O. Howard, Sept. 23, 1873, Howard Papers, Bowdoin College Library; *HMM*, x (Nov. 1888), 283; James Weldon Johnson, *The Autobiography of an Ex-Coloured Man*, Boston, 1912, pp. 60-61; Du Bois, "Atlanta University," in *From Servitude to Service*, 181.

Then comes the care of their rooms, which must be neat and tidy." The dining together of faculty and students provided an occasion for the missionaries to teach table manners. Alumni remembered these inter-racial meals as one of the most important experiences of their school years because, as one alumnus put it, "first of all it generated self-esteem; it set a high example in religious devotion; it was a practice three times a day in propriety of speech, in tidiness of person, in exer-cising courtesy."[24]

Since most of the missionary teachers were women, their relation-ship to students is best described as maternalism rather than paternal-ism. When James Weldon Johnson arrived at Atlanta University, he "found the matron even more motherly than the president was father-ly." To unmarried teachers the students sometimes became their sur-rogate families. One such teacher said proudly that her work was her husband and children. Several white teachers took black foster chil-dren into their homes and brought them up almost as their own children. A Baptist missionary who may have held the record for longevity of service (1863–1916) told Du Bois in 1907 that "my forty four years of work among the colored people of the South gives me the privilege of being a mother to them." Black people often reciprocated this sentiment; the Boston lawyer and civil rights leader Butler Wilson said that his race felt toward the AMA "as a man should toward his mother."[25]

Missionary maternalism was in some ways more important outside the schools than in them. Most students below the college level lived at home. It was "with heavy hearts" that teachers "oftentimes watch some of our scholars returning to their homes in the evening, for we know that there everything tends to overthrow the religious and moral teaching received during the day." Girls all too often went home to mothers who did not know the meaning of chastity, and "sometimes those most promising, those for whom we have entertained bright hopes for the future, fail us, and we are almost constrained to cry out, 'This is greater than I can bear.' "[26]

The mission societies became increasingly concerned about these

[24] Delia E. Emerson, in Isabel C. Barrows, ed., *First Mohonk Conference on the Negro Question*, Boston, 1890, pp. 60-61; *AM*, xxxix (Jan. 1885), 12; George A. Towns, "The Sources of the Tradition of Atlanta University," *Phylon*, iii (Sec-ond Quarter, 1942), 118, 122.

[25] Johnson, *Autobiography of an Ex-Coloured Man*, p. 61; Maria Waterbury, *Seven Years Among the Freedmen*, Chicago, 1890, p. 7; Helen Griffith, *Dauntless in Mississippi: The Life of Sarah A. Dickey, 1838-1904*, n.p., 1965, p. 94 and passim; Joanna P. Moore to Du Bois, Mar. 4, 1907, from the Du Bois Papers formerly in the custody of Herbert Aptheker, quoted with permission; address by Wilson published in *AM*, xxxvi (Oct. 1882), 294-96.

[26] *AM*, xli (Jan. 1887), 19-22.

"counteracting influences in the homes" that effaced "the good impressions of the school." Women teachers at first spent a great deal of time visiting their pupils' homes, instructing mothers in health care, sanitation, and chastity. But with the shift of emphasis to secondary schools and colleges in the 1870s, teachers had to spend more time on campus and the societies appointed full-time home visitors in some cities. The Baptists and Methodists moved first to institutionalize this missionary maternalism. In 1880 several local Baptist women's groups affiliated to form the Women's Baptist Home Mission Society. The same year Elizabeth Rust and Jane Hartzell, wives of the current and future secretaries of the Methodist Freedmen's Aid Society, organized the Women's Home Missionary Society of the Methodist Episcopal Church as an auxiliary of the Freedmen's Aid Society. In 1883 the AMA formed its Bureau of Woman's Work, followed by the Woman's Executive Committee of the Presbyterian Board of Missions for the Freedmen in 1884.

The home visitors sponsored by these women's auxiliaries made daily rounds trying to extend the "home" atmosphere of the schools into the students' real homes. They did the same kind of work among freedmen as charity visitors and social workers did in northern cities. They read the Bible to the aged, tried to aid the sick and comfort the dying, and implored mothers and daughters to live upright lives and keep clean, comfortable homes for their families. They were on the front line of the missionary effort to inculcate middle-class values and Victorian morality in black communities.

But despite the work of home visitors, the mission societies' direct influence was limited pretty much to students and their families. Teachers lamented their inability to reach more than a fraction of the black population. Our schools, they declared in a variety of metaphors, are "like a beacon" sending out "a ray of light toward those sitting in the darkness" or "*oases* sparsely planted in the great desert." Those in the schools received sustenance and light, but the condition of the rest in the desert beyond the rays of the beacon was deplorable. Of the nearly seven million southern blacks in 1890, declared the head of the AMA's Woman's Bureau, "we think of the few thousands . . . that we have reached, and we must see that there is an immense work to be done among them yet."[27]

On the whole, however, the mission societies more often accentuated the positive than the negative. They congratulated themselves for uplifting at least some of the freedmen from "poverty, helplessness and vice" to "Christian civilization and culture." The problem facing mis-

[27] *AM*, XLV (Oct. 1891), 355; *Friends' Review*, Feb. 13, 1875; Barrows, ed., *First Mohonk Conference on the Negro Question*, pp. 62-63.

sionary educators at the time of emancipation, wrote Morehouse in 1888, was "how to bring the lilies of the Christian graces out of the mire of semi-barbaric and servile degradation." Those who "regarded the negroes as essentially an inferior race doubted the solution. But who among us today doubts it?" A Methodist educator pronounced freedmen's education "the grandest success ever achieved by our Church," while the secretary of the Presbyterian Board of Missions for Freedmen considered it "a modern miracle" achieved "very largely by the efforts of the Christian men and women who have gone south to preach and teach."[28]

In fact, some abolitionists wondered if the missionaries might have been *too* successful in molding the black talented tenth in their own image. A third-generation abolitionist who attended the Atlanta University commencement in 1905 questioned whether the graduates "should have life made [so] much more serious to them than it [is] to others," though she was aware of "the greater difficulties they will meet than other young people, and the need they will have for a Puritan ability to endure hardness." Secretary Harlan Paul Douglass wrote in 1909 that he found in many black alumni of AMA schools "a gravity of manner, a sobriety of expression, a restraint of religious utterances which I think overdoes the matter." The traditional warmth and spontaneity of black religion were lacking. "In this particular our brother has ceased to be a negro and has become a mere Congregationalist. It has been a change for the worse."[29]

In his book *The Mis-Education of the Negro* (1933), Carter G. Woodson indicted the mission societies for giving blacks a white-oriented education unsuited to their needs. Founder of the Association for the Study of Negro Life and History and of *The Journal of Negro History*, Woodson stressed the African cultural heritage of black Americans and the need for Negro education to inculcate race pride. The missionary colleges, he said, had ignored the black man's heritage, constructed a curriculum centered on European languages and history, and imposed white middle-class values on the black elite, producing graduates who "do not like to hear such expressions as 'Negro literature,' 'Negro poetry,' 'African art,' or 'thinking black.'" The chief shortcoming of missionary education, he asserted, was that "it has been largely imitation" of white education "resulting in the enslavement of

---

[28] *HMM*, x (Nov. 1888), 300-301; *New England Methodist*, II (July 1881), 8; *Church at Home and Abroad*, VIII (Dec. 1890), 529.

[29] Mary White Ovington to W. E. B. Du Bois, June 27, 1905, from the Du Bois Papers formerly in the custody of Herbert Aptheker, quoted with permission; Douglass, *Christian Reconstruction in the South*, Boston, 1909, p. 379.

[the Negro's] mind." It sought to "transform the Negroes, not to develop them."[30]

These are legitimate criticisms. The goal of missionary education *was* a one-way acculturation of black people to "white" values and institutions. Because they wanted to prove the Negro equal to the Caucasian, the missionaries worked to make him just like the white man. Despite occasional references by romantic racialists to the special contributions black people could make to American culture, these contributions (except the spirituals) were ignored or even suppressed in missionary schools—in part because the educators feared that black differences would be branded black inferiority. Thus Fisk University's music department concentrated on classical European music, encouraged students to join the "Mozart Musical Society," and refused to allow them to play ragtime on school pianos. It was not from Fisk but from the black belt and the vice districts of southern cities that blues and jazz emerged. Few courses in black history were offered in Negro colleges before World War I. The image of Africa imparted to black students was often one of a benighted continent in need of Christianity and Westernization.[31]

On the other hand, several graduates of mission schools used their training to preserve and promote black culture, not to repudiate or ignore it. One needs only to cite the contributions of James Weldon Johnson, Langston Hughes, Zora Neale Hurston, W. E. B. Du Bois, and Woodson himself (a Berea graduate) to make this point. And although the number of Negroes in missionary schools was relatively small, an extraordinary proportion of the twentieth-century leaders of civil rights movements, black community organizations, and the church were educated in these schools. From Du Bois, Johnson, Ida Wells-Barnett, and Walter White to A. Philip Randolph, James Farmer, Thurgood Marshall, and Martin Luther King, these leaders have laid the groundwork for most of the progress toward racial justice in this century.[32]

The testimony of black alumni to the value of their education is important. Du Bois was unhappy with the heavy religious emphasis of

[30] Woodson, *The Mis-Education of the Negro*, Washington, 1933, pp. 5-6, 17, 19, 134.

[31] Joe M. Richardson, "History of Fisk University," unpublished ms. cited with the author's permission, p. 129; John Hope Franklin, "Courses Concerning the Negro in Negro Colleges," *Quarterly Review of Higher Education Among Negroes*, VIII (July 1940), 138-44.

[32] See Richard Bardolph, *The Negro Vanguard*, New York, 1959, esp. p. 188: "The importance of these New England heirs of the old Puritan-Abolitionist tradition in the molding of Negro leadership over several decades can scarcely be exaggerated."

missionary schools and contemptuous of the textbook on "Christian Evidences" he was compelled to memorize at Fisk. On the other hand, President Erastus M. Cravath's course in moral philosophy "opened vistas" in Du Bois's mind and "made me determine to go further in this probing for truth. Eventually it landed me squarely in the arms of William James of Harvard." Du Bois considered his other teachers at Fisk "excellent and earnest. . . . I did not find better teachers at Harvard, but teachers better known." He also praised Fisk's music program and the Mozart Society, which "did great things for my education. . . . No student ever left Fisk without a deep and abiding appreciation of real music." Looking back on the freedmen's education movement, Du Bois thought it the "finest thing in American history." The missionary teachers "came not to keep the Negroes in their place, but to raise them out of the defilement of the places where slavery had wallowed them. The colleges they founded were social settlements; homes where the best of the sons of the freedmen came in close and sympathetic touch with the best traditions of New England. . . . In educational power it was supreme."[33]

The distinguished sociologist Charles S. Johnson, a graduate of Virginia Union who in 1947 became the first black president of Fisk, wrote in an unpublished autobiography that his New England teachers had opened "a new world" to him. "Here were good men who thought it no sacrifice to devote their lives completely to the fashioning of Negro youth" in "a tradition that was one of the richest and most mature in America." In his 1938 study of *The Negro College Graduate*, Johnson had a good word for the piety and paternalism of mission schools. "No less stern rectitude and concern," he wrote, "could have broken the grip of habits adjusted to a now out-moded life of irresponsibility, and reshaped them to a new and more serious purpose." James Weldon Johnson testified that "in spite of petty regulations and a puritanical zeal," Atlanta University "was an excellent school. . . . The breadth of the social values that it carried out practically was, perhaps, unequaled. . . . For me there was probably no better school in the United States." Walter White, Johnson's successor as secretary of the NAACP and also an Atlanta alumnus, wrote in his autobiography that the "selfless devotion" of his New England teachers "saved me from the defeatist belief that all whites are evil and bigoted." And Mary McLeod Bethune, a graduate of the Presbyterians' Scotia Seminary, wrote that "I can never doubt the sincerity and wholehearted-

33 Du Bois, *Dusk of Dawn: An Essay Toward an Autobiography of a Race Concept*, New York, 1940, pp. 33, 184; *The Autobiography of W. E. B. Du Bois: A Soliloquy on Viewing My Life from the Last Decade of Its First Century*, New York, 1968, p. 123; Du Bois, *The Souls of Black Folk*, New York, 1903, p. 100.

ness of some white people, when I remember my experience with those beloved, consecrated teachers who took so much time and patience with me when patience and tolerance were needed."[34]

Such testimony suggests that the missionaries did indeed instill neo-Puritan ideals in their best students. But what of E. Franklin Frazier's thesis that the missionary colleges were nurseries of the black bourgeoisie, whose imitative customs, crass materialism, conspicuous consumption, and empty achievements Frazier satirized so sharply? Frazier's treatment of this question was ambivalent. In effect he distinguished between two types of bourgeois values. The first included the "ideals of Puritan morality" and "the Yankee virtues of industry and thrift." These were the values of the first generation or two of missionary educators, and though Frazier criticized their emphasis on "inspiration" at the expense of "information" he admired their "humanity and idealism." But with the decline of the missionary impulse, the replacement of white teachers with black, the northward migration and urbanization of Negroes after 1915, and the consequent secularization of black middle-class values, the colleges underwent a change of goals "from the making of men to the making of money-makers." Middle-class "respectability became less a question of morals and manners and more a matter of the external marks of a high standard of living." Greek-letter societies, dances, and card-parties replaced chapel services and prayer meetings as the social centers of campus. Students and faculty were no longer concerned with the state of their souls or their duty to society but with "social status and economic security."[35]

This contrast between the heroic age of missionary idealism and the later era of black Babbittry is a major theme in the recollections of several black scholars who graduated from college during the missionary era (which came to an end in the decade before World War I). A black educator writing in 1939 praised the "great old New Englanders who wrought miracles upon and with crude Negro youths. . . . There is something bordering on holiness in the old Fisk and the old Atlanta University where great men and women joined with God in man-making." Their achievements were all the more impressive in contrast with the "pathetically empty and shallow, and tragically narrow and cowardly" nature of Negro education in the post-missionary era. Kelly Mil-

[34] Charles S. Johnson, "A Spiritual Autobiography," quoted in Ralph L. Pearson, "Charles S. Johnson: The Urban League Years. A Study of Race Leadership," Ph.D. Dissertation, Johns Hopkins Univ., 1970, pp. 38-39 (I am indebted to Professor Nancy J. Weiss for this reference); Johnson, *The Negro College Graduate*, Chapel Hill, 1938, pp. 280, 286-87; James Weldon Johnson, *Along This Way*, 83-84; Walter White, *A Man Called White*, New York, 1948, p. 27; Bethune quoted in Edwin R. Embree, *13 Against the Odds*, New York, 1944, p. 14.

[35] Frazier, *Black Bourgeoisie*, Collier Books ed., New York, 1962, pp. 56-57, 71-76.

ler, a graduate of Howard and a professor and dean there for more than 40 years, lauded the missionary teachers who came out of the abolitionist tradition and "touched the lethargic faculties of the first generation of Negro college youth, as it were with a live coal of fire." But these saints passed from the scene and "left no successors." The northern teachers had been "indoctrinated in the Puritan cult which believed that character could be inspired only through religious consecration. . . . As they began to withdraw, this influence began to wane. The Negro colleges were shifted from a Puritan to a pagan basis." Writing in 1933, Miller deplored this change. "Painful observation convinces us that the later crop of college output falls lamentably short of their elder brothers. . . . The inducing process was cut short before the induction had become permanently effective."[36]

To some modern readers, Miller's words may prove only that the missionaries enslaved a generation of black leaders in a new intellectual bondage. The paternalism and deculturization that Miller and his black contemporaries praised are now regarded in many quarters as negative educational achievements, a form of cultural genocide. Several recent studies of American education have been critical of its efforts to impose a straitjacket of middle-class values on lower-class children, white or black, for whom many of these values are alien and useless if not harmful. The schools, in this interpretation, have been instruments of social control to keep the masses in line and perpetuate the class structure by the inculcation of capitalist values and the socialization of children to a soul-deadening discipline. The missionaries' belief that hard work, thrift, piety, and respectability would win prosperity and respect for the Negro is now viewed by some as at best naive and patronizing, at worst reactionary and racist.[37]

It is true that the missionaries socialized their students in the values of capitalism. But their purpose was not to keep the poor content in

[36] Lewis K. McMillan, "Negro Higher Education as I Have Known It," *Journal of Negro Education*, VIII (Jan. 1939), 1-12; Miller, "The Higher Education of the Negro Is at the Crossroads," *Educational Review*, LXXII (Dec. 1926), 273-74, and "The Past, Present and Future of the Negro College," *Journal of Negro Education*, II (July 1933), 413-14.

[37] See especially Michael B. Katz, *The Irony of Early School Reform*; Katz, *Class, Bureaucracy, and Schools: The Illusion of Educational Change in America*, New York, 1971; Colin Greer, *The Great School Legend: A Revisionist Interpretation of American Public Education*, New York, 1971; Joel Spring, *Education and the Rise of the Corporate State*, Boston, 1972; James D. Loerner, *Who Controls American Education?* Boston, 1968. For the black rebellion against "white" values, see Nathan Hare, *The Black Anglo-Saxons*, New York, 1965; Philip Mason, "The Revolt Against Western Values," in John Hope Franklin, ed., *Color and Race*, Boston, 1968; and several articles over the past few years in *The Black Scholar*.

their humble station; rather, it was to lift them into the middle class. Of course social stability was one of the goals of missionary education, but for the missionaries social *stability* was synonymous with social *mobility*. They did not want to change the system, but to give blacks a chance to participate more fully in it. Education was the great leveler, and it leveled upward. The function of the school, as the missionary educators viewed it, was to equip its graduates with both the character and skills necessary for a useful Christian life and for upward mobility in a competitive, capitalist, democratic society.

It is also true that the missionaries believed in the superiority of Western Christian culture and thought all men would be better off when they had assimilated it. Yet those who have described this attitude as racism are confusing their terms. Most of the northern educators were not racists, at least not consciously; they were *culturalists*. As one of them put it, "we are not indebted to our whiteness for our civilization, but to Christianity." They "proceeded upon the theory," explained Morehouse, "that the black man has essentially the same nature and endowments as the white man" and "that it is the duty of the race that has attained to the highest degree of civilization to help its unfortunate brothers onward and upward."[38] In this faith that blacks were capable of cultural assimilation as equals, the missionaries departed radically from the established wisdom of the age.

It is of course arguable that cultural paternalism and racism are the same thing. But such a notion would have been foreign to the champions of both racial equality and white supremacy a century ago. The Mississippi demagogue James K. Vardaman spoke more truly than he realized when he denounced the missionaries with the words: "What the North is sending South is not money, but dynamite; this education is ruining our Negroes. They're demanding equality." It was no accident that so many black leaders of twentieth-century civil rights movements graduated from missionary schools. Although the *means* of missionary education were often paternalistic, its *ends* were egalitarian, and in the final analysis the ends proved more important than the means. While the missionaries looked upon the first generation of freedmen as children, they expected these children to grow into adults. At its best, missionary paternalism involved warm human relationships that were egalitarian in their impact. Perhaps the best way to illustrate this is to quote a letter written in 1886 by a black man to his former teacher, a white abolitionist who had helped him through

---

[38] *The Friend*, Jan. 19, 1901, quoted in Philip S. Benjamin, "The Philadelphia Quakers in the Industrial Age, 1865-1920," p. 229, unpublished ms. cited with permission of the author; Morehouse quoted in Lewis G. Jordan, *Negro Baptist History, U.S.A., 1750-1930*, Nashville, 1930, p. 296.

Howard University. Addressing his mentor as "Father," the black man recalled "with great pleasure the night [20 years earlier] that you invited me to your room . . . and gave me such encouraging words about study, and when leaving I said good night—but you extended me your hand and I said I will see you in the morning but you still held out your hand and said good night a second time, and took my hand. You do not know what tender love it kindled in my heart towards you at that moment. And to-day I love you and my mother with parental tenderness."[39]

[39] Vardaman quoted in Ray Stannard Baker, *Following the Color Line*, New York, 1908, p. 247; Simon P. Smith to Edward F. Williams, Sept. 7, 1886, Williams Papers, Amistad Research Center, Dillard University.

Chapter Twelve

Detour or Mainstream? The Curriculum of Missionary Schools

The missionary educators brought south the academic tradition as well as cultural values in which they had been reared. Graduates of New England-type academies and Protestant colleges, they tried to reproduce in black schools the curriculum they had known as students and teachers in the North, from the three R's to Latin and Greek. This attempt to plant the New England college in the South was ridiculed by critics from both races. The anecdote about the black student who asked her roommate, "Mandy, is yo' did yo' Greek yit?" never failed to get a laugh. The story of the Negro college graduate who sat in his tumble-down cabin reading French while his property went to seed was a staple in Booker T. Washington's repertory. An historian of Hampton Institute paid homage to the "generous motives" and "sincerity" of missionary teachers, but considered their effort to establish a New England curriculum in the black belt as quixotic "as if they had persisted in planting winter-wheat in the cotton belt." Other white critics spoke contemptuously of the "misguided statesmanship and philanthropy" that offered courses in Latin and Greek to people who needed "the practical training that would teach them how to mend a mule harness." The liberal arts curriculum "wholly disregarded . . . the aptitude and capabilities and needs of the Negro" by aiming "to bring the race per saltum to the same plane with their former masters and realize the theory of social and political equality."[1]

These critics, of course, favored the program of industrial education pioneered by Samuel C. Armstrong at Hampton and carried on by his protégé Booker T. Washington at Tuskegee. Some modern historians, on the other hand, have condemned the missionaries' alleged retreat from their original academic curriculum to vocational training. After the end of Reconstruction, according to this thesis, philanthropists worked out an educational compromise by which southern whites agreed to support Negro education in return for a northern concession

[1] Francis G. Peabody, *Education for Life: The Story of Hampton Institute*, Garden City, 1918, pp. 290-91; *Journal of Social Science*, XXXIV (1896), 75-76; Albert Shaw in *Review of Reviews*, XX (Aug. 1899), 131-32; J. L. M. Curry, quoted in Dwight O. W. Holmes, *The Evolution of the Negro College*, New York, 1934, pp. 44-45.

that it should be limited largely to elementary and industrial training. This concept of "special" schooling marked the beginning of a "great detour" in black education that served the ends of white supremacy. As agents of the Slater Fund from 1882 to 1903, Atticus G. Haygood and Jabez L. M. Curry defined the terms of this compromise by favoring industrial training in their grants to black schools. The creation of the Southern Education Board in 1901 ratified the bargain by institutionalizing a system that channeled northern philanthropy to industrial schools and left black colleges to limp along on a pittance. By 1900, therefore, missionary schooling had become "consistent with the prevailing Southern philosophy. . . . Northern educators had . . . decided to sell the idea of Negro education to white Southerners by sacrificing the principle of racial equality."[2]

Both this argument and the opposing indictment of missionary educators for trying to teach Greek to a people illiterate in English contain grains of truth. But like most half-truths, they obscure more than they reveal. Missionary colleges did try to offer a New England curriculum, and many teachers did see this curriculum as the path to racial equality. In practice, however, the schools tailored their offerings to fit students' needs and preparation. But this does not mean that they detoured onto a second-class road. Most of them continued on the main road toward equal education despite obstacles that made the going rough. To chart the course of Negro education in the half-century after the Civil War, we will examine first the scope of academic programs in the schools and then describe the rise and impact of the industrial education movement.

Missionary educators had few illusions about their "universities," which they compared to infants who were christened with adult names even though many years must pass before they grew up to the status conferred by these names. And while it is true that within a few years of emancipation several former slaves were studying Latin and Greek, this was not so absurd as it seemed to some observers. The classical languages formed the core of the liberal arts curriculum in the nineteenth century; missionary educators intended a B.A. from a black college to mean as much as a B.A. from a white school. They quoted John

---

2 Henry Allen Bullock, *A History of Negro Education in the South from 1619 to the Present*, Cambridge, Mass., 1967, chaps. 3-6, quotations from pp. 91, 93. See also Louis R. Harlan, *Separate and Unequal: Public School Campaigns and Racism in the Southern Seaboard States, 1901-1915*, Chapel Hill, 1958, pp. 7-8, 75-101; Richard M. Drake, "Freedmen's Aid Societies and Sectional Compromise," *Journal of Southern History*, XXIX (1963), 175-86; and Kenneth James King, *Pan-Africanism and Education: A Study of Race Philanthropy and Education in the Southern States of America and East Africa*, London, 1971, chaps. 1-2.

C. Calhoun's sneering remark, "Show me a negro who knows Greek syntax and I will then believe that he is a human being and should be treated like a man." The missionaries meant to train men who would be treated like men.

But while the college catalogues listed courses in philosophy, rhetoric, mathematics, and the sciences as well as Latin and Greek, these schools concentrated for a long time mainly on the three R's. Rather than trying to impose a top-heavy New England curriculum on a people incapable of absorbing it, the missionaries slowly built an educational pyramid whose apex rested on a broad base. A synopsis of enrollment statistics will underscore this point. In 1880 only 9 of 21 institutions bearing the name of college or university actually offered college degrees. By 1895 this number had risen to 20, but fewer than 750 of their 9,100 students were enrolled in college classes. Of the remainder about 5,600 were in primary and grammar grades and 2,750 were studying at the secondary level. Twenty years later, fewer than 2,000 of the 12,900 students in 27 colleges and universities founded by the mission societies were studying college subjects. Even the best black schools enrolled only a handful of students at the college level for many years. Fewer than 5 percent of Atlanta University's students studied college subjects in the school's first 25 years. As late as 1908 only 15 percent of the students at Atlanta, 22 percent at Fisk, and 27 percent at Howard were in college classes (another 35 percent at Howard were in the law and medical schools). Talladega and Tougaloo did not enroll their first college students until 1892 and 1897, a quarter-century after they were chartered as colleges. Atlanta Baptist College (later renamed Morehouse) awarded its first B.A. in 1897, Spelman in 1901. As one abolitionist educator wrote, these figures showed that the missionary colleges "have served conditions rather than theories."[3]

[3] Quotation and the 1908 figures for Atlanta, Fisk, and Howard from Harlan Paul Douglass, *Christian Reconstruction in the South*, Boston, 1909, pp. 240-41. See also Holmes, *Evolution of the Negro College*, pp. 98-99, and W. E. B. Du Bois, *The College-Bred Negro*, Atlanta Univ. Publication no. 5, Atlanta, 1900, p. 14. The careful reader may note some apparent discrepancies between the number of students listed in Appendix B and the figures cited in the text. This is because three of the institutions in the table, Meharry Medical College, Gammon Theological Seminary, and Richmond Theological Seminary, were not colleges and did not require a college degree for admission. Some of the students in these schools were college graduates or were taking college courses in affiliated institutions but others were not—hence the apparent discrepancy. Several of the students taking professional courses at other colleges were also not taking college courses—college training was not then necessary for graduation from law or medical school. Lincoln University's students are included among the 750 college students cited in the text, but Lincoln is not included in the table because it was not a "missionary" college in the same sense as were those founded or sustained by the

The practice of combining preparatory and college divisions in the same school was not unique to black colleges. Before the spread of public high schools throughout the North, most white colleges had included secondary grades. After 1870 the better northern colleges dropped these grades as the high schools took over much of their function. But as late as 1900 nearly half of the students in land-grant colleges were taking preparatory rather than college courses, and in Alabama, to cite only one example of a southern state, all white colleges except the state university still enrolled preparatory classes.[4]

But most black colleges contained primary as well as secondary grades for several decades and enrolled a much smaller percentage of students in college courses than did contemporary white institutions. The poor quality of black public education and the virtual absence of public high schools for Negroes in the South before 1900 forced the missionary colleges to prepare their own students in the lower grades. Only 46 black public schools offered courses beyond the 8th grade in 1900; five states provided no high school education for Negroes at all. In 1909, only 6,443 southern blacks were in public high schools compared with 142,837 whites. Not until 1916 did the number of black secondary students in public schools exceed those in private schools, and most of the former were not in four-year programs. In that year the number of three- and four-year public high schools for Negroes in the entire South was 65, compared with 85 secondary schools founded or supported by the northern white Protestant mission societies. North Carolina and Louisiana had no public high schools for blacks; Atlanta did not build a four-year black high school until 1924.[5]

By 1880 most of the missionary schools had organized themselves in the familiar divisions of primary (grades 1–4 or 1–5), intermediate or grammar (grades 5–8 or 6–8), secondary, and college. The secondary division was divided into two basic classifications: a three- or four-year college preparatory course and a two- to four-year normal course. About three-fourths of the secondary students took the normal course.

---

northern mission-education societies. Lincoln was founded before the Civil War as Ashmun Institute by the Old School Presbyterians and was governed by an independent board of trustees unconnected with the Presbyterian Board of Missions for the Freedmen.

[4] Frederick Rudolph, *The American College and University: A History*, New York, 1962, pp. 281-84; Frank Bowles and Frank A. DeCosta, *Between Two Worlds: A Profile of Negro Higher Education*, New York, 1971, p. 31.

[5] Earl Edgar Dawson, "The Negro Teacher in the South," M.A. Thesis, University of Iowa, 1931, pp. 47-48; Horace Bumstead, *Secondary Higher Education in the South for Whites and Negroes*, New York, 1910, pp. 4, 8, 9; Thomas Jesse Jones, ed., *Negro Education: A Study of the Private and Higher Schools for the Colored People in the United States*, 2 vols., Washington, 1917, I, 41-42.

By 1910 all secondary programs were four years and a few black colleges had upgraded their teacher-training course to a two- to four-year college program leading to a diploma or a Bachelor of Pedagogy degree. Some schools offered theological training ranging from simple Bible courses to a full-fledged B.D. program requiring Greek and Hebrew. Howard University had a law school, and small or short-lived law departments also existed at five other black colleges. The Howard University Medical School and the Meharry Medical College offered degrees in dentistry and pharmacy as well as medicine, and smaller medical schools functioned for a time at three other black colleges. A college education was not a prerequisite for admission to the professional schools (in 1910 Howard began requiring one year of college for entering medical students), though the most advanced theological course leading to the B.D. required previous college training.[6]

The three R's, geography, and American history dominated the course of study in the elementary and grammar grades. The college preparatory curriculum included Latin, Greek, mathematics, rhetoric, literature, and a few science courses, while the normal curriculum dropped Greek (and in most cases Latin) and emphasized geography, civics, and basic English as well as teaching methods. The college curriculum varied slightly at different institutions, but in general the "classical" course leading to the B.A. required Latin, Greek, mathematics, science, philosophy, and in a few cases one modern language. Some colleges also offered a "Science" or "English" curriculum leading to a B.S., B.Lit., or B.Phil., which omitted Greek (and in rare cases Latin) but after 1890 usually required one modern language. Most students took the B.A. program. W. E. B. Du Bois's survey of 10 representative Negro colleges in 1899 found that, on the average, their B.A. curriculum consisted of 38 percent ancient languages, 15 percent mathematics, 15 percent natural sciences, 17 percent "Political Science, History, and Philosophy," with the remaining 15 percent divided between English (usually including rhetoric) and modern languages. Nearly all colleges incorporated Bible study into this program in some fashion.[7]

While the curriculum of black colleges was similar to that of northern Protestant colleges, the quality of most black schools fell below the white average. Howard University and the colleges founded by the

[6] The information in this and the following paragraph is based on the annual reports of the mission societies and especially on an examination of 267 annual catalogues of 19 colleges covering the years from 1869 to 1917. I am indebted to Timothy Bird for allowing me to use his superb collection of black college catalogues for this period.

[7] Calculated from Du Bois, *College-Bred Negro*, 28.

American Missionary Association, especially Fisk and Atlanta, deserved their reputations as the best institutions; the schools of the northern Baptist, Methodist, and Presbyterian societies generally ranked a notch or two lower; the institutions supported by the black denominations and the "colored" land grant colleges belonged with two or three exceptions near the bottom of the list. A college degree from the latter meant little more and sometimes less than a diploma from the average northern high school. On the other hand, while the level of work in the top black colleges was not up to the best northern standards it was equal to that of many southern white colleges. A southern white educator admitted in 1889 that students at Atlanta University sometimes scored higher on state examinations for teaching permits than students at the University of Georgia. W. E. B. Du Bois entered Harvard as a junior after graduating from Fisk in 1888; William Pickens graduated from Talladega in 1902 and entered the junior class at Yale; several Atlanta University graduates in the early 1900s earned B.A.'s from northern colleges after one additional year of study; E. Franklin Frazier was accepted for graduate study at Clark University (Worcester, Mass.) in 1919 with a B.A. from Howard.[8]

The traditional curriculum with its emphasis on ancient languages and the rote-recitation method of instruction tended to persist longer in black than in northern white colleges. The last third of the nineteenth century saw the beginnings of a movement in American higher education away from the classical languages, moral philosophy, and theology toward a liberalized curriculum with greater scope for the physical and social sciences. Lectures, seminars, the elective system, and open-minded questioning of ancient dogmas began to replace the old methods of rote learning. These changes percolated down from the major universities and came last to small, church-related colleges. Most of the black schools were too poor to afford the faculties or libraries necessary for many of the new courses even if they had wanted to offer them. Trained in the old tradition, missionary educators often distrusted the secular orientation of the new approach with its loosening of control over the moral as well as mental development of students. Black colleges also continued to strive for the status traditionally associated with classical education; they still thought it important

---

[8] This assessment of the quality of black colleges is based on data and evaluations in Du Bois, *College-Bred Negro*, 17; Du Bois and August G. Dill, *The College-Bred Negro American*, Atlanta University Publication no. 15, Atlanta, 1910, p. 22; Du Bois, "Atlanta University," in *From Servitude to Service*, Boston, 1905, p. 172; and Jones, ed., *Negro Education*, passim, esp. I, 58-59. The southern educator who compared the graduates of Atlanta University to those of the University of Georgia was J. A. Clark, a professor at Emory University, in a pamphlet titled *The Races and Their Future*, cited in *Independent*, Mar. 21, 1889.

to meet John C. Calhoun's challenge to prove the Negro's manhood by demonstrating his ability to master Greek.[9]

Nevertheless the secular and progressive trends did not entirely by-pass black colleges. An increasing number of M.A.'s and even a few Ph.D.'s began in the 1890's to join the B.D.'s and D.D.'s alongside faculty names in the catalogues. At about the same time a few of the better black schools modernized their science offerings and introduced new courses in the social sciences. Some of the larger institutions relaxed the prescribed curriculum and offered a modest range of electives. By 1915 more than a third of the black colleges allowed students to substitute German or French for Greek in the B.A. program. Between 1899 and 1909 the proportion of class hours devoted to ancient languages dropped from 38 to 20 percent, mathematics declined from 15 to 11 percent, natural sciences remained about the same (16 percent), English and modern languages increased from 15 to 21 percent, social sciences and philosophy rose from 17 to 25 percent, with "miscellaneous" (mostly Bible study) accounting for the remaining 7 percent in 1909.[10]

Several black colleges also emphasized social service to local communities in their academic programs. A Talladega instructor gave lectures on rents and contracts to students and nearby tenant farmers; Straight University operated a night school in bookkeeping and commercial law; Shaw University opened a night grammar school for working-class adults in 1899. Atlanta University established a kindergarten association in 1905, instituted a special course to train kindergarten teachers in 1912, and built a model playground on the campus in 1914. Atlanta also initiated sociological research on racial problems when President Horace Bumstead organized the Atlanta University Conference in 1896. Bumstead brought Du Bois to Atlanta the following year to carry on this program and to build up the college's social science offerings. At Fisk University George E. Haynes, one of the founders of the National Urban League, organized a department of

---

[9] For the changes in American higher education, see Lawrence R. Veysey, *The Emergence of the American University*, Chicago, 1965; Richard Hofstadter and Walter P. Metzger, *The Development of Academic Freedom in the United States*, New York, 1955, pp. 277-479; and R. Freeman Butts, *The College Charts Its Course*, New York, 1939, chap. 9-13. These studies tend to overemphasize the contrast between the old and the new. For an account of the sometimes painful adjustment of small colleges to the new order, see George E. Peterson, *The New England College in the Age of the University*, Amherst, 1964. Charles S. Johnson, *The Negro College Graduate*, Chapel Hill, 1938, pp. 272-74, discusses the time lag before changes in university curricula reached black colleges.

[10] This paragraph is based on an examination of 267 annual catalogues of 19 black colleges from 1869 to 1917, and on Du Bois and Dill, *The College-Bred Negro American*, 20-21.

social science in 1910 and began the first academic program to train black social workers.[11]

Thus despite the continuing religious emphasis and the partial survival of the traditional curriculum, some missionary schools were moving toward modernity. But one aspect of this movement—the increasing commitment to vocational training—provoked more controversy than any other issue in Negro education. Missionary educators became major protagonists in the great debate over academic versus industrial education.

"Industrial education" is a concept of great plasticity, capable of many meanings. Its origins lay in educational reforms that had nothing to do with race. Persistent misconceptions of industrial training as a unique form of second-class education for blacks, however, make necessary a review of these origins.

The early nineteenth century witnessed a ferment of educational reform in Europe. Johann Heinrich Pestalozzi, Phillip Emmanuel von Fellenberg, and their followers undertook to bring education closer to the everyday lives of students, to emphasize learning by doing rather than merely by reading, and to instruct pupils in manual trades. These ideas crossed the Atlantic with the industrial revolution and the wave of utopian romanticism in the 1820s and 1830s. At the same time, economic changes in the United States produced demands for a more utilitarian college curriculum and prompted the establishment of technical schools to keep pace with the need for specialized skills. The founding of Rensselaer Polytechnic Institute in 1824, the creation of the Lawrence and Sheffield scientific schools at Harvard and Yale in the 1840s, and the chartering of Massachusetts Institute of Technology in 1861 were followed by a rapid proliferation of technical schools after the Civil War. Many colleges introduced new courses in applied science, agronomy, and "the mechanic arts." The Morrill Act of 1862 authorized land-grant agricultural and mechanical colleges in every state, giving a boost to this movement.[12]

11 A. A. Safford to Erastus M. Cravath, Oct. 17, 1874, AMA Archives; John W. Blassingame, *Black New Orleans, 1860-1880*, Chicago, 1973, p. 129; *Twenty-Sixth Annual Catalog of the Officers and Students of Shaw University*, Raleigh, N.C., 1900; Clarence A. Bacote, *The Story of Atlanta University: A Century of Service, 1865-1965*, Atlanta, 1969, pp. 131-39, 153-54; Nancy J. Weiss, *The National Urban League, 1910-1940*, New York, 1974, pp. 74-75.

12 The best account of the historical context of black industrial education is August Meier, "The Beginning of Industrial Education in Negro Schools," *Midwest Journal*, VII (1955), 21-44. Other studies on which this paragraph has drawn are: Hugh M. Pollard, *Pioneers of Popular Education, 1760-1850*, London, 1956; Butts, *The College Charts Its Course*, chap. 8; Rudolph, *The American College and University*, chaps. 11-12; Earle D. Ross, *Democracy's College: The Land Grant*

A short-lived enthusiasm for "manual labor" colleges had also led to the founding of several such schools in the 1830s and to the grafting of the manual labor concept onto existing institutions. Associated with the reform movements of the decade, the manual labor schools included Oneida Institute, Knox College, and Oberlin College, all of them hotbeds of abolition. Students worked several hours a day on school farms or in carpentry, printing, or blacksmith shops. The purpose was to enable them to earn part of their expenses, teach the dignity of labor, instill habits of industry, and build character; the teaching of specific trades was a distinctly subordinate goal. The manual labor movement was something of a fad and soon died out. But many abolitionists had participated in it, and they revived the idea in southern schools they founded after the Civil War.[13]

By 1890 the successful example of a combined vocational and liberal arts program at Cornell University, the growth of technical and business schools, and the strengthening of the land-grant colleges by the second Morrill Act insured the success in higher education of what Cornell's president described as "our plan of Industrial Education and scientific instruction kept on equality in every respect with literary instruction."[14] At the same time, proponents of industrial training turned their attention to the public schools. The achievements of German and Russian trade schools and technical institutes helped inspire a crusade for manual training in American secondary education. Programs in wood- and metalworking, home economics, and other vocational subjects were introduced in urban high schools in the 1880s. The next decade saw the beginnings of agricultural courses in rural schools. Although traditionalists decried what they considered the cheapening of education to mere trades-training, the idea of combining academic and "practical" education had captured most leading educators by 1900. It fit perfectly with the "education for life" theme of progressive reformers, and it incorporated the Pestalozzian method of learning by doing into the progressive revolt against the classical curriculum. The industrial education movement reached its zenith in the decade before World War I. The National Society for the Promotion of Industrial Education was organized in 1906 to coordinate state programs and to

---

Movement in the Formative Stage, Ames, Iowa, 1942; and Oscar J. Chapman, "A Historical Study of Negro Land-Grant Colleges in Relationship with Their Social, Economic, Political, and Educational Background," Ph.D. Dissertation, Ohio State Univ., 1940, pp. 10-29.

[13] Elisabeth S. Peck, *Berea's First Century, 1855-1955*, Lexington, Ky., 1955, pp. 109-14; Robert Samuel Fletcher, *A History of Oberlin College from Its Foundation Through the Civil War*, 2 vols., Oberlin, 1943, I, chap. 5.

[14] Andrew Dickson White to Gerrit Smith, July 21, 1874, Smith Papers, Syracuse University Library.

lobby for federal aid; these efforts paid off with the passage of the Smith-Lever Act (1914) and the Smith-Hughes Act (1917) providing federal aid for agricultural, vocational, and home economics courses.[15]

Industrial education for Negroes was thus part of a general trend rather than an isolated enterprise. Of course there were differences of emphasis between the national movement to adapt education to a technology-based society and the narrower effort to train an emancipated people in the skills necessary to raise themselves by their bootstraps. And it is true that by the 1880s some educators and philanthropists had begun to see industrial education as something particularly applicable to blacks; this in turn provoked a counteraffirmation of the value of academic and higher education. These conflicting viewpoints formed the poles of a debate whose dialectics offer insights into the nature and problems of Negro education during this period.

Although the abolitionist missionaries who founded freedmen's schools were staunch defenders of higher education, some of them also pioneered early developments in industrial training. Drawing on their own experience, they saw no necessary conflict between the two. In their effort to inculcate the Protestant ethic, missionary teachers stressed the importance of work in practice as well as theory. Some of them sought to revive the manual labor idea of their own college days. Field Superintendent Joseph E. Roy of the AMA wrote in 1878 that the freedmen "need to be held to the Puritan doctrine of the dignity of labor. . . . The idea of our old Manual Labor Colleges has come around again under the new name, Industrial. It failed before; the freedmen bring a new element into the experiment."[16] More than half of the missionary colleges required boarding students to work at least an hour a day at the school farm, grounds, kitchen, or shops. Besides teaching the dignity of labor, this helped make these colleges one of the best bargains in American education. The average annual expense per student (including tuition, room, board, laundry, and books) at 19 colleges was $97 in the 1870s, dropping to $84 in the deflationary 1890s, and rising to $101 by 1910. Costs for nonboarding students averaged less than $20 during most of the period. Some students (especially those planning to enter the ministry) received scholarship support up

[15] Lawrence A. Cremin, *The Transformation of the School: Progressivism in American Education, 1876-1957*, New York, 1961, chap. 2; Berenice Fisher, *Industrial Education: American Ideals and Institutions*, Madison, Wis., 1967, pp. 83-124; Arthur G. Wirth, *Education in the Technological Society: The Vocational-Liberal Studies Controversy in the Early Twentieth Century*, Scranton, 1972; Marvin Lazerson, *Origins of the Urban School: Public Education in Massachusetts, 1870-1915*, Cambridge, 1971, chaps. 3-7; Sol Cohen, "The Industrial Education Movement, 1906-1917," *American Quarterly*, xx (1968), 95-110.

[16] Roy to Michael E. Strieby, Dec. 10, 1878, AMA Archives.

to $50 per year. Whether on scholarship or not, a student could often earn the balance of his expenses by working extra hours on campus and/or teaching in a rural public school for two or three months a year.[17]

Until the 1880s, industrial education at most mission schools consisted mainly of student work programs. But these programs planted the seeds of systematic vocational instruction. The AMA took the lead in this direction. Talladega and Atlanta offered limited training in horticulture and homemaking in the 1870s; Tougaloo, situated on a 500-acre farm, had more extensive programs in both agriculture and shop instruction. And though Hampton Institute had become independent of the AMA in 1872, the association applauded its development into the outstanding example of industrial education for Negroes.

Encouraged by Hampton's success, the trustees of the Slater Fund decided to concentrate their grants on industrial education. Perhaps more than anything else this caused several schools to initiate vocational programs in the 1880s. The readiness of some missionary educators to embrace industrial training may also have grown out of their desire to cultivate southern white support. By 1890 most of the black colleges and many of the secondary schools offered at least a smattering of vocational courses. Agriculture, building trades (especially carpentry), metalworking, and printing for boys, and home economics (then called "domestic science") for girls dominated the industrial curriculum. Normally these courses were offered in the secondary or grammar grades, and occasionally in college B.S. programs. Some B.A. students also took manual training courses, though usually as part of working their way through school.[18]

The main purpose of industrial education was the building of Christian character and self-discipline. While "the motive of our work is not to make carpenters, harness-makers, and machinists," explained the AMA in 1885, "nevertheless, while men live on earth, industry will be the handmaid of religion. . . . Missionary influences radiate from a carpenter's shop now as in the Lord's day." Though the freedmen espe-

[17] These expenses are calculated from the catalogues (which listed student costs) of the following colleges: Atlanta, Atlanta Baptist, Benedict, Bishop, Central Tennessee, Claflin, Clark, Howard, Knoxville, Leland, Morgan, Philander Smith, Roger Williams, Rust, Shaw, Straight, Tougaloo, Virginia Union, and Wiley.

[18] Meier, "The Beginning of Industrial Education," 29-44, and "The Vogue of Industrial Education," *Midwest Journal*, VII (1955), 241-66; Willard Range, *The Rise and Progress of Negro Colleges in Georgia, 1865-1949*, Athens, Ga., 1951, pp. 66-75; Frank K. Pool, "The Southern Negro in the Methodist Episcopal Church," Ph.D. Dissertation, Cornell University, 1939, pp. 94-102; *HMM*, VI (July 1884), 182-83; *AM*, XXXVII (Dec. 1883), 382, XXXIX (Feb. 1885), 51-53 (Nov. 1885), 304-309; *Report of the U.S. Commissioner of Education for the Year 1899-1900*, Washington, 1901, II, 2522-31.

cially needed the drilling in "orderliness and method" provided by industrial education, manual training should become part of everyone's education regardless of color or class. "A young man who can frame a school-house or make a table, a girl who can make a dress," wrote the AMA's field superintendent in 1892, "has gained in dignity and self-respect . . . and the same thought process which enabled them to do these things well will help materially in the study-room."[19]

In more direct economic terms, industrial education would train the artisans and farmers who formed the backbone of all stable, progressive communities. Without such a class of skilled workers, argued missionary educators, black people would never get out of economic bondage. While the race must have "the first quality of [higher] education in its preachers, professors, lawyers, doctors, journalists, scientists," declared the AMA, the masses needed vocational training to avoid being "forced back to be mere hewers of wood and drawers of water. . . . Not only should every calling be open to them, but they should be trained for every calling." Southern whites wanted to "monopolize the upper stratum of skilled labor" themselves, warned one missionary educator. Until the black man broke this monopoly, said another, until he became less often "a laborer, a porter, a waiter" and more often "a cabinet maker, a machinist, a watch maker" he would remain in "modified serfdom." Just as New England's greatness rested on her sturdy yeomen, skilled workers, and Yankee merchants, so must "educated carpenters, guilders, machinists, engineers, painters, draughtsmen, contractors, brokers, bankers, merchants and inventors [develop] among the negroes of the South. . . . With this state of affairs the chain gang and the plantation credit system must go, and crime and misery decrease."[20]

Black abolitionists voiced similar arguments. The antebellum Negro convention movement had repeatedly urged mechanical training for black youth. In the 1850s Frederick Douglass worked with Harriet Beecher Stowe on a projected industrial school for Negroes (which never materialized). Douglass continued after the war to support industrial education. "Get your sons into mechanic trades," he told blacks. The race needs "more to learn how to make a good living than to learn Latin and Greek." In 1892 Douglass delivered the commencement address at Tuskegee; three years later he praised the school as a "great and leading educational institution."[21]

19 *AM*, xxxix (Nov. 1885), 309-10, xl (Nov. 1886), 313, xlvi (Oct. 1892), 330-31.
20 *Ibid.*, xxxvi (Oct. 1882), 292-93, xxxviii (Nov. 1884), 338-40 (Dec. 1884), 376; *Sixteenth Annual Report FASME*, Cincinnati, 1883, pp. 15-18; *BET*, Feb. 13, 1884.
21 Meier, "The Beginning of Industrial Education," 24-28; Douglass, *Life and Times of Frederick Douglass*, New York, Collier Books ed., 1962, reprinted from

If industrial training was necessary to fit men for a range of skilled occupations, it was equally needed to prepare women for homemaking and practical nursing. In an 1885 editorial entitled "A Sanitary View of Industrial Education," the *American Missionary* cited improper diet, ignorance of hygiene, and inadequate medical care as major causes of the high black mortality rate. "To avert such evils from the coming generation is a part of the work of this Association." The women's auxiliaries of the mission societies established "model homes" on black campuses where teachers lived with women students and instructed them in nutrition, cooking, sewing, housekeeping, hygiene, sanitation, and nursing. From these activities grew courses in home economics and nursing to parallel the better-publicized agricultural and mechanical courses for male students. Several black leaders praised this work and urged even more attention to home economics. "I would have these girls taught to do accurately all domestic work, such as sweeping floors, dusting rooms, scrubbing, bedmaking, washing and ironing, mending and knitting . . . dress-making, millinery," wrote Alexander Crummell, one of the race's foremost clergymen and intellectuals. The AMA thought Crummell went too far in the direction of downgrading academic education, "which these Negro women need as much as any women in the world," but assured him that they were expanding their home economics offerings.[22]

Although enrollment in women's vocational programs continued to grow, many schools found in the 1890s that they could not afford the increasingly expensive equipment for men's shop courses. The 1893–1897 depression and the Slater Fund's new policy after 1892 of giving large grants to only a few schools (mainly Hampton and Tuskegee), instead of small subsidies to many, forced several institutions to curtail their industrial offerings. Increasing uncertainty about whether the primary purpose of industrial education should be to teach the dignity of labor or to prepare students for specific trades also weakened manual training programs at some schools. At the same time the provision of the 1890 Morrill Act requiring a prorated share of federal funds for black schools led to the founding of "Colored" A. & M. colleges that took over part of the vocational training once provided by missionary schools. By 1899 the industrial offerings for male students had been cut to the bone or eliminated at several black colleges.[23]

---

the rev. ed. of 1892, p. 283; Samuel R. Spencer, Jr., *Booker T. Washington and the Negro's Place in American Life*, Boston, 1955, p. 108.

[22] *AM*, XXXIX (Feb. 1885), 38-39, XLII (Apr. 1888), 105-107. See also *HMM*, VIII (June 1886), 129; *Church at Home and Abroad*, VI (Sept. 1889), 249-50; Pool, "The Southern Negro in the Methodist Episcopal Church," 102-108.

[23] Chapman, "Negro Land-Grant Colleges," 64-72; Meier, "Vogue of Industrial

But industrial education remained alive and well at other schools, including those like Berea, Talladega, and Claflin, which simultaneously offered a good college program and extensive vocational-agricultural training. As time went on, the missionary justification for industrial education evolved from the idea of instilling self-discipline or of training students for trades to a more general progressive concept of providing a well-rounded education. The Methodists explained that their schools tried not to let manual training "degenerate into the learning of a trade in the cheapest, shortest, and most imitative way" but rather to combine "practical work" with "a fine literary education" to prepare students "for the all-around positions of life." The AMA maintained that industrial courses "must ascend from mere hand techniques to engineering and industrial planning and the application of scientific and technical knowledge to the problems of work and wages."[24]

Around 1900, missionary educators began trying to apply these ideas in practice. One problem with certain manual-training courses such as harness making, wheel-wrighting, blacksmithing, and the like was their obsolescence in a modern industrial economy. Realizing this, several schools instituted courses in architecture and rudimentary civil engineering. Fisk established a "Department of Applied Science" in 1906 which, in the words of Fisk's president, "does not expect to make farmers, carpenters, masons, laundrywomen, dressmakers of its college graduates" but to teach them "the underlying principles of chemistry and physics as applied to modern industry and agriculture."[25] In his inaugural address as president of Howard in 1907, Wilbur P. Thirkield said that "practical scientific and industrial training" had become mandatory in "progressive" universities. "To every race it gives broad basis for industrial freedom and foundation for permanent life and progress. In a generation it has lifted Germany to economic and industrial supremacy in Europe." Thirkield made the modernization of Howard's curriculum his top priority. He raised funds for a science and engineering building and for new courses in physics and mechanics. The engineering program began in 1910, and until 1949, when Tuskegee opened an engineering department, Howard was the only black school to offer degrees in this vital discipline.[26] Thus it was Fisk and Howard

---

Education," 261-62; *Report of the U.S. Commissioner of Education for 1899-1900*, pp. 2522-31.

24 *NWCA*, Feb. 13, 1901; AMA quoted in Bacote, *The Story of Atlanta University*, 179.

25 Douglass, *Christian Reconstruction*, 250-51, 289-91; *AM*, LVI (Jan. 1902), 22, LX (Sept. 1906), 203.

26 Thirkield, "The Meaning and Mission of Education," *Howard University*

rather than Hampton or Tuskegee that first provided modern scientific and technical education for Negroes.

The notion of industrial education as a special kind of training for a backward race is associated mainly with Hampton and Tuskegee. The Hampton idea was the creation of Samuel C. Armstrong, one of the most successful educational salesmen in American history. Armstrong had spent his first 21 years in Hawaii, where his father was a missionary. Having no connection with the abolitionist movement, he was not, in the words of an admiring southern historian, motivated by "merely emotional sympathies." Armstrong did not set foot in the United States until he came to Williams College in 1860 to complete his education. When the Civil War broke out, he enlisted; becoming interested in the Negro, he obtained a commission as colonel of a black regiment. As an agent of the Freedmen's Bureau after the war he was soon active in education; when the AMA appointed him principal of its new school at Hampton, Virginia, he seized the opportunity to build the institution into an independent normal and industrial school.[27]

Armstrong believed that the freedmen should eschew concern with "social equality" and concentrate on overcoming the shiftlessness of slavery through the discipline of work while acquiring the vocational skills to function efficiently in the southern economy. Although at first he emphasized the complementary nature of industrial and academic education and spoke of the ultimate egalitarian goals of both, these themes grew faint in the 1880s. Exponents of white supremacy could read into Armstrong's statements their own conviction that the Negro must remain subordinate to the white man. Instead of industrial education providing a lever for upward mobility, they expected it to keep the Negro in his place and supply a stable pool of docile labor. This was certainly not the undesrtanding of abolitionists who gave money to Hampton and probably not Armstrong's intended meaning, but this interpretation of his message became orthodoxy in the South. It accounted for Hampton's popularity with southern whites and conservative northern philanthropists. And the Hampton idea, which became

---

Record, 1 (Nov. 1907), 10-14; Rayford W. Logan, Howard University: The First Hundred Years, New York, 1969, pp. 154-56; Howard University Catalogue, 1909-10, Washington, 1910, p. 158; Meier, "Vogue of Industrial Education," 249-50; Fisher, Industrial Education, 158.

[27] Suzanne Carson, "Samuel Chapman Armstrong: Missionary to the South," Ph.D. Dissertation, Johns Hopkins Univ., 1952; the admiring southern historian was Charles W. Dabney, Universal Education in the South, 2 vols., Chapel Hill, 1936, 1, 463-64. A fresh and provocative perspective on Armstrong is provided by Edward K. Graham, "A Tender Violence: The Biography of a College," unpublished ms., cited by permission of the author.

in the 1880s also the Tuskegee idea, formed the basis of the Atlanta Compromise announced by Booker T. Washington in 1895.[28]

While most missionary educators considered academic and industrial education to be complementary, some conservatives in both South and North began to argue that vocational training was the *only* kind of schooling appropriate for blacks. This put the exponents of higher education on the defensive. One of the most frequent charges they had to answer was that higher education taught black people to despise work and led them into lives of "idleness, dissipation and vice." This accusation should have been beneath notice, but it gained such wide currency that missionary educators spent much of their time refuting it. They kept careful records of alumni occupations, publishing them in school catalogues and using them as the basis for many speeches and newspaper articles. These data showed that about three-fifths of the alumni went into teaching, one-sixth were ordained into the ministry, and most of the rest became doctors, lawyers, businessmen, or civil servants. To cite just one example of missionary efforts to publicize this information, in 1885 Wilbur P. Thirkield sent questionnaires to the 176 living graduates of seven colleges and the three best academies owned by the Methodist Freedmen's Aid Society. Sixty-four of these were college graduates, 26 had completed the college preparatory course, and 86 were normal school graduates. Of the 160 who replied, 24 were clergymen, 81 teachers, 6 school principals, 3 college professors, 14 were physicians or medical students, 5 lawyers or law students, 3 editors, 2 members of state legislatures, 4 held civil-service jobs, 2 were music teachers, 10 were wives of professsional men, 3 were in business, and only 3 did not report an occupation. These facts, said Thirkield, should be sufficient to refute the idea that higher education for blacks produced only "vagabonds, loafers, useless members of society."[29]

The best defense was a good offense, and some missionary educators attacked critics of black higher education with as much gusto as they had assailed slaveholders in the old days. Just as slavery had been "based upon the assumption that the white man had the right to determine the place in the scale of being that the black man should occupy," so was industrial training exclusive of academic education "a form of training that encourages a system of thinly-disguised slavery or peonage" based on the assumption that "the Negro is to be a 'hewer of wood and a drawer of water.' " The 1899 report of the Methodist Freedmen's

---

[28] Armstrong, "How to Educate the Negro Race," *Independent*, Apr. 3, 1873; Meier, "The Beginning of Industrial Education," 246-49; Bullock, *History of Negro Education*, 76-85. Graham, "A Tender Violence," chaps. 3-4, stresses Armstrong's continuing liberalism and argues that Tuskegee more than Hampton conformed to the idea of limiting black educational horizons to vocational training.

[29] *Christian Advocate*, Apr. 2, 1885.

Aid Society pointed with pride to both its industrial and academic programs, adding that "the schools of this society have never encouraged the training of servants only; it has never been taught that God made all the people of one race to be nothing more than the servants of another."[30]

No one defended black higher education more vigorously than William Hayes Ward, for many years chairman of the AMA's executive committee as well as editor of the *Independent*. The "philosophy of education which will restrict the Negro schools to Industrial Training," he wrote in 1895, "is a denial of the manhood of the Negro. . . . There is no reason either in the constitution of the Negro mind . . . or in the teaching of ethics, religion or history, which will justify any such truncating and dwarfing of his education." When Theodore Roosevelt stated in 1906 that "of course, the best type of education for the colored man . . . is such education as is conferred by such schools as Hampton and Tuskegee," Ward rebuked the president. "That kind of education is no better for the colored man than the white man. . . . Just as President Roosevelt does not send his children to industrial schools . . . so colleges like Harvard or Yale or . . . Howard and Fisk and Atlanta are better for those colored youth who can go to them."[31]

Ward's reference to the "constitution of the Negro mind" touched a key point in the debate about black higher education. Ward did not believe there were any racial differences in mental capacity. An AMA official who had worked with him on the Association's executive committee said that he was a "tiger" on this question: "I have heard him tear apart anyone who spoke of 'the Negro mind.' " When President William McKinley visited Tuskegee in 1898 and praised the school for not "attempting the unattainable," Ward commented acidly: "What there is 'unattainable' to the Negro, or what school offers the unattainable, we do not know."[32]

But other whites thought they did know. By 1900 the thesis of Negro mental inferiority had become almost a scientific axiom. The applicability of this thesis to education was obvious. Since the Negro "is by birth and natural capacity fitted only for manual labor," wrote a journalist, it was foolish to teach those who have "no capacity [for] such things" how to "solve intricate problems in mathematics" or to read Plato. Author Charles Dudley Warner's presidential address to the American Social Science Association in 1900 was a long exposition of

[30] *AM*, xxxv (May 1881), 165-66; *Christian Educator*, viii (Apr.–May 1897), 75-76; annual report of the Freedmen's Aid Society quoted in *NWCA*, Nov. 22, 1899.
[31] *Independent*, Sept. 26, 1895, Dec. 13, 1906.
[32] Lura Beam, *He Called Them by the Lightning: A Teacher's Odyssey in the Negro South, 1908-1919*, Indianapolis, 1967, p. 117; *Independent*, Dec. 22, 1898.

the black man's inferiority and the absurdity of anything above elementary and industrial education for the race.[33]

For missionary educators to admit this inferiority would stultify their whole enterprise; like most other abolitionists, therefore, they rejected it. Secretary Thomas J. Morgan of the Baptist Home Mission Society insisted that "culture is colorless. The fundamental endowments of the human mind . . . the memory, imagination, and the reasoning powers . . . belong in common to Indians, Negroes, Chinese, as well as to Caucasians." Since "there is not one multiplication table for the whites and another for the blacks," Negro schools "should provide exactly the same courses" as white schools. To be sure, the heritage of slavery handicapped the race, but this was an argument for *more* education, not less. "The disabilities of the past," said President Henry De Forest of Talladega, "make the more urgent the demand for superior training."[34]

Missionary educators continued to cite their own classroom experiences to refute the racists' *a priori* assumptions. "Many who think they know all about the negro have yet to learn that they know very little," said Berea's President Edward H. Fairchild. In his 35 years of teaching blacks and whites in the same classes at Oberlin and Berea, Fairchild had found "no such dissimilarity between white and colored that they need to be educated differently." Looking back in 1895 on 25 years of teaching black students after a previous career teaching whites at the University of Michigan, Adam K. Spence recalled the introduction of a college curriculum at Fisk. "Like early navigators, we were out on new seas of discovery," he wrote. "Would we come to the charmed circle beyond which the Negro mind could not go? We would try and when we came to that fatal place, we would stop . . . but we never came to [it]."[35]

Thus the Negro race no more than the Caucasian could "receive its best development through handicraft." When the time came that white students who planned to become doctors, lawyers, ministers, and professors "should learn to hoe and plow and lay bricks rather than go to literary and classical schools," wrote President James G. Merrill of Fisk in 1901, "it will be the right policy to shut off all our literary and

[33] James R. Gilmore, "How Shall the Negro be Educated?" *Independent*, Nov. 1, 1883; Warner's address in *Journal of Social Science*, XXXVIII (1901), 1-14.

[34] *HMM*, XVI (Aug. 1894), 325; Morgan, *The Negro in America and the Ideal American Republic*, Philadelphia, 1898, pp. 88-90; De Forest in *AM*, XLI (Mar. 1887), 71.

[35] Fairchild, *God's Designs for and through the Negro Race*, New York, 1882, pp. 17-18; Spence quoted in Joseph N. Patterson, "A Study of the History of the Contribution of the American Missionary Association to the Higher Education of the Negro," Ph.D. Dissertation, Cornell Univ., 1956, pp. 245-46.

classical schools for negroes in the South." Nor could blacks any more than whites live by bread alone. "Education is not simply for 'practical' purposes," insisted Henry L. Morehouse; "it is to enlarge the soul of man." As a slave the Negro "was trained not to think," said President Horace Bumstead of Atlanta University; what he needed most in freedom was the kind of education that developed "the power of rational and consecutive thinking," including the much maligned courses in Greek and Latin.[36]

Liberal arts colleges would also stimulate ambition and improve black people's self-image. "The great danger of our colored youth is not that they will cherish aspirations that cannot be realized," wrote Fairchild, "but rather that they will lack encouragements." President William W. Patton of Howard was convinced that blacks could never overcome the prejudice "which so sadly limits their progress unless they can first make a favorable impression by presenting the evidence of ability and culture which comes only with higher education." Or as the AMA put it: "A race that *is* inferior in attainments . . . will be looked down upon by others, and be themselves permanently discouraged." It was the purpose of AMA colleges, therefore, "to show the colored people the possibilities of their own race, and inspire in them, by visible and living examples, a noble ambition. This, sooner than anything else, will remove unworthy prejudice against them, and raise them to respectability and influence."[37]

Booker T. Washington and other exponents of industrial training argued that Negro schools must begin at the bottom to build a solid foundation for the eventual spire of higher education. Not so, replied most missionary educators. "The fountainhead of learning is not the common school, but the college," wrote Thirkield. "The college not only furnishes the trained teacher, but gives motive and inspiration for the common school." Just as the early New England town schools could not have existed without Harvard, so public schools in the South were dependent upon missionary colleges. A majority of black teachers at Hampton and Tuskegee themselves had graduated from Fisk, Atlanta, and similar institutions. "Advancement comes by a pull from above, much more than by a push from below," declared Ward. "The

---

[36] *BET*, Apr. 25, 1900; Merrill in *Outlook*, May 11, 1901; Morehouse in *HMM*, VIII (Dec. 1886), 279; Bumstead, "The Higher Education of the Negro—Its Practical Value," in *Report of the U.S. Commissioner of Education for the Year 1901-02*, Washington, 1903, I, 225-26.

[37] Fairchild, *What Career for the Negro?* undated pamphlet, probably 1878, in Fairchild Papers, Berea College Library; Patton in *Independent*, July 7, 1887; *AM*, XLVI (April 1892), 104-105; Augustus F. Beard, *A Crusade of Brotherhood, A History of the American Missionary Association*, Boston, 1909, pp. 155-56.

academy lifts the common school; the college lifts the academy; the university lifts the college, and never the reverse."[38]

From almost the beginning of their work, the mission societies had emphasized this image of a pull from above rather than the Hampton-Tuskegee idea of a push from below as a central theme in defense of higher education. In 1896 Henry L. Morehouse became the first to use the words "talented tenth" to describe this philosophy of education; Du Bois would soon make the concept central to his writings on higher education. As Morehouse put it, "in all ages the mighty impulses that have propelled a people onward in their progressive career, have proceeded from a few gifted souls." This elite should be "trained to analyze and to generalize" by an education that would produce "thoroughly disciplined minds."[39]

How did the talented tenth theory work out in practice? Missionary educators frequently affirmed that it was working well. In 1892, AMA secretary Augustus Beard spelled out the Negro's progress since emancipation. A generation earlier southern blacks had been forbidden by law to learn to read; now there were 20,000 black schoolteachers instructing a million students. A thousand black ministers had received training beyond the high school level. Twenty-seven years earlier there had been two black newspapers; now there were 154; in 1865 there were two Negro lawyers, now there were 250; then there had been three black physicians, now there were 749. "Verily this is a grand record for one generation, unparalleled in human progress," wrote Beard. The leaven of higher education was lifting the race, giving "old abolitionists" cause for "joy and thanksgiving" and promising to "bear the next generation onward to even greater success."[40]

But on other occasions the missionary educators' rhetoric was less euphoric. They were aware that, while the national rate of black illiteracy had declined from 80 percent in 1870 to 45 percent in 1900, the number of illiterate Negroes was the same in 1900 as 30 years earlier and equaled the number of slaves freed in 1865. Not until the twentieth century did the absolute number of illiterate blacks begin to decrease. The 1,000 clergymen in 1892 with some college or professional training represented only 8 percent of the black ministry. Two decades later, the ratio of black physicians to the total Negro population was 1 to 3,194 compared with 1 to 553 among whites; for lawyers the black ratio was 1 to 12,315 compared with 1 to 718 among whites; for college professors 1 to 40,611 among Negroes and 1 to 5,301 among whites;

38 Thirkield, *The Higher Education of the Negro*, Cincinnati, 1904, pp. 6-7; *Independent*, Mar. 13, 1902.

39 Morehouse, "The Talented Tenth," *Independent*, Apr. 23, 1896.

40 *Independent*, June 16, 1892; *AM*, XLVII (Aug. 1893), 241.

and in the teaching profession generally there was one black teacher for every 334 black persons compared with a ratio of 1 to 145 for whites. And nowhere near a tenth of the Negro population benefited from higher education. In 1909–1910 there were approximately 3,000 black students in colleges and professional schools and probably not more than 3,500 living college graduates in a total black population of nearly 10 million. Less than 1/3 of 1 percent of college-age blacks were attending college in 1910 compared with more than 5 percent among whites. However aggressively they reacted to outside criticism, many people connected with Negro higher education admitted to themselves that their schools had defects and that the average standard of black colleges was considerably below that of white institutions.[41]

Yet on balance the positive accomplishments of black higher education were impressive. Of all the evaluations that could be cited, the most eloquent was penned by Du Bois, who praised the early missionary educators as "men radical in their belief in Negro possibility." By 1900 the black colleges had "trained in Greek and Latin and Mathematics, 2,000 men; and these men trained full 50,000 others in morals and manners, and they in turn taught thrift and the alphabet to nine millions of men, who today hold $300,000,000 of property. It was a miracle—the most wonderful peace-battle of the 19th century, and yet today men smile at it, and in fine superiority tell us that it was all a strange mistake." The missionary schools were far from perfect, concluded Du Bois, but "above the sneers of critics" stood "one crushing rejoinder: in a single generation they put thirty thousand black teachers in the South" and "wiped out the illiteracy of the majority of the black people of the land."[42]

[41] For data on illiteracy and on the proportion of professionals in the population, see *Negro Population: 1790-1915*, U.S. Dept. of Commerce, Bureau of the Census, Washington, 1918, chap. 16 and pp. 510-11, 385. The data for Negro college students and graduates and for white college students were calculated from Du Bois and Dill, *The College-Bred Negro American*, 14-15, 45-52; *Negro Population: 1790-1915*, p. 164; and *Historical Statistics of the United States: Colonial Times to 1957*, U.S. Dept. of Commerce, Bureau of the Census, Washington, 1960, p. 211.

[42] Du Bois, "Negro Education," a *Crisis* editorial (Feb. 1918) reprinted in Meyer Weinberg, ed., *W.E.B. Du Bois: A Reader*, New York, 1970, p. 167; Du Bois, "The Talented Tenth," in *The Negro Problem: A Series of Articles by Representative American Negroes of Today*, New York, 1903, p. 33; Du Bois, *The Souls of Black Folk*, Premier Americana paperback ed., Fawcett, Greenwich, Conn., 1961 (1903), 79-80.

Chapter Thirteen

The Segregation Issue

The freedmen's education societies inherited the abolitionist commitment to racial integration. Two of the most spirited spokesmen for integration were William Hayes Ward and Edward H. Fairchild. "Caste is a sin which springs from prejudice, and sin, we know, can be overcome," declared Ward in the best evangelical tradition. Fairchild insisted that the race problem could never be solved until whites "learn to treat negroes as we do white people. They must ride in the same cars, stop at the same hotels, sit at the same tables, attend the same schools and churches, meet in the same social circles, sing in the same choirs, and mingle as equals everywhere."[1]

But while continuing to insist that the "caste devil" was the "masterpiece of Satan," abolitionists and educators admitted that for the time being segregationist sentiment was so strong in the South that "neither logic nor Christianity" could overcome it. Although "prejudice will, of course, give way in the end," said Ward, "we must, meanwhile, submit to the absurd." But the missionary schools and churches themselves must set an example of biracialism that would show the way toward the final goal of an integrated society. The existence of southern prejudices, stated the AMA, "is no reason why we should not attempt to build up the educational work in the South on true Republican principles. . . . It is well that some white pupils should somehow be secured in every one of our schools, even if special pains have to be taken, or inducements offered."[2]

All of the missionary schools were open to both races. But few *southern* whites attended any of them except Berea. Several white students were enrolled in a Quaker freedmen's school at Maryville, Tennessee, a liberal community where a few blacks also attended the predominantly white Maryville College (supported by northern Presbyterians) until state law banned biracial education in 1900. Some whites studied law at the AMA's Straight University in New Orleans. The first four students admitted to Howard University in 1867 were white women, and the medical and law schools of the university had many white stu-

[1] *Independent*, Mar. 18, 1886; Fairchild, *God's Designs for and through the Negro Race*, New York, 1882, p. 19.

[2] Ward in *Advance*, Nov. 2, 1882, and in Joseph C. Hartzell, ed., *Christian Educators in Council*, New York, 1883, p. 67; *AM*, xx (Jan. 1876), 15.

dents until the 1890s. Indeed, through 1896 slightly more whites than blacks graduated from the medical school. In 1884 the highest graduate in pharmacy at Howard was a white man, in dentistry a black man, and in medicine a white woman. After 1900, however, the Howard student body became almost entirely black. At several other mission schools a few whites were enrolled, but these were nearly always the children of teachers. The racial climate in most parts of the South prevented anything more than this token white attendance at what became known as "Colored" schools. The same was true of churches established by the mission societies, whose only white members were teachers at nearby denominational schools.[3]

Tokenism or no, the presence of white students in mission schools led twice to major confrontations between northern educators and southern states. In 1887 the Georgia board of visitors suddenly discovered the presence of whites in Atlanta University classes (they had been there for years), whereupon the governor informed the legislature that the state's annual $8,000 appropriation was being used to promote social equality. Newspapers drummed up excitement over the issue; the lower house responded by passing a law making anyone who taught a racially mixed class liable to a fine of $1,000 and a sentence of one year on the chain gang. Predictably, this aroused a furor in the North. The *Independent* denounced it as "barbaric" and asked Henry Grady how it squared with his "pretty speeches about the reconstructed New South." Atlanta's President Horace Bumstead made it clear to Georgia officials that if the bill became law the state would have to enforce it or back down; the university would not be frightened into excluding white students. Faced with the prospect of sending graduates of Yale, Andover, and Oberlin to the chain gang for teaching their own children, the Georgia Senate passed a substitute bill merely cutting off the state appropriation, and the House concurred. Branding this "practically as wicked" as the original measure, northern abolitionists held fund-raising drives to make up the deficit, and white students continued to attend Atlanta until 1910.[4]

In 1891 the AMA established the Orange Park Normal and Indus-

[3] *Friends' Review*, Jan. 13, 1872; Alexander Bartlett to James H. Fairchild, Nov. 4, 1878, Fairchild Papers, Oberlin College Library; *AM*, XIV (Jan. 1870), 16, XXXVI (Dec. 1882), 362, XLI (Nov. 1887), 317; Walter Dyson, *Howard University: The Capstone of Negro Education: A History, 1867-1940*, Washington, 1941, pp. 36-37. Evidently the Quakers established a second school in Maryville in the 1880s, creating a situation in which the first became all black and the second all white. *Independent*, May 24, 1883.

[4] Quotation from *Independent*, July 21, 1887. The *American Missionary* was full of stories and editorials on the subject in the latter half of 1887. See also Clarence A. Bacote, *The Story of Atlanta University: A Century of Service 1865-1965*, Atlanta, 1969, pp. 86-101.

trial School in Orange Park, Florida. Within a year one-third of the students were white, children of northern families wintering in Florida who came to the AMA school because there was no other in the vicinity. In 1895 the state superintendent of education, William W. Sheats, pushed through the legislature a law banning interracial schools and also prohibiting teachers and students of different races from eating together. Sheats explained that "the intent of the law is to nip in the bud *social equality* and *miscegenation*. . . . Those of us who love the Anglo-Saxon race . . . are willing to do almost anything to preserve race purity."[5]

Southern newspapers picked up this theme and began referring to the AMA as the "American Miscegenation Association." Undaunted, the AMA decided to challenge the law in the courts and so opened its 1895–1896 term with white and black students in the same classes. Realizing the shaky constitutional grounds on which his law rested, Sheats hesitated until April 1896 before arresting seven teachers and closing the school. This action came as a relief to the AMA, which wanted a definitive settlement of the legal principles involved. "If the Bull Run battle in the local court goes against us," said Secretary Michael Strieby, "we shall appeal from court to court until we reach the highest tribunal, and thus we hope to win an Appomattox decision." When the case came before the Florida circuit court the AMA's lawyers actually helped the prosecution to frame its indictment in an effort to make sure the case was not quashed on a technicality. But perhaps because the matter had already become embarrassing to the state, the prosecuting attorney and the judge agreed to dismiss it on a technicality. Sheats tried to persuade the legislature to pass a new and sounder law, but with an eye toward the AMA's continued eagerness to test the issue, the Senate killed the measure.[6]

Although the AMA won the battle, Florida and the South won the war. Within a few years a new public school at Orange Park attracted the white students from the AMA school, and in 1904 Kentucky passed a segregation law aimed at Berea College that was eventually upheld by the U.S. Supreme Court. This ruling symbolized the hardening lines of segregation that by 1910 brought a virtual end to the presence of white students in black schools. Meanwhile the northern churches and mission societies had fought out the issue of segregation on a different plane within their own ranks, with ambivalent results.

[5] Sheats to Joseph C. Hartzell, July 2, 1895, copy in FASME Archives. See also *Independent*, Aug. 4, 1892, June 13, 1895; *AM*, XLIX (Aug. 1895), 250-51.

[6] Strieby quoted in *Independent*, Oct. 29, 1896. See also *ibid.*, Aug. 29, Sept. 19, Oct. 10, Nov. 28, 1895, Apr. 16, Oct. 29, 1896; *AM*, XLIX (Dec. 1895), 379-80, L (May 1896), 146-47 (Dec. 1895), 379-80.

It was one thing for a handful of whites to attend missionary schools or churches predominantly black; it was quite another for blacks to be admitted to churches and schools established for whites. When the northern Methodists moved into the South after the war, their most radical leaders, bred in the antislavery tradition, insisted that the church must come as the enemy of caste. Many Methodist abolitionists went South as missionary pastors of freedmen's churches, presiding elders of episcopal districts, or teachers in black schools. It was these men and women who became the strongest advocates of an anticaste church; their national spokesman was Gilbert Haven, the militant Boston abolitionist who from 1867 to 1872 edited *Zion's Herald*, organ of New England Methodism. The church must "cast off these filthy rags of self-righteous caste," thundered Haven, and must *"entirely ignore the idea of color in the organization of our Churches and Conferences throughout the whole land."* Haven challenged the self-styled realists who argued that the church should accommodate itself to the facts of life and organize segregated congregations in the South or give up its efforts to win white members. "Did our Church conquer sin by yielding to it?" he asked. "Where she yielded, as in the matter of slavery, was she not weakened and well-nigh ruined by the complicity?" If a nonsegregation policy drove all southern whites over to the southern Methodist Church, said Haven, so be it. Let that Church "have a monopoly of iniquity, and let us continue powerless until we can do our work right."[7]

At its 1872 General Conference, the Methodist Episcopal Church elected four new bishops. Haven was New England's candidate for the bishopric and was backed by abolitionist and black delegates from every part of the country. Conservatives regarded Haven as a fanatic and tried everything to defeat him, even culling his writings for quotations favoring interracial marriage and circulating them in pamphlet form to the convention. The year 1872 was the high point of radicalism in the church, however, and after a hard fight Haven was elected with a bare majority on the third ballot.[8]

The General Conference assigned Haven to Atlanta, where he could put his integrationist ideas into effect on the front lines. This was precisely what conservatives had feared. Numerous Yankee entrepreneurs had migrated to Atlanta after the war and had organized a Methodist church affiliated with the northern denomination. When they got wind

[7] William B. Gravely, *Gilbert Haven, Methodist Abolitionist: A Study in Race, Religion, and Reform, 1850-1880*, Nashville and New York, 1973, pp. 182-94; *ZH*, Mar. 12, 1868; Haven, *National Sermons, Speeches, and Letters on Slavery and Its War*, Boston, 1869, pp. 514-15; *Christian Advocate*, May 25, 1865.

[8] Gravely, *Haven*, 198-99; George Prentice, *The Life of Gilbert Haven*, New York, 1883, pp. 376-78.

of Haven's assignment as their bishop, letters of protest piled up on the desk of Matthew Simpson, senior bishop of the Church. Haven "would seriously embarrass our white work in Ga. if not in the entire South," wrote a northern-born railroad superintendent in Atlanta. He "would instantly revive with increased intensity all the old antagonisms that we have been trying for years—and with some success—to *live down.* . . . Scores of good men will be compelled to abandon the Church of their choice or give up their business." The leading pastor in the Holston Conference, which comprised a predominantly white area in eastern Tennessee and western North Carolina, warned Simpson that "our people . . . repudiate Bishop Haven. . . . Can there not be a change?" To have granted this request would have alienated northern radicals, however, so Simpson sent Haven to Atlanta, admonishing him to behave circumspectly. Haven replied that while he would do nothing contrary to Christ's teachings, "if I should change my principles" it would be "a cowardly desertion. . . . The South needs N[ew] E[ngland] money" but "it also needs N[ew] E[ngland] ideas more."[9]

The conservatives' worst fears were confirmed on the very day of Haven's arrival in Atlanta. The northern Methodist church there held a reception for him at the city's best hotel but neglected to invite any black pastors. Haven remedied this by walking into the hotel arm in arm with a black clergyman. Atlantans had hardly recovered from this before Haven and his daughter rode through the streets with black ministers and invited Negroes to their boardinghouse for social visits. The Georgia press quickly made Haven its favorite target, calling him a "distinguished skunk . . . a rancid old ecclesiastical goatherd" who "allows his daughter to ride out with buck niggers." Haven lived up to his reputation for brusqueness by giving as good as he got. In an article titled "Tinted Venuses" he described the beautiful quadroon women he had seen in his southern travels. "What exquisite tints of delicate brown; what handsome features; what beautiful eyes; what graceful forms," he wrote provocatively. "No boorish Hanoverian blood, but the best Plantagenet. Here are your Pinckneys and M'gills . . . your Rhetts, Barnwells, and Calhouns. . . . It is an improved breed, the best the country has." This article became instantly notorious through wide reprinting and called down on Haven's head a heavier shower of abuse than ever. "We shall never think the small-pox or Asiatic cholera have performed their duty as purifiers of civilization," said the *Savannah News,* "until they have had a rastle with old Gil."[10]

9 J. C. Kimball to Simpson, June 17, 1872, John F. Spence to Simpson, Sept. 5, 1872, Haven to Simpson, Aug. 6, 1872, Simpson Papers, Library of Congress.

10 Prentice, *Haven,* 418-19, 433; Gravely, *Haven,* 204-206, 218-19; William Haven Daniels, *Memorials of Gilbert Haven,* Boston, 1880, p. 87; Hunter D. Farish, *The Circuit Rider Dismounts: A Social History of Southern Methodism, 1865-1900,*

When Haven came to Atlanta, northern Methodists there worshipped in two congregations: the white church founded by northern immigrants, and the mostly black church connected with Clark University. In 1874 Haven ordered a merger of the two congregations, but to his mortification this interracial experiment lasted only a few months. Half the whites left the northern Methodist denomination altogether; the remainder formed a new congregation. Even some of the blacks protested Haven's action and went over to the AME Church. In less than a year Haven's home church as bishop had become all black except for a few whites from his own staff and from Clark.[11]

In New Orleans a similar controversy plagued northern Methodists. The Missionary Society established a half-dozen black churches in the city; northern-born white Methodists organized one small and struggling congregation, Ames Chapel. Fifteen or twenty blacks also worshipped at Ames, but when a new church edifice was dedicated in 1868 the black members were restricted to the gallery, which roused strong protests from black and white radicals. In 1870 Joseph C. Hartzell came to New Orleans as pastor of Ames Chapel. He ended all restrictions, and for the next three years blacks attended the church and theoretically sat where they chose, though in practice they seem usually to have sat in the gallery. Hartzell also opened the Sunday School to children of both races, invited black pastors to preach at Ames, and entertained them in his home. After Hartzell left the pulpit in 1873 to become presiding elder of the southern Louisiana district and to found the *Southwestern Christian Advocate*, his successor at Ames again confined black worshippers to the gallery. This time the resulting furor raged for more than a year, with the *Southwestern* leading the attack on the "sin of race caste." Hartzell drafted resolutions unanimously passed by the district Preachers' Meeting asserting that the color line in the Methodist Church "must be wiped out." This was "not to be argued, but accepted by those who believe in the Bible." Although Ames Chapel perforce ended its seating restrictions, few Negroes came where they were made to feel unwelcome. Conflict between Hartzell and a succession of Ames pastors continued until the former resigned as presiding elder in 1881 to become assistant secretary of the Freedmen's Aid Society. Ames Chapel was thereafter lily white.[12]

Richmond, 1938, p. 220; *Independent*, July 22, Aug. 26, 1875. The "Tinted Venuses" article originally appeared in *ZH*, July 24, 1873. *Savannah News* quoted in *ibid.*, Mar. 16, 1876.

[11] Ralph E. Morrow, *Northern Methodism and Reconstruction*, East Lansing, 1956, pp. 187-88; Edmund J. Hammond, *The Methodist Episcopal Church in Georgia*, Atlanta, 1935, pp. 131, 137; Gravely, *Haven*, 229; *ZH*, Mar. 11, 1876; *Independent*, June 10, 1875.

[12] Quotations from a Hartzell sermon printed in *NWCA*, Oct. 7, 1874, and resolu-

The dwindling hosts of radicals mustered their strength and persuaded the 1884 General Conference to pass a resolution stating that no person should be excluded from any Methodist Episcopal Church. But "realities" had long since made such resolutions meaningless, and the radicals had retreated to the next line of defense: nonsegregated annual conferences.

In the tightly structured Methodist polity, delegates to the quadrennial General Conference were elected by the annual conferences, which were geographical jurisdictions whose boundaries usually coincided with state or regional lines. The annual conferences were in turn divided into districts, each supervised by a presiding elder who had a number of local and traveling preachers under his charge. The antislavery radicals who went South after the war organized the new mission conferences on a nonsegregated basis. The 1868 General Conference recognized these as full-fledged conferences, but defeated Haven's attempt to merge three all-black conferences in the border states with geographically overlapping white conferences.[13]

For eight years the radicals staved off attempts to segregate the new conferences in the ex-Confederate states, but the tide was running against them. Pressures for separation came from three sources. The first and strongest was from southern whites who had joined the northern Church but disliked the mingling of black and white churches in the same conferences. Their argument that mixed conferences hindered the Church's growth in the South won a hearing among northern conservatives. Second, some of these conservatives wished to explore the possibility of reunion with the southern Methodist Church, and segregated conferences would be a prerequisite to reunion. Third and most perplexing to radicals was the preference of many blacks for separate conferences. In 1872 more than half the black ministers in the Georgia Conference joined their white counterparts to petition the General Conference for racially separate conferences in the state.

Conservatives pointed to this as proof that blacks wanted their own

---

tions of the Preachers' Meeting in *ZH*, May 13, 1875. See also an 1868 pamphlet, *Matters in New Orleans*, a fragment of a ms. autobiography of Hartzell, and undated clippings (probably 1875) of the *Weekly Louisianian* and *SWCA*, all in the Hartzell Papers, Drew University Library; *Weekly Louisianian*, July 17, 1875; *ZH*, Feb. 25, 1875, July 1, 1880; *SWCA*, June 3, 1880, Feb. 10, Mar. 3, 1881; E. Heath to Matthew Simpson, Feb. 21, 1880, George R. Bristor to Simpson, Mar. 24, Dec. 30, 1880, Simpson Papers; and Barbara Myers Swartz, "The Lord's Carpetbagger: A Biography of Joseph Crane Hartzell," Ph.D. Dissertation, S.U.N.Y., Stony Brook, 1972, pp. 226-55, 312-21.

[13] Frank K. Pool, "The Southern Negro in the Methodist Episcopal Church," Ph.D. Dissertation, Cornell University, 1939, pp. 66-67; Gravely, *Haven*, 182-87; *ZH*, June 11, July 9, 1868.

organizations; radicals countered with the argument that Negroes would prefer integrated conferences if allowed equal status therein, and only asked for separation to preserve their self-respect. "Our colored brethren," said Haven, "will not refuse to dwell with their white brethren if they are treated as brethren." Many Negroes agreed, but cited the paternalism of white missionaries themselves as another reason for black separatism. During Reconstruction many of the presiding elders and conference delegates in the South were white, and one of the missionary arguments for integrated conferences was that the freedmen needed white leadership until they were uplifted to white standards. Black preachers "coming up from slavery and the lonely cotton plantations without preparation," said missionaries, would need for several years "the benefit of the experience and culture of the white preachers," not because they were white but because they represented "what education, wealth, and higher civilization do for a people after generations of experience and opportunity." A growing number of black pastors, however, thought they would come up faster if they got out from under white leadership and gained experience on their own. Since integrated conferences seemed to mean white leadership, they pushed for separation. This had been the main reason for the desire of northern black Methodists for their own conferences before the war; during Reconstruction the pattern was repeated in the South.[14]

The example of the AME and AME Zion Churches, which offered talented blacks a scope for their ambitions from presiding elder up to bishop, gave a fillip to the separatist movement. AME preachers chided their brethren in the ME Church for being "a mere cipher" with "the shadow of the white man resting upon them." Thus when black clergymen from the Georgia Conference petitioned in 1872 for a separate conference they stated that segregation "will relieve us from the taunts and sneers of designing men" and "enable us to demonstrate our capacity for self-government. . . . It will make us feel as men, and the peers of our white brethren."[15]

[14] Quotations from *ZH*, Oct. 1, 1868, Sept. 1, 1881, Feb. 15, 1877, and *SWCA*, Oct. 3, 1895. See also Charles Swaney, *Episcopal Methodism and Slavery*, Boston, 1926, pp. 197, 213-15.

[15] *Christian Recorder*, May 3, 1888; Daniel A. Payne, *A History of the African Methodist Episcopal Church*, Nashville, 1891, pp. 9-12; James W. Hood, *One Hundred Years of the African Methodist Episcopal Zion Church*, New York, 1895, pp. 12-13, 16-17; *Journal of the General Conference of the Methodist Episcopal Church . . . 1872*, New York, 1872, pp. 92-94. Appeals to race pride lured thousands of black members from the ME Church into the all-black denominations. By 1890 the combined membership of the AME and AME Zion Churches was more than three times the black membership of the ME Church. On this matter see especially Lewis M. Hagood, *The Colored Man in the Methodist Episcopal Church*, New York, 1890, pp. 76, 88, 197.

But the role of black separatism in the movement for segregated annual conferences should not be overstated. The primary impetus came from southern whites and their northern sympathizers. A majority of black delegates to the 1872 General Conference united with the white radicals to condemn segregation as a manifestation of caste. The fate of petitions for separate conferences was decided when they were referred to the committee on boundaries chaired by Lucius Matlack, an old abolitionist who believed that "colored conferences every-where foster a feeling of caste, begotten of American slavery." Matlack's committee recommended not only the denial of the petitioners' request but also the re-absorption of the three existing black conferences into mixed conferences. The General Conference upheld the former recommendation but voted down the latter.[16]

This by no means settled the issue. In fact, Haven's integrationism as bishop produced a backlash that increased the pressures for separate conferences. Haven presided over seven annual conferences in the South during 1873–1874; on each occasion he made sure that the sessions were integrated in fact as well as theory. He administered the sacrament impartially without asking black clergymen to wait their turn until whites had received it first. He ordained new ministers in alphabetical order rather than by race, and had black presiding elders assist with the ordination of white pastors. He required integrated seating at conference sessions and prayer services. He asked black ministers to offer opening prayers or benedictions at some of the conferences. In Alabama, where "the prejudice against the colored brother was immense," Haven insisted on inviting blacks to a committee meeting held in a white minister's home. When some white preachers in Tennessee threatened to leave the conference, Haven told them that "their places would be filled in six weeks. Secession is as vain a threat in Church as in State."[17]

Haven's actions helped make the 1876 General Conference a showdown between pro- and antisegregation forces. In the Church press and on the floor of the conference itself the debate was passionate and prolonged. Former abolitionists charged that anyone who favored separate conferences was "disloyal to his Church, his conscience, and his God." In a moving speech, Hartzell warned that "we stand at a pivotal point in the history of the Church. Let us do right, and our children will commend us. Separate on the color line, and we stab our friends in the South." The most rousing plea was uttered by Robert M. Hatfield, a veteran of many abolitionist battles. "This is the old question

---

[16] Pool, "The Southern Negro in the Mehodist Episcopal Church," 69, 225-28; Matlack, "Conferences of 'Colored Members,'" *Christian Advocate*, Apr. 4, 1872.

[17] Gravely, *Haven*, 207-14; Prentice, *Haven*, 414-17.

between slavery and freedom," he declared. "Shall the great Methodist Episcopal Church put under ban and ostracize the colored people? (Several voices—'No! No! No!') . . . I stand here to-day, in the name of Methodism and humanity, to enter my protest against this great wrong" which "will bring crimson blushes of shame to the cheeks of our children."[18]

Each side in the debate claimed that a majority of blacks supported its position. The truth is difficult to ascertain. Black and white ministers in the Alabama Conference voted unanimously to request division into separate conferences. A majority of black preachers in the Georgia Conference now voted against separation on the *color* line but supported a motion for separation on geographical lines, which would have accomplished almost the same thing. Two influential black spokesmen, T. B. Snowden and Hiram Revels, opposed separation with arguments that would be called paternalistic if put forth by whites. "The mental development of our people depends largely upon the association of those who have had opportunities which the most of us have not," said Snowden, while Revels maintained that blacks in mixed conferences had benefited from "coming in contact with their more learned and intelligent white brethren. . . . There are colored churches in Mississippi where you will find as the result of intelligent instruction and leadership, the same order and decorum in worship that you will find in any white church." On the other hand a black delegate urged segregation because he and his colleagues 'wish to be recognized as men able to manage their own affairs, and not looked upon as children." The General Conference finally voted by a margin of 199 to 94 to allow annual conferences to divide when a majority of both white and black ministers requested it. Most of the opposing votes were cast by delegates from New England, upstate New York, and the northern tier of the Midwest—the old antislavery strongholds of the Church—and by the white missionary delegates from the deep South. Black delegates divided almost evenly, with a slight majority against the proposal.[19]

The General Conference vote set off a chain reaction of conference separations. The Alabama, Georgia, Florida, and West Texas conferences divided in 1876. White missionaries and black clergymen in Tennessee defeated the first attempt for separation in 1876 but were

[18] Henry J. Fox, "Our Work at the South," *Methodist Quarterly Review*, LVI (Jan. 1874), 41; *Christian Advocate*, June 8, 1876.

[19] Quotations from *Christian Advocate*, June 8, 1876, and William B. Gravely, ed., "Hiram Revels Protests Racial Separation in the Methodist Episcopal Church (1876)," *Methodist History*, VIII (Apr. 1870), 19-20. See also *Journal of the General Conference of the Methodist Episcopal Church . . . 1876*, New York, 1876, pp. 113, 130, 135, 164, 170, 188-89, 195, 201, 206, 245, 280, 287-88, 326-32.

beaten the second time a year later when several blacks changed sides. The same scenario was repeated in the Arkansas Conference, where separation was accomplished in 1880 after defeat the previous year. Four additional annual conferences, each with a membership barely adequate to maintain one respectable conference let alone two, split between 1880 and 1886. By the latter year the only integrated conferences were Louisiana, South Carolina, and Mississippi, which contained a handful of white members most of whom were presiding elders or teachers in black schools. The presence of even these few whites stirred resentment among black pastors whose ambitions for promotion were blocked, and within a decade nearly all the white presiding elders had retired from the remaining "mixed" conferences.[20]

Well before this time the issue had shifted from segregated conferences to segregated schools. On this question the Methodist radicals, stronger in the Freedmen's Aid Society than in the Church as a whole, won a victory in principle but conceded defeat in practice.

The original charter of the Freedmen's Aid Society authorized it to establish schools for the freedmen "and others," with the others understood to be blacks who had been free before the war. In 1866 the predominantly white Holston Conference founded a school in Athens, Tennessee, and in the next decade other white conferences also set up small schools. These institutions were supported by their conferences, though the Freedmen's Aid Society gave temporary assistance to at least two of them. By 1880 there were as many southern whites as blacks in the northern Methodist Church, and the Holston Conference petitioned the General Conference to apportion at least 25 percent of the society's proceeds to white schools. Several black delegates and white abolitionists opposed this proposal. But John M. Walden, a founder of the Freedmen's Aid Society and a future bishop, maintained that he had drafted the "and others" clause with whites as well as free Negroes in mind and that the Church had an obligation to educate all its people regardless of race. Walden introduced a resolution authorizing such funds for white schools as could be expended "without embarrassment to the schools among the freedmen." He assured the conference that this would boost the society's income by more than the amount spent for white schools by increasing contributions from white conferences that had not shown much interest in black education. In an eloquent speech urging "malice toward none and charity for all," he carried the conference with him. During the next decade

20 *ZH*, Feb. 20, 1879; *SWCA*, Jan, 23, 1879, Apr. 7, Dec, 9, 1880, Apr. 15, 1886; Pool, "The Southern Negro in the Methodist Episcopal Church," 49, 56, 62, 64; Joel Williamson, *After Slavery: The Negro in South Carolina during Reconstruction, 1861-1877*, Chapel Hill, 1965, pp. 187-88.

the Freedmen's Aid Society spent about one-sixth of its funds for white schools while its total income doubled, so Walden's assurances proved true although the increase probably owed as much to recovery from the 1870s depression as to larger contributions because whites as well as blacks were being helped.[21]

Although the question of segregation in white schools did not come up in the 1880 debate, it must have been on the minds of many. Nevertheless, officials of the Freedmen's Aid Society and the Holston Conference went ahead with plans for a new college in Chattanooga as if no racial issue existed. Residents of the city raised $15,000 for the school, the society put up the rest, and construction began in 1884. Rumors soon circulated that blacks would be admitted to the school, but local Methodists denied them. They pointed to the recent founding of Philander Smith College for blacks and Little Rock University for whites in the same city as evidence that the Freedmen's Aid Society would not wreck the experiment of white schools by trying to force blacks into them. It was true that the two Little Rock colleges had been established without any open reference to the matter of segregation. But in Chattanooga there would be only one school, and by 1884 Methodist radicals were determined to force the segregation issue to a resolution.[22]

"Better a hundred-fold" not to build Chattanooga University at all than to make it a caste school, thundered Massachusetts-born abolitionist L. P. Cushman, who edited the *Southwestern Christian Advocate* from 1881 to 1884. If the Church gave in to "expediency, which is made of ninety-nine planks of race prejudice and one of Christian brotherhood," it would sell its soul for a mess of pottage. Cushman admitted that "public opinion all through the South justifies caste churches and caste schools. But men and women have to answer at the judgment day not for their conformity to public opinion, but to the law of God." If the Church stood firm it would eventually triumph over caste. "It may take fifty years, it may take a hundred, with that we have nothing to do. We must stand by the fatherhood of God and the brotherhood of man and work on."[23]

Cushman's words were echoed by the two other abolitionist-edited Methodist papers, *Zion's Herald* and the *Northwestern Christian Ad-*

[21] Morrow, *Northern Methodism and Reconstruction*, 113-18; Pool, "The Southern Negro in the Methodist Episcopal Church," 234-35; Minutes of the Exec. Comm. of the Freedmen's Aid Society, meetings of Feb. 19 and Dec. 3, 1868, FASME Archives; *SWCA*, June 3, 10, 1880; *Thirteenth Annual Report FASME*, Cincinnati, 1880, pp. 11-13.

[22] Gilbert E. Govan and James W. Livingood, *The University of Chattanooga: Sixty Years*, Chattanooga, 1947, pp. 10-37; Hagood, *The Colored Man in the Methodist Episcopal Church*, 19-20.

[23] *SWCA*, May 3, 24, 1883, Mar. 13, 1884.

vocate, and by protests from the Boston Preachers' Meeting and the New England Conference. These tactics forced the Freedmen's Aid Society and the Church to take a stand. Speaking for the former, Hartzell declared that "our Society would see any one or any dozen of its schools in the South closed . . . rather than commit itself to the policy, that no freedmen should be admitted to what are known as white schools. . . . *No principle will be allowed to suffer* in the administration of our Southern educational work." Although this sounded unequivocal, the italicized phrase contained a hint of the approach eventually adopted: integrated schools in principle but segregated ones in fact. After long debate and sharp parliamentary maneuvering at the 1884 General Conference, the "New England fanatics" won their point in one resolution only to lose it in another. The General Conference first declared "that no student shall be excluded from instruction in any and every school under the supervision of the Church." This seemed clear enough. But the conference then considered the report of the Freedmen's Aid Committee, which stated that, since the subject of mixed schools was "beset with peculiar difficulties," whenever one or both races desired separate schools they should be allowed to have them so long as the facilities were equal. The conference thereupon passed a resolution stating that "the question of separate or mixed schools we consider one of expediency, which is to be left to the choice and administration of those on the ground."[24]

These Janus-faced resolutions puzzled a good many observers, including William Hayes Ward, who commented that "the General Conference is more mixed than the schools. . . . It would be easier to interpret an edict of Asoka." Meanwhile back in Chattanooga the white Methodists went ahead with plans for the opening of Chattanooga University, confident that the second resolution gave them control over admissions. When classes began, five blacks applied. The dean turned them down, explaining that if he admitted them the white students would walk out. Soon after this came news that one of the professors had refused to shake hands with a black clergyman to whom he had been introduced.[25]

The moment of truth had come for the Freedmen's Aid Society. Preachers' meetings in the Church's old antislavery strongholds passed angry resolutions threatening to cease all collections for the society if it endorsed Chattanooga's action. "It were better that all the school buildings erected for the whites should be burned to the ground," said

24 *NWCA*, July 25, 1883, May 28, 1884; *ZH*, Feb. 27, June 4, 1884; *Independent*, May 15, 29, June 5, 1884.

25 *Independent*, June 5, 1884; Govan and Livingood, *The University of Chattanooga*, 37-39.

abolitionist John W. Hamilton of Boston, "than that we should misrepresent the Lord Jesus to the people who are poor and nearer His own color than your color or mine." And Arthur Edwards insisted that the Church had "no right to close to colored students the doors of one single school in north or south, even if they first build forty equally fine colleges for colored men."[26]

After an investigation of the charges against the professor who had refused to shake hands, the Freedmen's Aid Society instructed the university's board of trustees to fire him. This was fine so far as it went, said abolitionists, "but it leaves the main question untouched. . . . Shall the Society sustain *exclusive* schools?" When the trustees refused to dismiss the professor, the Society's Board of Managers met in a special three-day session in February 1887 and finally voted by a margin of 18 to 4 to terminate its contract with the university unless the trustees forced the professor to resign *and* agreed to admit black students beginning in September 1887. Financially unable to sustain the school themselves, the trustees had no choice but to comply. Radicals were jubilant; they had finally secured "the triumph of principle over expediency." Such "decisive action," said *Zion's Herald*, "will prove an epochal event . . . in our Southern work."[27]

But celebrations were premature, for in the end expediency once again triumphed over principle. Although the 1888 General Conference upheld the Freedmen's Aid Society in the Chattanooga case, it also changed the name of the society to "The Freedmen's Aid and Southern Education Society." This was an implicit endorsement of separate schools. As Hartzell interpreted it, "there is to be no exclusion on account of race," but "separation in schools, as in conferences is to be the voluntary choice of the people themselves." No Negroes came to Chattanooga when it reopened. A black clergyman published a statement in the local newspapers explaining that since black attendance might destroy the university and since the ME Church sustained many fine colleges for Negroes, the race should work to strengthen these schools instead of agitating the segregation question. *Zion's Herald* praised the "manly and Christian" spirit of this statement, but added: "The shame is, that [there exists] a prejudice that would make a man of this type and education seek, in sheer self-respect, to avoid forcing himself upon its society and his children into its schools."[28]

26 *ZH*, Dec. 15, 1886; *NWCA*, Oct. 27, 1886.
27 Govan and Livingood, *The University of Chattanooga*, 39-42; Minutes of the Exec. Comm. of the Freedmen's Aid Society, meetings of Oct. 26, Dec. 20, 23, 30, 1886, Jan. 11, 13, Mar. 30, 1887; Minutes of a special meeting of the Board of Managers of the Society, Feb. 22-24, 1887, FASME Archives; *Independent*, Jan. 6, Feb. 3, 10, 17, Mar. 3, 31, 1887; *ZH*, Jan. 5, Feb. 16, Mar. 2, 1887.
28 Govan and Livingood, *The University of Chattanooga*, 43-48; Hartzell in *NWCA*, Mar. 27, 1889; *ZH*, Dec. 7, 1887.

Although in 1893 John W. Hamilton, now associate secretary of the
Freedmen's Aid and Southern Education Society, said that none of the
schools "would dare reject a colored man if he sought admission," no
Negroes were then attending any of the 21 white schools receiving
support from the Society. Several black clergymen defended this *de
facto* segregation. "*It is an utter impossibility* for any Church, indeed
for the United States government, to mix promiscuously, perforce, the
schools in the South," they said. "For this sort of radicalism we are not
yet prepared."[29]

Since the American Baptist Home Mission Society made no attempt
to establish schools or churches for whites in the South, segregation
never became an issue in its work. Nor did the problem confront the
Presbyterian Board of Missions for the Freedmen, since its educational
efforts were also confined to blacks. But in their desire for an enlarged
southern membership, northern Presbyterians did finally accept segregated presbyteries and synods in the South 30 years after northern
Methodists had trod the same path.

During Reconstruction the Presbyterian Church in the U.S.A. gathered a small number of black and white southern churches into its
fold. Despite pressures from whites the Church's governing body, the
General Assembly, refused to allow separate presbyteries and synods.
This matter came to a head in the 1880s when a committee worked out
a plan for reunion with the Presbyterian Church in the U.S. (the
southern Church, which had seceded with the Confederacy) that included a provision for segregated jurisdictions. The old antislavery
elements in the Church, the *Independent* (which had a large circulation among Presbyterians), and black Presbyterians themselves led a
spirited effort to defeat this move. "Better, a thousand-fold, that reunion be delayed till the millennium than that caste be ordained," proclaimed the *Independent*. The General Assembly defeated the proposed reunion in 1889, to the jubilation of liberals.[30]

But in the end, liberals went down to defeat. Early in the nineteenth
century most of the Presbyterian churches in Kentucky and Tennessee
had separated from the main body over questions of theology and education and had organized the Cumberland Presbyterian Church. By
1902 these differences had diminished and the northern Presbyterians
opened negotiations for reunification with the Cumberland body,

[29] Hamilton to I. G. Pollard, Oct. 31, 1893, FASME Archives; Hagood, *The
Colored Man in the Methodist Episcopal Church*, 283-84, 286-88; *SWCA*, Dec. 2,
1886.
[30] David M. Reimers, *White Protestantism and the Negro*, New York, 1965,
p. 137; *Independent*, Mar. 22, 1888, May 30, 1889.

which demanded segregated presbyteries and synods. For the sake of gaining 180,000 new white members, the northern Church now appeared ready to place its 21,000 black members in Jim Crow jurisdictions. The reunification committee reported to the 1904 General Assembly that "while there must be no yielding of principles, it is also true that there is a wise expediency in their application." Black churchmen aided by the *Independent* again fought the issue, but this time they lost. Reunion with segregation was approved and one more denomination was added to the list of those that had bowed to the "realities" of race.[31]

Although Congregationalists counted few communicants of either race in the South, they also went through a long dispute over segregation. In some ways this was a continuation of a conflict with roots in the antislavery movement. A principal reason for the founding of the American Missionary Association in 1846 had been the unhappiness of Congregational abolitionists with the American Home Missionary Society's neutrality toward slavery. After the war the AMA and AHMS had an implicit understanding concerning the division of mission activities, with the AMA working in the South and the AHMS in the rest of the country. But in 1882 a group of white Congregationalists in Atlanta organized the Piedmont Congregational Church and applied for assistance from the AHMS, which responded favorably. The existing Congregational Church in the city, affiliated with Atlanta University and containing a biracial membership, petitioned through the AMA for a clarification of the Church's policy. This touched off a "color line" debate that consumed reams of copy in the Congregational press during the next two years.[32]

There were several white Congregational churches in the South, but the one in Atlanta was the first to be established in a community where another church already existed. If this pattern were repeated elsewhere, the Congregationalists would go the same way as the Methodists. "Are Northern Congregationalists," asked an angry Horace Bumstead of Atlanta University, "ready for the virtual establishment of a color line in our missionary operations?" The AMA answered with a resounding "No." The association "was born an opponent of slavery," said Secretary Michael Strieby. "It must oppose caste as it did slavery," for "caste is the tap root of slavery." It was "not enough to say

[31] Reimers, *White Protestantism and the Negro*, 137-39; Andrew E. Murray, *Presbyterians and the Negro—A History*, Philadelphia, 1966, pp. 196-200; *Independent*, May 5, 26, June 2, Dec. 8, 1904, Jan. 4, 1906.

[32] Reimers, *White Protestantism and the Negro*, 58-59; Richard Bryant Drake, "The American Missionary Association and the Southern Negro, 1861-1888," Ph.D. Dissertation, Emory University, 1957, pp. 142-44.

that we are to preach the Gospel, and if people are converted the caste question will take care of itself." The Church had made a fateful mistake when it adopted this attitude toward slavery. "Ten churches or schools that stand unequivocally against caste are more important than a thousand churches or schools that sustain caste."[33]

The AMA and AHMS appointed a conference committee that worked out an agreement meeting the AMA's conditions. It reaffirmed the "long-established" Congregational policy of nondiscrimination. The "principal" work of the AMA was to be in the South and that of the AHMS in the West; each society agreed not to trespass on the other's territory without prior consultation. All churches supported by either society were required to extend the hand of fellowship to other Congregational churches. The AMA immediately accepted this agreement; the AHMS did so unenthusiastically in June 1884, after six months of "acrimonious discussion." There the matter rested uneasily for several years.[34]

Meanwhile the AMA confronted the caste question in one of its schools. Although the association's main efforts had focused on the freedmen since 1861, it had sustained antislavery missions among whites in eastern Kentucky before the war and had originally founded Berea to serve this constituency. In the 1880s the AMA expanded its work for "mountain whites" by establishing a school and church at Williamsburg, Kentucky. When a black girl applied in 1885 the principal, fearing that her admission would destroy the school, asked the AMA's central office what to do. Back came a telegram: "Admit all applicants irrespective of color." The girl was admitted, and half of the white students walked out. But as at Berea two decades earlier, most of them came back and the school survived. Strieby could not resist the temptation to boast: "No regrets for having played the hypocrite . . . no regrets for having turned away one of Christ's little ones for whom He died, no regrets for having counseled her, while professing friendship, to go elsewhere." A few more black students attended during the next term. But whether by accident or design, none returned in 1886 nor did any blacks attend the half-dozen other schools the AMA founded in the Appalachians, most of which, of course, were located where few black people lived.[35]

---

33 Bumstead in *Congregationalist*, Mar. 8, 1883; *AM*, XXXVII (Apr. 1883), 100; (Sept. 1883), 257, 267-68; (Dec. 1883), 376-82.

34 *Independent*, Dec. 20, 1883, Jan. 31, June 12, 1884; James Powell to Edward F. Williams, Jan. 1, 1884, Williams Papers, Amistad Research Center.

35 Augustus F. Beard, *A Crusade of Brotherhood, A History of the American Missionary Association*, Boston, 1909, pp. 237-41; *AM*, XXXIX (Mar. 1885), 71-74; *ZH*, Feb. 2, 1887. See also the AMA Executive Committee Minutes, meetings of May 18, Dec. 12, 1882, Jan. 9, 1883, Apr. 9, 1888, Mar. 14, 1892, Amistad Research Center.

Except in Georgia the 1884 agreement between the AMA and the AHMS seemed to be working. Black and white Congregational churches belonged to the same state associations; clergymen of both races served together on committees, presided alternately as moderators of state meetings, and were elected delegates to the triennial meetings of the National Council of Congregational Churches. But in Georgia, 44 Congregational Methodist Churches (a denomination organized in 1852 by Methodists opposed to episcopal jurisdiction) joined the half-dozen white Congregational churches in 1888 to form the United Congregational Conference. The 15 predominantly black churches in the Georgia Congregational Association invited the conference to merge with them, but the white churches refused despite advice from the AHMS to do so. The issue came to a head at the 1889 meeting of the National Council, to which the United Congregational Conference applied for membership.[36]

The AMA and the *Independent* stood fast against compromise on this matter. "Once more we have with us the 'practical men,' who . . . urge us to be content with the 'half-loaf,' " declared the AMA. Though many who advised the same course toward slavery had lived to confess their error, again "there are wise and good brethren [who] say: 'Theoretically, caste is all wrong, but . . . if you wish to press your denominational work in the South, you must ignore that question and plant your churches on the color line.' Somebody will live to hear those who take this position confessing their mistake." Black delegates and old abolitionists at the National Council meeting in 1889 opposed the admission of the white churches from Georgia on any terms except organic union with the black group. But after some bewildering parliamentary maneuvers, the council finally adopted a compromise that proved in the end to be a defeat for the integrationists. All Congregational churches in Georgia were reorganized into geographic districts whose boundaries coincided generally but not precisely with racial boundaries on the understanding that in the future, churches within given boundaries would be members of their geographic district regardless of race.[37]

If faithfully carried out, this compromise might have preserved at least the token integration of the Georgia Association. But the more numerous white churches blocked the admission of black churches to "white" districts. This "treason to Christ," as the *Independent* put it, proved that the National Council had committed a "big blunder" in

[36] Drake, "The American Missionary Association and the Southern Negro," 144-48; *Independent*, Apr. 12, 1888, Apr. 18, June 6, 13, July 25, Aug. 1, 15, Oct. 3, 10, 1889; *Congregationalist*, Aug. 1, 15, Sept. 26, 1889.

[37] *AM*, XLII (Sept. 1888), 243, XLIII (Oct. 1889), 273-78; *Congregationalist*, Oct. 17, 1889; *Independent*, Oct. 17, 1889.

trusting to the good faith of Georgia whites. The Church must learn the hard lesson that "it should not yield the first inch. . . . The only right policy is eternal war against caste." Encouraged by Georgia's example, five white Congregational churches in Alabama united with a dozen Congregational Methodist churches in 1892 to form a state association separate from the black churches. The National Council refused to recognize this group and urged it to merge with the Negro churches, but the Congregational tradition of local autonomy left the National Council without power to enforce its edicts. Several years later the white churches in Florida also organized separately. Thus the Congregationalists like other denominations succumbed to the spread of Jim Crow, and by World War I separate Congregational associations existed in most southern states.[38]

Congregationalist Jim Crow reached into the North and affected even Oberlin College, once the abolitionists' proudest example of integrated education. Before the Civil War the proportion of black students at Oberlin averaged about 5 percent, hardly momentous by modern standards but unprecedented then. The percentage increased slightly after the war and then dropped back to about 6 percent for the rest of the century. Until the 1880s little discrimination existed at Oberlin; dormitories and eating facilities were integrated; some black students had white roommates; social organizations were generally mixed.

But as a new generation of students unconnected with the antislavery movement began coming to Oberlin, racial incidents increased. White girls at one dormitory refused to eat with black girls in 1883. President James H. Fairchild gave them a lecture on brotherhood and told them there would be no discrimination in eating facilities—and the girls obeyed. But when Fairchild retired in 1889, Oberlin was for the first time without an abolitionist president, and during the next decade retirements eroded away the antislavery topsoil of the faculty as well. Social segregation grew more common. In 1910 black students felt compelled to organize their own literary societies (these societies were becoming more like fraternities and sororities) because of white hostility toward them in existing organizations. Old alumni exploded in anger when they learned of this; a graduate of the class of 1851 denounced the new Oberlin as no better than Simon Legree, while an alumnus of the class of 1865 wrote: "Must we say that the 'Brotherhood of man' is all right as a doctrine for building up a college [only] until it becomes strong and wealthy?" Several of the older faculty also

[38] Reimers, *White Protestantism and the Negro*, 61-62; *Independent*, Sept. 4, Dec. 11, 1890, Apr. 14, May 19, 1892, Sept. 14, 1893, Oct. 8, 1896, June 4, 1903, Feb. 16, 1905.

condemned student racism. But President Henry Churchill King defended the white students as "merely representative of the attitude of the whole north toward the question. Of course they are not zealous advocates of equal rights for negroes as were the early students," for times had changed.[39]

Indeed they had. By 1910 the racial climate was so severe that almost none of the missionary schools or churches any longer enjoyed even token integration. For more than a generation abolitionists had been able to point to Berea College to refute the claim of "realists" that integration was impossible in the South. But in 1904 Berea itself fell victim to the realists. The complex story of the rise and fall of biracial education at Berea requires a separate chapter for the telling.

[39] W. E. Bigglestone, "Oberlin College and the Negro Student, 1865-1940," *Journal of Negro History*, LVI (July 1971), 199-209, quotations from 203-204.

Chapter Fourteen

Berea College

In 1842 a young Kentuckian named John G. Fee enrolled at Lane Seminary in Cincinnati. Converted to abolitionism there, he returned to his native state to preach freedom despite attacks by mobs and warnings from his slaveholding father, who finally disowned him. In 1848 Fee accepted a commission from the American Missionary Association to organize antislavery churches in Kentucky. Seven years later he founded a school in the village of Berea on land granted by another antislavery Kentuckian, Cassius M. Clay. In 1858 John A. R. Rogers came from Oberlin to help Fee transform the one-room school into a college "which would be to Kentucky what Oberlin is to Ohio, anti-slavery, anti-caste, anti-rum, anti-sin." But before they could get started they were driven out of the state by a proslavery mob. In 1866 the school reopened, and three years later Edward Henry Fairchild began his long tenure as president of Berea. Fairchild gradually ended the school's dependence on the AMA and made Berea into a respected four-year college (though like other missionary schools, most of its students were in the lower grades). He also presided over a racially integrated student body unique in American history.[1]

Berea was the child of Oberlin. Except for Fee, all of its early teachers were Oberlin alumni. The curriculum and even the architecture were modeled on Oberlin's. Every president up to the present has been an Oberlin graduate. And just as Oberlin was the first college in the North to welcome blacks, Fee and Rogers were determined to make Berea the first integrated school in the South. In 1866 three black students recruited by Fee were enrolled; half of the whites walked out, but since there was no other school in the vicinity most of them returned when Fee and Rogers made it clear that they must be educated with blacks or not at all. During its first year of operation, Berea had 96 black students and 91 whites. During its first decade (1866–1875) 61 percent of the students were black, a proportion that remained constant throughout the Fairchild era. Most of the black students were Kentuckians from outside the community of Berea; most of the whites were local children, though a few came from elsewhere in eastern Kentucky or from the North.[2]

[1] Elisabeth S. Peck, *Berea's First Century, 1855-1955*, Lexington, Ky., 1955, pp. 1-38.
[2] *Ibid.*, 38-46; *AM*, x (Dec. 1866), 279-80, xi (Oct. 1867), 247-48. The numbers

Integration went beyond the classroom. Both races sang in the choir, played on the football and baseball teams, belonged to the same literary societies, played in the band, sat indiscriminately at chapel, and ate in the same boarding halls. The dormitories were integrated, though since most white students resided in Berea village few whites lived in the dormitories. Black and white students were evidently never roommates; a black woman who had attended Berea in the 1880s said that this was by personal choice, not by college rule. "We ate together, walked to class together and there was never any unpleasantness about the situation while I was there," she recalled. A white alumnus who had attended Berea from elementary school through college wrote 30 years after he graduated: "Were I to make a list of former Berea students whom I would genuinely enjoy meeting again, and sitting down for an evening to chat over old times, I would find a majority of them colored."[3]

The miscegenation bugbear was Berea's main headache. This was no small matter, for the school could not have survived if the scurrilous rumors that dogged its existence had ever been substantiated. No scandal ever became public; Fairchild mentioned in private correspondence a few cases of sexual dalliance between students, though it is not clear whether any of these was interracial. White boys occasionally escorted black girls to college functions, but this became less common in the 1880s than earlier. In 1872 the trustees held a special meeting to discuss the question of intermarriage. After two days they laid down a remarkably liberal policy for that time and place. Interracial dating was acceptable, but if "in our judgment their going together would expose them to violence" or if couples were "seriously exposed to the charge of impure motives," the relationship would be stopped. Intermarriage was not forbidden, but the faculty in its function *in loco parentis* should warn the parties "of the dangers to which they will expose themselves and their parents" and should discourage betrothal while students were still in school. The trustees' balancing act worked reasonably well over the next two decades. The students exercised restraint, and whites in eastern Kentucky at least tolerated

---

of black and white students were calculated from President William G. Frost's *Report to the Trustees*, 1893, p. 6, in the Frost Papers, Berea College Library; Frost, *For the Mountains*, New York, 1937, p. 72n; and the research notes of Elisabeth Peck in the Negro Collection, Berea College Library.

[3] Quotations from Elgetha Bell to Mrs. M. S. Griffin, Jan. 13, 1946, Negro Collection, and Earnest G. Dodge to William G. Frost, Apr. 11, 1925, Frost Papers. See also Charles T. Morgan, *The Fruit of This Tree*, Berea, 1946, pp. 147-48; John G. Fee to Gerrit Smith, Nov. 18, 1873, Fee Papers, Berea College Library; and a fragment of a history of Berea, written in 1926 by Thomas J. Osborn, typescript in Frost Papers.

the institution if they did not approve of it. Only one interracial marriage is known to have originated at Berea: a light-skinned Negro graduate named John T. Robinson became engaged to a white teacher (a relative of Fee); she died before they could be married, but Robinson later married her sister.[4]

Berea's ability to survive in hostile territory without compromising its principles was due mainly to the courage and tact of Fee and Fairchild, especially the latter. Fairchild was not afraid to endorse social equality by name, and he practiced it in his home, where black servants and workmen as well as students and clergymen were guests at his table. Students both black and white remembered him with fondness and respect as a man of dignity but also warmth, with a quiet sense of humor. His dignity, wrote one alumnus, "did not keep him from being the most democratic of men. He was the confidant of every student. There was ease of approach. . . . He was one of the people from whom a student would borrow money for his current necessities." These qualities also helped this native of Massachusetts gain the respect of whites in the Daniel Boone country where Berea was located.[5]

Fairchild died in 1889. His successor after a three-year interim president was William Goodell Frost, who seemed to be cut from the same cloth as Fairchild. Descended from two generations of abolitionists, Frost promised to maintain integration at Berea as "an object lesson for the whole country." But at the end of his first year he reported to the trustees that the institution was in bad shape. In the seven years since Fairchild became ill in 1886, enrollment had declined by a sixth, the teacher-training program had been dropped, and the number of students in college classes had decreased so sharply that the college department was in danger of disappearing. The endowment had not increased for 12 years. "There is an air of dilapidation about the place," said Frost. Vacant classrooms, empty chapel seats, and a spirit of listlessness had led to a feeling that "Berea's race is run, and that it has sunk to the level of a common high-school for colored students." Especially "disheartening" was the small number of white students from

4 Edward H. Fairchild, *Berea College, Kentucky, An Interesting History*, Cincinnati, 1883, pp. 40-41; Fairchild to Erastus M. Cravath, Jan. 23, 1872, Dec. 12, 1873, AMA Archives; Minutes of the meetings of the Board of Trustees, June–July 1872, Trustee and Faculty Records, Berea College Library; Earnest G. Dodge to William G. Frost, Apr. 11, 1925, Frost Papers.

5 Quotation from a typescript by Edward F. White, written in the 1920s, in Edward H. Fairchild Papers, Berea College Library. See also Elgetha Bell to Mrs. M. S. Griffin, Jan. 13, 1956, Negro Collection, Berea; Bertha Lauder Fairchild, "A Child Remembers Berea in the 70's," and Frederick Hall to William G. Frost, Oct. 14, 1925, Fairchild Papers.

outside Berea. Since "our success in breaking down caste" was measured by the number of white students, it was imperative to recruit more of them from outside the town.[6]

Frost exaggerated the problem. True, enrollment had declined from its peak in 1886, but the total of 354 students in 1892–1893 was on a par with the average for the preceding decade. And while the number of white students from outside Berea had indeed dwindled, Frost's implication that the school was about to become all black was far from true. In fact, white enrollment had held steady during the preceding six years; the decline had occurred among black students, and the white percentage of the student body had increased from 39 to 46 percent.

Nevertheless, part of Frost's indictment was correct; Berea was in danger of becoming a local primary and secondary school. The new president attacked this problem vigorously. He increased the endowment even during the depression of the 1890s, doubled the enrollment within five years, reinstated the normal school, and reinvigorated the college division. But his actions provoked controversy among Berea's black constituency, since all of the increase in enrollment was white. In the 27 years before Frost became president, Berea's student body averaged 59 percent black; in the first 11 years of his tenure it averaged 80 percent white.[7]

Frost justified the increased white enrollment mainly on two grounds: first, since the population of Kentucky was six-sevenths white and Berea had been founded to serve the people of the state, its racial balance should reflect the state's; and second, the more whites Berea could educate *in an integrated setting* the more widely it could spread its egalitarian message. Frost emphasized the second argument especially in response to the charge that he was altering Berea's original purpose by making it predominantly white. "Our great work is to reconcile the two races, and to make friends for the colored people among the Southern whites," he wrote. "The education of the Negro alone can never solve the southern problem." For blacks "the opportunity to learn to be at ease among white students" and "to compete with the Caucasian in the class room" was invaluable. For whites, "it is no unimportant part of a white boy's education to see the Negro treated as a man."[8]

[6] *Independent*, Oct. 27, 1892; typescript of Frost's report to the Board of Trustees and the Faculty, June 22, 1893, copy in Frost Papers; *Synopsis of the President's Report, June 28, 1894*, Berea, 1894, p. 7.

[7] These data compiled from reports and catalogues, Berea College Library.

[8] *Synopsis of President's Report, June 28, 1894*, p. 9; speech by Frost in Boston, Nov. 21, 1894, typescript in Frost Papers; Frost, "Berea College," *Berea Quarterly*, 1 (May 1895), 25-26.

The president's dominant motive, however, was his desire to make Berea into an institution to serve the neglected whites of the southern Appalachians. In his first summer at Berea, Frost rode on horseback through the mountains of eastern Kentucky to recruit students. He fell in love with the mountain people and their land, "the Scotland of America." He admired their craftsmanship, their Elizabethan ballads, folklore, and language. But "our contemporary ancestors," as Frost called them, suffered from isolation, economic decline, and above all from lack of education. It was from this stock that Abraham Lincoln had sprung; Frost wanted Berea to become the training ground of future Lincolns and the means by which mountain culture could be revitalized and American culture enriched.[9]

The tragic irony of Frost's vision soon became apparent: instead of transforming Appalachian whites into racial egalitarians, Berea was transformed by them in the direction of racism. Students, alumni, and faculty whose experience spanned the 1880s and 1890s agreed that the latter decade saw a deterioration of race relations caused by the influx of white students. A white alumnus and son of a long-time Berea professor described what happened. Before 1892, he wrote, white students were a self-selected group who accepted Berea's philosophy— "anti-slavery folk from the Ohio River country and further North, local boys and girls who had heard Brother Fee's anti-caste preaching," and a few "mountaineers from further back . . . the least prejudiced members of their respective communities." But when the number of white students began to grow, "there was an inward change in the atmosphere." Many of the whites now began to think: "I am willing to go to that school because, little as I wish to treat niggers as equals and friends, I think I can to a great extent ignore the minority of them who are there, and keep them pretty nearly outside the circle of my real school life." When they graduated and returned home, they thought further: "Berea's a good school and surely has taught me a lot, but it's really a shame that I had to stoop to reciting with darkies in order to get its advantages. How nice it would be if my younger brothers and sisters could have the advantages without the disgrace."[10]

Considerable evidence exists to support this thesis. In 1897, 23 white students petitioned against the assignment of black practice teachers from the normal school to teach the lower grades. "We do not want to go back to our home," they said, "and tell that we had Negro teachers. . . . This would cause us to suffer much ridicule and also would injure the school." Two years later a group of mountain students refused to have their picture taken with a black classmate. Black visitors, seeing

9 Peck, *Berea's First Century*, 68-81.
10 Earnest G. Dodge to William G. Frost, Apr. 11, 1925, Frost Papers.

the races sitting at separate tables in the dining hall, reported that Frost had imposed segregated seating. This was not true; the segregation was voluntary, but that in itself was significant. One black alumnus wrote that "when I attended Berea 1889–1890, there was as little prejudice and friction between the races as I have ever seen anywhere. The last time I was in Berea, 1904, there was more of both than anywhere I have ever been."[11]

Despite his professed good intentions, Frost bore part of the responsibility for this situation. Not only did he fail to speak out forcefully against student racism until too late, but some of his efforts to recruit white students catered to the very prejudices he was pledged to overcome. He told applicants that Berea would not compel them "to think as we do nor to associate with our colored students more than they please. . . . White and colored students never room together and seldom board at the same places. It is no more for white and colored to meet in the same recitation room than it is for them to work together in the same field or in the same house."[12]

Such statements enraged black alumni who disapproved of the effort to increase white enrollment in the first place. "It counts for little how fair the president's theories and promises are so long as he sticks to his policy of condoning caste-prejudice as a means of overcoming it," wrote John T. Robinson, one of Frost's most outspoken critics. In 1895 a group of disaffected alumni led by Robinson presented to the trustees a lengthy indictment accusing Frost of intending to "squeeze" black students out of Berea and put them in a "colored annex." The president's irrelevant argument that whites outnumbered blacks in Kentucky "indicates the mental color line running through his policy." He had allowed his "ambition and vanity to override right and justice"; the trustees must overrule him to "save Berea College for Christ and Humanity." But a majority of the board including the one black trustee passed a resolution of confidence in Frost's administration.[13]

A controversy over Frost's refusal to promote a black teacher to a professorship added fuel to the dispute about racial balance. In 1884 Fairchild had appointed James S. Hathaway instructor of Latin and Mathematics. As the first black member of Berea's faculty, Hathaway did not find the going smooth. A white alumnus later recalled that

[11] Student petition in Negro Collection; E. M. Frost to W. G. Frost, Feb. 21, 1899, Frost Papers; *Union Herald*, July 22, 27, 1899, clippings in John G. Fee Papers, Berea College Library, and Frost Papers; statement by H. C. Tinsley, in Negro Collection.

[12] Frost to Melissa Parkinson, Mar. 6, 1901, Frost Papers.

[13] Article by Robinson in *Lexington Standard*, May 4, 1894, clipping in Negro Collection; John T. Robinson et al., *Save Berea College for Christ and Humanity*, n.p., 1895.

"many [students] whose prejudices were enough softened to let them accept colored as classmates were not yet ready to accept a colored man as a teacher." One girl's father "absolutely forbade her" to take classes from Hathaway. Unfortunately Hathaway's personality did not help matters. He rubbed some of his white colleagues the wrong way; he also spent a lot of time in Lexington where he had business interests, and sometimes left his classes to substitutes. When Frost became president in 1892, Hathaway requested promotion to professor. The president delayed his reply and finally told Hathaway that he could not qualify for a professorship without at least a year's postgraduate training at a northern university. When Frost refused to promise that this would automatically bring promotion, Hathaway resigned and accepted a professorship of agriculture at the Kentucky Normal School for Negroes, of which he later became president.[14]

Black dissidents considered the Hathaway affair proof that Frost was really a racist. Hathaway was sacrificed not only because his presence kept white students away, they charged, but also because Frost did not believe in the race's capacity for high positions. They quoted Frost as saying that he "knew of no Negro at all worthy of a position in Berea." Black Kentuckians "have as great grievance at the hands of President Frost," said one alumnus, "as they have at the hands of the advocates of 'Separate Coach Laws.' "[15]

Frost resented the accusation of racism and denied making the statements attributed to him. "I believe in the absolute equality of the races in their rights and possibilities," he said. "I expect the Negro to advance as rapidly as any other race has ever advanced." The appointment of a black professor "would certainly gratify our feelings," for Berea wished to prove that "the Negro can attain all that the Caucasian has attained." But the appointment of an unqualified man would retard rather than advance the cause. The real reason for Hathaway's nonpromotion was "incompetence." He was the poorest teacher on the faculty. "My eyes were opened by a conversation overheard among the colored students. After several had complained of him, one exclaimed, 'Well, he is one of our own people and we must stand up for him.' " Although Hathaway "thought he could get the professorship because he was a Negro, without the preparation," Frost insisted that "the Negro must expect to earn his promotion as every other man has to do." The state normal school had appointed him professor of agriculture even though "he has never so much as kept down the weeds in his own door yard, but Berea can not appoint men who have no special

[14] Peck, *Berea's First Century*, 46-47; Earnest G. Dodge to Frost, Apr. 11, 1925, Frost Papers; *New South*, Nov. 24, 1894, clipping in Negro Collection.
[15] *Lexington Standard*, Dec. 17, 1894, June 21, 1895, clippings in Negro Collection.

qualifications. . . . No school can allow its beneficiaries to dictate its appointments."[16]

Frost's assertion that Hathaway was unqualified did not reveal all the reasons for his nonpromotion. In a report to the trustees the president virtually admitted that the desire to attract white students had played a part in his decision. Since Berea "has an altogether unique opportunity to break down the caste prejudice of the whites," we "should do a poor service to the colored race if for the sake of having colored professors we should give up our opportunity of instructing the Southern whites." Frost still insisted that he favored the appointment of a black professor. But it "must be well timed and well managed," he told the trustees in 1894. "It cannot come with blare of trumpets. At some time when agitation has ceased, and the claim to have a 'representative' on the faculty is abandoned," a qualified individual could be appointed. White students would eventually accept him on his merits, "but they will never do so when they understand that he is appointed in response to the clamor of the colored people." The board backed Frost. In response to a petition urging appointment of a black professor, the trustees noted Berea's precarious position as a mixed school in the South and explained that "until our action in mingling white and colored students in the class-room is more widely approved . . . the time is not ripe" for a black professor.[17]

The time never did ripen, for racial conditions grew worse instead of better. Meanwhile the war between Frost and his critics escalated to the point where each side lost sight of the issues in its ill-tempered attacks on the other. The blacks' tendency to misquote Frost or quote him out of context infuriated the president. He privately branded Robinson a "monomaniac" and Frank L. Williams, his other chief opponent, a "reckless . . . liar." In a public fit of anger he once denounced "these crazy colored people" who "smell around to see if they can't find some evidence that the people who have sacrificed everything for the Negro race are not after all their enemies."[18]

Some of Frost's published and undenied utterances were irritating enough without misquotation. His reference to Hathaway's failure to keep down the weeds in his dooryard was rightly regarded as a gratuitous insult. When Frost said that "we must do what is best for the colored people, and not what they *think* is best," resentment was inevitable. Even some of Frost's less provocative statements were patroniz-

[16] *Synopsis of the President's Report, June 28, 1894,* pp. 9-13; letter from Frost in *Lexington Standard,* 1894, undated clipping in Negro Collection.

[17] *Synopsis of the President's Report, June 28, 1894,* pp. 12-13; petition from 26 black alumni and the trustees' reply, Berea College Archives.

[18] Frost to John G. Fee, June 30, 1895, Frost to "My Dear Friend," Sept. 10, 1895, Negro Collection; speech by Frost to Berea students, 1893, MS in Frost Papers.

ing. The "extreme sensitiveness and suspicion of the colored people" toward whites was hardly surprising in view of "their history and former condition," he once said. "This childishness . . . must in no wise discourage our efforts. . . . [It is] one of the things to be eradicated only by patience like that of our Heavenly Father." The black protesters responded that "by his own words and acts" Frost had proved that he was no different from southern whites who "claim to know what is best for the colored man." Though the president might be "well meaning," he seemed to expect Negroes to be "the most *dependent* and *spiritless* of mortals. . . . They should feel that they are objects of charity . . . and that any manly demur on their part is unbridled audacity and insolence."[19]

In a private letter Frost expressed "regret" for "some foolish and careless remarks." And in reply to a black committee's statement of grievances in 1895, the board of trustees while affirming its confidence in Frost declared that "we do not feel called upon to defend every word the President has uttered." These quasi-apologies, conveyed to friendly black alumni, helped rally most of Berea's black constituency to Frost's defense. A clergyman who had been half-persuaded that students were being segregated by fiat in dormitories, dining halls, and athletic teams visited the campus for a week in 1894 and fond none of these things true. He preached in the chapel, dined at Frost's home, and said he had felt welcome wherever he went. Two black students condemned "outsiders" like Robinson who did not know what was really happening on campus. Frost had taken command at a low point in Berea's history and had already worked wonders to revive the school, they said in 1895. "I can truly say of him, he sought the acquaintance and welfare of all the students." One of Berea's ablest graduates, James Bond '92, declared that only a reverse racist could object to the growth of white enrollment. To allay some of the discontent, Bond was elected a trustee in 1895 and given the task of recruiting more Negro students; his efforts achieved a slight increase in black enrollment.[20]

The black critics dismissed pro-Frost expressions as nothing more than the obsequiousness of the proverbial "good nigger." Nevertheless

19 *Synopsis of the President's Report, June 28, 1894*, pp. 7-9, 13; Frost's quarterly report to the Berea Faculty, Feb. 3, 1894, typescript in Frost Papers; Robinson et al., *Save Berea College for Christ and Humanity*, 11-12, 20.

20 Frost to Fee, June 3, 1895, Negro Collection; declaration by the Board of Trustees, June 25, 1895, from Elisabeth Peck's research notes, *ibid.*; letter from D. A. Walker, Nov. 20, 1894, in *Lexington Standard*, letter from M. T. Martin in *ibid.*, 1894, letter from Robert Lee Walden in *Cleveland Gazette*, June 11, 1895, letter from James Bond in *Lexington Standard*, 1894 or 1895, clippings in Negro Collection. For an account of James Bond's career, see Roger M. Williams, *The Bonds: An American Family*, New York, 1971, part II.

Frost enjoyed something of a respite after 1895 until a new storm broke around his head in the crisis of 1904. But it was during these years that white students became increasingly anti-Negro. It was also in this period that the national wave of racism crested, depositing on an already littered beach the flotsam of disfranchisement and the jetsam of Jim Crow laws. In 1900 Tennessee prohibited racial integration in private schools, a law aimed at the northern Presbyterian's Maryville College with its three or four black students. Although the AMA had successfully challenged a similar law in Florida four years earlier, Maryville did not take the issue to court but instead turned over $25,000 of its endowment to a black school.[21]

Tennessee's action spurred talk of passing a similar law in Kentucky. Democratic politicians eager to jump on the Negrophobia bandwagon and Berea businessmen who hoped that property values would rise if blacks were excluded from the school stirred up public sentiment. Frost was alarmed and began mobilizing Berea's allies to counter this movement, which he saw as part of "a conspiracy throughout the land to defame the colored man." If a law were passed, said Frost in 1901, Berea College might move to Ohio or West Virginia, where it could carry on its dual work for mountaineers and Negroes. Fee and Rogers had been driven out of Kentucky in 1859; another exodus "would be in the line of Berea's history, and would extend our influence while preparing for a triumphant homecoming." Whether Frost meant this seriously or was only using it as a threat to discourage hostile legislation is uncertain. In any event, Berea's friends quashed the effort to bring a segregation bill before the legislature in 1902.[22]

But by 1904 the wave of segregation could no longer be pushed back. One of Kentucky's foremost race-baiting legislators, Carl Day, introduced a bill to prohibit biracial education. Supporters of the measure depicted Berea as a hotbed of social equality. Not only did "white and colored girls and boys associate together in class-rooms, dining halls, in dormitories and on playgrounds," but "Mr. Frost entertains negroes at his home." One white Kentuckian blamed the increase of rapes and therefore of lynchings on "the principles which are being taught over at Berea." The opening phrase of Berea's constitution, "To break down the caste of race," was "a species of blasphemy," according to one legislator. "If there is one thing clear about the designs of Providence it is that the 'caste of race' shall be preserved. . . . No man can

---

[21] Andrew E. Murray, *Presbyterians and the Negro—A History*, Philadelphia, 1966, p. 201.

[22] Peck, *Berea's First Century*, 49-50; Frost to Newell Dwight Hillis, Oct. 12, 1901, Frost to William E. Barton, ca. Sept. 20, 1901, Frost, "Berea's Readjustment" (ca. 1910), typescript, Frost Papers.

have any right to outrage the sentiment of the people among whom he lives."[23]

The bill passed the lower house easily, but Frost hoped it could be defeated in the Senate. A hastily convened meeting of trustees voted unanimously to fight to the last ditch. As leader of this battle, Frost first tried a conciliatory approach. He told friends in the North to soft-pedal their rhetoric to avoid giving backers of the Day Law a chance to unite the state against "meddling Yankees." In letters to moderates in the legislature, Frost emphasized the good that Berea had done for the people of the state. Behind the scenes he also explored the idea of a compromise whereby Berea would accept the segregation of dormi-tories and dining halls if integrated classrooms could be preserved. But James Bond and the white abolitionist trustees vetoed any such compromise. "That course would drive away every colored student, humilate the entire race and strengthen prejudice by pandering to it," said Bond. And W. E. C. Wright, a trustee and former professor, in-sisted that "the commanding position of equal rights and privileges is more easily defended than any lower ground to which a retreat might be made."[24]

Although Frost dropped the idea of compromise, he continued to assure legislators that no student was compelled to associate with others outside the classroom and that "our arrangements have been such as to prevent any tendency toward intermarriage." At the same time he renewed the threat to take Berea out of Kentucky or convert it to an all-black school if the bill passed. And Frost could be eloquent in his defense of equal rights. The southern problem "is not much a Negro problem, but mainly a white problem," he told Berea students in a sermon that was published and circulated widely during the Day Law debate. Racism kept the black man down just as surely as slavery did. Berea had been trying for 40 years to help the state overcome the legacy of slavery, Frost told the legislature, "not by repressing the Negro, and calling him by humiliating names," but by "making the col-ored population more virtuous, efficient, law abiding, respectful and self-respecting" and by teaching both races to "cooperate for the gen-eral welfare." To prohibit Berea from carrying on this mission would be a violation of constitutional liberties, Frost warned the Kentucky

23 *Louisville Courier-Journal*, Feb. 2, 1904, quoted in Richard Allen Heckman and Betty Jean Hall, "Berea College and the Day Law," *Register of the Kentucky Historical Society*, LXVI (1968), 42; *NYEP*, Feb. 6, 1904; ms. of a speech by one Sullivan and clipping of a letter from F.W.H. Clay to the *Pittsburgh Times*, Mar. 2, 1904, in Day Law Papers, Berea College Library.

24 Ms. minutes of an emergency meeting of the Board of Trustees, Feb. 5, 1904, Berea College Library; Bond to Frost, Feb. 19, 1904, Wright to Frost, Feb. 21, 1904, Day Law Papers.

Senate. "Berea's cause, therefore, in this matter is the cause of academic freedom in the whole land."[25]

Although Frost's speeches could not prevent the Senate from passing the Day Law, they did win praise from Kentucky Negroes, including some who had criticized him a decade earlier. One of the latter wrote that Frost's fight against the Day Law had "caused me to see you in *quite a different* light. . . . You are a *true* friend to my people."[26] But some blacks remained hostile or at least suspicious. They believed that Frost's policy of making Berea predominantly white had spurred the drive to make it all white. If the president had spoken out as vigorously against racism in previous years as he did in 1904 he might have won more plaudits for sincerity even if he had not been able to stem the tide of segregation. And his course after the Day Law went into effect revived all the old acrimony with redoubled intensity.

Frost's initial step, however, won black approval. With the unanimous backing of the trustees he decided to contest the Day Law in the courts. Berea retained a corps of outstanding lawyers headed by Kentuckian John G. Carlisle, former speaker of the U.S. House of Representatives and secretary of the treasury under Grover Cleveland. They argued before the state circuit court in 1904 that the Day Law violated the 1st and 14th Amendments. But in early 1905 the court ruled that the law fell within the police powers of the state, which had granted Berea's charter and was free to amend it. A year later the state appeals court upheld this ruling. Berea's lawyers began the long process of appealing to the U.S. Supreme Court, which did not hand down a verdict until November 1908.[27]

Although at first confident that the courts would overthrow the Day Law, Frost nevertheless had to decide what to do in the meantime. From blacks and old abolitionists came impassioned pleas to fight "to the *bitter* end." W. E. C. Wright insisted that "to side-track the Colored race would be to yield just what our enemies desire, for we could never get the Colored race onto the main track again." John R. Rogers, Jr., recalled the Ku Klux Klan's attacks on Berea: "I have heard the bullets sing into our yard & strike the trees. . . . Now either Mr. Fee and Father were fools to imperil . . . the lives of their families . . . or they were heroes defending at all risks a noble, righteous, & glorious

[25] "Remember Them That Are in Bonds," a sermon at Berea College ca. Mar. 1, 1904, typescript in Frost Papers; Frost to Addison Ballard, Feb. 6, 1904, *ibid.*, Frost's testimony before the Senate committee published in *Berea Quarterly*, VIII (Apr. 1904), 18-29.

[26] Pharis A. White to Frost, Mar. 28, 1904, Day Law Papers.

[27] Minutes of a Special Meeting of the Board of Trustees, Mar. 30, 1904, Berea College Library; Heckman and Hall, "Berea College and the Day Law," 46-49.

principle. If they were heroic in '67-71, can we submit to anything except the irresistible thirty years later?"[28]

Fine sentiments, these, but they gave Frost little help with the hard choices confronting him. He, too, believed that Berea must "stand by its historic position of 'opposition to slaveholding and caste.' " The question was how to do it. Some abolitionists reminded Frost of his earlier references to making Berea a black school or moving it to Ohio. But the president now considered these proposals impracticable. The economic losses involved in moving the college would destroy it; the racial balance of 804 white and 157 black students made it almost inevitable that so long as the Day Law was in effect Berea would be a white school. Frost realized that he faced a Hobson's choice; no matter what he decided, "those who are willing to criticize will find excuse in saying that we have been partial, hypocritical, fanatical, or unwise." In the end the trustees backed Frost's plan to carry on as a white school pending the Court's decision, with the understanding that if the law were overturned the black students could return. In the meantime Berea would finance their attendance at other schools. Left unresolved was the question of what to do if the legal decision went against Berea.[29]

Berea College paid tuition and transportation for more than 80 of her former students to attend Fisk, Hampton, Tuskegee, Wilberforce, and other schools. Frost and the trustees also raised money to improve Berea's black public school, which absorbed the exodus of students from the college's lower grades. Would these students return if the courts nullified the Day Law? By the fall of 1904 Frost had begun to think it impossible. In October, before any court had rendered judgment on the case, he took the first step toward a decision that would lay him open to charges of duplicity. "The fanatical element which now controls Kentucky" would "harass us, law or no law," he told the trustees. Thus it was an open question whether integration could be reinstated even if the Day Law was revoked. Events during the next year strengthened his conviction that the old Berea could never be revived. Kentucky courts upheld the law, and while Berea's lawyers still thought they could win the case in the Supreme Court they informed Frost that such a decision would probably turn on technicalities that would allow the state to pass a tighter law. And in the spring of 1905 Andrew Carnegie promised Frost $200,000 toward the found-

28 Wright to Frost, Mar. 24, 1904, Rogers to Frost, Mar. 11, 1904, Day Law Papers.

29 Copy of a confidential letter from Frost to the trustees, Mar. 17, 1904, Memorandum for the Board of Trustees, Mar. 28, 1904, in Frost Papers; address by Frost to the Board of Trustees, Mar. 30, 1904, in Day Law Papers; Frost, "Hostile Legislation Against Berea," *Berea Quarterly*, VIII (Apr. 1904), 12-17.

ing of a new black school. The president thereupon informed the trustees of his "reluctant conclusion" that black students would not "return to Berea in any case," and he appointed a committee to consider the founding of a separate school.[30]

The abolitionist trustees opposed this course. To announce the creation of a separate school before the Supreme Court acted would be "both a legal and a moral surrender," wrote John R. Rogers, Jr., and if the law were then nullified "we should be in a very peculiar position." His father spelled it out plainly: "The colored people would say that such an early step showed that we did not wish them back any way" and would give Frost's critics "some show of foundation" for their "false and malicious" claim "that while outwardly opposing the Day Law you were secretly in favor of it."[31]

Frost might have saved himself a lot of grief if he had heeded this advice. But he believed that a delay of possibly several years until the case was decided would cripple the effort to raise funds for a new school. He also noted that many blacks now desired a separate institution. Announcing in late 1906 his intention to raise $400,000 for a new black school, Frost proclaimed Berea's eternal fidelity to its creed, "God hath made of one blood all nations of men." Berea "may have been too far ahead of the times" in its practice of this creed, "but if we back our horses it is to put the plowshares in more deeply."[32]

As predicted, this action stirred the wrath of many black Kentuckians. Frederick L. Williams, head of the black state teachers' association, raked up all the old charges of the previous decade and packaged them in a new pamphlet, *President Frost's Betrayal of the Colored People in His Administration of Berea College.* By increasing white enrollment and sanctioning social discrimination, said Williams, Frost "adroitly . . . paved the way to the condition which led up to the Act of the Legislature which simply legalized what had already taken place in spirit." Frost's apparent efforts to defeat the bill in 1904 were just for show. The evidence in its total context, said Williams, proved "the determined policy of President Frost to eliminate the colored people from Berea College."[33]

[30] Heckman and Hall, "Berea College and the Day Law," 46; Peck, *Berea's First Century*, 53; correspondence on the college's efforts to upgrade the public school, in Negro Collection; Frost, "Berea and the Negro," *Berea Quarterly*, IX (Oct. 1904), 24-25; Frost's Report to the Board of Trustees, May 24, 1905, Negro Collection; John G. Carlisle to Guy Mallon, Oct. 1, 1906, Day Law Papers; Frost to Eleanor M. Frost, Feb. 11, 1905, Frost Papers.

[31] J. R. Rogers to Frost, Nov. 20, 1905, J.A.R. Rogers to Frost, Oct. 2, Nov. 10, 1905, Negro Collection.

[32] *Berea Quarterly*, X (Jan. 1907), 19; speech by Frost in Boston, Feb. 14, 1907, reprinted from *Alexander's Magazine*, in Frost Papers.

[33] Copy in Negro Collection.

Several whites "of the old Oberlin-New England abolition contingent," as a friend of Frost described them, echoed Williams' accusations. Eugene P. Fairchild, son of Berea's former president, wrote a series of articles denouncing Frost's "deception." Some of the most damaging criticisms came from the Garrison brothers, Francis and William, Jr., and their nephew Oswald Garrison Villard. Frost had hoped that the Garrison-Villard families would help him raise money for the new black school. But they refused, believing that he had "forfeited all claim to consideration from those whose interest & support of Berea was based on the fact that it made no discrimination." Villard told Frost that his policy of opposing "an unjust law while openly announcing that the dictates of that law will be accepted" was "inexcusable." In his heart Frost did not have "the slightest friendship for the negro," Villard wrote to a friend of the president. "It was characteristic . . . that when the crisis came it was the colored people who were turned out to shift for themselves and not the whites." In private letters to his uncles, Villard said that Frost was "as false as they make them . . . a crawling creature, utterly contemptible. . . . It is another case of our being betrayed in the house of our friend."[34]

Though Frost may have been guilty of bad judgment, he scarcely deserved this much abuse. For one thing, he did not turn blacks out of Berea to shift for themselves; the college spent $25,000 to finance their education elsewhere. And Frost worked until his health almost broke down to raise $400,000 for the new black school. The accusation that he secretly welcomed the Day Law is unsupported by any hard evidence, while hundreds of letters, petitions, memoranda, and other materials testify to his efforts to defeat the bill. It is true that by making Berea mostly white Frost tempted Kentuckians to make it all white. But the Day Law or something like it would have come sooner or later anyway. And Frost was probably right in his belief that even without such a law the increasingly harsh racial climate would have made continued integration at Berea impossible. Of course he could have made Berea a black school. But his "heart was in the highlands," as one of his milder critics put it. Long before 1904 he had made the redemption of Appalachia his life work. As he said on several occasions, there were many colleges for Negroes but only one college for the mountain whites. When forced to make a choice, Frost chose the mountaineers.[35]

[34] Howard Murray Jones to Frost, Nov. 8, 1905, Day Law Papers; Francis J. Garrison to Villard, July 15, 1906, Villard to Frost, May 24, 1907, Villard to Charles F. Dole, Dec. 22, 1908, Villard to William Lloyd Garrison, Jr., Jan. 2, Feb. 23, 1907, Villard to Francis J. Garrison, Nov. 19, 1908, OGV Papers.

[35] Quotation from Albert E. Pillsbury to Frost, Apr. 27, 1907, Day Law Papers. The two scholarly studies of the Day Law crisis agree that there is no evidence

His very success in building Berea into a renowned college for Appalachian whites provided circumstantial evidence for those who wanted to believe in his duplicity. When Frost became president in 1892, Berea had 354 students and its plant and endowment were worth $200,000. At the time of the Day Law in 1904 these figures had grown to 961 and $750,000. When Frost retired in 1920, Berea had 2,780 students and a total value of $12,000,000. The ending of integration that freed the school from an unpopular encumbrance was partly responsible for this growth, and many people found it easy to assume that Frost had planned it that way.[36]

Frost felt deeply aggrieved by what he described as "flagrant misrepresentation which constitutes real slander." In contrast to the 1890s, however, he controlled his temper and his tongue. He worked out a complicated formula whereby $200,000 of Berea's estimated 1904 assets of $750,000 were sequestered for the new black school, to be named Lincoln Institute. Since this was not enough to create a good school from scratch, Frost persuaded the trustees to authorize an additional $200,000 to be raised by contributions. The initial $200,000 sequestered from Berea also had to be replaced, so in effect Frost needed to raise $400,000. Andrew Carnegie gave $200,000, an anonymous donor contributed $50,000 on condition that a matching sum be raised in Kentucky, and Frost hoped to obtain the remaining $100,000 in the North. But his black opponents in Kentucky and some abolitionists in the North demanded that *half* of Berea's *1907* assets of $900,000 be sequestered for the new school. They failed to make good their threat to sue Berea for this amount, but they did make Frost's task much harder by refusing to give any money themselves and discouraging others from doing so.[37]

At several fund-raising meetings for Lincoln Institute, the dissidents heckled Frost and tried to turn black audiences against him. But many Negroes rallied to his support and disavowed the critics as a dyspeptic minority. One man apologized for the treatment Frost had received at a Louisville meeting. "I trust you will be patient and remember that

---

to support the thesis of Frost's connivance in passage of the Day Law: Peck, *Berea's First Century*, 56; Heckman and Hall, "Berea College and the Day Law," 42-45.

[36] *National Cyclopedia of American Biography*, xxx, 355. The belief that Frost secretly abetted the passage of the Day Law long persisted among blacks. See H. G. Duncan to Frost, July 13, 1917, Day Law Papers; Carter G. Woodson to the Associated Harvard Clubs, Apr. 13, 1923, Woodson Folder, mss, Berea College Library; Isabella Black, "Berea College," *Phylon*, xviii (1957), 267-68.

[37] Frost, "Slanders Refuted," *Berea Quarterly*, xi (Oct. 1907), 20-27; Peck, *Berea's First Century*, 55-56; Howard Murray Jones to Frost, Nov. 8, 1907, Frost Papers; James M. Bond to Frost, Mar. 29, Apr. 6, 1907, Negro Collection; H. M. Penniman to Frost, Apr. 4, 1907, Day Law Papers.

as a race we have to face in every phase of life—in every day in the year, and in every street and corner some sort of discrimination against us as a race, so that it is inevitable that we should be suspicious and misjudge every white man no matter how pure his motives and how truly a friend."[38]

Frost's closest black ally and friend was James Bond. Well before the president announced his decision to establish a separate black school, Bond had concluded that this was the only practical course. "We face a condition, and not a theory," he told blacks. Frost and the trustees "have done what they could to change this condition and prevent this legislation. I know their efforts have been sincere." Once the Day Law had passed, Bond said, "the trustees might have thrown the Negro overboard by appropriating a few thousand dollars to some distant institution, and washed their hands of a troublesome matter," but their decision to raise $400,000 proved their sincerity. Frost appointed Bond financial secretary of the fund-raising campaign. Bond had no illusions about his task: "you know the radicals will be ready to mob me." His expectation of rough sledding was fulfilled. The "radicals" branded him as Frost's flunky and tried to break up his meetings. "I realize [now] in some degree what you have carried all these years," he told the president. "I know of few men who could have met and overcome these difficulties as you have. . . . The time is coming when the colored people of Kentucky and the country will understand and appreciate you as they do not now."[39]

In 1909 it appeared for a time that the whole Lincoln Institute enterprise might fail. The financial recession of 1907–1908 and the hostility of black and white radicals slowed contributions. Frost became ill from overwork. Carnegie had made his $200,000 gift conditional on the raising of matching funds by January 1, 1910. The northern goal of $100,000 was met, but the effort to raise $20,000 from blacks and $30,000 from whites in Kentucky was falling short. The problem, Bond informed Frost, "is that explain as we may, deep down in the colored man's heart is the feeling that Berea has been taken away from the race and that after taking away from us our own school, the white people are making us help them build another, when they ought to give it to us out right."[40] But a last-minute drive finally secured the needed funds. Lincoln Institute was chartered in January 1910, and Frost took a year's leave of absence to recover his health.

38 G. M. McLellan to Frost, June 29, 1908, Day Law Papers.

39 Bond to Frost, Mar. 9, 1907, published in *Alexander's Magazine*, offprint in Frost Papers; Bond to Frost, May 19, 1906, Nov. 20, Dec. 26, 1908, Negro Collection; Bond to Frost, Nov. 19, 1906, Dec. 31, 1907, Day Law Papers.

40 Bond to Frost, July 23, 1909, Negro Collection.

The Supreme Court's 7-2 decision on November 9, 1908, upholding the Day Law as a legitimate exercise of state police power came as an anticlimax. Second- and third-generation abolitionists condemned the verdict as "appalling," "vicious," "almost as bad as the Dred Scott decision," but their protests and Justice John Marshall Harlan's ringing dissent could do nothing to alter this confirmation of the South's right to stamp out the last vestiges of biracial education in mission schools.[41]

Lincoln Institute did not measure up to the hopes of its founders. The controversy over its conception stunted its growth. Orphaned from Berea and alienated from part of the black population, it never flourished. Lincoln's first principal was a white graduate of Oberlin who had succeeded Fee as pastor of the integrated Union Church in Berea. Black Kentuckians who had looked upon the Institute sourly from the outset were hardly mollified by the appointment of a white principal. Possibly disappointed at not being named principal, James Bond resigned as financial agent in 1914 and left Kentucky.[42]

The story of integration at Berea College is the story in microcosm of race relations in the half-century after Appomattox. The disputes over the appointment of a black professor in the 1890s and a white president of Lincoln Institute in the 1910s reflect the drive for a larger black role in missionary education, a subject taken up in the next chapter.

[41] Francis Garrison to Oswald Garrison Villard, Nov. 10, 1908, OGV Papers; William Channing Gannett to Frost, Nov. 23, 1908, Day Law Papers. The Court's ruling and Harlan's dissent are in *Berea College* v. *Kentucky*, 211 U.S. 45 (1908). Oliver Wendell Holmes wrote the majority opinion.

[42] "A Brief Historical Sketch of Lincoln Institute," Day Law Papers; Williams, *The Bonds*, 63-64.

Chapter Fifteen

The Struggle for Black Control

As the overthrow of Reconstruction and the intensification of Jim Crow blocked the assimilation of black people into the mainstream of American life, their ambitions turned inward and focused on the two institutions that offered some access to power, the church and the school. Many Negroes demanded a larger role in managing missionary schools. The conflicts this produced had little to do with the content, methods, or purposes of education; blacks desired not to change the system but to achieve greater participation in it as teachers, deans, presidents, and trustees. This chapter will deal mainly with the disputes over control of the schools. But since these disputes took place against a background of similar controversies in missionary churches and cannot be understood apart from that background, the churches will be discussed first.

Because the Congregational Church had high educational standards for its clergy, most of the early AMA missionaries and pastors of freedmen's churches were white. The AMA planned to follow the example of foreign missions by training a "native" ministry as fast as possible. But well before AMA schools could turn out enough preachers with the equivalent of even a high school education, the association was forced to bow to pressures from black congregations for ministers of their own race. "There *exists a strong prejudice against suffering white ministers to be pastors of colored churches*," wrote a white missionary in 1874. "Can you not find a colored man to put in my place?" asked the pastor of the AMA's church in Macon, while the missionary in Columbus, Mississippi, declared that "I dont think much can be done here unless we get a good colored brother to come & take my place. I have given up in despair." In response, the AMA moved more quickly than it had intended to place its churches under black pastors. By 1875, 33 of its 48 preachers in the South were black. Though most of these were in small rural churches, the congregations in Charleston, Macon, and Savannah also had black ministers.[1]

Complaints about some of these newly installed clergymen confirmed AMA apprehensions. The association's central office was de-

[1] Frank Haley to Erastus M. Cravath, June 15, 1874, E. E. Rogers to Cravath, Apr. 10, 1871, unknown to Edgar Ketchum, Sept. 27, 1875, AMA Archives; *Annual Report of the American Missionary Association*, New York, 1875, pp. 34-35.

262

luged with letters from black parishioners and ministers accusing each other of conspiracies, corruption, and sexual offenses. To judge from such letters, the black community was riven by jealousies and intrigues. "How does your ear endure the perpetual report of these bickerings?" one AMA executive asked another. With limited opportunities for exercising leadership and power, black people worked off their ambition and frustration by fighting among themselves. Refusing to respect each other, "they look *up* to whites, and regard them with greater respect," reported a missionary educator. He realized that this was a legacy of slavery, but argued that without white leadership to keep order while guiding them out of the wilderness the freedmen would never organize themselves to overcome this legacy. Some blacks agreed. "I am afraid the time is drawing near when we shall have to get an experienced white preacher," wrote a member of one of the small AMA churches near Savannah torn apart by factionalism.[2]

In 1877 the AMA decided to move more slowly than heretofore in the ordination of black ministers. Only those who had acquired sufficient education and proved their competence in small churches would be promoted to important pastorates. This caused resentment, especially when the association shifted preachers from one church to another without consulting them or their congregations. Letters of protest from black ministers grew increasingly tart. But the AMA continued to employ white pastors in some black churches for another decade. This was a major factor in keeping black Congregationalist membership small, but the association stuck to its professions of greater concern for quality than quantity.[3]

The Presbyterians also required advanced education for ordained ministers and moved slowly in the transition from white to black pastors. Unlike the Congregationalists, however, they had a base to work from. Several black Presbyterian congregations in the upper South with ministers already educated at Ashmun Institute (renamed Lincoln University in 1866) transferred to the northern Church after the war. By 1880, 40 of the 53 ordained ministers employed by the Presbyterian Board of Missions for Freedmen were black and nearly all of the pastors serving black churches were Negroes. But Presbyterian black membership also remained small, and the Church did not escape

---

[2] Samuel S. Ashley to Michael E. Strieby, Jan. 24, 1876, Joseph E. Roy to Strieby, Dec. 10, 1878, William Golding to Strieby, Dec. 3, 1875, AMA Archives.

[3] Thomas N. Chase to M. E. Strieby, July 30, 1877, Joseph E. Roy to Strieby, Nov. 18, Dec. 21, 1878, George W. Andrews to Strieby, July 6, 1878, J. D. Smith to George W. Andrews, Oct. 23, 1878, Deacons of the Macon Congregational Church to Strieby, Oct. 28, 1878, AMA Archives; Report of Secretary Augustus F. Beard to the Executive Committee, Apr. 14, 1890, AMA Exec. Comm. Minutes, Amistad Research Center, Dillard University.

the charge of paternalism. Black pastors occasionally complained that the Board of Missions treated them "with disrespect and too little consideration." These protests helped persuade the board to install black faculty in its schools more rapidly than the other mission societies after 1890.[4]

Although the black-power conflict disrupted the American Baptist Home Mission Society's educational work, the society avoided such problems in its purely religious activities. A large Baptist constituency already existed among the freedmen in 1865; the society sent missionaries to help them organize churches under ministers who in many cases had been slave preachers. By 1875 all of the 20 full-time and 50 part-time missionaries of the society were black. In 1887 a black district secretary was appointed to supervise the work of "general missionaries" in each southern state and to bring the black state Baptist conventions into closer harmony with the Home Mission Society.[5]

It was in the tightly organized Methodist Episcopal Church that the struggle over black representation was most intense. In its southern work the Church installed untutored black ministers and then tried to educate them on the job. By 1875 all the pastors of black churches were black, but few Negroes were represented at higher levels of Church government. For decades the question of electing a black bishop was the focal point of this issue. In 1870, eight bishops (the number was later increased as the Church grew) presided over annual conferences and supervised Church agencies. The three all-black Methodist denominations (AME, AME Zion, and CME) were also organized on episcopal lines and were headed, of course, by black bishops. From the outset of their rivalry with the ME Church these denominations used this as their trump card in efforts to entice blacks away from the white man's Church. To counter their rivals' attractions, black pastors and most of their white abolitionist allies in the ME Church worked for the election of a black bishop.[6]

Gilbert Haven led this effort in the first postwar decade. He managed to get the matter of a black bishop placed high on the agenda of

4 Robert E. Thompkins, "Presbyterian Religious Education among Negroes, 1864-1891," *Journal of the Presbyterian Historical Society*, XXIX (1950), 150-52; *Annual Report* of the Presbyterian Committee of Missions for Freedmen, 1880, p. 7; Andrew E. Murray, *Presbyterians and the Negro—A History*, Philadelphia, 1966, p. 192.

5 Henry L. Morehouse, "Historical Sketch of the American Baptist Home Mission Society," in *Baptist Home Missions in North America: Jubilee Volume, 1832-1882*, New York, 1883, pp. 419-20; *HMM*, VIII (July 1886), 159, IX (July 1887), 174 (Aug. 1887), 207, XV (July 1893), 218-19.

6 Frank K. Pool, "The Southern Negro in the Methodist Episcopal Church," Ph.D. Dissertation, Cornell University, 1939, pp. 240-58; Lewis M. Hagood, *The Colored Man in the Methodist Episcopal Church*, New York, 1890, pp. 167-91.

the 1872 General Conference, insisting that such a man presiding over conferences of both races, "making appointments, ordaining ministers . . . dedicating churches" would give "the miserable caste devil" its "death blow." Among prominent Methodist abolitionists, only Daniel Wise disagreed with this. "The idea that duty to the Colored race requires us to make one of their number a Bishop without strict regard to qualifications," said Wise in 1871, "is the offspring of an unreasoning colorphobia." It was the most insidious form of paternalism to push forward a black candidate on racial grounds alone. Not until Negroes could win office on their merits rather than their race, which Wise expected to happen within a decade, could they truly earn the respect of mankind. Ironically, whatever slim chance may have existed for the election of a black bishop in 1872 was erased by Haven's own election, which was more than enough for many white delegates to digest.[7]

In 1876 several *de facto* black conferences petitioned the General Conference for a bishop of their race; preoccupied with the issue of segregated conferences, however, the delegates decided to elect no new bishops and to pass the buck to the next General Conference. But as a sop to black requests for "recognition," the 1876 General Conference elected Hiram Revels editor of the Church's newest newspaper, the *Southwestern Christian Advocate* in New Orleans. This action resulted from a cynical maneuver by conservatives to embarrass white radicals. The *Southwestern* had been started in 1873 by Joseph C. Hartzell, who carried it for three years without General Conference support. An outspoken egalitarian and a thorn in the side of conservatives, Hartzell was ousted as editor of the now officially sanctioned *Southwestern* in 1876 by the votes of blacks and conservative whites. When Revels learned of the General Conference's action, he wrote Hartzell a magnanimous letter declining the post. "The colored members should have stood firmly by you," he told Hartzell who had earlier helped Revels at a critical time in his career. "While it is desirable to build up the colored race, we must not sacrifice our best and purest white friends." Hartzell remained editor, and the *Southwestern* remained the gadfly of conservatives.[8]

The General Conference of 1880 decided to elect four new bishops, enlarging the total to 12. Before the balloting began one of the black

[7] Haven in *ZH*, Jan. 18, Feb. 8, 29, May 2, 1872; Wise in *Christian Advocate*, Mar. 23, 1871, Feb. 8, 22, 1872.

[8] *Journal of the General Conference of the Methodist Episcopal Church . . . 1876*, New York, 1876, pp. 158, 188, 195, 301, 304; typewritten notes on the founding and early history of the *Southwestern*, including a copy of the letter from Revels to Hartzell, June 7, 1876, in the Hartzell Papers, Drew University Library. At the time he declined the editorial post, Revels probably knew that he was about to be appointed president of Alcorn College in Mississippi.

delegates, E. W. S. Hammond, made an eloquent speech. "We have reached the crisis, the Rubicon is before us," he told the conference. "You taught us a century ago that we were men. . . . You are teaching us to-day that we are brothers," and now was the time to prove it. Hammond's address brought him a standing ovation, but in the balloting for bishops only 75 (of a total of 390) votes could be mustered for black candidates. After four white bishops were elected, the conference appointed a special committee to consider the election of a black man as a 13th bishop. A majority of the committee reported in favor of this proposal. In the floor debate, however, it became clear that such a bishop would be assigned only to Negro conferences. Some black delegates were willing to accept this, but others and many of the white radicals did not want a Jim Crow bishop. "Every one understands that this would be but the first step toward another [separate] Colored Methodist Church," said Hartzell, who implored blacks not "to listen to the arguments of the white-liners who want to drive our colored people from us." In the end the committee report was laid on the table by a vote of 228 to 137.[9]

Several black ministers were embittered by this "slap in the face," and some of them left the Church.[10] For the next eight years, however, the issue of a black bishop faded into the background as the Church grappled with other problems. The appointment of black men to official Church positions also took the edge off the pressure for a bishop. Negroes served on several committees at the 1884 and 1888 General Conferences; one of the general secretaries at both conferences was William H. Crogman, a black professor at Clark University; one-fourth of the clerkships in 1888 went to Negroes; black men were secretaries of three standing committees and field agents of the Freedmen's Aid Society and the Missionary Society by 1892. In 1881 Hartzell appointed his black protégé, A. E. P. Albert, assistant editor of the *Southwestern Christian Advocate*. The General Conference of 1884 elected another black man, Marshall Taylor, as editor (Hartzell meanwhile had become assistant secretary of the Freedmen's Aid Society). A black minister wrote that Taylor's appointment as "the first colored editor [of] a religious or secular paper owned and controlled by whites" was "highly pleasing" to the race.[11]

When Taylor died in 1887, Albert succeeded him; in effect the *Southwestern* was now the organ of the black conferences. Since its

9 Hagood, *The Colored Man in the Methodist Episcopal Church*, 187-88; *SWCA*, May 27, June 3, 24, 1880; *ZH*, June 24, 1880.

10 *SWCA*, July 1, 15, 29, 1880; *Christian Recorder*, July 29, 1880.

11 *SWCA*, Dec. 15, 1881, June 19, July 10, 1884, June 14, Aug. 9, 1888; *Christian Educator*, IV (Apr. 1893), 110-11.

editor owed his position to the patronage of a predominantly white church, however, the paper usually took a cautious position on the black power issue. When AME clergymen taunted blacks in the ME Church for being "dictated to as our masters dictated to us in slavery times," Albert replied that the ME Church had spent three million dollars on black education, 10 times as much as all the black denominations combined, "and employs to-day in our schools more Negro professors than are employed by the A.M.E. Church, the A.M.E. Zion Church, and the C.M.E. Church all put together." Three-fourths of the AME and AME Zion clergymen with some higher education had gone to ME schools. Northern Methodists, concluded Albert, had done more for the race than "all the ungrateful wretches who are constantly calling us slaves in the Methodist Episcopal Church."[12]

But the question of a black bishop would not stay in the wings. In the 1890s black "restlessness and discontent" concerning this matter again flared up. The 1896 General Conference took some steps to allay the discontent. On the first ballot to elect a new bishop John W. E. Bowen, a black professor at Gammon Seminary, received the highest number of votes but fell short of the two-thirds majority now necessary for election and was finally defeated. In what one black clergyman wryly described as "a piece of political church diplomacy," the conference then elected Hartzell missionary bishop for Africa and named M. C. B. Mason, a black man, to succeed him as one of the two secretaries of the Freedmen's Aid Society. It is not clear whether Hartzell participated in the negotiations that produced this compromise. In any case he gracefully accepted the result and went to Africa. As secretary, Mason received the same salary as a bishop and shared authority with his white colleague over white as well as black schools.[13]

This alleviated but did not cure black discontent. In 1900 several Negro delegates to the General Conference, conceding that white racism was too strong for a black bishop to serve white conferences, signified their willingness for such a bishop to be assigned only to black conferences. But a coalition of southern whites who wanted no black bishop at all plus Negroes and northern liberals who still opposed this Jim Crow compromise voted down the proposal. Not until 1920 did the 350,000 Negroes in the Methodist Episcopal Church get

---

[12] *SWCA*, Mar. 27, Apr. 10, 17, 1890, June 11, 1891.

[13] *Christian Educator*, IV (Apr. 1893), 91-98, VII (Dec.–Jan. 1895-96), 1-2 (Apr.–May, 1896), 57-59 (June–July 1896), 85-86; Hartzell to M.C.B. Mason, Feb. 18, 1895, Hartzell to Isaiah B. Scott, Mar. 1, 1895, FASME Archives; *Christian Recorder*, May 21, 28, 1896. Barbara Myers Swartz, "The Lord's Carpetbagger: A Biography of Joseph Crane Hartzell," Ph.D. Dissertation, S.U.N.Y. Stony Brook, 1972, pp. 591-95, does not interpret the elections of Hartzell and Mason as being intentionally related actions.

their first black bishop; then they got two, one for the black conferences and one for Africa. This was "representation," but hardly black
power.[14]

While all Negro congregations had black pastors by 1890, the missionary schools had predominantly white faculties until about 1905
and remained under white control for several decades longer. This
became a matter of concern to some black leaders. "We are willing to
return thanks to the many friends who have assisted us in educating
ourselves," said D. Augustus Straker in 1883, "but we have now
reached the point where we desire to . . . build school houses,
churches, colleges and universities, by our own efforts . . . ere we sacrifice our manhood." Emmanuel K. Love told the all-black National Baptist Convention in 1896: "We can better marshal our forces and develop our people in enterprises manned by us. Negro brain should
shape and control Negro thought."[15]

The AME and AME Zion Churches carried out this self-help impulse by supporting five colleges, a dozen secondary schools, and
about 30 elementary schools. Black Baptists had also founded 50
schools by 1895, but only a few of them were above the elementary
level and these received subsidies from the northern Baptists. The
black community lacked the resources to sustain major projects; most
of the black-owned schools, though objects of racial pride, were poor
in quality and starved for funds. The AME Church spent $49,000 for
education from 1886 to 1890; during the same period the ME Church
expended $675,000 on black schools.[16]

The state-supported black A. & M. colleges afforded another quasi-
separatist outlet for black ambitions. In 1870 a district secretary of the
AMA reported that some Negroes in Mississippi, dissatisfied with
white control of Tougaloo College, were pressing the legislature for a
school "of *their own*" where nobody "but themselves run their machine." The legislature established Alcorn College the next year. Presi-

14 David M. Reimers, *White Protestantism and the Negro*, New York, 1965, pp.
73-75; Pool, "The Southern Negro in the Methodist Episcopal Church," 248-57.

15 Straker in *New York Globe*, Jan. 20, 1883; Love quoted by Lewis G. Jordan,
Negro Baptist History, U.S.A., 1750-1930, Nashville, 1930, p. 124.

16 *Christian Educator*, v (Oct. 1893), 12. The AME colleges were Wilberforce
University (Wilberforce, Ohio), Morris Brown College (Atlanta), Allen University (Columbia, S.C.), and Paul Quinn College (Waco, Texas). The AME Zion
school was Livingstone College (Salisbury, N.C.). Wilberforce had been founded
by northern white Methodists in 1856; it was sold to the AME Church in 1863.
The Colored Methodist Episcopal Church also sustained two secondary schools,
Lane Institute in Jackson, Tennessee and Paine Institute in Augusta, Georgia (both
later took the name of "College"), but they received much of their support from
the ME Church, South.

dent Edmund A. Ware of Atlanta University headed off a similar movement in Georgia by increasing the number of blacks on the school's board of trustees. In Virginia a decade later Senator William Mahone kept his promise to black political allies for a state college with "colored professors, colored teachers, and a colored Board of Visitors." By the end of the century every southern state supported some kind of institution of higher education for Negroes. Most presidents of these schools and all but a handful of teachers were Negroes, presenting a facade of black control. But the reality was far different, since the faculties and administrations were beholden to state legislatures. Moreover, all of the black state colleges in this period were woefully underfinanced and devoid of genuine college-level offerings.[17] The principal black colleges were, and are, those founded by northern missionaries. The struggle for black power and against white paternalism in education, therefore, took place primarily within these schools, not outside them.

As the colleges began turning out graduates who were denied positions of authority in a Jim Crow society, the schools themselves became the arena for black ambitions. The missionary educators yielded only gradually to Negro demands for greater control. There were both subjective and objective reasons for this. Subjectively, some missionaries shared the widespread conviction that blacks were deficient in administrative skills. They were especially hesitant to entrust Negroes with the control of funds contributed by northern philanthropy. Many teachers were slow to believe that the "grown-up children" under their tutelage had matured to the point of readiness for adult responsibilities. Objectively, a genuine desire to maintain high standards was an important reason for the slowness to replace white teachers with blacks. The first and even second generations of freedmen could not produce enough teachers to staff the schools with personnel equal in training and experience to northern teachers from middle-class achievement-oriented New England backgrounds. Black communities served by mission schools were themselves frequently divided on the question; many Negroes, especially parents of students, considered white teachers superior to black instructors and were opposed to the

[17] Edward P. Smith to Oliver O. Howard, Apr. 2, 1870, Edmund A. Ware to Erastus M. Cravath, Oct. 25, 1870, AMA Archives; *People's Advocate*, Mar. 25, 1882; Earl Edgar Dawson, "The Negro Teacher in the South," M.A. Thesis, University of Iowa, 1931, pp. 74-75; Oscar J. Chapman, "A Historical Study of Negro Land-Grant Colleges," Ph.D. Dissertation, Ohio State University, 1940. For a perceptive study of black pressures for Negro teachers in public schools, see Howard N. Rabinowitz, "Half a Loaf: The Shift from White to Black Teachers in the Negro Schools of the Urban South, 1865-1890," *Journal of Southern History*, XL (Nov. 1974), 565-94.

drive for black control of schools. The interplay of these various attitudes produced smoldering tensions in several communities.

The first freedmen's school, started by the AMA at Fortress Monroe, Virginia, in September 1861, was taught by a free black woman, Mary Peake. But at least three-quarters of the estimated 4,000 teachers in missionary schools from 1862 to 1870 were white. When the mission societies began to concentrate on secondary schools and colleges, most of the black teachers and their small primary schools were absorbed into the public school system. Those societies that continued to sustain elementary schools—the AMA, the Presbyterians, and the Quakers—kept black teachers in charge of many of them, and half of the Presbyterian and Quaker teachers in 1877 were black. Some of the higher-grade institutions also employed black teachers. The AMA's school in Charleston had an interracial faculty headed by a black principal in the 1860s. The trustees of Howard University made an effort to recruit black professors, and four Negroes were on the faculty in the early 1870s. The Methodist Freedmen's Aid Society stated in 1878 that, "as rapidly as we have been able to prepare our own students, we have introduced them . . . as teachers in our schools," and in 1882 one-fourth of the Methodist teachers were black. In 1881 the Baptist Home Mission Society pointed proudly to 10 black instructors in its secondary schools and colleges. Negro teachers joined the faculties of Claflin in 1870, Straight in 1871, Fisk in 1875, Clark in 1876, and Atlanta in 1881.[18]

But with the exception of Howard, most missionary colleges and secondary schools had only one or two Negroes each on their staffs by the early 1880s and some of them had none. This became a sore point in several black communities. "The employment of a colored teacher would increase the influence of the school," wrote the AMA's black minister in Mobile, and "shut the mouths of those who are murmuring." The all-black Virginia Educational and Historical Association published a paper in 1876 titled "Colored Teachers for Colored

[18] Semi-Annual Reports on Schools for Freedmen, 1867-1870, U.S. Bureau of Refugees, Freedmen and Abandoned Lands, Washington, 1867-1870; AM, XIV (June 1870), 128; Annual Report, Presbyterian Committee of Missions for Freedmen, 1875, p. 5; Minutes of the Executive Board of the Friends' Freedmen's Relief Association of Philadelphia, Apr. 8, 1879, Department of Records, Philadelphia Yearly Meeting (I am indebted to Philip Benjamin for this reference); South Carolina File, 1865-1868, AMA Archives; Walter Dyson, Howard University: The Capstone of Negro Education, Washington, 1941, pp. 348, 371; Eleventh Annual Report FASME, Cincinnati, 1878, pp. 19-20; HMM, III (Aug. 1881), 166; Jay S. Stowell, Methodist Adventures in Negro Education, New York and Cincinnati, 1922, pp. 179-80; Willard Range, The Rise and Progress of Negro Colleges in Georgia, 1865-1949, Athens, Ga., 1951, pp. 149-51; Joe M. Richardson, "A Negro Success Story: James Dallas Burns," Journal of Negro History, L (Oct. 1965), 275-78.

Schools" criticizing Hampton Institute for its lack of black teachers. A black lawyer in South Carolina demanded in 1883 that "Negro teachers exclusively be employed to teach Negro schools," while T. Thomas Fortune urged blacks to "repel the philanthropy which sustains colleges . . . where the rule is applied that the race can learn but cannot instruct or manage—worthy objects of charity but without ability to disburse the charity."[19]

This drive for more black faculty met a mixed response from white missionaries. Some urged a crash program to recruit and train Negro teachers. The secretary of the Baptist Home Mission Society wrote to the president of Richmond Institute in 1872: "You do not know how resolutely colored leaders have pressed us to employ and pay colored teachers. . . . I pray you take your strongest and ablest students . . . and drill them, and *drill* them, and DRILL them" until they are qualified for faculty positions. Several AMA principals urged the association's central office to hire more black instructors. Though Negroes "may not be the very best teachers," wrote one, "it seems to me when the object of the A.M.A. is to fit colored teachers & missionaries to work among their own people," blacks should be "recognized and encouraged" by appointment to responsible posts. The principal of Storrs School in Atlanta advised the AMA secretary to yield to black pressure: "It will be well for them to try to manage the school for they will never be satisfied until they do," she wrote, and if the board "is wise in its selection of teachers I think they will do well. Certainly we are not the ones to oppose them, for it is for this work that we have been educating them."[20]

But other white administrators counseled caution in hiring black teachers on the ground that few Negroes were yet qualified. Laura Towne wrote in 1873 that schools taught by blacks on the South Carolina sea islands "are always in confusion, grief, & utter want of everything. It is hard to imagine schools doing so little good." She kept white teachers at her own Penn School until their black replacements were thoroughly trained. The president of Straight University in New Orleans urged the AMA not to employ black teachers in the theological and law departments just because of "this clamor for colored teachers. . . . We can't have any humbug about this department for the sake of color. . . . Colored teachers are not generally successful."[21]

[19] William Ash to Michael E. Strieby, Feb. 26, Mar. 13, 1878, AMA Archives; *People's Advocate*, Aug. 26, 1876; *New York Globe*, Oct. 13, Aug. 11, 1883.
[20] James B. Simmons to Charles H. Corey, Dec. 27, 1872, in Corey, *A History of the Richmond Theological Seminary*, Richmond, 1895, pp. 97-98; E. C. Stickel to M. E. Strieby, Dec. 27, 1875, Amy Williams to Mrs. Thomas Chase, quoted in Thomas Chase to Strieby, Mar. 19, 1878, AMA Archives.
[21] Towne to William C. Gannett, Feb. 9, Dec. 14, 1873, Gannett Papers,

Some black leaders insisted that traditional academic standards should not be the main criteria for hiring teachers. The black poet and journalist J. Willis Menard believed that only black instructors could achieve true rapport with students "because their color identity makes them more interested in the advancement of colored children than white teachers, and because colored pupils need the social *contact* of colored teachers." A black preacher thought "it is not well to train colored youth too much with white people" for "they soon begin to think that their own people do not know anything." And Francis Grimké agreed that "the intellects of our young people are being educated at the expense of their manhood" when "in the classroom they see only white professors." In their slowness to appoint black teachers, the schools "are failing to use one of the most effective means in their power, of helping on this race."[22]

But Negroes were not united behind this viewpoint. A black woman, herself a teacher, condemned as a "peculiar error" the argument that blacks should be given jobs "without due regard to their fitness. . . . We do not wish the standard of excellence lowered for us. To admit the necessity is to insult the Negro. . . . We should not allow a mistaken race pride to cause us to impose upon [our youth] inferior teachers." The school inspector for the AMA reported in 1878 that blacks in Atlanta "have again, as last year, arrayed themselves on both sides of the question and each party has petitioned . . . one for colored teachers & the other for Northern whites." In a few cases after the mission societies had turned their schools over to black teachers, the decline in quality prompted black leaders to ask for a return of whites. "Since the cessation of your work among us," wrote one Negro, "the schools have degenerated, and the system as operated here is a mere farce."[23]

Divisions in black communities *pro* and *con* white teachers tended to follow a pattern. Clergymen, alumni, and younger people usually desired black teachers because of their own ambitions or their belief in race pride. Parents of school-age children generally favored white teachers, whom they considered more intelligent, more experienced, and better disciplinarians than blacks. When the AMA appointed

---

Rochester University Library; James A. Adams to Erastus M. Cravath, Nov. 17, 1874, Jan. 11, 1875, AMA Archives.

22 Menard in *Florida News*, Dec. 5, 1885, clipping in ABHMS Archives; Simon P. Smith to Edward F. Williams, June 28, 1880, Williams Papers, Amistad Research Center, Dillard University; Grimké, "Colored Men as Professors in Colored Institutions," *A.M.E. Church Review*, II (Oct. 1885), 142-44.

23 Josephine Turpin, "Teaching as a Profession," *A.M.E. Church Review*, V (Oct. 1888), 108; Thomas N. Chase to M. E. Strieby, July 5, 1878, AMA Archives; Henry L. Shrewsbury to Ednah D. Cheney, Feb. 19, 1886, Cheney Papers, Boston Public Library.

black teachers for the lower grades of Straight University, parents complained that there was no point in sending their children to Straight since they could go to colored teachers in the public schools. Personal jealousies also sometimes caused particular Negroes to prefer white teachers over blacks from a rival faction in the community. When the white teacher of a Quaker school in Salem, North Carolina, took on a black assistant, the parents called a protest meeting. Negroes were "so jealous of each other," wrote the northern Quaker, that they refused to allow one of their own to exercise authority. "She must not 'rule my child' for 'she's no better than mine.' "[24]

Because of divided opinion among both races on the issue of black teachers, the AMA decided in 1877 to "make haste slowly in this regard." In subsequent years the association emphasized "slowly" more than "haste." In 1890 the secretary reported after a tour of AMA schools that they "do far better with white teachers." As late as 1895 only 12 of 141 teachers in the association's 17 secondary schools were black; only four of 110 faculty members in its five colleges were Negroes. A black journalist wrote in 1901 that the AMA's small number of Negro teachers had long been an "eyesore" to the race and that "only the splendid work of the association has kept down an agitation of this matter."[25]

It was not only the high quality of AMA schools but also the tiny black constituency of the Congregational Church that muted criticism. The Baptist and Methodist societies, on the other hand, were under greater pressure from the large black memberships of their denominations. During Joseph C. Hartzell's secretaryship the Methodist Freedmen's Aid Society increased the proportion of black teachers in its schools from less than a third in 1888 to half in 1896. Hartzell maneuvered carefully in what he called "these delicate matters." To blacks who urged him to appoint more black teachers he replied with some asperity that "there is but one basis of judgment and that is, adaptability and capability . . . irrespective of color." But to white trustees he wrote that "the color question is one of very great significance. . . . The next man who comes in as Professor . . . must be a colored man."[26]

[24] C. H. Thompson to E. M. Cravath, Oct. 27, 1874, AMA Archives; Leah Dore to William H. Haines, Dec. 1, 10, 1888, Records of the Friends' Freedmen's Relief Association (I am indebted to Philip Benjamin for this reference).

[25] Thomas N. Chase to M. E. Strieby, Nov. 26, 1877, AMA Archives; Secretary Augustus F. Beard's report to the Executive Committee, Apr. 14, 1890, AMA Exec. Comm. Minutes, Amistad, Research Center, Dillard University; *Cleveland Gazette*, Jan. 19, 1901. The AMA required higher qualifications for teachers than the other mission societies. In addition to its 22 secondary schools and colleges, the association sustained about 50 elementary schools in 1895. Most of their teachers were black.

[26] Hartzell to W. Wesley, July 28, 1892, Hartzell to I. W. Joyce, Aug. 3, 1893, FASME Archives.

In 1887 only one-fifth of the Baptist teachers were black; by 1895 the proportion had risen to more than half, though the latter figure is slightly misleading. The salaries of 39 of the 136 black teachers in Baptist schools were paid by black state conventions, which owned 15 of the schools receiving Home Mission Society aid. Of the teachers supported directly by the society, two-fifths rather than half were black. The Presbyterians had the largest percentage of black teachers in their higher schools—three-fifths by 1895—despite the small black membership of the Church.[27]

In 1895 there were 93 schools for Negroes of nominal high school or college grade in the South founded and/or supported by the northern mission societies. In the 89 institutions for which data are available there were 1,028 teachers, of whom 370 (36 percent) were black.[28] Viewed in one way, this was real progress. A race one generation away from slavery and illiteracy had advanced to the point of supplying one-third of the teachers for the higher schools founded or supported mainly by another race. Yet this progress was less impressive than it seemed. Most students in these schools were still in elementary grades, and 90 percent of the black faculty were teaching these grades rather than secondary or college classes. Even in schools with a sizable black faculty, policy decisions were made by whites. Though blacks served on the boards of trustees of most colleges, these boards usually had little power. Ultimate control rested with the mission societies, on whose boards Negroes were only nominally represented. While most blacks who benefited from mission schools recognized that the greater experience and resources of whites made a large degree of white control inevitable at least for a time, a vocal minority dissented. From the outset they struggled for greater influence in the management of some schools.

27 *HMM*, IX (July 1887), 192, XVI (Aug. 1894), 321, XVII (Nov. 1895), 415; *Church at Home and Abroad*, IX (Mar. 1891), 248, X (Oct. 1891), 334.

28 In 1895 there were 29 colleges and professional schools and 64 secondary schools. For details, see Appendix B. Bennett College was not really a college-level institution in 1895, which places the percentage of black faculty in Methodist colleges lower than indicated in Appendix B. The Presbyterians, Quakers, and the AMA owned more than 100 elementary schools not included in these figures. Also not included are the following: schools supported by the Roman Catholic and Protestant Episcopal Churches, most of which were parochial elementary schools sustained by local parishes or dioceses rather than by northern mission societies; schools sponsored by the southern Presbyterians and Methodists; schools owned by the all-black denominations; independent institutions like Tuskegee, which were founded and conducted by Negroes, even though they received most of their support from the North; and Lincoln University in Pennsylvania, which had been founded before the war and was sustained by a Presbyterian agency independent of the Board of Missions for Freedmen.

This conflict first broke into the open during the search for a successor to General Oliver O. Howard as president of Howard University in 1874–1875. Most black trustees and many students supported Dean of the Law School and acting President John Mercer Langston for the job. But the white Congregationalists (most of them members of the AMA) who had founded Howard believed that Langston, despite his Oberlin degree and eminence as a black leader, lacked energy as a fund raiser and "was not the man to hold the institution to the religious and moral ideas on which it was founded." The board offered the presidency to three white men in succession; two of them declined and the third died before he could formally assume office. Embittered by what he considered the paternalism of white trustees and by the AMA's attempt to control the university, Langston resigned his positions and fired a parting shot at "this Sectarian and Denominational influence" that tolerated the Negro as trustee or professor "only as he serves to give color to the enterprise." The black man, he declared, "seeks release from such associations and their self-assumed control of his affairs."[29]

Meanwhile Howard University was sliding toward collapse. The cessation of Freedmen's Bureau support and the Panic of 1873 had reduced its annual budget from $87,000 in 1872 to $11,000 in 1877. Believing that only a white man of prominence and administrative experience could tap the springs of northern philanthropy and save the school, black and white trustees finally united to elect William W. Patton president in 1877. A Congregational minister and former district secretary of the AMA, Patton was a good administrator. He raised money in the North, persuaded Congress to make annual appropriations for the school, brought the university from the brink of disaster, and built it into a major institution. But his relations with the black community were strained. He ran Howard with a strong and sometimes domineering hand. Some of the five black trustees (there were 18 white trustees) and many alumni disliked his "overbearing ways." The *People's Advocate*, a black newspaper, declared in 1883 that "there are very few *white* men who possess the qualifications of a president of a college where *colored* men principally are educated," and Patton was not one of the few.[30]

[29] Quotations from *Congregationalist*, July 1, 1875; Langston, *Emancipation and Citizenship. The Work of the Republican Party*, Washington, 1875, pp. 7-8; interview with Langston published in *NYEP*, June 26, 1875. See also Edward P. Smith to Oliver O. Howard, Nov. 23, 1874, Apr. 13, June 9, July 16, Nov. 5, Dec. 1, 20, 1875, Jan. 14, 1876, Howard Papers, Bowdoin College Library; and *Independent*, July 29, 1875.

[30] Dyson, *Howard University*, 301-06, 386-88; *Advance*, May 3, 1877; *People's Advocate*, June 9, 1883; Jeremiah E. Rankin to Oliver O. Howard, Oct. 15, 1889,

The *Advocate*'s comment was prompted by a contretemps over the appointment of a black man as Professor of Greek. Patton opposed the candidate, Wiley Lane, on the ground that he was not qualified. On this occasion the black trustees outmaneuvered the president and the board elected Lane. Patton reacted with ill-advised remarks about black people pushing themselves into places for which they were not prepared, which provoked a storm among Washington Negroes. One black leader demanded Patton's resignation in favor of Frederick Douglass, who could "surround himself with a Faculty of brilliant and able colored men" and thereby "do more to demonstrate the capacity of colored men than anything we can think of." When Lane died of pneumonia in 1885, Patton forced the appointment of a white successor instead of another black man whom Negro trustees thought at least as well qualified. Francis Grimké, a member of the board, published an article blasting Patton as a "hypocrite" and a "pseudo-friend" of the black man. "If this is philanthropy," said Grimké, "then I, for one, think we have had quite enough of it. If this is the treatment we are to continue to receive from our friends, then it is time for us to begin to pray to be delivered from our friends."[31]

Regarded by many Negroes as their national university, Howard remained a center of controversy. When Patton retired in 1889, the board with enthusiastic black support elected Jeremiah E. Rankin as his successor. An abolitionist and pastor of the integrated First Congregational Church in Washington, Rankin had won wide respect in the black community. His goal as president was to "cultivate in colored people a sense of *independence* of the white race: not antagonism but independence." He tripled the number of black teachers in 13 years and promoted two black men to deanships. But he ran up against more independence or perhaps antagonism than he had bargained for. When he did appoint whites (including his own daughter) to staff vacancies he was criticized for not appointing blacks. Rankin also made the mistake of taking sides in the factional infighting on his fac-

Howard Papers. Patton was a kinsman of President Hayes and a one-time pastor of the church to which Congressman Joseph Hawley of Connecticut belonged; these relationships helped make him an effective lobbyist for Howard University in Congress.

31 Quotations from *Washington Bee*, Apr. 5, 1884; *People's Advocate*, June 30, 1883; Grimké, "Colored Men as Professors in Colored Institutions," 147-48. See also Rayford W. Logan, *Howard University: The First Hundred Years, 1867-1967*, New York, 1969, pp. 104-105; *People's Advocate*, June 2, 9, 1883; *New York Freeman*, June 6, 1885; Simon P. Smith to Edward F. Williams, July 12, 1883, Williams Papers, Amistad Research Center, Dillard University; John W. Cromwell to William S. Scarborough, Feb. 20, 1885, Francis Grimké to Scarborough, June 16, 1885, Scarborough Papers, Wilberforce University Library (I am indebted to David A. Gerber for calling the last two references to my attention).

ulty, thereby alienating the two leading black professors, Kelly Miller and James M. Gregory, the latter of whom resigned angrily in 1895. Editor Calvin Chase of the *Washington Bee* demanded Rankin's ouster. "What claim has Dr. Rankin to the presidency of that institution? Is it not set apart for colored people?" But when Rankin retired in 1903 the *Bee* apologized for earlier attacks based on misinformation and praised him for having "done more . . . for the negro" than any other man in the country. "You have been a faithful public servant," Chase told Rankin, "and to you the negroes owe a debt of gratitude."[32]

By this time the black deans had carved out their own spheres of power. Rankin's successor, John Gordon, tried to restrict the growing autonomy of the Teachers College under Dean Lewis B. Moore and the Commercial College under Dean George W. Cook. The *Bee* supported the president because editor Chase believed that inefficiency and intrigue in these colleges had grown to scandalous proportions. The affair escalated into a bitter power struggle that, while not racial in origin, took on racial overtones as it became a showdown between a white president and two black deans. Although Moore and Cook rallied many students and alumni behind them, the *Bee* continued to back Gordon and charged that "personal pique . . . selfishness, cupidity and ambition" motivated the deans' recalcitrance. When a hundred students demonstrated against Gordon and called for his resignation, the *Bee* urged the expulsion of the students and the firing of the "teachers who encouraged or inaugurated that disgraceful scene."[33]

But an outspoken group of alumni and faculty, charging that among other things Gordon had displayed racial prejudice by joining white clubs and sending his children to white schools, sided with the deans and finally forced the president's resignation. Some leaders of this movement were not above the suspicion that they wanted the job for themselves. The jockeying for the succession caused Chase to reverse his earlier demands for a Negro president and to ridicule the intrigues

[32] Quotations from Rankin to Albion W. Tourgée, Apr. 26, 1890, Tourgée Papers, Chatauqua County Historical Museum, Westfield, N.Y.; *Washington Bee*, July 3, 1897, Feb. 28, 1903. For the initial black support of Rankin, see Frederick Douglass to Rankin, Dec. 4, 1889, in *Washington Bee*, Jan. 4, 1890; Richard T. Greener to Francis J. Grimké, Dec. 27, 1890, in Carter G. Woodson, ed., *The Works of Francis James Grimké*, 4 vols., Washington, 1942, IV, 25; James M. Gregory to Oliver O. Howard, June 8, 1889, L. Deane to Howard, July 2, 5, 1889, Rankin to Howard, July 3, Oct. 15, 1889, Jan. 6, 13, 1890, Howard Papers. Rankin's contretemps with black faculty is described in Kelly Miller's unpublished autobiography, chap. 22, cited with the permission of his daughter May Miller Sullivan, and in *Washington Bee*, Sept. 7, 1895, Jan. 13, 1900. Rankin was perhaps the leading American sacred poet of his day and was the author of the world-famous hymn, "God Be With You Till We Meet Again."

[33] Dyson, *Howard University*, 64-65; *Washington Bee*, Nov. 18, 25, Dec. 9, 16, 30, 1905, Jan. 27, 1906.

among black aspirants for the post. Alluding to the alleged power struggles, backstabbing, and corruption in the Negro public schools of Washington under a black superintendent, Chase predicted that a similar situation would prevail at Howard under a black president. To the advocates of a "colored president for a colored school" the *Bee* stated: "If the existence of Howard University depended upon the colored people, the institution could not exist a day. . . . White men have done far more to ameliorate the condition of the negro, and to elevate him in the social scale than negroes themselves have ever done."[34]

After long discussions, the trustees decided to appoint an outsider free of factional allegiances. They unanimously called Wilbur P. Thirkield from his post as secretary of the Methodist Freedmen's Aid Society to become president of Howard. An able and sensitive administrator, Thirkield rode herd on his warring deans and retained the confidence of all parties. During his six years as president he persuaded Congress to double the annual appropriation to $100,000 and wrung an extra $150,000 from the lawmakers for a science and engineering building. He also obtained a gift of $50,000 from Andrew Carnegie for a new library. He modernized the curriculum and made Howard more widely respected than ever before.[35]

When Thirkield was elected a bishop of the Methodist Episcopal Church in 1912, an "unholy scramble" for his job took place between Moore, Cook, and Kelly Miller (who had been dean of the College of Arts and Sciences since 1907). Each of three factions in the black community backed a different dean. But while a majority of white trustees desired the election of a black president, only two of the eight Negro trustees supported any of the black candidates. If any two of the three deans had withdrawn from the contest in favor of the third, a black man would have been elected. Since each of them preferred a white man to one of his rivals, a white president was finally chosen. Although two-thirds of the faculty was black by this time, another 14 years passed before Howard had a black president.[36]

While events at Howard received wide publicity in the Negro press, the struggle over control of Methodist and Baptist schools was in some

[34] Quotations from *Washington Bee*, Dec. 30, 1905, Jan. 27, 1906. See also Miller, "Autobiography," chap. 25, and Charles Howard to Edward F. Williams, Apr. 11, 1906, Williams Papers.

[35] Logan, *Howard University*, 150-56; *Washington Bee*, May 26, 1906, May 25, 1912.

[36] "Unholy scramble" from *Washington Bee*, June 1, 1912. See also *ibid.*, June 8, 15, 22, July 6, 13, Aug. 3, 1912; Dyson, *Howard University*, 65, 375; Miller, "Autobiography," chap. 26.

respects more intense. Black militancy reached high tide in these churches between 1880 and 1900. Resentment at the failure of the ME Church to elect a black bishop spilled over into the work of the Freedmen's Aid Society and exacerbated tensions already existing. When Joseph C. Hartzell became secretary of the society in 1888 he promised that "a colored brother" would be appointed field agent as soon as a vacancy occurred. Three years later he named M.C.B. Mason field agent with the special duty of increasing the contributions from black conferences. But this did little to mollify black militants, who reacted angrily when the 1892 General Conference authorized a second secretary and elected a white man to the post. Within another year, however, the society had promoted Mason to assistant secretary and given him responsibility for raising money in white as well as black conferences. Hartzell had confidence in Mason and began grooming him for promotion to secretary.[37]

In 1889 Hartzell appointed Charles Grandison principal of Bennett Seminary in Greensboro, North Carolina. "I want him especially to make a first class success," said Hartzell, "because it is the first colored man appointed to an institution as important as that." Bennett was raised to the status of a college and its principal to president a few years later. Meanwhile the society appointed two more black principals of secondary schools and in 1893 chose Isaiah B. Scott as president of Wiley University in Marshall, Texas. This "gives an opportunity for another good colored man to come to the front and make a success," wrote Hartzell to a white professor at Wiley, "and I want him to have a good faculty to stand with him and by him in every particular." Scott took hold smoothly at Wiley; Hartzell was proud of the society's "first class work without any fuss in the way of giving a position to a reliable colored man."[38]

When some Negroes nevertheless accused Hartzell of applying stricter criteria to blacks than whites for teaching and administrative posts, the secretary replied that on the contrary he had often bent over backward to give blacks the benefit of the doubt. In 1891, for example, the society fired a black professor at Clark University who had been feuding for years with the white president. The latter claimed that the professor had refused to teach certain courses, had often missed classes, and had tried to stir up student antagonism toward the administration. The professor insisted that he was the victim of an "attempt

[37] Hartzell to J. M. Buckley, July 8, 1888, Hartzell to Isaiah D. Scott, Dec. 29, 1888, Hartzell to M.C.B. Mason, July 17, 1891, Hartzell to A.E.P. Albert, July 17, 1891, Hartzell to A. McDade, Mar. 6, 1895, FASME Archives.

[38] Hartzell to J.W.E. Bowen, May 10, 1889, Hartzell to B. L. Billups, June 16, 1893, Hartzell to M.C.B. Mason, June 16, 1893, FASME Archives.

to crush down negro manhood" and had been fired only because he refused to "stoop to low things in order to retain the favor and good will of men who have set themselves up as . . . big Negro bosses." Hartzell tried to prevent an open break, but finally concurred with the decision to fire the professor. "The question of color does not enter into it at all," Hartzell told black friends, "except that . . . I have personally interceded to secure his retention in the school for two years which would not have been done if he had been a white man."[39]

The most serious conflict in Methodist schools originated in an attempt by Claflin University's black trustees to wrest control of the school from the Freedmen's Aid Society. In this case the issue was complicated by South Carolina's annual $10,000 appropriation for vocational courses at Claflin, which made the state a third party in the struggle for control. One of the white faculty members paid by the state in 1890 was William J. De Treville, a member of an old South Carolina family. Two of the black professors paid by the Freedmen's Aid Society were black-power advocates who made no secret of their coolness toward whites. This was a formula for trouble, and trouble came in March 1890. For two years one of the black professors, J. N. Cardozo, had been bickering with De Treville. The pretext for their increasingly acerbic exchanges was religion—Cardozo charged De Treville with lacking piety, and De Treville accused Cardozo of distracting students from their work with noisy revivals—but the real issue was race. When President L. M. Dunton left the room during a faculty meeting in March 1890, a shouting match broke out between Cardozo and De Treville in which the former called the white man a liar and De Treville denounced Cardozo as a hypocrite. Dunton returned in time to stop the argument short of violence. But when the two professors met on campus the next day and again exchanged insults, De Treville lost his temper and began to beat Cardozo with his cane and did not stop until Dunton came running up to separate them.[40]

This affair caused an awful row. Dunton suspended De Treville

[39] R. T. Adams to the *Atlanta Times*, undated clipping, 1891, in Hartzell Papers, Drew University Library; Hartzell to F. A. Fortson, Sept. 3, 1891, Hartzell to Charles N. Grandison, Sept. 4, 1891, Hartzell to R. T. Adams, Sept. 22, 1891, FASME Archives. The professor was F. A. Fortson and the president was W. H. Hickman.

[40] This paragraph is based on newspaper clippings in Hartzell's scrapbook, Hartzell Papers, and on the following letters: Hartzell to Dunton, Mar. 8, 1890, Hartzell to J. S. Chadwick, Mar. 8, 1890, Hartzell to Cardozo, Mar. 20, 1890, Hartzell to A.E.P. Albert, Apr. 7, 1890, Hartzell to George W. Gray, Apr. 15, 1890, Hartzell to John W. Hamilton, Apr. 15, 1890, FASME Archives; Mrs. L. M. Dunton to William B. Claflin, Apr. 25, 1890, Claflin Papers, Rutherford B. Hayes Memorial Library, Fremont, Ohio.

immediately; Cardozo and his black colleague resigned and left campus the same day, hoping that enough students would follow them to break up the school and force its reorganization under black leadership. In this they were disappointed. By promising to fire De Treville, Dunton managed to calm the students. His next step was more difficult. With Hartzell's help he tried to persuade De Treville to resign and the state board to accept his resignation, but at first they refused. Dunton faced a dilemma: as he wrote to the school's Massachusetts patron, "if I should go against the State then I may lose the moral and financial support of the State. If I should go against the Claflin Board I give an offense to the colored people that no argument could correct."[41]

After more than a month of negotiations, Dunton and Hartzell finally persuaded De Treville to resign. But in the meantime, rumors circulated among students and alumni that Dunton was about to sell them out. Those "were dark days," Dunton's wife later wrote in a private letter. "No language could convey to you the wildness, the rashness . . . of a few colored leaders . . . There were days when it seemed impossible to get the best ones among them to speak truthfully about the most ordinary matters. The old untruthfulness and secretiveness inherited from slavery came to the surface in all its force." Dunton himself reflected, also privately, that "it is [not] wrong for them to aspire to teach their own schools and manage their own concerns, but unfortunately for them not one in 1,000 has enough executive ability to manage the concerns of his own household successfully. It is not really their fault, as they have had but little experience in independent management." The president feared that "an effort will be made to tear up things at our next trustee meeting. But they must not be allowed to have their own way in this matter. Until they furnish a considerable proportion of the funds necessary to conduct the school, they should be content to allow others to manage it."[42]

It is not hard to see why blacks responded to this attitude with the "old untruthfulness and secretiveness" of slavery. And though the Claflin crisis of 1890 was resolved and the school went on, unrest continued to fester. A black trustee declared that "we are no more than figure-heads. . . . It is only a question of time when there will be revolt." But President Dunton's last sentence quoted in the preceding paragraph stated an axiom of missionary education: power flowed

[41] Hartzell to Dunton, Mar. 15, 1890, Hartzell to J. F. Spence, Apr. 28, 1890, Minutes of the executive committee of the Freedmen's Aid Society, meetings of Mar. 17, June 7, 1890, FASME Archives; Dunton to William B. Claflin, Mar. 24, 1890, Claflin Papers.

[42] Mrs. L. M. Dunton to William G. Claflin, Apr. 25, 1890, L. M. Dunton to Claflin, Mar. 24, 1890, Claflin Papers.

from the purse. The Freedmen's Aid Society had been successful in raising money, said Arthur Edwards of the *Northwestern Christian Advocate*, because contributors had confidence in it. There would be no such confidence in 22 separate boards of trustees. "Liberal Methodists" in the North, Edwards warned, "will not risk $300,000 annually to the tender mercies of the rhythmical phrase, 'Home rule for our colored schools in the south.' They will give cash confidently [only] so long as the cash is wisely expended." Northern Methodists provided more than half of Claflin's operating funds, the state contributed almost a third, and blacks themselves only a sixth. "Nothing would please us better than that the South Carolina Conference could become responsible for the support of Claflin," wrote Hartzell to a black critic, "but until it does . . . those who are responsible for the support of the Faculties must have the chief voice in their selection."[43]

Another dispute at Claflin in 1894–1895 prompted some black Methodists to support a movement to end the school's state appropriation and to establish a separate A. & M. college in which the "professors and instructors shall be of the negro race." At the South Carolina constitutional convention of 1895, Benjamin Tillman cooperated with black delegates to achieve this goal. The Colored Normal, Industrial, Agricultural and Mechanical College of South Carolina came into being the next year with a black president and faculty. Thus with the aid of a racist politician who disfranchised them and publicly endorsed lynching, South Carolina blacks got a college free from northern control.[44]

As the power struggles in Methodist schools came to a head in the 1890s, black moderates tried to work out a compromise. E. W. S. Hammond, who had earlier led the drive for a black bishop and had been tempted toward separatism by the Church's failure to elect him to this post, now praised the "marvelous work" of missionary schools. "I can conceive of no calamity so appalling, so calculated to blast the hopes and retard progress in the great struggle for manhood, as to be let alone," cut off from white help. At the same time, Hammond gently reminded the Freedmen's Aid Society that as Negroes became "manly

---

[43] Trustee quoted in *SWCA*, July 25, 1895; *NWCA*, Aug. 7, 21, 1895; Hartzell to A. Middleton, June 29, 1889, FASME Archives. Hartzell applied the same policy to the society's white schools. During a dispute with the board of Little Rock University he declared that "we cannot for a moment submit to any such dictation from that quarter." Hartzell to C. E. Libby, July 20, 1889, *ibid.*

[44] George B. Tindall, *South Carolina Negroes, 1877-1900*, Columbia, S.C., 1952, pp. 229-30; *Journal of the Constitutional Convention of the State of South Carolina*, Columbia, 1895, pp. 580-81; Hartzell to Dunton, July 24, Nov. 3, 1894, Hartzell to J. W. Hamilton, Aug. 23, 1895, Hamilton to J. E. Wilson, Sept. 17, 1895, Hamilton to Dunton, Feb. 12, 1896, FASME Archives.

and strong" it was "perfectly natural" that they wanted more authority in "the appointment of teachers and other matters pertaining to the local management of our schools." In 1895 the Freedmen's Aid Society met this wish halfway. It promised enlarged powers to local boards in proportion to the increase in black support for the schools, with the ultimate aim of transferring ownership to the boards when the schools became largely self-sustaining. The percentage of black support grew from a quarter to more than two-fifths by 1915. The authority of local boards, especially in the hiring of teachers, increased in rough proportion to this rise in self-support, but in 1915 the society still owned and controlled most of the schools.[45]

Potential black dissatisfaction with this state of affairs was tempered by the election of M. C. B. Mason as secretary of the Freedmen's Aid Society in 1896; thereafter one of the two secretaries was always black, and he exercised authority over white as well as black schools until the former were placed under a separate agency in 1908.[46] Within a week of taking office, Mason was overwhelmed with applications from blacks for jobs. The harassed secretary published a reply: "I will be only too glad to help and encourage any young colored man or woman who has character, ability, and common sense," but "recommend no man [just] because he is colored." An efficient administrator, Mason also functioned as a lightning rod for black discontent. He could say no to black requests when similar action by a white secretary would cause trouble. He sometimes sided with white teachers in disputes with blacks, thus preventing the matter from becoming a racial confrontation. That Mason could do this and retain the confidence of both races during his 16 years as secretary was a tribute to his tact and ability.[47]

Ironically, during Mason's first years as secretary the policy of promoting blacks to administrative posts was actually suspended. The depression of the 1890s had run the society into a debt of $250,000. Two of the black college presidents and one of the secondary school principals appointed by Hartzell had made the problem worse by spending thousands of dollars without authorization or record. In the

[45] Hammond in *Christian Educator*, II (Apr. 1891), 106-08, and *SWCA*, Aug. 29, 1895; Minutes of the Board of Managers of the Freedmen's Aid Society, meetings of July 2, Oct. 23, 1895, FASME Archives; *Christian Educator*, VII (June–July 1896), 88.

[46] The society resisted pressure from some white schools to place themselves under John W. Hamilton, the white secretary, and to relegate Mason to supervision of black schools only. Hamilton to J. L. Fowler, June 14, 19, 1897, Mason to Frank Adkinson, Mar. 18, 1897, FASME Archives.

[47] This paragraph is based on a reading of Mason's letters in the FASME Archives. Quotation from *Christian Educator*, VII (June–July 1896), 99.

case of Bennett College the society was unaware of the expenditures until creditors threatened to sue for unpaid bills. "One of the most important prerequisites in connection with our Presidents is to be able to manage finances," wrote Mason's associate John W. Hamilton in 1896. Since black presidents had done badly in this regard, both Mason and Hamilton sought a white man of "tried financial ability" when the presidency of Clark became vacant in 1897. Not until the depression was over and black aspirants had been thoroughly trained in bookkeeping and fiscal efficiency were any more black principals or presidents appointed.[48]

By 1915, 10 of the 23 Methodist schools and colleges were headed by Negroes, 71 percent of their teachers were black, their boards of trustees exercised modest powers, and one of the secretaries of the Freedmen's Aid Society was black. Although black control was not yet a reality, progress in that direction was steady enough to quiet the black power controversy among Methodists.

The power struggle in Baptist schools was even sharper than in their Methodist counterparts. Many of the younger generation of black Baptist leaders who emerged in the 1880s grew restless in the leading strings of the northern-based Home Mission Society and the American Baptist Publication Society. These separatists (or progressives, as they sometimes called themselves) wanted to break free from dependence on whites. Black cooperationists, on the other hand, maintained that the race could not yet support its own schools or publication society. The shifting patterns of this debate led to the founding of several independent black agencies that came together to form the National Baptist Convention in 1895. After two stormy decades in which the original distinction between separatists and cooperationists became blurred, the National Baptist Convention split into two hostile conventions with almost the same name (the seceding faction added "of America" to its title).[49]

These events formed the context of the conflict over control of Baptist schools. The conflict was triggered in the early 1880s by incidents at two of the schools. Principal G. M. P. King of Wayland Seminary in Washington was a strict disciplinarian "inclined to rule slightly in love, but very *abruptly with a rod of iron*," as a black critic put it. In 1882

---

[48] Quotations from Hamilton to Matthew W. Dogan, Aug. 27, 1896, and Hamilton to A. J. Howard, Dec. 28, 1896, FASME Archives. There are many letters in the Archives concerning this problem.

[49] Carter G. Woodson, *The History of the Negro Church*, 2nd ed., Washington, 1945, pp. 235-41; James D. Tyms, *The Rise of Religious Education among Negro Baptists*, New York, 1965, pp. 148-66; Owen D. Pelt and Ralph Lee Smith, *The Story of the National Baptists*, New York, 1960, pp. 79-109.

he lost his temper with a 17-year old student and pushed her into a chair. Blacks reacted angrily to the news of this affair, which was exaggerated by repeated telling. Twenty students left school in protest; alumni petitioned the Home Mission Society for King's dismissal. Secretary Henry L. Morehouse investigated and found no grounds for dismissal, though he advised King to apologize. King did apologize privately to black ministers but refused to do so to the student unless she first apologized for cursing him. She not only refused, but had King arrested for assault. Although she later dropped the charge, the incident escalated into a *cause célèbre* that almost wrecked the school. One of the leading separatists, Walter Brooks, made this "Wayland outrage" the chief issue in his campaign for black independence. If King was not removed or forced to apologize, said Brooks, then "we, like our brethren in the African M.E. Church, must rise and build, and take management of our own schools."[50]

But King remained, and eventually Wayland returned to normal. Meanwhile a clash between President Charles E. Becker of Benedict Institute in Columbia, South Carolina, and the outspoken black minister Edward M. Brawley added fuel to the separatist fire. Becker was a man of mediocre ability and poor judgment. When Brawley began agitating for more black teachers and a local board of trustees, Becker saw it as a threat to his own authority. Brawley was willing to see it that way too and traveled around the state making black power speeches. "We do not wish any longer to be treated like children," he said, "but like men." In letters to Secretary Morehouse, Becker dismissed the idea of a board of trustees as "infinitely absurd. . . . There is not a single man [among the black preachers] aside from Brawley who can speak two consecutive sentences correctly. . . . If I see a little more of the *ignorance & degradation* of these people . . . I think I shall give up work in sheer despair."[51]

In this frame of mind Becker addressed the white South Carolina Baptist convention in December 1882, where he was quoted as saying: "The ignorance and degradation of the colored people appall me. . . . To-day their condition as to religion is immeasurably worse than it was in slavery." These well-publicized words played right into Brawley's hands. An exasperated Morehouse called both men onto the carpet at society headquarters in Philadelphia. Whatever he told them was effective, for they stopped battling in public. More important, the so-

[50] Quotations from *People's Advocate*, May 17, July 14, 1883. See also *ibid.*, Feb. 24, 1882, June 2, Aug. 11, 1883; *Washington Bee*, May 26, 1883; *New York Globe*, June 2, 1883, June 20, 1885.

[51] This paragraph is based on undated memoranda by Morehouse and on the following letters in the ABHMS Archives: Morehouse to Brawley, Apr. 20, 1881, Becker to Morehouse, Sept. 28, Oct. 5, Nov. 27, Dec. 4, 11, 12, 1882.

ciety in 1883 created an interracial board of trustees for Benedict with "advisory powers" and began to establish similar boards for its other schools to prepare for the time when blacks "may maintain and manage these institutions for themselves." Some black militants interpreted this as "a great victory. . . . Let us see more Brawleys in our midst."[52]

For several years this arrangement seemed to work smoothly. Becker remained at Benedict, and Brawley became a cooperationist. Pointing out that blacks were already represented on local boards and school faculties in larger proportion than their degree of financial support for the schools, Brawley told his former separatist allies in 1890 that if "we would like greater influence, we must afford larger support."[53]

The experiences of several schools founded by state Baptist conventions seemed to provide an object lesson in the need for northern assistance. Two such schools were State University in Louisville and Selma University in Alabama. Within a few years of their founding, both turned to the Home Mission Society for help. The society subsidized each with grants of a few thousand dollars a year. Not surprisingly, their presidents became cooperationists. When separatist Walter Brooks urged blacks in 1883 to rise up and build their own schools, the president of State University replied: "Does he not know that if our brethren rise, most of them will sit down again? . . . I state from positive knowledge that the colored people are not able to support the schools now maintained in the South." Five years later the president of Selma University asked separatists: "How many [schools] have we supported ourselves that have attained to anything? . . . It is all nonsense for any of us to say we can support them, and then will not do it."[54]

Eventually the Home Mission Society subsidized more than a dozen black-owned schools. Although separatists were "slow to admit this stubborn fact," said a black financial agent of the Society, "had it not been for [this] timely help . . . the schools would have been lost." But such support involved a degree of supervision that some separatists were unwilling to accept. "If Negro schools cannot get money from the Home Mission Society without making cowards and bootlicks of all the men connected with them," said one, "it were far better that they never get a dime." Ironically, some of the schools founded with a flour-

52 *Independent*, Jan. 11, 1883; *HMM*, v (Feb. 1883), 35; *New York Globe*, Jan. 20, Feb. 17, 1883.

53 Brawley, ed., *The Negro Baptist Pulpit: A Collection of Sermons and Papers*, Philadelphia, 1890, pp. 248-49.

54 President William J. Simmons of State University in *People's Advocate*, July 28, 1883; President Charles L. Purce of Selma University in *HMM*, x (Dec. 1888), 348.

ish of separatist rhetoric, such as Lynchburg Seminary in Virginia and Hearne Academy in Texas, were compelled a few years later to go hat in hand to the Home Mission Society for help. And in Georgia one of the leading separatist spokesmen, Emmanuel K. Love, was disillusioned by his failure to raise funds for an independent school. "We are simply attempting too much," said Love in 1887. "We are poorly prepared to control and manage high schools financially and intellectually."[55]

Trouble at two of the society's schools in 1887 and 1891 ushered in a decade of renewed black-white confrontation. The first eruption occurred at Roger Williams University in Nashville, where the authoritarianism of the president and the poor food provided by the bursar set off a student protest in 1887. As usual the grievances snowballed, as rumors of even worse white misdeeds ran through the black community. Two-thirds of the students threatened to walk out unless the president and bursar resigned. At the height of the controversy these hapless officials received anonymous notes warning that "this is our house and you dirty pup we will kick your ass out if you do not act better" and informing the bursar that his "daughter makes love to one of us niggers." The local black press cheered on the students. "The Race is Rising," proclaimed one newspaper. "We are not what we were twenty years ago. We think and act now."

The Home Mission Society investigated the affair and concluded that most of the charges against the president and bursar were "unfounded" or "trivial." Since these men had forfeited student and community support, however, Morehouse persuaded them to resign. At the same time the society overruled the board of trustees and expelled two student protest leaders. Four trustees thereupon resigned and issued an angry statement: "We declare ourselves unable to see how any good is to come from charters and boards of trustees" if the Home Mission Society planned "to disregard entirely the judgment of the faculties and to usurp or set aside, at will, the plainest functions of Trustees." Roger Williams never fully recovered from this affair and eventually merged with a Baptist school in Memphis.[56]

The Baptists seemed afflicted with more inept college presidents than any other mission society. At Bishop College in Marshall, Texas, a feud between President S. W. Culver and a black teacher, David Abner, kept the school in a turmoil for two years, 1889–1891. In his

---

[55] A. R. Griggs to Thomas J. Morgan, Oct. 3, 1900, undated clipping of an article in the *Christian Organizer*, and clipping of a letter from Love published in the *Georgia Baptist*, Nov. 24, 1887, all in ABHMS Archives.

[56] These two paragraphs are based on correspondence, clippings and other material in an envelope marked "Roger Williams University," ABHMS Archives. The two white officials were President William Stifler and Bursar Theodore Balch.

own account of the affair Culver comes across as almost paranoiac. As he described it, Abner was a poor teacher filled with "egregious vanity and self-conceit" who concocted "the basest plots and intrigues [with] the purpose of turning some at least of the students against me." Twelve parents and alumni sent a list of grievances to Morehouse complaining of Culver's dyspeptic temperament and his disciplinary harassment of teachers and students. "The people feel that neither theirs nor the rights of their children are respected, that their mildest rebukes are regarded as great rebellions and as a consequence they are put in a totally helpless attitude." Morehouse resolved this dispute by forcing both Culver and Abner to resign.[57]

The society's problems in Texas were not over. The black state Baptist convention was divided between separatists and cooperationists. In 1893 the separatist leader Richard Boyd denounced every black man "who would try to sell his race to a white man's soulless corporation" (the Home Mission Society) and formed a second state convention. The strife between the two conventions produced new crises at Bishop College. Some northern Baptists suggested that the school be turned over entirely to the Negroes, but the new white president feared that "they would only quarrel over the spoils until all was destroyed." "I am very much discouraged," he wrote in 1897. "Sometimes I think that these seven years of very hard labor, the best years of my life, will not amount to much in the future." He resigned a year later.[58]

The wave of separatism crested in the second half of the 1890s. It was during those years also that the black nationalism of AME Bishop Henry M. Turner won its largest following, among Baptists as well as Methodists. Morehouse confronted the separatists on their own ground in an address to the organizational meeting of the National Baptist Convention in 1895, where he followed Turner at the podium. Turner had told the delegates to spurn all white men and to worship a black God. "Talk of this sort," said Morehouse, "is the race spirit gone mad." He pleaded for the ideal of Christian brotherhood. "Don't reproach us, brethren, *because we are white*—we can't help it. . . . We may not be altogether lovely; you may not be altogether lovely; but we are to love one another even as Christ loved us."[59]

[57] Culver's undated statement, a clipping of the statement by parents and alumni dated May 30, 1891, a letter accompanying this statement from F. G. Davis and E.W.D. Isaac to Morehouse, an undated clipping from the *Southwestern Baptist*, and two letters from Culver to Morehouse dated June 14 and 15, 1890, are in the ABHMS Archives.

[58] Boyd in *Austin Herald*, Mar. 18, 1903, clipping in ABHMS Archives, N. Wolverton to Malcolm MacVicar, Sept. 16, 1897, *ibid.*

[59] *HMM*, xvii (Nov. 1895), 413-14. For Turner and black nationalism, see Edwin S. Redkey, *Black Exodus: Black Nationalist and Back-to-Africa Movements, 1890-1910*, New Haven, 1969.

In the next few years secretaries Morehouse and Thomas J. Morgan spoke out repeatedly against the "unreasoning racism" of black separatists and accused a "few noisy, ignorant, ambitious, self-seeking would-be leaders" of trying to turn the race against its northern friends. In reply, Richard Boyd said that "the race movement which you so much dread and stigmatize . . . is simply a determination on the part of the Negroes to assume control of their race life and evolve along such lines and such ways as their spirit and genius may dictate . . . and not as the Anglo-Saxon may outline. . . . Hitherto the Home Mission Society has led and the Negroes have followed; henceforth the Negroes must lead and the Home Mission Society may follow . . . if it will."[60]

Though the separatists talked of supporting their own schools, what they really seemed to want was control of the society's schools *and* of the northern money they hoped would continue to flow south to finance them. This was precisely what the Home Mission Society would not grant. Morgan sympathized "with their laudable desire to manage their own institutions." But in many of the schools owned by blacks, he said, funds had been stolen, bookkeeping was nonexistent, teachers were semiliterate and principals incompetent. "It is easy to judge from these facts what would become" of the 13 Home Mission Society schools if the society "should foolishly and recklessly, in deference to the demand of hot-headed leaders, turn over to them their entire financial control." The society was trying to train promising teachers in administrative methods for the day when they would be ready to take over without loss of efficiency. But so long as most of the money for the schools came from the North, "just so long will it be necessary to have their control and management vested in the Society. Any other course than this would justly fail to command the confidence of contributors." The most important question, said Morgan, was not whether the schools were under black, white, or mixed management, but "whether they are doing their work aright."[61]

Some of the separatists were willing to settle for mixed management, though they wanted the mixture mostly black. Georgia provided an opportunity for the society to bring together the cooperationists and moderate separatists. Black Baptists in the state had split into two conventions in 1893. In an effort to head off separatist talk of founding their own college in Georgia, Morgan presented to both conventions a plan whereby they would jointly form an education association to work with the Home Mission Society in the coordination of all educa-

[60] *HMM*, xx (Aug. 1898), 254, xxi (July 1899), 264; clipping of an open letter from Boyd to Morgan, in *Christian Banner*, Dec. 22, 1899, ABHMS Archives.

[61] Morgan to Malcolm MacVicar, May 7, 1897, from an undated clipping of an unnamed newspaper, ABHMS Archives; *HMM*, xvi (Aug. 1894), 321-23, xvii (Nov. 1895), 418, xxi (Dec. 1899), 446-47.

tional activities in Georgia. The board of trustees of Atlanta Baptist College would then be enlarged by the addition of more black members and given increased powers. If this was unsatisfactory, Morgan suggested as an alternative the lease of the college to the state's black Baptists for one dollar per year, providing they would assume its entire support. Scarcely anyone in Georgia was ready for this; a majority of both conventions agreed to Morgan's first proposal in 1897.[62]

The initial success of this plan encouraged the society to establish similar associations in other states. But the Georgia accord almost broke down in 1899 when the separatists, resentful of the race's continued subordinate position on the reorganized board of Atlanta Baptist and token representation on the Spelman board, carried out their threat to found a rival institution, Central City College in Macon. A dissident group of black Baptists in Virginia also denounced the Home Mission Society as paternalistic, demanded more influence in the running of Virginia Union University, carried a majority of the state Baptist convention with them in 1899, and dissociated the black-owned Virginia Seminary at Lynchburg from Virginia Union when the society refused to make the required concessions.[63]

Fearful that the separatists' antiwhite rhetoric would dry up northern support for Baptist schools, black moderates rallied to the society's defense. A flood of adulatory and sometimes sycophantic letters poured across Morgan's desk, many of which he published in the *Home Mission Monthly*. Several erstwhile separatists embraced the society with the fervor of converts. "The craze of Negro independence," wrote one, was a "blind infatuation of sentimentalism. . . . We are too poor, ignorant and inexperienced to try to set up a kingdom of our own." Those who denounced the Home Mission Society, wrote another, were "worse than a child that would destroy its own mother." The president of a black-owned school receiving aid from the society said that the separatists were motivated only by a "greed for office. . . . The fellow that makes the bitterest race speech gets the most applause, and he is honored as a champion of the rights of the race." The writer believed in self-help, "but it is possible to separate self help from self

---

[62] *HMM*, XIX (June 1897), 237-38 (July 1897), 271-72 (Oct. 1897), 342-43, XX (Jan. 1898), 27-30 (Apr. 1898), 109-17; Benjamin Brawley, *A History of Morehouse College, Atlanta*, 1917, pp. 88-92.

[63] Range, *Rise and Progress of Negro Colleges in Georgia*, 109-10; Ridgely Torrence, *The Story of John Hope*, New York, 1948, pp. 137-38; *HMM*, XXI (July 1899), 264 (Dec. 1899), 444, 450-51, XXII (Jan. 1900), 1-2. Hailed as a grand venture in self-help and independence, Central City College soon faded into a marginal secondary school and eventually collapsed. In Virginia the cooperationists split off from the separatists and formed a second state convention that continued to work with the Home Mission Society.

foolishness; it is possible to practice self help and yet receive the generous aid of abler friends." Black independence did not mean that Negroes could "take all we can get from the whites and abuse them as much as we please." He hoped the militants' conduct would not "discourage our white friends who have stood by us so loyally during the dark and bitter past." In 1902 President E. C. Morris of the National Baptist Convention expressed a desire that "all of the misunderstandings cease and all the hard sayings be left in the forgotten past."[64]

The society reciprocated these signs of good will by stepping up efforts to promote blacks to important positions. "I am not at all prepared to admit the false philosophy that a white man cannot teach a Negro," wrote Morgan in 1900, but "I recognize that race feeling is very strong, and that other things being equal, a Negro will have more influence upon his race than a white man." Atlanta Baptist College hired more black faculty and began grooming John Hope for its presidency. Hope assumed the office in 1906, becoming the first black president of a Home Mission Society college. By 1915 nearly half the faculty in the society's eight colleges was black, as were two of the college presidents, more than nine-tenths of the teachers in the secondary schools, and 15 of the 16 principals of these schools.[65]

The Presbyterian Board of Missions for Freedmen also moved quickly in this direction. In response to black complaints, the board began to phase out white teachers earlier than any other mission society. In 1891 Daniel J. Sanders, born a slave, was installed as president of Biddle University (later renamed Johnson C. Smith University). Several new black faculty members were also appointed in 1891, and within three years the Biddle faculty was entirely black. Some Presbyterians criticized this as a "rash experiment"; the Board of Missions conceded that it was a "bold experiment," but hoped it would not prove to be rash. In 1893 the board pronounced the venture a success; administrative control of Biddle was thenceforth in black hands, though major policy decisions were still made by the northern board.[66]

[64] *Virginia Baptist*, July 7, 1900, *Georgia Baptist*, June 27, 1901, clippings in ABHMS Archives; *HMM*, XXII (Apr. 1900), 123-24; pamphlet copy of Morris's address to the National Baptist Convention, 1902, ABHMS Archives.

[65] *HMM*, XXII (Dec. 1900), 336, XXX (Nov. 1908), 439-40; Brawley, *Morehouse*, 95; Torrence, *John Hope*, 142-57, 164, 185. Although the black power controversy in Baptist schools subsided after 1900, it did not disappear. In 1908 a separatist faction in South Carolina, angry with white paternalism at Benedict College, founded their own school at Sumter, Morris College. Like Central City College in Georgia, Morris never amounted to more than a third-rate high school. Lewis K. McMillan, *Negro Higher Education in the State of South Carolina*, Orangeburg, S.C., 1952, pp. 139-40.

[66] *Church at Home and Abroad*, IX (Mar. 1891), 248, XIII (Apr. 1893), 208-209. The other major Presbyterian college, Lincoln University, took a radically dif-

After 1900 the black power issue in Negro education subsided for two decades as the mission societies continued to increase the number of black teachers and administrators in their schools. The change was most dramatic in the AMA's secondary schools. In 1895 only 9 percent of the teachers in these institutions were black; by 1905 the proportion had risen to 53 percent, and seven of the 21 principals were Negroes.

As in the 1870s the main pressure for change came from alumni and young black teachers impatient with the continued presence of white veterans who blocked their promotions. One black male teacher wrote in a private letter: "If that old bitch from Massachusetts would ever die or get through here, I could begin to live." But resistance from parents of students once again helped bring a virtual halt for several years to the increase of black teachers in AMA schools, and in 1915 the ratio of black and white faculty was about the same as it had been in 1905. The AMA's assistant superintendent of education reported that, when black teachers replaced whites in some communities, enrollment declined as parents complained that "their Harvard was being taken from them and they were being pushed back into the log cabin school." On more than one occasion parents formed a "Committee to Save Our School" and circulated petitions urging the retention of white teachers. Intraracial color prejudice also played a role in resistance to black teachers. This was particularly true at Charleston's Avery Institute, which had long been the preserve of the city's light-skinned Negro aristocracy. When the AMA proposed to appoint a dark man (William Pickens) as principal of Avery, the opposition was so strong that the association assigned him elsewhere.[67]

W. E. B. Du Bois also hoped the AMA would not convert its faculties from white to black too fast. "The only remaining point of intimate sympathetic broad-minded contact between the white and black world in the South is through the white teachers of Negro schools," he wrote in 1906. "We must keep up this contact, plead for it and nurture it.

---

ferent position on the issue of black teachers and administrators. Lincoln's faculty and board of trustees remained almost entirely white until the 1930s. This caused resentment among Lincoln alumni and students. In 1916 Francis Grimké, an alumnus, said that Lincoln's lily white policy was "a standing argument against the professed friendship and Christian character of the men who have permitted this condition of things to continue as long as it has." On the other hand, a poll of 127 students at Lincoln in 1927 showed that 81 of them were opposed to having a black professor. Grimké to George Johnson, Mar. 25, 1916, in Woodson, ed., *The Works of Grimké*, I, 530-31; Francis L. Broderick, *W.E.B. Du Bois: Negro Leader in a Time of Crisis*, Stanford, Cal., 1959, p. 178.

[67] Lura Beam, *He Called Them by the Lightning: A Teacher's Odyssey in the Negro South, 1908-1919*, Indianapolis, 1967, pp. 89, 150-54; Frederick L. Brownlee, *New Day Ascending*, Boston, 1946, pp. 134-36; Harlan Paul Douglass, *Christian Reconstruction in the South*, Boston, 1909, pp. 74-75.

Every Negro school should have a mixed faculty, just as some day we hope every white school will have."[68] The cross-pressures from younger blacks ambitious for places in the schools, parents who wanted white teachers to stay, mulattoes who did not want dark-skinned principals, men like Du Bois who wanted to preserve mixed faculties, southern whites who equated mixed faculties with social equality, and black separatists who wanted to control Negro education caused many headaches for missionary educators. But the trend toward greater black representation continued.

By 1915, 60 percent of the teachers in all secondary schools and colleges founded by or receiving support from northern missionary sources were black. The proportion of black faculty in the colleges alone had nearly doubled from 27 percent in 1895 to 51 percent in 1915. Eight of the 30 college and professional school presidents were black, while 52 of the 85 secondary schools had Negro principals. But most of the schools and colleges, including those with black administrators, were still governed mainly by the mission societies or by white-dominated independent boards.

Thus despite gradual movement toward black control, white influence was still paramount. This was doubtless owing in part to the paternalism inherent in mission enterprises and to a reluctance by those in authority to give up power, but it was also the product of continued dependence on northern financial support and of a desire to maintain high standards. Adam Clayton Powell, Sr., recognized the importance of the first factor in 1930 when he estimated that "Negroes have paid only 10 per cent of the cost of their [higher] education during the last sixty-five years." Black people owed "our white friends a unanimous vote of thanks," said Powell, but "this kind of charity cannot and should not go on forever"; the race should do more to support its own institutions.[69]

Powell understated the race's financial contribution to its own education. Although precise figures are impossible to obtain, an educated guess would place the percentage of black self-support at one-third rather than 10 percent for the half century through 1915. Extrapolating from incomplete data in the mission society reports, it appears that the proportion of self-support in Baptist missionary schools rose from about one-quarter in the first part of the period to nearly half in later years, in Methodist schools from one-sixth to more than two-fifths, and in Presbyterian schools from one-quarter to at least one-third. It is hard to estimate the degree of black support for AMA and Quaker schools, but since the number of black Congregationalists and Quakers

[68] Article in *Moon*, reprinted in *Washington Bee*, Feb. 17, 1906.
[69] Article by Powell in Jordan, *Negro Baptist History*, 306.

was small it was probably less than for the other societies. Most of the black financing came from payments for board and room and tuition. In 1895–1896, $84,000 of the $107,000 contributed by black Baptists to Home Mission Society schools was from such fees and only $23,000 directly from black churches or individuals. In 1905–1906, about 10 percent of the support for Methodist schools came from black conferences and nearly 30 percent from tuition and fees. The level of black support for all of the white-founded mission schools from 1865 to 1915 rose from about 15 percent in the first decade to 40 percent in the last. This accords with several contemporary estimates. The Freedmen's Bureau calculated that blacks provided $785,000 (13 percent) of the total cost of $5,800,000 for freedmen's education from 1866 to 1870. President Horace Bumstead of Atlanta University estimated in 1891 that Negroes paid one-third of the cost of their higher education. The black educator Richard R. Wright concluded that blacks had paid 36 percent of the total cost of their schooling in Methodist institutions through 1907. And in 1915 the *Negro Year Book* estimated that of $81,000,000 spent for nonpublic black education since 1865, $57,000,000 had come from northern sources and $24,000,000 (30 percent) from blacks themselves.[70]

This was an impressive record for a people emerging from slavery. But it was still true, in Kelly Miller's words, that "as long as whites contribute the support they will continue to wield the dominant influence." Missionary reluctance to give blacks more responsibility in the formulation of policy and the control of funds may have been the result of an unjustified and patronizing distrust of the Negro's competence to manage things for himself. Some blacks certainly thought so. In 1923 William Pickens deplored the "absentee control" of many black colleges which suppressed black aspirations and prevented the race from acquiring administrative experience. And a black teacher maintained that on interracial faculties, white administrators "refused to take Negro members of the faculty into their confidence. They were given little meaningless jobs like keeping students of opposite sexes from kissing, seeing to it that lights were put out on time, watching the grounds so that nobody threw paper in the front yards, and the like."[71]

[70] For the Baptist figures of 1895-96, see *HMM*, XIX (July 1897), 260; for the Methodist data on 1905-06, see *Christian Educator*, XVII (Nov. 1906), 12. The contemporary estimates are from: Freedmen's Bureau reports summarized in Monroe Work, ed., *Negro Year Book, 1918-1919*, Tuskegee, 1919, p. 261; Bumstead cited in Samuel J. Barrows, "What the Southern Negro is Doing for Himself," *Atlantic Monthly*, LXVII (June 1891), 811; Wright, *Self-Help in Negro Education*, Cheney, Pa., 1908; and Work, ed., *Negro Year Book, 1915*, Tuskegee, 1915, p. 235.

[71] Miller, "The Education of the Negro," *Report of the U.S. Commissioner of Education for the Year 1900-01*, 2 vols., Washington, 1902, I, 836; Pickens, *Bursting*

At the same time some AME churchmen, while expressing pride in their schools as an example of the Negro's willingness to "paddle his own canoe," nevertheless confessed that "ofttimes it seems sorry paddling," for the schools were "weak and inefficient" and suffered from "a lack of stability." Many observers believed that the petty authoritarianism of black college presidents was at least as bad as that of their white counterparts. Kelly Miller, who had once urged a faster conversion from white to black control, had changed his mind by 1933 when he lamented the "failure of Negroes to handle successfully practical projects which they had assumed." He now believed that "the race is not yet sufficiently experienced . . . to justify assuming complete guardianship of higher institutions of learning. . . . This is not a race question, but only one of common sense." The change from white to black faculties had been "too sharp and sudden. It was a misfortune barely short of a calamity."[72]

It may be impossible to reach a consensus on whether the transition of power from white to black in Negro higher education was too fast, just right, or not fast enough. Evidence regarding administrative efficiency and the ability to impart skills and mastery of subject matter seems to indicate that white administrators and teachers were more successful than their black counterparts, at least before 1910. On the other hand, proficiency in these areas may have been achieved at the cost of restricting black initiative, self-reliance, and pride. It is not easy to say which goals should have been uppermost in Negro education. It can be said, however, that the missionary schools could not have been sustained by pride alone. Despite discord, these institutions survived and grew, keeping Negro higher education alive through difficult times. From the viewpoint of the black power movements of recent years, persistent white influence in Negro education perpetuated the blacks' colonial dependence on white liberals. But without this colonialism there would have been little black higher education; there would have been no Howard, no Fisk, no Lincoln, no Morehouse, no Spelman, no Atlanta University. And there would have been fewer educated leaders of black power movements.

Bonds, Boston, 1923, pp. 143-52; McMillan, "Negro Higher Education as I Have Known It," *Journal of Negro Education*, VIII (Jan. 1939), 11.

[72] *A.M.E. Church Review*, III (Oct. 1886), 218; *African Methodist Recorder*, July 1887, quoted in Hagood, *The Colored Man in the Methodist Episcopal Church*, pp. 305-306; Daniel A. Payne, *History of the African Methodist Episcopal Church*, Nashville, 1891, pp. 446-47; Miller, "The Past, Present, and Future of the Negro College," *Journal of Negro Education*, II (July 1933), 418-19.

Part Three

The Revival of Militancy

Chapter Sixteen

The Shattering of Hope

Missionary educators had founded their schools on the belief that education was the path to racial equality. While this faith never died, it suffered serious strains when the civil and political status of blacks, instead of rising, declined inversely with their educational growth after 1890. Although optimistic gradualism enjoyed a renaissance with the emergence of Booker T. Washington to national prominence, the dominant theme of the post-1890 generation of neo-abolitionists became pessimism leading eventually to the revival of militancy and the founding of the National Association for the Advancement of Colored People. As the NAACP's principal founder, Oswald Garrison Villard, said in 1911, it was now obvious that the race problem "will not work itself out by the mere lapse of time or by the operation of education. . . . There is only one remedy—that the colored people shall have every one of the privileges and rights of American citizens."[1]

The year 1890 marked a turning point in race relations: Congress backed away from the federal elections bill; Mississippi adopted a new constitution that disfranchised black voters; Benjamin Tillman was elected governor of South Carolina. In the next two decades all but a handful of southern Negroes were disfranchised by poll taxes, white primaries, and literacy or property qualifications enforced against blacks but seldom against whites. During the same years southern states enacted a host of Jim Crow laws that segregated blacks in virtually every aspect of public life. One state after another followed South Carolina's lead in ousting from power the old conservatives, whose white supremacy sentiments had sometimes been tempered by benevolent paternalism, and replacing them with a new breed of southern politician, the Tillmans and James Vardamans and Cole Bleases who represented the "redneck" voters and whose chief stock in trade was a virulent racism. Lynching reached its worst level in the 1890s and became increasingly a racial and southern phenomenon. At the same time the growth of scientific racism, the advent of imperialism, and the beginnings of the northward migration of blacks intensified anti-Negro sentiment in the North as well. Race riots in several cities completed the scenario of the two decades after 1890, years that

[1] *Boston Herald*, Apr. 2, 1911.

Rayford W. Logan has aptly described as "the nadir of the Negro's status."[2]

One sign of the Negro's deteriorating status was the epidemic of Jim Crow laws. Before 1890, segregation in public accommodations was widespread but not total in the South. One of its most common manifestations was the second-class or "smoking" car on passenger trains, where black women as well as men were often forced to endure cheap cigar smoke, saliva-smeared floors, and vulgar profanity even if they bought first-class tickets. Frequent protests won some concessions, and in three decisions from 1887 to 1889 the newly created Interstate Commerce Commission ruled that railroads must provide equal accommodations for both races. Some Negroes hailed this as a victory, but the ICC's ruling did not require *integrated* accommodations, only *equal* ones. This endorsement of separate but equal opened the floodgates for Jim Crow legislation. By 1891, eight southern states had passed laws requiring segregated railroad coaches. It soon became clear that in practice separate meant *unequal*. Railroad companies stretched a curtain across the middle of a smoking car and called half of the car "first-class" for blacks, or set aside their oldest and dirtiest coaches as "Colored" cars. Thus blacks paid "first-class price for third-class accommodation," said the *Independent*, and "no sane man imagined" that the "equal" provisions of the law were ever enforced. Separate but equal was "a mere sham."[3]

Most former abolitionists were as much opposed to segregation *per se* as to the unequal facilities it produced. "The plea that equal accommodations are furnished," said Joseph C. Hartzell, "even if the promise is fulfilled, does not remove the injustices of the discrimination. Division at all, based solely on color, is un-American and un-Christian." Francis Garrison declared that "it makes one's blood boil to see the restrictions swept away a generation ago being steadily & relentlessly re-enacted." In 1890 the United States Supreme Court decided that Mississippi's 1889 separate coach law did not violate the Constitution's interstate commerce clause; six years later the Court ruled in *Plessy* v. *Ferguson* that Louisiana's railroad segregation statute did not violate the 14th Amendment. "These decisions are a positive disgrace," said the Chicago *Inter Ocean*. "The spirit of Roger B. Taney seems to be the presiding genius of that tribunal. . . . Take all these cases together and they complete the denial [of] the fourteenth amendment."

[2] Logan, *The Betrayal of the Negro from Rutherford B. Hayes to Woodrow Wilson*, New York, 1965, p. 62.

[3] August Meier, *Negro Thought in America, 1880-1915*, Ann Arbor, 1963, pp. 71-72; C. Vann Woodward, *Origins of the New South, 1877-1913*, Baton Rouge, 1951, pp. 211-12; *Independent*, Dec. 26, 1889, Aug. 17, 1905.

Gloomy predictions that *Plessy* would encourage the extension of Jim Crow laws to every walk of life were fulfilled. By 1915 some southern courts required black and white witnesses to swear on separate Bibles, and Oklahoma mandated segregated telephone booths.[4]

The everyday consequences of Jim Crow went beyond the discomfort of dirty coaches or the humiliation of riding in the back of the streetcar. Many public libraries in the South excluded Negroes. After a vain attempt to open the new Carnegie Library in Atlanta to blacks, Wilbur P. Thirkield wrote in 1902 that southern whites "condemn the Negro for his indifference to those things that make for the higher moral and intellectual life, and then shut in his face the very doors that open into the larger and higher life." And the AMA's assistant superintendent of education pointed out that the exclusion of blacks from city parks forced the association's urban schools to give up nature study "because it was impossible to go where trees, birds, rocks, and flowers were."[5]

Degrading as Jim Crow was, it occupied less space in the abolitionists' catalog of southern crimes than disfranchisement. The denial of the ballot to blacks was nothing new; for more than a decade before 1890 every southern state had resorted to legal as well as extralegal means to maintain white political supremacy. Nevertheless, some blacks had continued to vote and even to hold office in many parts of the South. Beginning with Mississippi in 1890, however, one state after another took constitutional steps to reduce black political power to a cipher and insure permanent white supremacy.

The central feature of the new constitutions was a literacy qualification for voting. Eight states imposed this requirement; four of them adopted a property qualification as an alternative to literacy. On the face of it, these were not egregious conditions; six northern states also required voters to be literate. The idea of a literacy qualification appealed to several former abolitionists of mugwump outlook. A number of leading black spokesmen—including Fortune, Du Bois, and Langston as well as Washington—also came out in favor of such a requirement in the 1890s. If enforced without racial discrimination, they thought, it might do away with the intimidation, bribery, and cheating

[4] *SWCA*, Jan. 28, 1892; Garrison to Fanny Garrison Villard, Feb. 14, 1904, FGV Papers; *Louisville, New Orleans and Texas Railway Company* v. *Mississippi*, 133 U.S. 587 (1890); *Plessy* v. *Ferguson*, 163 U.S. 537 (1896); *CIO* (D) Mar. 6, 1890, May 20, 1896; C. Vann Woodward, *The Strange Career of Jim Crow*, 3rd rev. ed., New York, 1974, pp. 97-102.

[5] *Christian Educator*, XIII (May 1902), 7; Lura Beam, *He Called Them by the Lightning: A Teacher's Odyssey in the Negro South, 1908-1919*, Indianapolis, 1967, p. 76.

that had characterized southern politics since Reconstruction. Theoretically it could enlarge the black electorate in some states because the Negro literacy rate was approaching 50 percent while extra-legal suppression of black voters had reduced their numbers below that level. Several missionary educators predicted that a literacy requirement would stimulate increased school attendance by blacks. Even William Penn Nixon of the *Inter Ocean* considered such a qualification "not unreasonable," but warned that "the people of the North will watch the experiment to see that the new test is not made to apply to the colored race alone."[6]

The principle of manhood suffrage still had many abolitionist defenders, however, especially William Hayes Ward and William Lloyd Garrison, Jr. "We dread these tests of intelligence as a panacea for the ills and dangers" of republican government, said Ward. "The fact that a man cannot read is very far from proving that he is not intellectually competent to vote." Limited suffrage, said Garrison, would create "a sham democracy. . . . There is no class so poor or ignorant in a republic that does not know its own sufferings and needs better than can the wealthy or educated classes." Both Garrison and Ward pointed out that in the North and in Britain, mass education necessarily *followed* rather than preceded universal suffrage. The right to vote, said Garrison, "is the first and most important essential in a republic. It antedates the school of letters for it is itself the greatest school. Better that the door of every school-house in the South were closed, than that the ballot should be wrested from black hands. With the ballot sacredly guarded, school-houses will, in time, take care of themselves."[7]

So far as the South was concerned the debate about the abstract right of universal versus limited suffrage soon proved irrelevant. The new voting regulations, with such ingenious loopholes for illiterate whites as "understanding" clauses, "grandfather" clauses, and the like, were designed to eliminate virtually all black voters while preserving the franchise for every white man who cared to register and pay his poll tax. Southerners piously denied that they had violated the 15th Amendment, which prohibited disfranchisement only on grounds of race, color, or previous condition. Scarcely anyone was taken in by such protestations. Abolitionist newspapers denounced the franchise loopholes as "the most open and barefaced fraud," "illegal, unconstitu-

6 *HW*, Feb. 1, 1890; Meier, *Negro Thought*, 39-40; *AM*, XLIV (Dec. 1890), 426, LV (July 1901), 139; *CIO* (D), Dec. 8, 1888.

7 *Independent*, Oct. 17, 1889, Sept. 4, 1890, Mar. 26, 1908; speeches or letters by Garrison published in *Boston Sunday Globe*, Nov. 27, 1898, *Boston Telegraph*, n.d. (probably Dec. 1898), *Boston Globe*, May 15, 1900, and an unidentified Negro magazine, July 1900, clippings in WLG, Jr., Papers.

tional, and a sin," "reprehensible . . . infamous . . . vicious."[8] Branding the disfranchisers as "conspirators" who had carried out "a new nullification," abolitionists backed court cases to test the southern constitutions. But in *Williams* v. *Mississippi* (1898), the U.S. Supreme Court ruled that, since the Mississippi constitution did not discriminate *on its face* against blacks, it did not violate the 15th Amendment. With this decision, said William Garrison angrily, constitutional rights for blacks had reverted "practically to the Court of Roger Taney."[9]

As a cause of abolitionist anguish and protest, however, even disfranchisement took second place to lynching. Lynch law had existed in the South before 1890, of course, but in the 1880s it was almost as much a phenomenon of the frontier West as of the South, and more white men than black stretched hemp.[10] The number of lynchings reached an all-time recorded high of 255 (155 of them black) in 1892; thereafter the lynching rate declined, but the percentage of victims who were black rose sharply. From 1890 through 1899 the average number of lynchings per year was 188; this declined to 93 in the following decade, but while 82 percent of the lynchings had taken place in the South and 68 percent of all victims were black in the 1890s, these proportions increased to 92 percent southern and 89 percent black in the next decade. Even worse, lynching was becoming less a matter of furtive midnight hanging and more a public spectacle accompanied by torture and carried out by burning at the stake. A lynching bee sometimes became the occasion for a holiday, with railroads running special trains to the event and thousands of men, women, and children watching the saturnalia of mutilation, screams, and burning flesh. Even as the rate of lynching declined, therefore, the practice became more visible and vicious; most of all, it became more exclusively *racial*, a means of terrorizing black people. It was this that made lynching a major social issue in the 1890s; more than anything else, it was this that deflated the optimism of the 1880s and rekindled the militancy of such former abolitionists as the Garrisons, Edward H. Clement, and William Hayes Ward. The *Transcript* and the *Independent* along with the *Inter Ocean* became three of the foremost antilynching newspapers in the country.[11]

[8] *CIO* (D), Dec. 7, 1890; *NYEP*, Dec. 18, 1902; *BET*, Nov. 5, 1895, Mar. 26, 1898, Nov. 4, 1902.

[9] *BET*, July 15, Sept. 13, 1895; 179 U.S. 213 (1898); Garrison quoted in *Boston Telegraph*, Dec. ?, 1898, clipping in WLG, Jr., Papers.

[10] From 1882, when the *Chicago Tribune* first began keeping statistics on lynching, through 1889, 701 whites and 519 blacks were lynched. Calculated from the tables in Walter White, *Rope and Faggot: A Biography of Judge Lynch*, New York, 1929, pp. 230-31, and Arthur F. Raper, *The Tragedy of Lynching*, Chapel Hill, 1933, pp. 480-81.

[11] Data and percentages of lynchings calculated from the tables in *ibid.* The

"It is impossible . . . to speak with self-restraint on this subject," wrote Ward in 1892. Lynch mobs cared not whether their victims were guilty of any crime. "They wanted the sight of blood. . . . They were savages." Every participant in "such lawless orgies," declared Thomas J. Morgan, "is a murderer." Lynchings "debauch the public conscience; they subvert the foundations of society; . . . they degrade the blacks to the level of brutes and place the whites in the category of wild beasts." When a large meeting of blacks in Chicago protested lynching by refusing to sing "America," white abolitionists came to their defense against charges of un-Americanism. Who could be proud of a country where mobs burned black men with impunity? asked Arthur Edwards. "Sing it yourself if you want to," Edwards told critics; "we shall not."[12]

The un-Americanism theme emerged prominently in 1894 when the black antilynching crusader Ida B. Wells made a lecture tour of Britain illustrating the horrors of mob law with photographs and clippings from southern sources. Her speeches sparked the formation of a British Anti-Lynching Committee that included 18 members of Parliament and some of England's foremost clergymen and journalists. The *Inter Ocean* hired Wells as a correspondent and published her fiery dispatches from Britain. Outraged southerners accused her of exaggeration, distortion, and worst of all of stoking British anti-Americanism. But white abolitionists cheered her efforts and worked with blacks to organize antilynching committees in northern states to cooperate with the British group. This enterprise revived the transatlantic abolitionist alliance. Several leading members of the British Anti-Lynching Committee were descendants of British abolitionists. A mass meeting at Fanueil Hall in August 1894 to launch the Massachusetts Anti-Lynching League reminded the participants of an old-time antislavery gathering; the two main speakers were William Lloyd Garrison, Jr., and Moncure Conway, the Virginia-born abolitionist who had lived in England for two decades after the Civil War.[13]

One of the worst lynchings of all occurred at Newnan, Georgia, on a Sunday afternoon in the spring of 1899. A black man named Sam Hose had raped and killed a small white girl; the whites advertised their intention to burn Hose the following Sunday; the railroad ran

figures used by White and Raper were based on statistics initially compiled by the *Chicago Tribune* and later by the NAACP and by Monroe Work of Tuskegee. These figures probably understate the true number of lynchings, especially in the deep South.

12 *Independent*, May 26, 1892, Sept. 28, 1893; *HMM*, XXIV (Jan. 1902), 13-14; *NWCA*, Apr. 13, 1892.

13 Alfreda M. Duster, ed., *Crusade for Justice: The Autobiography of Ida B. Wells*, Chicago, 1970, pp. 125-87, 215-17; *Christian Register*, Sept. 6, 1894; *CIO* (W), June 26, 1894.

excursion trains to the site; two thousand people gathered for the ritual. Hose was chained to a tree and castrated; his ears and fingers were cut off one by one and distributed as souvenirs. After he was drenched with oil and burned alive, the mob cut his body to pieces with jackknives, took out the heart and liver, and divided up the relics. The Boston *Transcript* realized that "language is inadequate" for comment on this proceeding, but editor Clement tried anyway. "The whole country is disgraced for a generation to come before the civilized world," he proclaimed. When a group of clergymen pointed to Hose's crime in extenuation of the lynchers, the *Transcript* erupted in fury. "How ministers of the gospel, or in fact any other persons claiming to be Christian or even civilized, can ever justify themselves in that position" was beyond belief. "No crime of which any man can be capable, could extenuate the sickening savagery and lawlessness" of the affair. "Each member of the mob is before the highest judge a greater criminal than was the negro who was tortured and killed."[14]

The Hose lynching triggered some of the largest protest meetings in the North since the days of the Fugitive Slave Law. At one meeting in Boston a second-generation abolitionist got up and said that if such outrages could be tolerated, all the sacrifices of the Civil War (including for him the loss of his father on the battlefield) had been in vain. Albert E. Pillsbury, former attorney-general of Massachusetts and a nephew of Parker Pillsbury, noted that at the very moment of the Hose lynching, American troops were trying to impose the "blessings" of Anglo-Saxon civilization on the Philippines. An anti-imperialist, as were most of those in the audience, Pillsbury brought the crowd to its feet with the words: "Do you really think that we have any civilization to spare for the Philippines? And do you know of any better use we can make of our armies than to recall them from the islands . . . and see if they can suppress this rebellion against humanity?"[15]

Of all the rationalizations for lynching, the one that most incensed abolitionists was the assertion of its necessity to control black rape. Lynching statistics culled from newspapers and other sources by the *Chicago Tribune* showed that fewer than one-quarter of the mob victims were even accused of rape. Most were charged with murder; some were guilty of little more than alleged insolence toward whites or of being too prosperous for a "nigger." Antilynching crusaders cited these facts as proof, in Moncure Conway's words, that "all the hysterics about female honor . . . are ridiculous. . . . Lynchings are not for punishment of crime, but for terrorism of a race."[16]

While conceding that some black men committed rape, former abo-

14 *BET*, Apr. 24, 26, 1899.   15 *Ibid.*, May 10, 20, 1899.
16 *Christian Register*, Sept. 6, 1894.

litionists insisted that many more white men raped black women, whether the act was called by that name or not. In this respect, said Henry L. Morehouse, the "white problem" was greater than the "Negro problem" and "it is high time that this should receive the attention of reformers while the overworked 'Negro problem' should have a little rest." Mary White Ovington, a third-generation abolitionist, social worker, and a founder of the NAACP, made the same point in a short story entitled "The White Brute." Based on an actual incident, the story told of a black man and his new bride who were accosted by two white men while waiting for a train. The whites demanded the wife for their pleasure during the two hours before the train arrived. The black man clenched his fists and nearly attacked them, but subsided with the heartsick knowledge that if he did so he would be lynched and his wife raped anyway. The men took her off and returned her just in time for the honeymoon couple to make their train. It was incidents like this that outraged antilynching spokesmen and made them contemptuous of southerners who deplored lynching but blamed it on the black community for failing to restrain its young men from committing the "one unspeakable crime." Such talk, said Clement, only gave the "crazy crackers" license to "slash ears and carve roasted livers for keepsakes."[17]

The question was, what could be done about it? It was all very well for northerners to hold protest rallies and pass resolutions, but as the *Independent* confessed, the lynchers "do not hear our voice."[18] A similar problem had confronted abolitionists in the days of slavery, when southerners heard their voice all right but rejected its message. Abolitionists of those days had three strategies besides verbal protest to choose from: encouragement of slave insurrections; attempts to convert slaveholders themselves to abolition; or compulsory emancipation by the federal government. It was the last alternative that finally won out, but only at the cost of war. The same three alternatives faced antilynchers, who tested each only to meet failure. In the end the southern people themselves brought a halt to lynching by rope and faggot, but not until the 1930s.

Several abolitionists encouraged the idea of black retaliatory violence, especially after the Wilmington (N.C.) and New Orleans race riots of 1898 and 1900 added new dimensions to the horrors of mob violence. "History seems to teach that no people ever yet secured a

---

17 *HMM*, xvi (Mar. 1894), 87-88, xxv (Apr. 1903), 95-96; "The White Brute" reprinted in Mary White Ovington, *The Walls Came Tumbling Down*, New York, 1947, pp. 86-89; *BET*, May 31, 1899.
18 Aug. 9, 1894.

recognition of their rights . . . who were not willing, if need be, to fight for them," wrote Thomas J. Morgan who had commanded four regiments of black troops in the Civil War. In the midst of the North Carolina political campaign of 1898 which was climaxed by the Wilmington riot, the *Independent* advised blacks to "stand their ground and defend themselves under the divine law which bids him that hath no sword sell his garment and buy one." Although Negroes did not fight back at Wilmington, they did so on a few other occasions. "This is a cheering sign," thought Richard P. Hallowell, "full of hopeful significance."[19]

But most abolitionists were ambivalent on the issue of black counterviolence just as their fathers had been on the question of slave insurrections. Some like William Lloyd Garrison, Jr., inherited the Garrisonian philosophy of nonresistance. Most abolitionists, however, hesitated to endorse retaliatory violence for the same reason their forebears had hesitated to endorse insurrections—because they would provoke a backlash and fasten the chains of oppression more tightly. Black retaliation, said Arthur Edwards in 1895, would only "cause many a negro to fall into a bloody grave." Albert Pillsbury, on every other issue a militant, nevertheless thought it "idle to talk of retaliation, or blood for blood." It was "difficult to preach patience under such . . . great provocation," he told blacks, "but you must not put a weapon in the hands of your adversaries." While refusing to *advocate* violence, however, some abolitionists warned the South of the whirlwind its repression was sure to reap. When the race war came, they said, abolitionists would again be found on the Negro's side. "While it would be unwise for the negroes in the South to arm and fight," said Norwood P. Hallowell, another Civil War colonel of a black regiment, "they would have my sympathy. I should do what I could to help them. It might be foolish, but so was John Brown's raid."[20]

If counterviolence would not work, what would? Abolitionists had hoped at first to end slavery by appealing to the conscience of slaveholders. Despite the discouraging results of that effort, northern antilynchers of the 1890s repeated the attempt. Unwilling to believe that *"all* Southerners are bloody-minded," they thought that "a large and very influential class of people in the South deplore these outrages as much as any at the North." Abolitionists gratefully publicized every antilynching statement by a southern white. "More encouragement is

[19] Morgan, *The Negro in America and the Ideal American Republic,* Philadelphia, 1898, p. 138; *Independent,* Sept. 15, 1898; Hallowell, *The Southern Question,* Boston, 1890, p. 27.

[20] Edwards in *NWCA,* Oct. 9, 1895; Pillsbury in *BET,* May 10, 1899; Hallowell in *Boston Journal,* Apr. 28, 1899.

to be derived from these utterances," said Hartzell, "than from any possible denunciations . . . made in the North."[21]

But as lynchings continued, many former abolitionists became disillusioned with the "better class" of southern whites. Clement lamented that "the best citizens of the South never do anything more than 'deplore' such outrages." When Wilbur Thirkield spoke out strongly in Atlanta after the Sam Hose lynching, his life was threatened. A member of the local gentry wrote in the *Atlanta Constitution* that the teachings of Thirkield and other missionary educators had done "more to add to the insolence of the negro race than anything else," and proposed a 10-year prison sentence for any white person teaching in a black school.[22]

"A moral revolution is wanted" to be sure, wrote Oswald Garrison Villard, "but where is it to begin? . . . Editors can accomplish nothing by mere writing and printing. Nothing except the administration of law and the punishment of lynchers by death or long terms of imprisonment will ever put an end to the practice of lynching." Since state laws were impotent because juries rarely convicted lynchers and state governments were in the hands of men like Tillman who publicly condoned lynching for rape, the only answer seemed to be a federal antilynching law. Repudiating his earlier conviction that the race problem should be left to time and education, Edward Clement became one of the leading proponents of such a law. In the 1880s when the South seemed to be ruled by men of good will, said Clement, it had been right to give them a chance to carry out their promises of fair treatment. But now, in 1899, "there is nothing to justify it; for daily we read of her brutalities, practised under the pretext of protecting woman's virtue. . . . Some good people North plead 'time.' True, 'time' may do it; but, in the language of George W. Cable, 'it's likely to make bloody work of it.' "[23]

Albert E. Pillsbury, a constitutional lawyer of high repute, drafted an antilynching bill that was introduced in Congress in 1902. Designed to overcome the provisions of the federal system that placed murder under state rather than national jurisdiction, Pillsbury's bill was based mainly on the equal protection clause of the 14th Amendment. "Forbidding the state to deny equal protection is equivalent to requiring the state to provide it," he contended. The failure of a state to prevent a lynching "shall be deemed a denial to the citizen by the state of the equal protection of the laws." Under Pillsbury's bill every member of

21 *AM*, LI (Mar. 1897), 81; *Christian Educator*, VI (Oct. 1894), 204.

22 *BET*, Feb. 23, 1898; letter from B. M. Blackburn to the *Atlanta Constitution*, reprinted in *Independent*, June 15, 1899.

23 *NYEP*, Nov. 22, 1902; *BET*, June 26, Sept. 6, 1899.

a lynch mob and every state officer guilty of failing to protect the victim would be prosecuted in federal courts, and if necessary the army could be used to enforce the measure. As Pillsbury had feared, his bill was killed in the Senate Judiciary Committee on grounds of unconstitutionality. The idea of a federal law did not die, however, and Pillsbury's proposal became the basis of the Dyer antilynching bill in the 1920s (which was filibustered to death in the Senate).[24]

Frustrated by the apparent impossibility of doing anything about lynching, many abolitionists fell into a mood of despondency. Their belief in mankind's innate goodness had been burned out by the flaming pyres of the South. "The shrieks of burning human sacrifices to the revenges and mad passions of men" caused Clement to wonder if America was "a society sweeping towards the maelstrom." The lynch mob brought out "the wild beast in men" and "unless we can destroy the wild beast it will destroy us." Provoked to utter despair by the "blood-mania driving people frantic at the sight of black men charged with any offence whatever," Villard asked: "What have we left of civilization?" The old saying "scratch a Russian and find a Tartar," he said, must be "amended so as to read: 'Scratch an American and find a savage.' "[25]

Another reason for abolitionist despair was the deteriorating status of Negroes in the North. During the two decades before 1890 the northern black population had been relatively stable, with a higher percentage employed in middle-class occupations than earlier or later. Although discrimination was widespread, the passage of civil rights and school desegregation laws by many states at least held out the hope of progress. In some cities such as Boston and Cleveland, blacks exercised political power almost in proportion to their numbers and the black middle class was more thoroughly integrated into the social structure than at any time before or since. Although black slums and ghetto neighborhoods existed, they were generally small and scattered.

Ironically, just as a modest northward migration of blacks got under way in the 1890s, northern white attitudes became increasingly racist. In part this was a product of the migration itself, which skewed the black class structure downward and exacerbated racial tensions as the

[24] Pillsbury to Archibald Grimké, Oct. 27, 1899, Jan. 20, 1900, Pillsbury to Congressman William H. Moody, Jan. 20, 1900, Archibald Grimké Papers, Moorland Foundation Library, Howard University; Pillsbury, "A Brief Inquiry into a Federal Remedy for Lynching," *Harvard Law Review*, xv (May 1902), 707-13; Pillsbury to Mrs. George Ruffin, June 24, 1903, George L. Ruffin Papers, Moorland Foundation Library; Eugene Levy, *James Weldon Johnson: Black Leader, Black Voice*, Chicago, 1973, pp. 240-41.

[25] *BET*, Nov. 8, 1902, Aug. 6, 1895, Jan. 16, 1901; *NYEP*, Feb. 29, Mar. 9, 1904.

black population grew and spread. Although in 1900 only 10 percent of American Negroes lived in the North where they constituted but 2 percent of the total population, already the number of blacks in New York and Philadelphia exceeded 60,000. Their concentration into large ghettos had begun by 1900. Segregation in hotels, restaurants, and other places of public accommodation increased despite civil rights laws. Racial hatred festered, clashes between black and white became more frequent, and ugly riots flared in a half dozen northern cities between 1900 and 1908.[26]

Abolitionists did not ignore this beam in the eye of the North; quite the contrary. During the years 1882–1927, when an average of about 12 percent of the nation's black population lived in the North, less than 3 percent of the Negro lynchings took place there, yet abolitionist newspapers and orators hurled far more than 3 percent of their denunciations at these northern crimes, which "prove that we are worse than we . . . supposed we were," said William Hayes Ward. In 1901 a lynching described by the *Independent* as "one of the most atrocious in the history of the country" occurred at Leavenworth, Kansas. A mob took a black man from a jail, burned him before a crowd of five thousand, and allowed children to fight over the charred souvenirs. Race riots at Springfield, Ohio, in 1904 and Springfield, Illinois, in 1908 "marked a new and savage excess" in northern life, said Clement. And the infamous lynching at Coatesville, Pennsylvania, in 1911, in which a Negro who had killed a policeman was dragged from the hospital and burned alive, shook abolitionists more than any other lynching. "Such things come to us as the uncovering of the pit and the letting loose on earth of the awful creatures seen by Milton and Dante," wrote Villard. Though everyone knew the identity of the mob's leaders, a Coatesville jury acquitted them. "Tell it not in Charleston; publish it not in the streets of Atlanta," commented Ward and Villard bitterly. "What Northern State can hereafter criticise Southern leniency toward lynchers?"[27]

[26] These two paragraphs have drawn from a large number of secondary sources. Of particular value were Allan H. Spear, *Black Chicago: The Making of a Negro Ghetto, 1890-1920*, Chicago, 1967; Gilbert Osofsky, *Harlem: The Making of a Ghetto, Negro New York, 1890-1930*, New York, 1966; David M. Katzman, *Before the Ghetto: Black Detroit in the Nineteenth Century*, Urbana, Ill., 1973; John Daniels, *In Freedom's Birthplace: A Study of the Boston Negroes*, Boston, 1914, esp. 406-407; Mary White Ovington, *Half a Man: The Status of the Negro in New York*, New York, 1911, esp. 26-33, 214; Stephan Thernstrom, *The Other Bostonians: Poverty and Progress in the American Metropolis, 1880-1970*, Cambridge, Mass., chap. 8; and David A. Gerber, "Ohio and the Color Line: Racial Discrimination and Negro Responses in a Northern State, 1860-1915," Ph.D. Dissertation, Princeton Univ., 1971, to be published in 1976 by the Univ. of Ill. Press.

[27] *Independent*, June 9, 1892, Aug. 30, 1900, Jan. 24, 1901; *BET*, Mar. 9, 1904; *Nation*, Aug. 17, Oct. 12, 26, 1911; *Independent*, Aug. 24, Oct. 5, 1911.

De jure school segregation had come to an end in most of the North by the 1890s. But *de facto* segregation began to increase in that decade as urban ghettos grew. Ohio communities pioneered in the gerrymandering of school districts and the development of other quasi-legal devices for keeping the races separate. Abolitionists condemned these evasions as "wicked," "barbarous," "a miserable recrudescence of a dying injustice." In the new century several northern cities tried to reimpose *de jure* segregation; in Kansas they succeeded, aided by a state law of 1901 allowing cities with a population over 15,000 to provide separate schools. "This is a sad reactionary step," said Francis Garrison, "for the state preserved to freedom by John Brown."[28]

As the number of northern Negroes increased, their problems of making a living and finding a place to live grew more serious. Although white abolitionists probably paid less attention to these problems than they should have, they did open their newspaper columns to black writers on the subject and became involved after 1900 in social welfare and employment efforts for blacks in northern cities. They conceded that "in some respects" blacks were better treated in the South than the North. "In the South, for instance, a black man may enter the ordinary mechanical trades," said Clement, "whereas in the North he is practically debarred from being a carpenter, a bricklayer, or a painter." When northerners who criticized the South "exclude [Negroes] from societies, churches, theatres and what not [and] boycott them in business and refuse to let them houses except in the slums . . . it is a shame as well as an inconsistency."[29]

Although they deplored the "reactionary policy" of trade unions that excluded Negroes, abolitionist newspapers printed by union men—such as the *Independent*—were forced to deny jobs to black printers (the same was later true of the *Crisis* under Du Bois' editorship). On the other hand, the *Evening Post* and *Nation* under Villard were printed by nonunion workers, including a few blacks. Houghton Mifflin, where Francis Garrison was an editor, also employed several nonunion black printers in its plant. In the Quaker community of Salem, Ohio, abolitionist C. A. Bonsall had several black iron molders in his Buckeye Engine Company. Clement hired T. Thomas Fortune as an editorial writer for the Boston *Transcript*. On the whole, however,

---

[28] Leslie H. Fishel, "The North and the Negro, 1865-1900: A Study in Race Discrimination," Ph.D. Dissertation, Harvard University, 1953, pp. 310-51, 494-95; *Nation*, Sept. 29, 1887, Jan. 24, 1889, Feb. 15, 1894; *NWCA*, Oct. 6, 1897; *Independent*, July 29, 1886, Oct. 13, 1887, Oct. 7, 1897; *HW*, Apr. 13, 1889; Garrison to Booker T. Washington, Jan. 7, 1907, BTW Papers. For the Kansas law, see *General Statutes of Kansas, 1909*, Topeka, 1910, pp. 1633-34.

[29] *BET*, Nov. 8, 1889.

abolitionists did less than black critics thought they should have done to provide jobs rather than charity for the race.[30]

Although northern liberals expanded their work against discrimination in the North after 1900 through such organizations as the NAACP and the National Urban League, many of them stopped condemning the North for being as bad as the South. As Francis Garrison explained in 1906, northern self-criticism too often had "a back slant" when accompanied by the corollary, "What is the North that it should throw stones at the South? . . . The South interprets this as meaning 'It is not so bad after all,' or 'It is the right & proper thing everywhere.' " Edward Clement agreed. "If we all waited until we were perfect ourselves before speaking out against the evil that we might detect elsewhere," he wrote, "there would be a tremendous silence in the world."[31] The real problem was not that the North hypocritically criticized the South too much, but that she did not criticize it enough. From "the present subserviency and sycophancy of the North," lamented Francis Garrison and his brother William, "one would think that the Confederacy had conquered. . . . The utmost apathy exists regarding the rights of the colored people."[32]

Most distressing of all was the apostasy of several abolitionists and their descendants. William Garrison was shocked when a granddaughter of Lucretia Mott praised Thomas Dixon's racist novel *The Leopard's Spots*. After a visit to California in 1903, William came home shaking his head about anti-Negro and anti-Japanese feeling there among "men who are proud of anti-slavery connections." A granddaughter of John Brown who had trouble with black students in her Pasadena school told Garrison that she "had no use for niggers." (On the other hand, another of Brown's granddaughters, a schoolteacher in Portland, Oregon, was an active civil rights worker.) In 1911 a second-generation Quaker abolitionist in Philadelphia grieved that some of her contemporaries "have become discouraged because after the lapse of a generation those who inherited the weaknesses of slavery have not already outgrown or overcome them." A few even thought

---

[30] Edward Blyden to Francis J. Grimké, May 17, 1895, in Carter G. Woodson, ed., *The Works of Francis James Grimké*, 4 vols., Washington, 1942, IV, 39; Oswald Garrison Villard to William Lloyd Garrison III, July 27, 1907, Garrison to Villard, July 30, 1907, OGV Papers; Francis J. Garrison to Fanny Garrison Villard, Jan. 3, 1915, FGV Papers; C. S. Bonsall to Booker T. Washington, June 6, 1910, BTW Papers (I am indebted to David Gerber for this reference); Emma Lou Thornbrough, *T. Thomas Fortune: Militant Journalist*, Chicago, 1972, p. 188.

[31] Garrison to O. G. Villard, Mar. 4, 1906, OGV Papers; *BET*, Feb. 17, 1903.

[32] Francis Garrison to W. L. Garrison, Jr., Apr. 28, 1903, W. L. Garrison, Jr., to Caroline Putnam, Oct. 25, 1902, Sept. 24, 1903, WLG, Jr., Papers.

"the negroes are necessarily an inferior people and should be forever content to be hewers of wood and drawers of water."[33]

The most spectacular recantation came from Daniel H. Chamberlain in a series of public letters that defended disfranchisement and Jim Crow and came close to justifying lynching. These utterances were the final step on the road to reaction Chamberlain had been traveling for 25 years. In 1879 he had eloquently defended blacks against charges of political ineptitude; in 1904 he stated that "the negroes never, as a race, were fit to use the ballot. They are no more fit to-day." The "constant coddling of the negro by distant philanthropists" and the "inspiring in him of the hope or dream of . . . social or political equality" were the main causes of racial tension in the South. As for lynching (which Chamberlain did brand a "monstrous crime"), it would end only when blacks themselves put a stop to the "widely prevalent" raping of white women, "this hideous crime, crime more shocking, evidencing greater moral degradation and depravity, than any other crime in the catalogue."[34]

Published originally in the *Charleston News and Courier*, these letters were reprinted by many southern newspapers. Here was a Yankee who had seen the light, gloated the *News and Courier*. "Gov. Chamberlain has lived and learned"; his views were now "so luminous, so fearless, so unimpassioned, so just." Chamberlain's erstwhile abolitionist friends were appalled by his "lamentable fall from grace." In a public rejoinder William Lloyd Garrison, Jr., invoked the Chamberlain of 1879 to refute the Chamberlain of 1904, and ended by quoting Whittier's famous poem "Ichabod" written after Daniel Webster had spoken in support of the Compromise of 1850. Chamberlain responded to criticisms in long, rambling letters reiterating all of his original points and knifing home what he considered the final thrust: "That a man at 60 or 70 holds opinions . . . contrary to those he held at 30" proved first that "he is honest, and second, that he is more likely to be right than the man who has not changed."[35]

[33] W. L. Garrison, Jr., to Francis Garrison, Mar. 24, 1903, W. L. Garrison, Jr., to Caroline Putnam, Sept. 24, 1903, WLG, Jr., Papers; for John Brown's Portland granddaughter, see Agnes S. Brown to W.E.B. Du Bois, June 3, 1905, from the Du Bois Papers formerly in the custody of Herbert Aptheker, cited by permission; for the Quakers, Elizabeth Lloyd, "Race Hatred in Pennsylvania," *Friends' Intelligencer*, Aug. 19, 1911.

[34] Letters from Chamberlain published in *Charleston News and Courier*, June 12, 1903, Aug. 1, 1904, June 18, 1905, and in *Boston Herald*, Sept. 1, 1904. Chamberlain published some of these letters plus other writings in a pamphlet titled *Phases of Our So-Called Negro Problem. Open Letter to the Right Honorable James Bryce, M.P., of England*, 1904.

[35] *News and Courier*, Aug. 1, 1904; W. L. Garrison, Jr., to Francis J. Grimké, June 23, 1903, in Woodson, ed., *The Works of Francis J. Grimké*, IV, 80; Francis

The Chamberlain affair soon blew over; more significant in the long run were the thoughtful second-generation abolitionists who modified their ancestral opinions. This seemed to happen especially to those who traveled or lived in the South. On the first of many research trips to the South (1892), Harvard historian Albert Bushnell Hart found his "preconceptions" about the Negro "much disturbed." "The greater part of the race moves in a nether world of great ignorance and greater degradation," wrote this son of an Ohio abolitionist. Slavery was not "wholly responsible" for the degradation—the Negro seemed to suffer from some "defect in the character." Hart condemned southern whites for their repressive practices, but on a later visit (1908) he wrote privately that "I feel more sympathy with the Southerner than I did five years ago" because "the negro is such a tremendous problem." In 1900 a native of New England explained that while he shared his father's "views to the extreme in regard to the evil of slavery, my long residence in Washington has made me incline to a more Southern view of the negro than he would have taken." In 1913 a clergyman "of strong abolition ancestry" told Oswald Garrison Villard that although he still considered racial prejudice "infernal" and "always demanded equality of opportunity for black and white alike," he had found the race problem more complex than he realized before coming to Baltimore. "While my original convictions have not budged an inch, as to the next step, the practical solution of the difficulty, I am still in a condition of grave bewilderment. Frankly, I do not see the way out."[36]

The failure of some second-generation abolitionists to follow in their fathers' footsteps was not a unique phenomenon in the relations of sons to fathers. Nor should the later conservatism of several first-generation abolitionists come as a surprise, since youthful radicalism is often a casualty of age. "It is the stern souls that hold fast to obligation who must be depended upon to insist upon political and social rights for the Negro," wrote William Hayes Ward in 1896.[37] Ward was one of the sternest of those souls, but he had plenty of company. Indeed, the surprise is not that some old and more young crusaders fell by the wayside, but that so many kept pressing on. It is with these stern souls—who for clarity's sake shall be called neo-abolitionists—that most of the rest of this book is concerned.

Garrison to O. G. Villard, Aug. 4, 1904, OGV Papers; W. L. Garrison, Jr., in *Boston Advertiser*, Sept. 9, 1904; Chamberlain in *Boston Herald*, Sept. 15.

[36] Hart in *Nation*, Mar. 17, 1892; Hart to Mrs. Hart, Jan. 22, 1908, Hart Papers, Harvard University Archives; *NYEP*, May 26, 1900; Alfred R. Hussey to Villard, Oct. 21, 1913, OGV Papers.

[37] *Independent*, Apr. 2, 1896.

Southern whites were delighted by examples of northerners who changed their minds about the race problem after spending time in the South, for this seemed to prove their contention that only southerners really *knew* the Negro. "It is simply impossible for a northern man to understand the patriarchal character of a great portion of southern life," a southern woman told William Lloyd Garrison, Jr. The *Atlanta Journal* considered Villard "one of the northern anachronisms still believing in negro equality" who would soon learn better if he came South to make "a practical trial of his theories." A professor at the University of Georgia told Francis Garrison that no one in Boston could know as much about the Negro as those like himself who had "lived long in contact with the race." This Georgian had been nursed by a black mammy, "raised with negroes on a farm, played with them, went swimming with them." Alas, the postslavery generation had degenerated since the good old days; the masses of blacks were now "shiftless, vicious . . . thoroughly irresponsible, mannerless, lazy & immoral." Education had made the race worse instead of better. Northern men who denied these truths, the professor told Garrison, simply did not "know whereof they speak."[38]

Neo-abolitionists were infuriated by such talk. In truth, they retorted, it was white southerners blinded by stereotypes who "knew" the Negro least. They judged the whole race by the domestic servant, the street-corner loafer, and "the shuffling field-hand who lifts a subservient cap," all of whom wore a mask to conceal their true feelings, said Ward. The average southern white knew nothing of the black teacher, doctor, or lawyer. "He was never in his home, never shook hands with him, never called him 'Mister.'" How many southern whites "have ever visited a negro school or preached in a negro church?" asked Joseph Hartzell. A black man like Du Bois was far better known in the North than the South, and "the splendid work of his college—Atlanta University—is more appreciated and better understood in Boston than in its own city," said Villard truthfully. On a trip to the South to visit black schools, AMA Secretary Augustus Beard sat in the train next to a southern white man who, unaware of Beard's occupation, declaimed to him on the uselessness of higher education for Negroes. Beard asked a few questions that elicited the man's ignorance of what black college graduates were doing; when he inquired whether the work of Straight University in the man's own city of New Orleans did not count for something, the man first said he had never

[38] Bessie Bainbridge to W. L. Garrison, Jr., Apr. 9, 1909, WLG, Jr., Papers; *Atlanta Journal*, Oct. 28, 1906; A. H. Patterson to Francis J. Garrison, May 28, 1903, May 7, 1904, WLG, Jr., Papers.

heard of Straight and then insisted that it was a white school. In Richmond a white banker was amazed when Villard informed him that there were three black banks in the city, that the largest steam laundry in town was owned by a black man, and that doctors in the black hospital had been educated in New York, Paris, and London—indeed, the banker had not known there was a black hospital. "For absolute and colossal ignorance of the negro of the South," observed Ward, "look to his white neighbor . . . who never had a doubt that he knows it all."[39]

Since southern whites did not "know" the Negro and seemed to have learned little since 1861, some former abolitionists—including several who in the 1880s had urged a let-alone policy—became convinced that the old tactics of agitation must be revived to teach southerners the truth. Feeling betrayed by southern whites whom he had once trusted, 77-year-old Thomas Wentworth Higginson said in 1900 that "I wish I had the voice to take part in the new abolitionist contest that is coming." Some missionary educators who once had faith in the New South also felt betrayed. Henry L. Morehouse warned that the time might come when it would be necessary "to declare martial law again." And the AMA's New England district secretary proclaimed in 1890 that since "time" had failed to solve the race problem, "agitation is needed," and New England must once again take the lead "in solemn and earnest protest."[40]

Appeals for a rebirth of abolitionist organizations bore sparse fruit in the 1890s. There were the antilynching committees and the protest meetings in Faneuil Hall, of course, but these were hardly on the scale of the old antislavery societies. Aging abolitionists met occasionally for reunions at which they condemned "southern outrages." But the South seemed to pay even less heed to resolutions passed in Boston than in the days of slavery. The older generation of abolitionists was past the time when it could embark on a new crusade; their children and grandchildren seemed not yet ready for one.

Former abolitionists played little part in the two principal civil rights organizations of the 1890s, neither of which lasted long or achieved much. The first was the Afro-American League, founded in 1890 by T. Thomas Fortune. Although several neo-abolitionists wished the league Godspeed and offered to help, this all-black organization did not want white participation. By 1893 the league was defunct; it reappeared in 1898 as the Afro-American Council but soon came un-

---

[39] Ward in *Independent*, Mar. 12, 1903; Hartzell in *NWCA*, Jan. 15, 1896; Beard in *AM*, LVI (June 1902), 279-80; Villard in *NYEP*, Aug. 21, 1903, Feb. 17, Nov. 30, 1904.

[40] Higginson quoted in undated clipping, 1900, WLG, Jr., Papers, *HMM*, XI (Oct. 1889), 270-71; *AM*, XLIV (Mar. 1890), 80 (June 1890), 175.

der Booker T. Washington's influence and lost its initial militancy.[41] In 1891 the former carpetbagger Albion W. Tourgée, rebuffed in his attempt to work with the Afro-American League, founded his own interracial National Citizens' Rights Association. Numerous neo-abolitionists joined, but though the association was launched with impressive fanfare, it also collapsed within three years, largely because of Tourgée's autocratic insistence on running the whole show himself. Its one solid achievement, whose outcome was unhappy, was to initiate the legal action that led to the Supreme Court's *Plessy* v. *Ferguson* decision.[42]

The formation of an effective neo-abolitionist organization was still more than a decade away, with much backing and filling before it was accomplished. In the meantime, concern for Negro rights once again became intermixed with other reform causes, muddying the currents of protest activity.

[41] Thornbrough, *Fortune*, 105-22, 178-86, 226-29; Nancy J. Weiss, "From Black Separatism to Interracial Cooperation: The Origins of Organized Efforts for Racial Advancement, 1890-1920," in Barton J. Bernstein and Allen J. Matusow, eds., *Twentieth-Century America: Recent Interpretations*, 2nd ed., New York, 1972, pp. 58-60; *Independent*, Nov. 7, 1889; *CIO* (D), Jan. 17, 1890.

[42] Otto H. Olsen, *Carpetbagger's Crusade: The Life of Albion Winegar Tourgée*, Baltimore, 1965, pp. 207-31.

Chapter Seventeen

Women's Rights and Anti-Imperialism

The two reform movements in which former abolitionists were most deeply involved during the 1890s were woman suffrage and anti-imperialism. Garrisonian abolition and the women's rights crusade had been born together in the 1830s. But during Reconstruction wide cracks had begun to appear in the united front for women and blacks, and by 1900 the two causes had become separated. At the same time many anti-imperialists, heirs of the mugwumps who in the 1880s had all but deserted the Negro, discovered a connection between the oppression of nonwhite peoples at home and overseas and renewed their concern for Negro rights as part of their larger effort against colonialism. On balance these developments probably strengthened rather than weakened the pro-Negro cause, for the defection of suffragists was more than offset by the accession of anti-imperialists. The imperialism issue also helped convert the *Nation* into the influential spokesman for equal rights its founders had hoped it would be.

Just as they had fought simultaneously for the liberation of black people and white women from exploitation by white males, abolitionist-suffragists Elizabeth Cady Stanton, Susan B. Anthony, and many of their followers hoped to merge the movements for enfranchisement of Negroes and women during Reconstruction. But in 1865 most abolitionists, realizing that political exigencies made possible the enfranchisement of freedmen while no such pressures could be brought to bear for women, wanted to strike for Negro suffrage while the iron was hot and to postpone the drive for women's votes to a more opportune time. This tactical dispute escalated into a bitter internecine struggle that led to the founding of two rival suffragist organizations in 1870, the National Woman Suffrage Association led by Stanton and Anthony, and the American Woman Suffrage Association led by Lucy Stone and her husband, Henry B. Blackwell, who edited the major suffragist periodical, *Woman's Journal*.[1] Though Stanton and Anthony had initially opposed the 15th Amendment because it did not enfranchise women, both suffragist factions continued to pay at least lip service to the idea that the causes of women and Negroes were linked by a common oppression. But this position began to change after the two

[1] James M. McPherson, "Abolitionists, Woman Suffrage, and the Negro, 1865-1869," *Mid-America*, XLVII (Jan. 1965), 40-47.

factions merged in 1890 to form the National American Woman Suffrage Association (NAWSA), and by 1903 the suffragists had jettisoned
the Negro in an attempt to win support for woman suffrage in the
South.

In the 1890s the resurgence of the idea that voting was not a natural
right but an earned privilege endangered the cause of votes for women
as well as for blacks and immigrants, since the theory considered only
Anglo-Saxon males truly fit to exercise this privilege. Suffragists could
respond to the danger in one of two ways: they could reaffirm the
ideology of natural rights; or they could accept the theory of limited
suffrage based on demonstrated capacity, amending it to include qualified *women* as well as men. For several years they fluctuated between
the two responses. In an 1894 address titled *Suffrage a Natural Right*,
Elizabeth Cady Stanton replied to the argument that universal suffrage in the South had proved a mistake with the assertion that "our
mistake in the South . . . was not in securing the blacks their natural
rights, but in not holding those States as territories until the whites
understood the principles of republican government." Stanton's radicalism extended to all races and classes: "How my blood boils over at
these persecutions of the Africans, the Jews, the Indians, and the Chinese," she wrote in 1893. She supported the Populist party and the
Pullman strikers in 1894 and Henry George's campaign for the New
York mayoralty in 1897.[2]

At the same time, and without apparent awareness of her inconsistency, Stanton endorsed the concept of "educated suffrage." Every
year thousands of illiterate immigrants were enfranchised, she wrote
in 1894, "while intelligent, educated women, the pillars of our schools
and churches . . . are denied the representation accorded to the most
ignorant class of male foreigners!" Stanton recognized that an important obstacle to the enfranchisement of women was the fear that it
would double the ignorant vote. Thus she proposed that beginning in
1898 the ballot should be limited to citizens of either sex who could
read and write the English language. Later she modified this to apply
only to *new* voters, thus avoiding the disfranchisement of illiterates
who already possessed the ballot, and broadened the requirement of
literacy in English to include any language.[3]

This idea was not new, of course; the personnel of the woman suffrage movement was largely middle class and tinged with nativism,
and they had always expressed resentment that ignorant males could

[2] Aileen S. Kraditor, *The Ideas of the Woman Suffrage Movement, 1890-1920*,
New York, 1965, pp. 46-47, 199; Theodore Stanton and Harriot Stanton Blatch, eds.,
Elizabeth Cady Stanton, As Revealed in Her Letters, Diary, and Reminiscences,
2 vols., New York, 1922, II, 294, 306, 327.

[3] *Woman's Journal*, Dec. 8, 1894; *Independent*, Feb. 14, 1895.

vote while distinguished women could not. Suffragists frequently pointed out that literate women outnumbered the illiterate of both sexes and that native-born women were more numerous than foreign-born men and women combined. Therefore the enfranchisement of literate women would "settle the vexed question of rule by illiteracy, whether of home-grown or foreign-born production." In 1895 the NAWSA held its convention for the first time in the South (Atlanta), where Stanton's address on educated suffrage "was especially acceptable to a southern audience."[4]

But it was not acceptable to several suffragists of abolitionist background, including Stanton's daughter Harriot Stanton Blatch, who considered educated suffrage a "Golden Calf," or her friend Susan Anthony, who called it a "conservative . . . fad." William Lloyd Garrison, Jr., like his father a life-long champion of women's rights, was the most vocal opponent of educated suffrage. Reiterating the natural rights philosophy, Garrison insisted that the best way to learn the responsibilities of citizenship was to perform them. To require literacy was "to mistake the means for the end. . . . The talk of fitting people for the suffrage by forbidding them to exercise it is the old talk of fitting men for freedom." But this position gradually lost ground among suffragists. By 1903 the restrictionists had carried the day. A straw poll of delegates at the NAWSA convention in New Orleans that year revealed overwhelming support for a literacy restriction.[5]

This had obvious implications for Negro suffrage. The women's rights movement was weaker in the South than elsewhere partly because the opposition to doubling the "ignorant" vote was strongest there. Some northern suffragists hoped to overcome this opposition by urging the *enfranchisement* of literate southern women instead of the disfranchisement of black men as the best way to neutralize the illiterate black vote. This had long been Henry B. Blackwell's pet idea. It would immediately add four times as many whites as blacks to the southern electorate, he pointed out, and thereby solve "the political problems otherwise insoluble, of race and illiteracy." Blackwell defended his plan as being far more equitable than the actual suffrage provisions enacted by southern states in the 1890s, which in effect robbed nearly all blacks of the ballot, literate or not, while preserving the privilege for most white males and refusing it to women.[6]

[4] Kraditor, *Ideas of the Woman Suffrage Movement*, 130-34; Ida H. Harper, *The Life and Work of Susan B. Anthony*, 3 vols., Indianapolis, 1898-1908, II, 811.

[5] Alma Lutz, *Created Equal: A Biography of Elizabeth Cady Stanton*, New York, 1940, p. 314; *Woman's Journal*, Oct. 2, 9, 1897; Kraditor, *Ideas of the Woman Suffrage Movement*, 136-37.

[6] *Woman's Journal*, Nov. 15, 1890, for quotation. Blackwell reiterated his proposal frequently in the pages of the *Woman's Journal* during the decade.

But several neo-abolitionists condemned "that miserable old dodge of the Blackwells" because it sought to do subtly what the new southern constitutions did blatantly. And by 1903 Blackwell had dropped his earlier protests against the *racial* injustice of disfranchisement and now concentrated only on sexual discrimination. By disfranchising most blacks, he wrote, the South had eliminated "much of the dominant illiteracy and corruption" and had given "an impulse in the direction of honest and responsible government" that would hasten the enfranchisement of women. The NAWSA, announced Blackwell, "is seeking to do away with the requirement of a sex qualification for suffrage. What other qualifications shall be asked for, it leaves to each State."[7]

This capitulation to racism signified the demise of abolitionist principles in the women's rights movement. In part this reflected the death of prominent abolitionist suffragists themselves: Lucy Stone had died in 1893; Elizabeth Cady Stanton passed away in 1902; Susan B. Anthony retired as president of the NAWSA in 1900 and died in 1906. Several leaders of the new suffragist generation were southern whites. But some of the surviving abolitionists also played a role in the suffragists' retreat from racial egalitarianism. At the 1898 NAWSA convention, Susan B. Anthony dissuaded Frederick Douglass's widow from discussing the plight of black women in southern prison camps. The introduction of this issue, said Anthony, would only weaken suffragist forces in the South. The following year a black delegate from Michigan presented a resolution condemning the segregation of black women on southern trains. Several speakers objected to the resolution as extraneous to the NAWSA's goals. Only Alice Stone Blackwell (Lucy Stone's daughter) spoke in its behalf; if an injustice was done to women anywhere, she said, it was the association's duty to protest. But Anthony closed the debate and secured the tabling of the resolution by arguing that so long as women were a "helpless, disfranchised class" they should avoid divisive issues. Privately she denounced segregation, but publicly she was unwilling to jeopardize suffragist sectional unity.[8]

Several abolitionist suffragists not present at the 1899 convention deplored its action. As honorary president of the NAWSA, Elizabeth Cady Stanton could not agree that the indignities suffered by black women on trains were outside the scope of a woman suffrage association. "What would the sainted Lucretia Mott, Ernestine L. Rose, Lucy Stone and Angelina Grimké" have said, she asked, "had they been

[7] Caroline Putnam to Samuel May, Mar. 7, 1898, May Papers, Massachusetts Historical Society; *Women's Journal*, Mar. 28, Apr. 11, 1903.

[8] Kraditor, *Ideas of the Woman Suffrage Movement*, 169-73; Caroline Putnam to Samuel May, Mar. 7, 1898, May Papers; *Woman's Journal*, May 13, 1899.

present when one colored woman stood alone, pleading for the protection of her sex against the coarse speech and manners of ill-bred men?"[9]

But Stanton's invocation of departed spirits could not stay the trend toward a divorce of the woman suffrage and Negro rights movements—a trend she herself had encouraged with her advocacy of educated suffrage. As the new century began, the *Woman's Journal* announced that hereafter the battle for women's rights in the South must be fought "upon a different plane from our Northern point of view." This became official NAWSA policy when the 1903 convention resolved to allow "each State Association to determine the qualification for membership in the Association, and the terms upon which the extension of suffrage to women shall be requested of the respective State Legislatures"—an obvious concession to Jim Crow and black disfranchisement. Several neo-abolitionist suffragists were bitter about this surrender to the South. Francis Garrison described Henry Blackwell as a man "utterly without basic principles . . . ready to assent to almost anything for a short cut to woman suffrage." And William Lloyd Garrison, Jr., announced his resignation from the NAWSA with the words: "One who has regard for freedom and equal political rights belongs outside."[10]

Paralleling these developments was a general reaction against unrestricted immigration that not only helped convert some woman suffragists from universal to limited suffrage but also reinforced the rise of racism. The earliest restrictionist legislation, based frankly on racial grounds, was the prohibition of Chinese immigrtaion in 1882. And as the sources of European immigration shifted from northern to southern and eastern Europe in the 1890s, the growing restrictionist sentiment became increasingly racist in its assumptions. In New England, where Brahmin descendants of Puritans had been fighting a losing battle against Irish political power, the new waves of Italian, French-Canadian, and Jewish immigrants spurred the founding of the Immigration Restriction League in 1894.[11]

A few mugwump abolitionists favored restriction. In the last years before his death in 1892, George William Curtis retreated further than ever from his one-time egalitarianism. The increase of "undesirable"

[9] *BET*, May 3, 1899; Stanton in *Boston Investigator*, July 22, 1899.

[10] Kraditor, *Ideas of the Woman Suffrage Movement*, 165-66, 199-202; *Woman's Journal*, Oct. 13, 1900, Mar. 28, Apr. 11, 1903; Francis Garrison to Fanny G. Villard, May 3, 1903, FGV Papers; W. L. Garrison, Jr., in *Woman's Journal*, May 2, 1903.

[11] Barbara Miller Solomon, *Ancestors and Immigrants: A Changing New England Tradition*, Cambridge, Mass., 1956, chaps. 1-5.

immigrants, he wrote—"swarms of Poles, Bohemians, Hungarians, Russians, and Italians"—threatened American institutions. The "sturdy, intelligent, industrious, moral people sprung of English stock" were in danger of engulfment by "the refuse population of semi-civilized or barbarous lands." Other neo-abolitionists who were unwilling to go so far as to restrict immigration nevertheless wished to curb the newcomers' political power by extending the naturalization period. Moorfield Storey, a second-generation abolitionist and leader of the Massachusetts mugwumps, believed that the immigrants' "prejudices, their habits of thought, their entire unfamiliarity with American questions . . . unfit them to take an intelligent part in our political contests."[12]

But most abolitionists condemned anti-immigrant and anti-Negro sentiments as twin evils. No one was more vocal on this matter than William Lloyd Garrison, Jr. A universal reformer like his father, active in the movements for woman suffrage, free trade, temperance, anti-imperialism, and the single tax (he was a friend of Henry George and president of the Massachusettes Single Tax League), Garrison devoted an increasing share of his time after 1895 to the race question in its dual manifestations of anti-Negro and anti-immigrant prejudice. He branded the "Toryism" of restriction "a far greater reason for alarm in our country than the increase of immigration." The Italian-Americans of Boston who would have been excluded by the restrictionists' proposed literacy test were, he asserted, "an industrious, thrifty, and progressive people. Their children are eager and quick to learn. . . . Bright, ambitious, studious, they are a sight to stimulate faith in the ultimate regeneration of mankind." It was time for Americans to begin living up to the Declaration of Independence. "Our danger is not from the contamination of foreigners, but from the surrender of ideals upon which self-governments rest or die."[13]

Other neo-abolitionists joined the counterattack on restrictionism. William Hayes Ward deplored the new "know-nothing movement" growing out of "Anglo-Saxon arrogance." He defended the southeastern European immigrants: "The most progressive country in Europe is Hungary, and the Russians are of magnificent promise. . . . No people have more native genius than the Italians." By welcoming these people "we do ourselves a benefit," for they contributed to the cultural diversity that made America unique. Although of Brahmin descent, Thomas Wentworth Higginson denounced the bigotry of the Immigration Restriction League. The United States was a failure, said Higgin-

---

[12] *HW*, Sept. 6, 1890, May 16, 1891, Apr. 16, 1892; William B. Hixson, Jr., *Moorfield Storey and the Abolitionist Tradition*, New York, 1972, p. 24.

[13] *Woman's Journal*, Aug. 11, 1894; speech to the Massachusetts Reform Club, Apr. 10, 1896, clipping in WLG, Jr., Papers; letter in *NYEP*, Dec. 26, 1896.

son, "if it was only large enough to furnish a safe and convenient place for the descendants of Puritans and Anglo-Saxons. . . . We err in assuming that any one race monopolizes all the virtues."[14] Garrison, Ward, and Higginson spoke for more neo-abolitionists than did such restrictionists as Curtis. By 1900 the mutality of the anti-Negro and anti-immigrant reaction had become so clear that, for most abolitionists, concern for the rights of one group led them to defend the interests of the other.

At the end of the century the controversy over American imperialism helped spark a revival of egalitarianism among mugwump abolitionists. Since the 1870s, Americans had watched with interest as European nations extended their control over nearly all of Africa. Several abolitionists who expressed an opinion about European colonialism approved of it, applauding especially the British effort to abolish the Arab trade in Negro slaves. Overlooking the exploitation and brutality of colonial conquest, they saw it as a civilizing force bringing Christianity and Western culture to Africa.

Some evangelical abolitionists supported the American acquisition of Puerto Rico and the Philippines for the same reason. They envisaged only a temporary possession of these colonies until the natives were educated up to the level of self-government. They supported missionary schools on the islands for this purpose just as they sustained similar schools for southern Negroes. Imperialism meant "the extension of American liberty and government" to "the people of other lands," said Ward in 1898. "For Porto Ricans and Filipinos, as well as for the so-called Anglo-Saxons, our trust must be in territorial autonomy, such as we gave New Mexico or Hawaii. . . . We want no colonies to be governed like India or Java; we want territories to be educated into self-government." Fine sentiments these, but they suffered considerable strain when an insurrection against American occupation of the Philippines broke out early in 1899. Ward thought the Filipinos were not yet ready for self-government; he maintained that Emilio Aguinaldo's guerrillas did not represent a majority of Filipinos; he continued to insist that the Philippines must be given the blessings of American liberty even if at the point of a gun.[15]

But this was a minority position among neo-abolitionists. Of the 42 abolitionists and their descendants whose attitude toward American imperialism is known, 10 supported it and 32 were opposed. Of the

14 *Independent*, Dec. 25, 1902, Mar. 5, Aug. 27, 1903; Higginson, "More Mingled Races," in *Book and Heart: Essays on Literature and Life*, New York, 1897, pp. 155, 158. See also Solomon, *Ancestors and Immigrants*, 49-51, 176-80.

15 *Independent*, Sept. 15, 29, 1898, Jan. 5, Feb. 16, Mar. 23, Sept. 28, 1899.

former, eight were evangelicals connected with the freedmen's education movement; of the latter, about half were Garrisonians or their descendants and 22 lived in the Boston area.

The anti-imperialist movement was a disparate coalition of Democrats, the older generation of New England Republicans, mugwumps, intellectuals, and reformers of various stripes. With such varied backgrounds they disagreed among themselves on many other issues but forged a united front against colonial expansion. The roots of their opposition lay in repugnance to militarism and the big-navy policy, fears of a self-aggrandizing colonial bureaucracy, hostility to American involvement in international power politics, distaste for the Gilded Age's acquisitive materialism of which imperialism was the latest manifestation, and uneasiness at the addition of millions of non-Caucasians to a polity already burdened with seemingly insoluble race problems. But their single most important argument rested on the principle of self-government. If the American colonies deserved independence in 1776, said anti-imperialists, the Philippines deserved no less in 1899.[16]

Although Democrats provided most of the anti-imperialist votes, their motives were as much political as ideological and their participation in the movement was sometimes perfunctory. It was mainly the mugwumps who gave anti-imperialism its intellectual and moral leadership, especially Carl Schurz, Charles Francis Adams, Jr., Moorfield Storey, Edward Atkinson, and Edwin L. Godkin. Massachusetts was the center of anti-imperialism just as it had been of abolitionism, and many former abolitionists helped found the Anti-Imperialist League in Boston in November 1898. From there the impulse spread over the whole country, especially after the administration sent the first of 70,000 troops to the Philippines to suppress Aguinaldo's insurrection. As independents in politics, the mugwump anti-imperialists hoped to form a third party in 1900; frustrated in this effort, most of them supported William Jennings Bryan on an anti-imperialist platform despite their distaste for the Commoner's free silver views. McKinley's victory and the collapse of Filipino resistance took the steam out of anti-imperialism after 1900; by 1904 only the original Boston League was left. Though they failed to prevent the United States from becoming

[16] Fred Harvey Harrington, "The Anti-Imperialist Movement in the United States, 1898-1900," *Mississippi Valley Historical Review*, XXII (1935), 211-30; Richard W. Welch, Jr., "Motives and Objectives of the Anti-Imperialists, 1898," *Mid-America*, LI (1969), 119-29; E. Berkeley Tompkins, *Anti-Imperialism in the United States: The Great Debate, 1890-1920*, Philadelphia, 1971; and Daniel B. Schirmer, *Republic or Empire: American Resistance to the Philippine War*, Cambridge, Mass., 1972. The Welch, Schirmer, and Tompkins studies agree with the thesis presented below that a significant part of the anti-imperialist argument was anti-racist.

a colonial power, the anti-imperialists did put their opponents on the defensive, they helped bring about relatively restrained rule in the Philippines looking toward early independence, and after 1904 they focused glaring publicity on America's noncolonial imperialism in the Caribbean.[17]

Several historians have emphasized the underlying racist convictions of both imperialists and anti-imperialists. If expansionists talked of the white man's burden, opponents of expansion pointed with alarm to the dangers of bringing more nonwhite peoples into the republic. Southern anti-imperialists played on fears that Puerto Rico, the Philippines, and Hawaii (annexed in the midst of the Spanish-American War) would become states and send colored senators to Washington. Godkin deplored "the admission of alien, inferior, and mongrel races to our nationality" while Schurz warned of the "participation in the conduct of our government" by "Spanish-Americans, with all the mixtures of Indian and Negro blood, and Malays . . . animated with the instincts, impulses and passions bred by the tropical sun." A few former abolitionists expressed similar sentiments. Edward L. Pierce opposed the acquisition of Hawaii because "we don't want those mongrel races for the basis of a State," and Henry Blackwell said that to annex new "colored races is to add new elements of danger and discord."[18]

But while the thesis of anti-imperialist racism is partly correct, it has been exaggerated to the point of distortion. Far from exhibiting a "near unanimity" of racism, as one historian has written, many anti-imperialists condemned the racism of their opponents and made the equal rights of all people the main thrust of their argument. This was especially true of anti-imperialists from an abolitionist background. Wendell Garrison pronounced the theory of the white man's burden

[17] Hixson, *Storey*, chap. 2.

[18] *Nation*, Jan. 13, 1898; Schurz quoted in Christopher Lasch, "The Anti-Imperialists, the Philippines, and the inequality of man," *Journal of Southern History*, XXIV (1958), and James P. Shenton, "Imperialism and Racism," in Donald Sheehan and Harold Syrett, eds., *Essays in American Historiography*, New York, 1960, p. 238; Pierce to William Claflin, Mar. 12, 1893, Claflin Papers, Rutherford B. Hayes Library, Fremont, Ohio; Blackwell in *Woman's Journal*, Oct. 13, 1900. Lasch, Shenton, and Robert Beisner have cited such remarks as evidence that with "near unanimity" the anti-imperialists "shared entirely the expansionists' belief in the inferiority and incapacity of the world's colored races." Lasch maintains that there was "no important difference" between the northern and southern racist anti-imperialist arguments "except that Northern anti-imperialists did not dwell on the parallel with the Southern Negro problem—something they were by this time anxious to forget." (Shenton, "Imperialism and Racism," 233; Beisner *Twelve Against Empire: The Anti-Imperialists, 1898-1900*, New York, 1968, p. 21; Lasch, "The Anti-Imperialists, the Philippines, and the Inequality of Man," 325-26.) This is nonsense. Not only were many of the northern anti-imperialists *anti*-racists, but a number of them dwelt very much on the parallel with the race problem in their twin campaigns against racism at home and overseas, as explained below.

a "vulgar conceit" based on the "spirit of caste." Imperialism "rests upon no better moral foundation than the heathen maxim, 'Might makes right,' " said Moorfield Storey, while the anti-imperialist conviction "that every people has an equal right to govern itself rests upon justice." Even Schurz's and Godkin's arguments carried an implicit egalitarian message. "We cannot deny to the Cubans and the people of the Philippines the right to govern themselves," said Schurz, "without denying the assertions of our own Declaration of Independence." Godkin considered it a "ridiculuous pretence" for Americans "to decide whether a people is worthy to be free. Any people proves its fitness to be free" by fighting for freedom, as the Filipinos were doing. Imperialism rested on the "old Taney Democratic doctrine that the dark-skinned natives have no rights that white men are bound to respect."[19]

As for the anti-imperialist reluctance to take on new race problems abroad before solving those at home, this was often an antiracist rather than racist viewpoint. It would be tragic, wrote Wendell Garrison, "to have the inhabitants of the Philippine Islands treated as our Indians have been treated, to have the people of Cuba ruled as the negroes in the Southern States are ruled." We should "remedy our own scandalous abuses rather than to extend the system under which they have arisen to other peoples." The earliest anti-imperialist meeting (June 15, 1898) resolved that "our first duty is to cure the evils in our own country," including the denial of "the rights of . . . the colored race."[20]

Since imperialism and racism reinforced each other, many anti-imperialists attacked both simultaneously. "In declaring that the principles of the Declaration of Independence apply to all men," resolved an anti-imperialist convention in 1900, "this Congress means to include the negro race in America as well as the Filipinos." The United States was "attempting to enslave the countrymen of Aguinaldo," William Lloyd Garrison, Jr., told a meeting of black anti-imperialists, therefore Aguinaldo "was fighting in the same cause for which John Brown died." The racism that rationalized imperialism was "the same race prejudice that justified your enslavement." The "old enemies of freedom" had brought on "another and more desperate conflict" than that of 1861, said Garrison in 1899. "To-day the same crucial issue is at the front, the old battle is in full swing."[21]

[19] *Nation*, Feb. 23, 1893; W. P. Garrison to Francis J. Garrison, Mar. 18, 1894, WPG Papers; Storey, *What Shall We Do with Our Dependencies?* Boston, 1903, pp. 4-5, 19; Schurz in *HW*, Oct. 1, 1898; Godkin in *Nation*, Mar. 2, 1899, Dec. 16, 1897. The last sentence quoted here may have been written by Wendell Garrison, but it was consistent with Godkin's sentiments.
[20] *Nation*, Aug. 25, 1898; Tompkins, *Anti-Imperialism*, 125.
[21] Mark A. DeWolfe Howe, *Portrait of an Independent: Moorfield Storey, 1845-*

If most anti-imperialists did not quite share Garrison's vision of Armageddon, several echoed his fear that "proslavery" imperialist theories would intensify racism at home. Once "the American people take up the policy of subjugating black men abroad," said Albert Pillsbury, "there will be no chance for the black man at home." Most discouraging of all, it was the party of Lincoln that had taken up the mantle of the new slavery. Imperialism had "paralyzed the conscience of the Republican party," said Moorfield Storey and Wendell Garrison, for while southern Democrats disfranchised blacks with impunity the McKinley administration was "disfranchising another colored race in another part of the world." Edward Clement saw a connection between the annexation of Hawaii and the Supreme Court's decision upholding Mississippi disfranchisement within a few days of each other. This "practical re-establishment of semi-slavery," said Clement of *Williams* v. *Mississippi*, "looks almost as if it were a part of the imperializing programme."[22]

Anti-imperialism catapulted some lukewarm neo-abolitionists back into the thick of civil rights agitation; the prime example was Moorfield Storey. Born into an antislavery family, Storey had been influenced in his youth by Charles Sumner, whom he served as secretary for two years during Reconstruction. After 1870, however, Storey all but lost interest in the Negro as he rose to the top of the legal profession (he was president of the American Bar Association in 1896) and became a prominent mugwump. Imperialism provoked his anger as nothing else had ever done and convinced him that racial oppression was the worst danger confronting the republic. "No man of antislavery antecedents can fail to regard with horror the treatment of the colored race," he said in 1900, especially since "the Southern Press directly justifies the acts of the South by the acts of the Administration in the Philippines." "We must," he told Carl Schurz in 1903, "for the sake of negroes and Filipinos both rouse again the anti-slavery feeling." It was no coincidence that Storey was president of the Anti-Imperialist League and the NAACP at the same time. His concern for the rights of brown and black men also produced a friendlier attitude toward immigrants. In the 1900s he became an eloquent critic of anti-Japanese, anti-Catholic, and anti-Semitic phobias. "The absurd prejudices of race

---

1929, Boston, 1932, p. 199; pamphlets and clippings of speeches by Garrison on June 10, July 7, 1899, and Jan. 21, Apr. 7, 1900, WLG, Jr., Papers.

22 Pillsbury to Francis J. Grimké, July 3, 1899, in Carter G. Woodson, ed., *The Works of Francis James Grimké*, 4 vols., Washington, 1942, IV, 66; Storey quoted in William B. Hixson, Jr., "Moorfield Storey and the Struggle for Equality," *Journal of American History*, LV (1968), 539; *Nation*, Dec. 16, 1897; *BET*, July 12, 1898.

and color," he said at an NAACP celebration of the centenary of Sumner's birth in 1911, must be countered "whether they bar the Negro from his rights as a man, the foreigner from his welcome to our shores, the Filipino from his birthright of independence, or the Hebrew from social recognition."[23]

The "deep-lying unities" between racism at home and abroad also helped turn the neo-abolitionist editors of the *Evening Post/Nation* into crusaders for racial equality on both fronts. "The new movement against the negro is a . . . necessary reflex of the wave of Imperialism and conquest," declared Oswald Garrison Villard in 1903. "Unless our skirts are clean in Manila, we cannot assume moral indignation towards Charleston."[24]

Actually, Villard and his uncle Wendell Garrison had begun to reshape the *Post/Nation* along egalitarian lines even before the Spanish-American War, which only speeded the process. In 1881 the railroad magnate Henry Villard had bought the *New York Evening Post* and the *Nation*; from then until 1918 the *Nation* was in effect the weekly edition of the *Post*. Villard's purchase strengthened the abolitionist lineage of the *Nation* in one sense, for his wife was William Lloyd Garrison's daughter. But Villard gave editorial freedom to the new trio of *Post* editors—Schurz, Godkin, and Horace White. Wendell Garrison was promoted to editor of the *Nation*, but except for book reviews his editorship was little more than nominal, since most of the *Nation*'s editorials appeared first in the *Post*. Schurz left the staff in 1883; thereafter until 1899, when he retired, Godkin was editor-in-chief and Horace White his top associate. Henry Villard's acquisition of the two papers made no difference in their treatment of racial issues; indeed, with the addition of Edward P. Clark to the editorial staff in 1885 the *Post/Nation* became even more conservative on the race question. But as Wendell Garrison and his brothers grew increasingly radical, Clark's conservatism exasperated them and finally drove Wendell to take the first steps to convert the papers into genuine neo-abolitionist spokesmen.[25]

Garrison was shaken out of his earlier complacency by the racial retrogression of the 1890s and the racist rationale for imperialism. The "horrible and sickening" increase of lynching, the wave of disfranchisement, and the exploitation of Hawaiians, he wrote, were signs of

[23] Hixson, *Storey*, 101, 112; Storey to Schurz, June 10, 1903, Schurz Papers, Library of Congress.

[24] *NYEP*, Feb. 16, 1903; *Nation*, Feb. 26, 1903.

[25] Allan Nevins, *The Evening Post: A Century of Journalism*, New York, 1922, chap. 20; Villard, "The 'Nation' and Its Ownership," *Nation*, July 8, 1915; W. P. Garrison to Villard, July 14, 1901, OGV Papers.

"the unchanged spirit of slavery." This "whirligig of reaction" must be met by a "counter wave of conscience." Garrison repeatedly invoked the memories of abolitionism as he called for a new crusade: "The great debate of the last century will be renewed in our latter years as it seemed settled in Father's," he declared in 1903. "It is now nearly a hundred years since my father was born, more than 70 years since he founded the *Liberator*. If we are silent now about the great reaction, where shall we be 100 years hence?"[26]

Before 1900 Garrison was not in a position to influence the tone of the *Evening Post* because, as he admitted to his brother, "I have been second fiddle on the political side" of editorial policy. But if he could do little about the *Post*, he could make the *Nation* rise higher than its source. He censored racist comments out of book reviews, justifying this practice to one angry reviewer with the explanation that "we ought to be very careful not to foster race and color prejudice." He excluded many of Clark's *Post* editorials from the *Nation* and revised others in a liberal direction; for example, he once changed a reference to the 15th Amendment from "unfortunate" to "indispensable."[27] Garrison also began writing editorials on racial matters that he printed in the *Nation* without prior publication in the *Post*. Unlike Clark's and Godkin's continuing tendency to blame blacks themselves for their problems, Garrison returned to his abolitionist conviction that white racism was "the core of the so-called Negro Problem." Unless the South repealed all discriminatory legislation and began practicing "even-handed justice," he said, "there will never be an end to the inherited cruelty of slavery."[28]

From 1895 to 1902 the *Evening Post/Nation* vacillated between mugwump conservatism and neo-abolitionist liberalism on the race issue. In 1897 Oswald Garrison Villard joined the *Post*'s editorial staff. Though he was raised on conventional mugwump principles that six years at Harvard (culminating in a history M.A. in 1896) did little to modify, young Villard never forgot—or allowed others to forget—that he was William Lloyd Garrison's grandson. As early as 1898 he told his uncle Francis that when he gained control of the *Post/Nation* he intended "to make it a worthy follower of the 'Liberator.' " The Spanish-American War propelled young Villard into anti-imperialism and paci-

26 *Nation*, Nov. 21, 1895; Garrison to Francis J. Garrison, Feb. 28, May 3, 1903, WPG Papers; Garrison to James Bryce, Mar. 2, June 29, July 23, 1903, Bryce Papers, Bodleian Library, Oxford University.

27 Garrison to Francis J. Garrison, May 14, 1899, Mar. 26, 1893, WPG Papers; Garrison to Goldwin Smith, July 29, 1895, Smith Papers, Cornell University Library; compare the *NYEP* editorial of May 12, 1900, on the Montgomery Race Conference with the condensed version of same in *Nation*, May 17, 1900.

28 *Nation*, Jan. 31, 1895, May 11, 1899.

ficism while sharpening his previously vague commitment to racial justice, and he began writing editorials linking imperialism and racism.[29]

At the end of 1899 Godkin retired as editor of the *Post*; a few months later Henry Villard died, leaving ownership of the *Post/Nation* to his wife and eldest son Oswald. While her husband was alive, Fanny Garrison Villard had been a house-bound mother and homemaker; after his death she blossomed into a vigorous reformer in her father's mold. She contributed a great deal of time and money to the woman suffrage movement, helped found the NAACP in 1909, organized the Woman's Peace Society in 1919, and served as its president until her death in 1928. She reinforced Oswald's growing radicalism. "By means of the 'Liberator' your grandfather found a way to rouse the conscience of his country," she told him. "May you do likewise."[30]

With the help of Wendell Garrison and Rollo Ogden (the best editorial writer on the *Post*'s staff), Villard set out to do just that. But even though he and his mother owned the paper, the tradition of editorial independence hampered their efforts so long as holdovers from the Godkin era remained in the top editorial positions. Horace White, who despite his youthful radicalism had subsided into genteel mugwumpery after 1870, succeeded Godkin as editor, and Edward P. Clark also remained with the *Post*. Thus from 1900 to early 1903 the papers veered sharply between the old and new positions on the race question. After Clark died in January 1903, Villard persuaded White to retire. With Ogden now editor of the *Post* and Garrison continuing as editor of the *Nation*, Villard proceeded to make the papers into unequivocal crusaders for racial justice. "All the Garrison blood in me has been moving me to bear testimony," he declared. "We are in this fight to stay."[31] Although it had taken a long time, the *Nation* finally fulfilled William Lloyd Garrison's desire that it become a successor of his *Liberator*.

Thus while the vain hope of winning the South for woman suffrage impelled several suffragists to drop out of the movement for Negro rights, the debate over imperialism infused other abolitionists with

[29] D. Joy Humes, *Oswald Garrison Villard, Liberal of the 1920's*, Syracuse, 1960, pp. 1-9; Michael Wreszin, *Oswald Garrison Villard: Pacifist at War*, Bloomington, Ind., 1965, pp. 7-24; Villard to Francis Garrison, Apr. 28, 1898, OGV Papers.

[30] Oswald Garrison Villard, *Fighting Years: Memoirs of a Liberal Editor*, New York, 1939, pp. 17-22; F. G. Villard to O. G. Villard, Aug. 3, 1901, OGV Papers.

[31] Quotations from Villard to Booker T. Washington, July 11, Aug. 4, 1903, BTW Papers. See also W. P. Garrison to F. J. Garrison, Nov. 5, 12, 1899, Apr. 14, 1901, Nov. 29, 1902, Feb. 21, 1903, WPG Papers; O. G. Villard to F. J. Garrison, Aug. 28, 1901, Mar. 18, 1902, OGV Papers; F. J. Garrison to Fanny Garrison Villard, Jan. 1, 5, 1902, FGV Papers.

new energy for the ancestral cause. The cause needed these reinforce-
ments, for the racial reaction of the 1890s continued unabated into the
new century. Not only did lynching, riots, disfranchisement, and Jim
Crow remain a part of the American scene, but racist versions of history and science that rationalized these practices gained increasing
acceptance and challenged neo-abolitionists to defend their egalitarian
assumptions.

Chapter Eighteen

History and Biology

"All you know is the ethics" of the race question, a southerner told William Hayes Ward in 1904, "and the ethics is one thousand years ahead of the facts."[1] The accepted "facts" of history and science supported the prevalent belief in the mental inferiority of black people. This conviction gained greater respectability than ever from 1890 to 1920, as the newly professionalized social sciences, backed by genetics, seemed to provide convincing evidence of Negro inferiority. Though some neo-abolitionists accepted this evidence, most of them rejected it in whole or in part, seeing it as only a more sophisticated version of the "Cursed be Canaan" mythology that had sanctioned white supremacy for centuries.

By 1900 the Road to Reunion had reached its destination. North and South cemented the new nationalism in the Spanish-American War. Yankees and Southrons charged together up San Juan Hill under generals who had fought for the Confederacy as well as the Union. In school textbooks, popular histories, and novels about the Civil War, the issues of slavery and secession were obscured by the romanticism of the Lost Cause. Former abolitionists were disgusted by this "sentimental sophistry." In the hands of historians who maintained "that there really never were any points of difference between the North and South, no question of right or wrong, no question of human liberty or serfdom," wrote Oswald Garrison Villard, "all history becomes foggy." It was high time, wrote a friend of Villard's grandfather, "for truth to be spoken about Lee, & Jeff Davis—in Garrison's spirit—of being *harsh* as truth—as uncompromising as justice! . . . The School Histories ought to be explicit—in this Anti-Slavery instruction, which the South is desperate to hide."[2]

But the conservative interpretation dominated Civil War historiography for many years. Reconstruction became the historians' chief whipping boy; it was "the nadir of national disgrace," the "most soul-sickening spectacle that Americans had ever been called upon to behold," in the words of John W. Burgess of Columbia University.

[1] *Independent*, Dec. 1, 1904.
[2] Norwood P. Hallowell, "The Meaning of Memorial Day," Address at Harvard University, May 30, 1896, in *Selected Letters and Papers of Norwood P. Hallowell*, Peterborough, N.H., 1963, pp. 58-59; *Nation*, Feb. 24, 1910; Caroline Putnam to Samuel May, Feb. 20, Nov. 30, 1897, May Papers, Mass. Hist. Society.

Burgess's colleague William A. Dunning trained a generation of graduate students whose published dissertations reinforced their mentor's influential writings on Reconstruction. James Ford Rhodes spread the same message in his popular history of the Civil War era. Radical Reconstruction, said Rhodes, was an "uncivilized" scheme that "pandered to the ignorant negroes, the knavish white natives and the vulturous adventurers who flocked from the North." Negro suffrage produced "an agglomeration of incompetence and corruption at which the world stood aghast." Northerners all, Burgess, Dunning, and Rhodes fashioned the southern white version of Reconstruction into a national consensus. No northerner could read this story of "injustice and misery," confessed Lyman Abbott in 1904, "without a profound sense of humiliation."[3]

Though some former abolitionists shared this view, most of them saw pro-southern historiography as an obstacle to racial justice. "We must rely on corrected teaching," wrote Mary White Ovington, to "stop the iniquitous so-called history that is coming out of the South."[4] This was easier said than done, since most historians accepted the southern version, and textbook publishers, fearful of alienating the super-sensitive southern market, shied away from anything that could be labeled a "northern" or "Negro" viewpoint. Neo-abolitionists thus relied mainly on journalism, lectures, book reviews, and the like to publicize their version of the past. In so doing they fashioned an interpretation of Reconstruction that anticipated the revisionist historiography of recent decades.

This interpretation fell into two parts, which can be labeled "defensive" and "positive." The defensive school consisted mainly of mugwump abolitionists who had themselves once subscribed to the negative view of Reconstruction. By 1900 their revived militancy seemed to call for a reexamination of the past. They developed a somewhat apologetic defense of radical Reconstruction, admitting its defects but insisting that postwar southern intransigence had made Negro suffrage necessary. "The fact of this necessity," wrote Thomas Wentworth Higginson in 1899, should have been obvious to anyone who studied the black codes passed by southern states after the war. Only with the ballot could freedmen have been "protected in their most ordinary rights from those who had tried to destroy [the Union]. Any-

---

[3] Burgess, *Reconstruction and the Constitution*, New York, 1902, p. 263; Rhodes, *History of the United States from the Compromise of 1850 to the Final Restoration of Home Rule at the South*, 7 vols., New York, 1893-1906, VII, 168; paper by Rhodes read before the Mass. Hist. Society, Dec. 1904, in the Society's *Proceedings*, 2nd Ser., XVIII, Boston, 1905, pp. 465-67; *Outlook*, June 29, 1901.

[4] Ovington to Archibald Grimké, Apr. 13, 1915, Grimké Papers, Moorland Foundation Library, Howard University.

thing less would have been an act of desertion on the part of the nation which would have disgraced it for ever." Negro suffrage had been "the only alternative to a far more serious evil," agreed Edward Clement. The Negro's condition in 1900 was bad enough; "it is not difficult to imagine how much more hopeless" it would be "if he had not had the ballot as an actual, efficient defense in reconstruction times and did not possess it at least as a potential defence today."[5]

Moorfield Storey was the best example of a mugwump neo-abolitionist whose growing concern about racial oppression changed his view of Reconstruction. In his early anti-imperialist speeches, he compared American colonial rule in the Philippines to carpetbag governments in the South. But as time went on he inverted the comparison, arguing that without the franchise the freed slaves would have been in the same position as the oppressed Filipinos. In a reply to Rhodes' indictment of Negro suffrage, Storey conceded its evils but argued that the purposes of Reconstruction were not limited to good government, social stability, or prosperity—all of which had existed under slavery. "Anything less than equality of rights . . . would mean slavery modified, but not abolished. . . . No people can learn self-government while governed by others." Higginson and Norwood Hallowell joined Storey in trying to persuade Rhodes to modify his anti-Negro interpretation, and failing, spoke out in criticism of it. And in 1915 Storey was one of the first white supporters of Carter Woodson's *Journal of Negro History*, an important vehicle for revisionist historiography.[6]

Several neo-abolitionists went beyond the mugwumps' defensive stance and portrayed Reconstruction as a positive good. They began by attacking the pro-southern account as a series of "exaggerations and falsehoods" that only proved, said Ward, that "if it is said loud enough or times enough, people can be made to believe almost anything." Ward and Richard P. Hallowell insisted that Negro suffrage was "not only a necessary act of justice" but "a magnificent and courageous piece of statesmanship." The Reconstruction governments rehabilitated the war-torn South, inaugurated social reforms, and most impor-

---

[5] Higginson in *Nation*, Mar. 2, 1899; *BET*, Mar. 19, 1901.

[6] Storey, *Anti-Imperialism: Speeches Delivered at Fanueil Hall, June 15, 1898*, Boston, 1898, and address by Storey at Saratoga, New York, Aug. 19, 1898 (I am indebted to William B. Hixson, Jr., for supplying me with these references); Storey, *What Shall We Do with Our Dependencies?* Boston, 1903, pp. 35-36; Storey, "Memoir of Charles Sumner," Mass. Hist. Society, *Proceedings*, 2nd Ser., xx (Jan. 1907), 545; Storey, *Negro Suffrage Is Not a Failure*, Boston, 1903, pp. 7, 16; Rhodes to Higginson, Oct. 24, 1905, Higginson Papers, Houghton Library, Harvard University; address by Higginson to the Mass. Hist. Society, cited in Robert Cruden, *James Ford Rhodes*, Cleveland, 1964, p. 97; Hallowell to George Haven Putnam, Feb. 4, 1910, in *Selected Letters and Papers of Hallowell*, 80; "Notes," *Journal of Negro History*, xvi (Jan. 1930), 123.

tant of all built a public school system. Ward and Hallowell admitted the existence of corruption but maintained that whites were more responsible for it than blacks. Even in South Carolina, said Hallowell, the Negro's record was "certainly as good as that of the white men of the state during the same period and better than that of the whites since then." When the true story of Reconstruction was written, it would show that in spite of being "persecuted, mobbed, flogged, and murdered," the freed slave "demonstrated his capacity for self-government, not only by what he accomplished as a citizen, but by showing what he could and surely would accomplish under more favorable conditions."[7]

These arguments had little impact on the leading professional historians of the day, with the ambivalent exception of Harvard's Albert Bushnell Hart. Though conscious of his abolitionist heritage, Hart wrote in 1898 that the "mistaken" attempt during Reconstruction "to confer the suffrage on the most ignorant class" had been "doomed to failure from the beginning." It was Hart who, as editor of the *American Nation* historical series, persuaded William A. Dunning to write the volume on Reconstruction. When Dunning turned in his manuscript in 1907, Hart declared himself "immensely pleased with it. . . . You are going to have a very strong effect on the future attitude of Americans toward this troublous period."[8]

But Hart also suggested revisions that modified Dunning's interpretation in a more positive direction. "I doubt very much whether reconstruction can be fairly convicted of all the evils with which it is charged," Hart told Dunning. "I should be sorry to have your volume give currency to the exaggerated ideas on this subject that fly through the South." He persuaded Dunning to place more emphasis on the beginnings of both public and missionary education and the constructive role of several black political leaders. Believing that "Reconstruction did many good things for which it has never been credited," Hart invited his former student W. E. B. Du Bois to read a paper at the 1909 meeting of the American Historical Association that was published in the *American Historical Review* the next year as "Reconstruction and Its Benefits." Du Bois's paper was the first expression in a professional journal of ideas that became standard revisionist themes a half century later.[9]

---

[7] Hallowell, *The Southern Question*, Boston, 1890, pp. 14-15, 2; Hallowell, *Why the Negro Was Enfranchised. Negro Suffrage Justified*, Boston, 1903, pp. 15, 31-32; *Independent*, June 29, 1899, May 2, 1901, Jan. 23, Mar. 20, 1902, May 4, Dec. 28, 1905.

[8] Hart's review of Dunning's *Essays on the Civil War and Reconstruction*, in *Book Reviews*, v (Jan. 1898), 203-207; Hart to Dunning, Jan. 15, 1902, Jan. 17, June 1, 1907, Hart Papers, Harvard University Archives.

[9] Hart to Dunning, Jan. 17, Apr. 8, 1907, Hart Papers; Hart to Oswald Garrison

In 1906 Hart himself had published a balanced appraisal of Reconstruction in the *Boston Evening Transcript,* of which Du Bois thought
well enough to have it reprinted as a Niagara Movement pamphlet.
The popular belief that "from 1865 to 1875 the whole South was governed by an unrighteous combination of Negroes with a few 'scala-
wags' . . . and 'Carpetbaggers' is badly warped," wrote Hart. On the
contrary, most of the Reconstruction governments were led by able
men; public schools and progressive state constitutions were positive
and permanent achievements; Boss Tweed's Democratic machine in
New York stole more public money than all the Reconstruction governments combined; and of all the evils associated with Reconstruction, the Ku Klux Klan was the worst.[10]

If Hart's historical writings were a partial antidote to the anti-Negro
interpretation of Reconstruction, the same cannot be said of his excursion into the no-man's land of racial differences. At the core of the race
problem, he wrote in 1905, was the question: "Has the negro the intellectual and moral power to raise himself out of his present inferiority
into a position of equality of achievement with the white man?" Re-
viewing the literature purporting to demonstrate black inferiority,
Hart conceded that "if provable, it is an argument that not only justifies slavery, but now justifies any degree of political and social dependence." In 1905 Hart thought Negro deficiencies could be explained
by environment, lack of opportunity, poor education, and the short
time since slavery. There was plenty of evidence, he said, to indicate
that when given a chance blacks measured up to whites. Hart had
taught more than 20 black students at Harvard, all of whom had done
well; he had studied first-hand the all-black communities at Mound
Bayou, Mississippi, and on St. Helena Island, South Carolina, which
were "a standing refutation of the statement often made that Negroes
have not the capacity to combine and build up a new town in the same
way that white people build theirs."[11]

But Hart moved toward a belief in Negro inferiority during the next

Villard, Dec. 4, 1909, OGV Papers; Du Bois to Hart, Nov. 30, Dec. 6, 1909, Jan.
8, 1910, cited in Francis Broderick's research notes for a biography of Du Bois,
Schomburg Library, New York City; Du Bois, "Reconstruction and Its Benefits,"
American Historical Review, xv (1910), 781-99.

[10] Hart, "The Realities of Negro Suffrage," *BET,* Mar. 24, 1906, reprinted by
the Niagara Movement as *Negro Suffrage.*

[11] Hart, "Is the Southern Negro Degenerating?" *BET,* Mar. 18, 1905; Hart,
"The African Riddle," *Saturday Evening Post,* CLXXVIII (Oct. 28, 1905), 15; Hart's
review of two books on the race question in *Nation,* Oct. 5, 1905; Hart to his
wife, Jan. 25, 1908, Hart Papers; Hart, "Mississippi, the State and the River,"
BET, Feb. 5, 1908.

three years. His latent Anglo-Saxonism seems to have undermined his determination to preserve an open mind on the question of racial differences. Hart had done his graduate study at the University of Freiburg, where he was drilled in the "germ theory" of the Teutonic origins of northern European civilization. Like most American scholars of his generation, he taught that British and American institutions marked the highest development of the Teuton's native genius for government and social organization. Hart favored immigration restriction because he believed southern European immigrants incapable of full assimilation to Anglo-American institutions; it was perhaps inevitable that this conviction would broaden into a thesis of racial differences.[12]

In the winter of 1907–1908 Hart made another of his many trips to the South for research on race relations. This time he concentrated on the rural black belt, where the poverty and pathology of black life depressed him and apparently convinced him of the Negro's inferiority. Hart gave the Lowell Institute Lectures in Boston in 1908, which became the basis for his book *The Southern South* (1910). Scholarly in tone, this book criticized the South for its extreme racism expressed in lynchings, disfranchisement, and neglect of black public schools. At the same time, however, Hart conceded the central argument that underlay these policies: the Negro was "permanently inferior to the white race in capacity." Hart did not arrive at this conclusion lightly. Through many pages he painfully balanced the pros and cons of the argument; he noted all the environmental constrictions that prevented black people from realizing their full potential. But even after making allowances for these disadvantages, the failure of Negroes to do better since emancipation was "frankly discouraging." The "main issue must be fairly faced by the friends" of the race, insisted Hart. "The negroes as a people have less self-control, are less affected by ultimate advantages, are less controlled by family ties and standards of personal morality, than the average even of those poor white people, immigrants or natives, who have the poorest chance. . . . Race measured by race, the Negro is inferior, and his past history in Africa and in America leads to the belief that he will remain inferior."[13]

At least one southern reviewer pointed out the inconsistency between the "abolitionist bias" of Hart's criticism of the South and his

---

[12] Barbara Miller Solomon, *Ancestors and Immigrants: A Changing New England Tradition*, Cambridge, Mass., 1956, p. 95; Edward N. Saveth, *American Historians and European Immigrants, 1875-1925*, New York, 1948, p. 25. See also correspondence between Hart and numerous genealogists, immigration restrictionists, and the like, in Hart Papers.

[13] Hart, "Outcome of the Southern Race Question," *North American Review*, July 1908, pp. 50-51; Hart, *The Southern South*, New York, 1910. pp. 99-105, 134-35.

admission of Negro inferiority.[14] So did some of Hart's neo-abolitionist colleagues, who thought that this concession stultified his efforts for racial uplift and his support of the NAACP. But Hart believed that, while the Negro would never equal the Anglo-Saxon, the race was capable of much improvement and certainly deserved justice. And to some extent the apparent paradox of his racial attitudes can be explained by the tension between egalitarian faith and the "truths" of science taught in his day. Faced with an apparent conflict between science and faith, some neo-abolitionists reacted as did Hart with a perplexed effort to reconcile the two; others accepted science; several remained romantic racialists; but an impressive number worked out an egalitarian argument strikingly modern in its methods and conclusions.

By the beginning of the twentieth century the thesis of Negro inferiority was pandemic in both scientific and popular thought. Weighty tomes based on research in physical and social sciences offered apparently irrefutable evidence of racial differences. "The sanction of science for the inferiority of the Negro," concluded one historian, was so overwhelming especially among biologists and physicians that "arguments to the contrary were simply not to be found in the transactions and journals of the medical societies." Racist sentiments prevailed not only among the large audiences who read Thomas Dixon's anti-Negro novels or watched the Broadway play *The Clansmen* and D. W. Griffith's 1915 movie *The Birth of a Nation* based on Dixon's books, but also among the writers and political leaders who molded national opinion. "As a race and in the mass," wrote Theodore Roosevelt in 1906, Negroes "are altogether inferior to the whites." Three years earlier the president's younger cousin Franklin had remarked during his junior year at Harvard: "Yes, Harvard has sought to uplift the Negro, if you like has sought to make a man out of a semibeast." During a congressional debate in 1904, a representative from Massachusetts stated that "of course I recognize the supremacy of the Caucasian race. I suppose everybody does." The Left in American politics thought no differently. "Almost all socialists," writes an historian of the Socialist Party of America, regarded the Negro "as occupying a lower position on the evolutionary scale than the white."[15]

---

14 Review by William Garrott Brown in *Nation*, Aug. 4, 1910.

15 John S. Haller, Jr., *Outcasts from Evolution: Scientific Attitudes of Racial Inferiority, 1859-1900*, Urbana, Ill., 1971, pp. 207, 68; Theodore Roosevelt to Owen Wister, Apr. 27, 1906, quoted in Wister, *Roosevelt: The Story of a Friendship, 1880-1919*, New York, 1930, p. 253; Franklin D. Roosevelt quoted in James MacGregor Burns, *Roosevelt: The Lion and the Fox*, New York, 1956, p. 20; Congressman Fred Gillett quoted in Richard M. Abrams, *Conservatism in a Progres-*

With "everybody" recognizing white superiority, it is hardly surprising that some former abolitionists did so. A few like Daniel Chamberlain made no apology for their conversion to racism. Others like Hart wrestled with the problem before taking a definite position. Two men whose fathers had been friends of John Brown looked back on their own youthful idealism with some embarrassment. Citing an abolitionist tribute to black achievement, journalist Joseph E. Chamberlin wrote in 1899 that "at this late day, we who are the children of the ardent abolitionists of that earlier period can only sigh when we read such a glorious paean." Russell H. Conwell, founder of Temple University, expressed disappointment that so few of the black students at Temple had graduated. "In the primary grades, and in parrot learning by rote," Conwell was quoted as saying, Negroes "did fairly well; but . . . in the higher intellectual levels demanding original powers of thought, the race as a race seemed largely incompetent."[16]

More surprising was the number of educated black people who seemed to accept their own inferiority. Thomas Inborden, principal of a black school in North Carolina, praised the great achievements of Anglo-Saxons wrought from "the handsome endowment of their own brains" while "the Negro was roaming the deserts and wilds of Africa [in] . . . a condition of savagery." William J. White, editor of the leading black religious periodical in the South, the *Georgia Baptist*, explained the superiority of mulattoes to pure blacks: "This mixture of blood supplies the quality in which the full-blooded Negro is deficient . . . that kind of ambition that causes us to reach out after higher and better things." Such opinions were not confined to accommodationists or Uncle Toms. A correspondent of the militant *Cleveland Gazette* wondered if the failure of black businesses was proof that Negroes were "a scrub race of born servants." The novelist Sutton Griggs, a one-time champion of black nationalism who later joined the integrationist Niagara Movement, wrote that the Negro whose "grandfather was a savage" could hardly be expected to compete "in a highly complex civilization . . . with the most cultured, aggressive and virile type of all times, the Anglo-Saxon."[17]

---

sive Era: Massachusetts Politics, 1900-1912, Cambridge, Mass., 1964, pp. 25-26; R. Laurence Moore, "Flawed Fraternity—American Socialist Response to the Negro, 1901-1912," *The Historian*, XXXII (1969), 12. For detailed studies of the pervasiveness of racism at the turn of the century, see Idus A. Newby, *Jim Crow's Defense: Anti-Negro Thought in America, 1900-1930*, Baton Rouge, 1965, and Helen Knuth, "The Climax of American Anglo-Saxonism, 1898-1905," Ph.D. Dissertation, Northwestern University, 1958.

16 Chamberlin, *John Brown*, Boston, 1899, pp. 41-45; Conwell quoted in *Friends' Intelligencer*, Oct. 5, 1912, Supplement.

17 Inborden in *AM*, LVIII (Mar. 1904), 79-83; White in *Independent*, May 14,

All of the men quoted in the previous paragraph were of mixed blood, and the cultural milieu that denigrated a black heritage may have influenced them subconsciously to reject that heritage. This was almost certainly true of the mulatto William H. Thomas, whose 1901 book *The American Negro* was one of the most extreme racist polemics of its time. Thomas had grown up in a black abolitionist family, fought in the Union army, went to South Carolina as a schoolteacher after the war, and served in the state legislature during Reconstruction. In those days he was an egalitarian, but he eventually grew disillusioned with the "insensate follies of a race blind to every passing opportunity." The Negro, he said in 1901, was a "sensuous savage" who resembled a "rational human creature" only in proportion to his admixture of white blood. He could imitate but never create; his mind could grasp facts but not concepts; his idea of education was "to imitate mechanically what he only succeeds in caricaturing." Morally the Negro was the victim of his "imperious sexual impulse" which was "the main incitement to the degeneracy of the race." The average black man was "immersed in poverty, steeped in ignorance, stifled with immorality, inherently lazy, and a born pilferer." Such a cancerous growth in the body politic must be removed even if it meant the race's "virtual extermination." But Thomas did not really propose genocide; what he envisaged was a new form of compulsory labor to replace slavery. "The Negro has neither the intellect nor will to institute self-redemptive measures," so it was up to whites to do so. "The only effective and efficient agencies are the shalls and shall-nots of command, backed up by imperative force."[18]

Virtually all black people and white neo-abolitionists who read or heard of Thomas's book repudiated this product of a sick mind that sought to escape blackness by identifying with the most virulent white stereotypes of Negroes. Thomas was a living illustration of the "tragic mulatto," a favorite theme of nineteenth-century novelists. Often the vehicle for tear-jerking sentimentality, fictional treatments of mulattoes who suffered from cultural schizophrenia could become in the hands of skillful writers an instrument to attack racism and to plumb the psychological depths of self-hatred. William Dean Howells did this in his short novel *An Imperative Duty* (1892). The heroine, Rhoda Aldgate, is engaged to a prominent Bostonian when she learns that her

---

1891; *Gazette* correspondent quoted in David A. Gerber, "Ohio and the Color Line: Racial Discrimination and Negro Responses in a Northern State, 1860-1915," Ph.D. Dissertation, Princeton University, 1971, p. 365; Griggs, *Overshadowed, a Novel*, Nashville, 1901, p. 5.

[18] Thomas, *The American Negro*, New York, 1901, pp. xi-xviii, 106, 112, 177, 180, 136, 384, 363, 390.

mother was an octoroon. Revolted by the discovery, she indulges in an orgy of self-pity during a walk through Boston's black neighborhoods where she views with new eyes the people for whom she had previously felt only a vague sympathy. "She never knew before how hideous they were, with their flat wide-nostriled noses, their out-rolled thick lips, their mobile, bulging eyes set near together, their retreating chins and foreheads." She met a girl so light-skinned she could have passed for white, and thought: "I am like her, and my mother was darker, and my grandmother darker, and my great grander like a mulatto, and then it was a horrible old negress, a savage stolen from Africa, where she had been a cannibal." Rhoda could not cope with "the horror of the wrong by which she came to be. . . . She grovelled in self-loathing and despair. . . . She seemed to see herself and hear herself stopping some of these revolting creatures, the dreadfulest of them, and saying, 'I am black, too. Take me home with you, and let me live with you, and be like you in every way.' " When her fiancé (who eventually married Rhoda) tried to talk her out of this mood, she could only respond: "I can't help it. It's burnt into me. It's branded me one of *them*. I *am* one. No, I can't escape. And the best way is to go and live among them and own it. Then perhaps I can learn to bear it, and not hate them so. But I *do* hate them. I do, I do! I can't help it."[19]

Although *An Imperative Duty* reveals Howells' sensitivity to the impact of racism on black self-perception, he was not a thoroughgoing egalitarian. Rather he was (in George Fredrickson's terminology) a romantic racialist who like several other neo-abolitionists believed in the Negro's special artistic or temperamental qualities. In 1896 Howells helped to launch Paul Laurence Dunbar's career with a favorable review of the black poet's privately printed volume *Majors and Minors*. Howells also found a publisher for Dunbar's *Lyrics of a Lowly Life* and wrote an introduction for the book, in which he expressed the hope that "the hostilities and the prejudices which had so long constrained his race were destined to vanish in the arts; that these were to be the final proof that God had made of one blood all nations of men." Howells thought these dialect poems illustrated "a precious difference of temperament between the races which it would be a great pity ever to lose." The Negro's "natural gaiety and lightness of heart," he said, contrasted favorably with the Anglo-Saxon's materialism and aggressiveness. "If the negroes ever have their turn—and if the meek are to inherit the earth they must come to it," spoke Howells through one of his fictional characters, "we shall have a civilization of such

---

[19] Howells, *An Imperative Duty*, New York, 1892, pp. 85-87, 144.

sweetness and good-will as the world has never known yet. Perhaps we shall have to wait their turn for any real Christian civilization."[20]

The tradition of romantic racialism stretched back at least to Harriet Beecher Stowe's Uncle Tom; it has come down to the present in the form of a "black aesthetic" or "soul culture" whose expressive life style is seen as superior to that of whites. Some neo-abolitionists at the turn of the century talked of "Negro traits" in ways similar to both Stowe and the modern proponents of a black aesthetic. The Negro's special genius, said Mary White Ovington and Edward Clement, lay in his "feeling for rhythm, for melodious sound," his "intensity of sentiment and emotion" that accounted for black success in music and vaudeville. Black people would enrich Western culture, said Michael Strieby, because their "amiability and joyousness will supplement the fierceness and energy of European and American life." Most neo-abolitionist romantic racialists repudiated the thesis of Negro mental inferiority; the racial differences they perceived were cultural or temperamental, and these gave blacks an edge on whites in certain areas. Mentally there was "as much variety of original endowment in the Afro-American as in the Anglo-American," said President Jeremiah E. Rankin of Howard University, but blacks were superior in "aesthetic culture."[21]

Then as now, romantic racialism was more common among black spokesmen than among their white sympathizers. The Negro's "fervid oratory" and "sensuous poetry," wrote scholar Benjamin Brawley, proved that there was "something very elemental about the heart of the race, something that finds its origin in the African forest." Several black romantic racialists conceded Anglo-Saxon superiority in the world of business, politics, and science. "The black man has not the grim, dogged determination and bull dog tenacity of purpose of the white man" nor his "daring, adventurous spirit [and] ability to fight a hard, uphill battle," wrote William H. Ferris, the first black man to call Booker T. Washington an "Uncle Tom" and later the editor of Marcus Garvey's *Negro World*. But the Negro, continued Ferris, possessed special gifts, among which were "poetic imagination . . . a lovable nature, a spiritual earnestness and a musical genius." The black nationalist Edward Blyden asserted that "the African is a spiritual and minis-

[20] Dunbar, *Lyrics of a Lowly Life*, with an Introduction by Howells, New York, 1897, p. xvii; Howells, *An Imperative Duty*, 91, 29. See also James B. Stronks, "Paul Laurence Dunbar and William Dean Howells," *Ohio Historical Quarterly*, LXVII (1958), 95-108.

[21] Clement quoted in *AM*, LXII (Apr. 1908), 102; Ovington, *Half a Man: The Status of the Negro in New York*, New York, 1911, pp. 124, 129; Strieby in *AM*, XLIV (Dec. 1890), 373; Rankin, "The Aesthetic Capacity of the Afro-American," *Our Day*, XIII (July–Aug. 1894), 293, 295.

terial race. The European is . . . the statesman, the soldier, the sailor, the policeman of humanity. The Negro is the protégé, the child, the attendant, the servant, if you like of this dominant race."[22]

The black man's special qualities more than compensated for his inferiority to the dour Anglo-Saxon. The race's artistic "gifts and inspiration," said Blyden, would enable him to "attain to heights as yet inaccessible" to the "materialistic" white man. James Weldon Johnson rhapsodized: "Warmed by the poetic blood of Africa," the Negro possessed a "racial genius" that America needed. "Extreme rhythm, color, warmth, abandon, and movement" were the elements of this genius. Especially was the black woman "with her rich coloring, her gaiety, her laughter and song, her alluring, undulating movements" a "more beautiful creature than her sallow, songless, lipless, hipless, tired-looking, tired-moving white sister." Du Bois eulogized the race's "innate love of harmony and beauty." "Will America be poorer if she replaced her brutal dyspeptic blundering with light-hearted but determined Negro humility?" he asked. "Or her coarse and cruel wit with loving jovial good-humor? or her vulgar music with the soul of the Sorrow Songs?" The black man's "sense of meekness," said Du Bois, "has breathed the soul of humility and forgiveness into the formalism and cant of American religion."[23]

Such expressions of romantic racialism could play into the hands of white supremacists, who were quite willing to concede to blacks a racial genius for rhythm and gaiety. Nobody recognized this better than William Hayes Ward, who consistently rejected theories of racial differences. When Du Bois published a paper entitled "The Conservation of Races" in which he discussed the "products of the Negro mind," Ward criticized this idea as "nonsense. There is no special difference between a white mind and a Negro mind." Since Du Bois was a Harvard graduate, "we presume he has a Harvard mind."[24]

But Ward rightly considered white racism more dangerous than romantic racialism. He was in the vanguard of the numerous white neo-abolitionists who defied the racist consensus. "There is no slightest evidence that there is a lower level above which the negro cannot rise,"

[22] Brawley quoted in August Meier, *Negro Thought in America, 1880-1915*, Ann Arbor, 1963, p. 268; Ferris, "Typical Negro Traits," *AM*, LXII (Apr. 1908), 99-102; Ferris, *The African Abroad*, New Haven, 1913, quoted in S. P. Fullinwider, *The Mind and Mood of Black America: 20th Century Thought*, Homewood, Ill., 1969, p. 24; Edward Blyden to Augustus F. Beard, Oct. 20, 1899, quoted in Edith Holden, *Blyden of Liberia*, New York, 1966, pp. 698-99.

[23] Holden, *Blyden*, 698-99; Johnson and Du Bois quoted in Fullinwider, *Mind and Mood of Black America*, 89, 57-58, 60, and Du Bois, *The Souls of Black Folk*, Premier Americana paperback ed., Greenwich, Conn., 1961, p. 18.

[24] *Independent*, May 20, 1897.

stated Ward flatly. "There is no such essential, invincible inferiority." If given a chance, black people would "prove themselvs equal to the best the world has yet produced. We expect to see men of that blood occupying the highest positions in this country, all conceited Caucasian or Anglo-Saxon assumption and resistance to the contrary notwithstanding. . . . We believe that a succeeding generation will see great black republics in Africa, producing statesmen, philosophers, poets and orators worthy to be counted beside Homer and Plato and Cicero and Dante and Shakespeare."[25]

In their rebuttals of racist arguments, neo-abolitionists borrowed ideas from abolitionists of an earlier generation, cited anthropologists of their own day, and anticipated modern environmentalist hypotheses. Horace Bumstead put together a number of these themes in his 1908 rejoinder to Albert Bushnell Hart's Lowell Institute lectures. The average level of present Negro achievement was of course inferior to that of whites, said Bumstead, but the important facts were the wide range of individual capacities *within* each race and the overlap of both races at all levels. The disproportionate number of blacks at the lower end of the scale "can reasonably be accounted for by factors of past history and present environment for which the negro is not responsible." It was unreasonable to expect a people only 40 years out of slavery "to unlearn the bad lessons and overcome the handicap of two hundred and fifty!" Moreover, many of the Negro's alleged traits, said Bumstead, were white stereotypes derived from cartoons, minstrel shows, and darkey stories. "Let us rid our minds of the picture of the Negro as he is burlesqued in the comic papers and on the cover of the shoe-blacking box," he pleaded, "and get a higher conception of him." As for the claim that Africans were a barbarous people who had never accomplished anything, Bumstead dismissed this also as a stereotype. White people were "still too much under the sway of antiquated teaching in regard to the negro in Africa. From childhood we have been fed with stories of the ignorant and lazy savages. . . . But more recent investigations are presenting a very different picture." Drawing on the research of anthropologists, particularly Franz Boas, Bumstead cited the early development of iron smelting, domesticated animals, flourishing cities, trade networks, and empires in pre-modern Africa.[26]

Egalitarian neo-abolitionists worked out many variations on these

[25] *Ibid.*, Feb. 19, 1903, May 10, 1906, July 18, 1907.
[26] Bumstead, "Handicaps of the Negro Race," *NYEP*, Apr. 25, 1908. See also Bumstead, "The Freedmen's Children at School," *Andover Review*, IV (Dec. 1885), 550-51; and Bumstead's remarks at the Second Lake Mohonk Conference on the Negro, in Isabel Barrows, ed., *Second Mohonk Conference on the Negro Question*, Boston, 1891, p. 54.

themes in the generation after 1890. The first line of defense of racial equality lay athwart the old debate over nurture versus nature. Darwinism had given the proponents of hereditary determinism a shot in the arm; the eugenics movement at the turn of the century re-emphasized the importance of "breeding" in determining character. In reply, several neo-abolitionists reasserted their environmentalism with renewed vigor. "Matters of education, culture, character," said Ward, "depend not on physical, but on social heredity." Wilbur P. Thirkield confessed that "I used to stand dazed before the problem of heredity" until he learned that people "may be transformed by the power of Christian influences." Since "environment counts for more than heredity," we must "distinguish between the intellectual capacity, with which God has endowed every race, and the mental and moral acquirements, which are the outcome of civilization and environment." Other missionary educators insisted that whatever Negro inferiority still existed could be "traced to the lack of education in the early years, and to previous environments [rather] than to essential intellectual differences. . . . Those who are on the path to the future have not yet made their proper environment."[27]

This Christian environmentalism blended the evangelical reform tradition with the new currents of the social gospel. A dominant strain in both movements was the emphasis on the Church's mission to reform society as well as to redeem individuals. The social gospel's crusade against poverty, slums, and industrial exploitation was a broadening of the evangelicals' crusade against slavery. After Reconstruction the missionary educators, who were the connecting link between evangelicalism and social Christianity, had concentrated more on instilling the elements of Christian manhood into the freedmen than on altering the environment in which they lived. Though this emphasis continued, the rise of hereditary determinism sparked a counter-revival of environmentalism among missionary educators that paralleled the social gospel's concern with the environmental causes of urban poverty.[28]

The individual who best personified this fusion of evangelical aboli-

27 *Independent*, July 28, 1904; two speeches by Thirkield published in William N. Hartshorn, *An Era of Progress and Promise, 1863-1910*, Boston, 1910, p. 56, and *Proceedings of the First Capon Springs Conference for Education in the South*, Capon Springs, W. Va., 1898, p. 17; *AM*, LI (Apr. 1897), 126, LXII (Dec. 1908), 323. For the eugenics movement, see Mark H. Haller, *Eugenics: Hereditarian Attitudes in American Thought*, New Brunswick, N.J., 1963.

28 Three recent doctoral dissertations have begun to revise the long-standing assumption that social Christianity largely ignored the race problem: Curtis Robert Grant, "The Social Gospel and Race," Stanford University, 1968; Ronald C. White, "Social Christianity and the Negro in the Progressive Era," Princeton, 1972; and Ralph E. Luker, "The Social Gospel and the Failure of Racial Reform, 1885-1898," Univ. of No. Car. at Chapel Hill, 1973.

tionism and the social gospel was Harlan Paul Douglass. Born after the Civil War into a family whose abolitionism was two generations deep, Douglass graduated from Grinnell College, entered the Congregational ministry, did graduate study in sociology and psychology at Harvard, Columbia, and the University of Chicago, and taught psychology at Drury College in Missouri for six years before becoming the AMA's superintendent of education in 1906 and its secretary from 1910 to 1918. Thereafter Douglass filled a number of executive and editorial posts in Christian social agencies until his death in 1953. Perhaps the most important of his 12 books was *Christian Reconstruction of the South*, published in 1909 as an exposition of the *AMA*'s social mission to the Negro. [29]

Douglass considered scientific racism a threat to both Negro education and social Christianity. "When Jesus says, 'Make learners of all nations,' does God say, 'No, some haven't brains enough'?" he asked. "When the voice sounds, 'Feed my sheep,' must we reply, 'yea Lord, thou knowest that we love thee, but what you take for sheep are only goats'?" Christians could not shrug off these questions with platitudes about brotherhood. "The alleged findings of science [must] be met on their own ground," said Douglass. "These Philistines also are men, and as such we may fight them."[30]

Douglass' credentials as a social psychologist gave him greater authority than other neo-abolitionists in this battle of ideas. He maintained that "social heredity" accounted for racial differences in achievement. By social heredity (a term borrowed from Lester Ward), Douglass meant something akin to what modern sociologists have called the culture of poverty—a physical environment lacking proper diet, sanitation, and medical care and a closed system of values in which education, ambition, and planning for the future have no place. This locked many children of the poor into a self-perpetuating cycle of poverty. "If the children of one generation grow up in ignorance," wrote Douglass, "it goes without saying that the children of the next generation will grow up in ignorance." If this "hard and cramping tradition is not challenged and broken through by new and energizing beliefs, social heredity works out human destiny as relentlessly as if it were true physical heredity." Though middle-class children—black and white—performed better in school than lower-class children, "there is not a vestige of scientific proof that these contrasts in any wise register the distribution of natural capacity by physical heredity." The poor, especially the black poor, "are simply normal human beings whose average capacities are socially suppressed; partly through un-

[29] Biographical data in the Douglass Papers, Amistad Research Center.
[30] *Christian Reconstruction in the South*, Boston, 1909, pp. 372-73.

dernourishment and other environmental handicaps . . . and partly through paralyzing beliefs in natural inferiority which forbid them to hope for themselves and prevent society from doing its best in their behalf."[31]

Douglass drew upon his visits to southern cities where the AMA maintained schools for data to illustrate his points. Consider the high mortality rate among urban blacks, he said—this was the result not of hereditary weaknesses (a popular Darwinian belief of the time) but of the confinement of blacks in slums without adequate sanitation, water supply, garbage removal, or public health facilities, and of an economic structure that compelled black mothers to work long hours leaving their children to fend for themselves. As for occupational patterns, if the Negro "falls back on the servile callings, it is because he is pushed down by man, not pulled down by his own nature. . . . The instability of the negro family, too, its excessive marital infidelity and frequent divorce, are due to specific social causes." Despite these handicaps, said Douglass, the black community had done more than whites realized to organize itself for stability and progress. Citing Du Bois' Atlanta University studies of the black church, Negro business, and black fraternal and social agencies, Douglass asserted that these institutions belied the notion of organizational incapacity.[32]

"The deep-seated determination of the American people to give a racial explanation to [the Negro's] deficiencies and to act accordingly," Douglass concluded, was "one of the cruelest of his environing facts." Thus "at the core of the negro problem lies the problem of the Anglo-Saxon, a difficulty not of the blood of Africa, but of the spirit of America." It was time to recognize that the Negro's lack of achievement was the product of "conditions which men can control." Even in Darwinian terms of the survival of the fittest, "the negro has a fighting chance . . . and it is the duty of just men to help him in his fight."[33]

The development of intelligence testing struck a hard blow at the egalitarian position. By 1905 the French psychologist Alfred Binet had worked out a series of tests to measure intelligence, and this forerunner of the famous IQ tests soon caught on in the United States. In 1913 a University of South Carolina psychologist, Josiah Morse, tested black and white school children in Columbia to determine comparative racial intelligence. The first in a long line of such comparisons, these tests showed that 29 percent of the black children performed more than a year below their age compared with 10 percent of the whites. Attempting to control for environment, Morse compared Negroes with

31 Ibid., 374, 380-83.   32 Ibid., 174-79, 186, 193, 131-51.
33 Ibid., 206-207, 170-71.

the white children of textile mill workers, whose economic conditions and school facilities, he maintained, were similar to those of blacks, and found that 18 percent of the mill children performed below their age level. These results, Morse believed, indicated that heredity accounted for part of the white superiority over blacks.[34]

In a critique that could as well have been written in 1974 as in 1914, Oswald Garrison Villard's *Evening Post* rebutted Morse's conclusions. Morse had offered no proof of his dubious claim that black schools were "as good" as the mill children's schools. And "when we come to the child's environment outside of school, the influence of a difference in the whole mental atmosphere of the child is quite incalculable." Morse had contended that the mill children's environment was "little if any better" than that of blacks, but the *Post* would not accept this. It was "far from being solely a question of economic condition or material surroundings," the paper declared. "It is a question of the presence or absence of those thousand momentary contacts with a broad and stimulating life to which the child's impressionable nature responds so readily. . . . The white cotton-mill family is not cut off from the general life of the community . . . in any such complete way as is the colored family." But even if the black and white child's environments were *exactly* the same, "the chief home influence of all, that of the parents, is affected by the environment under which *they* grew up," and Morse had not even pretended to control for that.[35]

The proponents of black inferiority attributed the high crime rate among Negroes to genetic traits. Neo-abolitionist environmentalists dealt with this issue at two levels by arguing that: 1) discriminatory treatment by newspapers, police, and courts accounted for part of the apparently higher black crime rate; and 2) to the extent that blacks did commit more crimes than whites, the causes were sociological rather than racial.

In the first place, said Villard, the press's habit of identifying criminals by race and giving inordinate publicity to black crimes did as much as anything else to create a false image of Negro criminality. "Let us be fair in such matters," he declared in launching a crusade for less newspaper sensationalism. In Chicago, Villard pointed out, more men were convicted of rape in 1898 than blacks charged with it in the entire South; in New York City 148 persons were arrested for rape in 1902 as against 50 blacks accused of this crime in the rest of the coun-

[34] Morse, "A Comparison of White and Colored Children Measured by the Binet Scale of Intelligence," *Popular Science Monthly*, LXXIV (Jan. 1914), 75-79. For the early history of intelligence testing, see Frank N. Freeman, *Mental Tests: Their History, Principles, and Applications*, rev. ed., Boston, 1939, chaps. 2-5.

[35] *NYEP*, Jan. 14, 1914.

try. But "nobody comments on the New York or Chicago offenders . . . while the whole country is informed of the 'black scourge.' "[36]

Villard and Wendell Garrison ran articles and editorials in the *Evening Post/Nation* documenting racial discrimination by police and courts. Francis Garrison maintained that statistics of black crime were "worthless" because of "the five or tenfold greater harshness in arresting & fining & imprisoning the blacks." A courageous white Episcopal clergyman from Louisiana, Quincy Ewing, agreed with Garrison and sent him in 1905 a long manuscript titled "The Criminality of the Southern Negro: An Essay in Explanation and Rebuttal." Though the manuscript was poorly organized and badly written, Garrison tried to get Houghton Mifflin, where he worked as an editor, to publish it. Fearing a southern boycott of its textbooks, Houghton as well as several other publishers refused to touch even a revised manuscript. Garrison then formed a committee headed by himself and his nephew Oswald to publish the book on commission, but they were unable to raise enough money. Finally in 1909 Garrison helped persuade the *Atlantic Monthly* (published by Houghton Mifflin) to print an article by Ewing, "The Heart of the Race Problem," which set forth his indictment of southern racial justice.[37]

The foremost abolitionist expert on crime was Franklin B. Sanborn, who served for many years as secretary of the Massachusetts Board of Charities, helped found the National Prison Association, and won praise for his work in behalf of criminal rehabilitation. In 1904 Sanborn gave the opening address at the Atlanta University Conference on Negro Crime. He demonstrated statistically that while the per capita ratio of sentenced criminals was nearly three times greater among blacks than whites, when these figures were weighted for seriousness of offense, length of sentence, and for the tendency of courts to impose heavier penalties on Negroes than whites for the same crime, the *actual* black crime rate was probably only 1½ times the white rate. Sanborn traced the double standard of justice to the convict lease system, which encouraged courts to sentence Negroes to long prison terms for petty offenses or trumped-up charges in order to provide lessees with a large labor supply. Convict leasing and its successor the chain gang perpetuated a vicious cycle under which black prisoners of all ages, both sexes, and all degrees of criminality were thrown to-

36 *Ibid.*, June 4, 30, 1904, Jan. 13, 1903; *Nation*, June 9, July 7, Oct. 13, 1904, Jan. 8, 1903; W. P. Garrison to Francis J. Garrison, Jan. 10, 1903, WPG Papers.
37 F. J. Garrison to Booker T. Washington, Nov. 6, Dec. 27, 1905, BTW Papers; Ewing to F. J. Garrison, Oct. 12, 1905, Jan. 6, 1906, F. J. Garrison to Villard, Jan. 4, 9, Apr. 12, 1906, May 26, 1907, Sept. 12, 1908, OGV Papers; *Atlantic Monthly*, CIII (Mar. 1909), 389-97.

gether under brutalizing conditions. The result was inevitable, said Sanborn: "The innocent were made bad, the bad worse; women were outraged and children tainted." Since it was white oppression that "led to that sort of social protest and revolt which we call crime," concluded Sanborn, "we must look for remedy in the sane reform of these wrong social conditions, and not in intimidation, savagery, or the legalized slavery of men."[38]

Other neo-abolitionists expressed variations on these themes. "Brutality begets brutality," said Moorfield Storey, so it should surprise no one that whites had "succeeded in brutalizing" black people. After describing the life of black teenagers shut up in ghettos and denied a future, Harlan Paul Douglass asked who could wonder "that the negro child becomes a delinquent, whom our medieval law mistakenly classes as a criminal?" Of course Negroes committed crimes, said Villard. "What else is to be expected when one industrial opportunity after another is closed to them . . . when every place of decent resort, every decent concert hall or place of theatrical entertainment is closed to them," when the streets where they lived were "neglected, filthy and unsanitary, badly policed? . . . What incentive remains" for hard work and obedience to the law? It was the worst kind of hypocrisy for whites to compel the Negro "to roam in slum streets, and then if he grows up an animal [to] say the responsibility is his, that that proves him a beast, and his race is inherently criminal."[39]

While the dominant thrust of the life sciences and most of the social sciences in the early twentieth century was in a racist direction, anthropology gave more comfort to egalitarians. Some neo-abolitionists were acquainted with work in this field. As far back as 1861, abolitionists had publicized the work of Armand de Quatrefages, professor of natural history and ethnology at the Museum of Natural History in Paris. Quatrefages was still publishing in the 1890s; his major work, *The Introduction to the Study of the Human Races*, was translated into English in 1893. According to Michael Strieby and Joseph Hartzell, this book would force all racists to "reconstruct their anthropol-

[38] W. E. B. Du Bois, ed., *Some Notes on Negro Crime, Particularly in Georgia*, Atlanta University Publication no. 9, Atlanta, 1904, pp. 1-18, esp. 4-5, 8-9. For Sanborn's career, see Benjamin B. Hickok, "The Political and Literary Career of F. B. Sanborn," Ph.D. Dissertation, Mich. St. Univ., 1953.

[39] Storey to Charles Francis Adams, Jr., Aug. 14, 1905, Storey Papers, Mass. Hist. Society (I am indebted to William B. Hixson, Jr., for this reference); Douglass, *Christian Reconstruction*, 199-200; Villard, "Color Hysteria," *Crisis*, 1 (Apr. 1911), 26; MS of a Villard speech to the Ethical Culture Society, 1911, OGV Papers; report of Villard's speech to the Baltimore convention of the NAACP, in *NYT*, May 6, 1914.

ogy," for it dispelled "the unscientific prejudice" that drew "invidious distinctions" among the races of mankind.[40]

Other French anthropologists including Jean Finot, whose *Race Prejudice* appeared in English in 1907, published studies puncturing the myth of Anglo-Saxon supremacy. These works, said one neo-abolitionist, demonstrated that "there is no such thing as permanency in either the constituent elements or the superiority or inferiority of races." Even a few German ethnologists repudiated the concept of innate racial differences. In 1905 Oswald Garrison Villard, fluent in German, wrote a long editorial summarizing the work of Ludwig Stein and Friedrich Mueller, who argued that "the term 'race,' as often used, is merely a pseudo-scientific or political catchword." When ethnologists could not even agree on a definition of the term, said Villard, it was clear that for measuring mental differences the concept of race was "ethnological claptrap . . . humbug pure and simple." Villard dismissed the scientific racists as "astrologers of sociology"—they had many followers, "but so had phrenology and other spurious sciences in their day."[41]

A number of American anthropologists began making important contributions to the egalitarian position in the first decade of the century, especially Franz Boas and Livingston Farrand of Columbia University. Neo-abolitionists read and quoted their work. Farrand addressed the National Negro Conference (forerunner of the NAACP) in 1909, and Boas spoke at the first official NAACP Conference in 1910. Citing one of Farrand's articles, William Hayes Ward rejoiced that it "utterly cuts the ground out from under" the white supremacists. And in a review of several anthropological studies in 1907, the *American Missionary* proclaimed that "the ethnological doctrines for which the American Missionary Association has stood for more than half a century are now prevailing among the most advanced and trusted thinkers upon the races. We found our inspiration in the teachings of Jesus Christ which the scientists are now asserting to be the conclusions of the best ethnological knowledge."[42]

Whether grounded in Christianity or anthropology, racial egalitarianism seems to have been the majority opinion among neo-abolitionists

[40] *AM*, XLVII (Sept. 1893), 273-76; Hartzell to D. Appleton & Co., Jan. 7, 1895, FASME Archives; *Christian Educator*, VI (Aug.–Sept. 1895), 95.

[41] W. L. Garrison, Jr., to F. J. Garrison, May 15, July 14, 1908, WLG, Jr., Papers; *AM*, LXI (Oct. 1907), 248-49; *BET*, Oct. 20, 1905; *NYEP*, Mar. 25, 1905; *Nation*, Jan. 28, 1904.

[42] *Independent*, Mar. 26, 1903; *AM*, LXI (Oct. 1907), 248-49. See also *Nation*, May 3, 1906; *Independent*, Mar. 26, 1903; *Proceedings of the National Negro Conference 1909*, New York, 1909, pp. 14-21; and Charles Flint Kellogg, *NAACP: A History of the National Association for the Advancement of Colored People*, Baltimore, 1967, p. 45.

in the generation from 1890 to 1915, just as it was earlier. Of the 48 abolitionists and their descendants for whom evidence has been found, nine took a basically racist position, four were primarily romantic racialists, and 35 denied the existence of significant innate racial differences. To be sure, five of these 35 made statements at one time or another indicating some leanings toward racism and another five occasionally sounded like romantic racialists (which was not necessarily inconsistent with egalitarianism). On the other hand, two of the racists and one romantic racialist expressed their convictions cautiously and on some occasions took a strong environmentalist position. It is possible that many of those who left no record of their thoughts were at least latent racists, or that even some of the egalitarians harbored private doubts. But it is significant that in an age of overwhelming racist consensus, more than three-quarters of the white neo-abolitionists took a public stand in agreement with William Hayes Ward's assertion that notions of racial inferiority were "false in science, ruinous in government, and intolerable in morals."[43]

[43] *Independent*, Oct. 25, 1900.

Chapter Nineteen

Booker T. Washington and the Reaffirmation of Gradualism

"I feel as if we had already got beyond the necessity for proving the capacity of the colored people for full citizenship," wrote Richard P. Hallowell in 1903. "Hereafter less defensive and more aggressive warfare will be needed."[1] Hallowell's call to arms was premature. Eventually neo-abolitionists would take the offensive with the founding of the NAACP, but meanwhile they floundered from one approach to another. The indifference of the federal government and the courts to Negro rights forced some of them back on their shopworn faith in gradualism, education, and the goodwill of southern moderates. Again these proved frail reeds, but around the turn of the century they seemed the only alternatives to unconditional surrender to racism. Under the leadership of Booker T. Washington, black people and their white allies tried to salvage some hope from the wreckage of egalitarian aspirations.

In 1899, Republican Congressman Edgar Crumpacker of Indiana introduced a resolution directing the Census Bureau to determine the number of male citizens denied the ballot in specified southern states, with an eye toward enforcement of Section 2 of the 14th Amendment providing for the proportional reduction of congressional representation from such states. Neo-abolitionists at first hailed this proposal. "The Constitution of Some Use After All," ran a typical headline in the *Boston Evening Transcript*. "If the South does not set about correcting the manifest evil," predicted Villard, "the North will at least demand that the South take the Constitutional consequences."[2]

Although Crumpacker reintroduced his resolution in various forms at subsequent sessions of Congress, it was always buried in committee. The difficulty of determining the number of male ctiizens mandatorily disfranchised (contrasted with those who failed to register for voluntary or indeterminate reasons) plus an apprehension that any attempt to enforce Section 2 would in effect nullify the 15th Amendment by

---

1 Hallowell to Du Bois, Aug. 11, 1903, from the Du Bois Papers formerly in the custody of Herbert Aptheker, cited with permission.

2 *BET*, Feb. 21, 1899; *NYEP*, Dec. 8, 1904. For a brief discussion of the Crumpacker resolution, see Rayford W. Logan, *The Betrayal of the Negro from Rutherford B. Hayes to Woodrow Wilson*, New York, 1965, pp. 102-104.

conceding the constitutionality of disfranchisement caused many black leaders and white liberals to come out against the Crumpacker resolution by 1903. Edward Clement of the *Transcript* now realized that "what the South has done would not be undone; it would be confirmed"; the *Independent* feared that "the political rights of the negro would be even more hopelessly eclipsed than at present." For this reason T. Thomas Fortune and Booker T. Washington helped persuade President Roosevelt to oppose the Crumpacker resolution, which killed any slim hopes of passage.[3]

In the meantime several neo-abolitionists were involved in court challenges to disfranchisement. Two of these cases originated in Alabama, two in Virginia, and one (which never made it to the federal courts) in Louisiana. Their main targets were the grandfather clause and the exclusion of qualified blacks by registrars. In four decisions in 1903–1904 the U.S. Supreme Court threw out the challenges on technicalities. Villard denounced the rulings as "agile shuffling" to avoid confronting the issues, while Moorfield Storey expressed neo-abolitionist discouragement when he described the first Alabama decision (*Giles* v. *Harris*) as "a very serious blow to freedom, for if a man deprived of his vote has no remedy except to sue for damages before a white jury in the Southern states he is entirely without a remedy."[4]

These rulings seemed to seal the fate of Negro suffrage in the South. But even if the Court had decided the other way or if Congress had bestirred itself to pass new enforcement legislation, many neo-abolitionists expected that the South would only find new means of evasion. "When a total ruling community is determined that a law shall not be enforced, or that justice shall not be done, they are sure to nullify any laws," said William Hayes Ward. "Our liquor laws are an example." Clement added that "Force bills, Federal election laws and all that class of legislation have proved ineffective in the past because no statute is stronger than the juries which have to enforce it." For 30 years the North had tried various ways of securing black political rights in the South, but nothing had worked. "Since force bills fail and letting the South manage its own affairs fails, what will succeed?" The whole business seemed hopeless. "As matters stand," concluded Clement despairingly in 1904, "we see little hope for the colored voter at the South in the near future."[5]

[3] *BET*, Dec. 8, 1904; *Independent*, Dec. 31, 1903; Emma Lou Thornbrough, *T. Thomas Fortune: Militant Journalist*, Chicago, 1972, p. 272.

[4] *NYEP*, May 4, 1903; Storey to Erving Winslow, May 5, 1903, Storey Papers, Mass. Hist. Soc. (I am indebted to William B. Hixson, Jr., for this reference). The four decisions were *Giles* v. *Harris*, 189 U.S. 475 (1903); *Giles* v. *Teaseley*, 193 U.S. 146 (1904); *Jones* v. *Montague*, 194 U.S. 147 (1904); and *Selden* v. *Montague*, 194 U.S. 147 (1904).

[5] *Independent*, Dec. 17, 1903; *BET*, Feb. 6, 1902, Feb. 24, 1904.

These words reflected a strain of pessimism among neo-abolitionists that had been growing since 1890. Clement himself vacillated between optimism and despair, gradualism and militancy. One day he would cite the actions of Booker T. Washington as "full of hopeful significance"; on another he would point to a lynching as evidence that "the prospect is appalling." For abolitionists whose memories stretched back to the 1850s, the South's aggressive racism at the turn of the century was reminiscent of King Cotton's arrogance. "Oh! how it recalls the days before the war, when we had all the same miserable fallacies and falsehoods to contend with," wrote a 75-year-old abolitionist in 1899. Neo-abolitionist writings around 1900 were full of warnings of another Armageddon unless the South mended its ways. "If a nation cannot be half free and half slave, neither can it be half a democracy and half an oligarchy," declared Villard. If lynching continued unabated, said Clement, "then a death grapple is inevitable." Some abolitionists would welcome "the day of just wrath" if racism could be overthrown in no other way. "We are approaching a crisis and cannot get there too soon," wrote Richard Hallowell in 1901, while an old Garrisonian thought that "perhaps blood alone will settle" the race question in 1901 as it had settled slavery in 1861.[6]

More common than apocalyptic visions were feelings of helplessness. Letters from neo-abolitionists to each other were sprinkled with such words as "melancholy," "gloomy," "painful," "disheartening," "intensely depressing," "pervading gloom."[7] Such despondency could lead to a paralysis of will, a feeling that the whole abolitionist crusade had turned to ashes. If it were possible "to resurrect the old anti-slavery guard," said William Lloyd Garrison, Jr., in 1901, "they would behold [in the South] a race contempt unabated by emancipation, and lynching cruelties that exceed in savagery the deeds of Simon Legree." In the North "instead of indignation and protest, they would see the old pro-slavery prejudice against color revived" and would wonder whether "Lee and not Grant dictated the terms of surrender at Appomattox."

[6] *BET*, Nov. 7, 1901, Aug. 10, 1899; Ednah D. Cheney to Francis J. Grimké, May 18, 1899, in Carter G. Woodson, ed., *The Works of Francis James Grimké*, 4 vols., Washington, 1942, IV, 63; *Nation*, Mar. 3, 1904; *BET*, Oct. 29, 1901; *NWCA*, Sept. 5, 1900; Hallowell to Booker T. Washington, May 9, 1900, BTW Papers; William I. Bowditch to Francis J. Grimké, Nov. 11, 1901, in Woodson, ed., *Works of Grimké*, IV, 74.

[7] Fanny G. Villard to Francis J. Garrison, May 10, 1902, FGV Papers; Albert Bushnell Hart to William Garrott Brown, Sept. 23, 1903, Brown Papers, Duke University Library; Hart to B. T. Washington, Sept. 25, 1903, BTW Papers; F. J. Garrison to Helen B. Clark, Mar. 17, 1904, WLG, Jr., Papers; Mary White Ovington to Archibald Grimké, June 26, 1905, Grimké Papers, Moorland Foundation Library, Howard University; Albert Bushnell Hart, *The Southern South*, New York, 1910, p. 69.

Abolitionist-type protest meetings in Faneuil Hall no longer made any impact on public opinion, said Garrison's brother Wendell, "one of the signs of the changed times since we grew up." Most pessimistic of all was the Virginia-born abolitionist Moncure Conway. "All that I once hoped for and laboured for seems turning to dead sea fruit," wrote Conway at the end of the century. "The negro's freedom means disfranchisement. . . . They are under a chronic reign of terror. . . . This is what we gave up the best years of our lives for. . . . I see no ray of hope at all."[8]

Such hopeless resignation was contrary to the spirit of abolitionism, however, so most of the old crusaders publicly reaffirmed their faith in the ultimate triumph of right. God was on the side of the angels; He would eventually bring victory if His children kept the faith. Out of the reaction of the 1850s had come the war for freedom; out of the reaction of the 1890s would come a new regeneration. "The darkest hour is the herald of the coming dawn," the *Independent* reminded its readers in 1899. Though there was much cause for "discouragement and sometimes despair," wrote Secretary Augustus M. Beard of the AMA, "we must work on, believing in God. . . . The movements of Providence . . . can not be permanently hindered."[9] In editorials with such titles as "The Bright Side," "Hopeful Signs," and "Is the Problem Insoluble?" (to which the answer was No), neo-abolitionist journalists tried to counter the pessimism that threatened to cause some of the old guard to give up in despair.

As part of their effort to sustain commitment by looking on the bright side, neo-abolitionists publicized black accomplishments on every possible occasion: propertyless and illiterate in 1865, more than half the race was literate in 1900; blacks owned one-quarter of the farms (totalling more than 12 million acres) on which they worked and paid taxes on nearly half a billion dollars of property; the race had produced doctors, lawyers, educators, poets, novelists, scholars, and inventors; it had crossed the Red Sea, survived its ordeal in the desert, and was ready to enter the Promised Land as soon as God made up His mind to humble the Philistines. "The progress made by the negro during the few years of freedom has been marvelous," "a marvel to all candid observers," "one of the marvels of history," ran typical neo-abolitionist comments. Henry L. Morehouse considered black progress "greater than that of any other people similarly handicapped by un-

[8] William L. Garrison, Jr., in *Boston Globe*, Dec. 3, 1901; Wendell P. Garrison to F. J. Garrison, Mar. 31, 1901, WPG Papers; Conway to Charles Eliot Norton, May 3, 1898, Norton Papers, Houghton Library, Harvard University; Conway to W. L. Garrison, Jr., July 22, 1899, WLG, Jr., Papers.

[9] *Independent*, Jan. 5, 1899; *AM*, LVI (Jan. 1902), 24-25, LII (Dec. 1898), 202-203.

favorable conditions." Franklin Sanborn proclaimed that "there is no instance in the world's history of another race that has risen faster from illiteracy and dependence," and Francis Garrison agreed that this was reason for "renewed faith & enthusiasm as to the future of the race."[10]

The desire to combat theories of Negro inferiority was another reason for the neo-abolitionist paeans to black achievement. Since pointing in alarm at deteriorating conditions seemed to play into the hands of those who insisted that the Negro was losing the Darwinian struggle for survival, there was a need to accentuate the positive "to silence calumniators of the race." In 1893 the monthly magazines of the AMA and the Methodist Freedmen's Aid Society began to publish columns titled "Successful Colored People" and "The Negro in Art and Literature" to demonstrate that "the race has talent and energy."[11] In later years the *Boston Transcript* and the *New York Evening Post* ran many feature articles on outstanding black people.

All of this emphasis on black accomplishments ran the risk of distorting the reality of the Negro's desperate and in many respects worsening plight. Most neo-abolitionists were aware of this; their writings on the subject often ended by chastising white racism. "For a people who fifty years ago were themselves assessed as 'real estate,' " said Villard in a 50th anniversary article citing black economic progress since the Emancipation Proclamation, "it is certainly an astounding showing which by itself gives the lie to those who declare that the negro cannot be compared in efficiency with the white man." But so much more could have been accomplished had blacks not been forced to fight "against odds great enough to discourage any race."[12]

For many abolitionists, especially missionary educators, both optimism and pessimism reinforced gradualist convictions. In their optimistic moods, they pointed to what education and uplift had already done and pressed on confidently toward final victory. When their spirits dipped, the only alternative to defeat seemed to be greater efforts for uplift. "The re-actionary sentiment in the Nation and the Church against the Negro," wrote Joseph C. Hartzell in 1892, "only makes it more imperative that our work should be pushed to its utmost

[10] *NWCA*, June 23, 1897, Jan. 9, 1901; ms. of a speech by W. L. Garrison, Jr., ca. 1900, in WLG, Jr., Papers; *HMM*, XXIV (Sept. 1902), 249-50; speech by Sanborn, Jan. 26, 1913, ms. in Sanborn Papers, American Antiquarian Society; F. J. Garrison to Helen B. Clark, Dec. 12, 1894, WLG, Jr., Papers.

[11] *Mass. Spy*, Aug. 25, 1893; *AM*, XLVII (Jan. 1893), 4; *Christian Educator*, IV (Jan. 1893), 83.

[12] *NYEP*, Jan. 4, 1913; address by Villard to a Chicago meeting of the NAACP, Jan. 12, 1912, ms. in OGV Papers.

limit." The "frightful recrudescence of barbarism" in the South, said an AMA official, was but the symptom of a deep-seated disease. "The disease is ignorance. Education, Christian education . . . is the only successful warfare against the barbarism which so terribly infests the South."[13] Although "we must stand for equal privileges for all men without wavering, evasion, or apology," reiterated missionary educators, it was still true that race prejudice "cannot be overcome by arms or argument. . . . It can only be done by the black man's lifting himself up." Our mission "is to help the black man to the education and character that will make him worthy of all civil rights," and once worthy he would attain them.[14]

This bootstrap theory of racial progress was of course the credo preached by Booker T. Washington. Thus it is not surprising that most neo-abolitionists endorsed Washington's work. Many of them dissented from his emphasis on industrial training or found distasteful his sometimes obsequious praise of southern whites and his reluctance to speak out strongly against injustice. But these were faults that became more apparent after 1903 than before. For a long time Washington retained the support of even militant abolitionists such as the Garrison-Villard family, who realized that he had to proceed cautiously in the super-heated racial atmosphere of the South. Washington's perennial optimism buoyed the spirits of abolitionists who did not want to give up the cause as hopeless. When this great leader "can look behind the clouds which now lower so portentously and find the sun shining," said Clement in 1899, "there is certainly no excuse for those who are less in the thick of the fight giving way to despair."[15]

Washington's address at the Atlanta Exposition on September 18, 1895, was more than an event; it was a phenomenon. His appeal to both races to work together for mutual progress, his rejection of "social equality," and his insistence that while the Negro would ultimately achieve his rights he would do so by "severe and constant struggle rather than [by] artificial forcing" struck just the right note for the age. The man and the times had found each other; Washington's speech before a predominantly white audience in the heart of the New South was printed and commented on by nearly every major newspaper in the country, and a new race leader was born.

Joining the chorus of praise for Washington's address were the voices of neo-abolitionists, old and young, white and black. Mary E.

[13] Hartzell to W. H. Rider, Dec. 14, 1892, FASME Archives; Frank P. Woodbury, *The Feudal South*, New York, 1898, pp. 9, 12.
[14] Annual Report of the Methodist Freedmen's Aid Society, in *NWCA*, Nov. 21, 1900; *AM*, XLVII (Oct. 1893), 307-308; *Independent*, May 17, 1900.
[15] *BET*, Sept. 26, 1899.

Stearns, widow of a man who had aided John Brown, considered the speech "glorious! One of the historic speeches of the century, worthy to rank with Lincoln's 'Gettysburg.'" Less effusive, Joseph Hartzell approved the "plain, philosophic common sense" of the address. William Penn Nixon compared Washington to Benjamin Franklin, who had also urged "industry, thrift, morality" as the basis of citizenship and who rightly believed that a man possessing these virtues would win respect and rights.[16] The venerable black abolitionist William Still wept tears of joy as he read Washington's speech, by which "our cause was absolutely advanced many degrees." Similar words of congratulation came from T. Thomas Fortune, Francis J. Grimké, J. W. E. Bowen, and other black men who were leaders in the drive for civil rights and higher education, some of whom would later turn against Washington. Du Bois wrote to Washington after reading the speech, "Let me heartily contratulate you upon your phenomenal success at Atlanta—it was a word fitly spoken," and publicly endorsed the Tuskegeean's effort to win southern white support for black uplift as the basis for a real racial settlement.[17]

Though most blacks and white neo-abolitionists seem to have approved of Washington's address, some did not. Among white abolitionists, the veteran Caroline Putnam, still teaching at a black school in Virginia, was distressed by Washington's "acquiescence in leaving out . . . the very foundation principle of *citizenship! political* equality of *rights.*" From Boston both Richard Hallowell and Ednah Cheney, financial supporters of Tuskegee for many years, wrote to Washington in "friendly criticism" pointing out that his deprecation of social equality sounded like approval of segregation. Anxious not to alienate his friends in New England, Washington replied that nothing could be further from his mind than acceptance of Jim Crow. "If anybody understood me as meaning that riding in the same railroad car or sitting in the same room at a railroad station is social intercourse," he told Cheney, "they certainly got a wrong idea of my position."[18]

Washington's reply was disingenuous, for he must have known that his "separate as the fingers" simile would be understood in the South as an endorsement of Jim Crow. Yet with his genius for the apt phrase that seemed to say what each listener wanted to hear, Washington

[16] Stearns to Washington, Sept. 19, 1895, BTW Papers; *Christian Educator*, VI (Oct.–Nov. 1895), 136; *CIO* (D), Sept. 19, 24, 1895.

[17] Still to Washington, Sept. 19, 1895, Du Bois to Washington, Sept. 24, 1895, BTW Papers; Du Bois, *Dusk of Dawn*, New York, 1940, p. 55. There are many letters in the BTW Papers praising the speech.

[18] Putnam to Samuel May, Sept. 30, 1895, May Papers, Mass. Hist. Society; Hallowell to Washington, Oct. 3, 17, 1895, BTW Papers; Washington to Cheney, Oct. 15, 1895, Cheney Papers, Boston Public Library.

managed for several years to keep together his coalition of blacks, northern liberals, southern moderates, and wealthy philanthropists. Neo-abolitionist supporters sometimes defended his lack of militancy by pointing out that a man sitting on a powder keg does not play with matches; or they read into his statements a different interpretation than did southern whites. William Hayes Ward believed that Washington "did not say at Atlanta all he felt, for it would not be agreeable or wise." Whereas most southerners considered the speech's central image to be the separate fingers, northern liberals found the keynote in Washington's statement that "it is right and important that all privileges of the law be ours" but even more important "that we be prepared for the exercise of these privileges." With these words, said Clement, Washington "abates nothing of the ultimate claims of manhood and womanhood to social respect and privilege; he merely advises against pressing those claims until they can be backed up."[19]

Especially important to Washington was the support of the Garrisons, which helped him neutralize radical critics. In 1900 Washington scored a coup by securing William Lloyd Garrison, Jr., as a featured speaker at the first convention of the National Negro Business League. Garrison's brother Francis became a good friend of the Tuskegeean. In the spring of 1899 when Washington was on the verge of exhaustion from overwork, Francis Garrison raised a subscription to send him abroad for a vacation, arranged steamship passage (after protracted negotiations to make sure he suffered no racial discrimination on board), and provided him with introductions to a wide circle of Garrison friends in England. The trip restored Washington's health and enhanced his already large reputation.[20]

For several years after 1895 Washington also continued to enjoy the support of most segments of the black population. Even as he wrote hell-fire editorials damning the white South, T. Thomas Fortune became Washington's confidant and began ghosting some of his articles. Defending Washington's reluctance to alienate sympathetic whites by rash speech, Fortune even boasted in 1899 of having persuaded him to tear up the draft of a letter protesting the Sam Hose lynching. Du Bois remained an ally of Washington until 1903. In 1896 he tried to get a teaching position at Tuskegee; in 1897 he said that black people must earn their rights by "a vast work of self-reformation. . . . A little less complaint and whining, and a little more dogged work and manly striving would do us more credit and benefit than a thousand Force or

[19] *Independent*, Oct. 3, 1895; *BET*, Sept. 21, 1895.
[20] W. L. Garrison's speech to the National Negro Business League was published in *NYEP*, Aug. 24, 1900. There are many letters between Francis Garrison and Washington in the BTW Papers concerning the latter's European trip.

Civil Rights bills"; in 1899 he praised Washington as "one of the great-est men of our race." Black critics of Washington continued to speak out, of course, and in the late 1890s they became more vocal. But For-tune advised Washington that these "hot-headed" Negroes could be ignored since they had "neither the capacity nor force to accomplish anything," and Francis Grimké assured him that "there are some Negroes in this country who are never satisfied unless they are trying to run some body down."[21]

Some of Washington's white abolitionist friends, however, began gently to warn him that his conciliatory statements seemed to sound "the same old false note of compromise . . . so familiar to our ears be-fore the War." It was "painful," they said, to "find the advocates of a white man's government counting Mr. Washington on their side." Ward criticized the Tuskegeean's tendency "to avoid all mention of wrongs done to the Negroes by others and to speak only of those which they do to themselves either through ignorance, laziness or vice." Clement told Washington privately that while his "reserve" might be "the course of wisdom in the thickening difficulties which be-set the upward path of your race," he wondered if the time had come for bold words against "the new outburst of intolerance" before it was too late to arrest the reactionary trend. Though they continued to sup-port Washington, Clement and Ward also began to publicize the words of his black critics.[22]

Even as he arranged Washington's trip to Europe, Francis Garrison urged him to speak out against lynching and disfranchisement. "Par-don this frank expression," wrote Garrison, but "I only want that your quiet & consistent assertion of equality of rights . . . shall never be lack-ing, & thus give color to the assertion that you are silently assenting to inequity." In reply, Washington described an occasion a year earlier when he had publicly criticized racism as a "cancer gnawing at the heart of the Republic" and had urged an end to segregation in "our business and civil relations." This caused such an uproar in the south-ern press that Washington had felt it necessary again to deny that he favored social equality. "I could stir up a race war in Alabama in six

[21] The best treatment of the relationship between Washington and other black spokesmen is August Meier, *Negro Thought in America, 1880-1915*, Ann Arbor, 1963, chaps. 11-12. Fortune and Du Bois are quoted in Thornbrough, *Fortune*, 191, and Howard Brotz, ed., *Negro Social and Political Thought, 1850-1920: Representative Texts*, New York, 1966, p. 490; Grimké to Washington, Jan. 20, 1898, BTW Papers.

[22] Ednah D. Cheney to Margaret J. Washington, Jan. 26, 1899, Richard P. Hallowell to Emmett J. Scott, June 28, 1899, Hallowell to B. T. Washington, Feb. 15, 1900, Clement to Washington, Jan. 2, 1898, BTW Papers; *Independent*, Mar. 11, 1897, Dec. 8, 1898; *BET*, Apr. 25, 1899, July 24, 1901.

weeks if I chose," he told Garrison, but it was vital to avoid provoking a reaction that would "wipe out the achievements of decades of labor." Washington did finally release a public letter against lynching in 1899, but only after he had arrived in Europe and only in careful language that would not offend southern whites. Although not entirely happy with Washington's caution, the Garrisons accepted his argument that he could carry on his work "only by keeping his mouth shut about his inner convictions."[23]

Neo-abolitionist awareness of Washington's quiet and sometimes secret activities against disfranchisement made it easier for them to accept his public reticence. After returning from Europe, Washington led a successful effort to prevent the Georgia legislature from enacting disfranchisement. This victory brought praise from Francis Garrison for Washington's "earnest and tactful efforts . . . wisdom and statesmanship. . . . I can see . . . the firm path which you are treading." Garrison predicted that this defeat of disfranchisement would bring "a halt in the rising tide of hostile legislation"; the *Independent* said that it "raised the first great barrier against the tide of suppression of the negro ballot"; Washington himself thought it "means the turning point in the South."[24] Overlooked in this chorus of congratulation was the hard truth that Georgia Negroes were already pretty well disfranchised by a poll tax and white primary (the latter adopted in 1898 without fanfare). Moreover, the tide of disfranchisement rolled on across Louisiana in 1898 and North Carolina in 1900, reaching Washington's own state of Alabama in 1901. As he had done in Louisiana, Washington sent to the Alabama constitutional convention a softspoken appeal for justice. He won the sympathy of moderates, but could do nothing to stem the tide in either state.[25]

Having failed to stop disfranchisement with open efforts, Washington went underground and secretly backed the court tests of suffrage provisions in Louisiana and Alabama. Several neo-abolitionists knew about this, since they took part in the activities. Washington asked Richard Hallowell and Francis Garrison to raise money in Boston for

[23] Garrison to Washington, May 8, June 13, Sept. 18, 1899, BTW Papers; Washington quoted in F. J. Garrison to Wendell P. Garrison, Aug. 20, 1899, FGV Papers; Louis R. Harlan, *Booker T. Washington: The Making of a Black Leader, 1856-1901*, New York, 1972, pp. 236-37, 262-63; W. P. Garrison to James Bryce, Bryce Papers, Bodleian Library, Oxford University.

[24] Garrison to Washington, Nov. 18, 1899, BTW Papers; Garrison to Helen B. Clark, Dec. 9, 1899, WLG, Jr., Papers; *Independent*, Dec. 7, 1899; Washington to Francis J. Garrison, Nov. 29, 1899, Washington-Garrison Correspondence, Schomburg Library, New York City.

[25] Edwin C. Silsby to Washington, June 25, 1901, BTW Papers; F. J. Garrison to F. G. Villard, Aug. 8, 1901, FGV Papers; Harlan, *Washington*, 290-92, 298-302.

legal fees. Hallowell at first refused unless Washington allowed his name to be used openly, but finally relented and joined Garrison in soliciting funds. Washington also recruited the constitutional lawyers Albert E. Pillsbury and Arthur A. Birney (grandson of the old Liberty party leader James G. Birney) to help prepare the briefs. The Louisiana case bogged down in squabbles among the parties sponsoring it and never reached the federal courts. The ultimate fate of the Alabama cases was no better, for as noted earlier the Supreme Court ruled against the plaintiff on technicalities.[26]

Washington's secret activities against disfranchisement were a minor part of his strategy for racial progress. Far more important was his open courting of the "better element" of southern whites. The rise of redneck racism drove blacks closer to their traditional "best friends" in the south who could hopefully provide some protection from reactionary radicals. As an antidote to pessimism and despair, neo-abolitionists also welcomed the rise of noblesse oblige progressivism in the South. They hoped that the southern crusades for better schools, prison reform, public health, and the abolition of child labor would lead to a better life for both races and reduce tensions by mitigating the South's grinding poverty.[27]

Southern humanitarians of the early 1900s—the clergymen-reformers Edgar Gardner Murphy and Alexander J. McKelway, educator Edwin A. Alderman, expatriate editor Walter Hines Page, to name only a few—were the spiritual heirs of George W. Cable, Atticus Haygood, and other southern moderates of whom much had been expected in the 1880s. Although these expectations had not been fulfilled, neo-abolitionists continued to hope. "There must be good people of the

[26] Harlan, *Washington*, 297-98, 302; Robert L. Factor, *The Black Response to America: Men, Ideals, and Organization from Frederick Douglass to the NAACP*, Reading, Mass., 1970, pp. 238-41; Meier, *Negro Thought*, 110-14; Washington to F. J. Garrison, Feb. 27, Mar. 11, 1900, Washington-Garrison Correspondence; F. J. Garrison to Washington, Mar. 2, 1900, Hallowell to Washington, Mar. 2, Oct. 10, 1900, Archibald Grimké to Washington, Aug. 27, 1900, Pillsbury to Washington, Apr. 26, May 16, 1902, Feb. 20, 1903, Washington to Pillsbury, Feb. 27, 1903, BTW Papers; *BET*, Oct. 10, 1900.

[27] Good accounts of southern liberalism in this period are C. Vann Woodward, *Origins of the New South, 1877-1913*, Baton Rouge, 1951, chap. 15; Hugh C. Bailey, *Liberalism in the New South: Southern Social Reformers and the Progressive Movement*, Coral Gables, Fla., 1969; Bailey, *Edgar Gardner Murphy: Gentle Progressive*, Coral Gables, 1968; and H. Shelton Smith, *In His Image, But . . . Racism in Southern Religion, 1780-1910*, Durham, 1972, chap. 6. For critical analyses of the racial attitudes of southern liberals, see George M. Fredrickson, *The Black Image in the White Mind: The Debate on Afro-American Character and Destiny, 1817-1914*, New York, 1971, chap. 10, and Bruce Clayton, *The Savage Ideal: Intolerance and Intellectual Leadership in the South, 1890-1914*, Baltimore, 1972.

white South," wrote one in 1900, but "they are never heard from. . . . If they only would give some sign, protest in some form, it would have telling effect." They were soon heard from, though how tellingly is uncertain. In 1902 an Emory University professor named Andrew Sledd wrote an article attacking lynching and advocating racial moderation; the resulting furor forced him to resign his professorship. The next year a professor at Trinity College in Durham, John Spencer Bassett, criticized race-baiting demagogues and praised Booker T. Washington as next to Robert E. Lee the greatest southerner of the last hundred years. A majority of Trinity trustees lukewarmly supported Bassett when the head-hunters came after him, but three years later Bassett pulled up stakes and joined George W. Cable in the friendlier environs of Northampton, Massachusetts.[28]

Though this was hardly an auspicious beginning, neo-abolitionists regarded Sledd's and Bassett's articles as harbingers of better times. "We see frequent accounts of the better feeling of Southern white people toward their colored brethren," wrote Ward. "The solid, decent and intelligent middle class . . . are not, we are convinced, in sympathy with such ranters as Senator Tillman." Clement thought that President Roosevelt's appointment in 1901 of the patrician conservative Thomas G. Jones as a federal judge in Alabama heralded the dawn of the new day. Described by Clement as a "clear-visioned and conscientious" man, Jones was Booker T. Washington's personal choice for the judgeship. His appointment marked the fruition of the Tuskegeean's efforts to build a coalition with southern moderates and the beginning of Washington's influence on federal patronage in the South.[29]

For their part, southern moderates welcomed neo-abolitionist sympathy so long as it eschewed criticism of southern shortcomings. "I beg of you," said a southern clergyman to the AMA, "that when sometimes you hear of things that try your patience, you will . . . be careful as to what you may say" because "we who are seeking to help you may be hindered sometimes by an incautious utterance." Several neo-abolitionists took this advice to heart. "The lesson of the hour is not that of impatience and denunciation," declared an AMA district secretary, "but of mutual sympathy and co-operation." Clement urged northerners to avoid "harsh and bitter speeches" and "anything like a 'patronizing' attitude" toward the South.[30] Although Clement did not always follow his own counsel, he and other neo-abolitionist editors

[28] Quotation from Emily Howland to B. T. Washington, Oct. 7, 1900, BTW Papers. Sledd's and Bassett's essays are reprinted in Charles E. Wynes, ed., *Forgotten Voices: Dissenting Southerners in an Age of Conformity*, Baton Rouge, 1967, pp. 91-120.

[29] *Independent*, Nov. 3, 1904; *BET*, Oct. 11, 1901; Harlan, *Washington*, 305-10.

[30] *AM*, XLVII (Dec. 1893), 434, LIV (Jan. 1900), 2-3; *BET*, July 11, 1903.

often bent over backward to exonerate the South as a whole from the racial crimes of its worst element.

More than any other neo-abolitionist in the early 1900s, Oswald Garrison Villard worked to cement the alliance between northern philanthropists, southern moderates (whose privately expressed views, he once said, "encourage me more than anything else"), and Booker T. Washington. This alliance was ratified by the creation of the Southern Education Board in 1901, which became the spearhead of an educational awakening in the South. Intersectional in membership and largely northern in financing, this board was the brainchild of Robert C. Ogden, a New York merchant-philanthropist who had long been a trustee of Hampton and Tuskegee. In 1901 Ogden sponsored the first of his annual "millionaires' specials"—chartered Pullman trains carrying philanthropists through the South to visit schools and plan future bequests. John D. Rockefeller, Jr., was on the 1901 special. Already interested in Negro education through his abolitionist mother Laura Spelman, young Rockefeller persuaded his father to set up the General Education Board in 1902 as a clearinghouse for educational philanthropy. Following an initial gift of $1,000,000 to this board, the senior Rockefeller granted $33,000,000 over the next decade, most of it for southern education, and another $96,000,000 by 1921. In theory, the functions of the Southern and General Boards were different. The Southern Board concentrated on arousing southern support for public schools, while the General Board disbursed grants to schools and other educational agencies. In practice, though, the membership of both boards was almost the same, and in the public mind they constituted a single organization. In 1914 the General Education Board absorbed the Southern Board.[31]

Some neo-abolitionists hoped for great things from this educational crusade. From 1901 to 1903 Villard in particular earned Ogden's gratitude for the favorable publicity he gave the movement in the *Evening Post/Nation*. "They are on the firing line in a battle for civilization," Villard wrote of the two boards. "The educational path is the only way out of the South's overwhelmingly difficult social and industrial problems." When his uncle Francis Garrison expressed concern about the conservatism and industrial-education orientation of the boards, Villard reassured him that while this movement must begin cautiously it would soon grow broader and more liberal.[32]

[31] Woodward, *Origins*, 396-406; Louis R. Harlan, *Separate and Unequal: Public School Campaigns and Racism in the Southern Seaboard States 1901-1915*, Chapel Hill, 1958; Raymond B. Fosdick, *Adventure in Giving: The Story of the General Education Board*, New York, 1962.

[32] Villard, *Fighting Years: Memoirs of a Liberal Editor*, New York, 1939, pp.

But Garrison's skepticism was well founded, and it was shared by an increasing number of neo-abolitionists including Villard himself after 1903. The boards represented the "best North" and the "best South," in Ogden's words, but they contained virtually no representation of neo-abolitionists or missionary educators. Nor did they have any black members—Booker T. Washington was the agent of the Southern Board for black schools, but out of deference to southern sensibilities he never attended Board meetings. Secretary Wallace Buttrick of the General Board had once been chairman of the Baptist Home Mission Society's education committee, but he was a racial conservative who channeled the General Board's resources mainly into white education. "The Negro is an inferior race," he wrote. "There cannot be any question about that." What little money the General Board did earmark for Negro education went mainly to industrial schools. Railroad executive William H. Baldwin expressed the boards' philosophy in the words: "The Negro should not be educated out of his environment. . . . Except in the rarest of instances, I am bitterly opposed to the so-called higher education of Negroes."[33]

The General and Southern Boards did a great deal for southern education. The General Board granted millions of dollars directly to schools, and the Southern Board deserved much credit for the three-fold increase in southern public school appropriations from 1900 to 1910, which gave the South the beginnings of a modern educational system. But while black schools shared in this largesse, they usually received only the crumbs that fell from the white man's table. The disparity between black and white public schools in per capita expenditures was greater in 1910 than 1900 in every southern state. Thus the educational awakening, southern liberalism's proudest achievement in the first decade of the century, only fastened the shackles of educational inferiority more firmly around the ankles of blacks trying to lift themselves by their bootstraps.

These developments helped to sow a new crop of neo-abolitionist doubts about the "better class" of southern whites and even about Booker T. Washington. As it became clear to Villard and his associates that the Murphys and Aldermans and Pages of the South and the Baldwins and Ogdens of the North, while not as racist as Tillman or Vardaman, nevertheless wished to keep blacks in their place, Washington's accommodationism seemed increasingly to serve the ends of white supremacy. After 1903, neo-abolitionists searched for a new strategy, which led six years later to the founding of the NAACP.

172-75; Ogden to Villard, Nov. 11, 1901, May 12, 1902, OGV Papers; *NYEP*, Jan. 10, 1903; Villard to Garrison, May 16, 1902, OGV Papers.
[33] Quotations from Fosdick, *Adventure in Giving*, 11.

Chapter Twenty

The Rejection of Gradualism and the Founding of the NAACP

The year 1903 marked a turning point in the strategy of northern liberals of both races. Du Bois published *The Souls of Black Folk* containing the essay "Of Mr. Booker T. Washington and Others," which signified his conversion to the anti-Bookerite viewpoint. Though Du Bois was never as hostile to Washington as was William Monroe Trotter, the acerbic Bostonian who founded the *Guardian* in 1901, the two men became allies in a revival of black militancy. At the same time several white neo-abolitionists were growing disillusioned with Washington and moving toward Du Bois. Their break with the Tuskegeean was not sharp or sudden; the Garrison-Villard families in particular remained friendly to Washington even as they became impatient with him. But in the end it was the Garrisons and especially Oswald Garrison Villard who took the lead in founding the NAACP and launching a crusade for racial justice that looked back to the abolitionist radicalism of the 1860s and forward to the civil rights movement of the 1960s.

A number of events made 1903 a watershed in the shift from accommodation to protest. In Mississippi, Texas, and Georgia an "organized reign of terror" known as whitecapping broke out, in which bands of white tenant farmers drove land-owning blacks off their farms and took the land for themselves. The most racist political campaign yet brought James K. Vardaman the governorship of Mississippi. In Louisiana a black principal of an AMA secondary school was murdered and his successor driven away by threats on his life. The Supreme Court's decision in *Giles* v. *Harris* put the stamp of approval on disfranchisement and encouraged reactionaries to step up their campaign for repeal of the 15th Amendment. President Roosevelt's appointments of blacks to civil service posts in the South became a national issue when a Senate filibuster blocked the confirmation of William Crum as Collector of the Port of Charleston and the whites of Indianola, Mississippi, drove out a black postmistress who had served there several years. The tide of racial hatred also continued to sweep northward. Race riots growing out of lynchings occurred at Wilmington, Delaware, and Evansville, Indiana, while in Maryland the Democrats campaigned for black disfranchisement in a state where Negroes were only 20 percent of the population. In New York one of the most popular Broadway plays of 1903 was Thomas Dixon's racist *The Leopard's Spots*, and pressure from expatriate southerners living in the city caused the school board to remove copies of *Uncle Tom's Cabin* from school libraries because the book "distorted" slavery.[1]

All of these things happening in one year were bad enough; even worse were the peonage revelations of 1903. Investigations by the Justice Department uncovered scores of cases in which black debtors were forced or "persuaded" to sign labor contracts, held to service beyond the terms of their contracts, worked as literal slaves at turpentine camps or plantations, housed in stockades under armed guards, and tracked by bloodhounds if they tried to escape. An 1867 federal statute (aimed at New Mexico) had prohibited peonage as a violation of the 13th Amendment; as 1903 progressed, federal grand juries in Alabama indicted 18 men under this law. Only seven were convicted and sentenced to light fines or short jail terms; the others escaped conviction by reason of hung juries or were never brought to trial. The northern press played up the issue; Villard's *Evening Post/Nation* plunged into the anti-peonage campaign with greater energy than any other newspaper. Villard made this crusade against "the new slavery" a springboard for his drive to mold the *Post/Nation* in the image of his grandfather's *Liberator*. While praising the courage of southern whites who aided the prosecution, he denounced the failure of some juries to convict, printed atrocity stories, and maintained that without the pressure of federal officials and northern newspapers most cases of peonage would have remained unexposed and southern whites would have got away with their claim that the practice was isolated and exceptional.[2]

Things went from bad to worse after 1903. Theodore Roosevelt retreated from the occasional racial liberalism of his first term. In a tour of the South in 1905 he made much of his Confederate relatives and spoke softly on racial matters. "His repetition of the cant assertion that the South must be left to solve the 'problem,'" wrote Francis Garrison in disgust, "is already interpreted by the Southern press as a conver-

---

[1] For the alarm of neo-abolitionists over these and other developments in 1903, see especially *Independent*, Feb. 5, 1903; *NYEP*, May 27, June 24, 1903; *Nation*, July 2, 1903; *BET*, Oct. 29, 31, Nov. 2, 1903; *AM*, LVIII (Oct. 1904), 251-56; Francis J. Garrison to Fanny Garrison Villard, Feb. 8, July 11, 1903, FGV Papers; F. J. Garrison to Oswald Garrison Villard, July 10, 1903, OGV Papers.

[2] *NYEP*, May 26, June 16, 24, 29, 30, July 2, 3, 6, 8, 15, Nov. 30, 1903; *Nation*, June 18, July 2, 9, 23, Dec. 3, 1903, May 10, 1906. An excellent treatment of peonage is Pete Daniel, *The Shadow of Slavery: Peonage in the South, 1901-1969*, Urbana, Ill., 1972.

sion to their claim that they must be let alone to disfranchise or do whatever they choose."[3]

A year later the president ordered the dishonorable discharge of three companies of a black regiment stationed at Brownsville, Texas, after unidentified members of these companies allegedly shot up the town and killed a white man. Roosevelt acted on the basis of a superficial investigation by a southern white officer; when none of the soldiers would confess guilt or inform on their fellows, the president discharged every one of the 167 men, the innocent along with the possibly guilty. Neo-abolitionists were infuriated by this wholesale punishment without even a court-martial. They interpreted it as "a sop to the white South . . . another sacrifice of law & legal rights, of which we have seen so many in the last dozen years." The Constitution League, an interracial civil rights organization, undertook its own investigation, which turned up evidence suggesting that the whole affair was a frameup by local whites. The league's report prompted Senator Joseph Foraker of Ohio, a political foe of Roosevelt, to head an official inquiry by the Senate Committee on Military Affairs. Although the committee's majority report upheld the president, a stinging minority report by Foraker and three other senators maintained that no proof of guilt had been offered. For many historians as well as contemporaries, the evidence was inconclusive and certainly insufficient to prove guilt. [4]

Coming less than two months after the Atlanta riot of September 1906, the Brownsville affair seemed to fit the pattern of reaction plunging the country toward a racial precipice. For many neo-abolitionists the accumulating horrors of these years destroyed the last shreds of faith in time and education. They shifted their main concern from uplift to protest; they began to emphasize the need for social change more than the need for black self-improvement, rights more than duties, opportunity more than preparation.

The hope that blacks would earn equality by achievement had proved false; indeed the opposite had occurred, for the race steadily lost civil and political rights after 1890 even as its literacy and wealth increased. And it was the blacks who had forged ahead who aroused

[3] Garrison to Booker T. Washington, Oct. 25, 1905, BTW Papers.

[4] Quotations from F. J. Garrison to O. G. Villard, Nov. 8, 1906, OGV Papers, and Albert E. Pillsbury to Archibald A. Grimké, Nov. 15, 1906, Grimké Papers, Moorland Foundation Library, Howard University. See also John D. Weaver, *The Brownsville Raid: America's Black Dreyfus Affair*, New York, 1970; Ann J. Lane, *The Brownsville Affair: National Crisis and Black Reaction*, Port Washington, N.Y., 1971; and Emma Lou Thornbrough, "The Brownsville Episode and the Negro Vote," *Mississippi Valley Historical Review*, XLIV (1957), 469-83. In 1973 the U.S. Government made a belated gesture of justice by retroactively granting the Brownsville soldiers honorable discharges.

the most hatred from lower-class whites whose only source of status was their color. The "policy of drift" had not worked, said Villard in 1903. "While philanthropists and teachers are laboring to raise the negro to the full level of citizenship," the South was doing its best "to thrust him back into serfdom. . . . It is exactly against these educated negroes that feeling in the South is now running highest." Ward described as a "system of half truths" the philosophy that "says to the aspiring Negroes: 'Work, wait, acquire property, be patient, and live decently,'" for "as fast as he approaches this standard . . . he is thrust back." And the AMA acknowledged in 1904 that "never since emancipation has race prejudice in the South come so near race hatred, and part of it is because the Negro people are advancing rather than because they are not." It was now clear that if blacks "simply 'get ready and wait' upon the purely voluntary friendship of another race to bestow upon them the privileges and dignities of manhood," said the AMA, they "will tarry outside in the cold until after the arrival of the millennium."[5]

These were important statements, for despite their frequent militancy the AMA and the *Independent* had for 30 years advocated something similar to what they now rejected as a half-truth. They realized that even education itself would die on the vine if rights and opportunities were long restricted. It was senseless for blacks to make sacrifices to obtain schooling if they could look forward only to "a horizon bounded on the north by a future as a porter in a Pullman car, on the south by one as a 'washlady,' and on the east and west by that of a cook or stevedore. . . . How can they be expected to want to rise when they see the ordinary recognition and reward of ability and character withheld from a man who has risen?"[6]

And without political power, blacks would never get decent public schools anyway. Several of the state constitutional conventions that disfranchised Negroes also considered proposals to apportion to the schools of each race the percentage of taxes each paid. Southern moderates managed to head off these efforts to starve the already emaciated black schools, but ironically the Southern Education Board's public school crusade achieved a similar result by bringing about a much greater increase of appropriations for white than black schools. In 1909 the southern states spent 2½ times more per white student than black; by 1915 the disparity had grown to 3½ to 1. In at least four states, according to neo-abolitionist interpretations of ad-

---

[5] *NYEP*, Apr. 15, Sept. 30, Dec. 24, 1903; *Independent*, Dec. 29, 1910; Ward to A. W. Anthony, Aug. 6, 1908, Anthony Autograph Collection, Manuscript Room, N. Y. Public Library; *AM*, LVIII (Oct. 1904), 246-48, LXI (Apr. 1907), 99-103.

[6] *Independent*, Sept. 18, 1913; *NYEP*, Feb. 13, 1903.

mittedly ambiguous statistics, black schools by 1909 were receiving *less* than the proportion of taxes paid by Negroes. Little could be done about this so long as blacks were politically powerless. "Strip the black man of his political rights," said Villard, "and you cut the nerve of negro education."[7]

Of course neo-abolitionists, especially missionary educators, continued to believe that "good Christian schools where youth are trained in righteousness . . . good homes with Christian parents, good, honest industry" were vital to Negro progress. The shift in emphasis from education to rights, patience to agitation, was neither sudden nor total. But a shift there was. "We cannot trust to time to remedy wrongs, which by time, are continually growing stronger," declared the AMA. "If we consent now to the postponement of justice we consent to a more difficult and more nearly hopeless future." "What this country now needs," wrote one septuagenarian abolitionist in 1905, "is a revival of Abolitionism."[8]

The Garrisons were ready for such a revival. "There is too much agitator blood in me," said Villard, to "fall back upon educational influences and trust to the healing spread of knowledge." If the original abolitionists could come back, he told Tuskegee students in 1906, they would be gratified to see how the race had "fought its way upward with magnificent courage in the face of seemingly insuperable obstacles," but they would also find "grave injustices to denounce with all the vigor of their fiery language of old." It was time, said William Lloyd Garrison, Jr., after the Brownsville affair, for "colored people to organize for lawful self-defense and for white lovers of liberty to stand up for equal rights." The "recrudescence of slavery . . . must be met with the undaunted purpose that the abolitionists displayed, for the conflict is the same irrepressible one."[9]

The first casualty of this rejuvenated radicalism was the coalition of neo-abolitionists and southern moderates. The basis for this coalition

[7] Quotation from *NYEP*, Feb. 13, 1903. See also *Nation*, Aug. 1, 1907, Sept. 16, 1909, Apr. 24, 1913; *Independent*, Mar. 10, 1910, July 25, 1912; Horace Bumstead, *Secondary and Higher Education in the South for Whites and Negroes*, New York, 1910; AMA, *As Others See Us in Our Southern Field*, New York, 1917; and Louis R. Harlan, *Separate and Unequal: Public School Campaigns and Racism in the Southern Seaboard States, 1901-1915*, Chapel Hill, 1958, pp. 255-56.

[8] *AM*, LX (Jan. 1906), 3-4, LVIII (Mar. 1904), 69; John F. Hume, *The Abolitionists*, New York, 1905, p. 86.

[9] Villard to Ray Stannard Baker, Aug. 29, 1908, Baker Papers, Library of Congress; Villard's address to the NAACP's annual convention, Jan. 12, 1912, typescript in OGV Papers; *Tuskegee Student*, Apr. 28, 1906; speeches by Garrison published in *Washington Evening Star*, Feb. 24, 1906, and *Springfield* (Mass.) *Republican*, Nov. 17, 1906.

had always been shaky. Whenever the southerners showed signs of backsliding, neo-abolitionists found their doubts confirmed. The "glib and jaunty" expressions of white supremacy at a conference of southern reformers in 1900, said Edward Clement, were "enough to shake one's faith in the probity and sincerity of the Southern people's oft expressed desire to solve the race problem in accordance with the rules of fair play and humanity." And Francis Garrison concluded sadly: "Father's belief that the new generation of whites would materially differ from the old, 'since they would no longer have slavery to tie to,' proved too optimistic."[10]

Cooperation between neo-abolitionists and the Southern Education Board began to break down within two years of the latter's founding. In 1902 the board declared its first priority to be the education of whites, since the race problem could be settled only by "educated intelligent white men . . . teaching the negro to work." This "muddled nonsense," said Ward, should be condemned for what it was by those "who believe in equal rights and privileges for everybody, equal education and equal work." Villard also soon joined the opposition. He attended the board's annual meeting at Richmond in 1903, where speakers from both North and South talked of the need to preserve white political supremacy. Distressed by this "truckling to Southern fraud in disfranchisement," Villard was particularly angered by Lyman Abbott's address approving the suffrage clauses of southern constitutions. Abbott was an influential spokesman of northern Progressivism and a friend of President Roosevelt; his widely publicized statement that "manhood suffrage means manhood first and suffrage afterwards" was taken as an official northern endorsement of disfranchisement. "To express sympathy with the South in its difficult problems is both wise and just," wrote Villard in a rejoinder, but "to allow one's sympathy with the South to blind one to its wrongdoings" only gladdened reactionaries by "justifying any amount of repression of the negro."[11]

Villard's editorials brought a pained response from his friend Edgar Gardner Murphy, who grieved that neo-abolitionists failed to appreciate "the sincere and adequate forces of conscience" in the South. Why must northern papers carry "ten editorials on wrong at the South to one editorial on the wrongs of any other section?" asked Murphy. "There is not a day in which the actual status of the negro in Alabama does not show progress . . . through the kindly cooperation of his white neighbor." If Villard would write about this he could help the forces

[10] *BET*, May 14, June 4, 1900; Garrison to F. G. Villard, Jan. 18, 1903, FGV Papers.

[11] *Independent*, Apr. 24, 1902; Wendell P. Garrison to Francis J. Garrison, Apr. 24, 1903; *NYEP*, Apr. 25, 27, 1903.

of progress, but "censorious and intemperate criticism . . . can only intensify resentment [and] solidify the forces of prejudice."[12]

In reply to this and other charges by southern friends that he had become an "extremist," Villard insisted that extremism in the cause of virtue was no vice. "I believe thoroughly in extremists, when their views are based upon the principles of the teachings of Christ." The race question was a national and not an exclusively southern responsibility. "These peonage cases," Villard instructed Murphy in 1903, "illustrate very clearly the need of outside criticism." Or consider lynching. Southern whites had finally awakened to the evil, but "this awakening would never have come about if the Northern newspapers had not fitted the proper language to the deeds in season and out of season." Just as "the *Liberator* . . . threw the whole South into convulsions," said Villard, "so the advocate of political and civil equality of the races [today] . . . may feel that his words will fly straight to the mark."[13]

Though some neo-abolitionists continued to believe that only the South could solve the race problem, most of them by 1905 agreed with Villard that the let-alone policy was played out. Moorfield Storey best expressed their sentiments. The South "had the full charge of the Negro problem for a great many years," he wrote, "and they made a great mess of it." Now it was time "to bring to bear all the public opinion that we can muster in favor of justice to the Negro."[14]

If one incident more than any other finally convinced neo-abolitionists that alliance with southern moderates was hopeless, it was the furor aroused by a Cosmopolitan Club dinner in 1908. An interracial group in New York City, the club occasionally held dinner meetings to discuss social problems. Three of its leading white members were Villard, Mary White Ovington, and Hamilton Holt (Lewis Tappan's grandson, who had been managing editor of the *Independent* since 1897), the foremost third-generation abolitionists in the city. On April 27, 1908, the club met for dinner at a Manhattan restaurant, where its black president Owen Waller presided and Villard and Holt, among others, made brief speeches. In his remarks, Holt referred to the question of racial intermarriage and said in the usual abolitionist fashion that while he did not necessarily *advocate* it, neither did he oppose it. An uninvited reporter for a Hearst paper had somehow got into the banquet room; the next day his paper ran a lurid story about

12 Murphy to Villard, May 2, 22, 29, June 10, 1903, OGV Papers.

13 Villard to Murphy, Feb. 23, 1906, OGV Papers; *NYEP*, June 2, July 24, 1903; Villard, "Northern Criticism of the South," ms. of a 1905 speech, OGV Papers.

14 Storey to Charles Francis Adams, Jr., Nov. 19, 1908, Storey Papers, Mass. Hist. Society (I am indebted to William B. Hixson, Jr., for this reference).

the "social equality dinner" where white women sat next to leering Negro men while the editor of the *Independent* urged miscegenation as a solution of the race problem.[15]

Several newspapers had a field day with this story. The *New York Times* denounced the participants in this "odious exhibition" as socialists seeking "by revolution if necessary, to destroy society, and with it the home and religion." As the news traveled South, the dinner turned into an orgy and became a sensation rivaling Booker T. Washington's dinner with President Roosevelt seven years earlier. Some of the sharpest southern reaction came from three men soon to be key figures in national politics. The social equality dinner, said Albert Burleson of Texas, was "unbelievable, abhorrent." Josephus Daniels' *Raleigh News and Observer* roasted "the miscegenation club" for putting "fool notions in the heads of uppish young negroes." Carter Glass's *Lynchburg News* gave big headlines to this "race orgy," which had countenanced the mongrelization of "the white race of the South—the proudest and highest strain of people that ever sprung from the loins of time." Glass reserved the hottest fire in hell for Villard who "with the bitter abolition blood . . . coursing in his veins, has . . . profaned things that are sacred in Southern thought and life."[16]

These newspaper comments were nothing compared with the avalanche of obscene mail that descended on participants in the dinner. Ovington fled to her sister's house for a week to escape the filth, and for the next six weeks her brother opened her letters. Villard ignored his hate mail but did respond privately to some of the criticisms from southern acquaintances. A Washington lawyer told him that with friends like the Cosmopolitan Club the Negro did not need enemies. The black man "is being educated, encouraged and well cared for" by the South, said this long-time friend of Villard, "but he must stay in the position that public opinion has put him." Villard replied testily that he would continue to dine with whom he pleased, and "if that means encouraging social equality, I expect to encourage it as long as I live." To the faculty of a preparatory school in Virginia who censured him because dining with blacks was "especially obnoxious to us," Villard recommended the Bible verse 1 John 4:20, in which Jesus said that unless a man loved his brother he could not love God. Villard asked the school "whether in deference to your wishes I should eschew all

[15] Villard, *Fighting Years: Memoirs of a Liberal Editor*, New York, 1939, pp. 196-98; Ovington, *The Walls Came Tumbling Down*, New York, 1947, pp. 43-46; Warren F. Kuehl, *Hamilton Holt: Journalist, Internationalist, Educator*, Gainesville, Fla., 1960, pp. 47-48.

[16] Burleson quoted Ovington, *Walls Came Tumbling Down*, 45; clippings from the *Raleigh News and Observer*, May 1, 1908, and *Lynchburg News*, May 2 and undated, OGV Papers.

my colored friends, or whether I may except from your decree those in whose veins flows some of the noblest blood of . . . 'the proudest and best people that ever sprung from the loins of time.'" This provoked the headmaster to berate Villard as a "South-hating . . . fanatic" in the mold of his grandfather whose effort to place the black race over the white was "the most diabolical crime ever conceived in all the annals of history."[17]

This whole affair only confirmed Villard's feeling that unless southern moderates were willing to stand up for racial justice they were only slightly better than the Vardamans. Thus he continued the course which an unhappy southern friend described as "very irritating & very harmful, & which has given the Post the nickname of the 'most bitter South-hating paper in the country.'" Things got to the point that on one occasion after the *Post/Nation* had praised Edgar Gardner Murphy the latter privately asked Villard to stop doing so. "Deeply as I value your approval," wrote Murphy, "I would rather have you fight me than to have you praise me to the prejudice of my position among my people."[18]

This did not stop the neo-abolitionist search for white allies in the South. Convinced that genuine egalitarians existed there but were muzzled by public opinion, abolitionists began to argue that "outside agitation," instead of frightening true liberals into silence as Murphy claimed, would embolden them to speak out by assuring them of northern support. Neo-abolitionists befriended the "radical and un-flinching" Quincy Ewing, helped him obtain lecture engagements in the North, and placed his article "The Heart of the Race Problem" in the *Atlantic Monthly*. They worked with the Kentucky-born socialist William E. Walling, one of the principal founders of the NAACP. Several other southern whites joined the NAACP; two of them, John Spencer Bassett (now living in the North) and Joseph C. Manning, spoke at the founding meeting of the association. An organizer of the Alabama Populist party, a former member of the state legislature and leader of a Populist-Republican fusion, Manning had long fought the Bourbons. In his speech to the National Negro Conference in 1909 he charged that those who denied the Negro his full rights were "as much in revolt against the letter and the spirit" of the Constitution as their

[17] Paul E. Johnson to Villard, May 2, 1908, Villard to Johnson, May 4, 1908, Villard to Hampden Wilson, May 5, 1908, Wilson to Villard, May 28, 1908, OGV Papers. Ironically, Villard could not entertain Negroes in his own home. Like Hamilton Holt and Moorfield Storey, he had married a southern woman. Mrs. Villard and Mrs. Storey did not agree with their husbands' racial views and refused to have black people as guests in their homes.

[18] W. D. Hooper to Villard, Dec. 9, 1904, Murphy to Villard, Jan. 5, 8, 1905, OGV Papers.

ancestors of 1861. "The treacherous cry of 'let the South alone,'" he thundered, "is as ungodly, as infamous today as was that anti-abolition and copperhead sentiment of the North detestable in 1860."[19] By 1909, neo-abolitionist hopes for the white South no longer rested on the benign paternalism of ex-Confederates but on the radicalism of the spiritual heirs of the Grimké sisters, James G. Birney, John Fee, and other southerners who had joined the abolitionist crusade.

The revived emphasis on rights over education reversed Booker T. Washington's priorities. Veteran Garrisonians from Boston with roots sunk deep in the radical tradition were the first to break with the Tuskegee educator. They were particularly upset by Washington's 1903 endorsement of southern suffrage laws requiring literacy or property ownership. Such requirements, said Washington, placed a premium on intelligence, character, and thrift that would spur black self-improvement. Richard Hallowell considered this statement "disgraceful." "Premium upon intelligence and education forsooth!" he said. "Washington knows . . . that those constitutions . . . are villainous frauds." Hallowell did not deny "the good side of Washington and his magnificent work. None the less I sadly admit that he is a temporizer and a trimmer." A few years later Albert Pillsbury summed up the radical neo-abolitionist indictment of Washington. "I have neither sympathy nor respect for the trimmer or temporizer," he wrote, "who is willing to crook the knee for thrift or barter principle for a job, who preaches patience and silence under wrongs that cry to Heaven for justice."[20]

Most neo-abolitionists did not go this far in disapproval of Washington. The *Transcript* and the *Independent* continued to steer a middle course between the Tuskegeean and his more outspoken critics. While higher education for the elite was necessary, they said, so was industrial education for the masses; while agitation for equal rights was vital, so was uplift of the poor. If Washington seemed silent in the presence of wrong, those who lived in the North should keep in mind that Tuskegee was not Boston. Both Washington and Du Bois were right; both were needed.

None was more adept at this balancing act than the Garrison-Villard families. For five years after 1903 they maintained their ties with Washington despite growing alienation from his gradualist strategy

[19] Villard to Lulie Jones, Feb. 9, 1906, OGV Papers; F. J. Garrison to F. G. Villard, Mar. 17, 1907, FGV Papers; Manning's speech published in *Proceedings of the National Negro Conference, 1909*, New York, 1909, pp. 207-10.

[20] Hallowell to W. L. Garrison, Jr., Apr. 7, 1903, WLG, Jr., Papers; speech by Pillsbury published in *NYEP*, May 13, 1910.

and his southern white allies. Their awareness that Washington's real attitude was to the left of his public stance was an important reason for their loyalty. Washington used Villard as a proxy spokesman for positions he could not afford to take publicly. He sent Villard information on southern racial developments and sometimes suggested the editorial use that might be made of this material. When Vardaman won the Mississippi governorship, Washington was alarmed by the potential threat to the state's black public schools. "Now is the time, it seems to me, for strong action and brave words," he told Villard—but it was Villard, not Washington, who was to utter the words. Washington sent the *Evening Post* clippings on lynchings and whitecapping. "Terrible as these details are," he wrote in a typical instance, "I think in some way they ought to be given to the public," and the *Post* published them. With regard to peonage and disfranchisement, Washington on another occasion said to Villard: "What a relief it is to know that there is a paper of respectability and wise influence through which matters that ought to be known can get before the public." In 1906 Villard and Washington collaborated in the hiring of a private detective to investigate the Atlanta riot; his findings formed the basis for Ray Stannard Baker's article on the riot in the muckraking *American Magazine*. Washington informed Villard and Francis Garrison that he had done his best to dissuade Roosevelt from discharging the black soldiers after Brownsville; Washington could not criticize Roosevelt openly, but he was not unhappy with the *Post/Nation*'s denunciations of the president.[21]

Washington's strongest black opposition came from Boston. In 1904 the Boston Literary and Historical Association, a black society dominated by anti-Bookerites, invited Villard to give an address. Knowing that he was going into the lion's den, Villard asked Washington for advice on what he might say to put the Tuskegeean in the right light. Washington's reply outlined the image he wished to project among northern liberals. Somehow, he told Villard, the notion had got abroad that "I was willing to surrender all the rights of the colored people and cater to all the unreasonable wishes of the Southern whites." Nothing could be further from the truth. In the matter of higher education "I do not believe in placing any limitation upon the mental development of the black man"; indeed, Tuskegee employed "more college and university graduates than is true of any other similar institution in the world." As for voting rights, in every case where states had disfranchised blacks "I have spoken out frankly and directly to the people in

[21] Quotations from Washington to Villard, Aug. 31, 1903, Feb. 26, Oct. 10, 1904. See also Washington to Francis J. Garrison, Dec. 3, 1906, Washington-Garrison Correspondence, Schomburg Library.

that state through the public press regarding the injustice of not making the same conditions for one race as for the other." Washington had
been charged with cowardice for not denouncing lynching more vigorously. This he resented more than anything else. "When I think the
proper season has come I never fail to speak out and rebuke the lynchers in every part of the country." In sum, Washington wanted Villard
to tell the radicals that he was just as "restless and impatient over conditions which the race has to endure" as they were. Since both he and
his critics were "aiming at the same thing" although "pursuing different methods," Washington thought there was "no necessity for quar-
relling." Villard used these points as a guide for his speech. He gained
few converts, but if his words made little impact on Washington's
critics they did reinforce Villard's own confidence in the Tuskegeean.[22]

In 1906 the 25th anniversay celebration of Tuskegee's founding provided Washington with an unplanned opportunity to use a Garrison
as a front for egalitarian sentiments. Villard and his uncle William
attended the celebration, where one of the invited speakers was the
president of the University of Alabama, James Abercrombie. With
poor taste, Abercrombie used the occasion to say that slavery had been
a benefit to the Negro by freeing him from barbarism and teaching
him work, discipline, and Christianity. The enactment of Negro suffrage during Reconstruction, he went on, had been a "stupendous
error." Outwardly unruffled but inwardly seething at this display of
bad manners, Washington calmly went to the podium after Abercrombie sat down and called on the son and namesake of the *Liberator's*
editor to stand and be recognized. Amid cries of "speech, speech,"
Garrison came forward and gave a brief but powerful lecture on racial
equality. "I cannot speak to you as one of the superior race," he said
pointedly. As a white man, he felt humiliated by membership in a race
that had enslaved others. God knew no distinction of races, and he
hoped the day would come when mankind could say the same. As for
Negro suffrage, it had been a measure of wise statesmanship, and to-
day as 40 years earlier the black man's right to vote was as good as the
white man's. Garrison sat down to the loudest applause of the day;
afterwards dozens of blacks thanked him effusively, and Washington
expressed quiet satisfaction.[23]

The founding of the Niagara Movement in 1905 confronted neo-
abolitionist friends of Washington with a dilemma. For two years they

[22] Washington to Villard, Nov. 16, 1904, OGV Papers; Stephen R. Fox, *The
Guardian of Boston: William Monroe Trotter*, New York, 1971, pp. 77-78. No
official report of Villard's speech has survived.

[23] *Tuskegee Student*, Apr. 28, 1906; W. L. Garrison, Jr., to Ellen Wright Garrison, Apr. 4, 5, 1906, WLG, Jr., Papers; Washington to Francis J. Garrison, Apr. ?,
1906, Garrison to Washington, Apr. 14, 1906, BTW Papers.

had hoped to prevent a total break between Washington and Du Bois. In February 1904 Villard and Ward along with other whites had attended a unity conference at Carnegie Hall between Du Bois, Washington, and their followers. This meeting formed the Committee of Twelve (all blacks) to coordinate racial efforts. But Du Bois soon became disillusioned and resigned from the committee because it was dominated by Bookerites, who refused to give the radicals a fair hearing. Out of this failure grew the Niagara Movement, which issued a stirring declaration of principles in July 1905 demanding voting rights, equal educational opportunities, and "the abolition of all caste distinctions."[24]

Few neo-abolitionists disagreed with the goals of the Niagara Movement. Francis Garrison considered the declaration of principles "a very able and forcible presentation"; the *Independent* endorsed "every word" of the platform; the AMA thought "the positions taken cannot be controverted. . . . It is the right and duty of all men everywhere . . . to agitate for the right."[25] At the same time some neo-abolitionists were chary of the anti-Bookerite animus of the movement and continued to praise Washington as a statesmanlike leader whose goals if not methods were the same as Niagara's. Villard sent Mary White Ovington as a special *Evening Post* correspondent to the 1906 conferences of both the National Negro Business League and the Niagara Movement, and gave equal billing to each in the *Post*. But Ovington, originally an admirer of Washington, had gone over to Du Bois. Her articles on the 1906 and 1907 Niagara Movement conferences were the fullest and most sympathetic to appear in the white press; in 1907 she accepted Du Bois' invitation to join the movement, becoming the only white person so honored. Her action was a straw in the wind; within two years most other neo-abolitionists followed her into the anti-Bookerite camp.[26]

But the Garrisons and Villards were slow to desert Washington. Partly this was because some of Washington's critics seemed so shrill and personal in their attacks on him while the Tuskegean gave the impression of remaining above the battle, going about his important work without rancor toward his adversaries. That he could sustain this image for so long is testimony to his tactical genius, for in reality he infiltrated the ranks of his enemies, used his influence over white philan-

24 Elliott M. Rudwick, *W. E. B. Du Bois: A Study in Minority Group Leadership*, Philadelphia, 1960, chap. 4; Fox, *Guardian of Boston*, 82-92.

25 Garrison to Washington, Sept. 25, 1905, BTW Papers; *Independent*, Aug. 23, 1906; *AM*, LIX (Sept. 1905), 202.

26 *NYEP*, Aug. 17, 20, 1906, Sept. 3, 1907; Ovington to Du Bois, Sept. 10, 1906, Apr. 20, Aug. 7, 1907, from the Du Bois Papers formerly in the custody of Herbert Aptheker, cited with permission.

thropy and patronage to silence his critics, and subsidized part of the black press to control it. These were the methods of what Du Bois called the "Tuskegee machine"; it was Washington's manipulation of this machine against other black leaders that transformed ideological differences into an open schism.

Du Bois did his best to expose the workings of the Tuskegee machine. In January 1905 he published an article accusing Washington of having subsidized a half-dozen black newspapers with "hush money." The *Evening Post* reproved Du Bois for making such a charge without offering proof. President Horace Bumstead of Atlanta University also questioned the wisdom of the hush money accusation. It "may be a thing of which we are morally certain," he told Du Bois, "yet in the nature of the case, it is one that is almost impossible to prove." It was not worth the risk of alienating Villard and the Garrisons, who while friendly to Washington "are heartily in sympathy with us in nearly all the things that we are contending for."[27]

Villard and William Hayes Ward privately asked Du Bois to furnish proof of his charges. In reply, Du Bois pointed out that Tuskegee advertised heavily in several black newspapers; Washington's private secretary, Emmett Scott, sent out canned editorials praising Washington that often appeared simultaneously in these papers; two or three black editors had testified that they or someone they knew had been offered loans or outright bribes by Washington or his intermediaries. Villard and his uncles went over the evidence carefully. They decided that some of it raised ethical questions about Washington's or at least Scott's activities, but on balance they found most of it too flimsy to constitute proof. Scott's literary bureau "has been extremely injudicious," Villard admitted to Du Bois, and "it also looks as if money aid had been given" in the form of advertisements and perhaps loans, but "it will take a great deal more than the evidence you have presented to shake my faith in Mr. Washington's purity of purpose."[28]

While Villard promised to "speak to Mr. Washington about Scott's activities," he also lectured Du Bois on his duties. "I greatly regret . . . your attitude towards Mr. Washington," he wrote. "I do not think that there are any essential differences between your positions." Du Bois replied that this was not a "petty squabble of thoughtless self-seekers" as Villard seemed to think. Washington "represents today in much of his work and policy the greatest of the hindering forces in the line of

[27] Rudwick, *Du Bois*, 88-89; *NYEP*, Jan. 23, 1905; Bumstead to Du Bois, Jan. 24, 1905, Du Bois Papers.

[28] Ward to Du Bois, Feb. 18, 1905, Du Bois Papers; Du Bois to Ward, Mar. 10, 1905, in Herbert Aptheker, ed., *The Correspondence of W. E. B. Du Bois: Vol. I*, Amherst, Mass., 1973, p. 96; Villard to Du Bois, Feb. 7, Mar. 13, 1905, Du Bois to Villard, Mar. 24, 1905, Villard to Du Bois, Apr. 18, 1905, OGV Papers.

our true development." His subsidies of the black press "are not 'in-judicious,' Mr. Villard, they are *wrong*. I do not believe you can make Mr. Scott the scape goat for them." "In the trying situation in which we Negroes find ourselves," concluded Du Bois, "we specially need the aid and countenance of men like you," but even without it, unmuzzled black people would go on fighting for their rights.[29]

Among themselves, Villard and his uncles were more upset with Washington than they admitted to Du Bois. Although the evidence of hush money was circumstantial, "I fear that there is truth in the charge," wrote Francis Garrison. The Tuskegeean might legitimately "justify his course on the grounds that a division of his race into two warring camps would be a serious danger," but nevertheless such methods were "regrettable" and showed "bad taste." "It may be that the time has come," the Garrisons agreed, when Washington's "best friends should utter a word of caution [in] . . . plain speech." But Washington allayed the Garrison-Villard suspicions in a long letter whose disavowals were disingenuous to say the least (modern scholars have confirmed many of Du Bois's accusations). Pronouncing Washington's explanations "absolutely satisfactory," Villard wished he could show the letter to Du Bois "and shut him up. I am afraid that there will yet be a nasty explosion there which will hurt the race."[30]

Despite their reaffirmation of faith in Washington, this affair planted seeds of doubt in neo-abolitionist minds. They became more aware of the Tuskegee machine, more unhappy with some of its operations. While their relations with Washington for the next three years remained cordial if a trifle cooler than in the past, they moved closer to Du Bois and the Niagara Movement. They might have joined forces with Du Bois sooner had it not been for the prominence of William Monroe Trotter in the anti-Bookerite camp.

Trotter frequently labeled Washington the Benedict Arnold of his race, the Great Traitor, an Imperial Caesar with a lust for power; on one occasion Trotter's newspaper, the *Boston Guardian*, portrayed Washington as a man with "dull and absolutely characterless" eyes, "leonine jaws into which vast mastiff-like rows of teeth were set" and an

[29] Villard to Du Bois, Apr. 18, 1905, Du Bois to Villard, Mar. 24, Apr. 20, 1905, OGV Papers.

[30] Francis J. Garrison to Villard, Apr. 7, 9, 1905, OGV Papers; Garrison to Washington, May 8, 23, 24, 1905, Washington to Garrison, May 17, 18, 1905, Villard to Washington, May 20, 1905, BTW Papers; Villard to Garrison, May 23, 1905, OGV Papers. For modern studies of Washington's efforts to influence the black press, see August Meier, "Booker T. Washington and the Negro Press, with Special Reference to the *Colored American Magazine*," *Journal of Negro History*, XXXVIII (1953), 68-82; Emma Lou Thornbrough, "More Light on Booker T. Washington and the New York *Age*," *ibid.*, XLIII (1958), 34-49; and August Meier, *Negro Thought in America, 1880-1915*, Ann Arbor, 1963, pp. 224-36.

overall appearance "that would leave you uneasy and restless during the night if you had failed to report to the police such a man around." Many neo-abolitionists considered this a despicable defamation of a man working selflessly for his race. Even Mary White Ovington, who agreed with Trotter's radicalism, was put off by his style. Since she had begun reading the *Guardian*, she wrote half-jokingly, "I have grown more fond of Mr. Washington every day!" Trotter's role in the "Boston Riot" of July 30, 1903, earned him particular notoriety. On that evening the anti-Bookerites came in force to an address by Washington, shouted hostile questions from the floor, threw red pepper stink bombs onto the stage, started fights in the aisles, and finally provoked the police to arrest them. Though Norwood Hallowell was a character witness for Trotter at the latter's trial for disturbing a public meeting, most neo-abolitionists approved of Trotter's conviction and 30-day jail sentence. But Du Bois was impressed by Trotter's energy and dedication. He joined the *Guardian* editor in the efforts that led to the founding of the Niagara Movement two years later.[31]

The Garrisons could not understand how Du Bois could ally himself with such an "unmitigated nuisance" as Trotter. They resented Trotter's attempt to upstage the William Lloyd Garrison centenary celebration they had organized (with Washington's help) in Boston on December 10, 1905, by holding a rival celebration of his own. Significantly, however, several white neo-abolitionists including Moorfield Storey, Albert Pillsbury, and Franklin Sanborn spoke at Trotter's meeting.[32] And as the Garrisons and Villards moved toward a more radical position during the next two years, Trotter was emboldened to portray them as coming over to his side. In 1907 William Lloyd Garrison, Jr., spoke at a Faneuil Hall meeting to commemorate the 70th anniversary of Elijah Lovejoy's martyrdom. Garrison stressed as usual the importance of voting rights and agitation. Under the headline "William Lloyd Garrison vs. Booker T. Washington" the *Guardian* juxtaposed several quotations from this speech with some statements by Washington deprecating agitation. Angered by this "yellow journalism of the most unscrupulous sort," Garrison tried to set the record straight in a letter to the *Guardian*, but Trotter refused to print it. Garrison thereupon published it in the *Transcript*. With respect to the "uncompromising demand" for equal rights and "the value of agitation to rectify wrongs," Garrison said he agreed with Trotter. It was easy

[31] Fox, *Guardian of Boston*, 38-39, 49-64; Ovington to Du Bois, Sept. 2, 1905, Du Bois Papers; Elliott M. Rudwick, "Race Leadership Struggle: Background of the Boston Riot of 1903," *Journal of Negro Education*, XXXI (1962), 16-24.

[32] Quotations from Villard to Du Bois, Apr. 18, 1905, F. J. Garrison to Villard, Dec. 29, 1907, OGV Papers. For the contretemps over the Garrison centenary, see F. J. Garrison to Washington, Nov. 29, 1905, and Fox, *Guardian of Boston*, 99-100.

enough to utter radical sentiments in Boston, but Washington was "working in the most inflammable portion of the South . . . where a whisper at times precipitates the avalanche." Hence his methods could not be Trotter's methods, and Garrison deplored the use of his words against a man whom he considered "the most remarkable living American." Villard approved of his uncle's rebuke to the "unbalanced" Trotter. "It is a terrible pity," he added, "that Du Bois lends his name to that crowd."[33]

At just this time, however, Du Bois had a falling out with Trotter that paved the way for a new coalition between neo-abolitionists and black militants. In a quarrel between factions of the Massachusetts branch of the Niagara Movement in 1907, Du Bois sided with the anti-Trotter group. The wrangling became so intense that this branch, the most important in the organization, virtually collapsed. Du Bois attacked Trotter as a man impossible to work with unless he was in command; Trotter in turn dismissed "Du Bois and his crowd" as "self-seekers." This feud was partly responsible for the early demise of the Niagara Movement.[34]

It was probably more than coincidence that, as Du Bois split from Trotter, Washington's neo-abolitionist supporters began to criticize the Tuskegeean more openly than ever before. In 1908 the *Independent* said that the Niagara Movement contained "some of the ablest and best" black men in the country. The paper agreed with their belief that "it does no good to excuse or explain away the laws which somehow exclude the negro vote, or to talk optimistically of the future." *Evening Post* editorials declared that the trouble with Washington's policy was that "in thus concentrating upon material progress, [the Negroes'] political and social rights will slip from them." The white South liked Washington "because he seems to be teaching the South's own doctrine that the negro shall remain 'a hewer of wood and a drawer of water.' " Villard privately expressed growing impatience with Washington's speeches. "It is always the same thing, platitudes, stories, high praise for the Southern white man who is helping the negro up, insistence that the way to favor lies through owning farms, etc. etc." He feared that Washington "is lost for the righting of any of the spiritual, or civil, or legal wrongs of his people."[35] From 1909 on, the friendship between Washington and the Garrison-Villard families cooled rapidly. As

[33] Fox, *Guardian of Boston*, 119-20; F. J. Garrison to Washington, Dec. 30, 1907; W. L. Garrison, Jr.'s letter in *BET*, Jan. 13, 1908; Villard to F. J. Garrison, Jan. 15, 1908.

[34] Fox, *Guardian of Boston*, 103-14; Rudwick, *Du Bois*, chap. 5.

[35] *Independent*, Mar. 26, 1908; *NYEP*, Apr. 25, 1908; *Nation*, Mar. 18, 1909; Villard to W. L. Garrison, Jr., Feb. 24, 1909, OGV Papers.

Washington's stock went down, Du Bois's went up. While Washington "counsels his people to submit to disfranchisement," wrote Villard in the *Post*, Du Bois was "living up to the highest traditions of American life" by refusing to "sit silent in the presence of wrong." When William Lloyd Garrison, Jr., died in September 1909, it was Du Bois rather than Washington who was invited to give the memorial address.[36]

In 1911 Washington complained that "it used to be the Southern white man who pretended that the Negro was not making progress," but now "some of the rank abolitionists are loudest in their claims that the Negro is not making progress. In response, Villard said that Washington's speeches describing the race's achievements were fine "as far as they go, but they do not go far enough to satisfy any Garrison. . . . You record cases of [white] friendliness, but are silent about the increasing prejudice and injustice." What good did farm ownership or small businesses to for a people who "read almost every week of men of their race burned at the stake" or who looked at their children and asked "with panic fear if these are to be the children of the ghettos now being established . . . with one avenue of advancement after another closed to them." Speaking for the revived neo-abolitionist militancy of the NAACP, Villard wished that Washington "could take to heart the lesson of my grandfather's life and know no such thing as compromise with prejudice or with evil. Then a nation of whites and blacks would rise up and call you blessed."[37]

Whether or not Washington agreed with Villard, he was locked into his public stance of accommodation by dependence on conservative northern philanthropists and moderate southern whites. Thus the foremost Negro rights organization of the twentieth century, the NAACP, began without his blessing and soon incurred his opposition. And the man who for years had served as a link between Washington and the abolitionist past was more than any other person responsible for the founding of the NAACP: Oswald Garrison Villard.

After the Atlanta riot of 1906, Villard began to discuss with black and white associates a plan for a national organization to work for equal rights. This "Committee for the Advancement of the Negro Race" would establish a research and publicity bureau, a monthly magazine, a legal division to challenge discrimination in the courts,

[36] *NYEP*, Apr. 1, 1910; typescript of Du Bois's memorial address in WLG, Jr. Papers.
[37] Washington to Villard, Jan. 10, 1911, Washington to James Dillard, June 8, 1911, Villard to Washington, Feb. 7, 1911, BTW Papers; Villard, "If Lincoln Could Return," *Century*, LXXXV (Nov. 1912), 153-54; Villard to Washington, Apr. 4, 1913, BTW Papers.

and special committees to investigate lynchings, peonage, and violations of civil rights; it would send lobbyists to Washington and state capitals and would organize mass protest meetings. The time for "national agitation" had come, wrote Villard. "Justice and right must triumph now as they triumphed in Abolition days." Other neo-abolitionists endorsed his proposal. "You and I were brought up on stories of heroism for a cause," Ovington told Villard, "and dreamed dreams of doing something ourselves some time."[38]

Of course the NAACP did not spring full-blown from Villard's mind. Several forces converged to produce the National Negro Conference of 1909 from which grew the NAACP a year later. The first was organized black protest. Although by 1908 the Afro-American Council had died of internal conflict, several other protest organizations existed in the early twentieth century. Trotter established a bewildering succession of them, beginning with the Boston Suffrage League in 1904 and continuing with the New England Suffrage League, the National Negro Suffrage League, and the Negro-American Political League. The last was founded in 1908 as a splinter group from the Niagara Movement; it went through several reorganizations, finally settling down as the National Equal Rights League. All of these were dominated by Trotter and had little impact beyond the flurries created by his own crusading personality. The Niagara Movement started with great promise but collapsed from internal factionalism within five years. Overlapping with Niagara was the interracial Constitution League, founded in 1904 by the white industrialist John E. Milholland. The league's main contribution was its investigation of the Brownsville affair; after 1908 it declined in importance and like the Niagara Movement was eventually absorbed by the NAACP.[39]

Another stream that fed the founding of the NAACP was the social settlement movement. Until about 1900 the only white-sponsored social agencies for blacks in northern cities were orphanages, employment bureaus, nursing homes, and mission stations run by Quakers. Concerned about the problems of employment, housing, health, and child care facing the growing number of black migrants from the

[38] Speech by Villard to the Afro-American Council, Oct. 10, 1906, in *Colored American Magazine*, undated clipping, OGV Papers; *NYEP*, Mar. 3, 1906, Feb. 6, 1908; Villard to Mary Church Terrell, Sept. 19, 1907, M. C. Terrell Papers, Library of Congress; Villard to Hugh H. Gordon, Jr., Sept. 19, 1906, Villard to Washington, Jan. 27, Sept. 7, 1908; Ovington to Villard, Oct. 8, 1906, May 6, 1908, OGV Papers.

[39] Meier, *Negro Thought*, 172-82; Emma Lou Thornbrough, *T. Thomas Fortune: Militant Journalist*, Chicago, 1972, chaps. 6-8; Fox, *Guardian of Boston*, chaps. 2-4; Rudwick, *Du Bois*, 101-20; Nancy J. Weiss, "From Black Separatism to Interracial Cooperation: The Origins of Organized Efforts for Racial Advancement, 1890-1920," in Barton J. Bernstein and Allen J. Matusow, eds., *Twentieth-Century America: Recent Interpretations*, 2nd ed., New York, 1972, pp. 58-67.

South after 1895, young social reformers in several cities established settlement houses, playgrounds, kindergartens, and the like in black neighborhoods just as they were doing in white immigrant neighborhoods. The names of some of these settlements recalled the earlier crusade for freedom: the Frederick Douglass Center and the Wendell Phillips Settlement in Chicago, the Lincoln Settlement in Brooklyn, and the Robert Gould Shaw House in Boston. Several second- and third-generation abolitionists were active in this movement: Mary White Ovington helped found the Lincoln Settlement, she lived in a model tenement for blacks in the San Juan Hill district of Manhattan, and she wrote a study of Negroes in New York titled *Half a Man*; Elizabeth Walton was a social worker at the Sojourner Truth House in New York; William Eliot Furness was treasurer of the Frederick Douglass Center; Quaker abolitionists in Philadelphia worked in a number of settlements; and so on.[40]

In 1906 Frances Kellor, a white social worker who was angered by the exploitation of black women migrants by unscrupulous employment agencies, founded in New York the National League for the Protection of Colored Women. In the same year several black and white reformers formed the Committee for Improving the Industrial Condition of Negroes in New York. The chairman of this Committee was William Jay Schieffelin, a third-generation heir of the Jay abolitionist family. In 1910 a third organization, the Committee on Urban Conditions among Negroes, was established to sponsor social research and to train black social workers. All three merged in 1911 to form the National League on Urban Conditions among Negroes (later shortened to National Urban League). In many ways the Urban League tried to do for Negroes in the North what Booker T. Washington was attempting in the rural South.[41] This was fine so far as it went, but for the more radical progressives, especially neo-abolitionists and socialists, it did not go far enough. From their desire for an organization that would fight disfranchisement, Jim Crow, and lynching came the impulse for the NAACP.

An historian of the settlement house movement has found that more than a third of the signers of the call for the National Negro Conference in 1909 were settlement workers, including Jane Addams, Florence Kelley, and Lillian Wald. At least nine of the 60 signers

[40] Allen F. Davis, *Spearheads for Reform: The Social Settlements and the Progessive Movement 1890-1914*, New York, 1967, 94-98; Gilbert Osofsky, *Harlem: The Making of a Ghetto*, New York, 1966, pp. 53-62; Nancy J. Weiss, *The National Urban League, 1910-1940*, New York, 1974, p. 51; *Woman's Journal*, July 30, 1904; *NYEP*, Oct. 23, 1903, Aug. 19, 1908; Ovington, *Half a Man: The Status of the Negro in New York*, New York, 1911, pp. 41-42.

[41] Weiss, *National Urban League*, chaps. 2-4.

considered themselves socialists at one time or another. And 16 of the 53 white signers were one-time abolitionists or their descendants, including Villard (who wrote the call), his mother and his uncle William, Mary White Ovington, Edward Clement, and William Hayes Ward. The forces that converged to form the NAACP, then, were black radicals whose organizations had foundered, white neo-abolitionists, social justice progressives, and socialists. These categories overlapped considerably: Du Bois was a member of the Socialist party; Mary White Ovington and Florence Kelley were social workers, abolitionist descendants, and socialists; Charles E. Russell was a socialist and a second-generation abolitionist.[42]

The story of the founding of the NAACP is familiar and needs little elaboration here. In August 1908 a race riot broke out in Springfield, Illinois, which the *Independent* described as "worse, if possible, than the horrible Atlanta riot" (though the loss of life was much less). Several weeks later the *Independent* published a special article on the riot by William English Walling, a Kentucky-born socialist who had previously written articles on Russian revolutionaries and now pleaded for a revolution in American racial attitudes. "Either the spirit of the abolitionists . . . must be revived and we must come to treat the negro on a plane of absolute political and social equality," wrote Walling, "or Vardaman and Tillman will soon have transferred the race war to the North." After reading this, Ovington arranged a meeting with Walling and Henry Moskowitz, a New York social worker, to discuss proposals for an equal rights association. Joining these three in subsequent meetings were Villard, Charles E. Russell, Lillian Wald, Florence Kelley, AME Zion Bishop Alexander Walters (the former head of the Afro-American Council), and black Baptist clergyman William Henry Brooks. This group chose Villard to draft a call for a National Negro Conference to establish a permanent organization. Villard's call, issued on the centenary of Lincoln's birth, proclaimed that " 'A house divided against itself cannot stand'; this government cannot exist half-slave and half-free any better today than it could in 1861. . . . [There must be] a renewal of the struggle for civil and political liberty."[43]

Villard, Ovington, and Russell carried out most of the arrangements for the National Negro Conference in New York on May 31 and June 1, 1909. Ovington was secretary of the planning committee, Russell was

[42] Davis, *Spearheads for Reform*, emphasizes the role of settlement workers. For the names of the signers of the call and of members of various committees of the early NAACP, see the Appendixes of Charles Flint Kellogg, *NAACP: A History of the National Association for the Advancement of Colored People, 1909-1920*, Baltimore, 1967.

[43] *Independent*, Aug. 20, Sept. 3, 1908; *NYEP*, Feb. 13, 1909. The most detailed account of the origins of the NAACP is Kellogg, *NAACP*, 9-19.

chairman of the committee on resolutions, and Villard was chairman of the organization committee. At the conference itself Ward, Russell, Villard, and Wendell Phillips Stafford chaired four of the six sessions; each of them was an abolitionist descendant. Villard reported to the conference a plan for permanent organization. During the next year he and Ovington shouldered nearly all of the work, and at the second annual meeting in May 1910 his proposals for a National Association for the Advancement of Colored People were put into effect. For the first three years of its existence, when the NAACP had only a few hundred members most of whom were white liberals and black professionals in New York and Boston, Villard as treasurer and then as chairman of the board of directors carried the association almost single-handedly, dipping into his own pocket to meet its frequent deficits and providing office space in the *Evening Post* building. Although Villard was often overbearing or condescending toward associates and clashed particularly with Du Bois, without his early leadership the NAACP would never have got off the ground.[44]

Garrisonian neo-abolitionists also dominated the Boston branch of the NAACP, the first and for two or three years the strongest branch outside New York. The roster of NAACP founders in Boston reads like a membership list of the old New England Anti-Slavery Society: Garrison, Hallowell, Pillsbury, May, Bowditch, Foster, Channing, Rogers, Jackson, Clarke, Storey, and Bumstead. Francis Garrison was president of the Boston branch, while Moorfield Storey was president of the national association. When the NAACP held its 1911 national convention in Boston it seemed, in the words of Albert Pillsbury, "like an old-fashioned anti-slavery meeting."[45]

[44] This paragraph is based on a study of the NAACP Records in the Library of Congress and on various other manuscript collections, especially the OGV Papers. The importance of Villard in the early history of the Association is also emphasized in Kellogg, *NAACP*, chaps. 1-3. From his grandfather Villard seems to have inherited a prickly ego that made it difficult for him to share authority. Like some of the missionary educators, he succumbed occasionally to the temptation to act in a paternalistic fashion toward black associates. In exasperation after a prolonged dispute with Negroes on the board of trustees of Manassas Institute, of which he was chairman, Villard exploded in a private letter: "Truly they are a child race still!" (Villard to Francis J. Garrison, Mar. 14, 1913, OGV Papers.) For a highly critical study of the paternalism of Villard and other white founders of the NAACP, see Victor M. Glasberg, "Black Liberation and White Liberalism: The Founders of the NAACP and American Racial Attitudes," unpublished manuscript, cited with the author's permission.

[45] Pillsbury quoted in a letter from F. J. Garrison to Ellen Wright Garrison, Apr. 6, 1911, OGV Papers. Information on the early history of the Boston branch comes mainly from Francis J. Garrison's letters to Oswald Garrison Villard, OGV Papers, and from a report by Butler Wilson, 1914, typescript in the NAACP Records. Ironically, the grand old man of Boston abolitionism, 86-year-old Thomas Wentworth Higginson, refused in 1909 to sign the call for the National Negro

Although abolitionist influence in the NAACP was nowhere else so strong as in Boston and New York, the sons and daughters of abolitionists also played significant roles in other branches, particularly Philadelphia. In the predominantly black branch at Washington, D. C., one of the few white members was Wendell Phillips Stafford, whose abolitionist parents had named him after the great orator. Chief Justice of the District of Columbia Supreme Court, Stafford (a native of Vermont) was probably the most liberal white man in Washington on the race question. "We who have united to demand of the American people the rights guaranteed by the Constitution," he said at the NAACP's celebration of the centenary of Wendell Phillips' birth in 1911, "have reason to believe that the master spirits of the earlier crusade are with us now. . . . In every charge we make against the forces of oppression we have a right to feel that Garrison and Phillips . . . are riding at our side."[46]

The main themes of the NAACP's first decade—its development into a mass-membership organization, the campaign against segregation in the federal civil service, victories in the Supreme Court over the grandfather clause and residential segregation laws, the growth of the *Crisis*, and tensions between whites and blacks in the association resulting from the collision between white paternalism and black pride —have been treated by several historians.[47] Nearly all of these studies also emphasize the self-conscious neo-abolitionism of the NAACP's founders, whether or not their ancestors had been abolitionists. In *Crisis* editorials Du Bois frequently referred to the association as the "New Abolition Movement." Several black newspapers took up this slogan, especially during the crusade against civil service segregation in 1913–1914. White newspapers described the NAACP in similar terms. "It is the fiery abolitionism as against the calm meliorism of Booker T. Washington," observed the *Chicago Evening Post* in 1914, "and it is important that these two sides of the movement to alter the colored man's status should be clearly discerned."[48]

Conference because he perceived it as a threat to Booker T. Washington, in whom he still had faith. But two years later, just before his death, Higginson apparently changed his mind and expressed a desire to join the NAACP. *New York Sun*, May 30, 1909; Francis J. Garrison to Ellen Wright Garrison, May 11, 1911, OGV Papers.

[46] Constance McLaughlin Green, *The Secret City: A History of Race Relations in the Nation's Capital*, Princeton, 1967, pp. 169-76, 194; Stafford, *Wendell Phillips: A Centennial Oration*, Boston, 1911, p. 27.

[47] See especially Kellogg, *NAACP;* Rudwick, *Du Bois;* Francis L. Broderick, *W.E.B. Du Bois: Negro Leader in a Time of Crisis*, Stanford, 1959; B. Joyce Ross, *J. E. Spingarn and the Rise of the NAACP, 1911-1939*, New York, 1972; William B. Hixson, Jr., *Moorfield Storey and the Abolitionist Tradition*, New York, 1972; and Glasberg, "Black Liberation and White Liberalism."

[48] *Chicago Evening Post*, quoted in *Crisis*, VII (Mar. 1914), 227.

Missionary educators continued to stress the calm meliorism of their work. For some of them, education still represented the best hope for racial progress, and in any case their sensitive position in the South made participation in the NAACP difficult if not impossible. Nevertheless a number of educators who had left the South were active in the association: Horace Bumstead, who retired as president of Atlanta University in 1907; James G. Merrill, who left the presidency of Fisk in 1908; and of course Du Bois himself. M. C. B. Mason, former secretary of the Methodist Freedmen's Aid Society, became an organizer for the NAACP in 1912, and Wilbur P. Thirkield was a member of an NAACP committee while he was president of Howard. William Hayes Ward was chairman of the AMA's executive committee when he took part in the National Negro Conference. The AMA was proud of Du Bois as the most illustrious graduate of one of its schools; the *American Missionary* frequently reprinted his *Crisis* articles and endorsed the NAACP's activities.

For neo-abolitionists in the NAACP, the association represented a triumphant revival of the immediatism and agitation so long subordinated to time and education. Appropriately, no one articulated this revival better than the grandson of the man who in 1831 had promised to be as harsh as truth and as uncompromising as justice. "Agitation is precisely what is needed," said Oswald Garrison Villard. Those who counsel "time and patience" are "blinded to the fact that thus far the negro's progress in material things has been coincident with his being stripped more and more of his civil and political rights." If this was fanaticism, Villard was proud to wear the label. "No one who has ever made an impress in a reform movement has ever done so without being called a fanatic, a lunatic, a firebrand, etc. If in this cause of human rights I do not win at least a portion of the epithets hurled at my grandfather in his battle, I shall not feel that I am doing effective work." The new abolition movement, like the old, must be "a fire bell in the night to alarm the conscience of the people. . . . People may talk compromise and peace to us all they please, but there can be no compromise and no peace in this country as long as injustice is done."[49]

Of the 26 abolitionists or their descendants active in the early NAACP who can be identified with any of the three abolitionist factions, 14 were Garrisonians, eight were connected with the political wing, and four were evangelicals. The prominence of Garrisonians was

[49] *NYEP*, May 13, 1910; Villard's address, "The Objects of the National Association for the Advancement of Colored People" at the NAACP's 1912 convention, pamphlet in OGV Papers; undated ms. of a speech (probably 1913) in OGV Papers; Villard to J. C. Hemphill, Nov. 6, 1913, OGV Papers.

consistent with the pattern that appears throughout this book. On four of six issues used to measure the persistence of militancy—the election of 1872, the Civil Rights Act of 1875, the army's intervention in Louisiana in 1875, Hayes's southern policy in 1877, the election of 1888, and the Federal Elections Bill of 1890—the Garrisonians had the largest percentage taking a "militant" or "radical" stand. On two issues (the 1888 election and the Federal Elections Bill) the evangelicals had the largest proportion. If one adds up all of the abolitionists who took a position on these questions, the Garrisonians were on the radical side 80 percent of the time, evangelicals 77 percent, and political abolitionists 58 percent.

Although crude and not necessarily representative, these samples provide a rough index of rates of radical persistence among abolitionists after 1870. They tend to confirm that those whose ideology was primarily moral or religious were more likely to persist in their radicalism than those who followed a political strategy. They also confirm that a substantial majority of all of the abolitionists dealt with in this book persevered in their concern for Negro rights after 1870. The majority would be even larger if we included the percentages on attitudes toward Hayes's southern policy after the 1878 congressional elections, on the Blair bill for federal aid to education, and on the question of the Negro's innate mental ability.

Of course these data are based on only those abolitionists who expressed an opinion in documents that have survived for the historian's scrutiny. It may well be that a Gallup poll of a representative sample would have changed the picture somewhat. On the other hand, a "conservative" stand on some of these issues did not necessarily mean abandonment of the Negro. This was especially true of the evangelicals, among whom most of the missionary educators were found. When they argued that education was the best long-range solution of the race problem, they were not just repeating an empty cliché, for many of them spent their lives in this work. Of course there is much debate today about the effectiveness of education in overcoming racial discrimination and socio-economic handicaps. Several missionary educators themselves had come to believe by the early 1900s that the schools alone could not do the job, and they began to view agitation more favorably than at any time in the previous 30 years. But they did not lose faith in education as a vital lever for upward mobility. They viewed education in the same way that modern economists view it—as a means of human capital formation, an investment that does not produce immediate or direct profits, but that creates the necessary basis for economic growth and social change. The missionary schools did help to provide black people with educational capital in the two generations after emancipation. It was the talented tenth trained in these schools who have led most of the twentieth-century civil rights movements and furnished much of the leadership for the black community. The values and skills imparted by the schools played no small part in these achievements.

An interesting cyclical pattern in the history of racial reform can be discerned in the two centuries since 1776. After the antislavery victories of the Revolution came the decline of southern liberalism and the failure of gradualism in the early nineteenth century. This led to the rise of militant abolitionism in the 1830s, which during the next generation broadened and grew until it won what appeared to be a complete triumph in the Civil War and Reconstruction. But the following generation experienced another cycle marked by the failure of gradualism and southern liberalism. With the call for a National Negro Conference in 1909 written by the grandson of the man who 76 years earlier had written the Declaration of Sentiments of the American Anti-Slavery Society, a new cycle of militancy began. This cycle also seemed to culminate in total victory after another war in the mid-twentieth century. It remains for some future historian to record whether the cyclical pattern has finally been broken.

Abolitionists on Whom This Book Is Based

Name and Generation	Birth/Death	Principal Residence	Faction	Occupation	Religion	Education
*Abbot, Francis E.	1836-1903	Boston	Polit.	Journalist	Free Religious Assoc.	Col. Gr.
Alcott, Amos Bronson	1799-1888	Concord, Mass.	Gar.	Educator	Transcendentalist	No Col.
Alexander, Walter S.	1835-1900	New Orleans/North	Evang.	Clergy/Educ.	Cong.	Col. Gr.
*Alvord, John W.	1807-1880	Washington, D.C.	Evang.	Clergy/Educ.	Cong.	Col. Gr.
Ames, Charles G.	1828-1912	Boston	Gar.	Clergy	Unitarian	Some Col.
*Andrews, George W.	1833-1910	Talladega, Ala./Ohio	Evang.	Clergy/Educ.	Cong.	Col. Gr.
*Anthony, Susan B. (2)	1820-1906	Rochester, N.Y.	Gar.	Lecturer/Reformer	Free Religious Assoc.	No Col.
*Ashley, Samuel S.	1819-1887	Wilmington, N.C. & Atlanta/Northboro, Mass.	Evang.	Clergy/Educ.	Cong.	Col. Gr.
*Atkinson, Edward	1827-1905	Boston	Polit.	Textile Mfr.	?	No Col.
Axtell, Seth J.	?	New Orleans/North	Evang.	Clergy/Educ.	Baptist	Col. Gr.
Baily, Joshua L.	1826-1916	Philadelphia	Evang.	Commission Merchant	Quaker	No Col.
Baldwin, Charles C. (2)	1835-1927	Worcester, Mass.	Polit.	Journalist	Cong.	?
Baldwin, John	1799-1884	Louisiana/Berea, Ohio	Evang.	Grindstone Mfr.	Methodist	No Col.
**Baldwin, John D.	1809-1883	Worcester, Mass.	Polit.	Journalist	Cong.	Col. Gr.
Baldwin, John S. (2)	1834-1909	Worcester, Mass.	Polit.	Journalist	Cong.	?
Ballou, Adin	1803-1890	Milford, Mass.	Gar.	Clergy	Universalist	No Col.
Bancroft, Frederic (2)	1860-1945	Washington, D.C.	—	Writer	Cong.	Col. Gr.
**Beard, Augustus F.	1833-1934	N.Y. City	Evang.	Clergy/Educ.	Cong.	Col. Gr.
Beecher, Edward	1803-1895	Brooklyn	Evang.	Clergy/Educ.	Cong.	Col. Gr.
Bennett, Henry S.	1838-1895	Nashville/Wakeman, Ohio	Evang.	Clergy/Educ.	Presby.	Col. Gr.
Bird, Charles S. (2)	1855-1927	Walpole, Mass.	Polit.	Paper Mfr.	Unitarian	Col. Gr.
Bird, Francis W.	c. 1810-1894	Walpole, Mass.	Polit.	Paper Mfr.	Unitarian	?
Birney, Arthur A. (3)	1852-1916	Washington, D.C.	Polit.	Lawyer	Episcopalian	Col. Gr.
Birney, William (2)	1819-1907	Washington, D.C.	Polit.	Lawyer	Freethinker	Some Col.
Blackwell, Alice Stone (3)	1857-1950	Boston	—	Journalist/Reformer	Unitarian	Col. Gr.
*Blackwell, Henry B. (2)	1825-1909	Boston	Polit.	Journalist & Realtor	Unitarian	No Col.
Blanchard, Jonathan	1811-1892	Wheaton, Ill.	Evang.	Clergy/Educ.	Cong.	Col. Gr.
Blatch, Harriot Stanton (2)	1856-1940	N.Y. City	—	Lecturer/Reformer	Free Religious Assoc.	Col. Gr.

Name	Dates	Residence	Occupation	Faction	Religion	Color
Bond, Elizabeth Powell (2)	1841-1926	Philadelphia	Educator	Gar.	Quaker	No Col.
Botume, Elizabeth Hyde	?	Beaufort, S.C./Boston	Educator	?	Unitarian	No Col.
Bourne, Theodore (2)	1821-1910	N.Y. City	Clergy/Educ.	Evang.	Presby.	Col. Gr.
Bowditch, Henry Ingersoll	1808-1892	Boston	Physician	Polit.	Unitarian	Col. Gr.
Bowditch, Vincent I. (2)	1852-1929	Boston	Physician	Gar.	Unitarian	Col. Gr.
Bowditch, William I.	1819- ?	Boston	?	Gar.	Unitarian	?
**Bowen, Henry C.	1813-1896	Woodstock, Conn.	Journalist	Evang.	Cong.	No Col.
Brisbane, Benjamin (2)	?	Beaufort, S.C./Wis.	Journalist	Evang.	Baptist	No Col.
Brisbane, William H.	1803-1878	Beaufort, S.C./Wis.	Physician & Clergy	Evang.	Baptist	?
Brown, Agnes S. (3)	?	Portland, Ore.	Educator	———	?	No Col.
**Bumstead, Horace (2)	1841-1919	Atlanta/Boston	Clergy/Educ.	Evang.	Cong.	Col. Gr.
Burleigh, Charles C.	1810-1878	Northampton, Mass.	Lecturer/Reformer	Gar.	?	No Col.
Burritt, Elihu	1810-1879	Conn.	Lecturer/Reformer	Polit.	"Liberal"	No Col.
Carpenter, Charles C.	?	Greenfield, Mass.	Clergy	Evang.	Cong.	Col. Gr.
Chace, Elizabeth Buffum	1806-1899	Providence, R.I.	———	Gar.	Quaker	No Col.
Chadwick, John White	1840-1904	Brooklyn	Clergy	Gar.	Unitarian	Col. Gr.
**Chamberlain, Daniel H.	1835-1907	South Car./N.Y.C.	Lawyer	———	Cong.	Col. Gr.
Chamberlin, Joseph E. (2)	1851-1935	Boston	Journalist	Gar.	?	?
Channing, William H.	1810-1884	Washington/London	Clergy	———	Unitarian	Col. Gr.
Chapman, John Jay (3)	1862-1933	N.Y. City	Writer	Polit.	?	Col. Gr.
Chapman, Maria Weston	1806-1885	Boston	———	Gar.	Unitarian	No Col.
Chase, Mary Tuttle	1837-1900	Atlanta/Vermont	Educator	Evang.	Cong.	No Col.
*Chase, Thomas Noyes	1898- ?	Atlanta/Vermont	Educator	Evang.	Cong.	Col. Gr.
Cheever, George B.	1807-1890	N.Y. City	Clergy	Evang.	Cong.	Col. Gr.
Cheever, Henry T.	1814-1897	Worcester, Mass.	Clergy	Evang.	Cong.	Col. Gr.

* Indicates "important."
** Indicates "very important" in this study.

Numbers in parentheses after a person's name designate second or third generation.

The symbol [/] between two places of residence indicates that the first place is where the individual lived in the South and the second is his home city or state in the North.

A [———] in the Faction or Occupation column indicates that so far as is known, the person was not identified with any faction or did not have a remunerative occupation.

A [?] in any column indicates that the information is unknown.

Name	Dates	Location		Occupation	Religion	Color
Diaz, Abby Morton (2)	1821-1894	Boston	?	Writer	Unitarian	No Col.
Dickey, Sarah	1839-1904	Clinton, Miss./Dayton, Ohio	Evang.	Teacher	United Brethren	Col. Gr.
*Dickinson, Anna E. (2)	1842-1932	Philadelphia	Gar.	Lecturer	Quaker	No Col.
**Douglass, Harlan Paul (3)	1871-1953	N.Y. City	Evang.	Clergy/Educ.	Cong.	Col. Gr.
Douglass, Helen Pitts (2)	1837-1903	Washington, D.C.	Polit.	Civil Servant	Cong.	Col. Gr.
Dow, Neal	1804-1897	Portland, Me.	Gar.	Lecturer/Reformer	Quaker	No Col.
Eastman, Zebina	1815-1883	Chicago	Polit.	Journalist/Printer	?	No Col.
**Edwards, Arthur	1834-1901	Chicago	Evang.	Journalist	Methodist	Col. Gr.
Elliott, Maud Howe (2)	1854-1948	Boston & Newport	Polit.	Writer	Unitarian	?
*Emerson, Delia E.	1899-1939	N.Y. City & Mass.	Evang.	Educator	Cong.	No Col.
Fairchild, Charles G. (2)	1843-1933	Berea/Oberlin	Evang.	Educator	Cong.	Col. Gr.
**Fairchild, Edward Henry	1815-1889	Berea/Oberlin	Evang.	Clergy/Educ.	Cong.	Col. Gr.
Fairchild, Eugene P. (2)	?	Berea/Oberlin	Evang.	Educator	Cong.	Col. Gr.
Fairchild, James H.	1817-1902	Oberlin	Evang.	Clergy/Educ.	Cong.	Col. Gr.
*Fee, John G.	1816-1901	Berea	Evang.	Clergy/Educ.	Presby.	Some Col.
Foster, Abigail Kelly	1811-1887	Mass.	Gar.	Lecturer/Reformer	Non-affil.	No Col.
Foster, Stephen S.	1809-1881	Mass.	Gar.	Farmer	Non-affil.	Col. Gr.
Fox, Henry J.	?	So. Car./North	Evang.	Clergy/Educ.	Methodist	Col. Gr.
Francis, Abby B. (2)	?	Richmond, Va./Cambridge, Mass.	Gar.	Educator	?	No Col.
French, W. M. (2)	?	Beaufort, S.C./N.Y. City	Evang.	Journalist/Businessman	Methodist	?
**Frost, William Goodell (3)	1854-1938	Berea/Oberlin	Evang.	Educator	Cong.	Col. Gr.
Frothingham, Octavius B.	1822-1895	N.Y. City	Polit.	Clergy	Unitarian	Col. Gr.
Furness, William Eliot (3)		Chicago	——	Lawyer	Unitarian	Col. Gr.
Furness, William Henry	1802-1896	Philadelphia	Gar.	Clergy	Unitarian	Col. Gr.
Gage, Frances D.	1808-1884	Greenwich, Conn.	?	Lecturer/Writer	?	No Col.
Gammon, Elijah J.	1819-1891	Illinois	Evang.	Farm Machinery Mfr.	Methodist	No Col.
Gannett, William Channing	1840-1923	Rochester, N.Y.	Gar.	Clergy	Unitarian	Col. Gr.
Gardner, Anna	?	Charlottesville, Va. & Newbern, N.C./North	?	Educator	?	No Col.
**Garrison, Francis J. (2)	1848-1916	Boston	Gar.	Editor	Non-affil.	No Col.
Garrison, Lloyd McKim (3)	1867-1900	N.Y. City	Gar.	Lawyer	Non-affil.	Col. Gr.
**Garrison, Wendell Phillips (2)	1840-1907	N.Y.C. (Orange, N.J.)	Gar.	Journalist	Non-affil.	Col. Gr.

Name and Generation	Birth/Death	Principal Residence	Faction	Occupation	Religion	Education
**Garrison, William Lloyd	1805-1879	Boston	Gar.	Journalist	Prog. Friends	No Col.
**Garrison, Wm. Lloyd, Jr. (2)	1838-1909	Boston	Gar.	Wool Wholesaler & Investment Broker	Non-affil.	No Col.
Garrison, Wm. Lloyd III (3)	1874-1964	Boston	Gar.	Investment Broker	?	Col. Gr.
Gay, Sydney Howard	1814-1888	N.Y. City	Gar.	Journalist	?	Col. Gr.
Gibbons, Abigail Hopper	1801-1893	N.Y. City	Gar.	Social Worker	Quaker	No Col.
Gibbons, James Sloan	1810-1892	N.Y. City	Gar.	Banker	Quaker	No Col.
Goff, Harriett	?	Mississippi/Brooklyn	Evang.	Educator	Cong.	?
Grew, Mary	1813-1896	Philadelphia	Gar.	Lecturer/Reformer	Unitarian	No Col.
Haley, Frank	?	Macon, Ga./Wolfboro, N.H.	Evang.	Clergy/Educ.	Cong.	Col. Gr.
Hallowell, Emily (3)	?	Calhoun Co., Ala./Boston	Gar.	Educator	?	?
Hallowell, James Mott (3)	?	Boston	Gar.	Lawyer	?	Col. Gr.
Hallowell, Norwood P. (2)	1839-1914	Boston	Gar.	Banker	Quaker	Col. Gr.
*Hallowell, Richard P. (2)	1835-1904	Boston	Gar.	Wool Merchant	Quaker	Col. Gr.
Hamilton, John W.	1845-1934	Boston & Cincinnati	Evang.	Clergy/Educ.	Methodist	No Col.
Hancock, Cornelia	1839-1926	Mt. Pleasant, S.C./Salem, N.J.	Evang.	Educator & Social Worker	Quaker	Col. Gr.
*Hart, Albert Bushnell (2)	1854-1943	Cambridge, Mass.	Polit.	Educator	?	Some Col.
Hart, William	?	Berea/North	Evang.	Educator	Cong.	No Col.
Hartzell, Jane Culver (2)	1844-?	New Orleans/Cincinnati	Evang.	Social Worker	Methodist	No Col.
**Hartzell, Joseph C.	1842-1928	New Orleans/Cincinnati	Evang.	Clergy/Educ.	Methodist	Col. Gr.
Hatfield, Robert M.	1819-1891	Cincinnati	Evang.	Clergy	Methodist	?
**Haven, Gilbert	1821-1880	Atlanta/Boston	Evang.	Clergy	Methodist	Col. Gr.
Haven, William I. (2)	1856-1928	Boston	Evang.	Clergy	Methodist	Col. Gr.
Haviland, Laura S.	1808-1898	Michigan	Evang.	Social Worker	Quaker	No Col.
Hawkins, Dexter A.	1825-1886	N.Y. City	Polit.	Lawyer	Cong.	Col. Gr.
Heinzen, Karl	1809-1880	Boston	Gar.	Journalist	Freethinker	Some Col.
*Higginson, Thomas Wentworth	1823-1911	Cambridge	Polit.	Writer	Unitarian	Col. Gr.
Hinton, Richard J.	1830-1901	N.Y. City & elsewhere	Polit.	Journalist & Labor Reformer	Non-affil.	No Col.
*Holley, Sallie (2)	1818-1893	Lottsburgh, Va./New York State	Gar.	Educator	Unitarian	Col. Gr.
Holt, Hamilton (3)	1872-1951	N.Y. City	Evang.	Journalist & Educator	Cong.	Col. Gr.

Name	Dates	Place	Evang.	Educator	Cong.	No Col.
Hosley, Mary A.	?	Summerville, S.C./Chesterfield, N.H.				
*Hovey, William A. (2)	c. 1840-1906	Boston	Gar.	Journalist & Engineer	?	No Col.
Howe, Julia Ward	1819-1910	Boston	Polit.	Lecturer/Reformer	Unitarian	No Col.
Howe, Samuel Gridley	1801-1876	Boston	Polit.	Physician	Unitarian	Col. Gr.
Howe, William	1806-1906	Cambridge, Mass.	Evang.	Clergy	Baptist	?
Howells, William Dean (3)	1837-1920	Boston	Polit.	Writer & Editor	Unitarian	No Col.
Howland, Emily (2)	1827-1929	Va./Cayuga Co., N.Y.	Gar.	Educator & Philanthropist	Quaker	No Col.
Hubbard, George W. (2)	1841- ?	Nashville/North	Evang.	Physician & Educator	Methodist	Col. Gr.
Hunn, John A.	?	St. Helena, S.C./Delaware	?	Missionary & Social Worker	Quaker	?
Hutchinson, John W.	1821-1908	Lynn, Mass.	Gar.	Singer	Baptist	No Col.
Jay, John (2)	1817-1894	N.Y. City	Polit.	Lawyer	Episc.	Col. Gr.
*Jocelyn, Simeon S.	1799-1879	N.Y. City	Evang.	Engraver	Cong.	No Col.
*Johnson, Oliver	1809-1889	N.Y. City	Gar.	Journalist	Prog. Friends	No Col.
Johnson, Samuel	1822-1882	Lynn, Mass.	Gar.	Clergy	Unitarian	Col. Gr.
Jones, Alfred H.	1835-1907	Danville, Va./China, Me.	Evang.	Educator	Quaker	?
Jones, Charles K. (2)		Danville, Va./China, Me.	Evang.	Educator	Quaker	?
Jones, Jesse H.	1836-1904	N. Abington, Mass.	Gar.	Clergy/Reformer	Cong.	Col. Gr.
Kelley, Florence (3)	1859-1932	N.Y. City	——	Social Worker	Quaker	Col. Gr.
Ketchum, Edgar	1811-1882	N.Y. City	Evang.	Lawyer	Presby.	No Col.
Leavitt, Joshua	1794-1873	N.Y. City	Evang.	Journalist	Cong.	Col. Gr.
Lee, Luther	1800-1889	Michigan	Evang.	Clergy	Methodist	No Col.
LeMoyne, Francis J.	1798-1879	Washington, Pa.	Evang.	Physician	Presby.	Some Col.
Lewis, Timothy Willard	?	South Car./Worcester, Mass.	Evang.	Clergy	Methodist	?
Livermore, Mary A.	1820-1905	Boston	Gar.	Lecturer/Reformer	Universalist	No Col.
Lloyd, Elizabeth (2)	1848-1917	Philadelphia	——	Journalist	Quaker	?
Loud, Maria Hallowell (3)	1860-1916	Boston	Gar.	?	?	?
Love, Alfred K.	1890-1913	Philadelphia	Gar.	Wool Merchant	Quaker	No Col.
Lowell, James Russell	1819-1891	Cambridge	Lapsed Gar.	Professor & Poet	Unitarian	Col. Gr.
Lowell, Josephine Shaw (2)	1843-1905	N.Y. City	——	Social Worker/Philanthropist	Unitarian	No Col.
McKim, James Miller	1810-1874	Philadelphia	Gar.	Educator	Presby.	Col. Gr.
McNeill, George E. (2)	1837-1906	Boston	Gar.	Labor Organizer & Reformer	?	No Col.

Name and Generation	Birth/Death	Principal Residence	Faction	Occupation	Religion	Education
Mahan, Asa	1799-1889	Adrian, Mich.	Evang.	Clergy/Educ.	Cong.	Col. Gr.
*Markham, Richard F.	1818-1897	Savannah/Oberlin	Evang.	Clergy	Cong.	Col. Gr.
Matlack, Lucius C.	c. 1808- ?	N. Orleans/Delaware	Evang.	Clergy	Methodist	?
Matson, Henrietta	?	Tennessee/Ohio	Evang.	Educator	Presby.	Col. Gr.
May, Joseph (2)	1836-1918	Philadelphia	Gar.	Clergy	Unitarian	Col. Gr.
*May, Samuel	1810-1899	Leicester, Mass.	Gar.	Clergy	Unitarian	Col. Gr.
Mead, Edwin D. (2)	1849-1937	Boston	——	Journalist/Lecturer	Free Religious Assoc.	Some Col.
Mead, Lucia True Ames (3)	1856-1936	Boston		Lecturer/Reformer	Unitarian	No Col.
Miller, Elizabeth Smith (2)	1820-1911	Geneva, N.Y.	Polit.	Philanthropist	Non-affil.	No Col.
Miner, Alonzo Ames	1814-1895	Boston	Polit.	Clergy	Universalist	Col. Gr.
*Monroe, James	1821-1898	Oberlin	Polit.	Educator & Congressman	Cong.	Col. Gr.
Moody, Loring	1813-1883	Boston	Gar.	?	?	?
Moore, Joanna P.	1832-1916	South/Illinois	Evang.	Missionary & Social Worker	Baptist	Some Col.
**Morehouse, Henry Lyman	1834-1917	Philadelphia	Evang.	Clergy/Educ.	Baptist	Col. Gr.
**Morgan, Thomas Jefferson (2)	1839-1902	Philadelphia & Washington	Evang.	Clergy/Educ.	Baptist	Col. Gr.
Mott, Lucretia	1793-1880	Philadelphia	Gar.	——	Quaker	No Col.
Munro, Abby	?	Mt. Pleasant, S.C./Bristol, R.I.	——	Educator	Quaker	?
Murray, Ellen	? -1908	St. Helena, S.C./Boston	——	Educator	?	?
Nixon, W. Oliver (2)	1825- ?	Chicago	Polit.	Journalist	Quaker	Col. Gr.
**Nixon, William Penn (2)	1833-1912	Chicago	Polit.	Journalist	Quaker	Col. Gr.
*Ovington, Mary White (3)	1865-1951	Brooklyn	——	Social Worker	Unitarian	Some Col.
Painter, Charles C.	1832-1895	Nashville/Conn.	Evang.	Clergy/Educ.	Cong.	Col. Gr.
Parker, Joseph W.	1805-1887	Boston	Evang.	Clergy	Baptist	Col. Gr.
Parmelee, Laura A.	? -1893	Georgia/Toledo	Evang.	Teacher	Cong.	?
**Patton, William W.	1821-1889	Washington/Chicago	Evang.	Clergy/Educ.	Cong.	Col. Gr.
*Peirce, Bradford K.	1819-1889	Boston	Evang.	Journalist	Methodist	Col. Gr.
Philleo, Prudence Crandall	1803-1889	Kansas	Gar.	——	Quaker	No Col.
**Phillips, Wendell	1811-1884	Boston	Gar.	Lecturer/Reformer	Cong.	Col. Gr.
Pierce, Edward L.	1829-1897	Boston	Polit.	Lawyer	?	Col. Gr.
Pike, Gustavus D.	1831-1885	Hartford, Conn.	Evang.	Clergy	Cong.	Col. Gr.
*Pillsbury, Albert E. (2)	1849-1930	Boston	Polit.	Lawyer	?	Some Col.

			Polit.			Col. Gr.
Pillsbury, Gilbert	1813-1893	Charleston, S.C./Ludlow & N. Abington, Mass.		Educator	?	Col. Gr.
*Pillsbury, Parker	1809-1898	New Hampshire	Gar.	Lecturer/Reformer	Free Religious Assoc.	Some Col.
Plumly, Benjamin Rush	1816-1887	Galveston, Tex./Philadelphia	Gar.	?	Quaker	No Col.
Porter, Samuel D.	?	Rochester, N.Y.	Polit.	?	?	?
Potter, William J.	1832-1896	New Bedford, Mass.		Clergy	Unitarian	Col. Gr.
Powell, Aaron M. (2)	1832-1899	N.Y. City	Gar.	Journalist & Reformer	Quaker	?
Pugh, Sarah	1800-1884	Philadelphia	Gar.		Quaker	No Col.
*Putnam, Caroline	1826-1917	Lottsburgh, Va./North	Gar.	Educator	?	Some Col.
Quincy, Edmund	1808-1877	Boston	Gar.	Journalist	Unitarian	Col. Gr.
*Rankin, Jeremiah E.	1828-1904	Washington	Evang.	Clergy/Educ.	Cong.	Col. Gr.
*Redpath, James	1833-1901	Boston & elsewhere	Polit.	Journalist	Non-affil.	No Col.
Rhoads, James E. (2)	1828-1895	Philadelphia	——	Physician	Quaker	Col. Gr.
Robert, Joseph T.	1807-1884	Atlanta	Evang.	Clergy/Educ.	Baptist	Col. Gr.
Robinson, William S.	1818-1876	Boston	Polit.	Journalist	?	No Col.
Rockefeller, Laura Spelman (2)	1839-?	Cleveland	Evang.	Philanthropist	Baptist	Some Col.
*Rogers, John A. R.	1828-1906	Berea/North	Evang.	Clergy/Educ.	Presby.	Col. Gr.
Rogers, John R., Jr. (2)	1856-1934	Brooklyn	Evang.	Engineer & Inventor	Cong.	Col. Gr.
Rogers, Joseph M. (2)	1861-1922	Philadelphia	Evang.	Journalist	Episc.	Col. Gr.
Rowe, Aaron	?-1875	Savannah/North	Evang.	Clergy	Cong.	?
*Roy, Joseph E. (2)	1827-1908	Chicago	Evang.	Clergy/Educ.	Cong.	?
Russell, Charles Edward (3)	1860-1941	N.Y. City	Polit.	Journalist	Non-affil.	No Col.
Rust, Elizabeth L.	?-1899	Cincinnati	Evang.	Social Worker	Methodist	No Col.
Rust, R. H. (2)	?	Massachusetts		Clergyman	Methodist	Col. Gr.
**Rust, Richard S.	1815-1906	Cincinnati	Evang.	Clergy/Educ.	Methodist	Col. Gr.
Salter, William M. (2)	1853-1931	Chicago		Lecturer/Writer	Ethical Culture	Col. Gr.
*Sanborn, Franklin B.	1831-1917	Boston	Polit.	Administrator, Social Institutions	Unitarian	Col. Gr.
Sargent, John T.	1808-1877	Boston	Gar.	Clergy	Unitarian	Col. Gr.
Schieffelin, William Jay (3)	1866-1955	N.Y. City	——	Chemist	Episc.	Col. Gr.
*Schofield, Martha	1839-1916	Aiken, S.C./Philadelphia	——	Educator	Quaker	No Col.
Sewall, Samuel	1798-1888	Boston	Gar.	Lawyer	Unitarian	Col. Gr.
Shaw, Francis George	1809-1882	N.Y. City	Gar.	Philanthropist	Unitarian	Some Col.

Name and Generation	Birth/Death	Principal Residence	Faction	Occupation	Religion	Education
Shaw, Sarah S.	1815- ?	N.Y. City	Gar.	Educator	Unitarian	No Col.
Silsby, Edwin C. (2)	1851-1923	Talladega/Beloit, Wis.	Evang.	Educator	Presby.	Col. Gr.
Silsby, John	?	Alabama/Beloit, Wis.	Evang.	Clergy/Educ.	Presby.	Col. Gr.
**Slack, Charles Wesley	1825-1885	Boston	Polit.	Journalist	Unitarian	No Col.
Smith, Edward P.	1827-1876	N.Y. City	Evang.	Clergyman	Cong.	Col. Gr.
Smith, Gerrit	1797-1874	Peterboro, N.Y.	Polit.	Philanthropist/Reformer	Presby.	Col. Gr.
*Spence, Adam K.	1831-1900	Nashville/Ann Arbor, Mich.	Evang.	Educator	Presby.	Col. Gr.
Stacy, George W.	1809- ?	Milford, Mass.	Gar.	Clergy	Universalist	?
Stafford, Wendell Phillips (3)	1861- ?	Washington, D.C.	Gar.	Lawyer	Universalist	Col. Gr.
*Stanton, Elizabeth Cady	1815-1902	N.Y. City	Gar.	Lecturer/Reformer	"Liberal"	No Col.
Stanton, Henry Brewster	1805-1887	N.Y. City	Polit.	Journalist & Lawyer	?	Some Col.
*Stearns, Charles	c. 1821- ?	Georgia/Boston	Gar.	Farmer	?	Some Col.
Stearns, Frank Preston (2)	1846-1917	Boston	Polit.	Writer	?	Col. Gr.
Stearns, Mary E.	? -1901	Boston	Polit.	Philanthropist	?	No Col.
Stebbins, Giles B.	1817-1900	Michigan	Gar.	?	Unitarian	No Col.
Stevens, Abram W.	1833-1924	Boston & elsewhere	Polit.	Journalist & Clergyman	Unitarian	Some Col.
Stone, Lucy	1818-1893	Boston	Gar.	Lecturer/Reformer	Unitarian	Col. Gr.
**Streby, Michael E.	1845-1899	N.Y. City (Newark)	Evang.	Clergy/Educ.	Cong.	Col. Gr.
*Storey, Moorfield (2)	1845-1929	Boston	Polit.	Lawyer	Unitarian	Col. Gr.
Swisshelm, Jane Grey	1815-1884	Swissvale, Pa.	Polit.	Journalist & Reformer	?	No Col.
Tappan, Lewis	1788-1873	N.Y. City	Evang.	Merchant	Cong.	No Col.
Thayer, E. O.	?	So. Car./Mass.	Evang.	Clergy/Educ.	Methodist	Col. Gr.
**Thirkield, Wilbur P. (2)	1854-1936	Atlanta/Franklin, Ohio	Evang.	Clergy/Educ.	Methodist	Col. Gr.
Thompson, James (2)	?	So. Car./Philadelphia	?	Journalist	?	?
Thompson, Ruth (3)	?	Pasadena, Calif.	—	Educator		No Col.
Thwing, Charles F. (2)	1853-1927	Cleveland	—	Clergy/Educ.	Cong.	Col. Gr.
*Tilton, Theodore	1835-1907	N.Y. City	Gar.	Journalist	Cong.	Col. Gr.
Tomlinson, Reuben	?	So. Car./Philadelphia	Gar.	Businessman	Quaker	No Col.
*Towne, Laura	1825-1901	So. Car./Philadelphia	Gar.	Educator	Unitarian	No Col.
*Villard, Helen Frances Garrison (2)	1844-1928	N.Y. City	Gar.	Philanthropist/Reformer	Non-affil.	No Col.
**Villard, Oswald Garrison (3)	1872-1947	N.Y. City	Gar.	Journalist	Non-affil.	Col. Gr.

Name	Dates	Location		Occupation	Religion	College
Walton, Elizabeth (2)	?	N.Y. City	——	Social Worker	Quaker	No Col.
**Ward, William Hayes (2)	1835-1916	N.Y. City	Evang.	Journalist	Cong.	Col. Gr.
Wardner, Nathan	1833-1898	Syracuse, N.Y.	Evang.	Journalist & Clergyman	Methodist	?
*Ware, Edmund A.	1837-1885	Atlanta/Norwich, Conn.	Evang.	Educator	Cong.	Col. Gr.
Ware, Edward T. (2)	1874-1927	Atlanta/Hartford, Conn.	Evang.	Clergy/Educ.	Cong.	Col. Gr.
*Warner, Yardley	1815-1885	N.C. & Tenn./Philadelphia	Evang.	Educator	Quaker	No Col.
Washburn, Elizabeth C.	1812-1893	Worcester, Mass.	Evang.	Philanthropist	Cong.	No Col.
Webster, Alonzo	?	Orangeburg, S.C./Mass.	Evang.	Clergy/Educ.	Methodist	Col. Gr.
Weld, Angelina Grimké	1805-1879	Boston	Evang.	Educator	Non-affil.	No Col.
Weld, Theodore	1803-1895	Boston	Evang.	Educator	Presby.	Some Col.
*Whipple, George	1805-1876	N.Y. City	Evang.	Clergy/Educ.	Cong.	Col. Gr.
White, Andrew Dickson	1832-1918	Ithaca, N.Y.	Polit.	Educator	Episc.	Col. Gr.
White, Horace	1834-1916	N.Y. City	Polit.	Journalist	Presby.	Col. Gr.
Whittier, John G.	1807-1892	Amesbury, Mass.	Polit.	Poet	Quaker	No Col.
Wilbur, Henry W. (2)	1851-1914	Philadelphia	——	Journalist & Writer	Quaker	No Col.
Williams, Amy	? -1895	Atlanta/North	Evang.	Educator	?	?
Williams, Edward F. (2)	1832-1919	Chicago	Evang.	Clergy	Cong.	Col. Gr.
Wise, Daniel	1813-1898	N.Y. City (Englewood, N.J.)	Evang.	Clergy	Methodist	No Col.
Woodworth, Charles L.	1820-1898	Boston	Evang.	Clergy	Cong.	Col. Gr.
Wright, Elizur	1804-1885	Boston	Polit.	Insurance Actuary	Free Religious Assoc.	Col. Gr.
Wright, Walter E. C.	?	Oberlin/Olivet, Mich.	Evang.	Educator	Cong.	Col. Gr.
Wyman, Lillie Buffum Chace (2)	1847-1929	Valley Falls, R.I. & Newtonville, Mass.	Gar.	Writer	Quaker	No Col.

Totals and Percentages for Variables
in the List of Abolitionists

GENERATIONS

First Generation	191	(67.2%)
Second Generation	70	(24.6%)
Third Generation	23	(8.1%)

SEX

Male	216	(76.1%)
Female	68	(23.9%)

FACTIONAL IDENTIFICATION

Garrisonians	79	(27.8%)	31.3%
Evangelicals	116	(40.8%)	46.0%
Political	57	(20.1%)	22.6%
Nonaffiliated or Unknown	32	(11.3%)	

FACTIONAL IDENTIFICATION OF WOMEN

Garrisonians	25	(36.8%)	50.0%
Evangelicals	19	(27.9%)	38.0%
Political	6	(8.8%)	12.0%
Nonaffiliated or Unknown	18	(26.5%)	

RESIDENCE

New England	95	(33.5%)
Mid-Atlantic	84	(29.6%)
Rest of North	31	(10.9%)
South	74	(26.1%)

NATIVE REGION FOR THOSE LIVING IN SOUTH

New England	25	(33.8%)
Mid-Atlantic	12	(16.2%)
Rest of North	25	(33.8%)
"North"	10	(13.5%)
"South"	2	(2.7%)

NATIVE REGION FOR TOTAL SAMPLE WITH THOSE
IN SOUTH CREDITED TO HOME STATES

New England	120	(42.3%)
Mid-Atlantic	95	(33.5%)
Rest of North	56	(19.7%)
"North"	10	(3.5%)
"South"	2	(.7%)

RESIDENCE BY FACTIONS

Residing in	Garrisonians		Evangelicals		Political		Nonaffiliated or Unknown	
New England	38	(48.1%)	14	(12.1%)	34	(67.6%)	9	(28.1%)
Mid-Atlantic	28	(35.4%)	27	(23.3%)	17	(29.8%)	12	(37.5%)
Rest of North	3	(3.8%)	19	(16.4%)	4	(7.1%)	5	(15.6%)
South	10	(12.7%)	56	(48.2%)	2	(3.5%)	6	(18.8%)
Totals	79	(100.0%)	116	(100.0%)	57	(100.0%)	32	(100.0%)

OCCUPATIONS

Clergy	39	(13.8%)	Total Clergy: 80 (28.2%)	
Clergy/Educ.	42	(14.8%)	Total Educators: 87 (30.6%)	Total Involved in
Educators	45	(15.8%)		Communication of
Journalists	45	(15.8%)		Ideas & Information:
Writers	12	(4.2%)		201 (70.8%)
Lecturers/			Total "Publicists": 75 (26.4%)	
Reformers	17	(6.0%)		
Editor	1	(.4%)		
Businessmen	17	(6.0%)		
Lawyers	17	(6.0%)		
Physicians	7	(2.5%)		
Philanthropists	9	(3.2%)		
Missionaries/				
Social Workers	11	(3.9%)		
Farmers	3	(1.1%)		
Civil Servants	2	(.7%)		
Others	5	(1.8%)		
None	6	(2.1%)		
Unknown	6	(2.1%)		

OCCUPATIONS OF WOMEN ALONE

Educators	24	(35.3%)	Missionaries/		
Journalists	3	(4.4%)	Social Workers	10	(14.7%)
Writers	6	(8.8%)	Civil Servant	1	(1.5%)
Lecturers/Reformers	11	(16.2%)	None	6	(8.8%)
Philanthropists	6	(8.8%)	Unknown	1	(1.5%)

RELIGION

(Percentages do not include the Religious Unknowns)

Denomination	Garrisonians		Evangelicals		Political		Nonaffiliated or Unknown		Total	
Congregationalist	4	(5.7%)	51	(45.1%)	6	(15.8%)	3	(12.0%)	64	(25.9%)
Methodist	0		26	(23.0%)	1	(2.6%)	0		27	(10.9%)
Baptist	1	(1.4%)	12	(10.6%)	0		1	(4.0%)	14	(5.7%)
Presbyterian	1	(1.4%)	12	(10.6%)	1	(2.6%)	0		14	(5.7%)
Episcopalian	0		1	(.9%)	3	(7.9%)	1	(4.0%)	5	(2.0%)
United Brethren	0		1	(.9%)	0		0		1	(.4%)
Quaker	18	(25.7%)	10	(8.8%)	3	(7.9%)	8	(32.0%)	39	(15.8%)
Unitarian	24	(34.3%)	0		19	(50.0%)	8	(32.0%)	51	(20.6%)
Universalist	3	(4.3%)	0		1	(2.6%)	0		4	(1.6%)
"Liberal"	7	(10.0%)	0		4	(10.5%)	4	(16.0%)	15	(6.1%)
No Affiliation	12	(17.1%)	0		1	(2.6%)	0		13	(5.3%)
Totals	70		113		38		25		247	

Religion Unknown 37

284

EDUCATION

	First Generation		Second Generation		Third Generation		Total	
College Graduates	88	(51.8%)	37	(63.8%)	14	(70%)	139	(56.0%)
Some College	15	(8.8%)	5	(8.6%)	1	(5%)	21	(8.5%)
No College	67	(39.4%)	16	(27.6%)	5	(25%)	88	(35.5%)
Totals	170		58		20		248	

Education Unknown 36

284

Appendix B

Southern Negro Colleges and Secondary Schools
Established by Northern Mission Societies[a]

	1894–95									1914–15									
Mission Societies and Schools (Date of the Founding of Colleges in Parentheses)	Faculty and Administration					Students				Faculty and Administration[b]					Students[e]				
	Total	Negro	White	% Negro	President or Principal	Total	Elementary and Grammar	Secondary	College and Professional	Total	Negro	White	% Negro	President or Principal	Total	Attended[d]	Elementary and Grammar[d]	Secondary[d]	College and Professional[d]
American Missionary Association: Colleges																			
Fisk University, Nashville, Tenn.[e] (1866)	31	1	30	3%	White	539	221	263	55	45	14	31	31%	White	505	505	112	205	188
Straight University, New Orleans, La. (1869)	24	2	22	8%	White	563	470	91	2	30	13	17	43%	White	758	578	364	203	11
Talladega College, Talladega, Ala. (1867)	20	1	19	5%	White	581	509	66	6	41	12	29	29%	White	668	561	382	124	55
Tillotson College, Austin, Tex. (1877)	13	0	13	0%	White	193	153	40	0	20	6	14	30%	White	314	223	135	70	18
Tougaloo College, Tougaloo, Miss. (1869)	22	0	22	0%	White	377	332	45	0	31	2	29	6%	White	455	444	275	149	20
Total	110	4	106	4%	Black: 0 White: 5	2,253	1,685	505	63	167	47	126	28%	Black: 0 White: 5	2,700	2,311	1,268	751	292

Notes: see p. 416.

Institution	1895									1915									
AMA Secondary Schools: 1895 (17); 1915 (22)f	141	12	129	9%	Black: 1 White: 16	4,327	3,743	584		246	132	114	54%	Black: 10 White: 12	5,977	4,743	3,892	851	
Total: All AMA Schoolsf	251	16	235	6%	Black: 1 White: 21	6,580	5,428	1,089	63	413	179	234	48%	Black: 10 White: 17	8,677	7,054	5,160	1,602	292
Freedmen's Aid Society of the Methodist Episcopal Church: Collegesf																			
Bennett College, Greensboro, N.C. (1873)	10	10	0	100%	Black	203	198	5	0	15	12	3	80%	Black	312	312	235	67	10
Clark University, Atlanta, Ga. (1870)	19	8	11	42%	White	341	246	91	4	24	14	10	58%	White	304	304	128	144	32
Claflin College, Orangeburg, S.C. (1869)	20	10	10	50%	White	570	473	74	23	27	21	6	78%	White	866	814	597	191	26
Gammon Theological Seminary, Atlanta, Ga. (1882)	4	1	3	25%	White	84	0	0	84	6	2	4	33%	White	78	78	0	0	78
Meharry Medical College, Nashville, Tenn.f (1876)					White					30	28	2	93%	White	505	505	0	0	505
Morgan College, Baltimore, Md. (1867)	9	2	7	22%	White	160	96	3	61	11	4	7	36%	White	128	81	0	55	26
New Orleans University, New Orleans, La. (1873)	24	12	12	50%	White	603	531	65	7	24	11	13	46%	White	557	432	298	125	9
Philander Smith College, Little Rock, Ark. (1883)	15	4	11	27%	White	312	259	37	16	18	17	1	94%	Black	491	439	268	132	39
Rust College, Holly Springs, Miss. (1866)	10	4	6	40%	White	230	127	97	6	18	10	8	56%	White	378	196	128	60	8
Samuel Houston College, Austin, Tex. (1900)	Founded in 1900									20	19	1	95%	Black	405	377	267	92	18

Southern Negro Colleges and Secondary Schools Established by Northern Mission Societies[a] (*Continued*)

Mission Societies and Schools (Date of the Founding of Colleges in Parentheses)	1894–95									1914–15									
	Faculty and Administration					Students				Faculty and Administration[b]					Students[c]				
	Total	Negro	White	% Negro	President or Principal	Total	Elementary and Grammar	Secondary	College and Professional	Total	Negro	White	% Negro	President or Principal	Total	Attendance[d]	Elementary and Grammar[d]	Secondary[d]	College and Professional[d]
Central Tennessee College, Nashville, Tenn.[g] (1865)	11	2	9	18%	White	326	115	158	53	17	8	9	47%	Black	107	107	30	77	0
Wiley University, Marshall, Tex. (1873)	12	3	9	25%	Black	284	89	139	56	30	28	2	93%	Black	439	384	176	170	38
Total	134	56	78	42%	Black: 2 White: 9	3,113	2,134	669	310	240	174	66	73%	Black: 5 White: 7	4,570	4,029	2,127	1,113	789
Methodist Secondary Schools: 1895 (11); 1915 (11)[f]	54	35	19	65%	Black: 4 White: 4 Unknown: 3	1,650	1,203	447		135	94	41	70%	Black: 5 White: 6	2,493	2,401	1,864	537	
Total: All Methodist Schools[f]	188	91	97	48%	Black: 6 White: 13 Unknown: 3	4,763	3,337	1,116	310	375	268	107	71%	Black: 10 White: 13	7,063	6,430	3,991	1,650	789
American Baptist Home Mission Society: Colleges																			
Benedict College, Columbia, S.C. (1871)	8	1	7	13%	White	135	0	135	0	30	12	18	40%	White	595	507	254	205	48

School																			
Bishop College, Marshall, Tex. (1881)	18	7	11	39%	White	368	270	65	33	22	10	12	45%	White	421	371	176	153	42
Hartshorn Memorial College, Richmond, Va. (1884)	9	2	7	22%	White	97	22	75	0	15	3	12	20%	White	188	169	73	96	0[h]
Morehouse College, Atlanta, Ga.[i] (1867)	11	6	5	55%	White	150	72	50	28	19	17	2	89%	Black	277	277	110	111	56
Richmond Theological Seminary, Richmond, Va. (1865)	4	2	2	50%	White	50	0	0	50	Merged with Wayland Seminary in 1899 to form Virginia Union University									
Roger Williams University, Nashville, Tenn.[j] (1867)	16	7	9	44%	White	227	141	67	19	17	17	0	100%	Black	123	107	27	80	0
Shaw University, Raleigh, N.C. (1865)	26	10	16	38%	White	362	129	175	58	30	16	14	53%	White	291	221	52	123	46
Spelman Seminary, Atlanta, Ga.[k] (1881)	38	4	34	11%	White	491	416	52	23	51	3	48	6%	White	631	595	330	254	11
Virginia Union University, Richmond, Va. (1899)	Formed in 1899 of merger between Wayland Seminary and Richmond Theological Seminary									16	7	9	44%	White	265	255	35	145	75
Total	130	39	91	30%	Black: 0 White: 8	1,880	1,050	619	211	200	85	115	43%	Black: 2 White: 6	2,791	2,502	1,057	1,167	278
Baptist Secondary Schools: 1895 (20); 1915 (16)[l]	122	97	25	80%	Black: 15 White: 5	2,392	1,951	441		208	195	13	94%	Black: 15 White: 1	4,040	3,009	2,243	766	
Total: All Baptist Schools[f]	252	136	116	54%	Black: 15 White: 13	4,272	3,001	1,060	211	408	280	128	69%	Black: 17 White: 7	6,831	5,511	3,300	1,933	278
Presbyterian College: Biddle University, Charlotte, N.C. (1867)	11	11	0	100%	Black	260	19	172	69	16	16	0	100%	Black	221	207	24	131	52

Southern Negro Colleges and Secondary Schools Established by Northern Mission Societies[a] (Continued)

Mission Societies and Schools (Date of the Founding of Colleges in Parentheses)	1894-95									1914-15									
	Faculty and Administration					Students				Faculty and Administration[b]					Students[e]				
	Total	Negro	White	% Negro	President or Principal	Total	Elementary and Grammar	Secondary	College and Professional	Total	Negro	White	% Negro	President or Principal	Total	Attendance[c]	Elementary and Grammar[d]	Secondary[d]	College and Professional[d]
Presbyterian Secondary Schools: 1895 (7); 1915 (20)[f]	75	41	34	55%	Black: 4 White: 3	1,515	953	562		218	173	45	75%	Black: 16 White: 4	4,798	4,197	3,516	681	
Total: All Board of Missions for Freedmen, Presbyterian Church in the U.S.A., Schools[f]	86	52	34	60%	Black: 5 White: 3	1,775	972	734	69	234	189	45	81%	Black: 17 White: 4	5,019	4,404	3,540	812	52
United Presbyterian College: Knoxville College, Knoxville, Tenn. (1875)	21	0	21	0%	White	317	186	114	17	29	5	24	17%	White	327	327	187	110	30
United Presbyterian Secondary Schools: 1895 (1); 1915 (5)	14	3	11	22%	White	686	622	64		77	57	20	74%	Black: 3 White: 2	1,726	1,344	1,137	207	
Total: All Board of Freedmen's Missions, United Presbyterian Church, Schools	35	3	32	9%	Black: 0 White: 2	1,003	808	178	17	106	62	44	58%	Black: 3 White: 3	2,653	1,671	1,324	317	30
Quakers: Secondary Schools: 1895 (3); 1915 (4)	37	20	17	54%	Black: 0 White: 2 Unknown: 1	655	297	358		64	54	10	84%	Black: 2 White: 2	1,464	1,243	924[m]	94[m]	30

Other Denominations:[n] Secondary Schools: 1895 (3); 1915 (4)	16	8	8	50%	Black: 1 White: 2	379	259	120		64	30	34	47%	Black: 1 White: 3	917	862	614[m]	142[m]	
Independent, Nondenominational Colleges																			
Atlanta University, Atlanta, Ga. (1867)	16	0	16	0%	White	217	66	131	20	33	4	29	12%	White	586	586	182	360	44
Howard University, Washington, D.C. (1867)	64	21	43	33%	White	587	129	151	307	106	73	33	69%	White	1,401	1,401	0	373	1,028
Leland University, New Orleans, La.[o] (1869)	13	4	9	31%	White	439	357	59	23	14	4	10	29%	White	298	298	203	91	4
Total	93	25	68	27%	Black: 0 White: 3	1,243	552	341	350	153	81	72	53%	Black: 0 White: 3	2,285	2,285	385	824	1,076
Independent Secondary Schools (including Hampton Institute):[p] 1895 (2); 1915 (3)	70	19	51	27%	Black: 0 White: 2	1,067	751	316		250	93	157	37%	Black: 0 White: 3	1,167	1,115	710	405	
Total: All Independent Schools	163	44	119	27%	Black: 0 White: 5	2,310	1,303	657	350	403	174	229	43%	Black: 0 White: 6	3,452	3,400	1,095	1,229	1,076
All Colleges and Professional Schools[q]	499	135	364	27%	Black: 3 White: 26	9,066	5,626	2,420	1,020	805	408	397	51%	Black: 8 White: 22	12,894	11,661	5,048	4,096	2,517
All Secondary Schools[q]	547	235	294	44%	Black: 25 White: 35 Unknown: 4	12,671	9,779	2,892		1,262	828	434	66%	Black: 52 White: 33	22,582	18,914	14,840	3,683	
Total: All Schools[q]	1,028	370	658	36%	Black: 28 White: 61 Unknown: 4	21,737	15,405	5,312	1,020	2,067	1,236	831	60%	Black: 60 White: 55	35,476	30,575	19,948	7,773	2,517

a These statistics have been garnered from *The Report of the U.S. Commissioner of Education for the Year 1894–95* (Washington, 1896), 1338–45, and from *Negro Education: A Study of the Private and Higher Schools for the Colored People in the United States*, ed. Thomas Jesse Jones (Washington, 1917), *passim*. The government figures for 1894–95 are not wholly reliable and have been checked and supplemented whenever possible by the scattered statistics available in the annual reports and other materials published by the mission societies, and in college catalogs. The statistics in this table do not include elementary schools.

b Includes clerical staff for a few schools.

c The Jones report applied stricter criteria for classifying students in secondary or college classes than the earlier reports of the Commissioner of Education, so there are fewer students listed in the higher grades than if earlier standards had been applied.

d Students in attendance on day of visit.

e Acquired an independent status in 1909.

f Statistics incomplete for 1894–95.

g Name changed to Walden University in 1900.

h Hartshorn was the girls' college of Virginia Union University; several students took college courses at Virginia Union.

i Named Atlanta Baptist Seminary until 1897, Atlanta Baptist College 1897–1913.

j Taken over by the state Negro Baptist convention in 1908; continued to receive some Home Mission Society aid.

k Supported mainly by the Woman's American Baptist Home Mission Society, an affiliate of the American Baptist Home Mission Society.

l Fifteen Baptist secondary schools in 1894–95 and fourteen in 1914–15 were owned by Negro state Baptist conventions and partly supported and supervised by the Home Mission Society.

m Statistics on students incomplete.

n Christian Missionary Society; American Christian Convention; Free Baptist Church; Reformed Presbyterian Church.

o Partly supported and controlled by the American Baptist Home Mission Society until 1887. Leland always maintained close ties with the Baptist Church.

p Hampton Institute was founded by the American Missionary Association, which continued to appropriate some funds to the school until 1894.

q Statistics on faculty incomplete or not available for one of the colleges and three of the secondary schools in 1894–95; statistics on students incomplete for one of the colleges and six of the secondary schools in 1894–95, and for two of the secondary schools in 1914–15.

A Note on Sources

The footnotes of this book constitute the best guide to the wide variety of primary and secondary sources on which it is based. The most important of these sources were the newspapers and periodicals edited by abolitionists, other newspapers and periodicals that published material by or about them, and manuscript collections or archives containing letters and other unpublished material. The following listings include only the most significant newspapers and periodicals consulted, with the years in parentheses indicating the period for which relatively complete and continuous runs were available and consulted. Where no dates are indicated, only scattered issues were consulted for all or part of the period covered by this book. No attempt is made to list the many newspapers and periodicals to which only a handful of citations are made, some of them from clippings collections; for references to these, the reader must depend on the footnotes. Since substantive information about important newspapers and their editors is contained in the text, that information is not duplicated here.

Daily Newspapers Edited by Abolitionists

Boston Evening Transcript (1876-1905)
Chicago Inter Ocean (1876-1896, weekly ed. used 1876-1883, 1887, 1892-1894)
New York Evening Post (1881-1890, 1898-1915)
Richmond State Journal (1871-1874)

Other Daily Newspapers

New York Times
New York Tribune
Springfield (Mass.) *Republican*

Weeky Newspapers and Other Periodicals Edited by Abolitionists

Advance (1870-1883), a Congregational weekly published in Chicago.
Atlantic Monthly (1871-1881), edited by William Dean Howells.
Boston Commonwealth (1870-1886)
Christian Register (1877-1880), a Unitarian weekly in Boston.
Friends' Intelligencer (1908-1912), a Hicksite Quaker weekly in Philadelphia.
Friends' Review (1870-1888), an Orthodox Quaker weekly in Philadelphia.
Golden Age (1871-1874)
Harper's Weekly (1870-1892)
Independent (1870-1915)
Index (1870-1885)

Massachusetts Spy (1870-1893), weekly ed. of *Worcester Spy*.
Nation (1870-1915)
National Anti-Slavery Standard (1870)
National Standard (1870-1872)
New England Magazine (1889-1901), a monthly edited by Edwin D. Mead.
North American Review (1886-1888), James Redpath, managing ed.
Northwestern Christian Advocate (1872-1901)
Orange (N.J.) *Journal* (1876-1879)
Our Country (1885-1887)
Revolution (1868-1870), a women's rights weekly edited by Elizabeth Cady Stanton and Parker Pillsbury.
Southwestern Christian Advocate (1878-1896)
Wesleyan Methodist (1880-1891), until 1883 *American Wesleyan*
Woman's Journal (1870-1908)
Zion's Herald (1867-1888)

Periodicals Concerning Negro Education

American Missionary (1863-1915)
Berea Quarterly (1895-1909)
Christian Educator (1889-1907), organ of the Freedmen's Aid Society of the Methodist Episcopal Church.
Church at Home and Abroad (1887-1894), organ of Presbyterian mission agencies.
Freedmen's Record (1865-1874), organ of New England Freedmen's Aid Society.
Home Mission Monthly (1878-1909), organ of the American Baptist Home Mission Society.

Periodicals to Which Abolitionists Were Frequent Contributors

Crisis (1910-1915)
Christian Union (1870-1878)
Congregationalist (1870-1890)
Lend a Hand (1886-1897)
Methodist Quarterly Review (1870-1894)
Old and New (1870-1874)
Outlook (1893-1915)

Black Newspapers

Cleveland Gazette
Indianapolis Journal
New York Age
New York Freeman
New York Globe
People's Advocate
Washington Bee

Manuscript Collections

The manuscript collections of individual abolitionists were of central importance for this study, especially for the two main periods of abolitionist activism in reform activities, the 1870s and the early 1900s. Of all abolitionist families, the three generations of Garrisons preserved the largest and most complete collections of private papers. The William Lloyd Garrison Papers in the Boston Public Library are of great significance for the 1870s; the William Lloyd Garrison, Jr., Papers in the Sophia Smith Collection at the Smith College Library span an active career of nearly half a century; the Wendell Phillips Garrison Papers at Houghton Library, Harvard University, contain much material on the *Nation* during the first 40 years of its existence; the Frances (Fanny) Garrison Villard and the Oswald Garrison Villard Papers (also at Houghton), especially the latter, are important for the years after 1900. Also significant for the 1870s are the large collection of Lydia Maria Child Papers in the Samuel J. May Antislavery Collection at the Cornell University Library; the Edward Daniels Papers at the State Historical Society of Wisconsin; the James Monroe Papers at the Oberlin College Library; and the Gerrit Smith Papers at the Syracuse University Library. The papers of two leading political figures in the 1870s also contain many letters from abolitionists: the Charles Sumner Papers at the Houghton Library; and the Rutherford B. Hayes Papers at the Hayes Memorial Library, Fremont, Ohio. The huge collection of Booker T. Washington Papers in the Library of Congress is important for the relationship between neo-abolitionists and Washington as well as for developments in Negro education.

By far the most important manuscript collection for this book was the beautifully organized archives of the American Missionary Association at the Amistad Research Center, Dillard University. Although most of the AMA correspondence for the period after 1878 is lost, the minute books of the executive committee, financial records, correspondence of some of the secretaries, pamphlets, and other fugitive materials go part way toward making up this gap. And for the years through 1878 the richness of the collection is unparalleled. The archives of the Freedmen's Aid Society of the Methodist Episcopal Church at the Interdenominational Theological Center at Atlanta University (microfilm copies of which I used at the Commission on Archives and History of the United Methodist Church, Lake Junaluska, North Carolina), are missing before 1888 but complete beginning in that year. Unfortunately the Interdenominational Theological Center has not yet organized the vast amount of incoming correspondence of the Freedmen's Aid Society, so I was only able to consult the letterbook copies of outgoing correspondence. The archives of the American Baptist Home Mission Society at the American Baptist Historical Society, Colgate-Rochester Theological Seminary, Rochester, New York, were very helpful for understanding the developments at Baptist Negro schools in the 1880s and 1890s. Of several collections in the Department of Special Collections at the Hutchins Library, Berea College, three were of major significance for my chapter on Berea: the William Goodell Frost Papers; the Negro Collection; and the Day Law Collection. Two other collections were also important for Part II on Negro education: the Ednah Dow Cheney Papers, Boston Public Library, and the William Claflin Papers, Hayes Memorial Library.

The following list includes the rest of the manuscript collections consulted for this book. It does not include scattered and isolated manuscript items, the locations of which are given in the footnotes, nor does it include collections that turned out to contain nothing of value for the study.

Alfred William Anthony Collection, New York Public Library
Susan B. Anthony Papers, Library of Congress
Susan B. Anthony Papers, Schlesinger Library, Radcliffe College
Susan B. Anthony Papers, Sophia Smith Collection, Smith College Library
Atlanta University Archives
Joshua L. Baily Papers, Quaker Collection, Haverford College Library
Ray Stannard Baker Papers, Library of Congress
Berea College Board of Trustees, Minutes, Hutchins Library, Berea College
Francis W. Bird Papers, Houghton Library, Harvard University
William H. Brisbane Papers, State Historical Society of Wisconsin
James Bryce Papers, Dept. of Western MSS., Bodleian Library, Oxford University
Horace Bumstead Papers, Atlanta University Library
William E. Chandler Papers, Library of Congress
John Jay Chapman Papers, Houghton Library, Harvard University
Cheever Family Papers, American Antiquarian Society
Charles Waddell Chesnutt Papers, Fisk University Library
Lydia Maria Child Papers, Library of Congress
James Freeman Clarke Papers, Houghton Library, Harvard University
Moncure D. Conway Papers, Columbia University Library
Marmaduke C. Cope Papers, Quaker Collection, Haverford College Library
George William Curtis Papers, Hayes Memorial Library, Fremont, Ohio
George William Curtis Papers, Houghton Library, Harvard University
Anna E. Dickinson Papers, Library of Congress
Frederick Douglass Papers, formerly at Douglass Memorial Home, Washington, D.C.
Harlan Paul Douglass Papers and Beam-Douglass Collection, Amistad Research Center, Dillard University

William E. B. Du Bois Papers, University of Massachusetts Library, Amherst (formerly in the custody of Herbert Aptheker)
Zebina Eastman Papers, Chicago Historical Society
Edward P. Evans Papers, Cornell University Library
Edward Henry Fairchild Papers, Hutchins Library, Berea College
James H. Fairchild Papers, Oberlin College Library
John G. Fee Papers, Berea College Library
Abby Kelly Foster and Stephen S. Foster Papers, American Antiquarian Society
Matilda Joslyn Gage Papers, Schlesinger Library, Radcliffe College
William Channing Gannett Papers, University of Rochester Library
Booker T. Washington-Francis J. Garrison Correspondence, Schomburg Library, New York City
Wendell Phillips Garrison Papers, University of Rochester Library
William Lloyd Garrison Papers, Massachusetts Historical Society
William Lloyd Garrison III Letterbooks, Baker Library, Harvard Business School
Joshua R. Giddings-George W. Julian Manuscripts, Library of Congress
Edwin L. Godkin Papers, Houghton Library, Harvard University
Archibald H. Grimké Papers, Moorland Foundation Library, Howard University
Albert Bushnell Hart Papers, Harvard University Archives
Joseph C. Hartzell Papers, Drew University Library
Thomas Wentworth Higginson Papers, Houghton Library, Howard University
Thomas Wentworth Higginson Papers, Henry E. Huntington Library, San Marino, Cal.
Thomas Wentworth Higginson Papers, Misc. MSS., New York Public Library
George F. Hoar Papers, Massachusetts Historical Society
Holt-Messner Papers, Schlesinger Library, Radcliffe College
Oliver Otis Howard Papers, Bowdoin College Library
Julia Ward Howe Papers, Schlesinger Library, Radcliffe College
Samuel Gridley Howe Papers, New York Historical Society
Samuel Johnson Papers, Essex Institute, Salem, Mass.
John Mercer Langston Papers, Fisk University Library
Loring Family Correspondence, Schlesinger Library, Radcliffe College
McKim-Maloney-Garrison Papers, New York Public Library
Samuel May, Jr., Papers, Boston Public Library
Samuel May, Jr., Papers, Massachusetts Historical Society
Samuel Chiles Mitchell Papers, Library of Congress
National Association for the Advancement of Colored People, Records, Library of Congress
New England Freedmen's Aid Society, Papers, Massachusetts Historical Society
Charles Eliot Norton Papers, Houghton Library, Harvard University
Leonora O'Reilly Papers, Schlesinger Library, Radcliffe College
Edward L. Pierce Papers, Houghton Library, Harvard University
Parker Pillsbury Papers, Sophia Smith Collection, Smith College Library

Edmund Quincy Papers, Massachusetts Historical Society
James Redpath Correspondence, New York Public Library
James E. Rhoads Papers, Quaker Collection, Haverford College Library
Robie-Sewall Papers, Massachusetts Historical Society
William S. Robinson Scrapbooks, Boston Public Library
John A. R. Rogers Papers, Hutchins Library, Berea College
George L. Ruffin Papers, Moorland Foundation Library, Howard University
Franklin B. Sanborn Papers, American Antiquarian Society
Franklin B. Sanborn Papers, Concord Public Library
William S. Scarborough Papers, Wilberforce University Library
Carl Schurz Papers, Library of Congress
Shaw Family Correspondence, New York Public Library
Matthew Simpson Papers, Library of Congress
Julius Skilton Papers, Collection of Regional History and Archives, Cornell
    University Library
Elizabeth Cady Stanton Letters, Library of Congress
Moorfield Storey Papers, Library of Congress
Moorfield Storey Papers, Massachusetts Historical Society
Mary Church Terrell Papers, Library of Congress
Albion W. Tourgée Papers, Chautauqua County Historical Museum, West-
    field, N.Y.
Henry Villard Papers, Houghton Library, Harvard University
Andrew Dickson White Papers, Cornell University Library
John G. Whittier Papers, Essex Institute Library, Salem, Mass.
John G. Whittier Papers, Henry E. Huntington Library, San Marino, Cal.
Pickard-Whittier Papers, Houghton Library, Harvard University
Edward F. Williams Papers, Amistad Research Center, Dillard University
Elizur Wright Papers, Library of Congress

Index

Abbot, Francis E., 46, 48
Abbott, Lyman, 334, 373
Abercrombie, James, 379
abolitionists, definition of, 4; classification of, 4-6; collective biography of,
6-10; ideology of, 53-54, 56-57, 71-72;
and Civil Rights Act of 1875, 13-14,
16-21; and Liberal Republican movement, 25; and election of 1872, 33;
on military intervention in Louisiana,
47-50; on racist theories, 67-71; on
Hayes's southern policy, 81, 87, 100,
102; evaluation of Reconstruction,
112-14; and 1884 election, 123-26; on
Blair bill, 131; and 1888 election, 134;
and federal elections law, 134;
importance of in Negro education,
3-4, 6, 7-8, 61, 72, 139, 143, 152-60;
persistence of, 392. See also Garrisonian abolitionists; neo-abolitionists
Adams, Charles Francis, 27
Adams, Charles Francis, Jr., 325
Addams, Jane, 387
African Methodist Episcopal Church,
65, 189; critical of AMA, 64; membership of, 150n; attracts blacks
from ME Church, 231 and n, 264,
267; and Negro education, 151, 268
and n, 285, 295
African Methodist Episcopal Zion
Church, membership of, 150n; at-
tracts blacks from ME Church, 231
and n, 264, 267; schools founded by,
268 and n
Afro-American Council, 316-17, 386,
388
Afro-American League, 316, 317
Agassiz, Louis, 69
Aguinaldo, Emilio, 324, 325, 327
Albert, A. E. P., 266-67
Alcorn College, 265n, 268
Alderman, Edwin A., 364, 367
Alvord, John W., 74
American Anti-Slavery Society, 4, 29,
153, 393; dissolution of, 13
American Baptist Home Mission
Society, 117, 150, 188, 220, 367; and
Negro education, 144, 145, 147, 149,
154; New England influence in,

161-62; relations with southern
whites, 180; schools burned by
arsonists, 182-83; on religion in
schools, 191, 193; quality of schools,
208; and segregation issue, 238;
and black churches, 264; and question of black control of missionary
schools, 278, 284-91; black financial
support of, 293-94. See also Morehouse, Henry Lyman; Morgan,
Thomas J.
American Baptist Publication Society,
284
American Freedmen's Union Commission, 144
American Home Missionary Society,
239-41
American Missionary, on freedmen's
condition, 60; urges black uplift,
65, 185; optimism toward New
South, 95; disillusionment with New
South, 114-15; on industrial education, 215; rejects racism, 352; on
NAACP, 391
American Missionary Association, 72,
95, 145, 152, 196, 222, 315, 357;
founding of, 153; Bureau of Woman's Work, 195; and abolitionist
movement, 9, 153; and gradualism,
53-56; supports Civil Rights bill,
56; on freedmen's condition, 59-60;
on black religion, 62-63, 189; urges
black uplift, 64-65; urges black
self-help, 71; optimistic toward New
South, 111, 365; disillusioned toward
New South, 114-15; on theories of
Negro inferiority, 118, 119, 347,
352; role of, in Negro education, 10, 143-44, 145n, 147, 148-49,
153, 274n, 348, 359; on education
as a missionary enterprise, 148, 150,
151; New England influence in,
161-62; and "Puritanism," 162-64;
and missionary spirit of teachers,
165-66, 169, 173; on Negroes' morals,
168, 184-86; on achievements of
Negro education, 179; relations with
southern whites, 172-78, 181-82,
368; and "social equality" issue,
180-82; gratitude of blacks toward,

Library of Congress Cataloging in Publication Data

McPherson, James M.
  The abolitionist legacy.

  Bibliography: p.
  Includes index.
  1. Negroes—Civil rights—History. 2. Abolitionists.
I. Title.
E185.61.M18   322.4'4'0973   75-22101
ISBN 0-691-04637-9